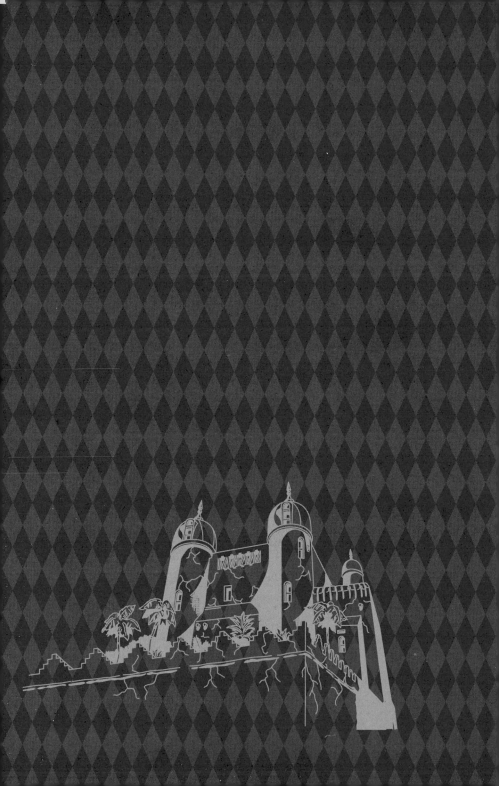

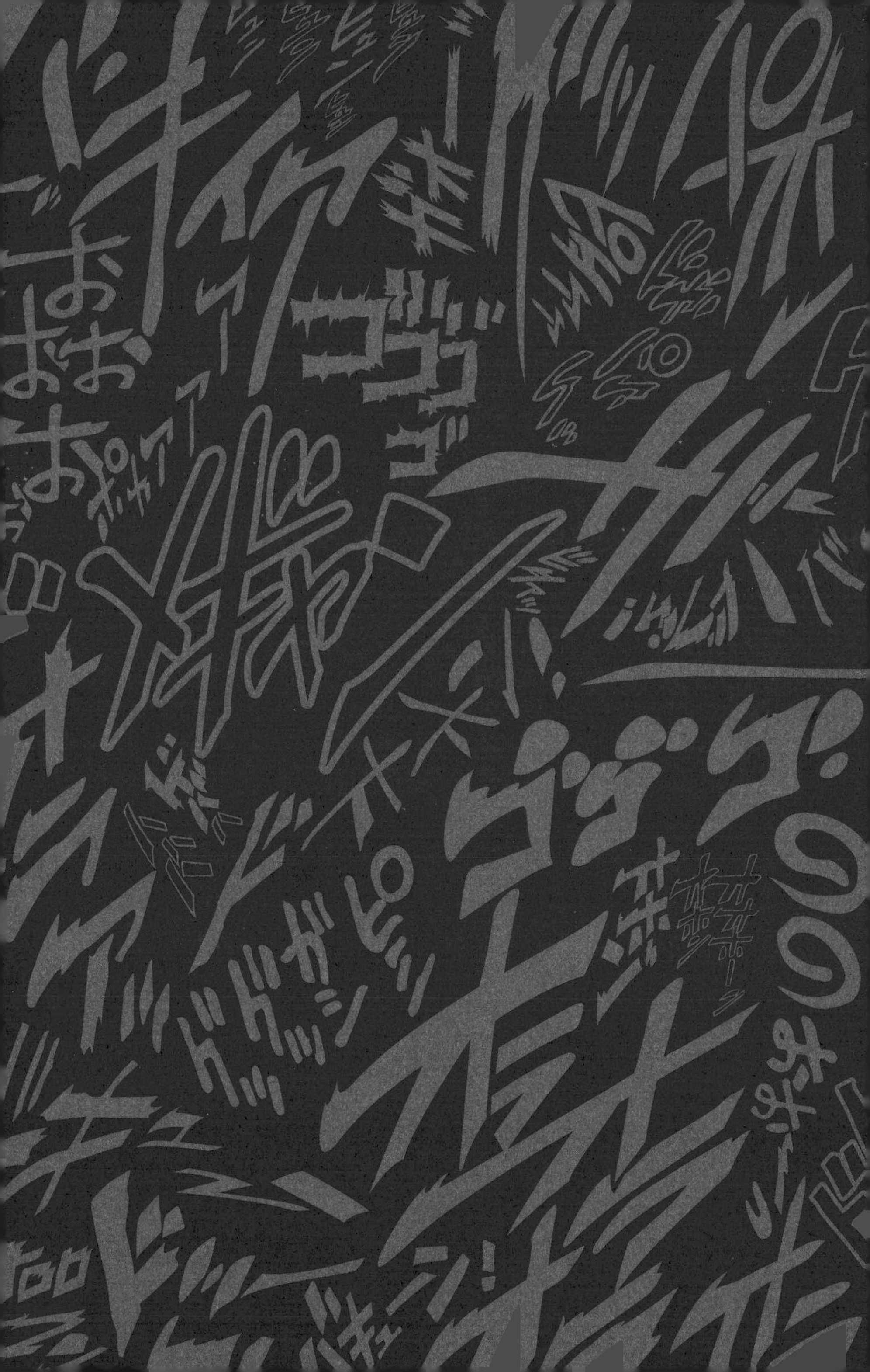

09

JoJo's

BIZARRE ADVENTURE

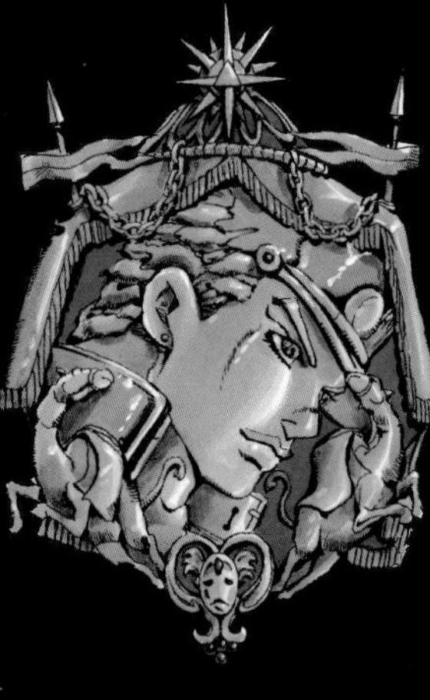

PART 3

STARDUST CRUSADERS

荒 木 飛 呂 彦

HIROHIKO ARAKI

JoJo's BIZARRE ADVENTURE
PART 3 STARDUST CRUSADERS

CONTENTS

CHAPTER 115: D'Arby the Player PART 2

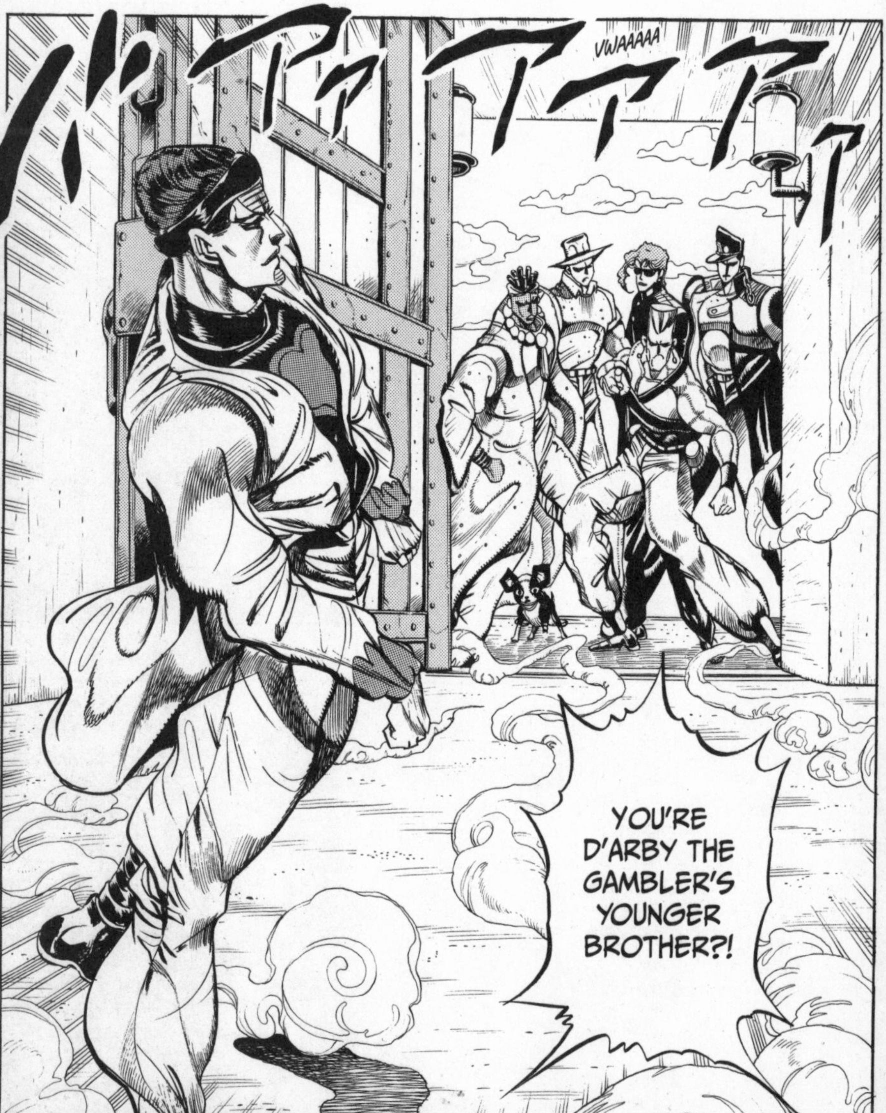
VWAAAAA
YOU'RE D'ARBY THE GAMBLER'S YOUNGER BROTHER?!

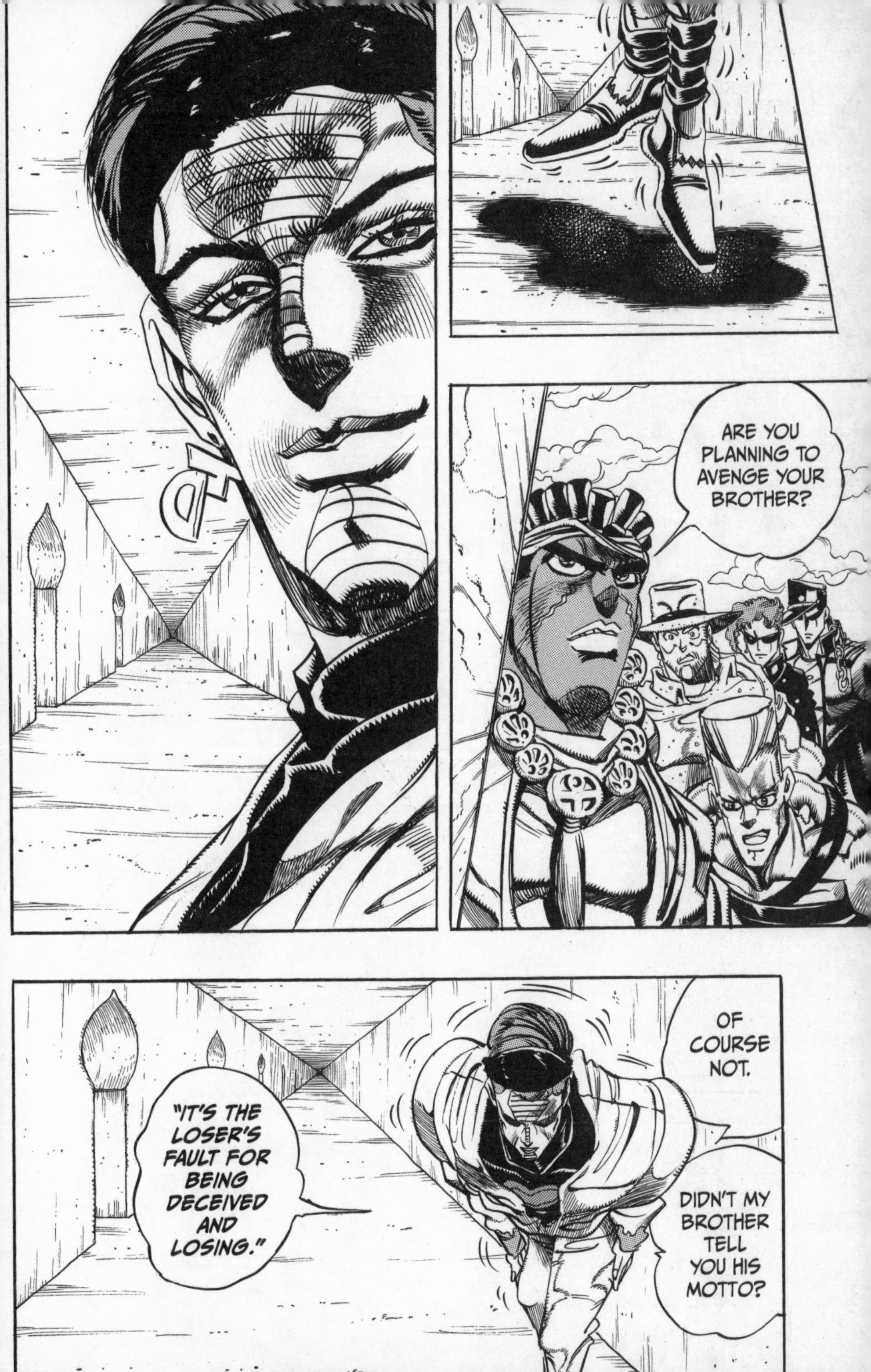
ARE YOU PLANNING TO AVENGE YOUR BROTHER?
OF COURSE NOT.
DIDN'T MY BROTHER TELL YOU HIS MOTTO?
"IT'S THE LOSER'S FAULT FOR BEING DECEIVED AND LOSING."

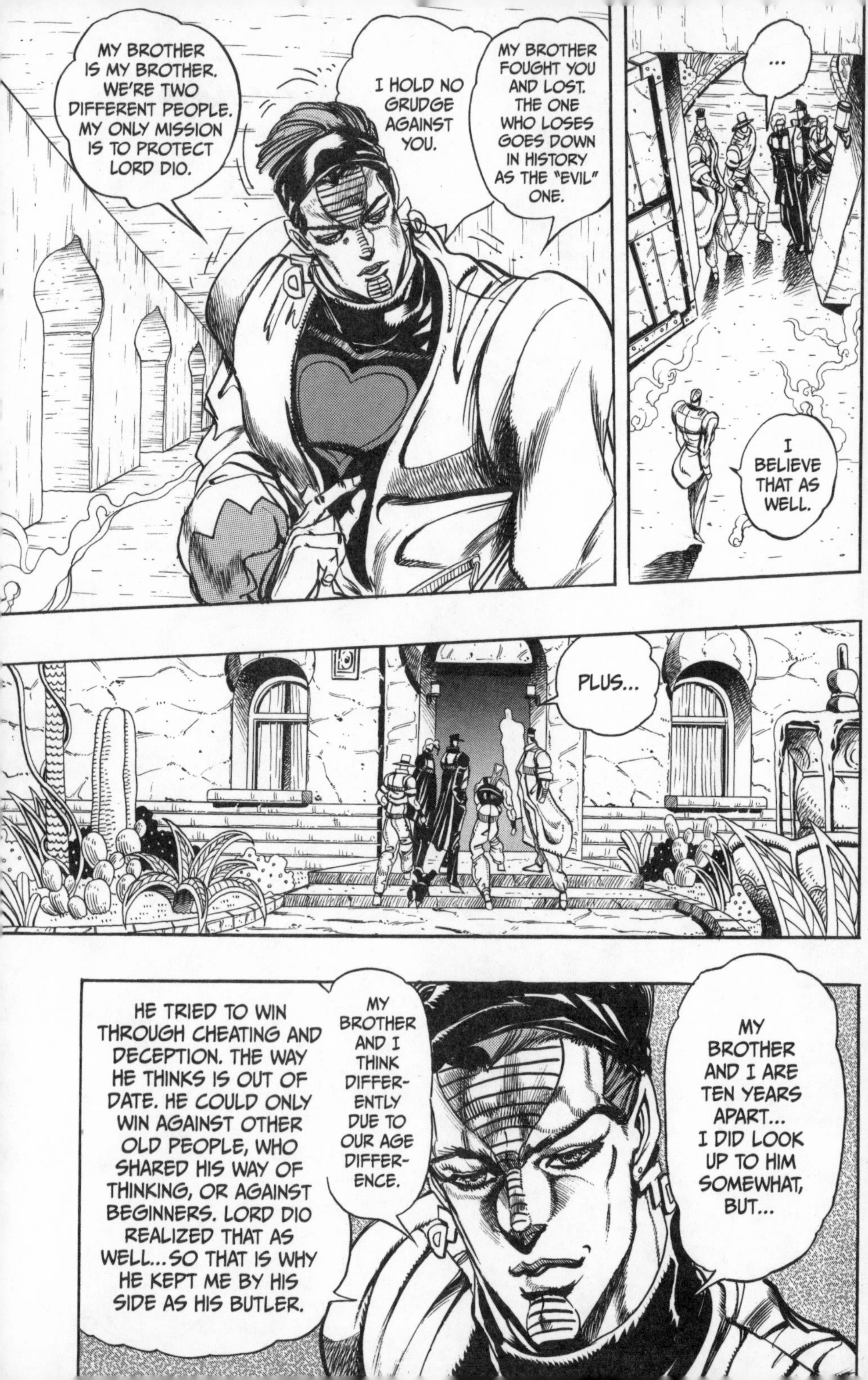
...
I BELIEVE THAT AS WELL.
MY BROTHER FOUGHT YOU AND LOST. THE ONE WHO LOSES GOES DOWN IN HISTORY AS THE "EVIL" ONE.
I HOLD NO GRUDGE AGAINST YOU.
MY BROTHER IS MY BROTHER. WE'RE TWO DIFFERENT PEOPLE. MY ONLY MISSION IS TO PROTECT LORD DIO.
PLUS...
MY BROTHER AND I ARE TEN YEARS APART... I DID LOOK UP TO HIM SOMEWHAT, BUT...
MY BROTHER AND I THINK DIFFER- ENTLY DUE TO OUR AGE DIFFER- ENCE.
HE TRIED TO WIN THROUGH CHEATING AND DECEPTION. THE WAY HE THINKS IS OUT OF DATE. HE COULD ONLY WIN AGAINST OTHER OLD PEOPLE, WHO SHARED HIS WAY OF THINKING, OR AGAINST BEGINNERS. LORD DIO REALIZED THAT AS WELL...SO THAT IS WHY HE KEPT ME BY HIS SIDE AS HIS BUTLER.

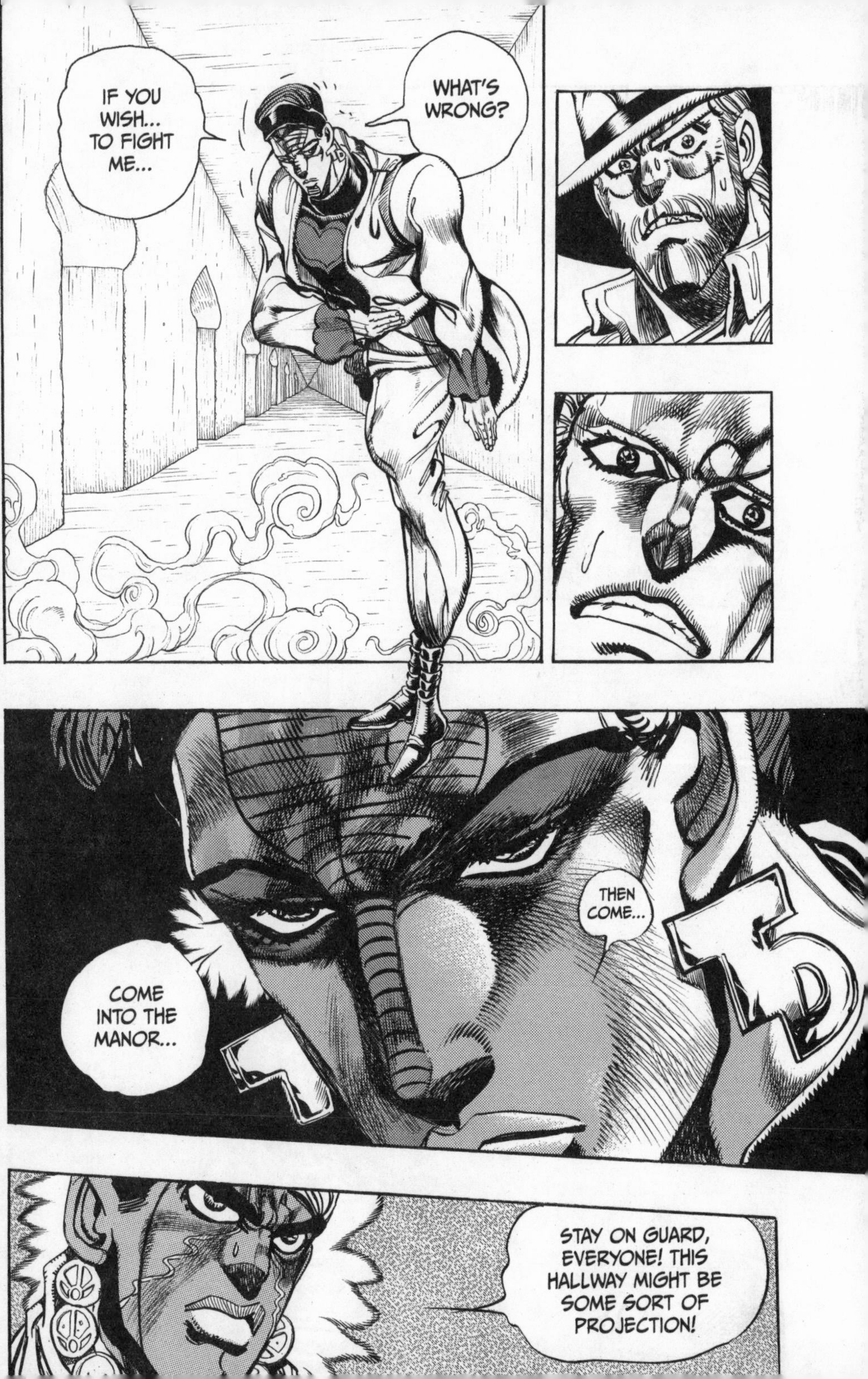
WHAT'S WRONG?
IF YOU WISH... TO FIGHT ME...
THEN COME...
COME INTO THE MANOR...
STAY ON GUARD, EVERYONE! THIS HALLWAY MIGHT BE SOME SORT OF PROJECTION!

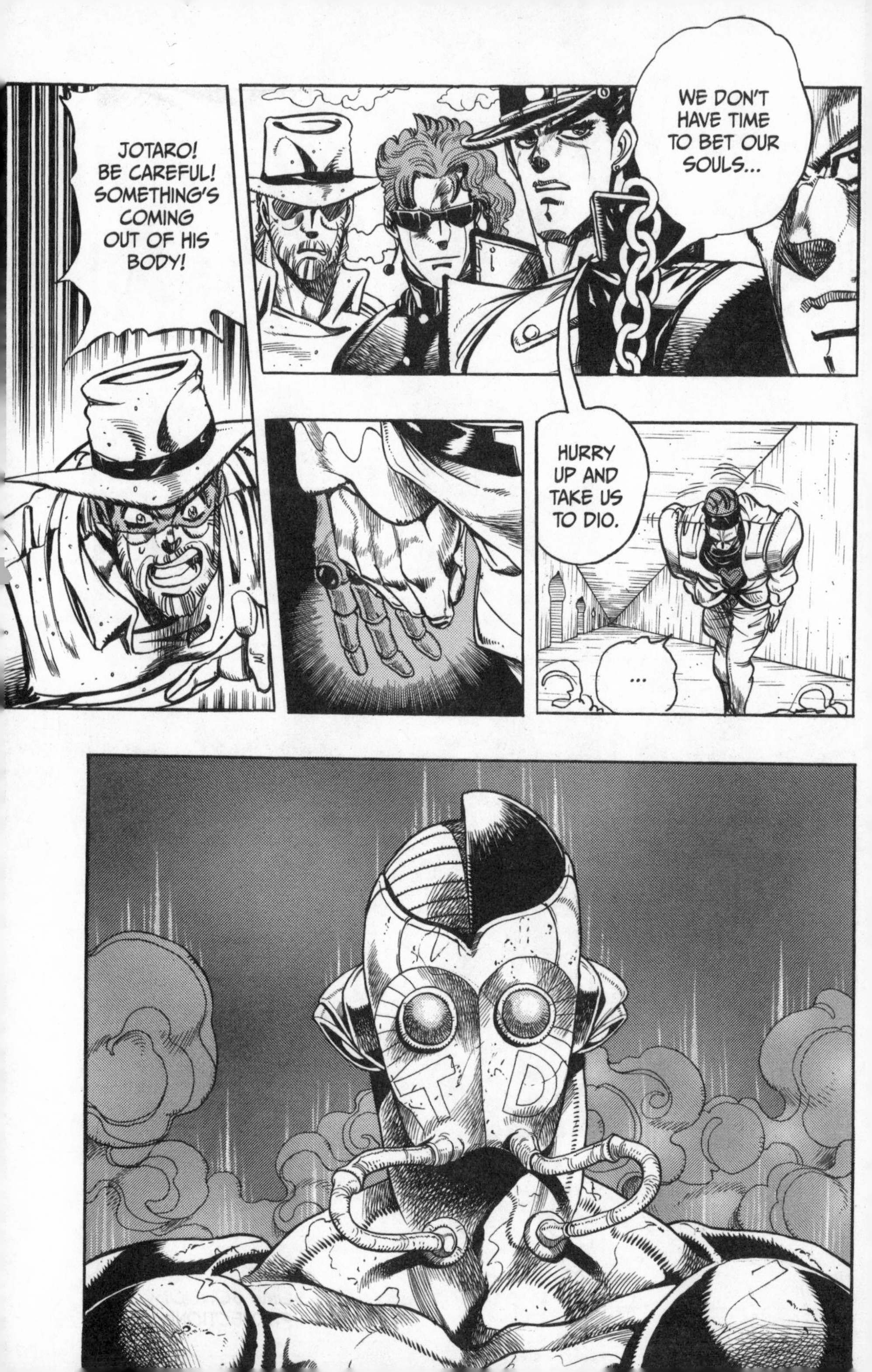
WE DON'T HAVE TIME TO BET OUR SOULS...
HURRY UP AND TAKE US TO DIO.
...
JOTARO! BE CAREFUL! SOMETHING'S COMING OUT OF HIS BODY!

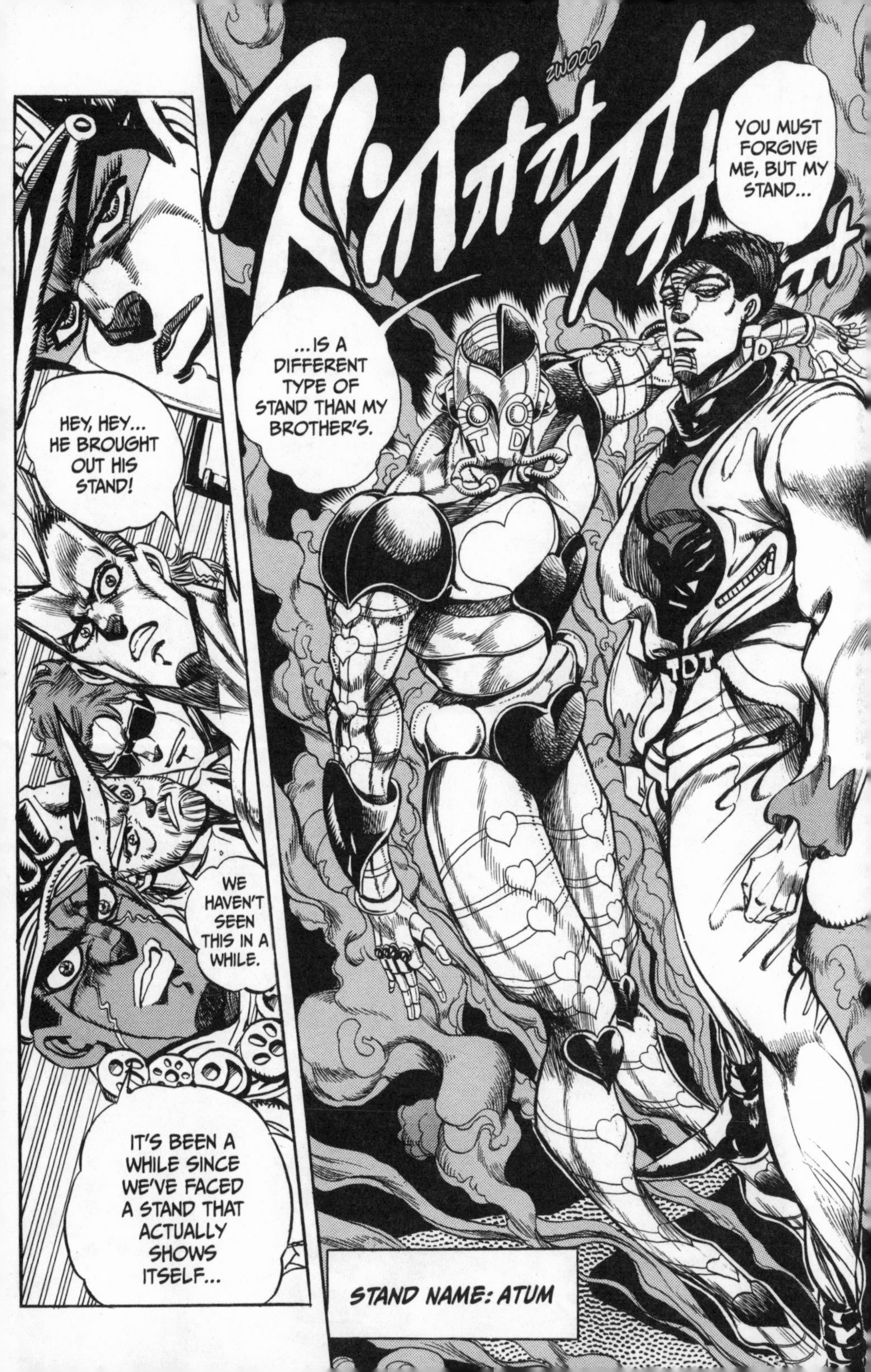
ZWOOO
YOU MUST FORGIVE ME, BUT MY STAND...
...IS A DIFFERENT TYPE OF STAND THAN MY BROTHER'S.
STAND NAME: ATUM
HEY, HEY... HE BROUGHT OUT HIS STAND!
WE HAVEN'T SEEN THIS IN A WHILE.
IT'S BEEN A WHILE SINCE WE'VE FACED A STAND THAT ACTUALLY SHOWS ITSELF...

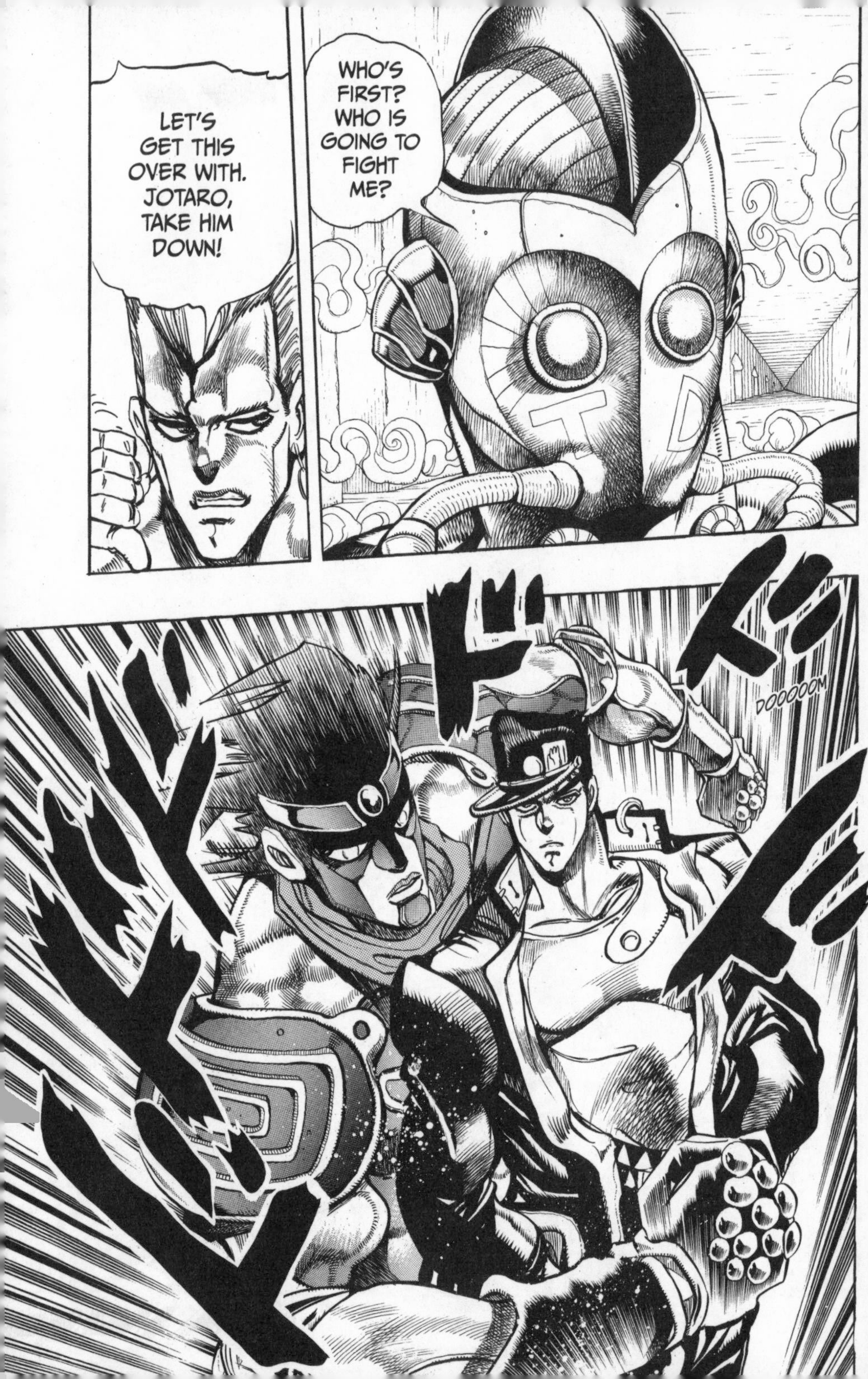
WHO'S FIRST? WHO IS GOING TO FIGHT ME?
LET'S GET THIS OVER WITH. JOTARO, TAKE HIM DOWN!
DOOOOOM

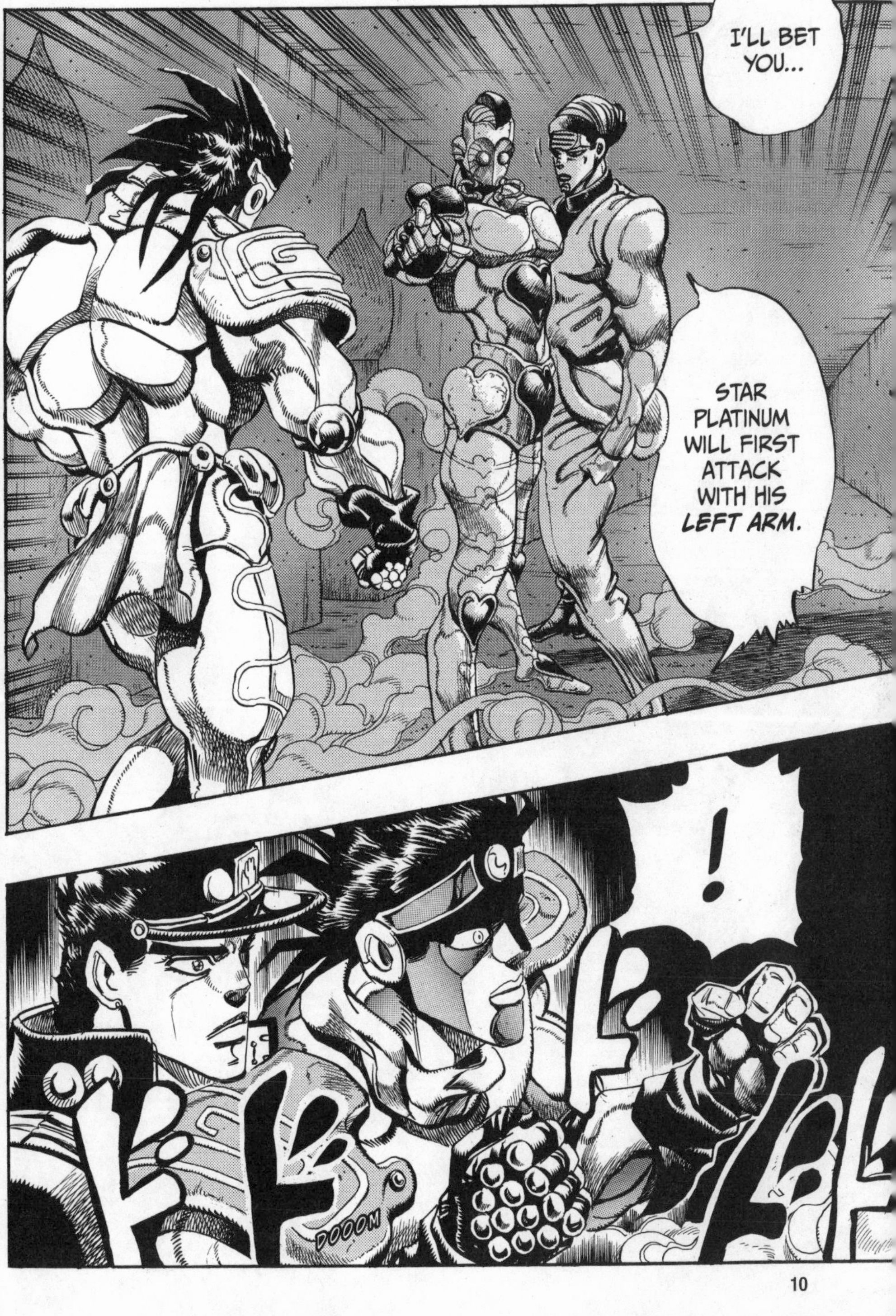
I'LL BET YOU...
STAR PLATINUM WILL FIRST ATTACK WITH HIS LEFT ARM.
!
DOOOM

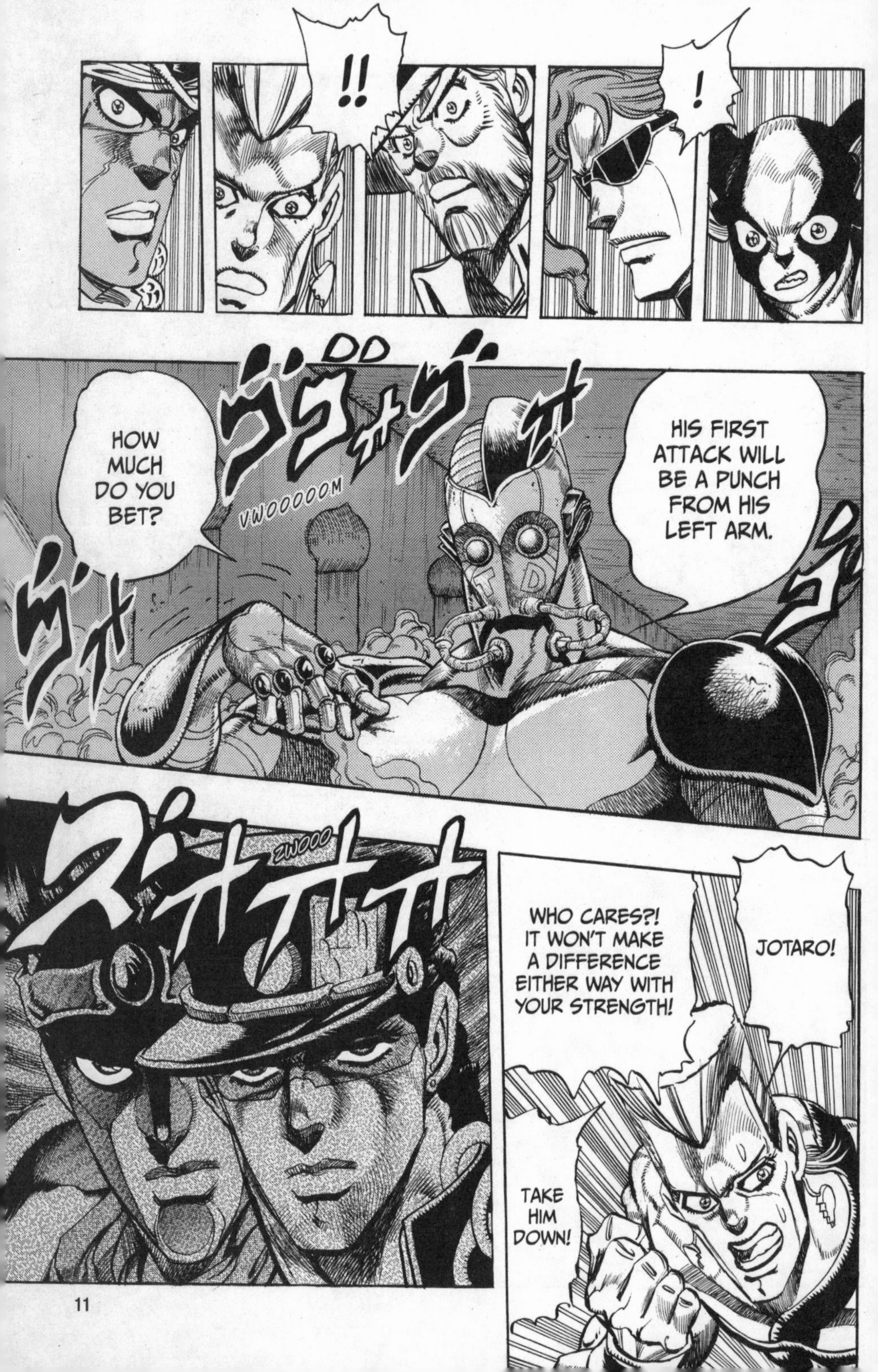

!
!!
HIS FIRST ATTACK WILL BE A PUNCH FROM HIS LEFT ARM.
DD
VWOOOOOM
HOW MUCH DO YOU BET?
JOTARO!
WHO CARES?! IT WON'T MAKE A DIFFERENCE EITHER WAY WITH YOUR STRENGTH!
TAKE HIM DOWN!
ZWOOO

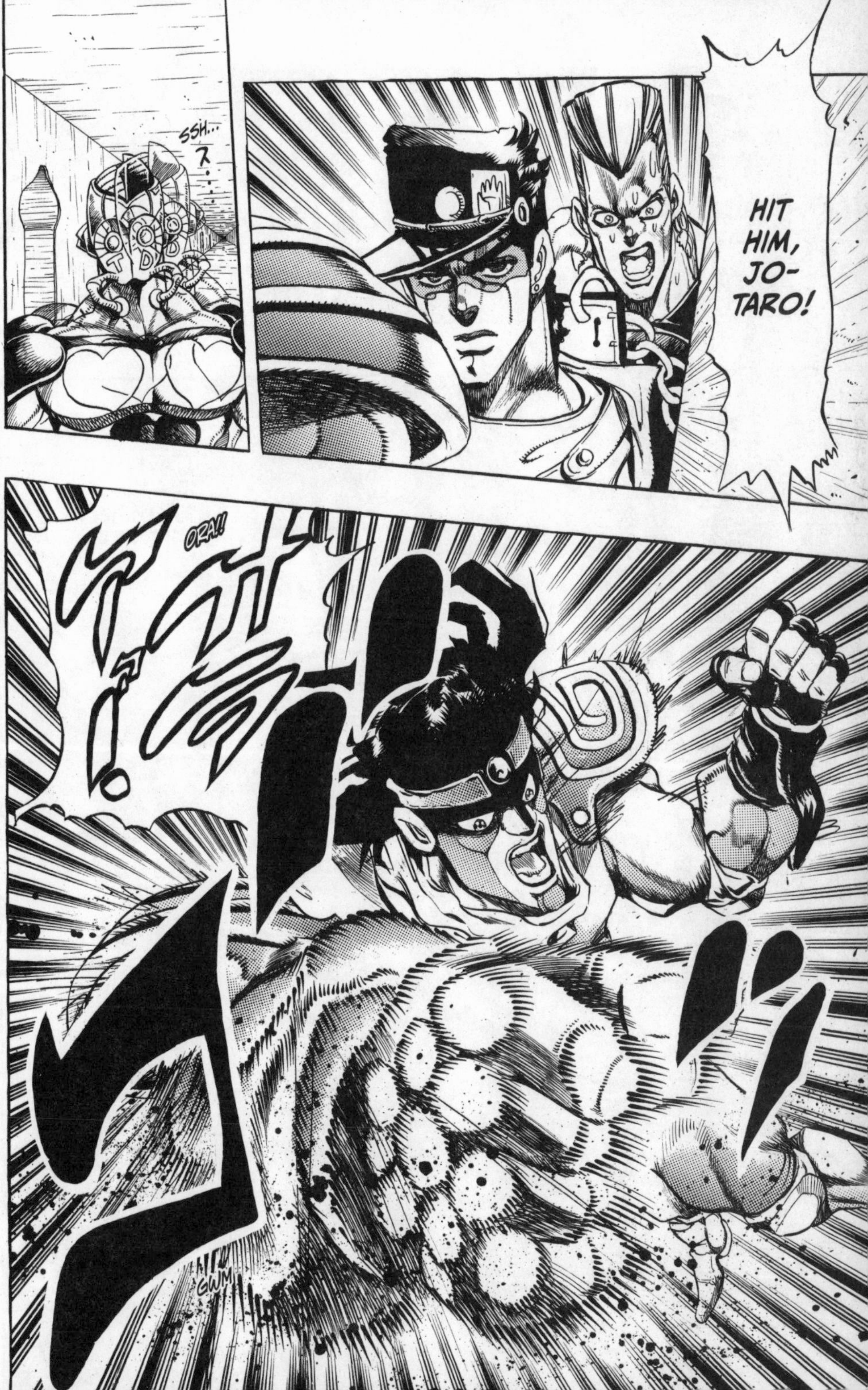
HIT HIM, JO-TARO!
...
SSH...
ORA!!
GWM

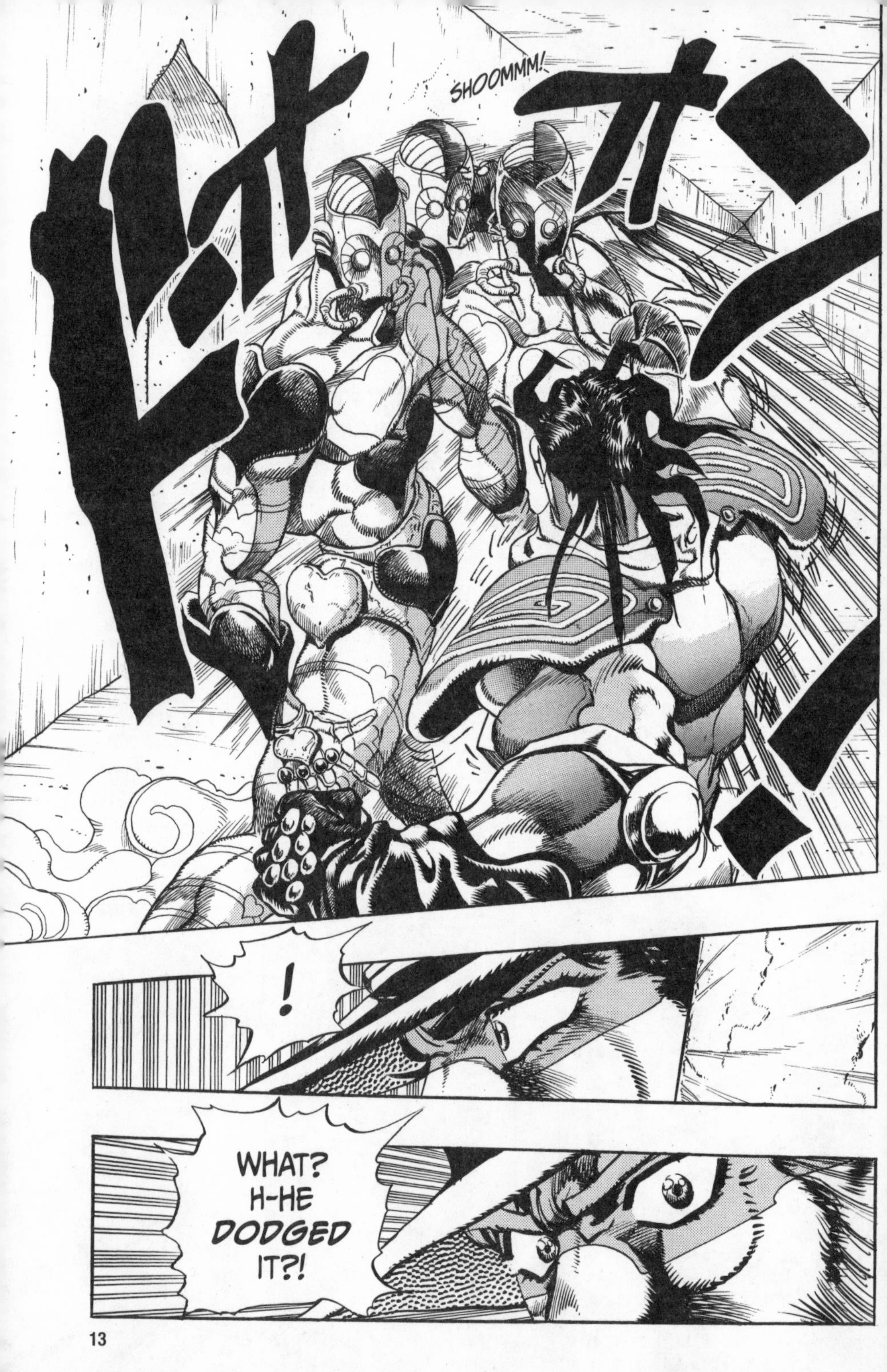
SHOOMMM!
!
WHAT? H-HE DODGED IT?!

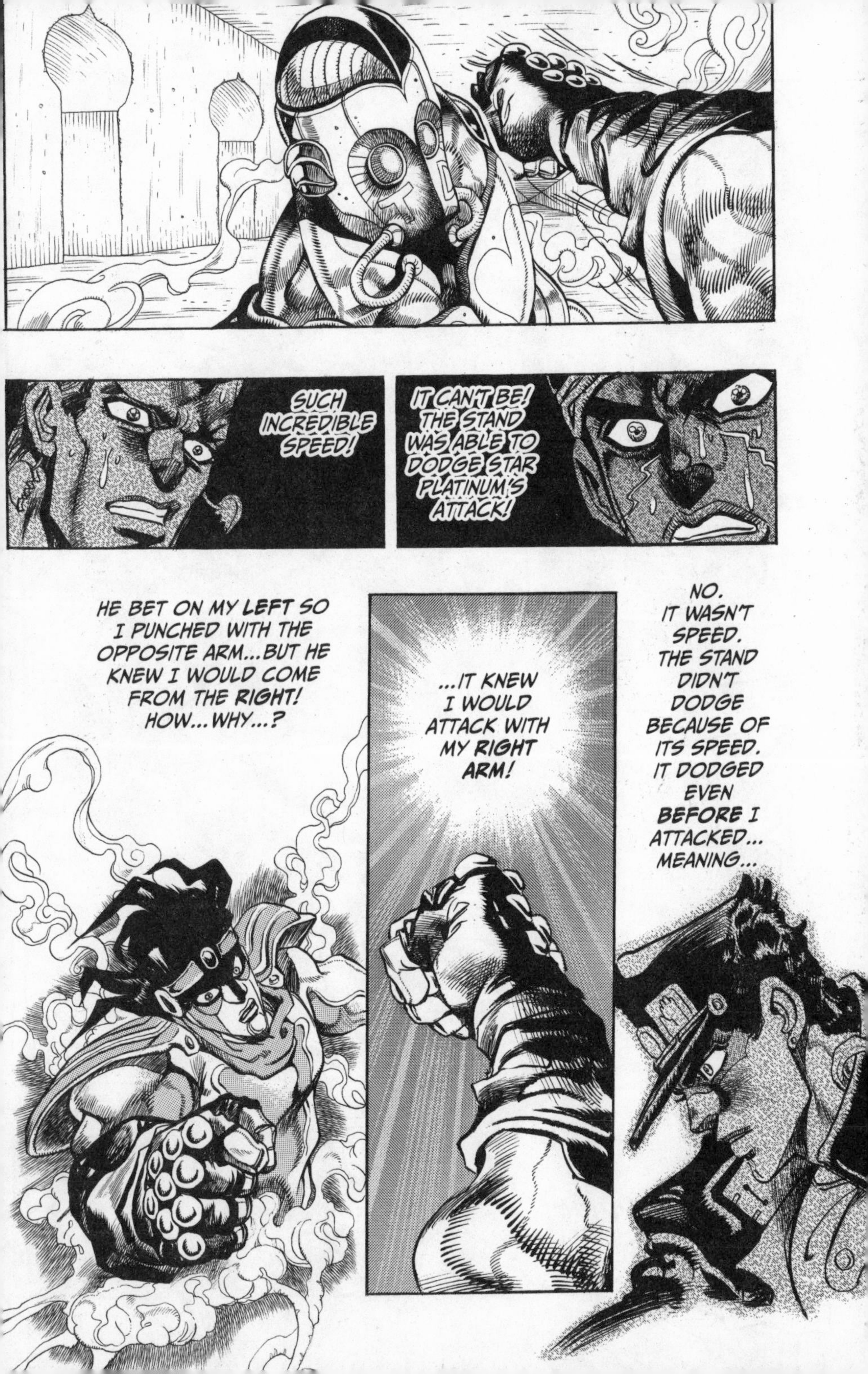
IT CAN'T BE! THE STAND WAS ABLE TO DODGE STAR PLATINUM'S ATTACK!
SUCH INCREDIBLE SPEED!
NO. IT WASN'T SPEED. THE STAND DIDN'T DODGE BECAUSE OF ITS SPEED. IT DODGED EVEN BEFORE I ATTACKED... MEANING...
...IT KNEW I WOULD ATTACK WITH MY RIGHT ARM!
HE BET ON MY LEFT SO I PUNCHED WITH THE OPPOSITE ARM...BUT HE KNEW I WOULD COME FROM THE RIGHT! HOW...WHY...?

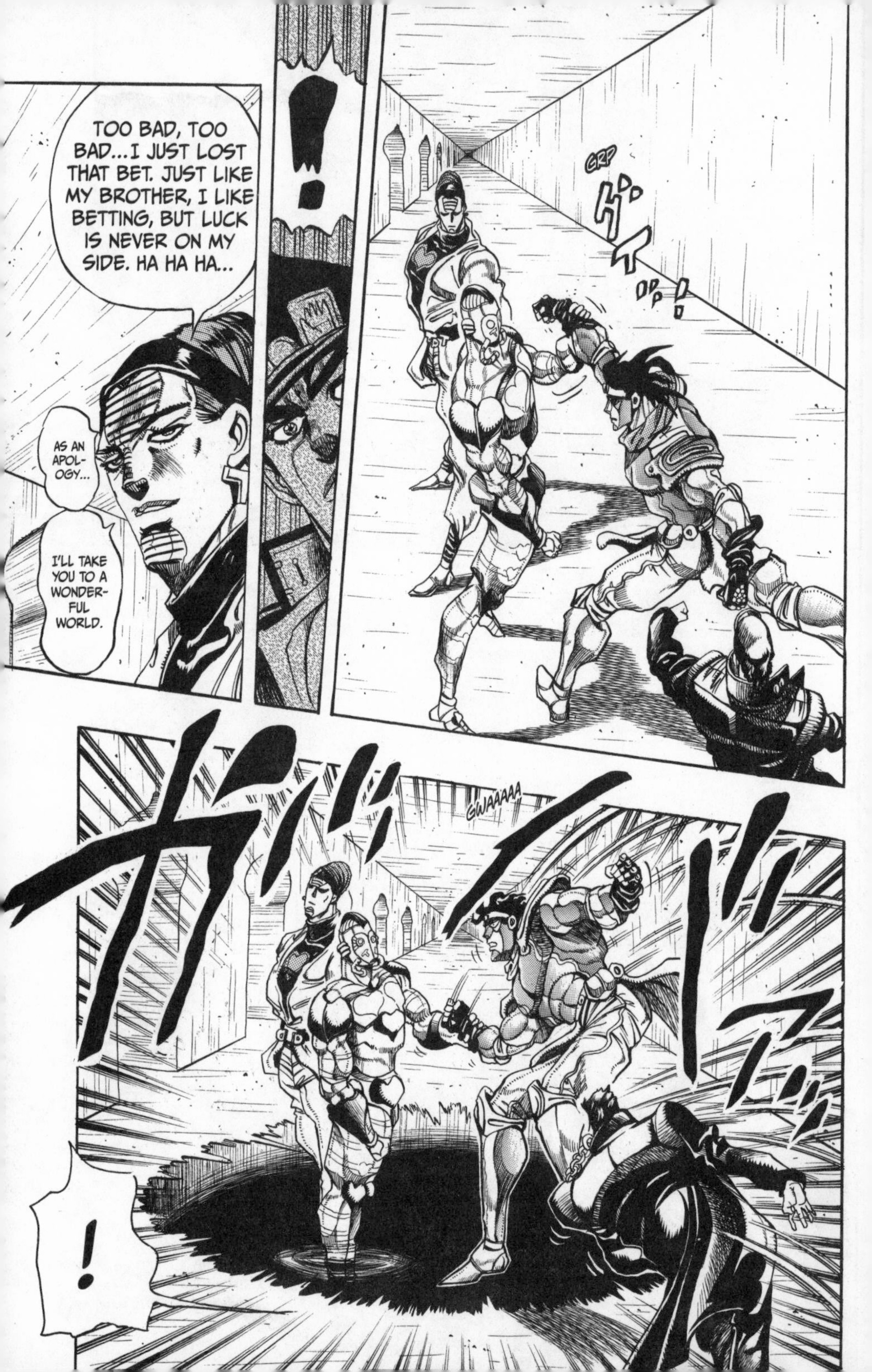
GRP
!
TOO BAD, TOO BAD...I JUST LOST THAT BET. JUST LIKE MY BROTHER, I LIKE BETTING, BUT LUCK IS NEVER ON MY SIDE. HA HA HA...
AS AN APOLOGY...
I'LL TAKE YOU TO A WONDERFUL WORLD.
GWAAAAA
!

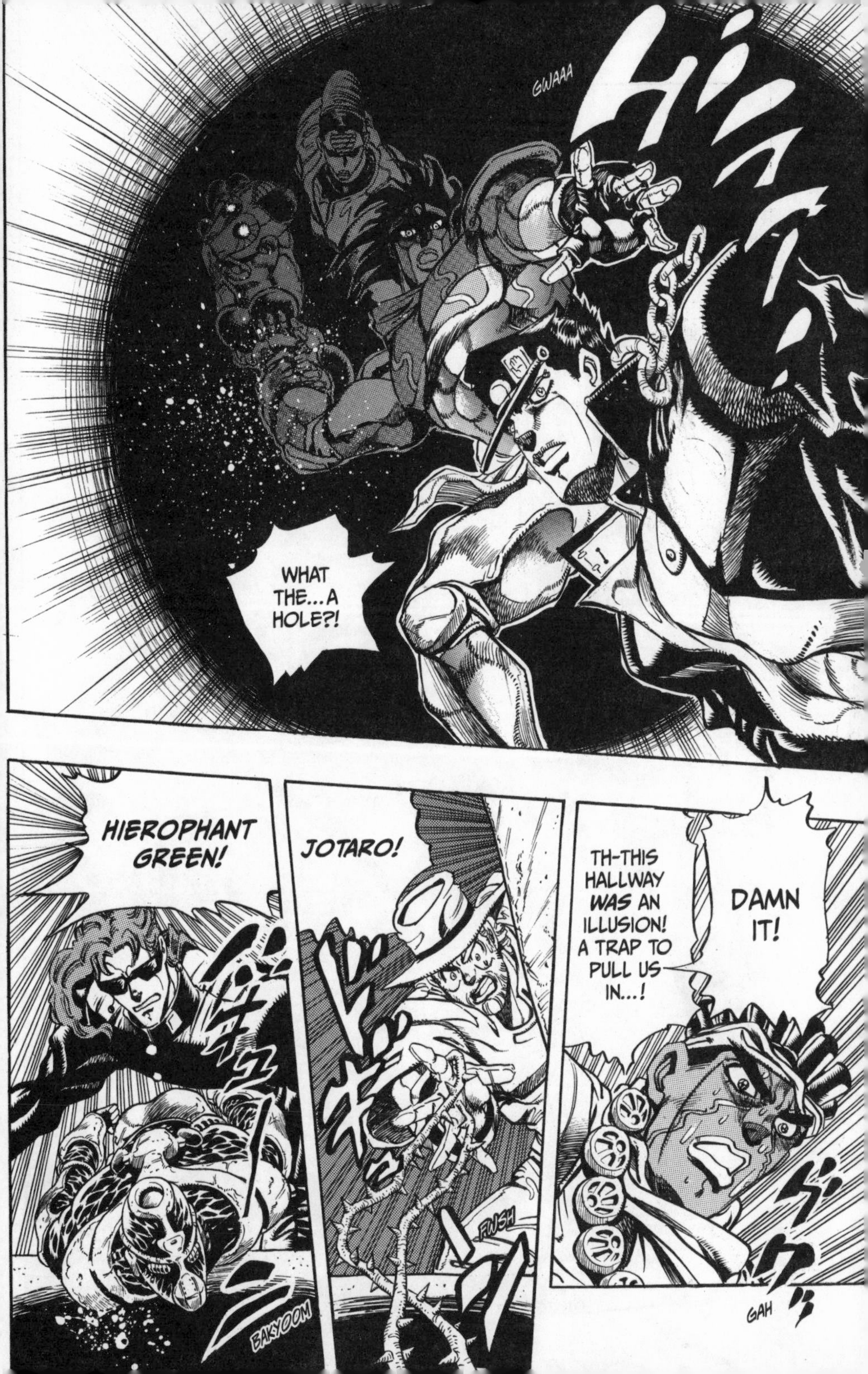
GWAAA
WHAT THE...A HOLE?!
DAMN IT!
TH-THIS HALLWAY WAS AN ILLUSION! A TRAP TO PULL US IN...!
GAH
JOTARO!
FWSH
HIEROPHANT GREEN!
BAKYOOM

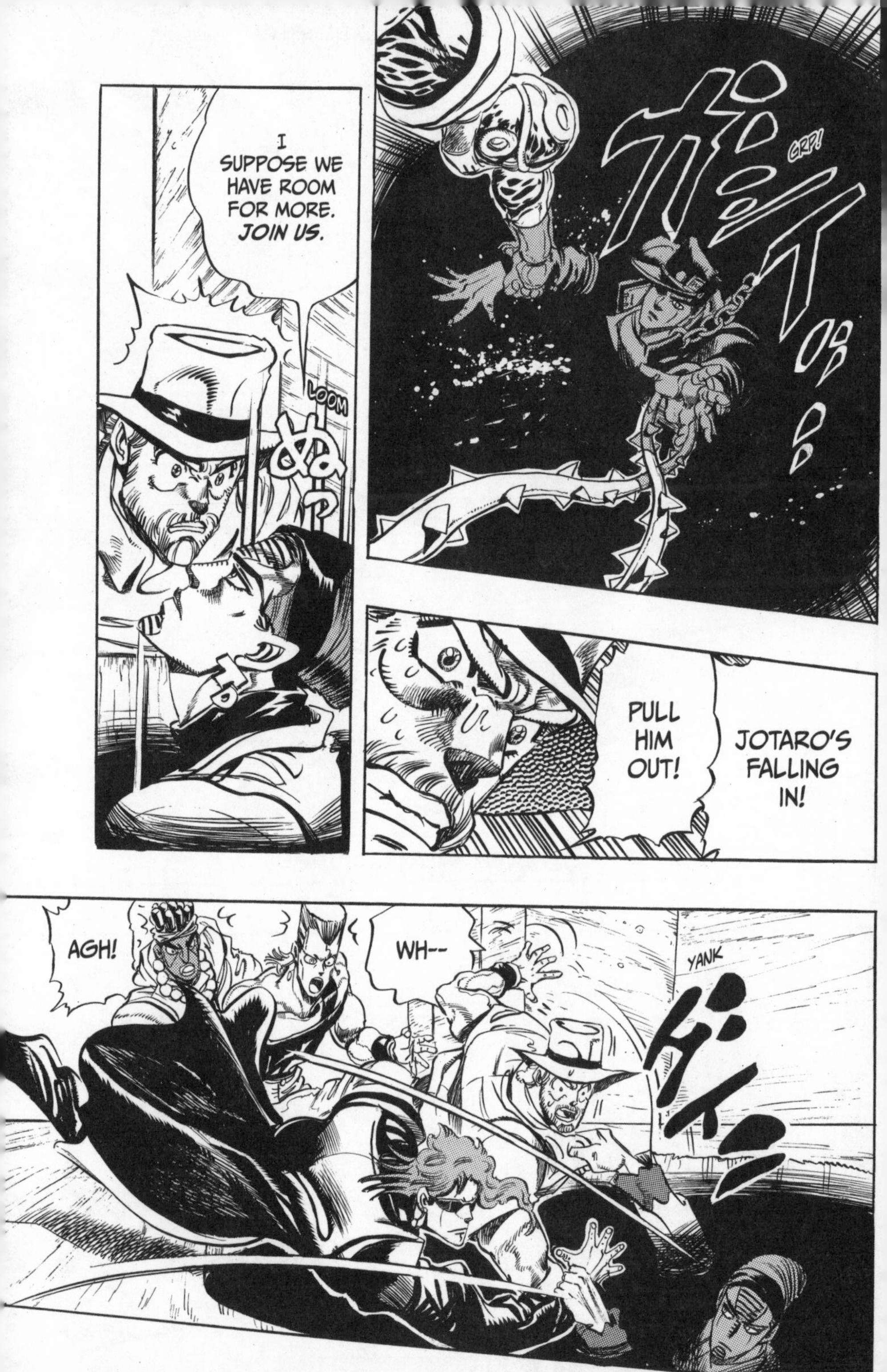
GRP!
JOTARO'S FALLING IN!
PULL HIM OUT!
I SUPPOSE WE HAVE ROOM FOR MORE. JOIN US.
LOOM
YANK
WH--
AGH!

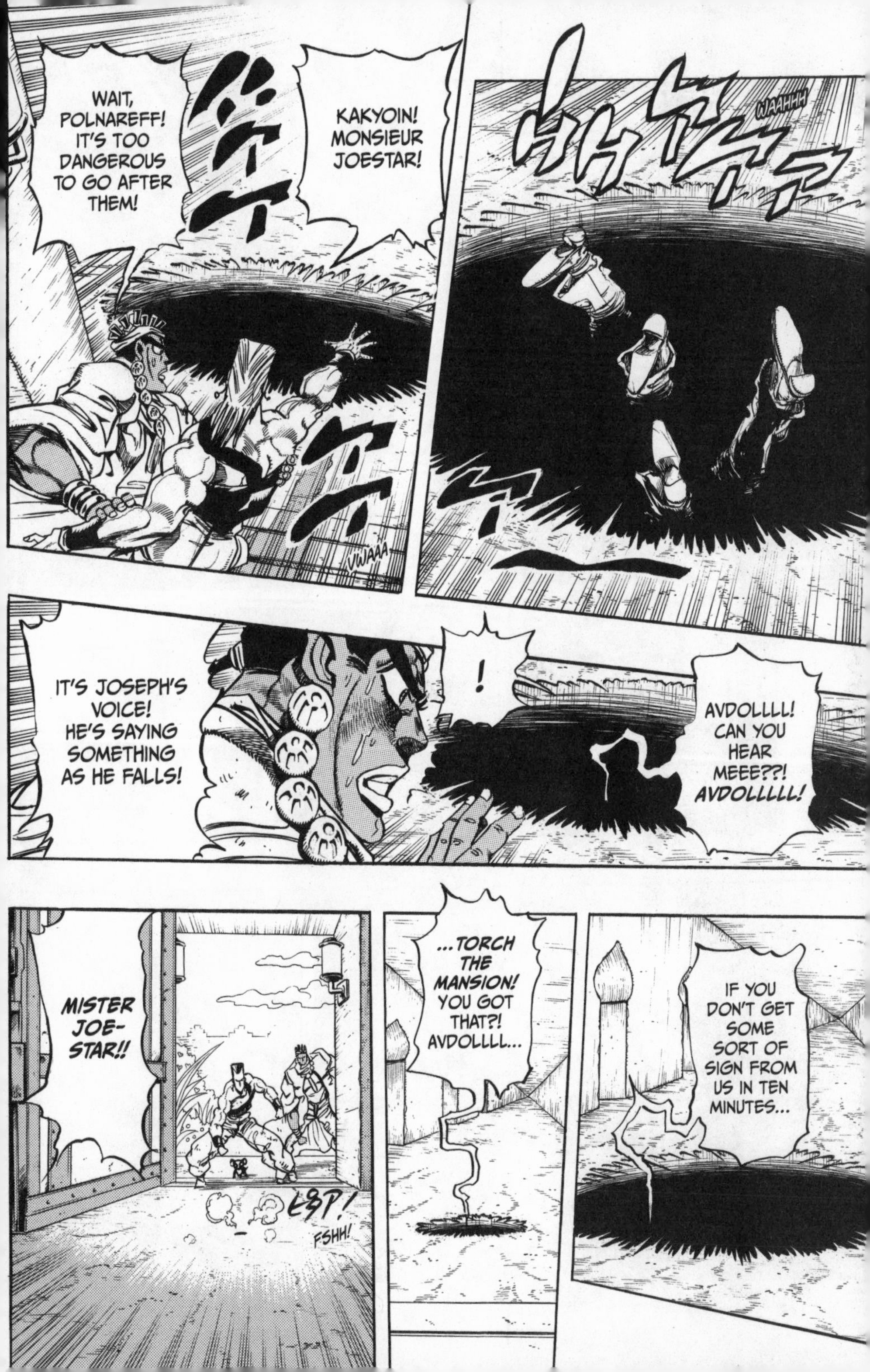
WAAHHH
KAKYOIN! MONSIEUR JOESTAR!
WAIT, POLNAREFF! IT'S TOO DANGEROUS TO GO AFTER THEM!
VWAAA
AVDOLLLL! CAN YOU HEAR MEEE??! AVDOLLLLL!
!
IT'S JOSEPH'S VOICE! HE'S SAYING SOMETHING AS HE FALLS!
IF YOU DON'T GET SOME SORT OF SIGN FROM US IN TEN MINUTES...
...TORCH THE MANSION! YOU GOT THAT?! AVDOLLLL...
MISTER JOE-STAR!!
FSHH!

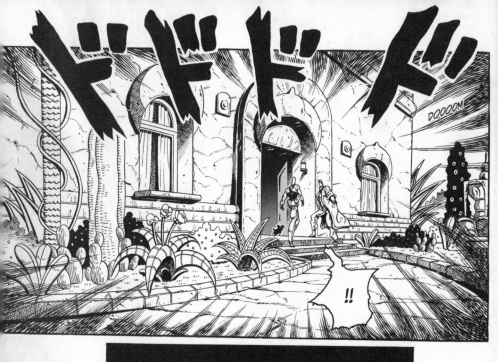

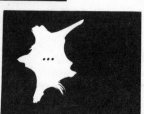

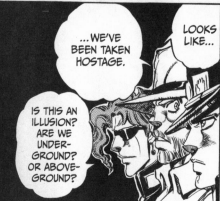

...WE'VE BEEN TAKEN HOSTAGE.

LOOKS LIKE...

IS THIS AN ILLUSION? ARE WE UNDER-GROUND? OR ABOVE-GROUND?

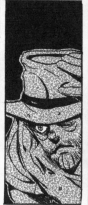

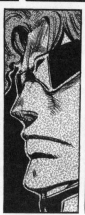

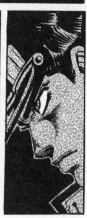

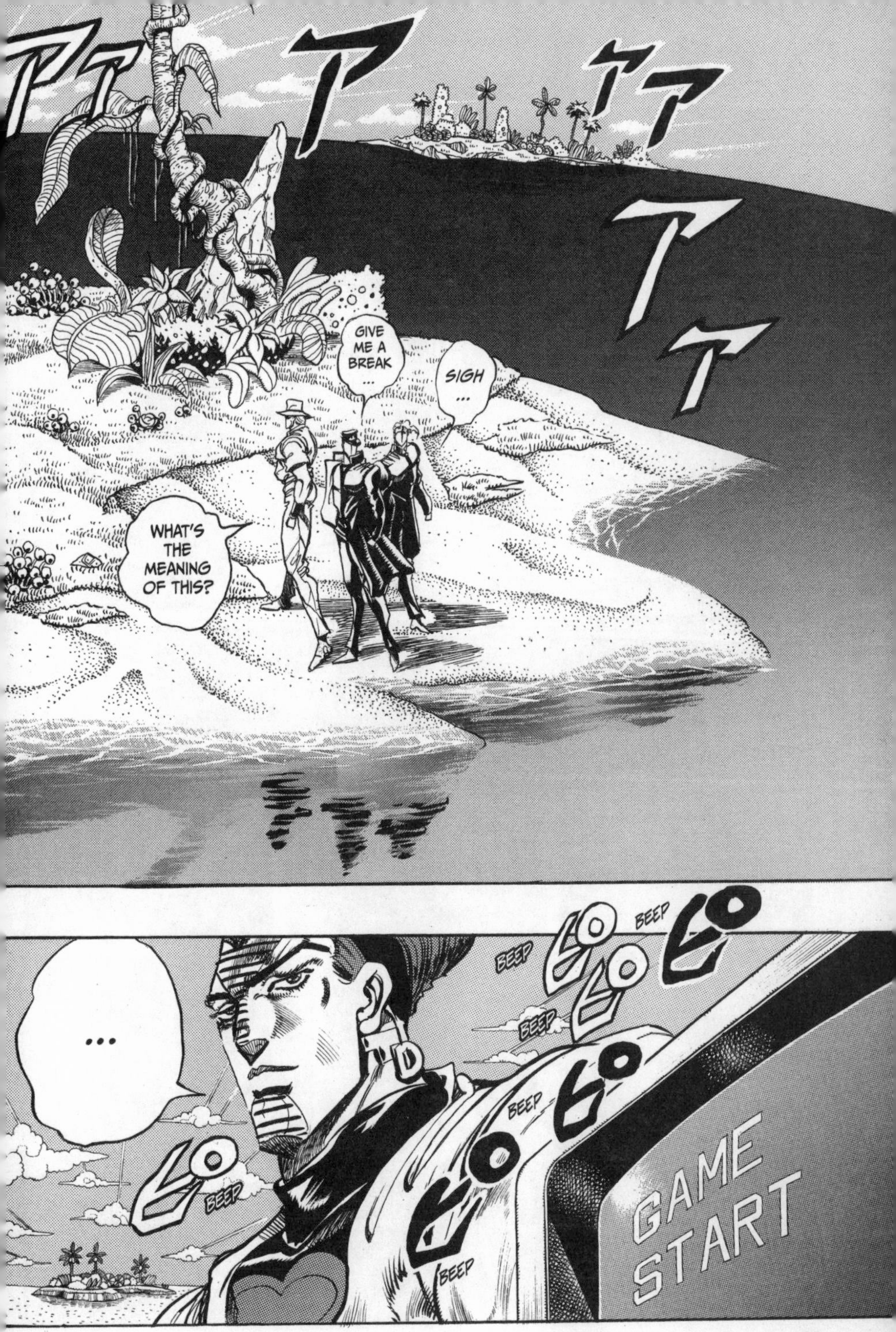
アアアアアアア
SIGH ...
GIVE ME A BREAK ...
WHAT'S THE MEANING OF THIS?
BEEP
BEEP
BEEP
BEEP
GAME START
BEEP
BEEP
...

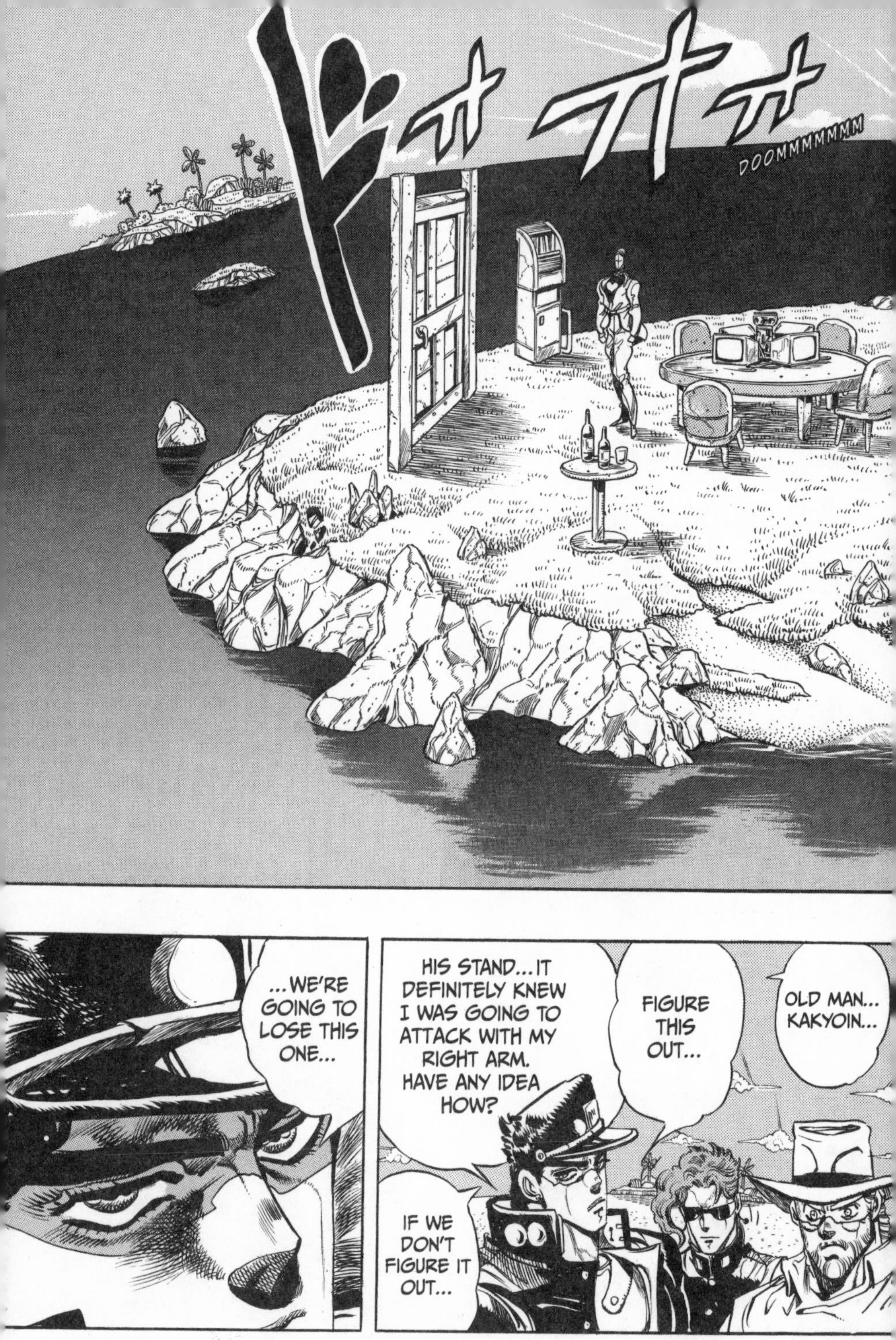
DOOMMMMMMM
OLD MAN... KAKYOIN...
FIGURE THIS OUT...
HIS STAND...IT DEFINITELY KNEW I WAS GOING TO ATTACK WITH MY RIGHT ARM. HAVE ANY IDEA HOW?
IF WE DON'T FIGURE IT OUT...
...WE'RE GOING TO LOSE THIS ONE...

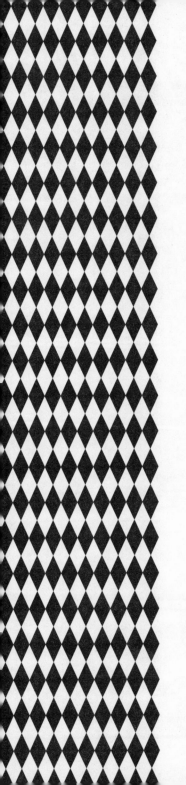

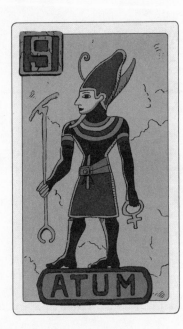

ATUM

CHAPTER 116: D'Arby the Player PART 3

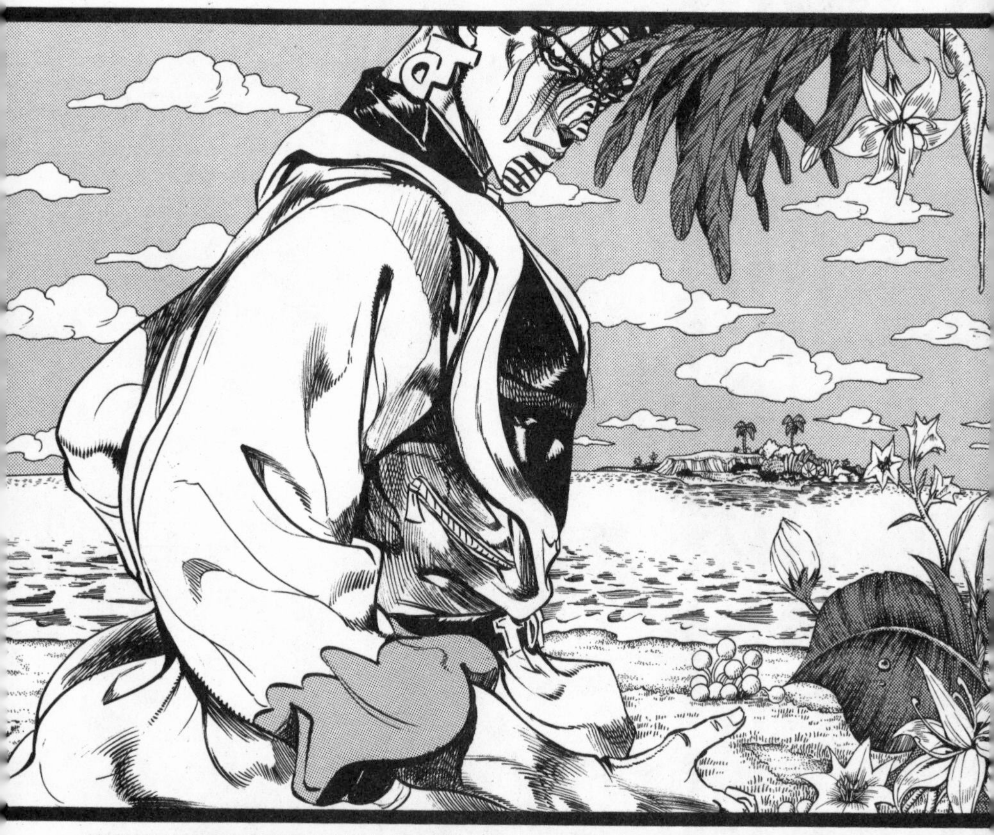

D'Arby the Younger

Nationality: American **Age:** 21

D'Arby the Elder's younger brother

As one of DIO's favorites, he serves as DIO's butler

Stand: The Egyptian god Atum

Stand Ability: Still a mystery, but its true power will soon be revealed

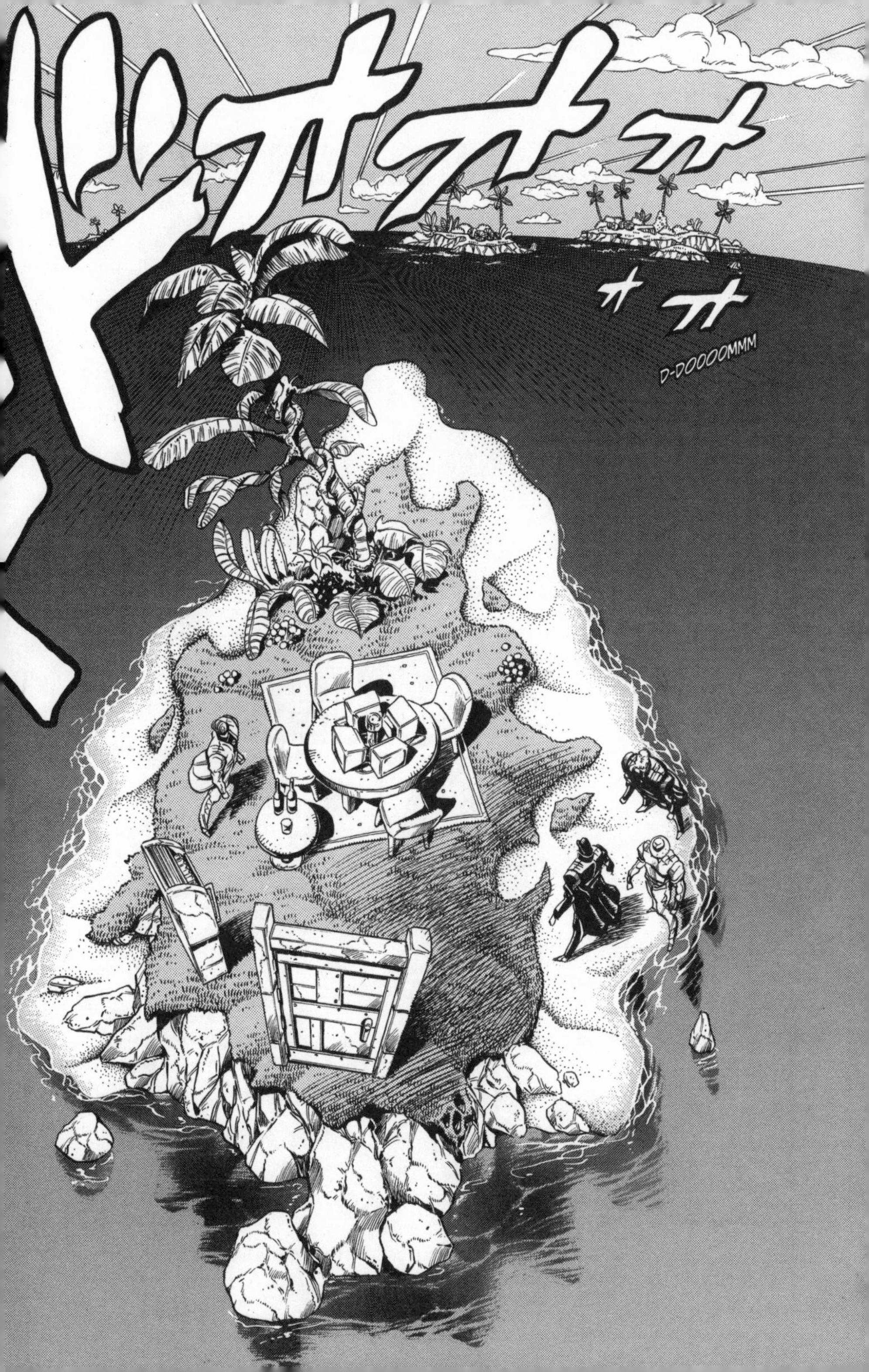
ドッオオオォォ
D-DOOOOOMMM

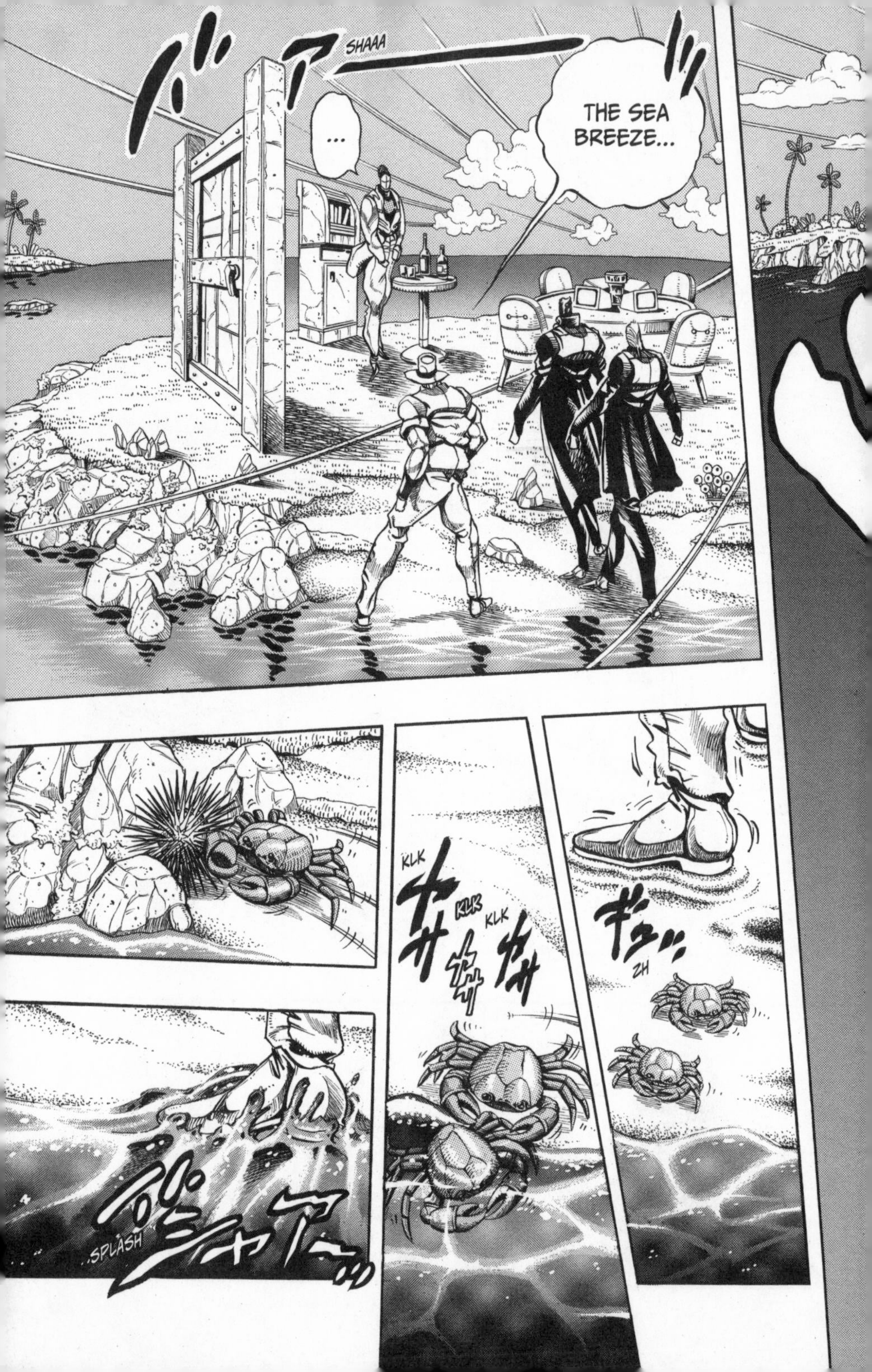
SHAAA
THE SEA BREEZE...
...
ZH
KLK
KLK
KLK
SPLASH

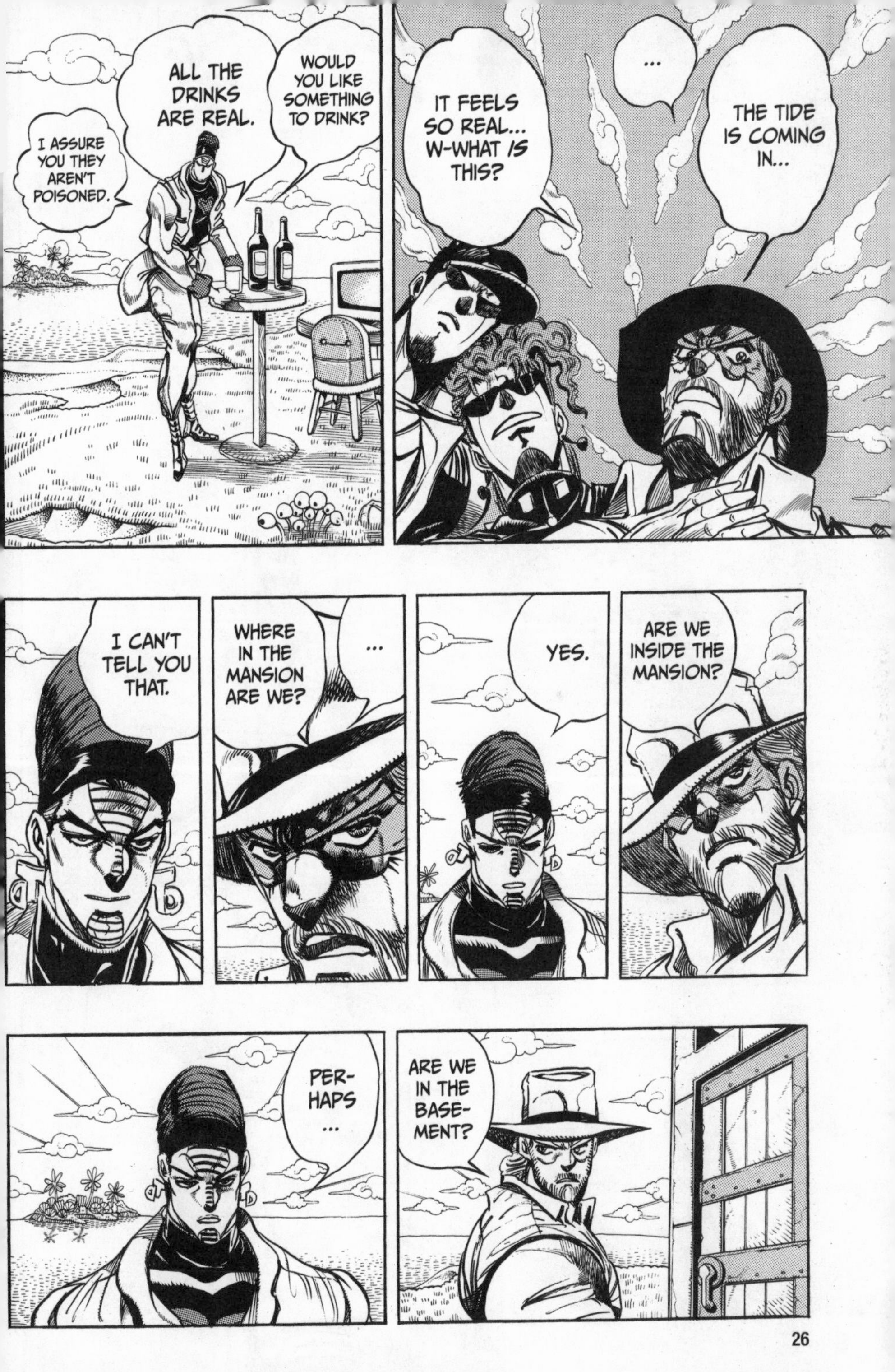
THE TIDE IS COMING IN...
...
IT FEELS SO REAL... W-WHAT *IS* THIS?
WOULD YOU LIKE SOMETHING TO DRINK?
ALL THE DRINKS ARE REAL.
I ASSURE YOU THEY AREN'T POISONED.
ARE WE INSIDE THE MANSION?
YES.
...
WHERE IN THE MANSION ARE WE?
I CAN'T TELL YOU THAT.
ARE WE IN THE BASE-MENT?
PER-HAPS ...

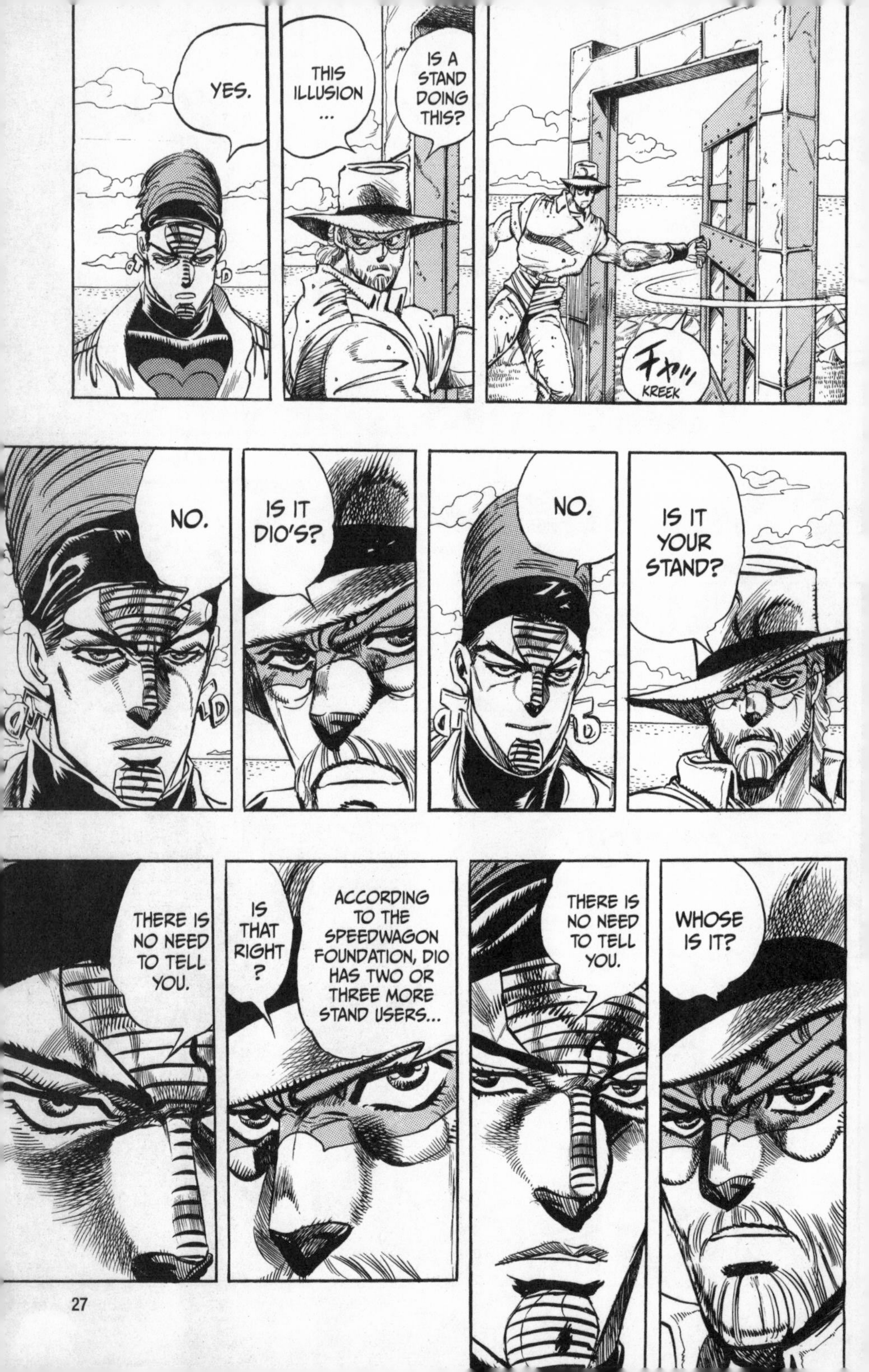
チャッ
KREEK
IS A STAND DOING THIS?
THIS ILLUSION ...
YES.
IS IT YOUR STAND?
NO.
IS IT DIO'S?
NO.
WHOSE IS IT?
THERE IS NO NEED TO TELL YOU.
ACCORDING TO THE SPEEDWAGON FOUNDATION, DIO HAS TWO OR THREE MORE STAND USERS...
IS THAT RIGHT?
THERE IS NO NEED TO TELL YOU.

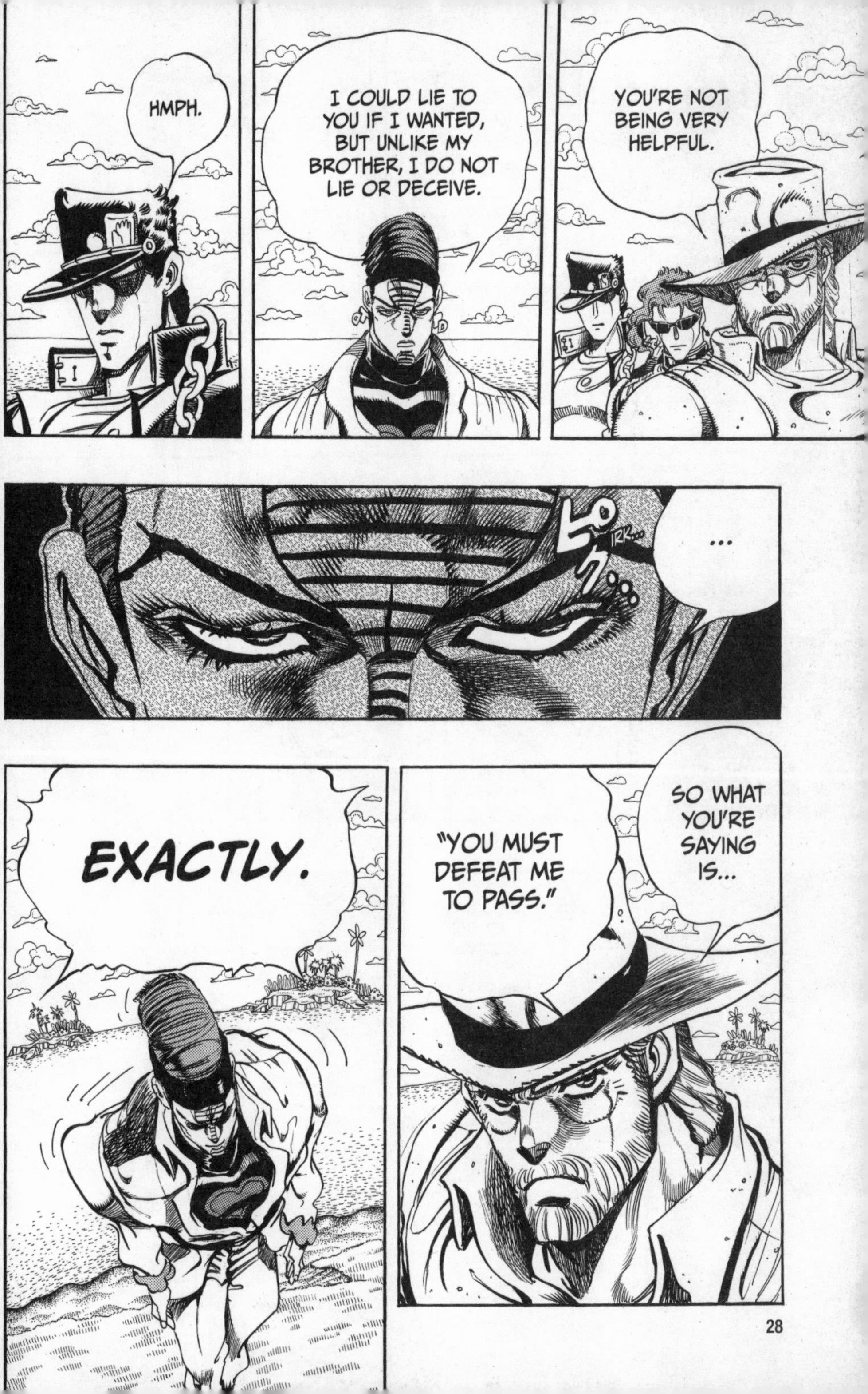
YOU'RE NOT BEING VERY HELPFUL.
I COULD LIE TO YOU IF I WANTED, BUT UNLIKE MY BROTHER, I DO NOT LIE OR DECEIVE.
HMPH.
...
TRK...
SO WHAT YOU'RE SAYING IS...
"YOU MUST DEFEAT ME TO PASS."
EXACTLY.

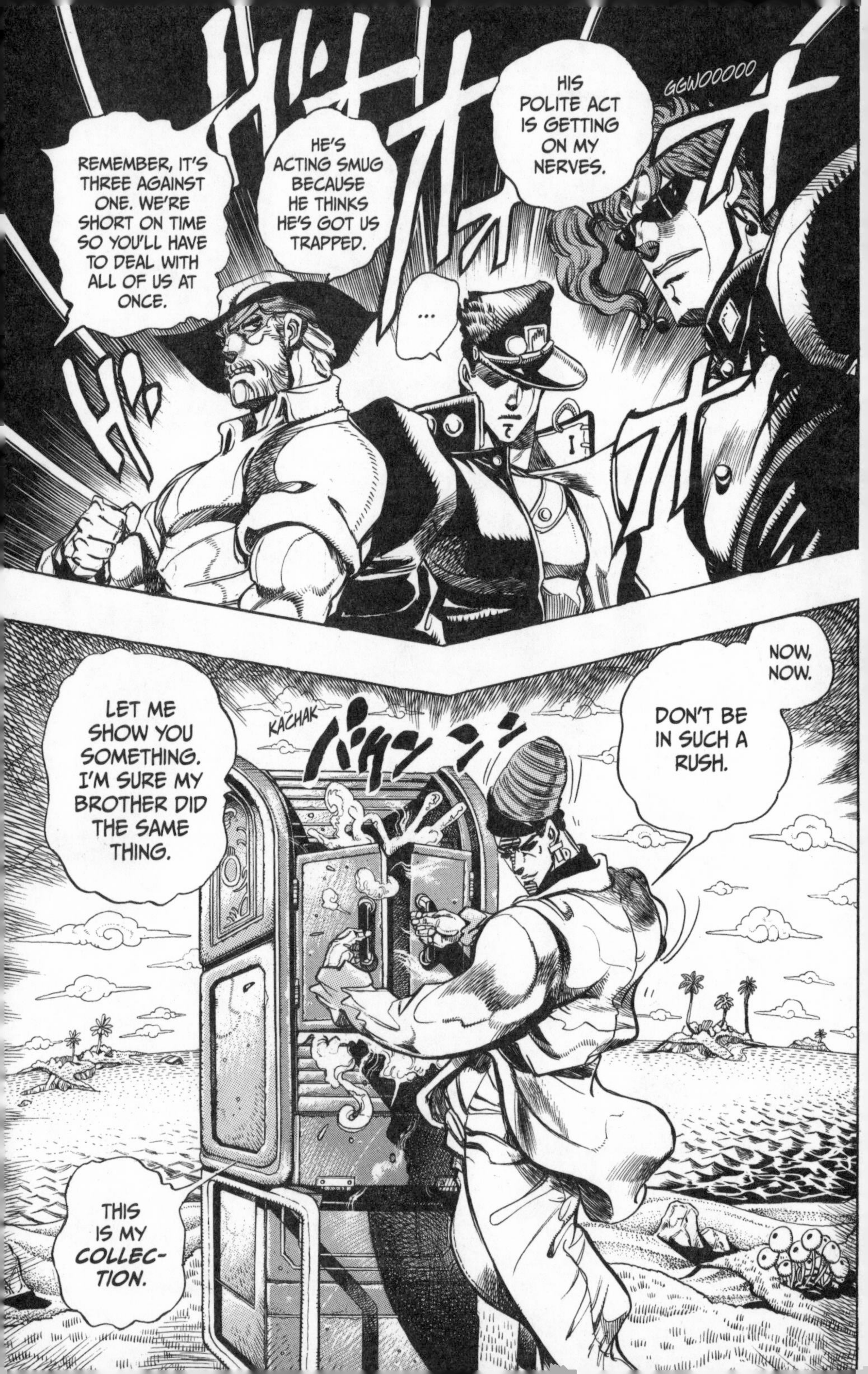
GGWOOOOO
HIS POLITE ACT IS GETTING ON MY NERVES.
HE'S ACTING SMUG BECAUSE HE THINKS HE'S GOT US TRAPPED.
...
REMEMBER, IT'S THREE AGAINST ONE. WE'RE SHORT ON TIME SO YOU'LL HAVE TO DEAL WITH ALL OF US AT ONCE.
NOW, NOW.
DON'T BE IN SUCH A RUSH.
KACHAK
LET ME SHOW YOU SOMETHING. I'M SURE MY BROTHER DID THE SAME THING.
THIS IS MY *COLLECTION.*

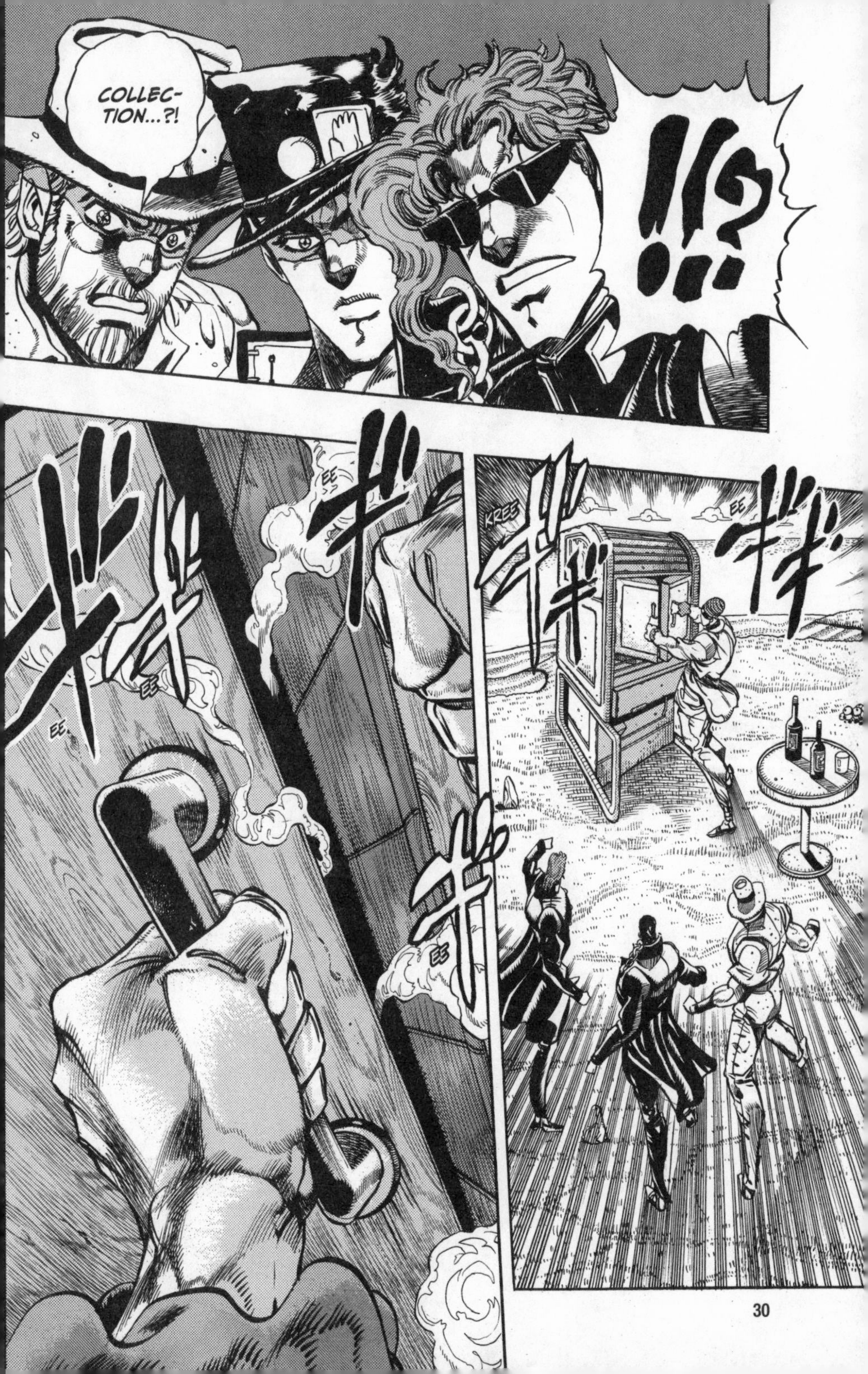
!!?
COLLECTION...?!
EE
KREE
EE
EE
EE
EE

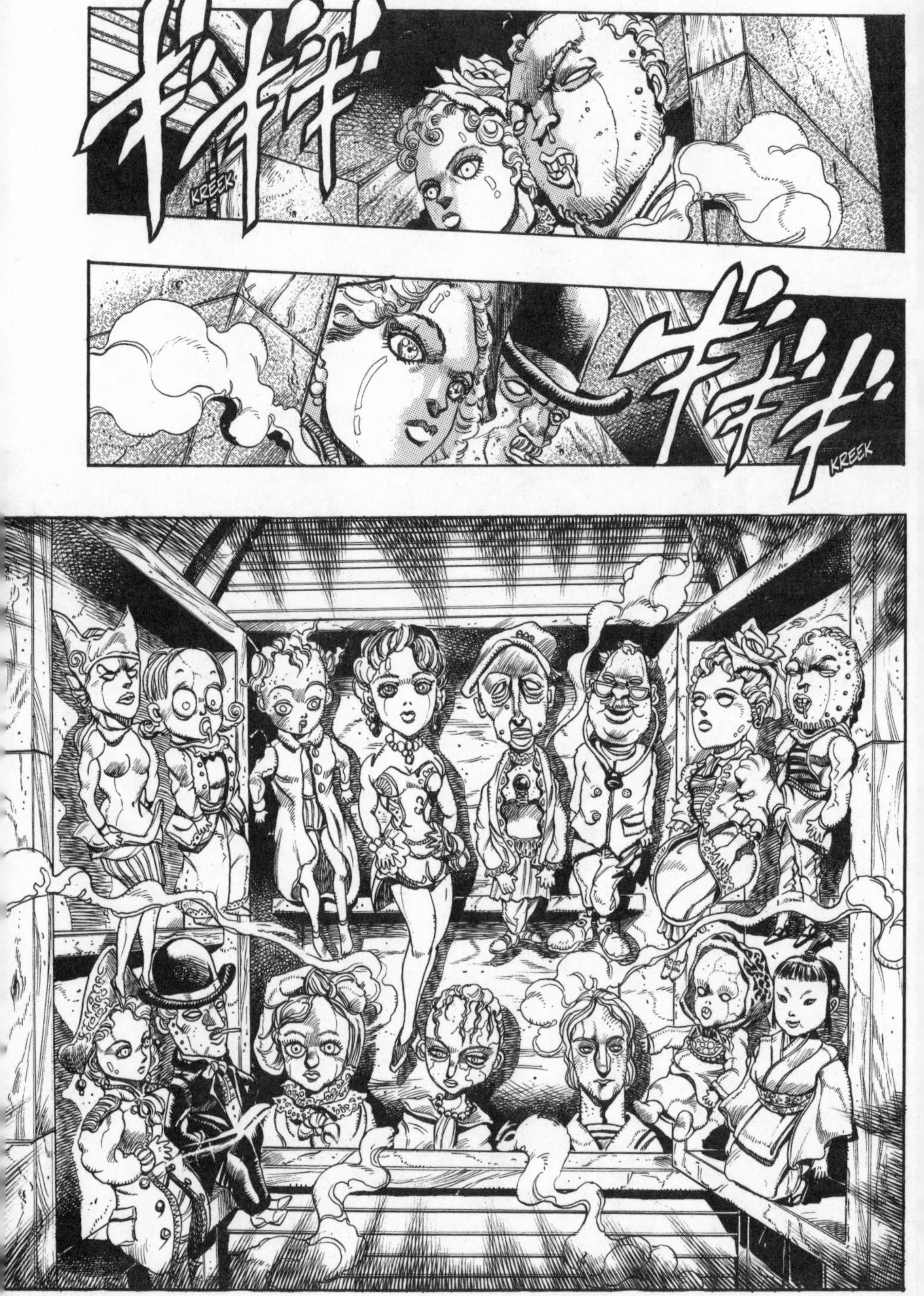
KREEK
KREEK

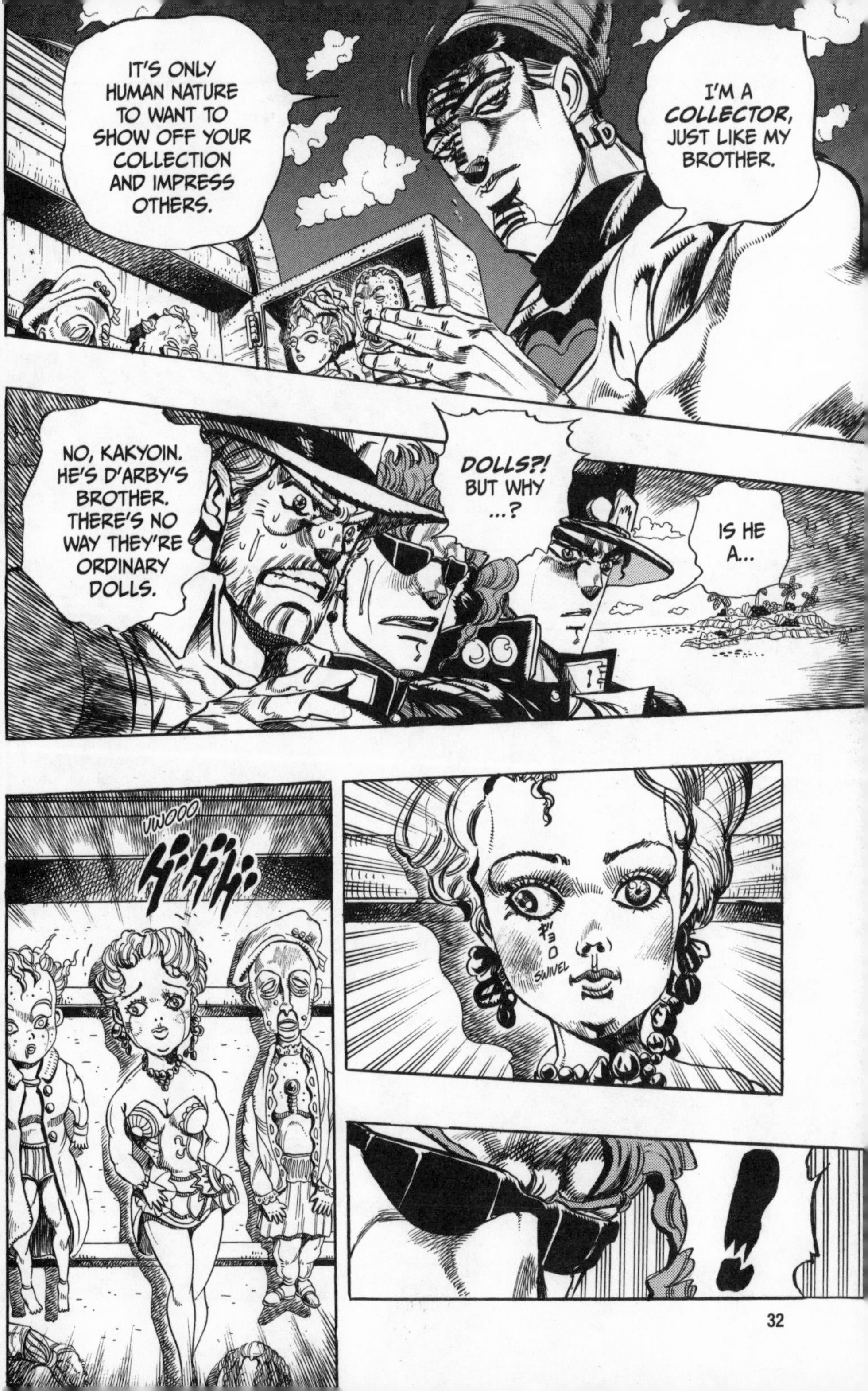
I'M A *COLLECTOR*, JUST LIKE MY BROTHER.
IT'S ONLY HUMAN NATURE TO WANT TO SHOW OFF YOUR COLLECTION AND IMPRESS OTHERS.
IS HE A...
DOLLS?! BUT WHY ...?
NO, KAKYOIN. HE'S D'ARBY'S BROTHER. THERE'S NO WAY THEY'RE ORDINARY DOLLS.
ギョロ
SWIVEL
!
UWOOO

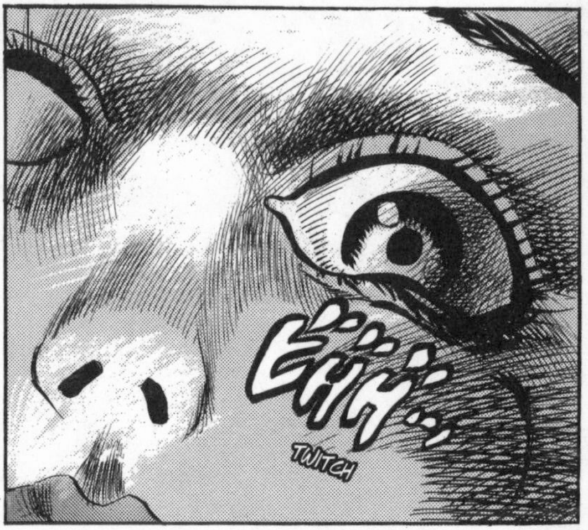
TWITCH
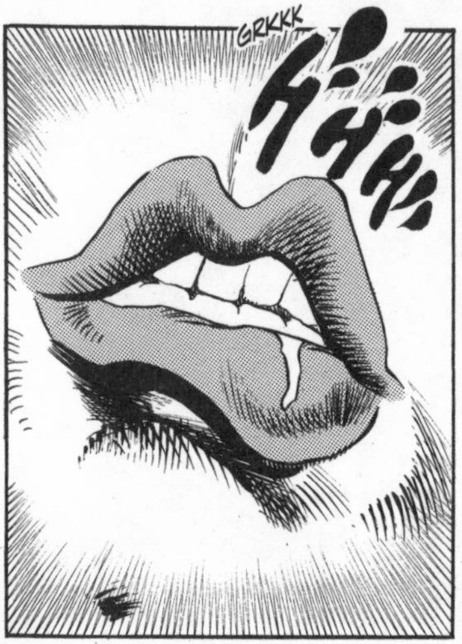
GRKKK
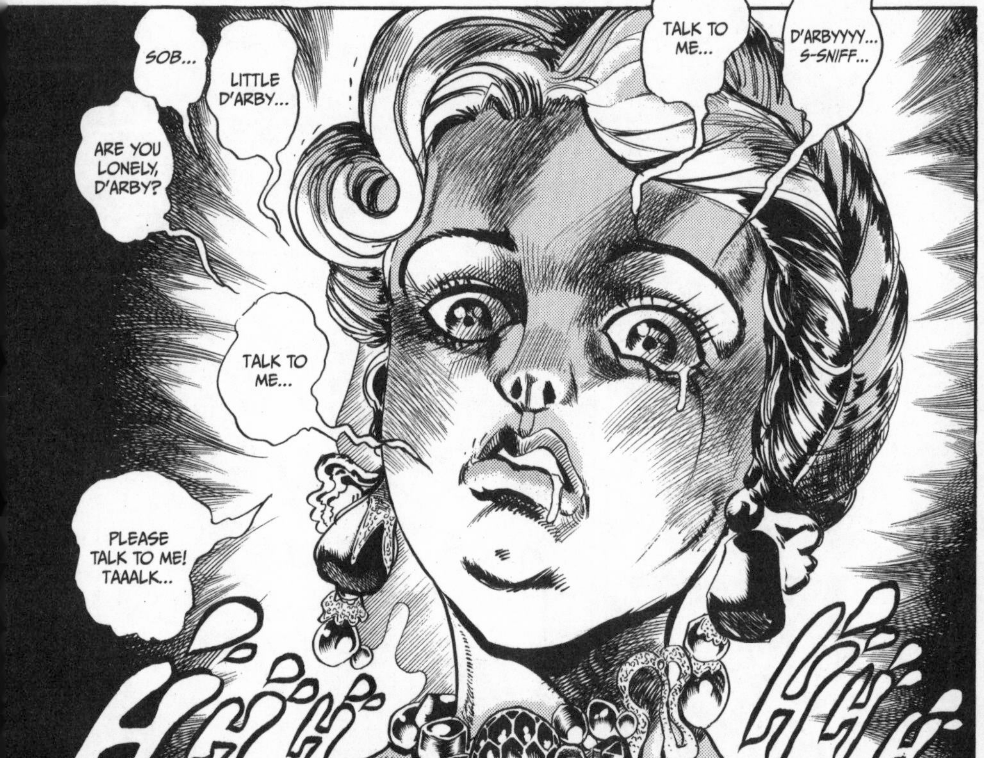
D'ARBYYYY... S-SNIFF...
TALK TO ME...
LITTLE D'ARBY...
SOB...
ARE YOU LONELY, D'ARBY?
TALK TO ME...
PLEASE TALK TO ME! TAAALK...
GRKKKKK

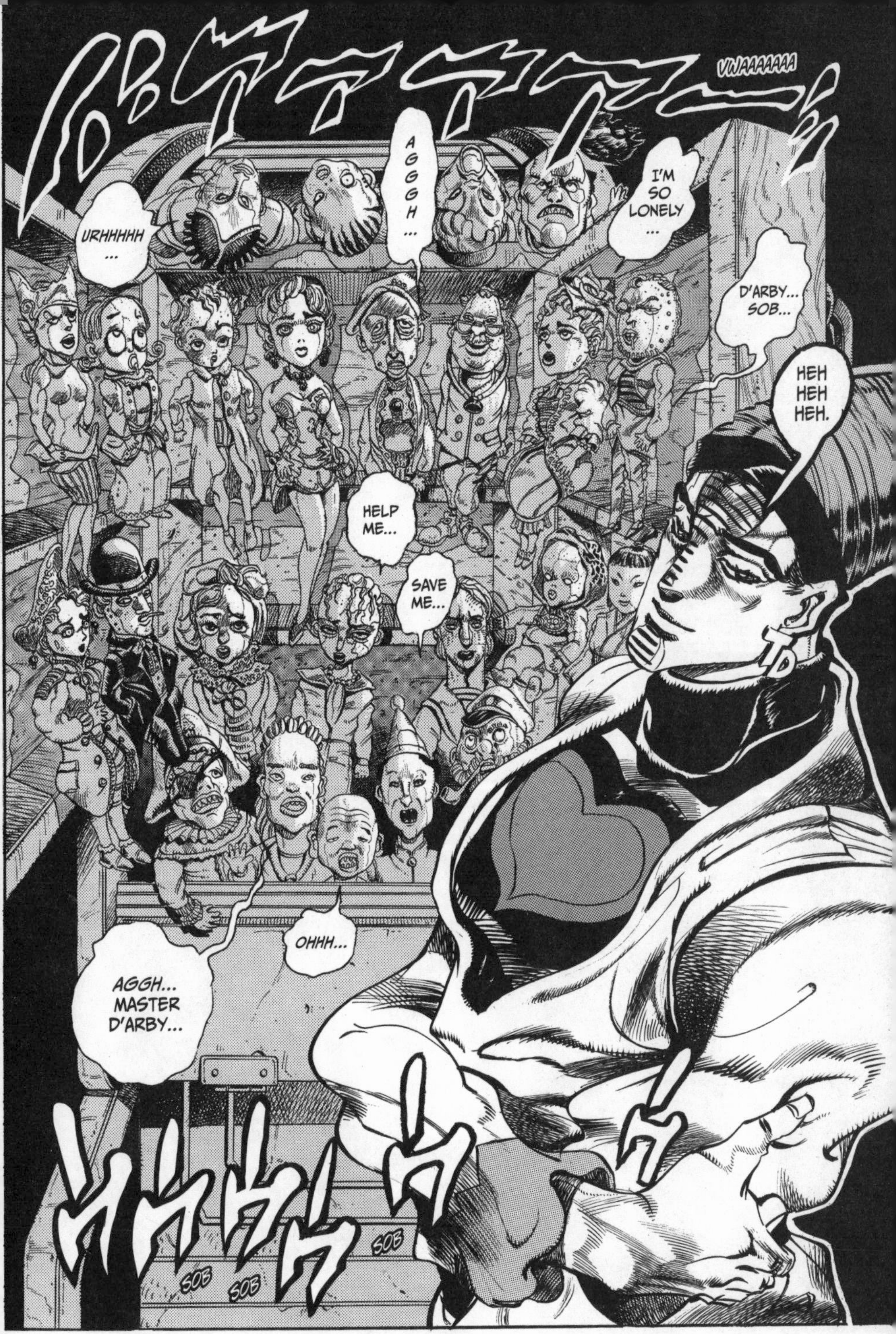
VWAAAAAAA
D'ARBY... SOB...
I'M SO LONELY...
AGGGH...
URHHHHH...
HEH HEH HEH.
HELP ME...
SAVE ME...
OHHH...
AGGH... MASTER D'ARBY...
SOB
SOB
SOB

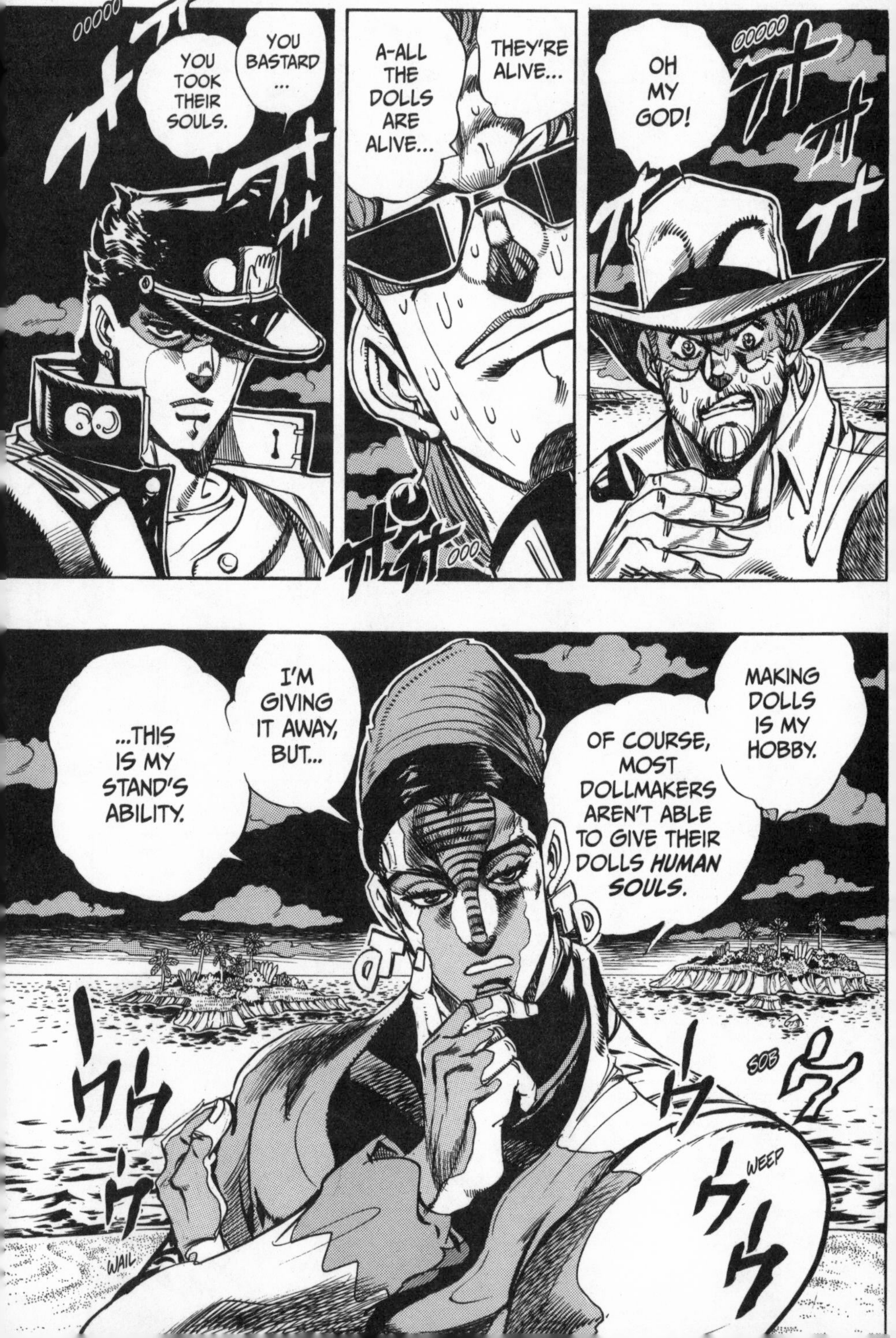
OOOOO
OH MY GOD!
THEY'RE ALIVE...
A-ALL THE DOLLS ARE ALIVE...
OOO
YOU BASTARD...
YOU TOOK THEIR SOULS.
OOOOO
MAKING DOLLS IS MY HOBBY.
OF COURSE, MOST DOLLMAKERS AREN'T ABLE TO GIVE THEIR DOLLS *HUMAN SOULS*.
I'M GIVING IT AWAY, BUT...
...THIS IS MY STAND'S ABILITY.
SOB
WEEP
WAIL

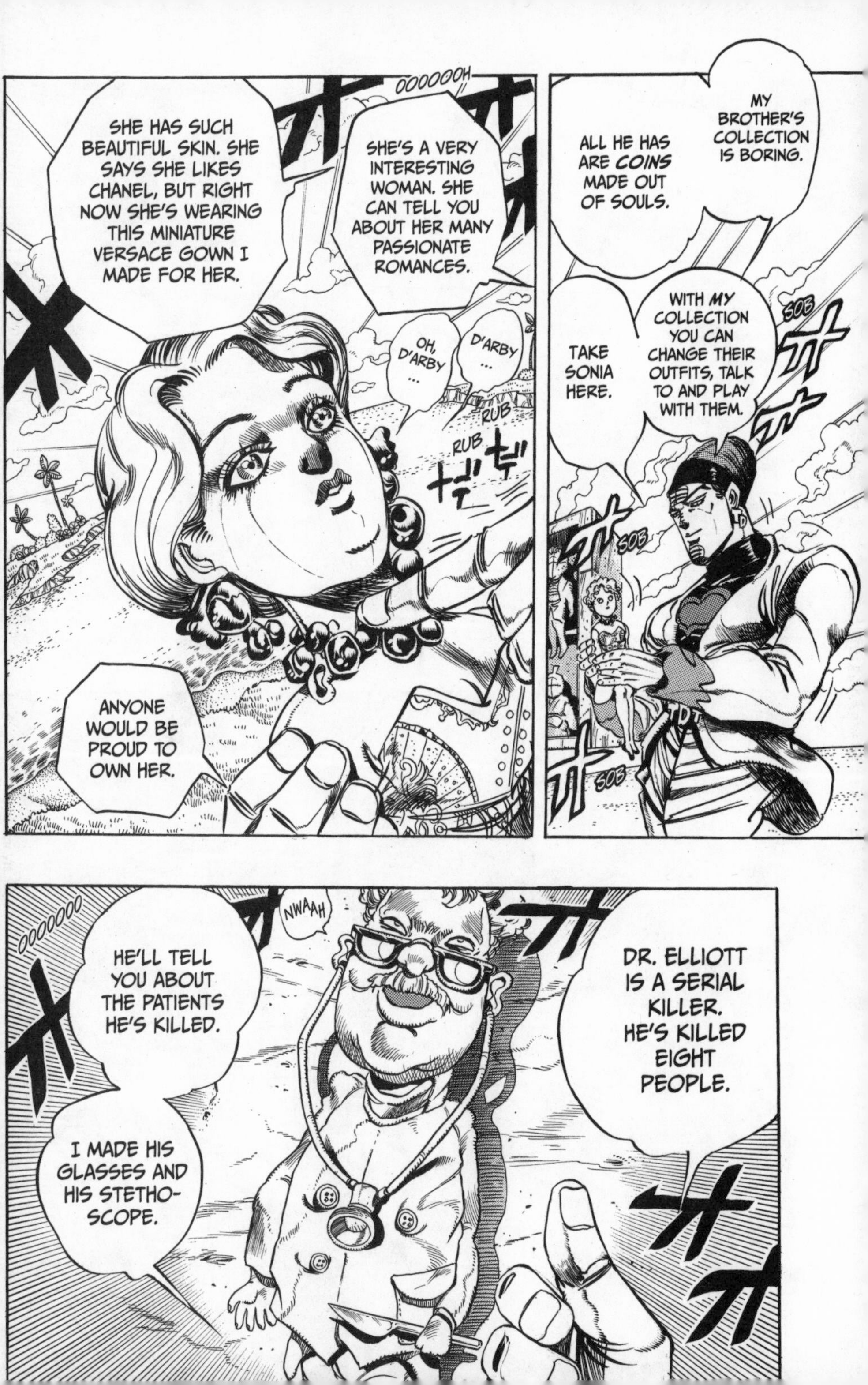
MY BROTHER'S COLLECTION IS BORING.
ALL HE HAS ARE *COINS* MADE OUT OF SOULS.
WITH *MY* COLLECTION YOU CAN CHANGE THEIR OUTFITS, TALK TO AND PLAY WITH THEM.
SOB
TAKE SONIA HERE.
SOB
SOB
OOOOOOOH
SHE'S A VERY INTERESTING WOMAN. SHE CAN TELL YOU ABOUT HER MANY PASSIONATE ROMANCES.
SHE HAS SUCH BEAUTIFUL SKIN. SHE SAYS SHE LIKES CHANEL, BUT RIGHT NOW SHE'S WEARING THIS MINIATURE VERSACE GOWN I MADE FOR HER.
D'ARBY ...
OH, D'ARBY ...
RUB
RUB
ANYONE WOULD BE PROUD TO OWN HER.
NWAAAH
DR. ELLIOTT IS A SERIAL KILLER. HE'S KILLED EIGHT PEOPLE.
OOOOOOO
HE'LL TELL YOU ABOUT THE PATIENTS HE'S KILLED.
I MADE HIS GLASSES AND HIS STETHO-SCOPE.

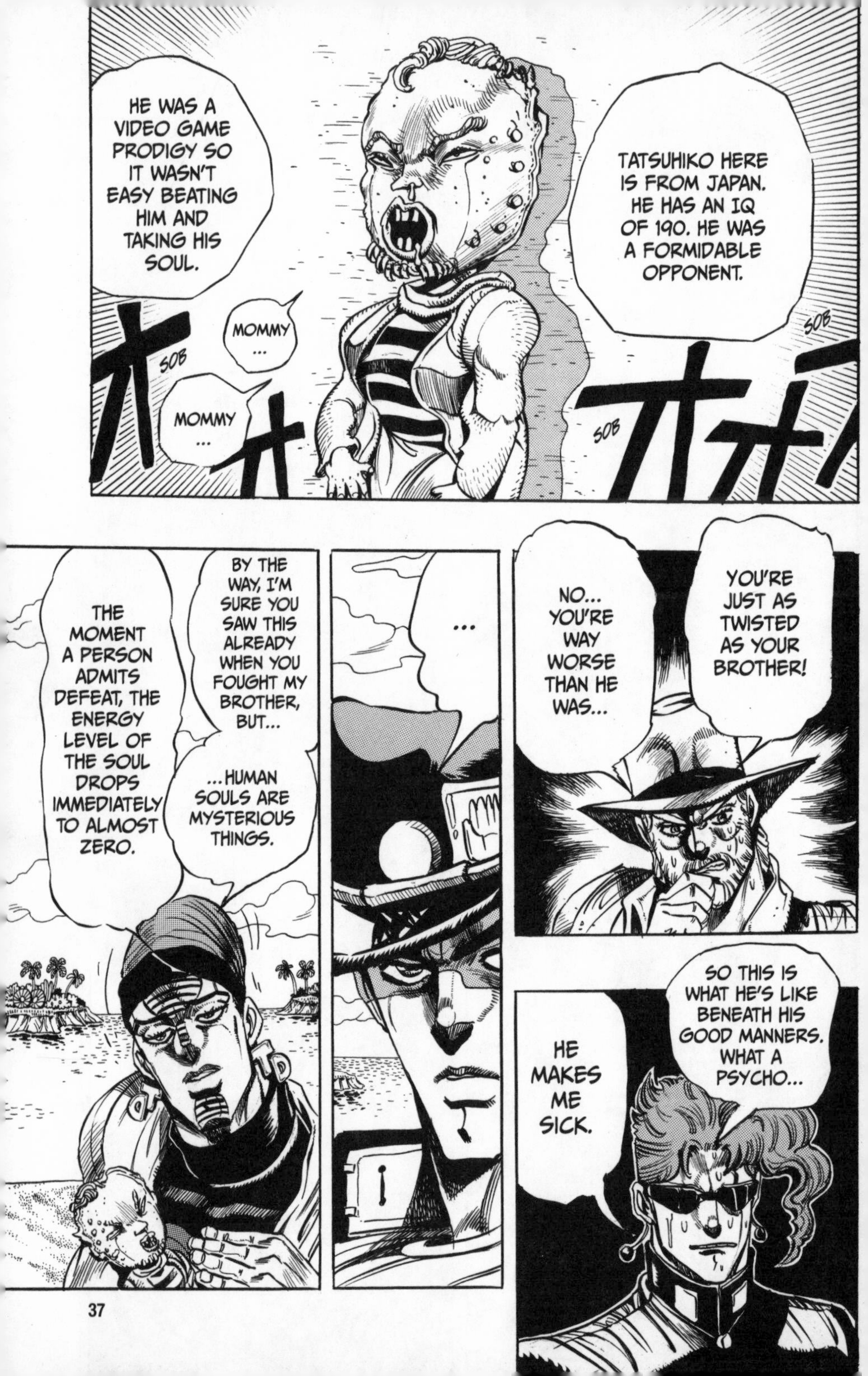
TATSUHIKO HERE IS FROM JAPAN. HE HAS AN IQ OF 190. HE WAS A FORMIDABLE OPPONENT.
HE WAS A VIDEO GAME PRODIGY SO IT WASN'T EASY BEATING HIM AND TAKING HIS SOUL.
SOB
SOB
MOMMY ...
SOB
MOMMY ...
YOU'RE JUST AS TWISTED AS YOUR BROTHER!
NO... YOU'RE WAY WORSE THAN HE WAS...
SO THIS IS WHAT HE'S LIKE BENEATH HIS GOOD MANNERS. WHAT A PSYCHO...
HE MAKES ME SICK.
...
BY THE WAY, I'M SURE YOU SAW THIS ALREADY WHEN YOU FOUGHT MY BROTHER, BUT...
...HUMAN SOULS ARE MYSTERIOUS THINGS.
THE MOMENT A PERSON ADMITS DEFEAT, THE ENERGY LEVEL OF THE SOUL DROPS IMMEDIATELY TO ALMOST ZERO.

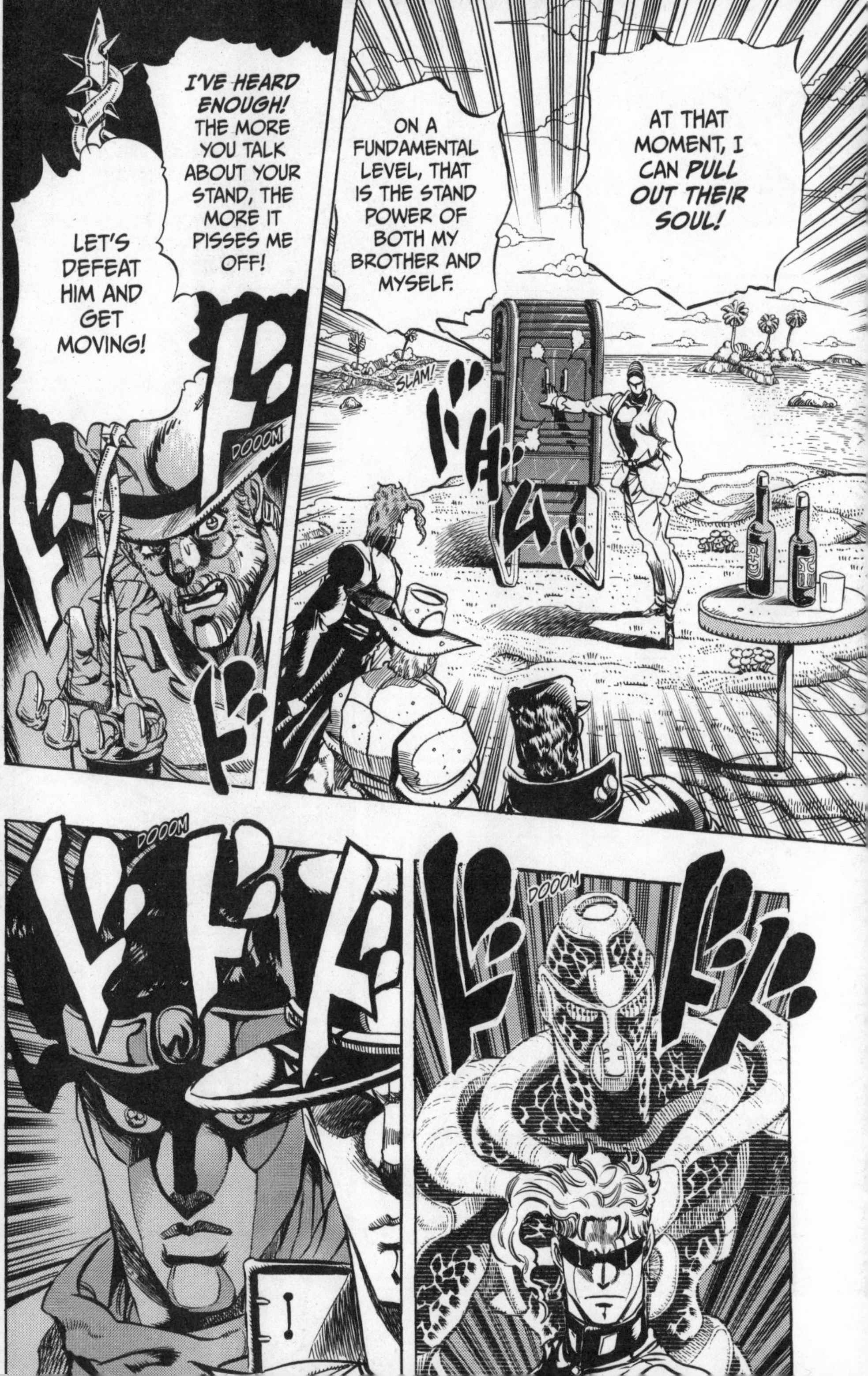

AT THAT MOMENT, I CAN PULL OUT THEIR SOUL!
ON A FUNDAMENTAL LEVEL, THAT IS THE STAND POWER OF BOTH MY BROTHER AND MYSELF.
SLAM!
I'VE HEARD ENOUGH! THE MORE YOU TALK ABOUT YOUR STAND, THE MORE IT PISSES ME OFF!
LET'S DEFEAT HIM AND GET MOVING!
DOOOM
DOOOM
DOOOM

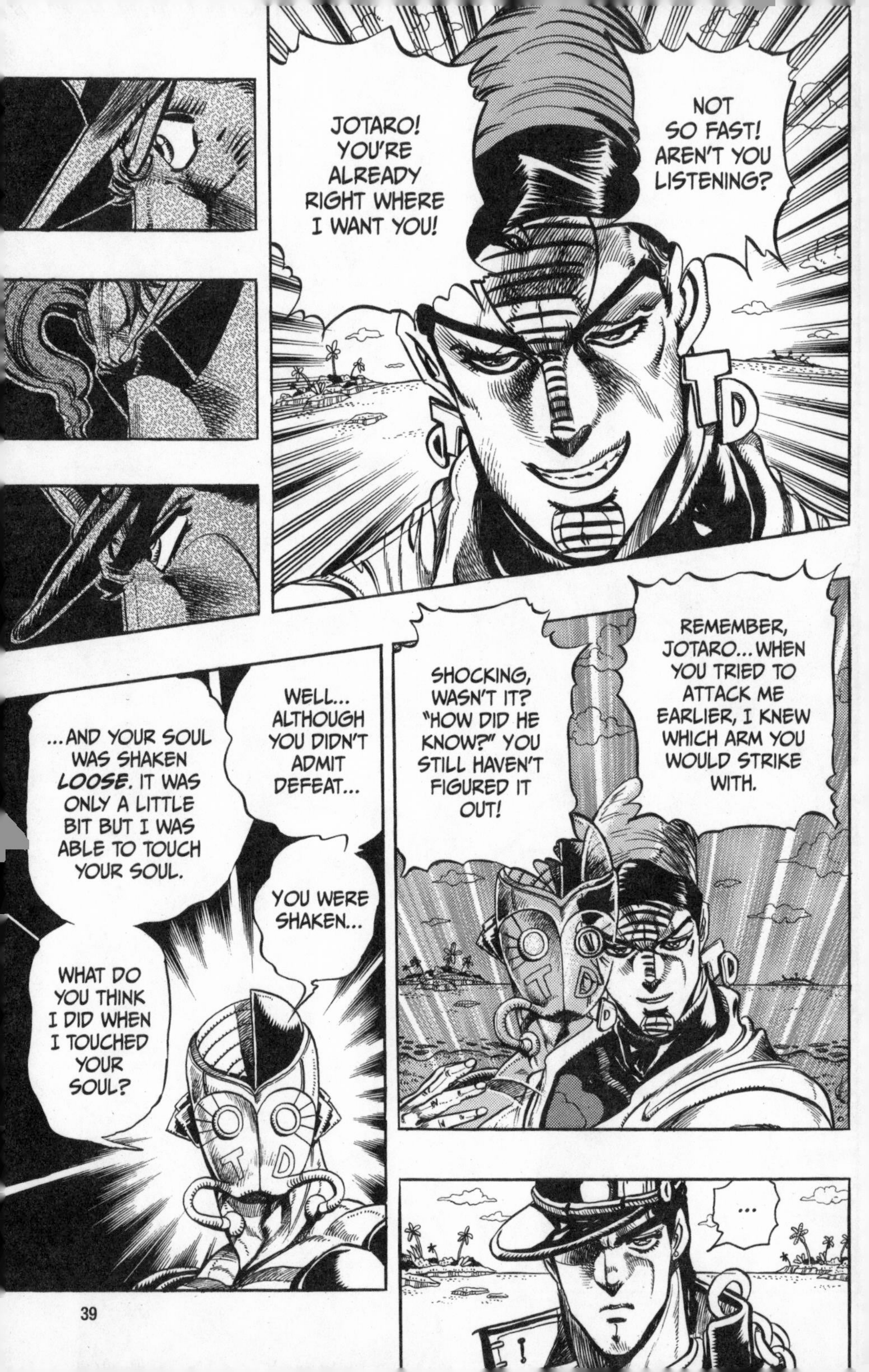
NOT SO FAST! AREN'T YOU LISTENING?
JOTARO! YOU'RE ALREADY RIGHT WHERE I WANT YOU!
REMEMBER, JOTARO...WHEN YOU TRIED TO ATTACK ME EARLIER, I KNEW WHICH ARM YOU WOULD STRIKE WITH.
SHOCKING, WASN'T IT? "HOW DID HE KNOW?" YOU STILL HAVEN'T FIGURED IT OUT!
...
WELL... ALTHOUGH YOU DIDN'T ADMIT DEFEAT...
YOU WERE SHAKEN...
...AND YOUR SOUL WAS SHAKEN *LOOSE*. IT WAS ONLY A LITTLE BIT BUT I WAS ABLE TO TOUCH YOUR SOUL.
WHAT DO YOU THINK I DID WHEN I TOUCHED YOUR SOUL?

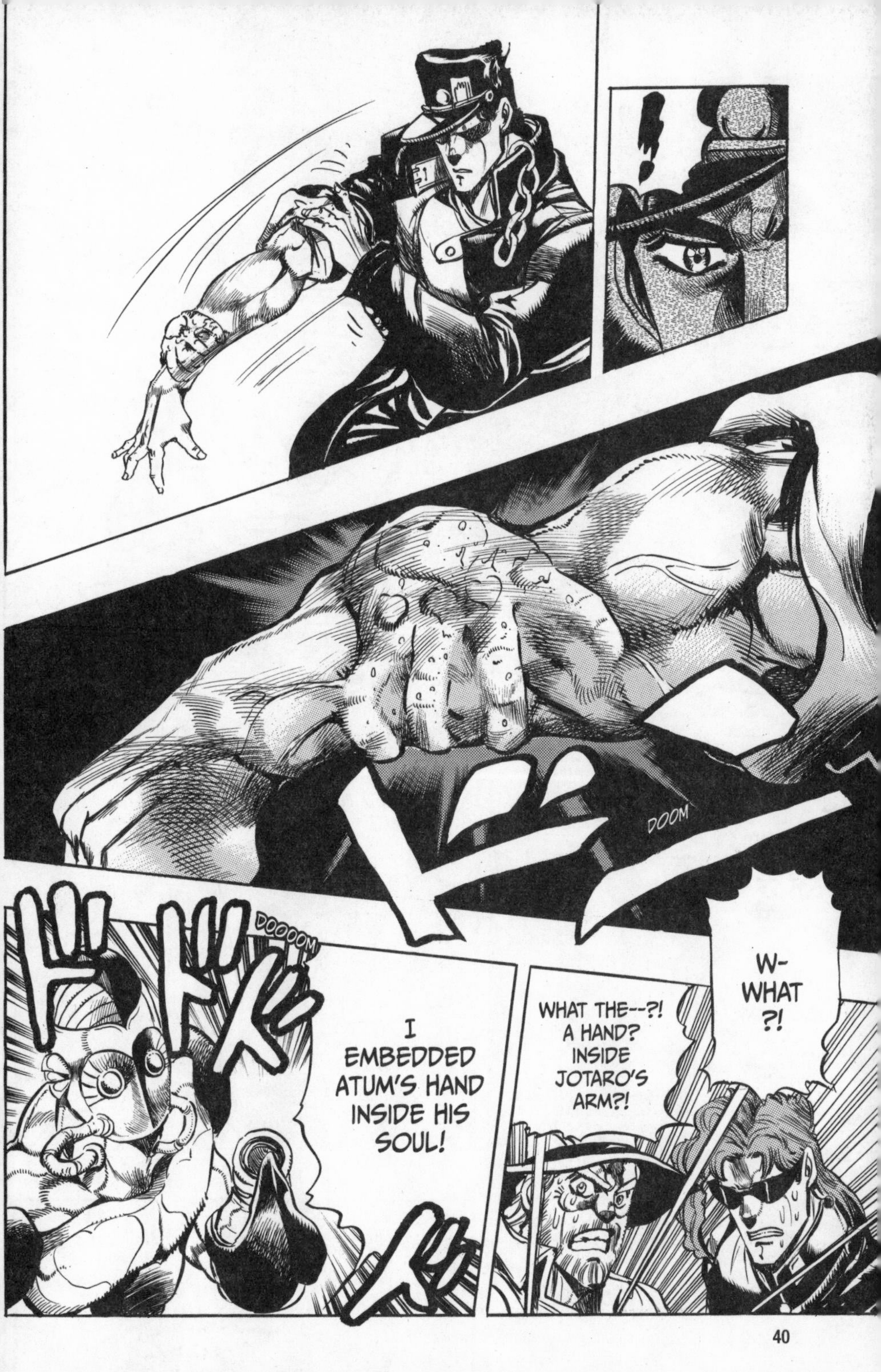
DOOM
W-WHAT?!
WHAT THE--?! A HAND? INSIDE JOTARO'S ARM?!
I EMBEDDED ATUM'S HAND INSIDE HIS SOUL!
DOOOOM
ドドド

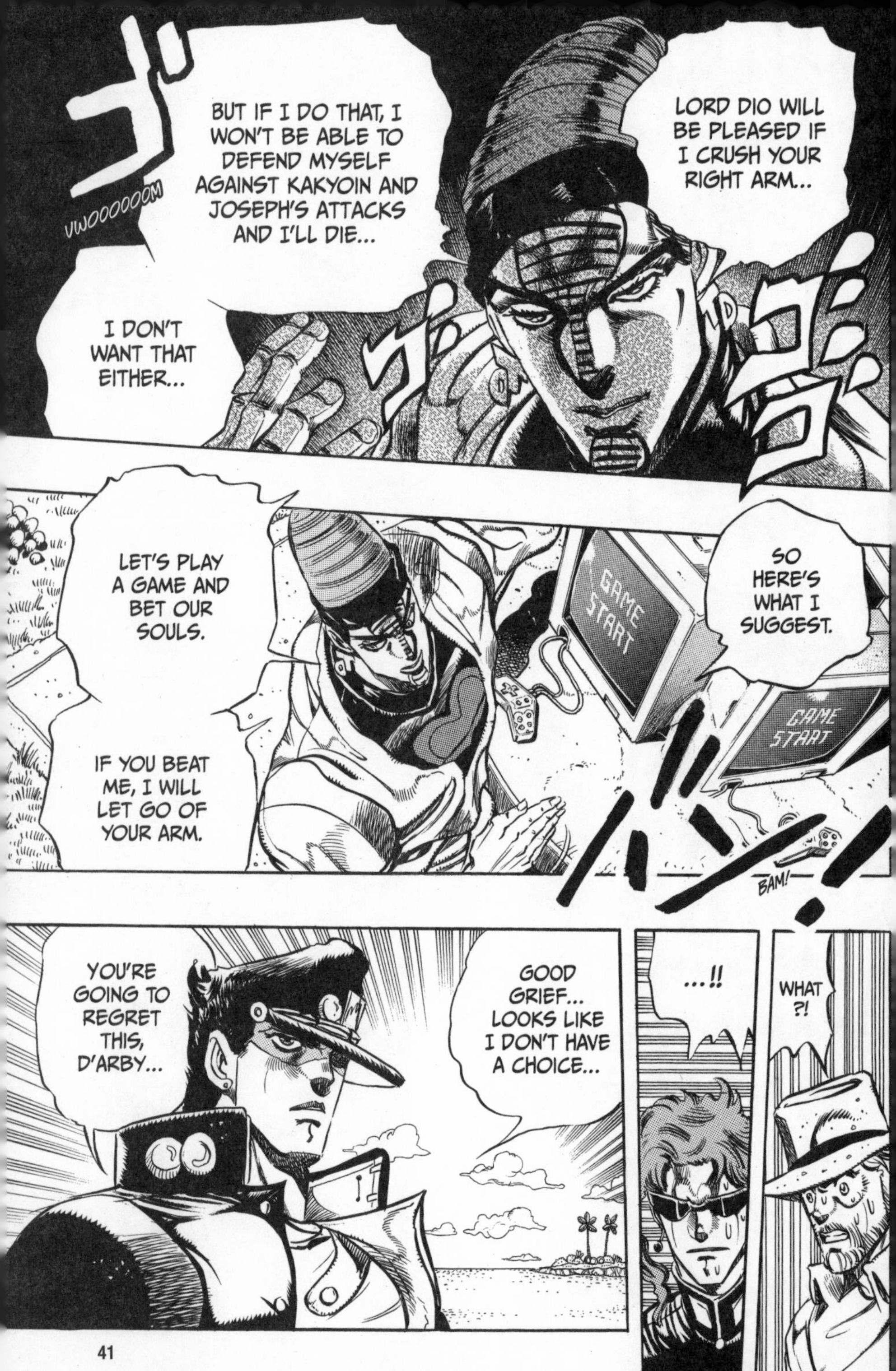
LORD DIO WILL BE PLEASED IF I CRUSH YOUR RIGHT ARM...
BUT IF I DO THAT, I WON'T BE ABLE TO DEFEND MYSELF AGAINST KAKYOIN AND JOSEPH'S ATTACKS AND I'LL DIE...
VWOOOOOOM
I DON'T WANT THAT EITHER...
SO HERE'S WHAT I SUGGEST.
GAME START
GAME START
LET'S PLAY A GAME AND BET OUR SOULS.
IF YOU BEAT ME, I WILL LET GO OF YOUR ARM.
BAM!
WHAT ?!
...!!
GOOD GRIEF... LOOKS LIKE I DON'T HAVE A CHOICE...
YOU'RE GOING TO REGRET THIS, D'ARBY...

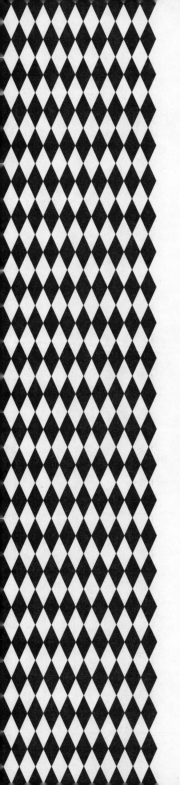
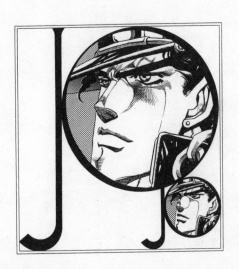

CHAPTER 117: D'Arby the Player PART 4

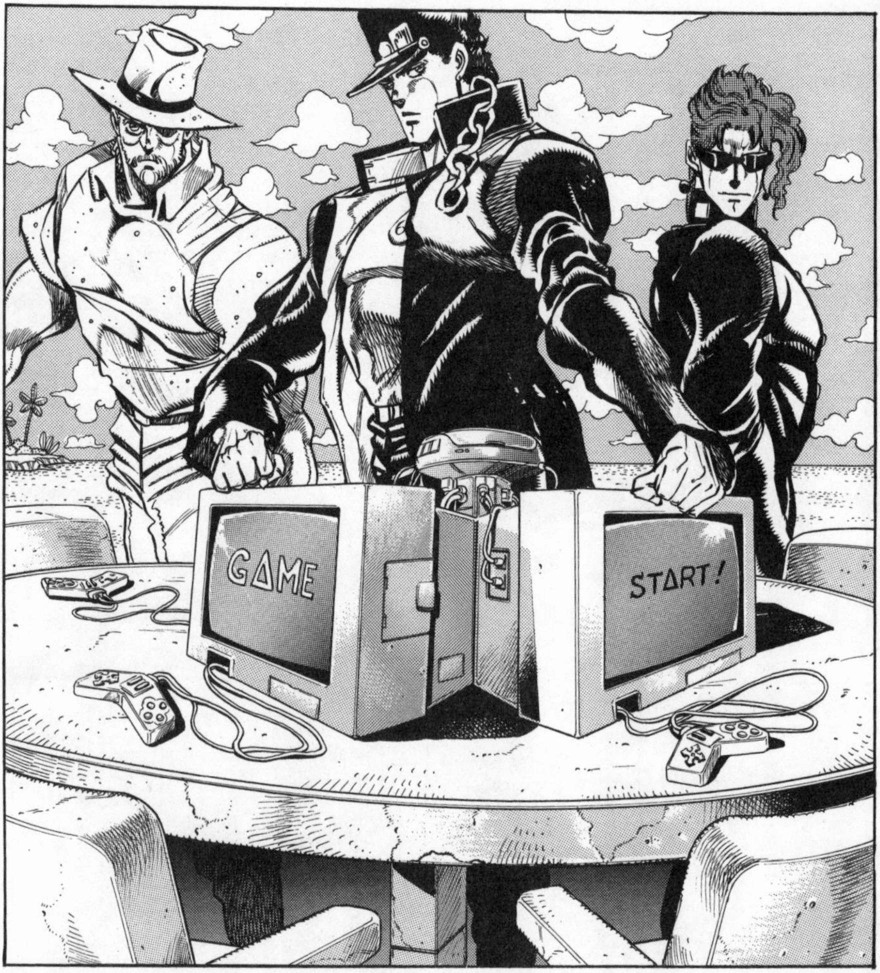
GAME
START!

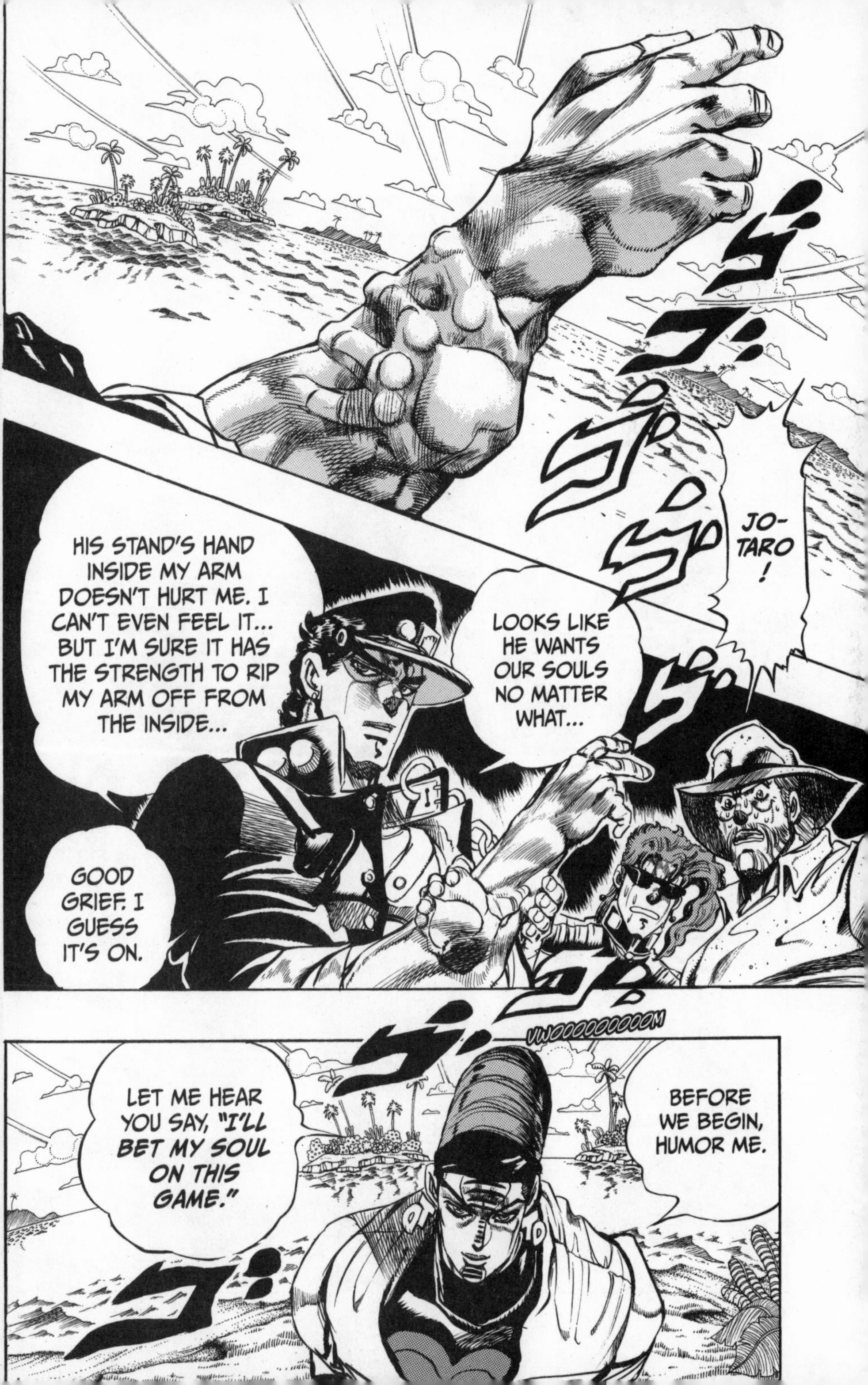
JO-TARO!
LOOKS LIKE HE WANTS OUR SOULS NO MATTER WHAT...
HIS STAND'S HAND INSIDE MY ARM DOESN'T HURT ME. I CAN'T EVEN FEEL IT... BUT I'M SURE IT HAS THE STRENGTH TO RIP MY ARM OFF FROM THE INSIDE...
GOOD GRIEF. I GUESS IT'S ON.
VWOOOOOOOOOOM
BEFORE WE BEGIN, HUMOR ME.
LET ME HEAR YOU SAY, "I'LL BET MY SOUL ON THIS GAME."

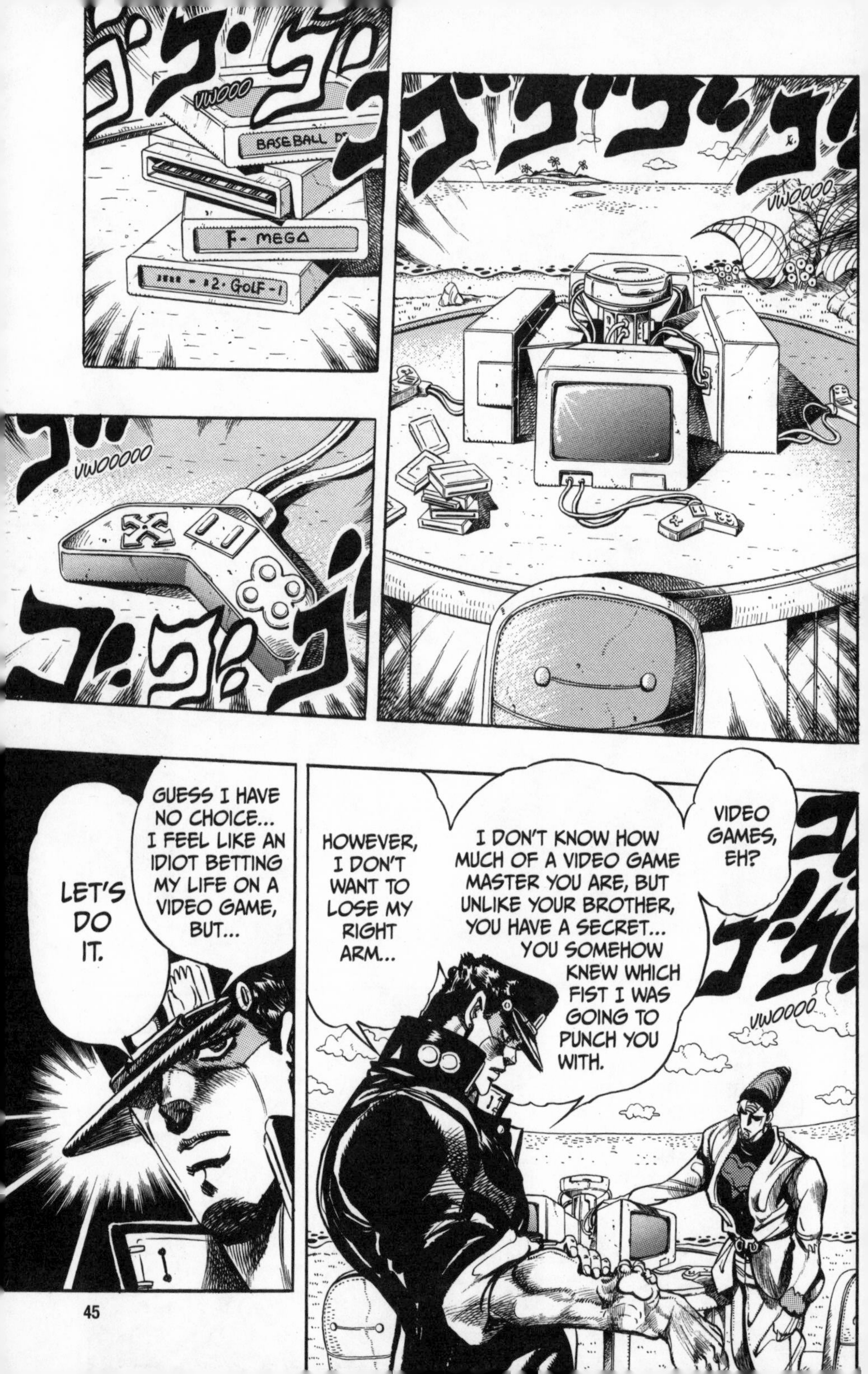
VWOOOO
VWOOO
BASEBALL
VWOOOOO
VIDEO GAMES, EH?
I DON'T KNOW HOW MUCH OF A VIDEO GAME MASTER YOU ARE, BUT UNLIKE YOUR BROTHER, YOU HAVE A SECRET... YOU SOMEHOW KNEW WHICH FIST I WAS GOING TO PUNCH YOU WITH.
HOWEVER, I DON'T WANT TO LOSE MY RIGHT ARM...
VWOOOO
GUESS I HAVE NO CHOICE... I FEEL LIKE AN IDIOT BETTING MY LIFE ON A VIDEO GAME, BUT...
LET'S DO IT.

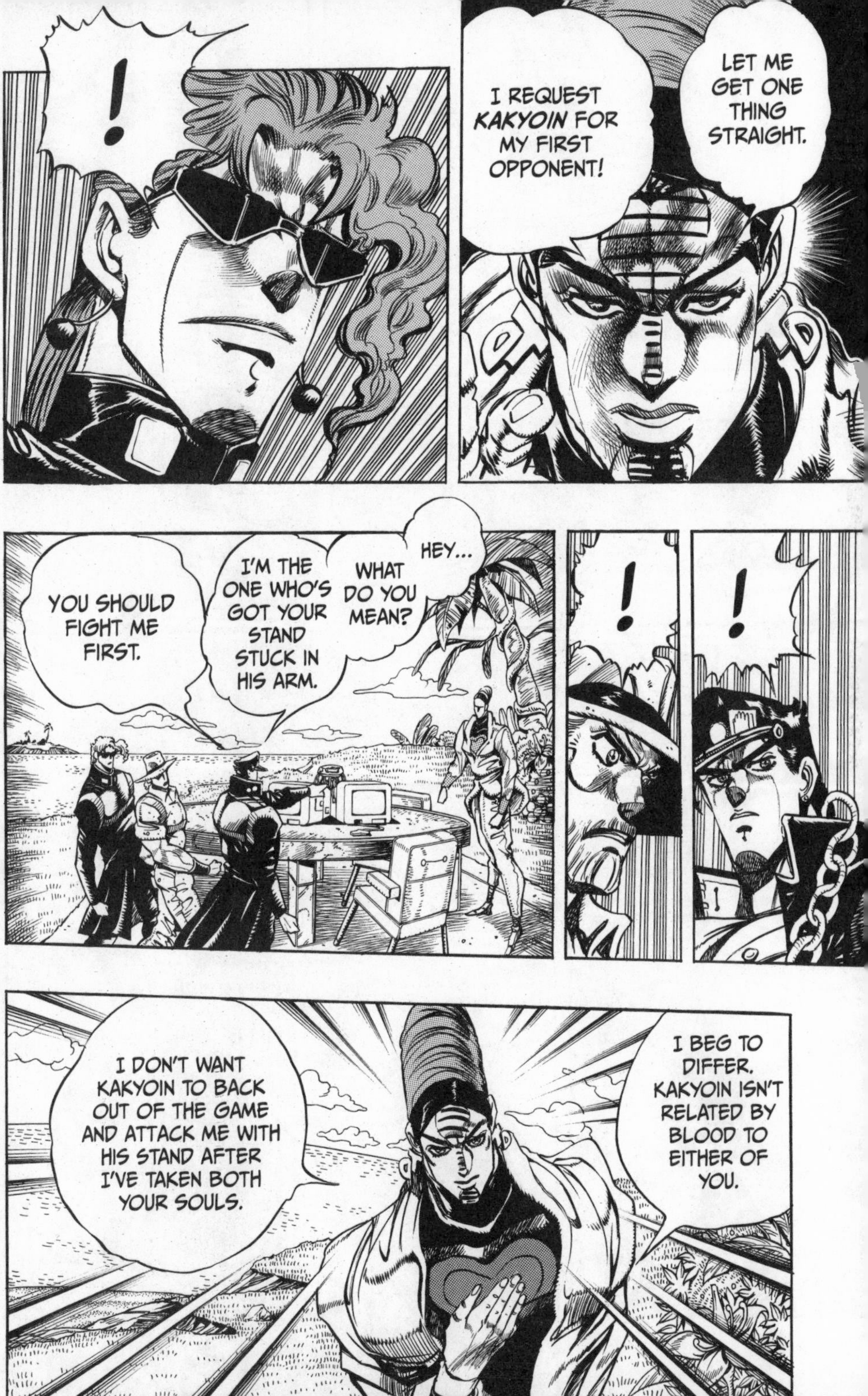
LET ME GET ONE THING STRAIGHT.
I REQUEST KAKYOIN FOR MY FIRST OPPONENT!
!
!
!
HEY...
WHAT DO YOU MEAN?
I'M THE ONE WHO'S GOT YOUR STAND STUCK IN HIS ARM.
YOU SHOULD FIGHT ME FIRST.
I BEG TO DIFFER. KAKYOIN ISN'T RELATED BY BLOOD TO EITHER OF YOU.
I DON'T WANT KAKYOIN TO BACK OUT OF THE GAME AND ATTACK ME WITH HIS STAND AFTER I'VE TAKEN BOTH YOUR SOULS.

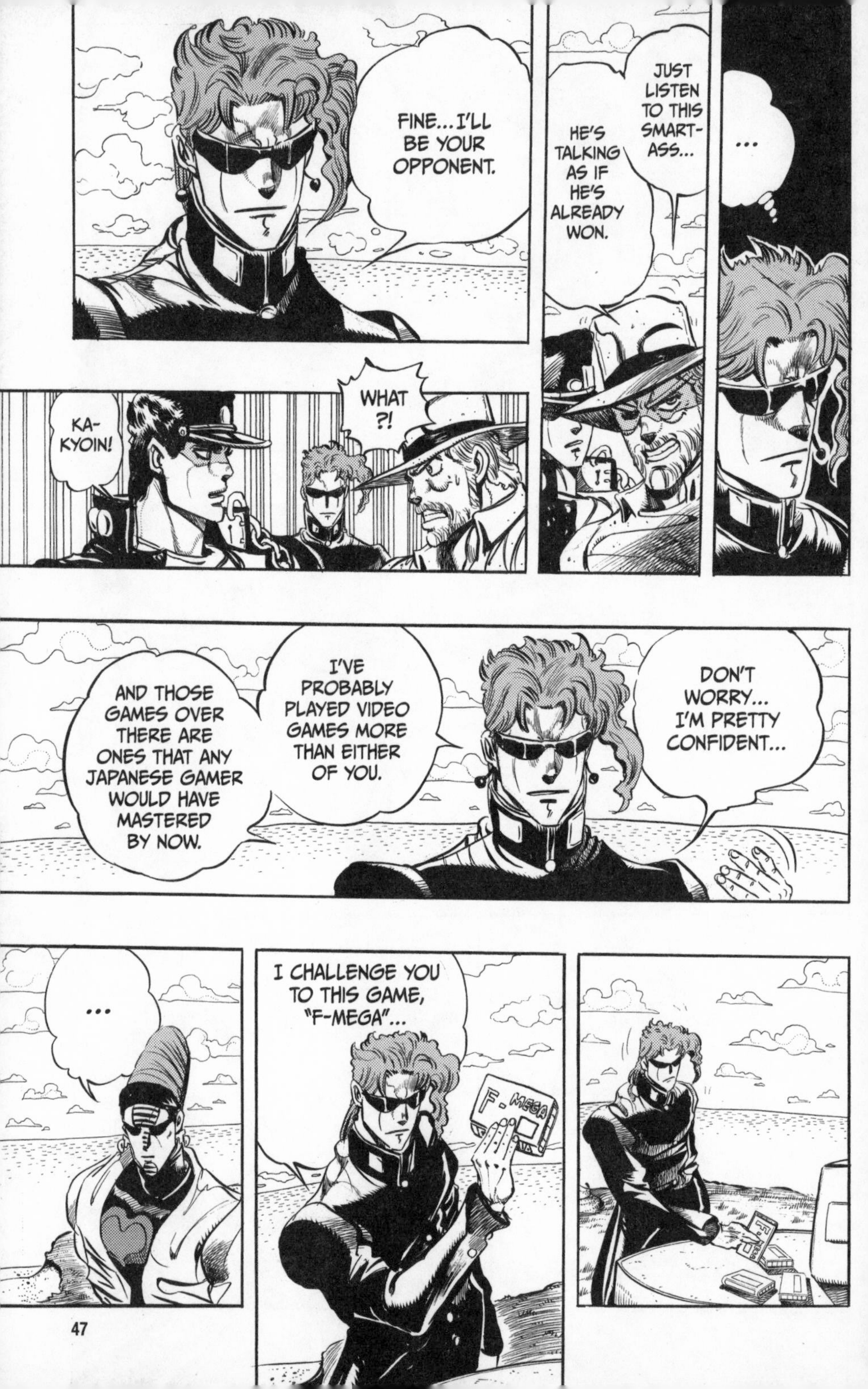
...
JUST LISTEN TO THIS SMART-ASS...
HE'S TALKING AS IF HE'S ALREADY WON.
FINE... I'LL BE YOUR OPPONENT.
WHAT ?!
KA-KYOIN!
DON'T WORRY... I'M PRETTY CONFIDENT...
I'VE PROBABLY PLAYED VIDEO GAMES MORE THAN EITHER OF YOU.
AND THOSE GAMES OVER THERE ARE ONES THAT ANY JAPANESE GAMER WOULD HAVE MASTERED BY NOW.
I CHALLENGE YOU TO THIS GAME, "F-MEGA"...
F-MEGA
...

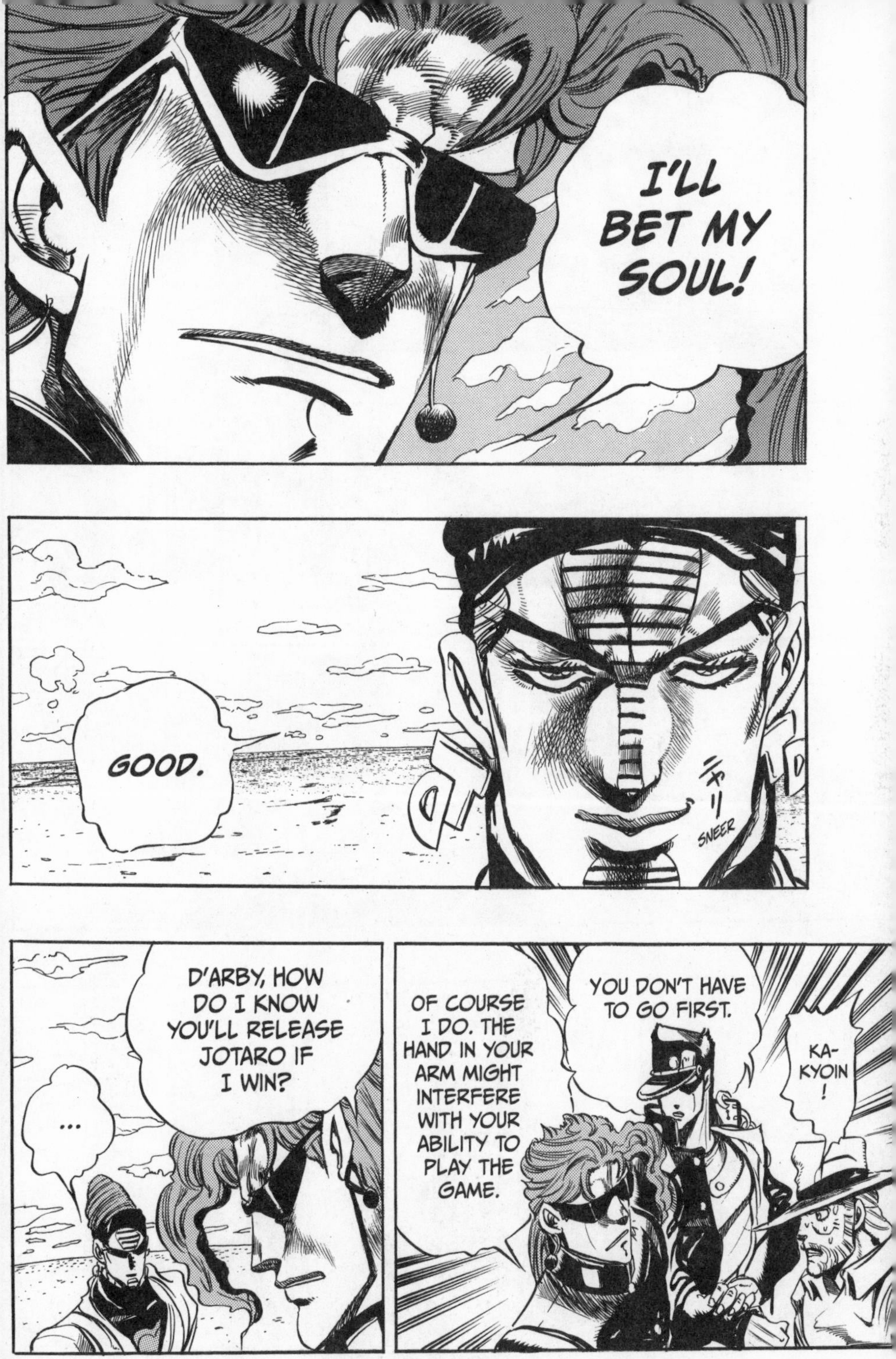
I'LL BET MY SOUL!
GOOD.
ニヤリ
SNEER
KA-KYOIN!
YOU DON'T HAVE TO GO FIRST.
OF COURSE I DO. THE HAND IN YOUR ARM MIGHT INTERFERE WITH YOUR ABILITY TO PLAY THE GAME.
D'ARBY, HOW DO I KNOW YOU'LL RELEASE JOTARO IF I WIN?
...

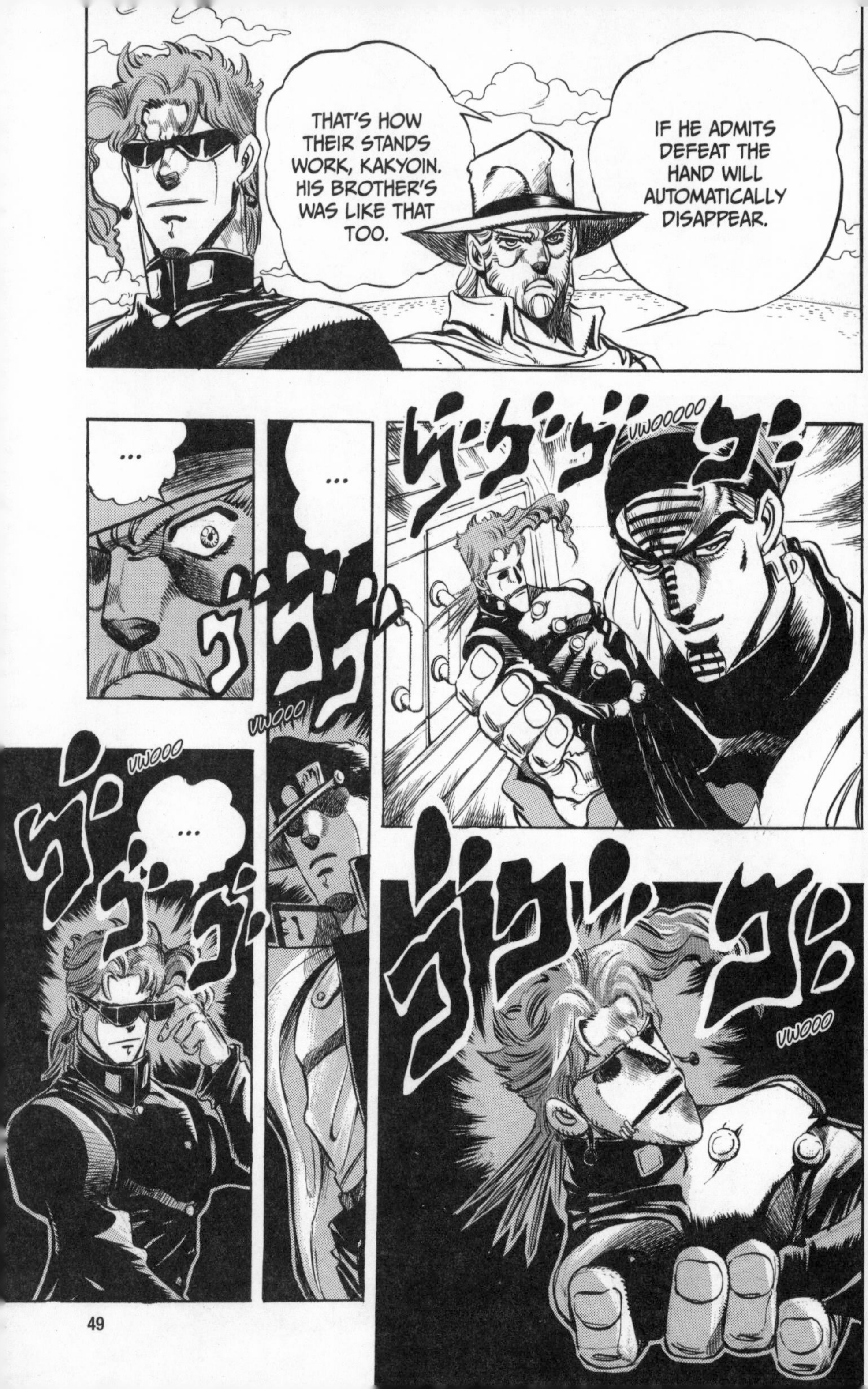
IF HE ADMITS DEFEAT THE HAND WILL AUTOMATICALLY DISAPPEAR.
THAT'S HOW THEIR STANDS WORK, KAKYOIN. HIS BROTHER'S WAS LIKE THAT TOO.
VWOOOOO
...
...
VWOOO
VWOOO
VWOOO
...

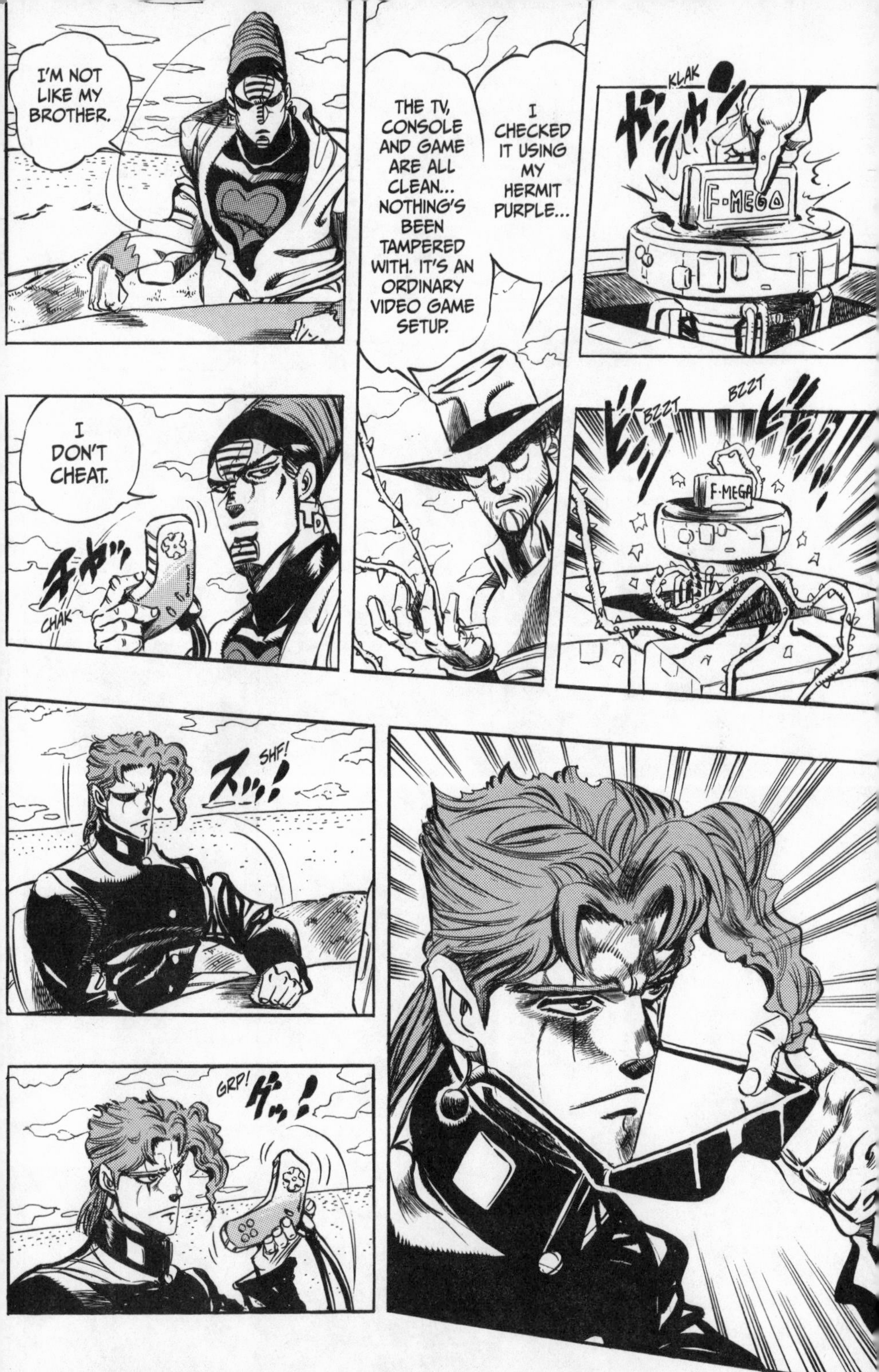
KLAK
BZZT
BZZT
I CHECKED IT USING MY HERMIT PURPLE...
THE TV, CONSOLE AND GAME ARE ALL CLEAN... NOTHING'S BEEN TAMPERED WITH. IT'S AN ORDINARY VIDEO GAME SETUP.
I'M NOT LIKE MY BROTHER.
I DON'T CHEAT.
CHAK
SHF!
GRP!

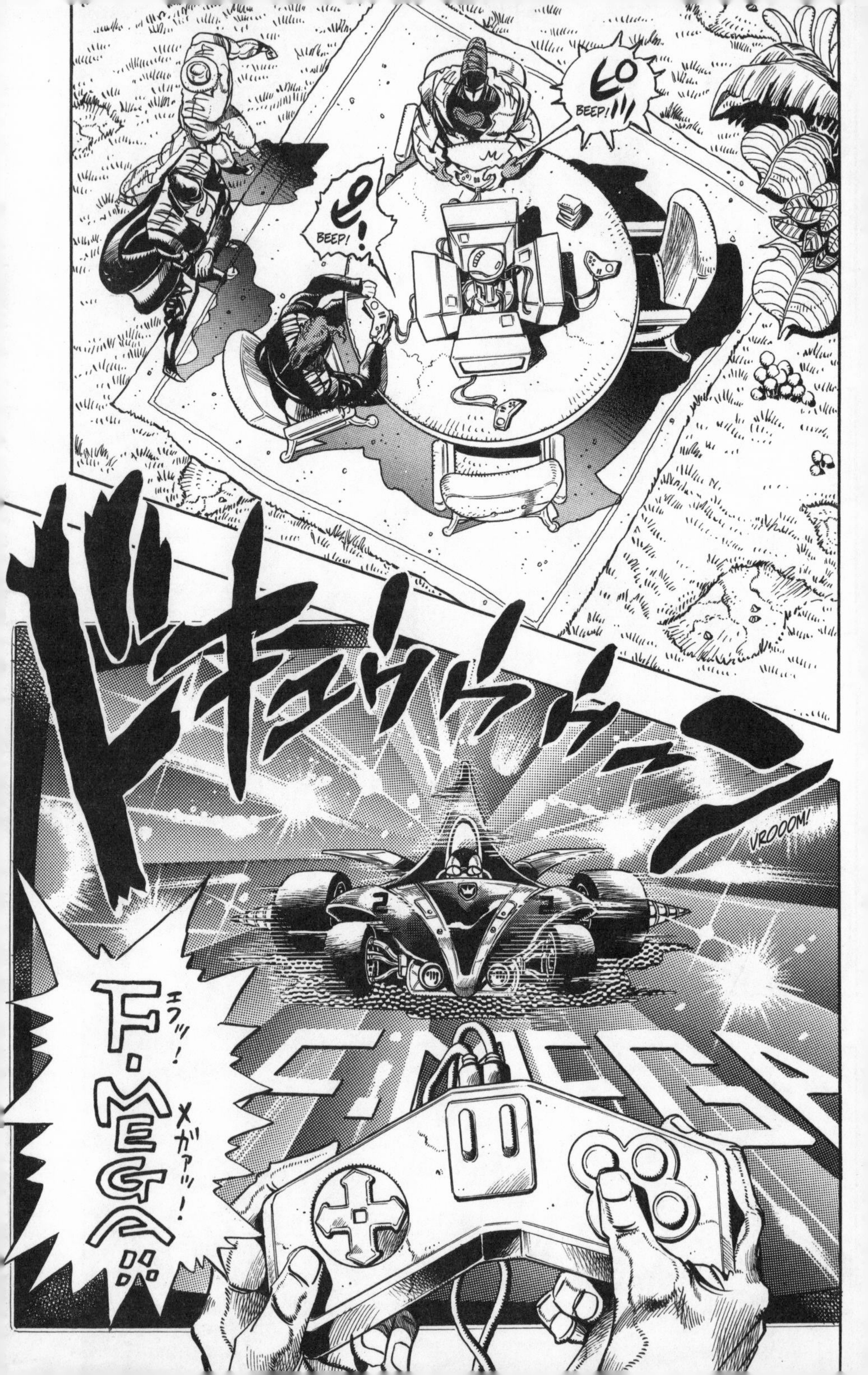
BEEP!
BEEP!
VROOOM!
F. MEGA

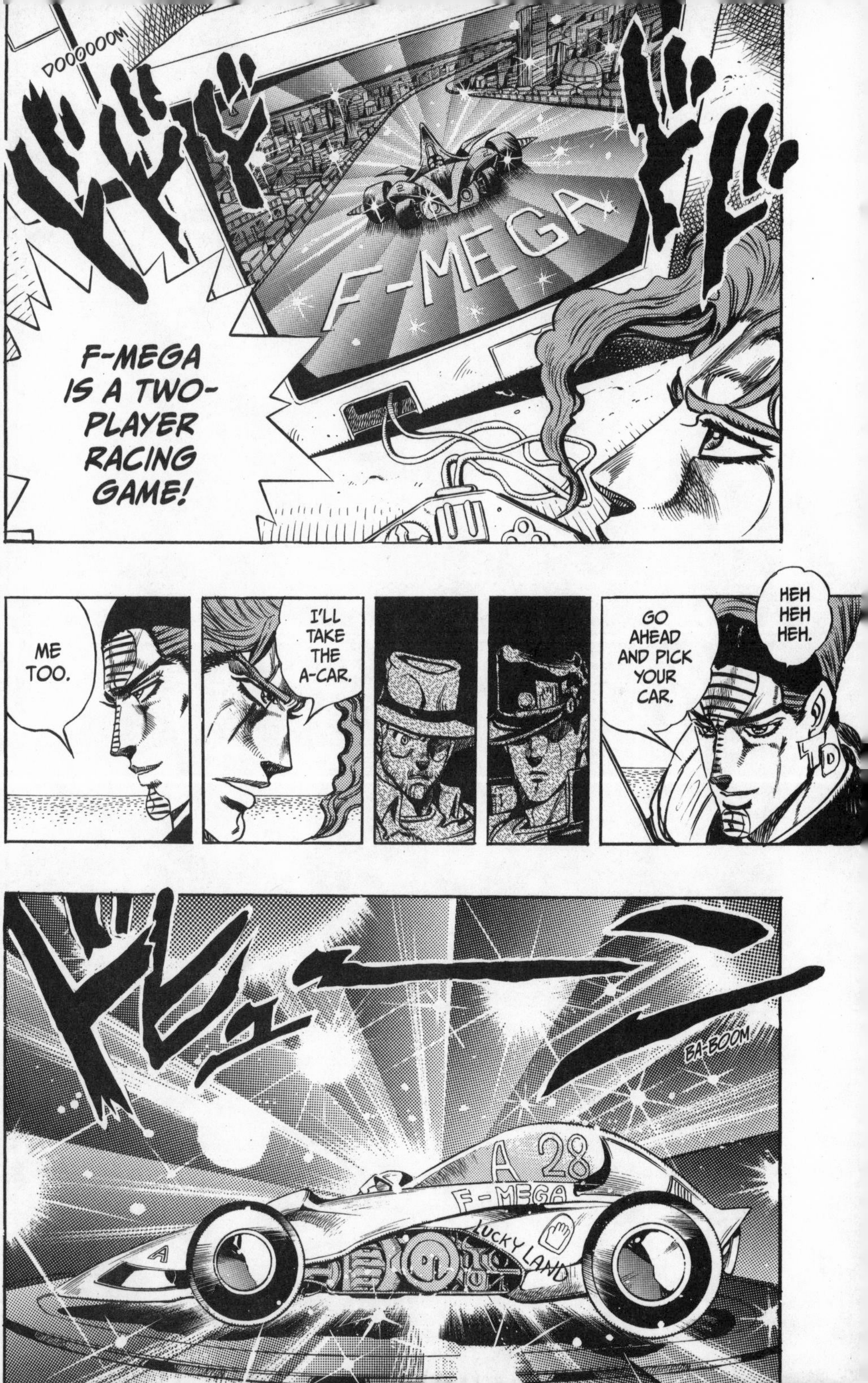
DOOOOOOM
F-MEGA
F-MEGA IS A TWO-PLAYER RACING GAME!
HEH HEH HEH.
GO AHEAD AND PICK YOUR CAR.
I'LL TAKE THE A-CAR.
ME TOO.
BA-BOOM
A 28
F-MEGA
LUCKY LAND

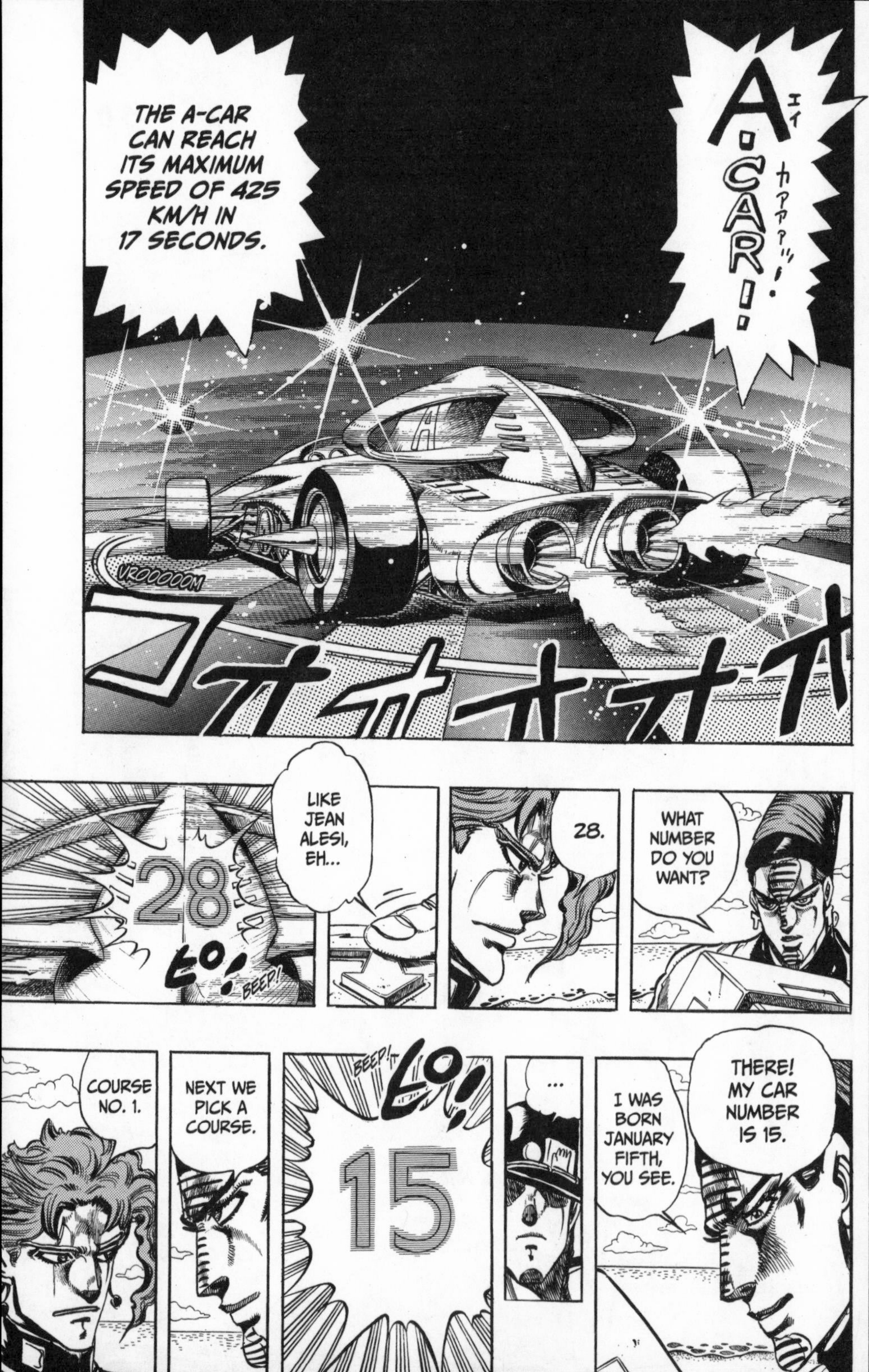
A-CAR!!
エイ カァァァッ!
THE A-CAR CAN REACH ITS MAXIMUM SPEED OF 425 KM/H IN 17 SECONDS.
VROOOOOM
コォォォォ
WHAT NUMBER DO YOU WANT?
28.
LIKE JEAN ALESI, EH...
28
ピッ!
BEEP!
THERE! MY CAR NUMBER IS 15.
I WAS BORN JANUARY FIFTH, YOU SEE.
...
BEEP!
ピッ!
15
NEXT WE PICK A COURSE.
COURSE NO. 1.

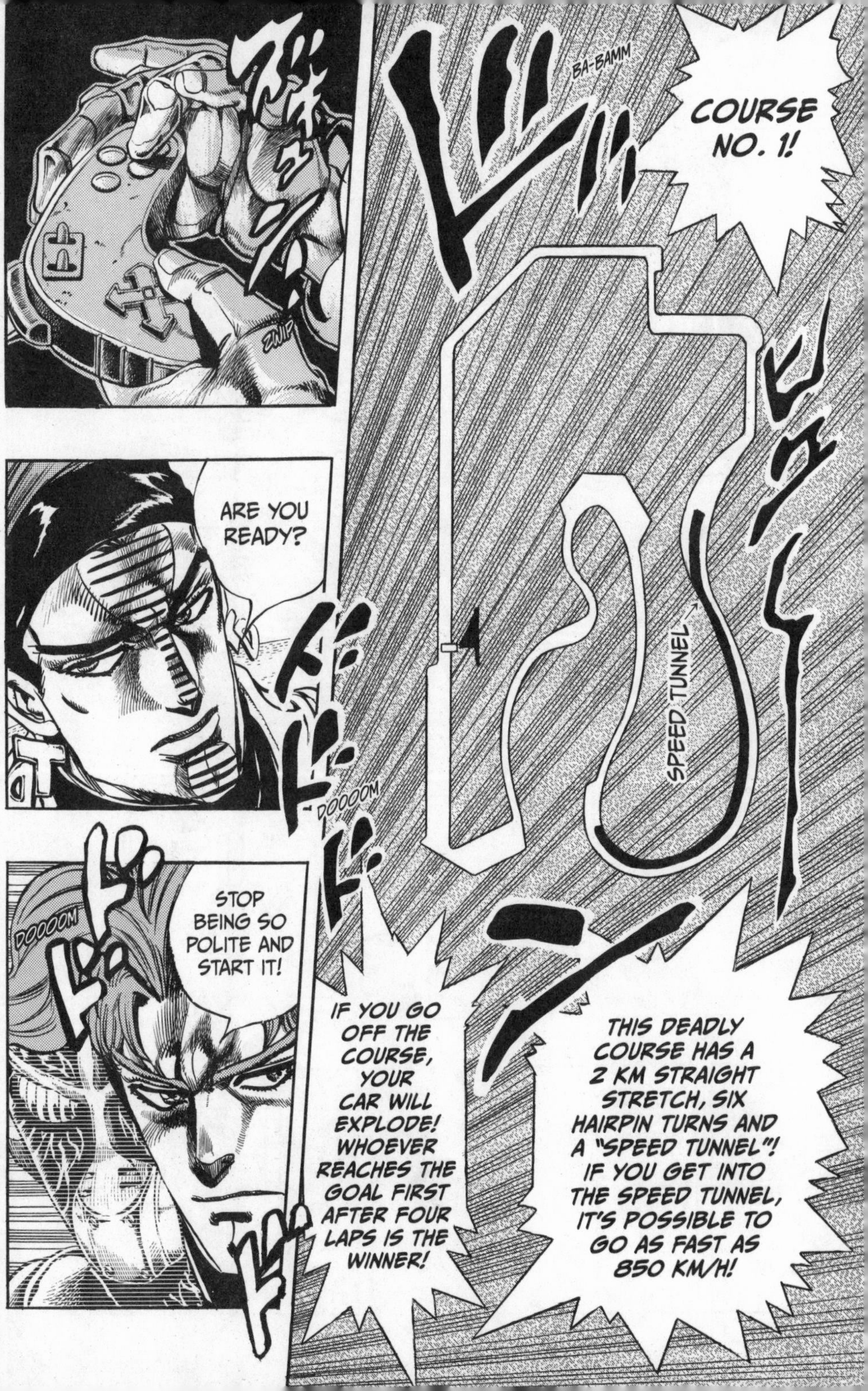
BA-BAMM
COURSE NO. 1!
SPEED TUNNEL
DOOOOM
THIS DEADLY COURSE HAS A 2 KM STRAIGHT STRETCH, SIX HAIRPIN TURNS AND A "SPEED TUNNEL"! IF YOU GET INTO THE SPEED TUNNEL, IT'S POSSIBLE TO GO AS FAST AS 850 KM/H!
IF YOU GO OFF THE COURSE, YOUR CAR WILL EXPLODE! WHOEVER REACHES THE GOAL FIRST AFTER FOUR LAPS IS THE WINNER!
ZWIP
ARE YOU READY?
STOP BEING SO POLITE AND START IT!
DOOOOM

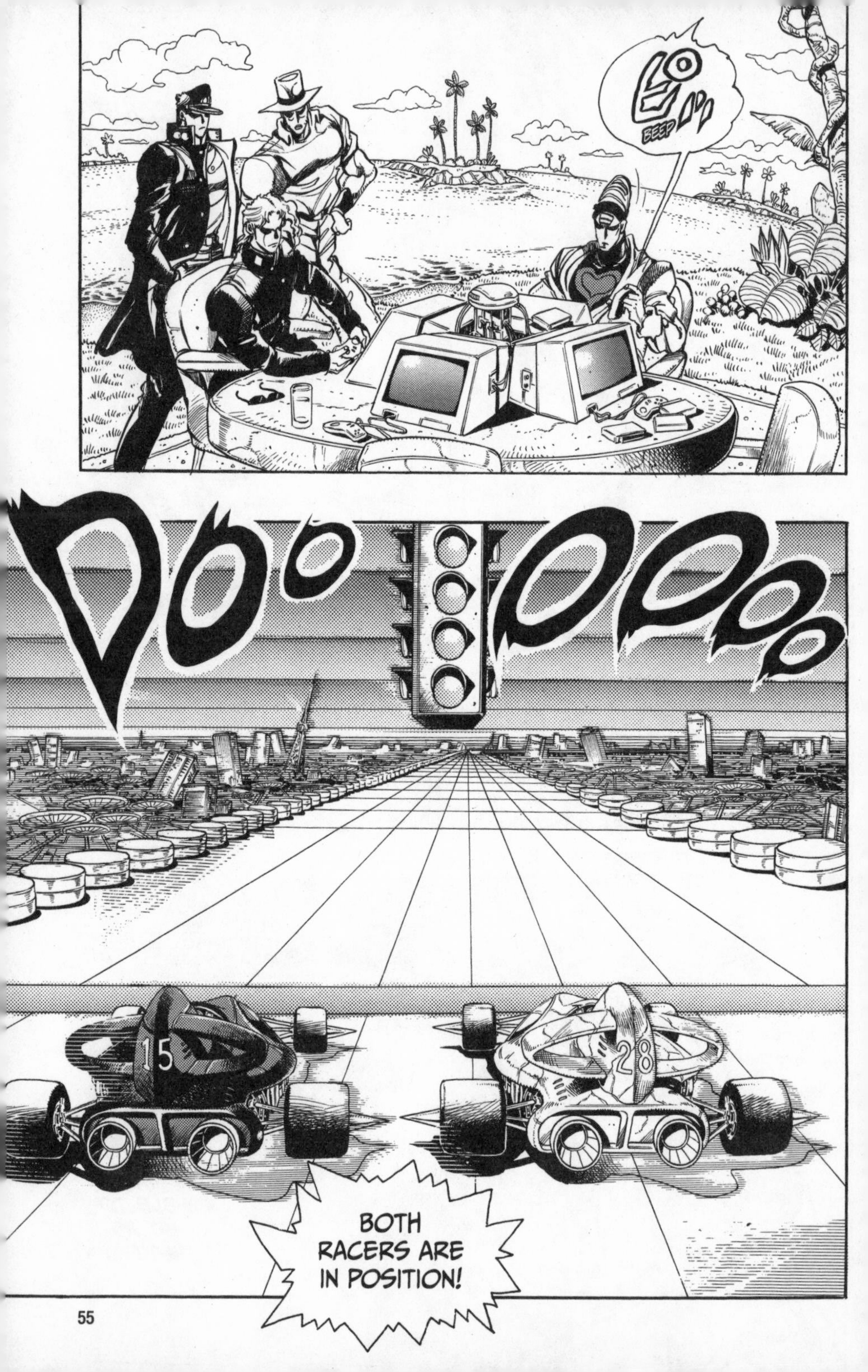
BEEP
DOOOOOOO
BOTH RACERS ARE IN POSITION!

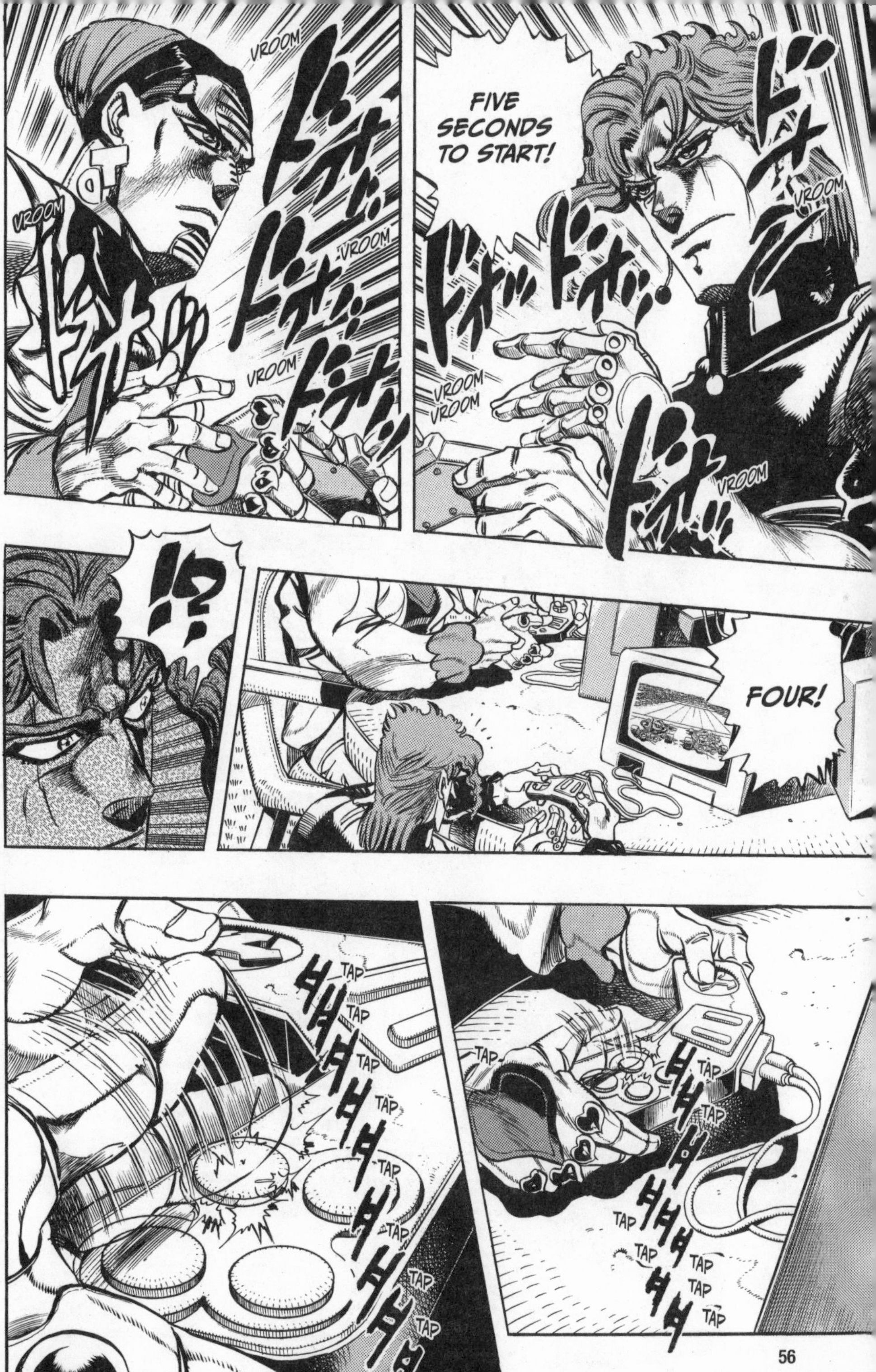
FIVE SECONDS TO START!
VROOM
VROOM VROOM
VROOM
VROOM
VROOM
VROOM
VROOM
FOUR!
!?
TAP TAP TAP TAP TAP TAP TAP TAP TAP TAP
TAP TAP TAP TAP TAP TAP TAP TAP TAP TAP

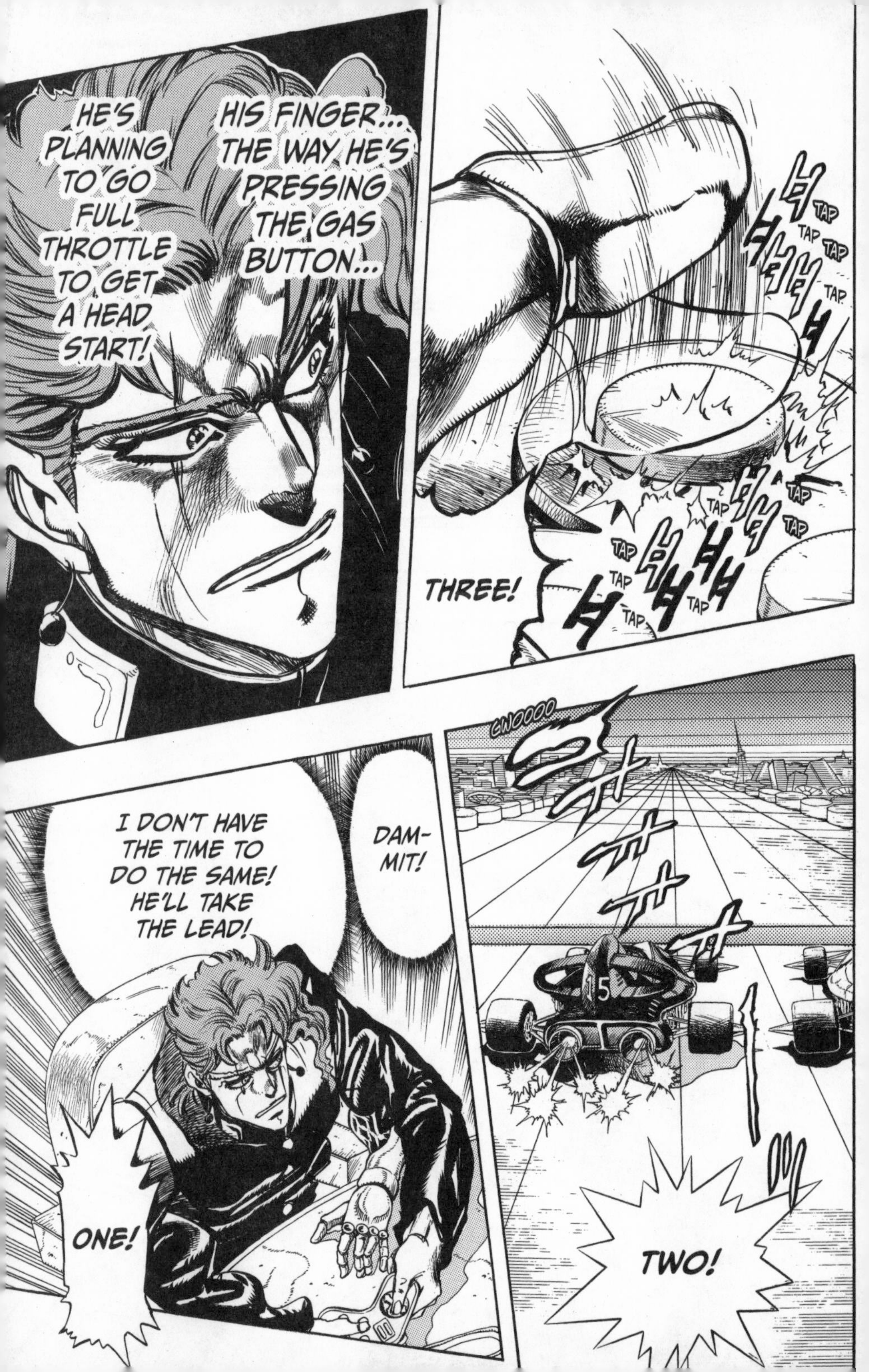
TAP TAP TAP TAP
TAP TAP TAP TAP TAP TAP TAP TAP
THREE!
HIS FINGER... THE WAY HE'S PRESSING THE GAS BUTTON...
HE'S PLANNING TO GO FULL THROTTLE TO GET A HEAD START!
GWOOOO
TWO!
DAM-MIT!
I DON'T HAVE THE TIME TO DO THE SAME! HE'LL TAKE THE LEAD!
ONE!

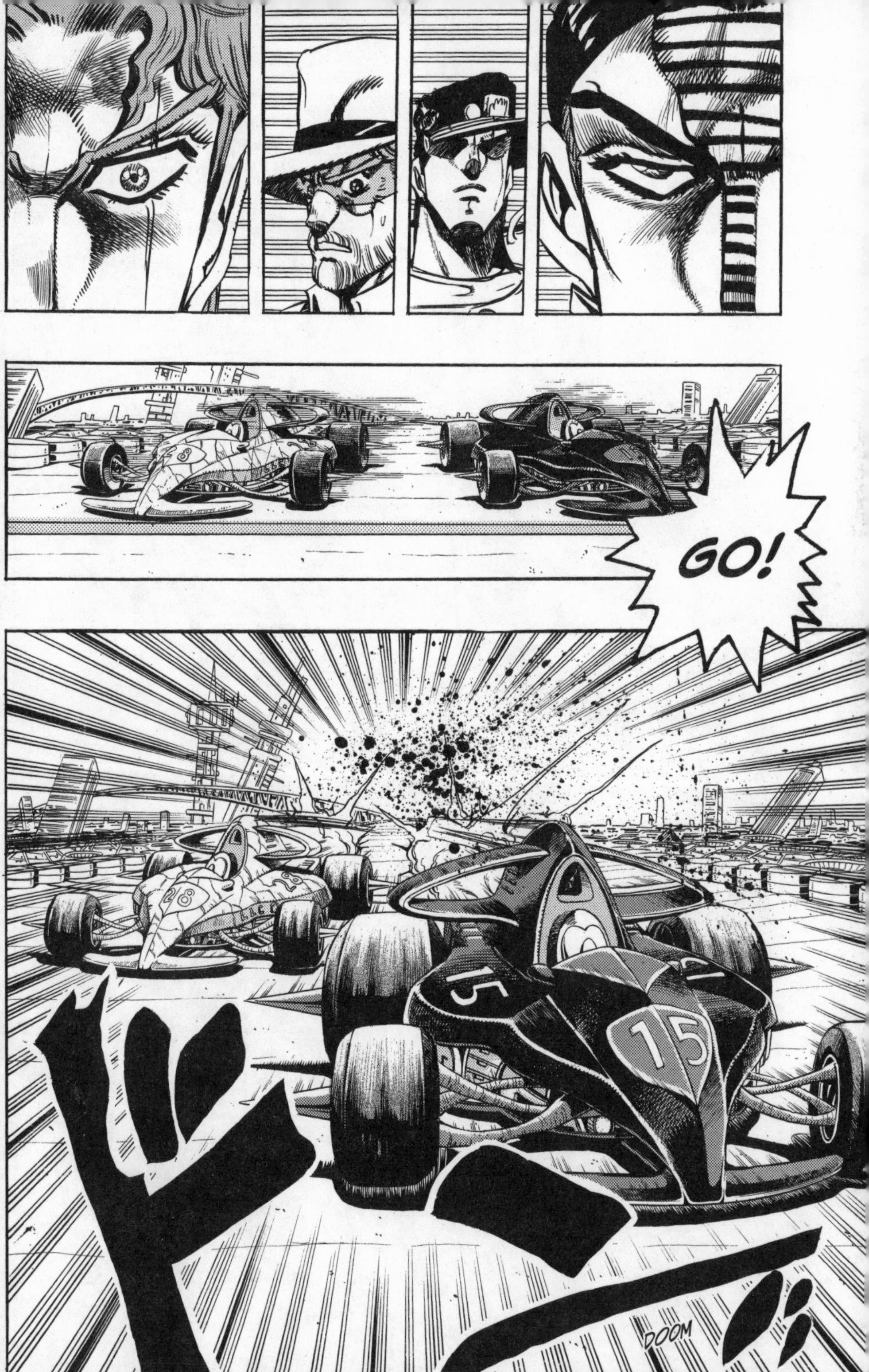
GO!
DOOM

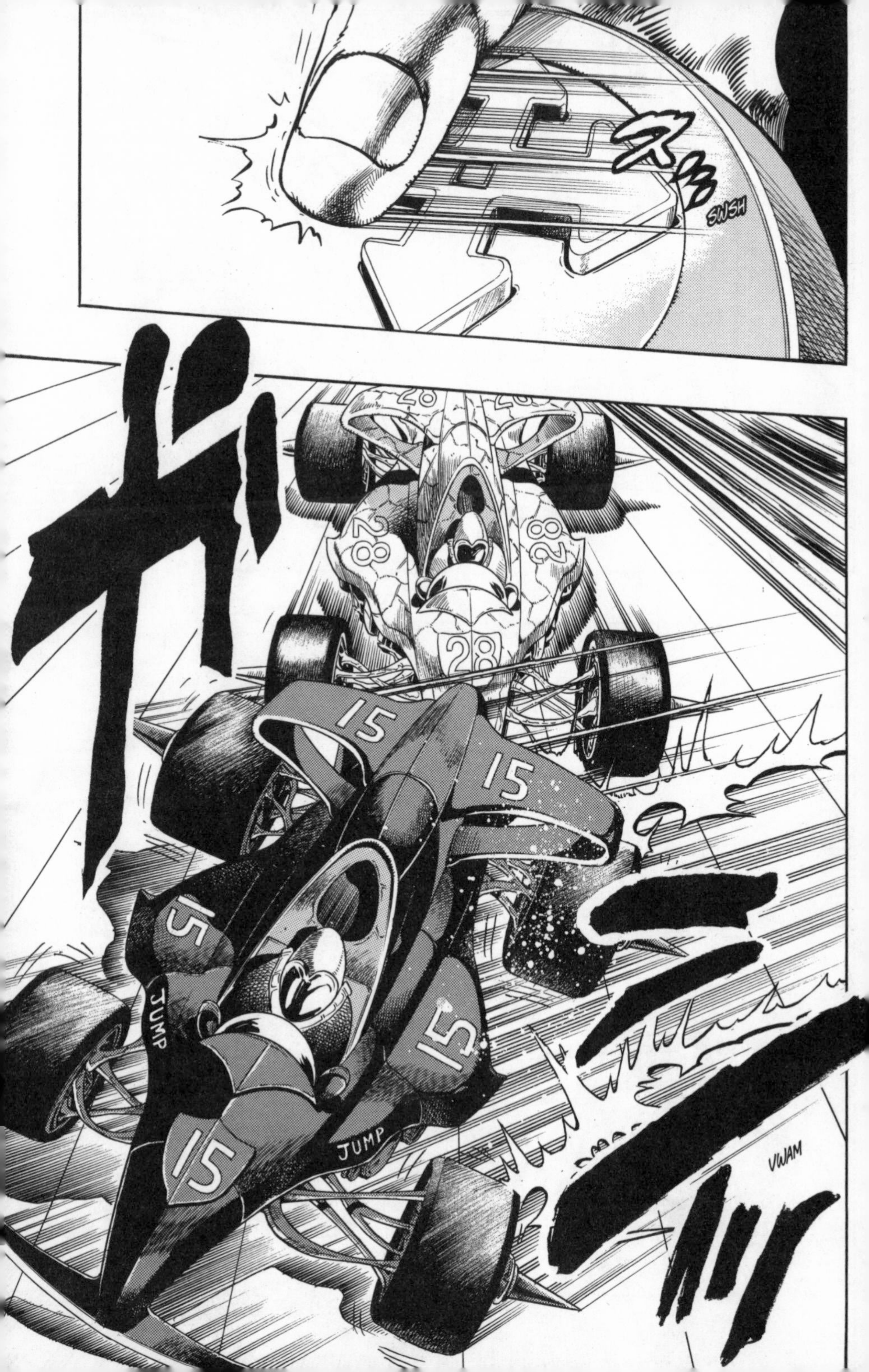
SWSH
VWAM

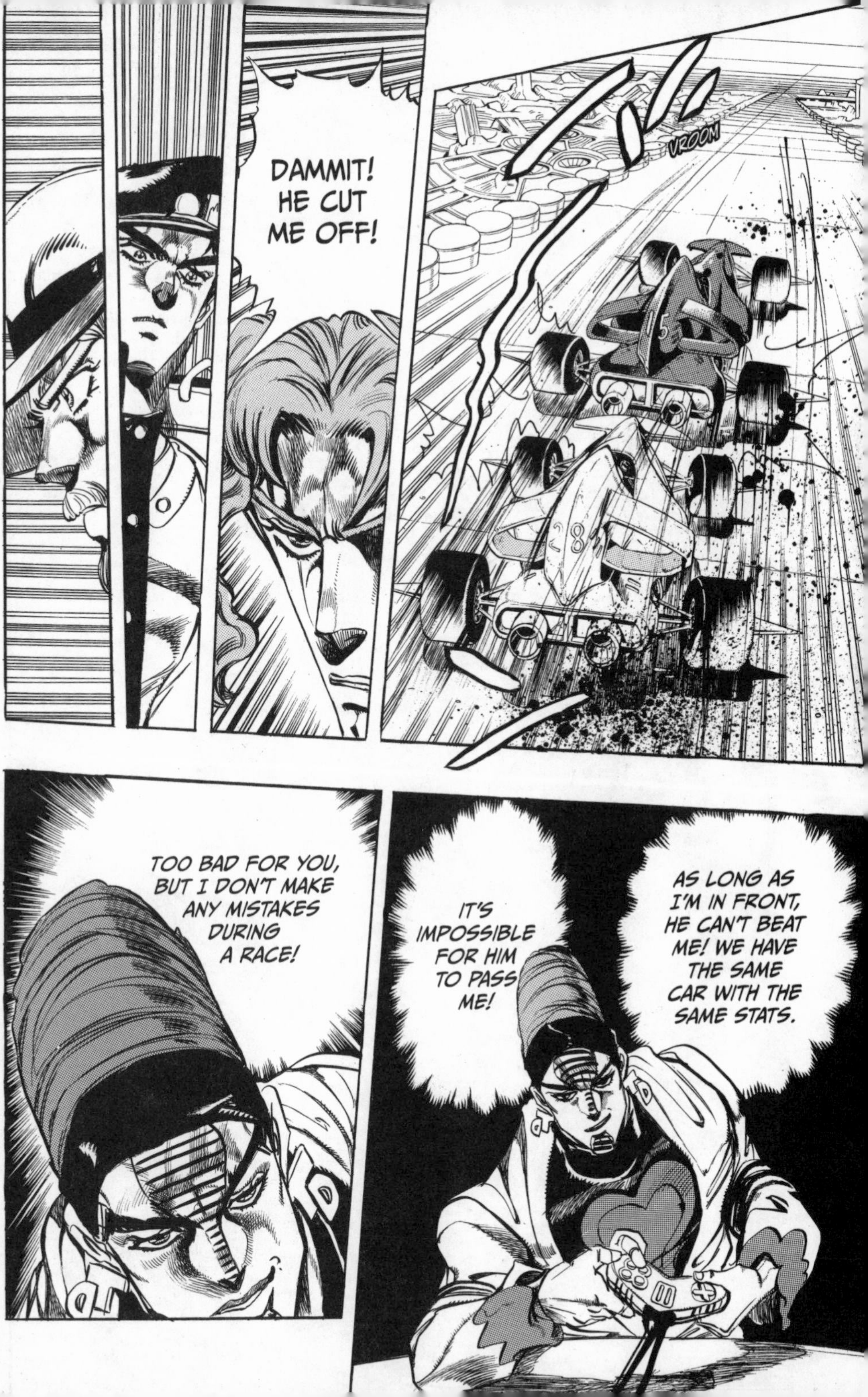
VROOM
DAMMIT! HE CUT ME OFF!
AS LONG AS I'M IN FRONT, HE CAN'T BEAT ME! WE HAVE THE SAME CAR WITH THE SAME STATS.
IT'S IMPOSSIBLE FOR HIM TO PASS ME!
TOO BAD FOR YOU, BUT I DON'T MAKE ANY MISTAKES DURING A RACE!

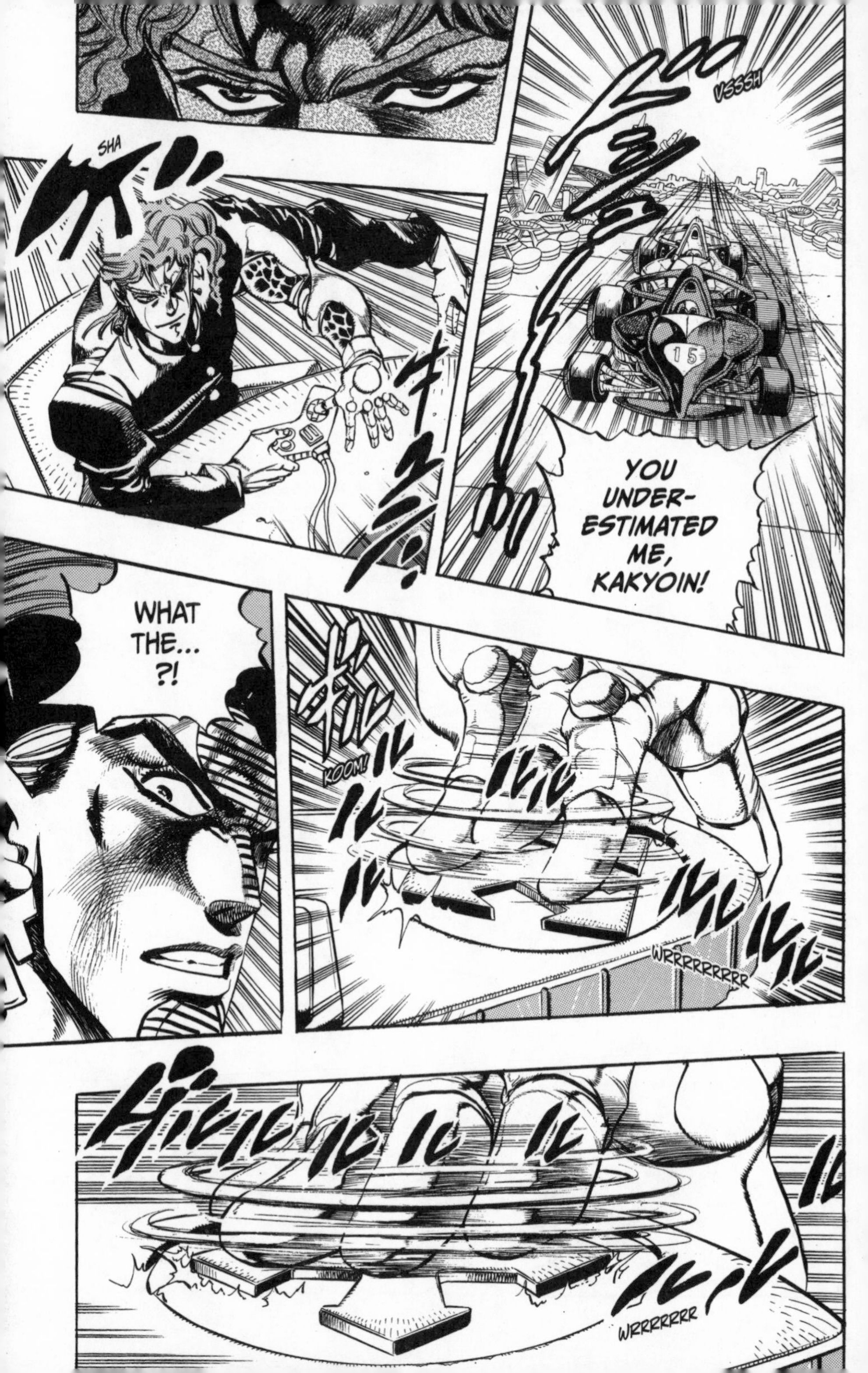
VSSSH
YOU UNDER-ESTIMATED ME, KAKYOIN!
SHA
KOOM!
WRRRRRRRRR
WHAT THE... ?!
WRRRRRRR

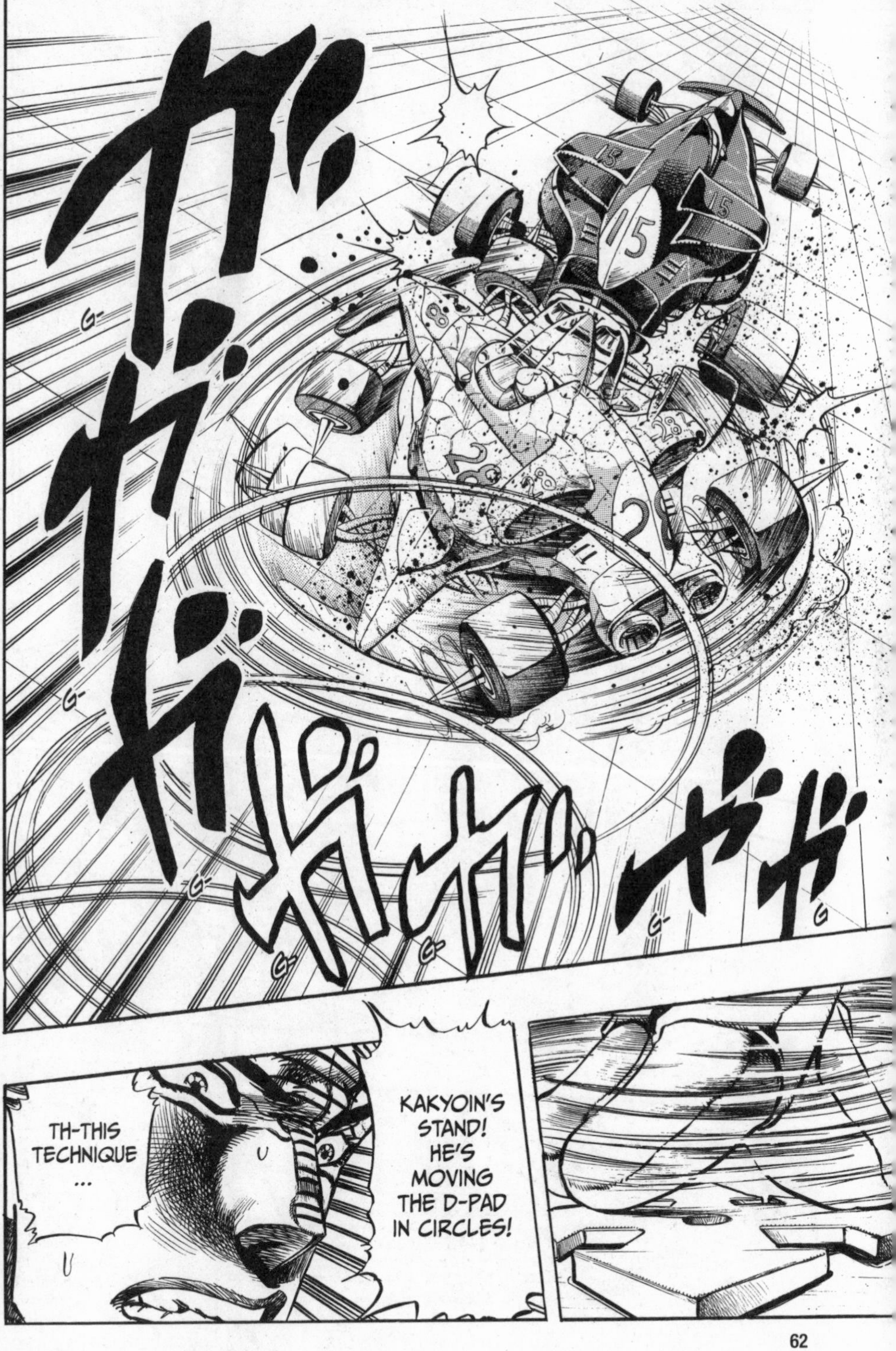
KAKYOIN'S STAND! HE'S MOVING THE D-PAD IN CIRCLES!
TH-THIS TECHNIQUE ...

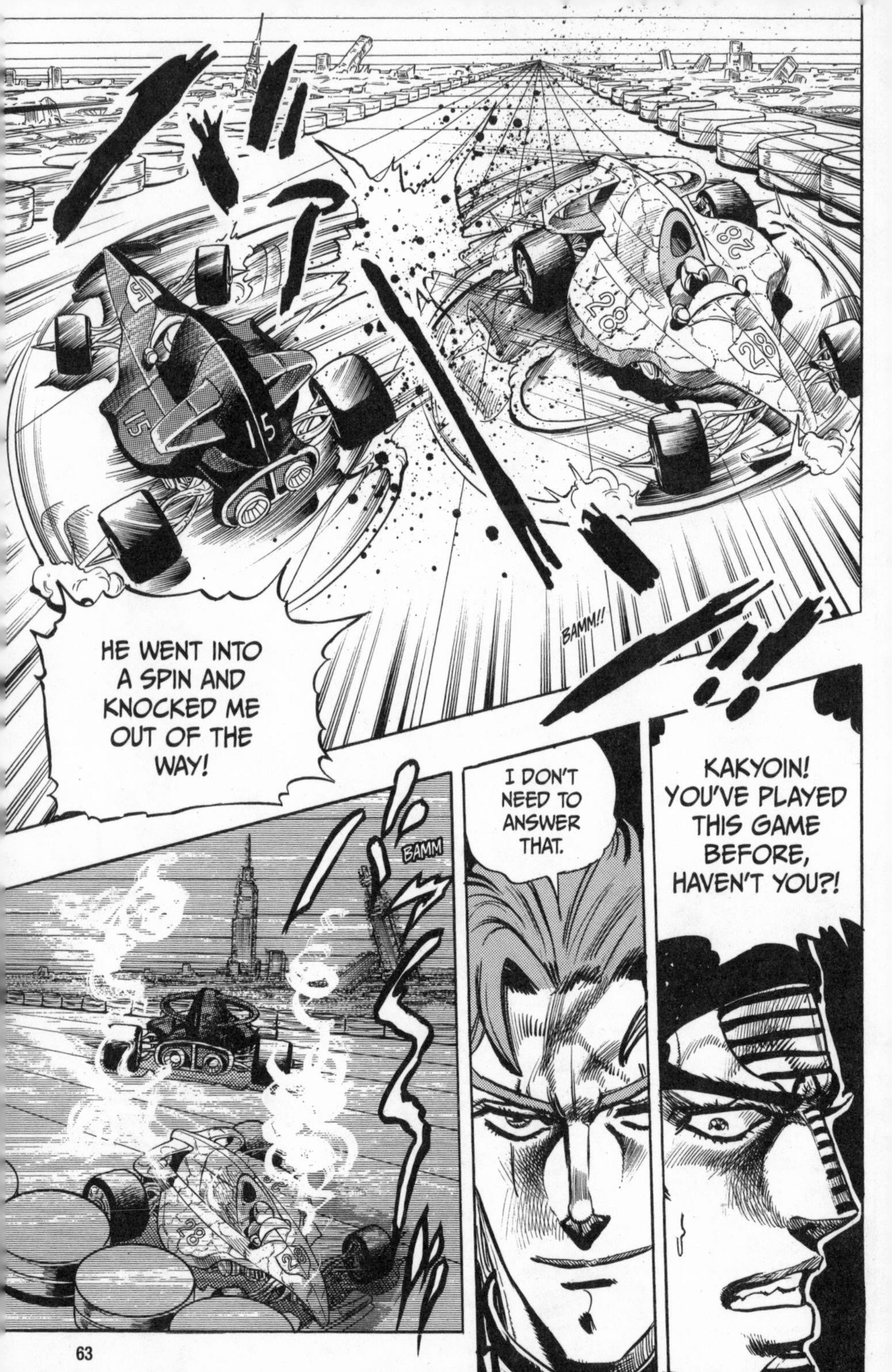
BAMM!!
HE WENT INTO A SPIN AND KNOCKED ME OUT OF THE WAY!
KAKYOIN! YOU'VE PLAYED THIS GAME BEFORE, HAVEN'T YOU?!
I DON'T NEED TO ANSWER THAT.
BAMM

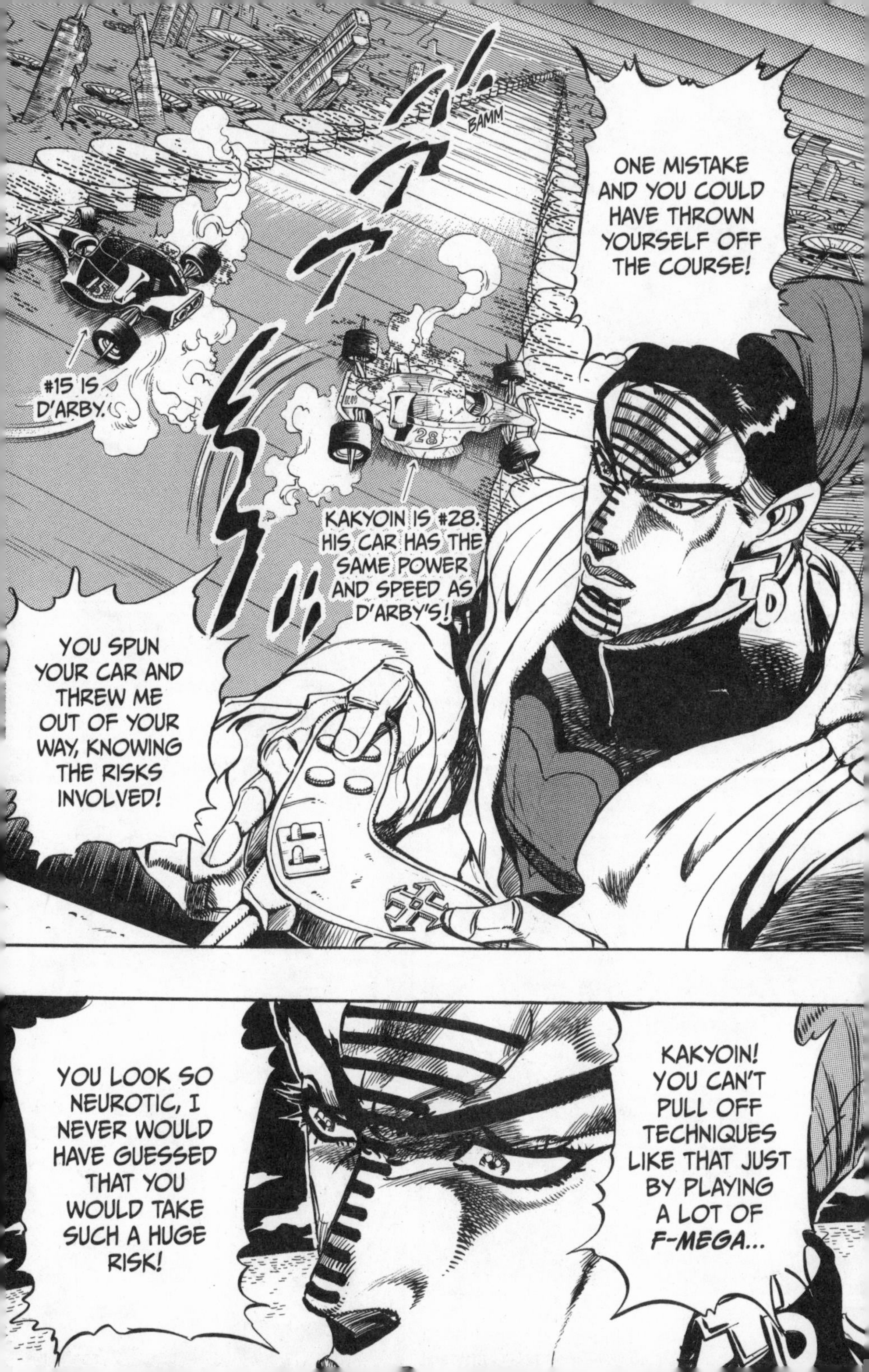
ONE MISTAKE AND YOU COULD HAVE THROWN YOURSELF OFF THE COURSE!
BAMM
#15 IS D'ARBY.
KAKYOIN IS #28. HIS CAR HAS THE SAME POWER AND SPEED AS D'ARBY'S!
YOU SPUN YOUR CAR AND THREW ME OUT OF YOUR WAY, KNOWING THE RISKS INVOLVED!
KAKYOIN! YOU CAN'T PULL OFF TECHNIQUES LIKE THAT JUST BY PLAYING A LOT OF *F-MEGA*...
YOU LOOK SO NEUROTIC, I NEVER WOULD HAVE GUESSED THAT YOU WOULD TAKE SUCH A HUGE RISK!

CHAPTER 118: D'Arby the Player PART 5

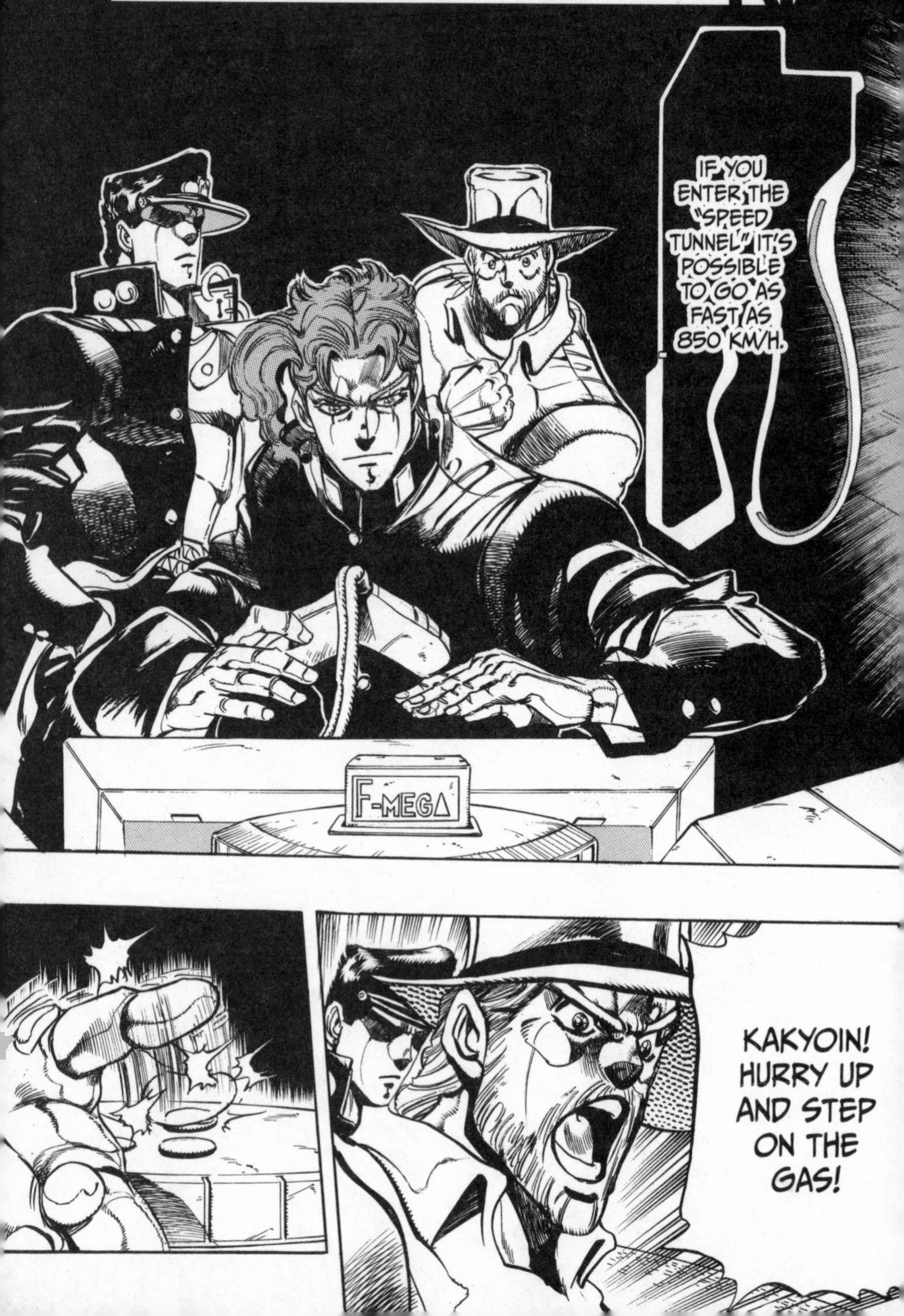
IF YOU ENTER THE "SPEED TUNNEL," IT'S POSSIBLE TO GO AS FAST AS 850 KM/H.
KAKYOIN! HURRY UP AND STEP ON THE GAS!

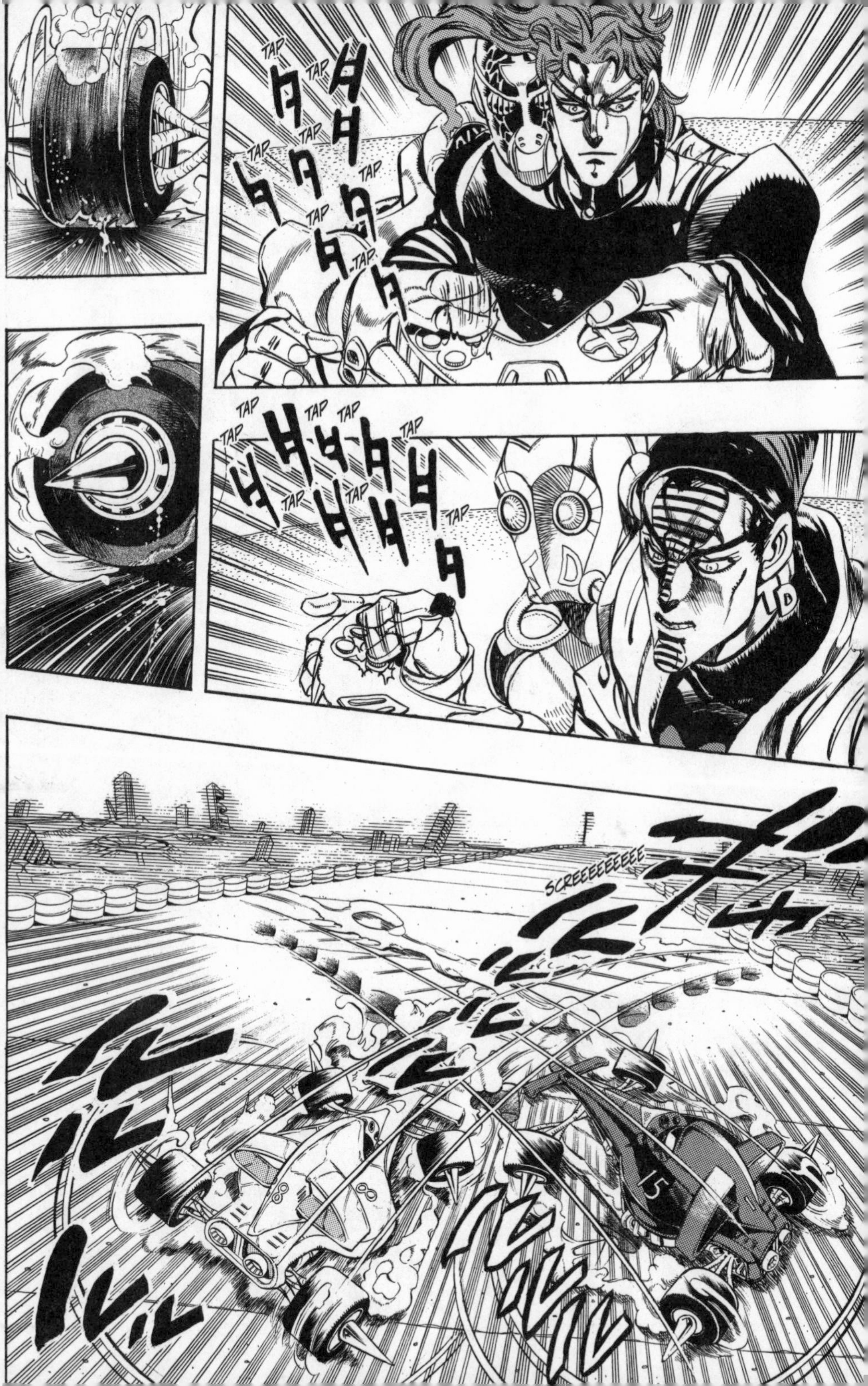
TAP
TAP
TAP
TAP
TAP
TAP
TAP
TAP
TAP
TAP
TAP
TAP
TAP
TAP
TAP
SCREEEEEEEEEE

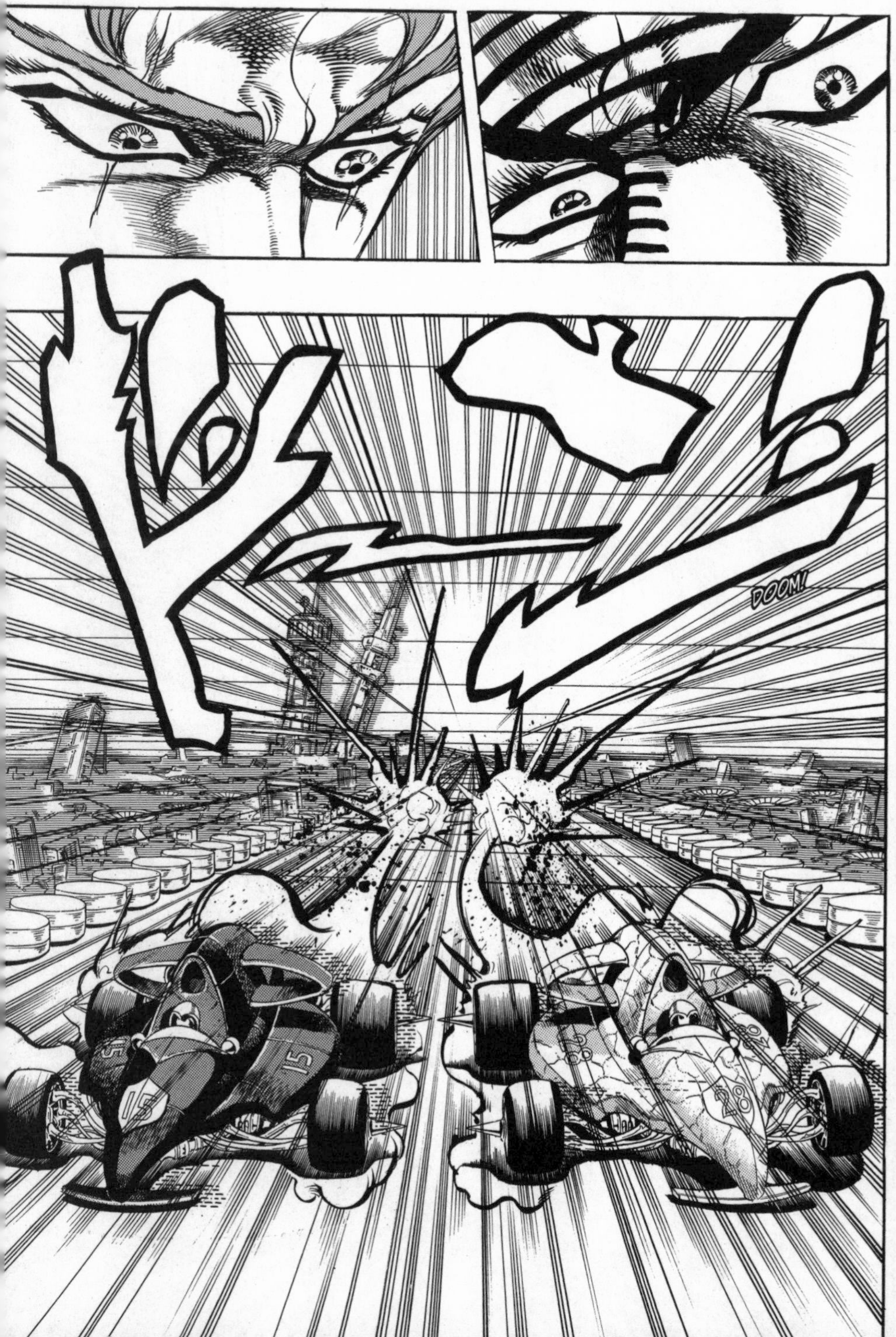
DOOM!

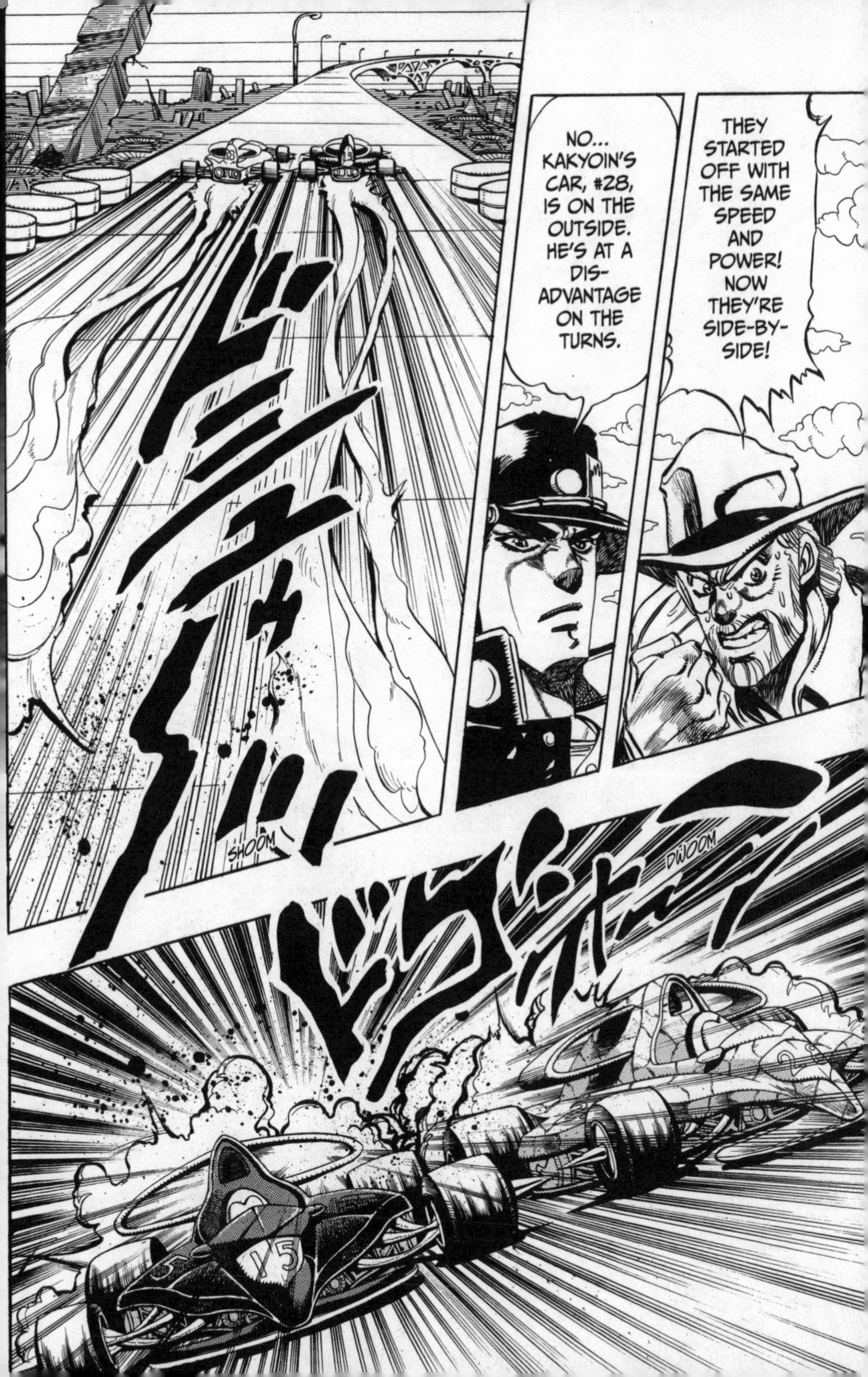
THEY STARTED OFF WITH THE SAME SPEED AND POWER! NOW THEY'RE SIDE-BY-SIDE!
NO... KAKYOIN'S CAR, #28, IS ON THE OUTSIDE. HE'S AT A DIS-ADVANTAGE ON THE TURNS.
SHOOM
DWOOM

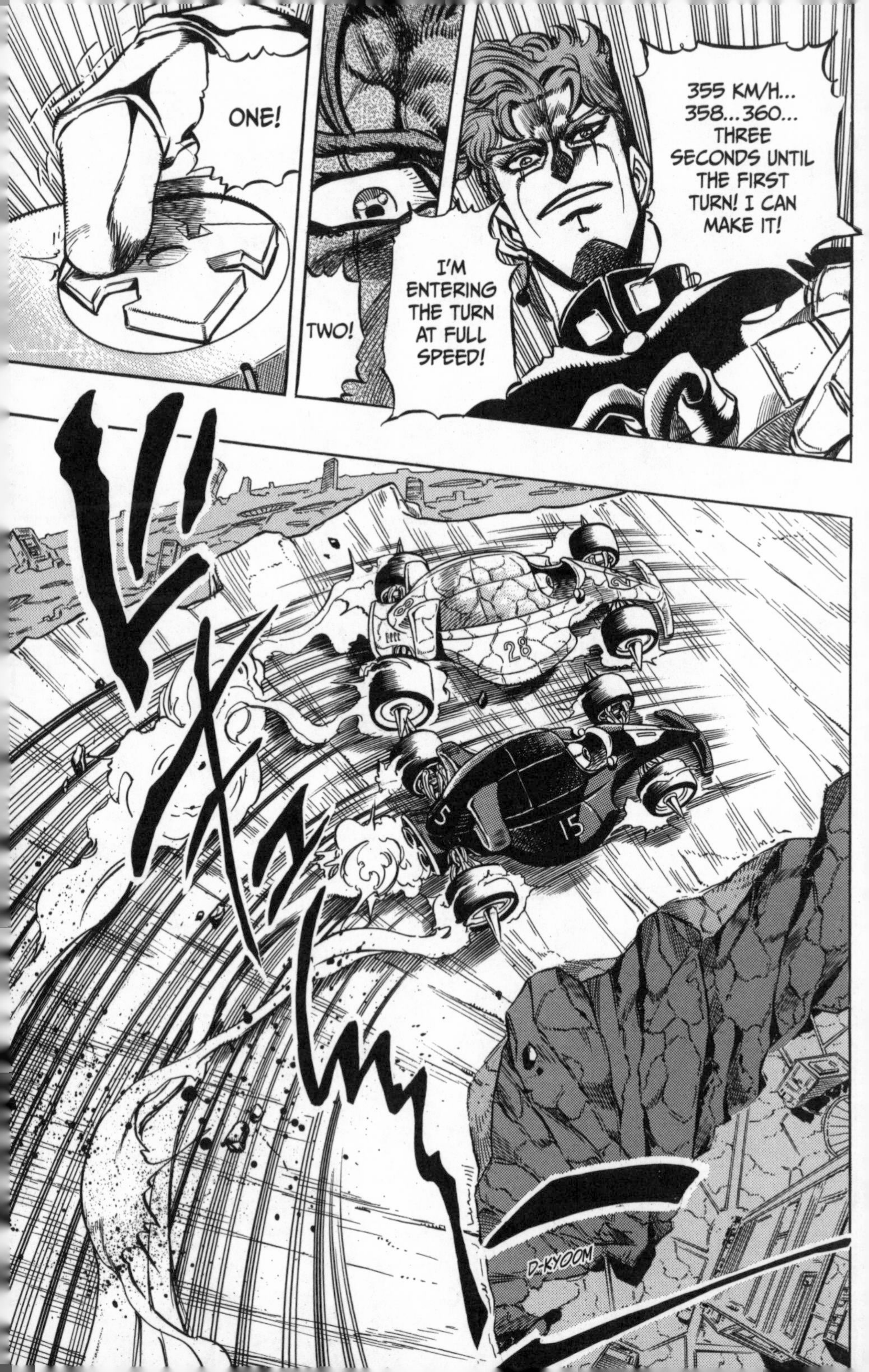
355 KM/H... 358...360... THREE SECONDS UNTIL THE FIRST TURN! I CAN MAKE IT!
I'M ENTERING THE TURN AT FULL SPEED!
TWO!
ONE!
D-KYOOM

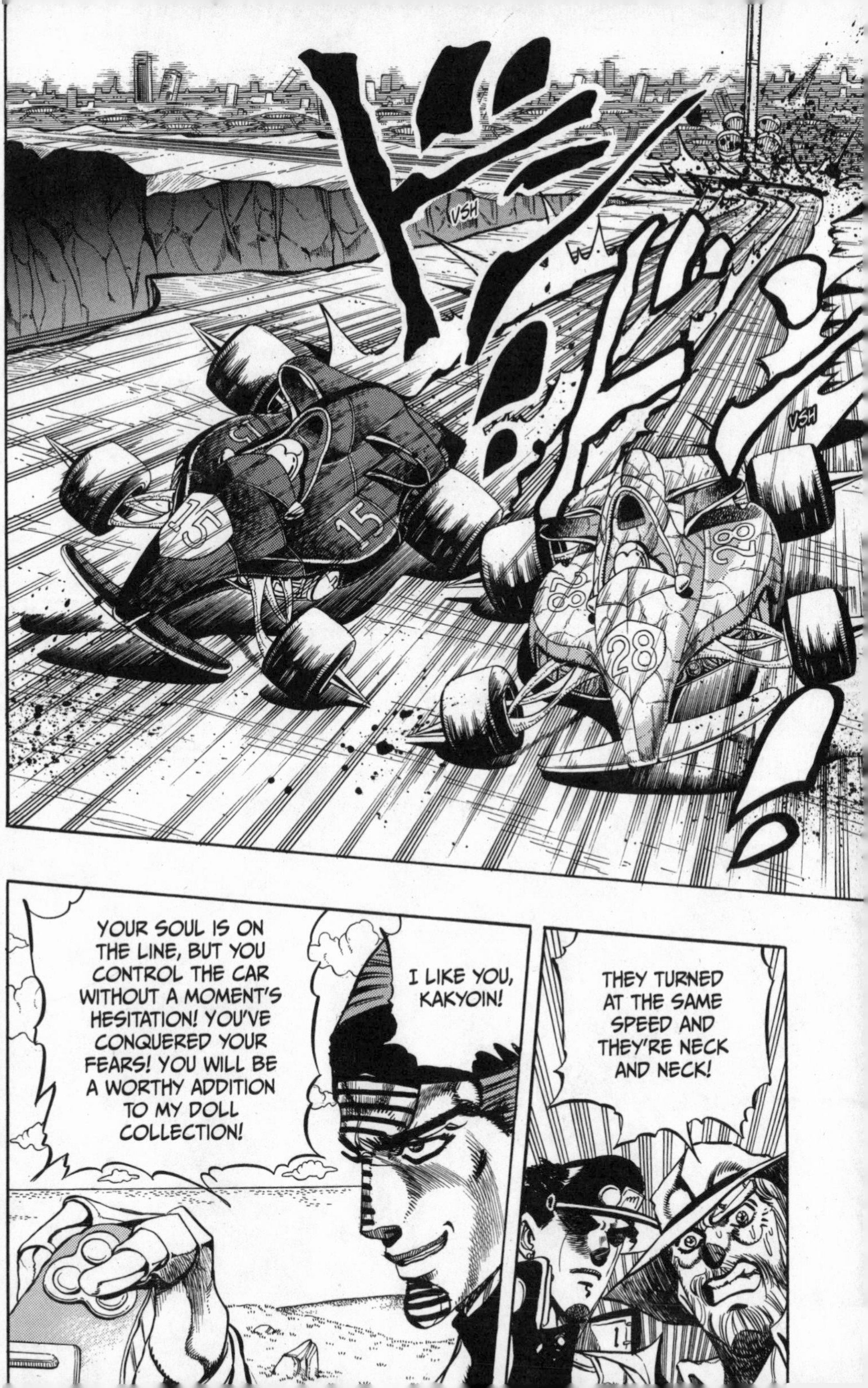
VSH
VSH
THEY TURNED AT THE SAME SPEED AND THEY'RE NECK AND NECK!
I LIKE YOU, KAKYOIN!
YOUR SOUL IS ON THE LINE, BUT YOU CONTROL THE CAR WITHOUT A MOMENT'S HESITATION! YOU'VE CONQUERED YOUR FEARS! YOU WILL BE A WORTHY ADDITION TO MY DOLL COLLECTION!

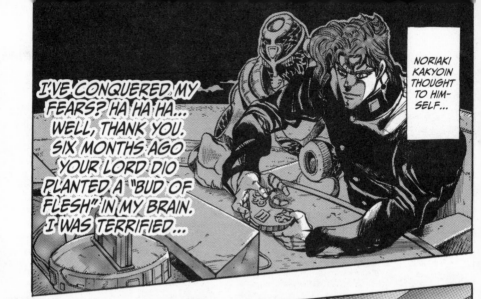

NORIAKI KAKYOIN THOUGHT TO HIMSELF...

I'VE CONQUERED MY FEARS? HA HA HA... WELL, THANK YOU. SIX MONTHS AGO YOUR LORD DIO PLANTED A "BUD OF FLESH" IN MY BRAIN. I WAS TERRIFIED...

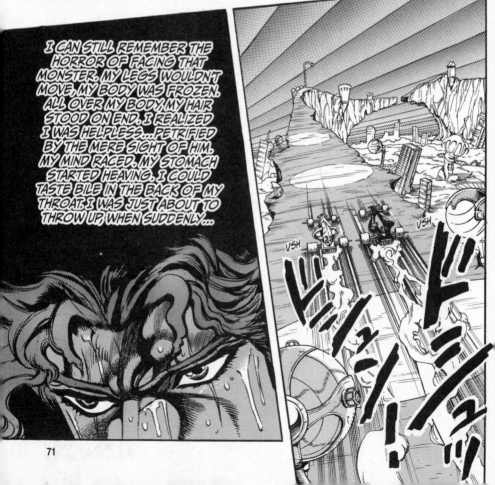

I CAN STILL REMEMBER THE HORROR OF FACING THAT MONSTER. MY LEGS WOULDN'T MOVE, MY BODY WAS FROZEN. ALL OVER MY BODY, MY HAIR STOOD ON END. I REALIZED I WAS HELPLESS...PETRIFIED BY THE MERE SIGHT OF HIM. MY MIND RACED. MY STOMACH STARTED HEAVING. I COULD TASTE BILE IN THE BACK OF MY THROAT. I WAS JUST ABOUT TO THROW UP, WHEN SUDDENLY...

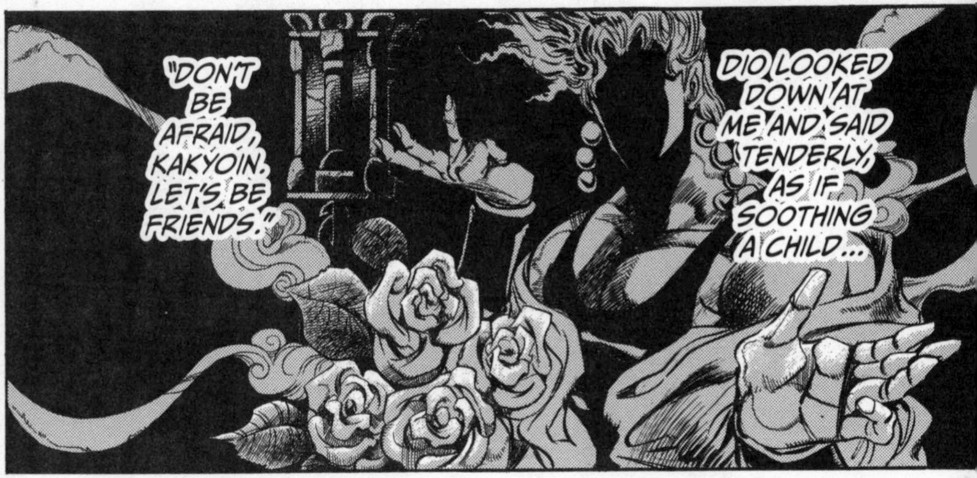
DIO LOOKED DOWN AT ME AND SAID TENDERLY, AS IF SOOTHING A CHILD...
"DON'T BE AFRAID, KAKYOIN. LET'S BE FRIENDS."

I CURSE MY-SELF!

I WAS SO RELIEVED TO HEAR THOSE WORDS...I WAS GRATEFUL FROM THE BOTTOM OF MY HEART. **"I CAN STILL LIVE!"** THAT'S WHAT WENT THROUGH MY MIND. BUT... IT WAS SUCH HUMILIATION. THE ULTIMATE HUMILIATION... **I CAN'T FORGIVE HIM! I CAN'T FORGIVE MYSELF!**

I CURSE MYSELF FOR SUBMITTING TO HIM. JOTARO SAVED ME AND THAT'S WHY I WENT ON THIS JOURNEY. I WILL NEVER AGAIN BECOME THE PATHETIC, COWARDLY KAKYOIN I WAS ON THAT DAY. AND THAT, D'ARBY, IS WHY I CAN FIGHT WITH MY VERY SOUL ON THE LINE!

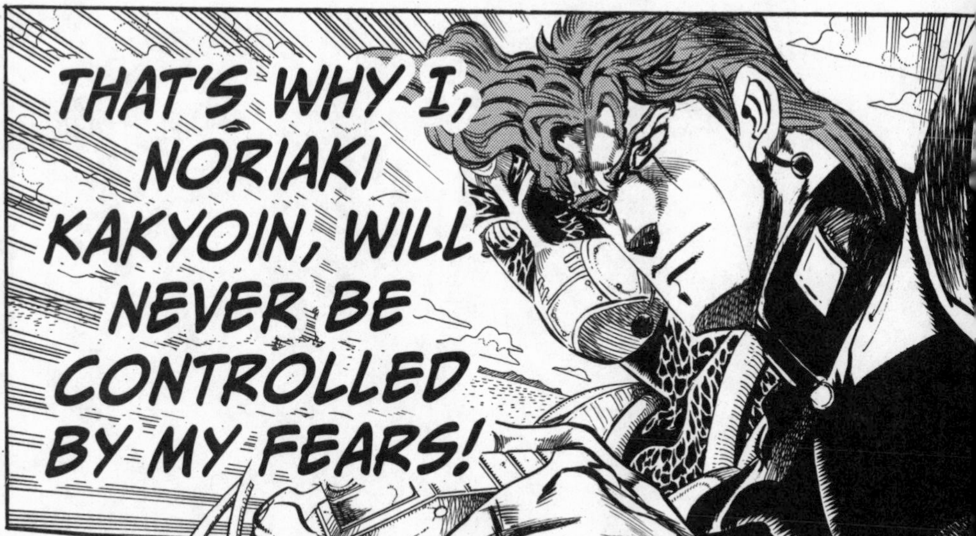
THAT'S WHY I, NORIAKI KAKYOIN, WILL NEVER BE CONTROLLED BY MY FEARS!

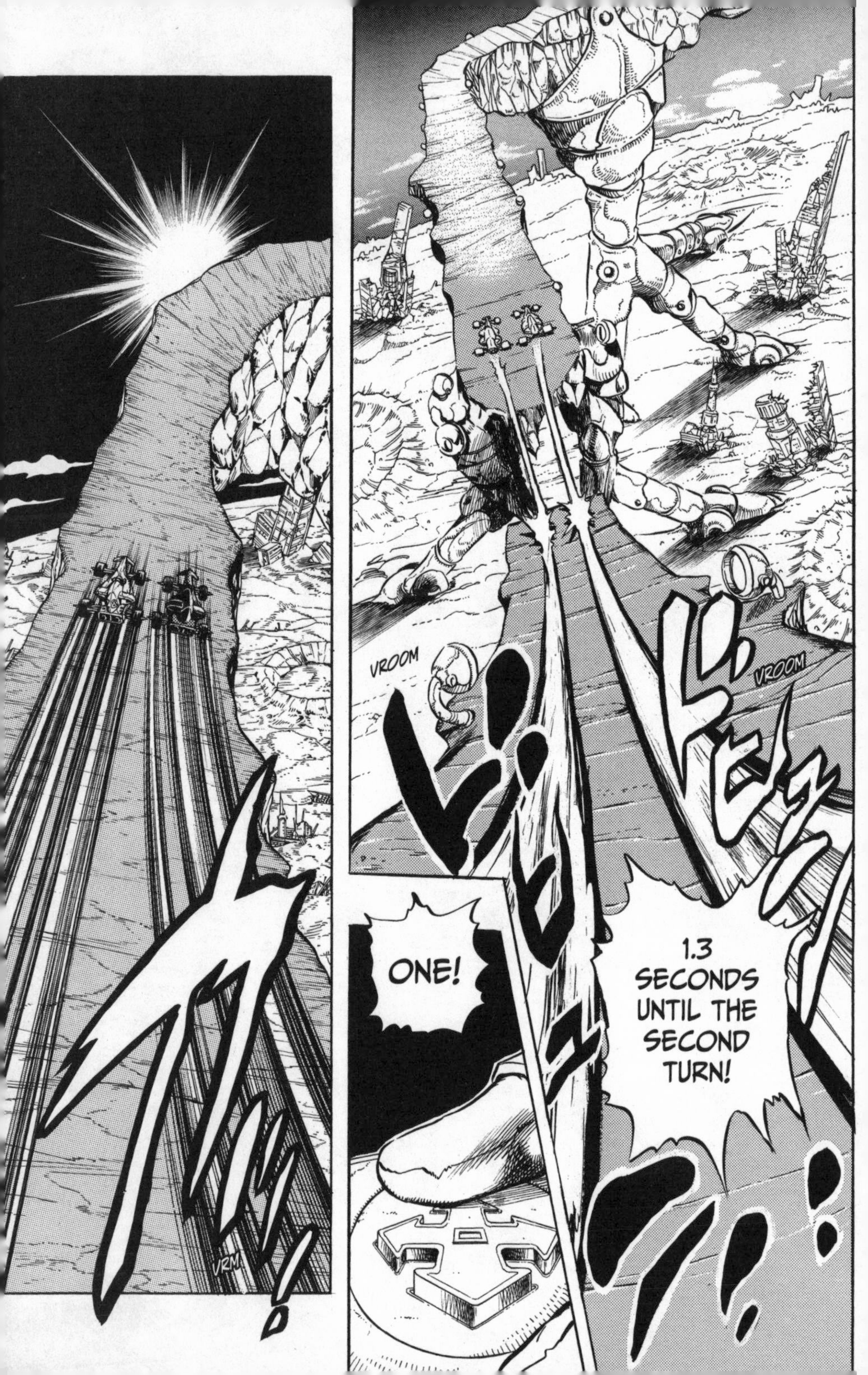
VROOM
VROOM
1.3 SECONDS UNTIL THE SECOND TURN!
ONE!
VRM

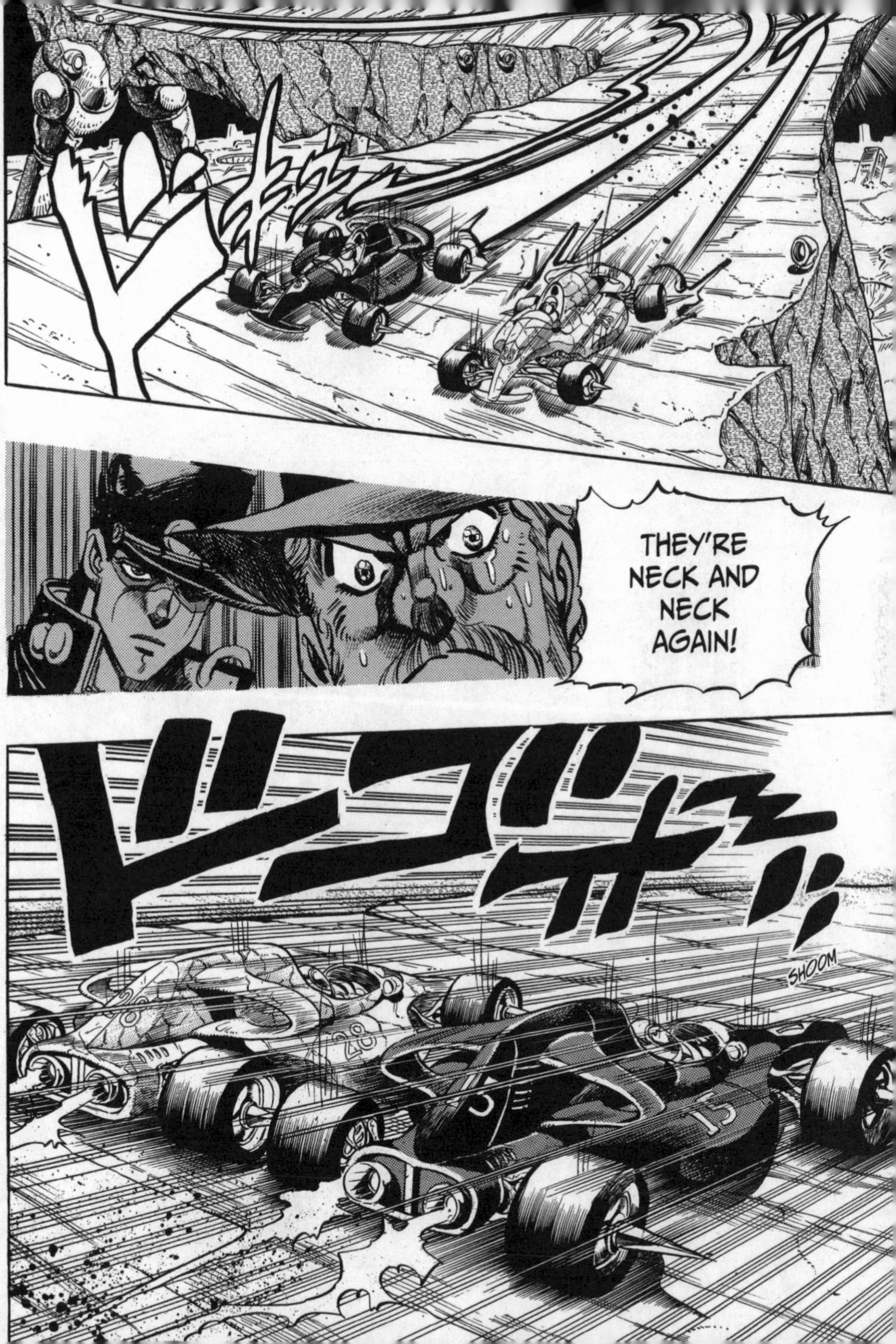
THEY'RE NECK AND NECK AGAIN!
SHOOM

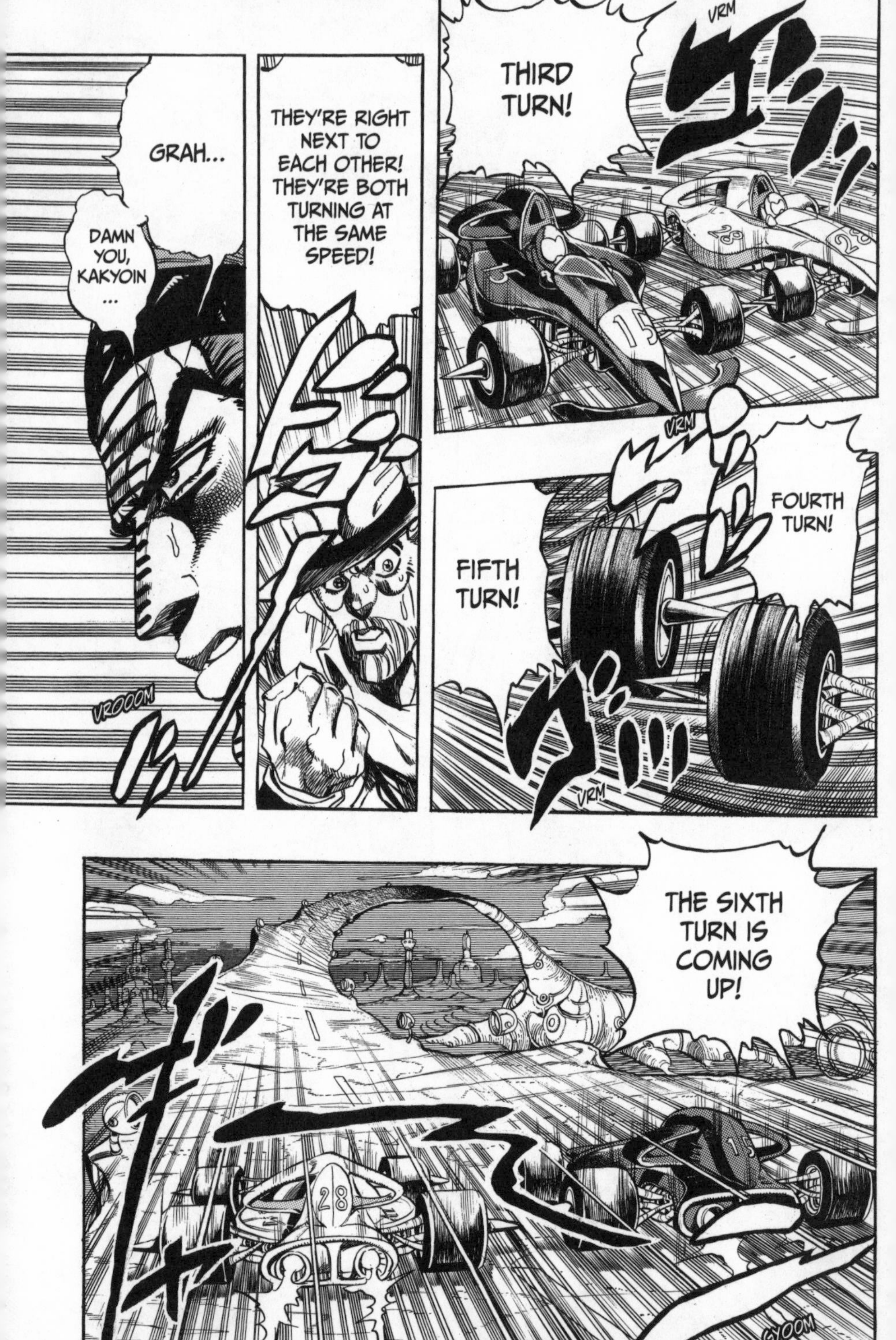
VRM
THIRD TURN!
VRM
FOURTH TURN!
FIFTH TURN!
VRM
THEY'RE RIGHT NEXT TO EACH OTHER! THEY'RE BOTH TURNING AT THE SAME SPEED!
GRAH...
DAMN YOU, KAKYOIN ...
VROOOM
THE SIXTH TURN IS COMING UP!
GYOOM

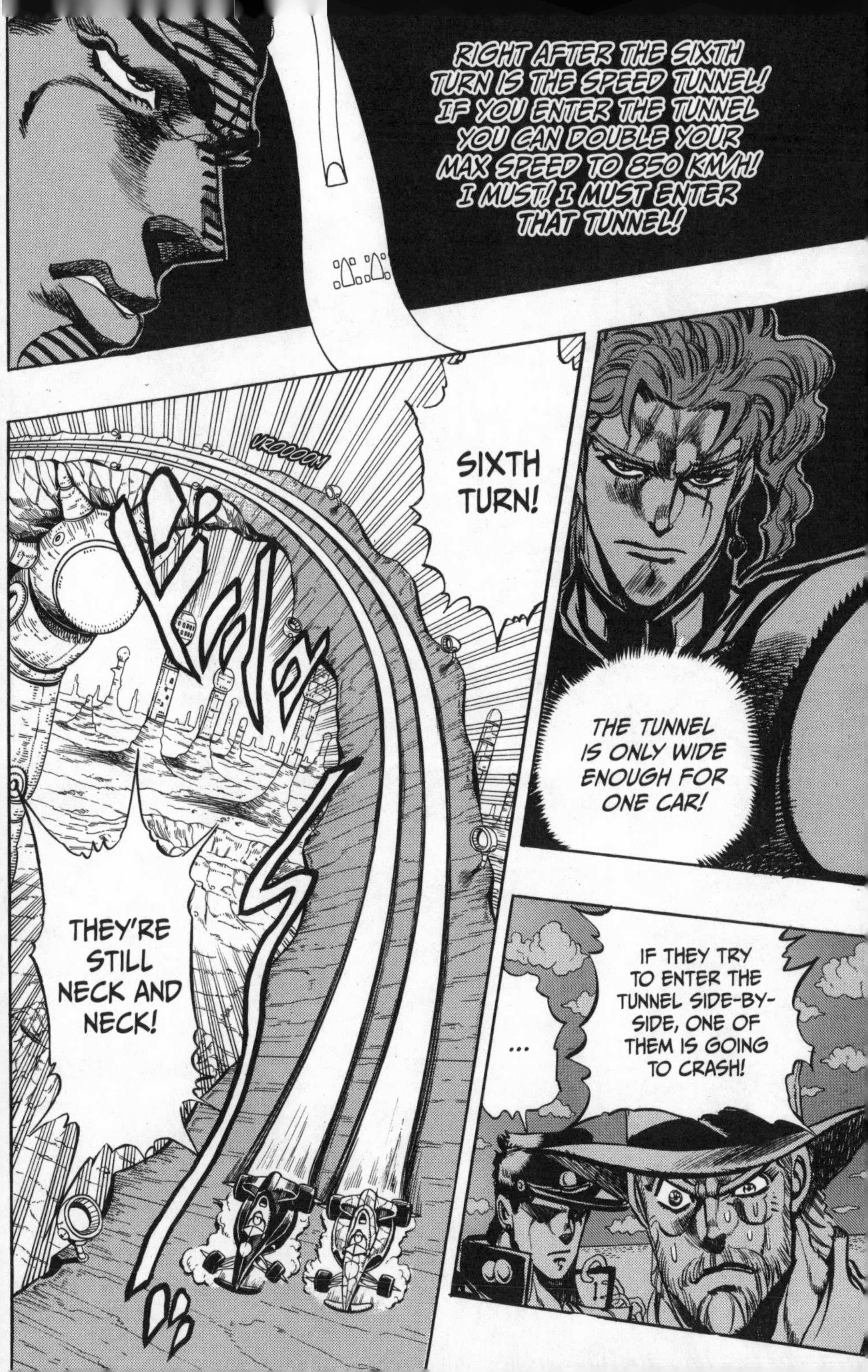
RIGHT AFTER THE SIXTH TURN IS THE SPEED TUNNEL! IF YOU ENTER THE TUNNEL YOU CAN DOUBLE YOUR MAX SPEED TO 850 KM/H! I MUST! I MUST ENTER THAT TUNNEL!
THE TUNNEL IS ONLY WIDE ENOUGH FOR ONE CAR!
IF THEY TRY TO ENTER THE TUNNEL SIDE-BY-SIDE, ONE OF THEM IS GOING TO CRASH!
...
SIXTH TURN!
VROOOOM
THEY'RE STILL NECK AND NECK!

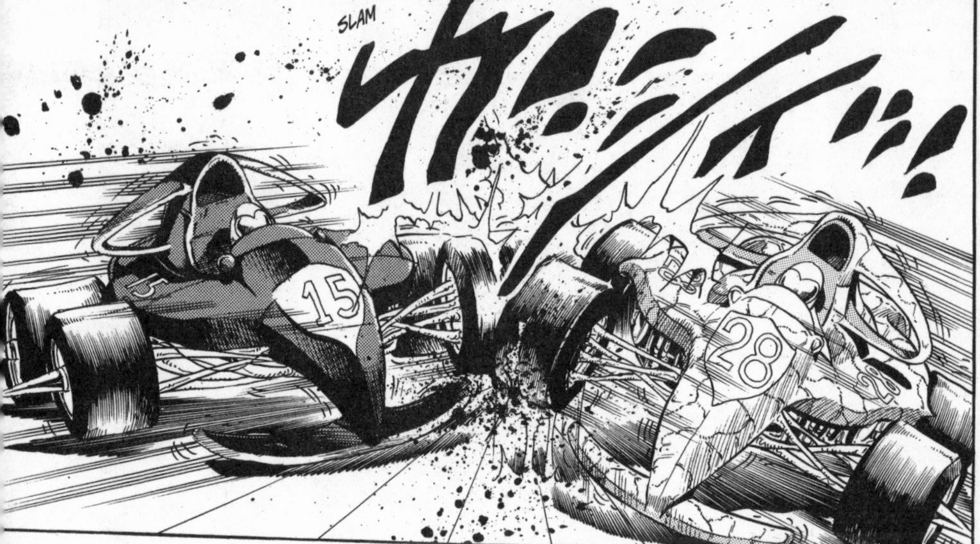
SLAM

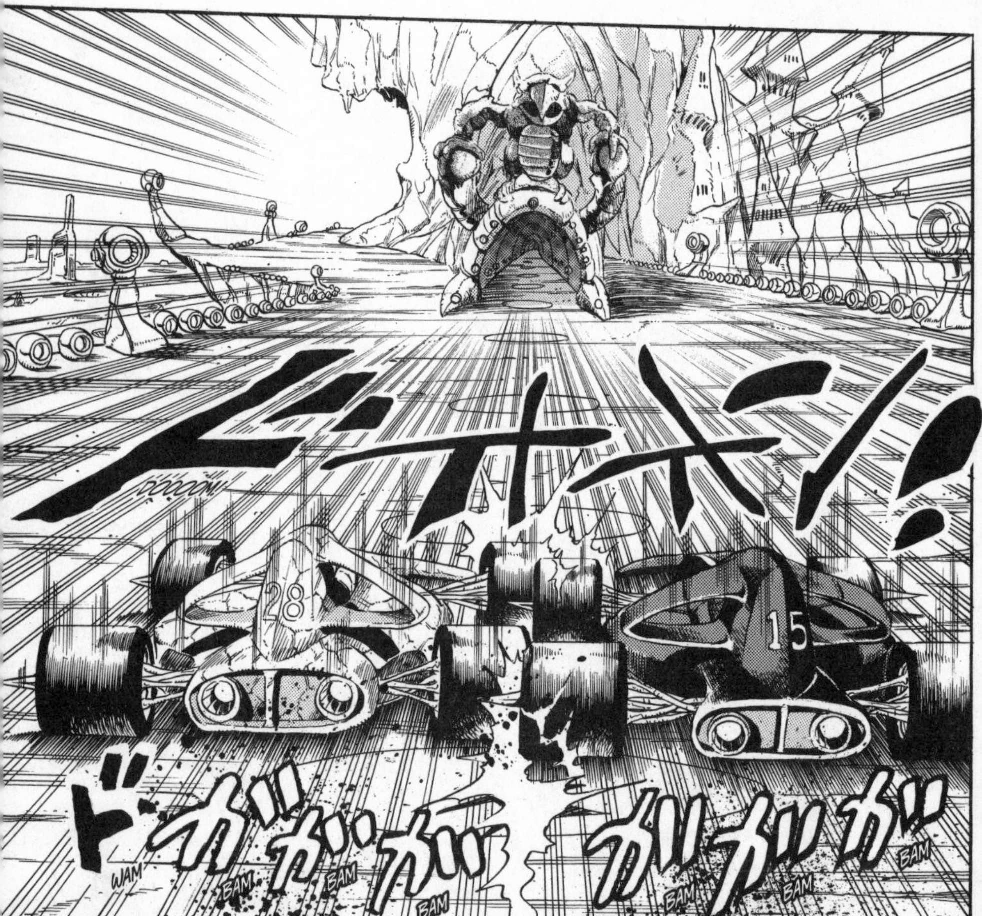
DOOOON!
WAM
BAM
BAM
BAM
BAM
BAM
BAM

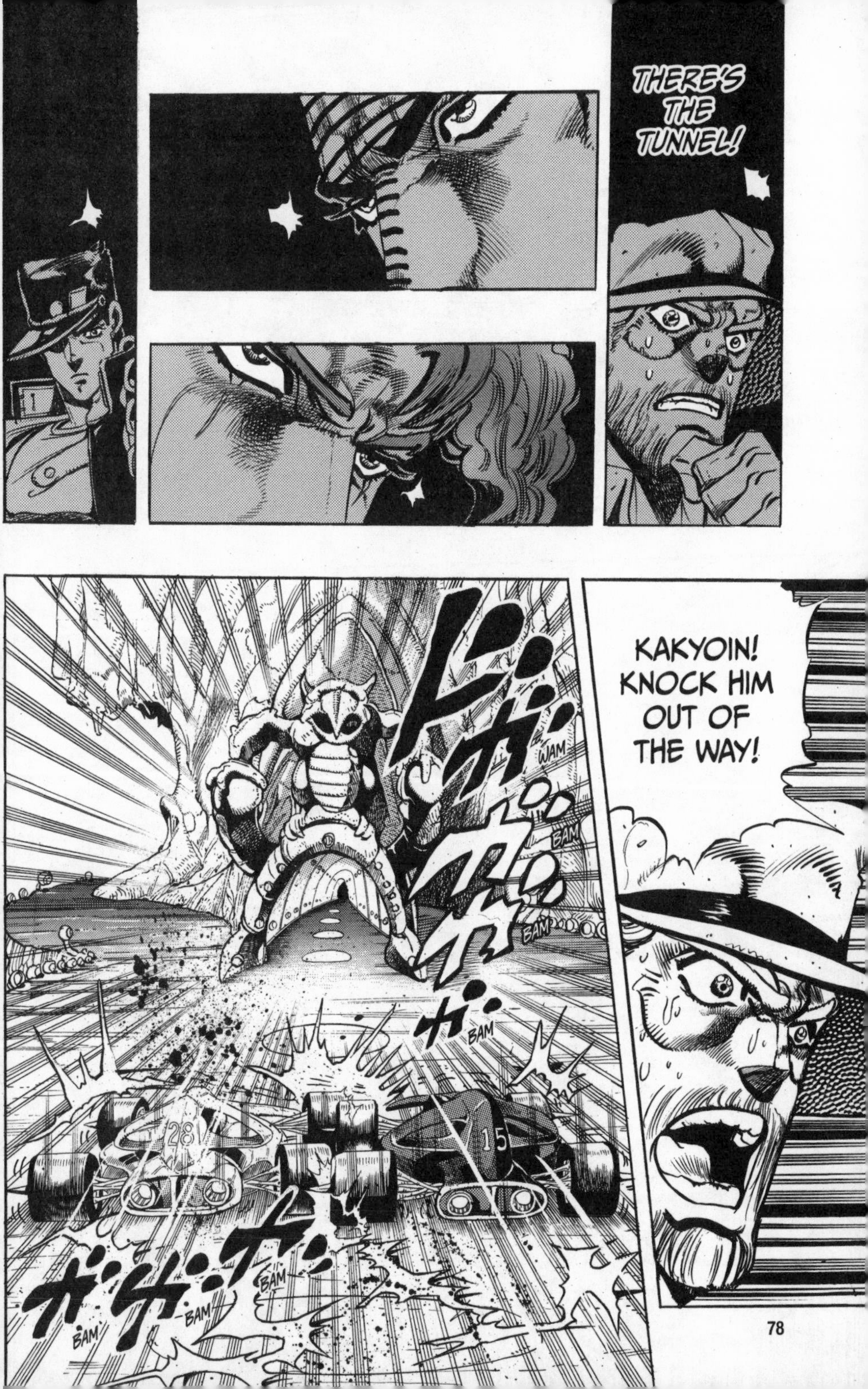
THERE'S THE TUNNEL!
KAKYOIN! KNOCK HIM OUT OF THE WAY!
WAM
BAM
BAM
BAM
BAM
BAM
BAM

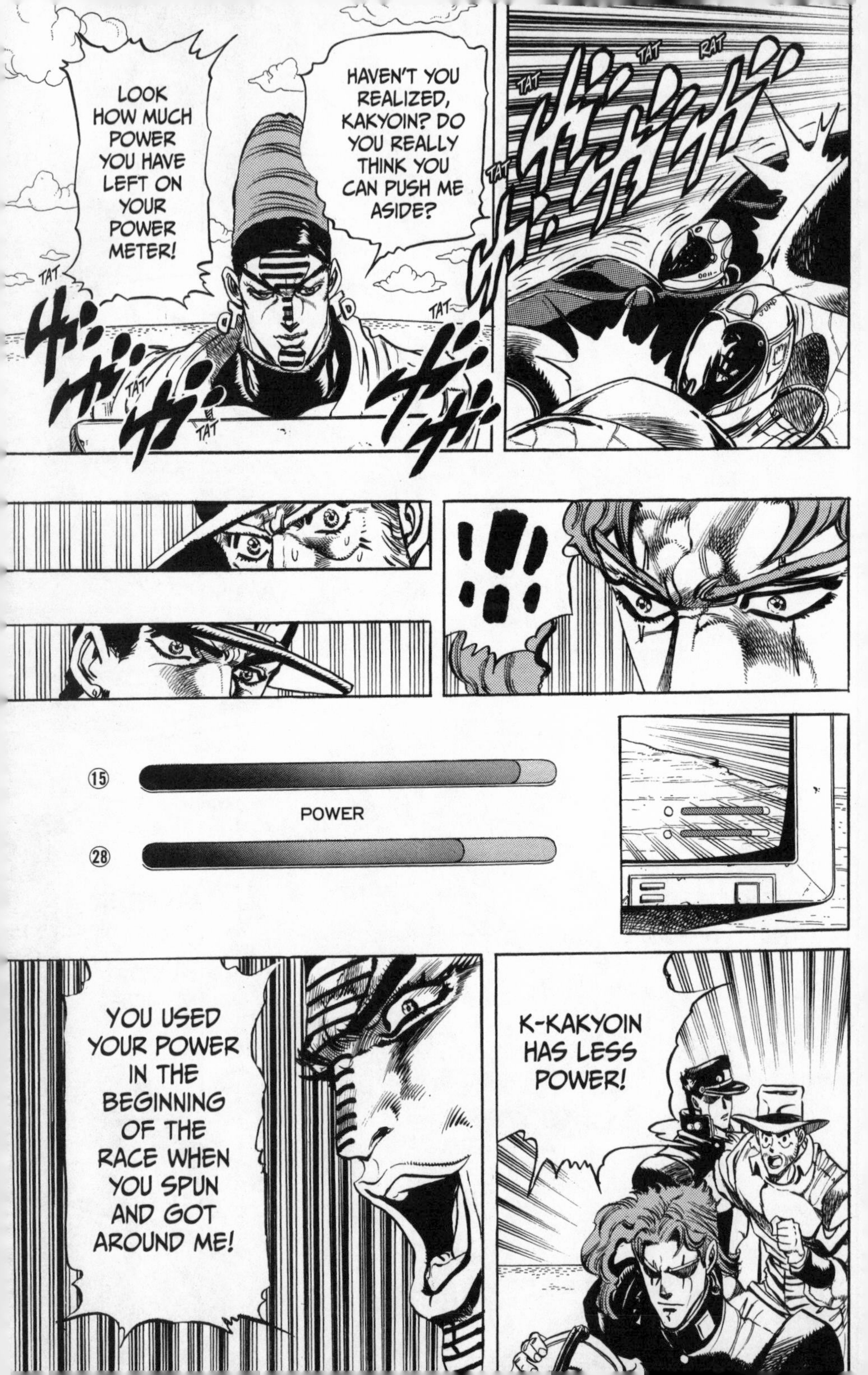
TAT
TAT
RAT
TAT
HAVEN'T YOU REALIZED, KAKYOIN? DO YOU REALLY THINK YOU CAN PUSH ME ASIDE?
LOOK HOW MUCH POWER YOU HAVE LEFT ON YOUR POWER METER!
TAT
TAT
TAT
TAT
15
POWER
28
K-KAKYOIN HAS LESS POWER!
YOU USED YOUR POWER IN THE BEGINNING OF THE RACE WHEN YOU SPUN AND GOT AROUND ME!

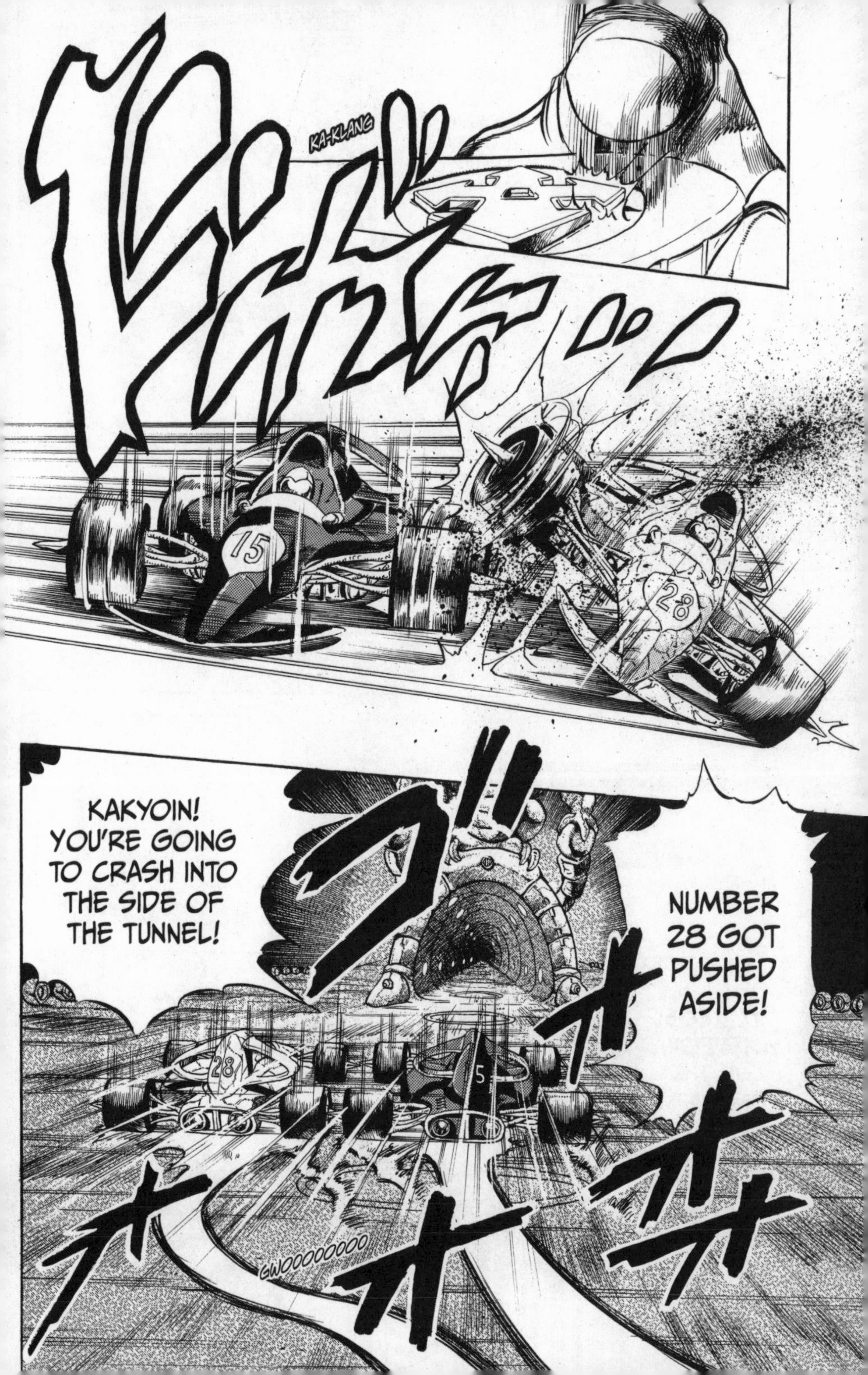
KA-KLANG
NUMBER 28 GOT PUSHED ASIDE!
KAKYOIN! YOU'RE GOING TO CRASH INTO THE SIDE OF THE TUNNEL!
GWOOOOOOOO

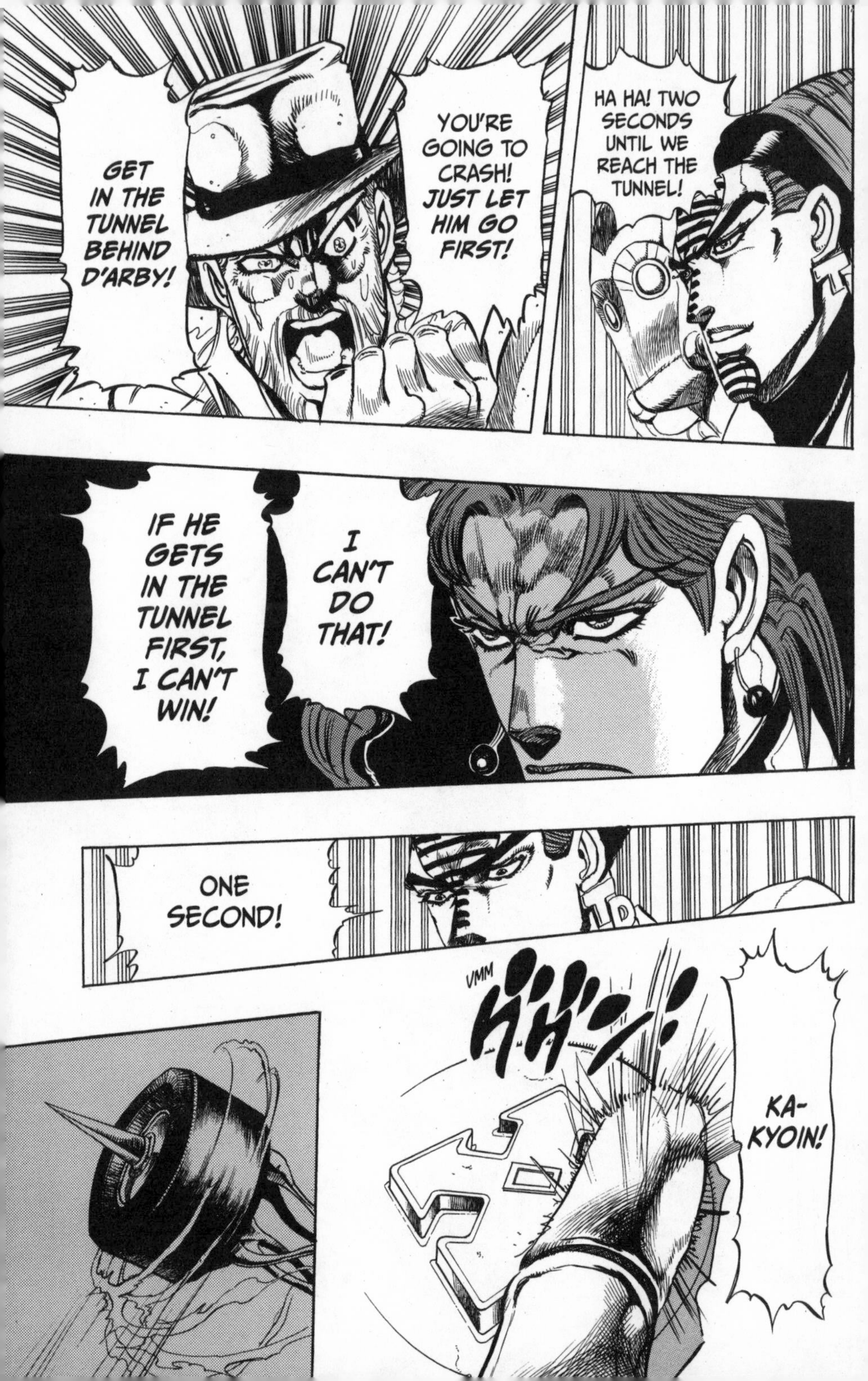
HA HA! TWO SECONDS UNTIL WE REACH THE TUNNEL!
YOU'RE GOING TO CRASH! JUST LET HIM GO FIRST!
GET IN THE TUNNEL BEHIND D'ARBY!
I CAN'T DO THAT!
IF HE GETS IN THE TUNNEL FIRST, I CAN'T WIN!
ONE SECOND!
VMM
KA-KYOIN!

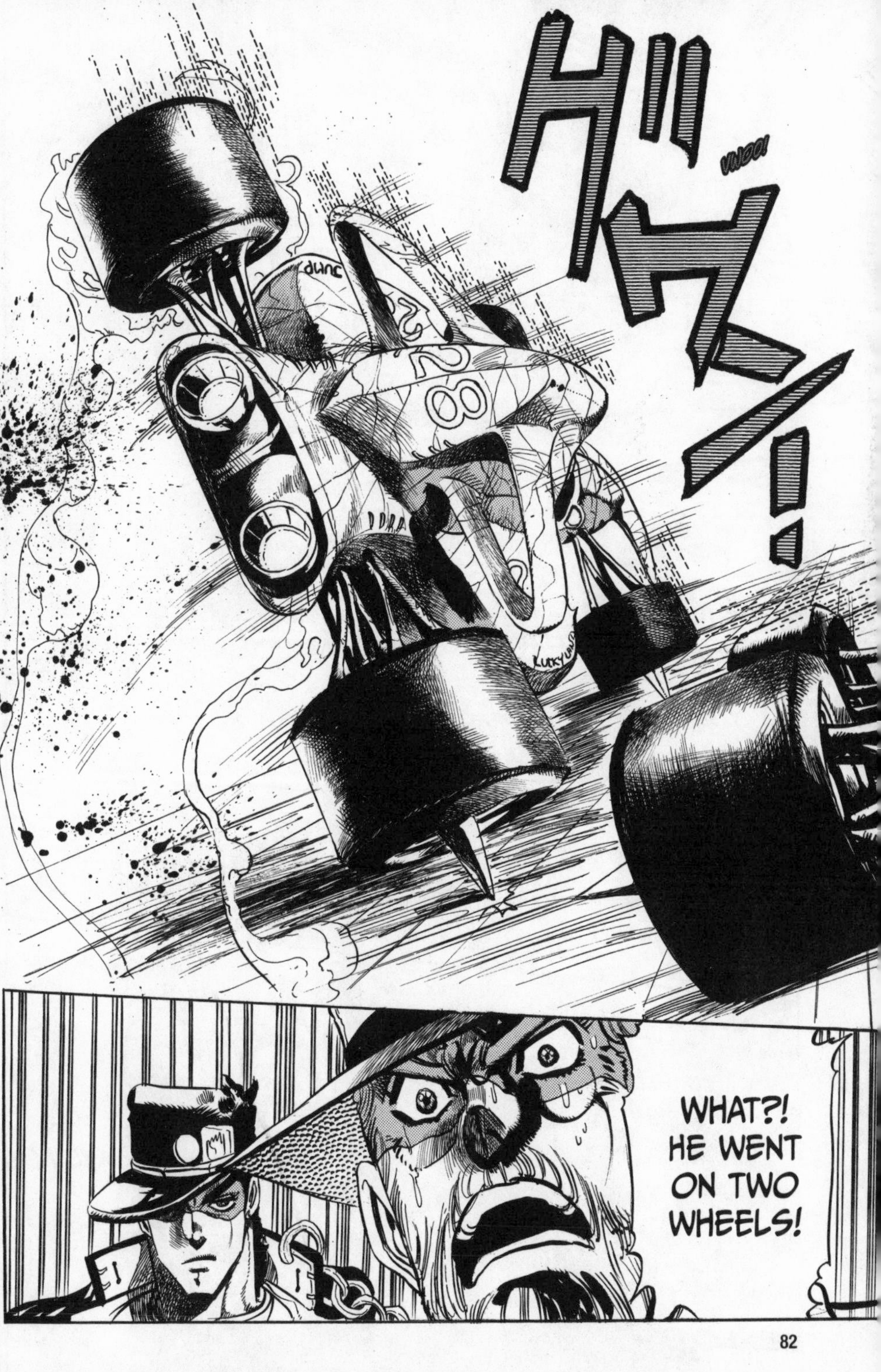
ヴォン!
VWOO!
WHAT?! HE WENT ON TWO WHEELS!

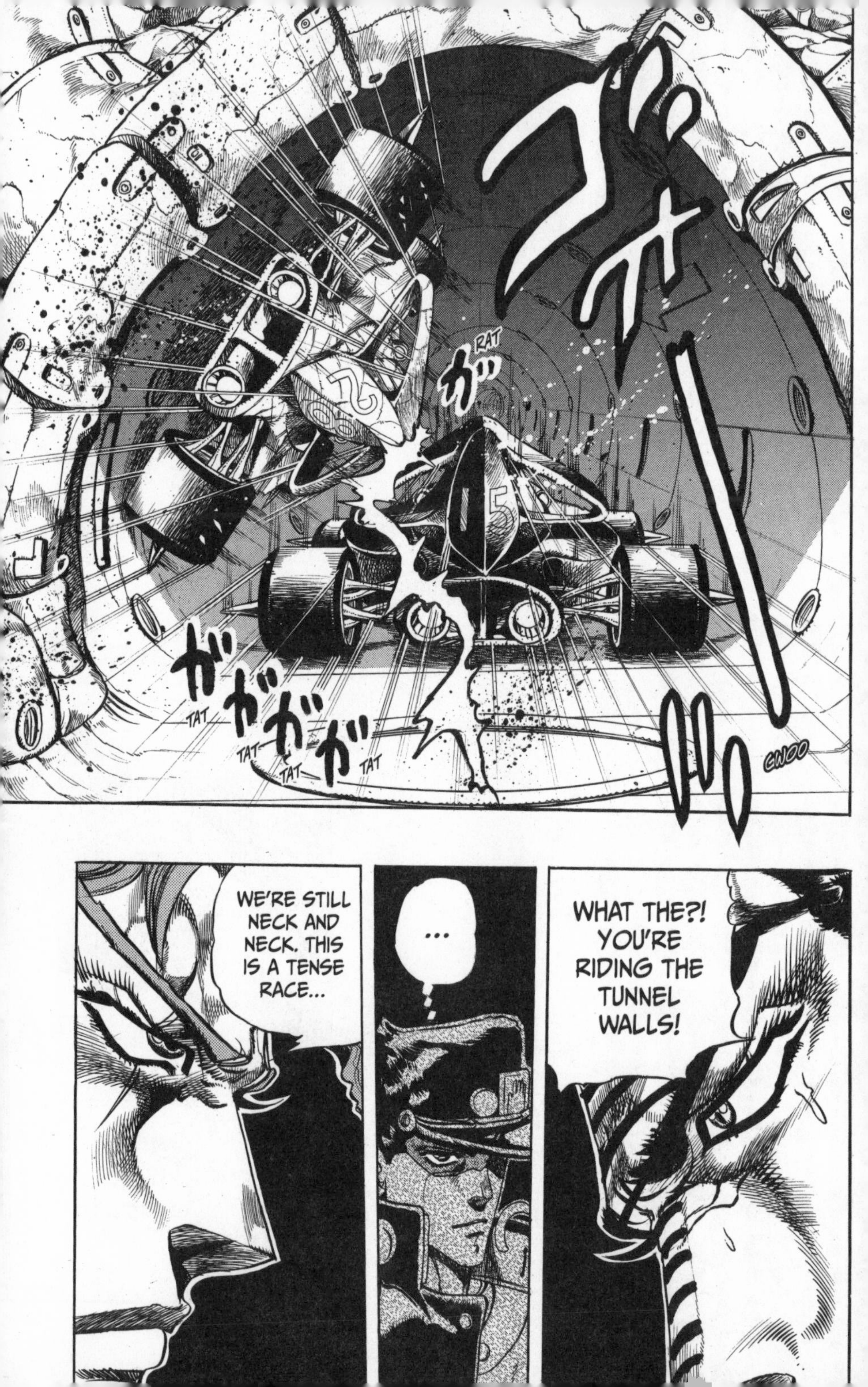
RAT
GWOO
TAT
TAT
TAT
TAT
WHAT THE?! YOU'RE RIDING THE TUNNEL WALLS!
...
WE'RE STILL NECK AND NECK. THIS IS A TENSE RACE...

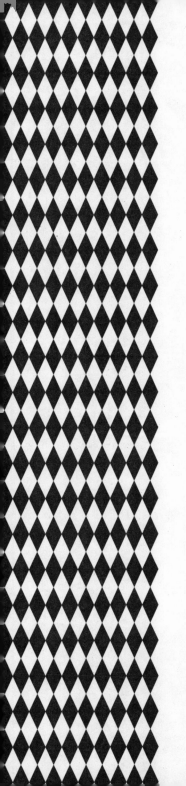

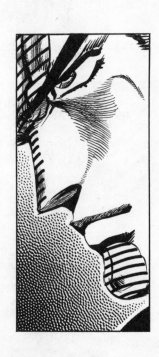

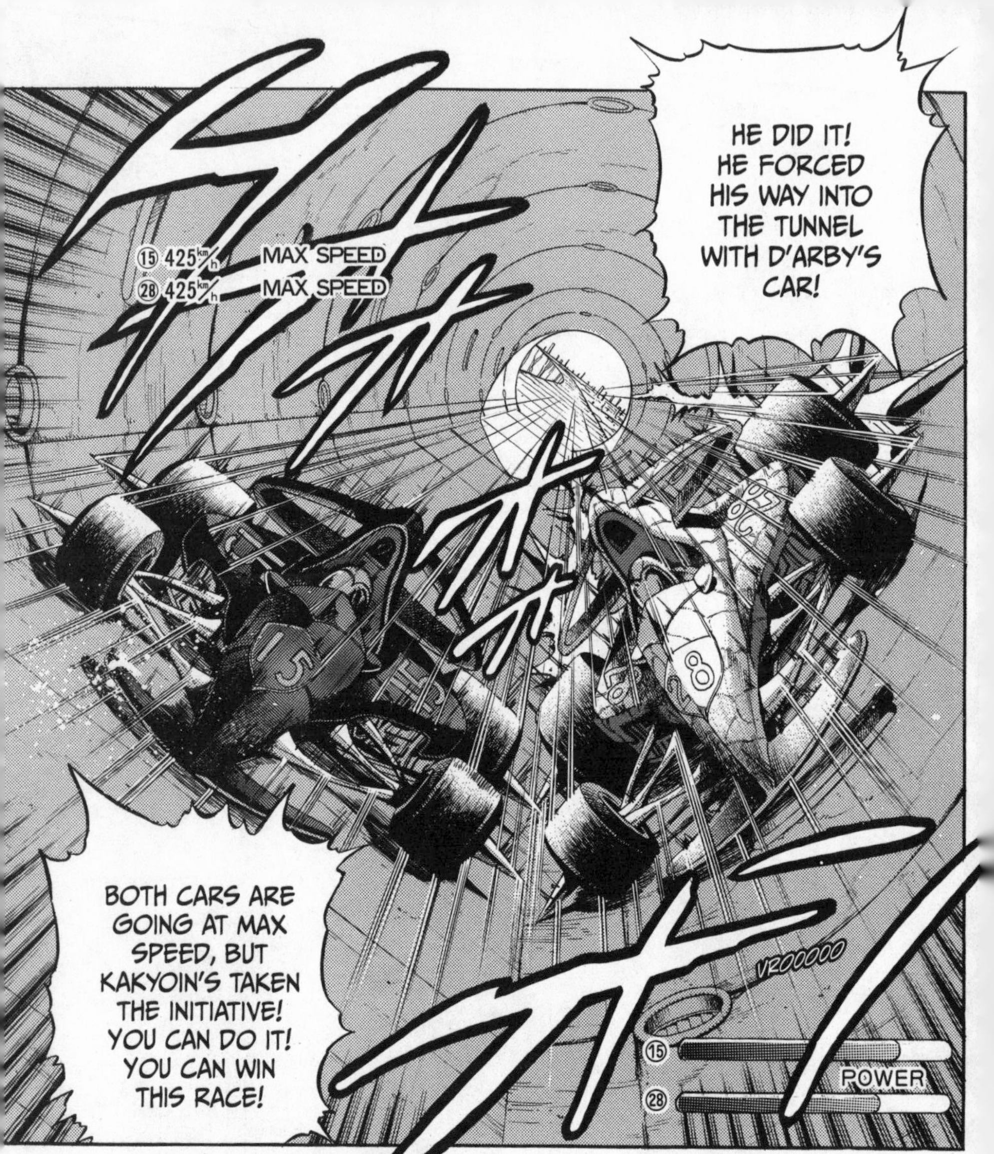
HE DID IT! HE FORCED HIS WAY INTO THE TUNNEL WITH D'ARBY'S CAR!
⑮ 425km/h MAX SPEED
㉘ 425km/h MAX SPEED
VROOOOO
⑮ POWER
㉘
BOTH CARS ARE GOING AT MAX SPEED, BUT KAKYOIN'S TAKEN THE INITIATIVE! YOU CAN DO IT! YOU CAN WIN THIS RACE!

CHAPTER 119: D'Arby the Player PART 6

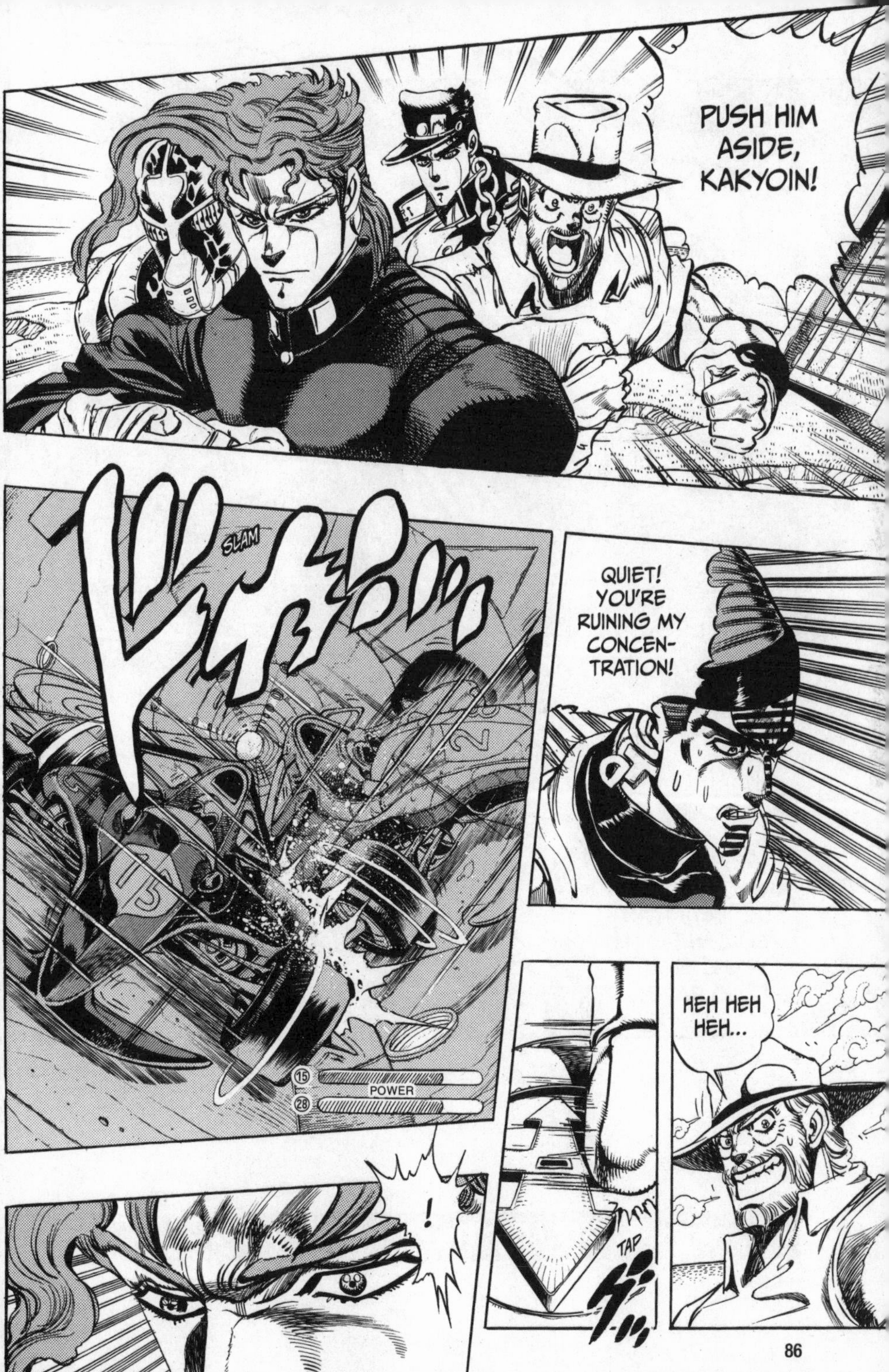
PUSH HIM ASIDE, KAKYOIN!
QUIET! YOU'RE RUINING MY CONCEN-TRATION!
SLAM
15
POWER
28
HEH HEH HEH...
TAP
!

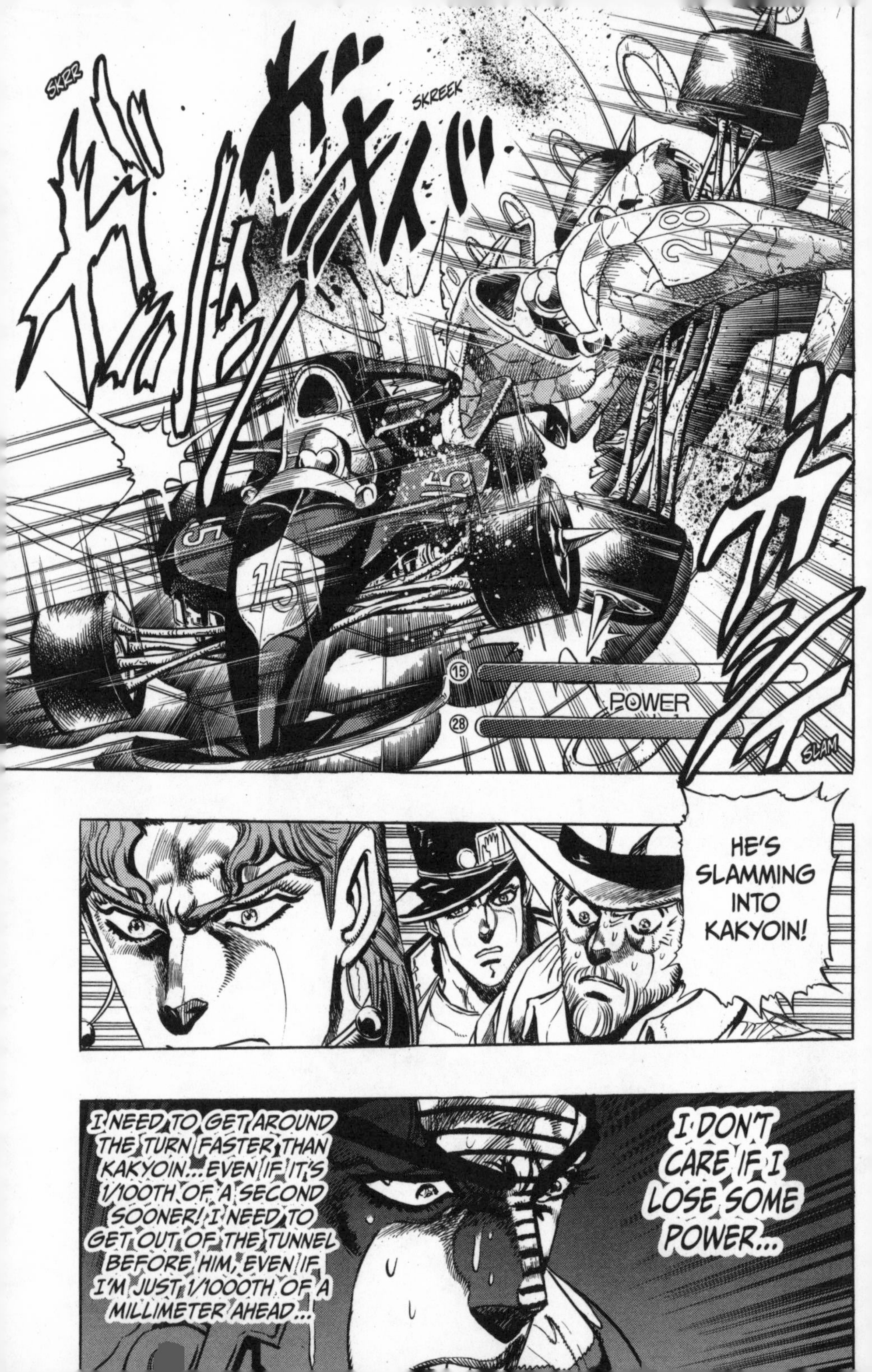
SKREEK
SKRR
15
28
POWER
SLAM
HE'S SLAMMING INTO KAKYOIN!
I DON'T CARE IF I LOSE SOME POWER...
I NEED TO GET AROUND THE TURN FASTER THAN KAKYOIN... EVEN IF IT'S 1/100TH OF A SECOND SOONER! I NEED TO GET OUT OF THE TUNNEL BEFORE HIM, EVEN IF I'M JUST 1/1000TH OF A MILLIMETER AHEAD...

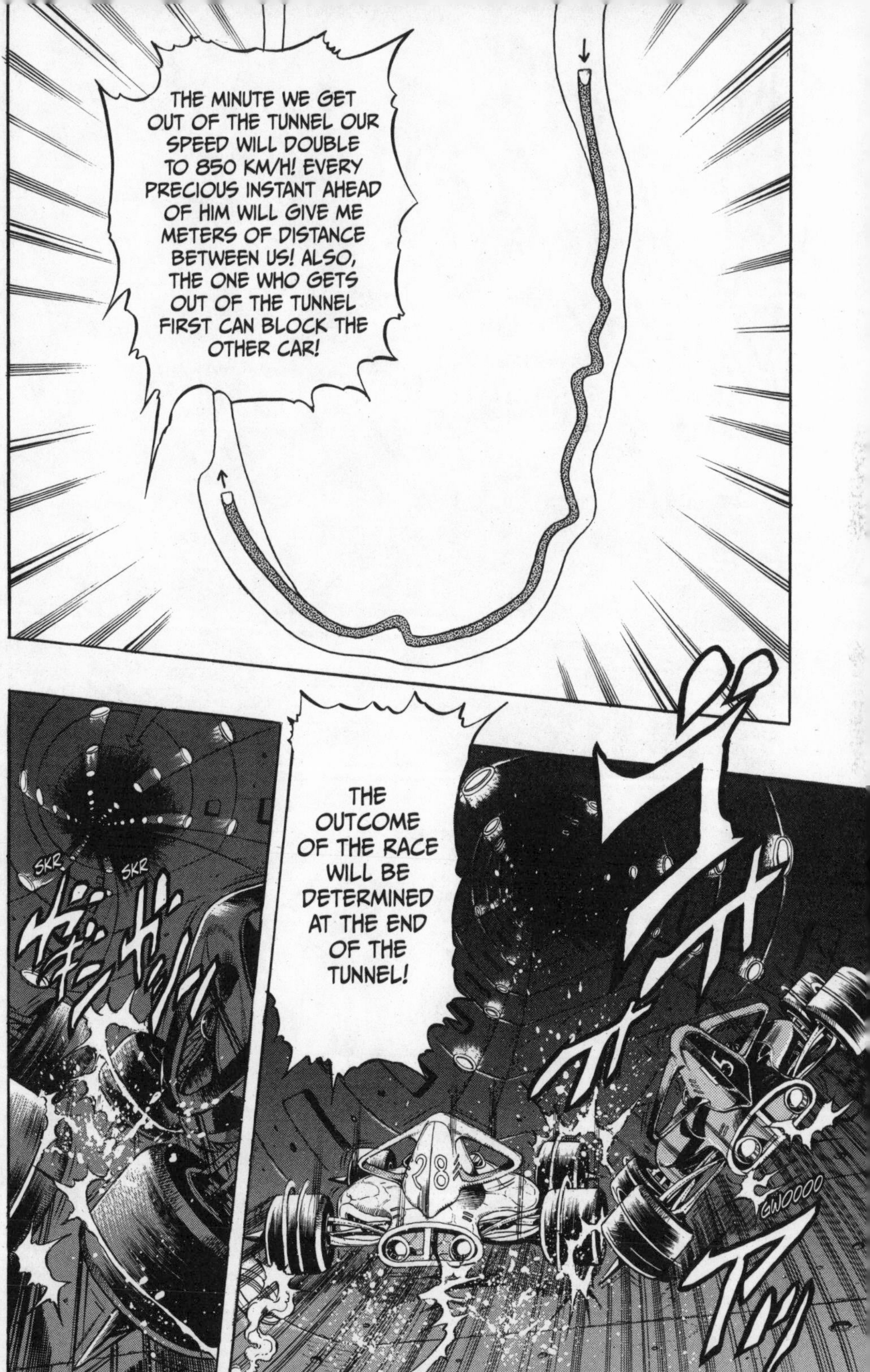
THE MINUTE WE GET OUT OF THE TUNNEL OUR SPEED WILL DOUBLE TO 850 KM/H! EVERY PRECIOUS INSTANT AHEAD OF HIM WILL GIVE ME METERS OF DISTANCE BETWEEN US! ALSO, THE ONE WHO GETS OUT OF THE TUNNEL FIRST CAN BLOCK THE OTHER CAR!
THE OUTCOME OF THE RACE WILL BE DETERMINED AT THE END OF THE TUNNEL!
GWOOOO
SKR
SKR

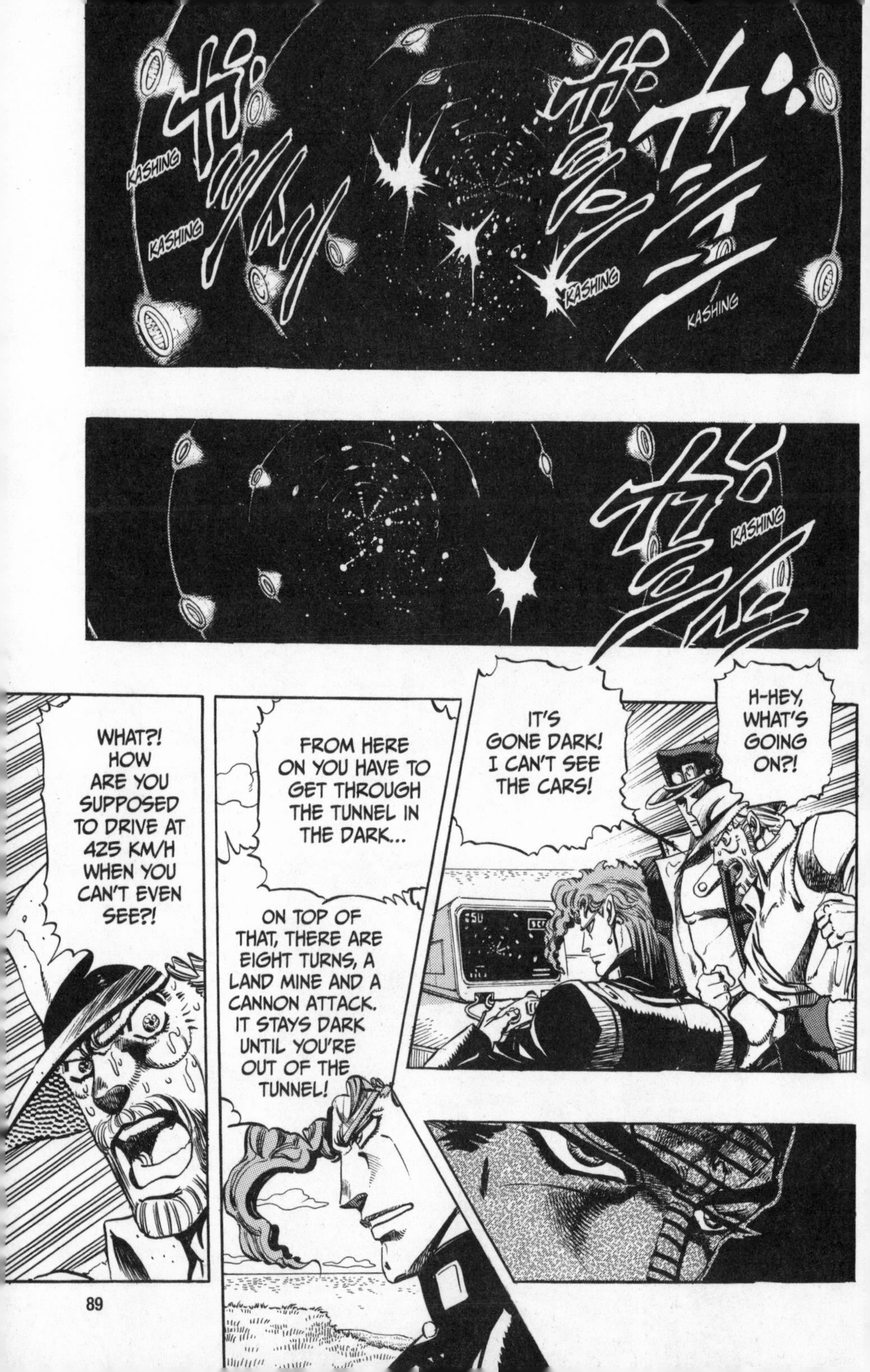
KASHING
KASHING
KASHING
KASHING
KASHING
H-HEY, WHAT'S GOING ON?!
IT'S GONE DARK! I CAN'T SEE THE CARS!
FROM HERE ON YOU HAVE TO GET THROUGH THE TUNNEL IN THE DARK...
ON TOP OF THAT, THERE ARE EIGHT TURNS, A LAND MINE AND A CANNON ATTACK. IT STAYS DARK UNTIL YOU'RE OUT OF THE TUNNEL!
WHAT?! HOW ARE YOU SUPPOSED TO DRIVE AT 425 KM/H WHEN YOU CAN'T EVEN SEE?!

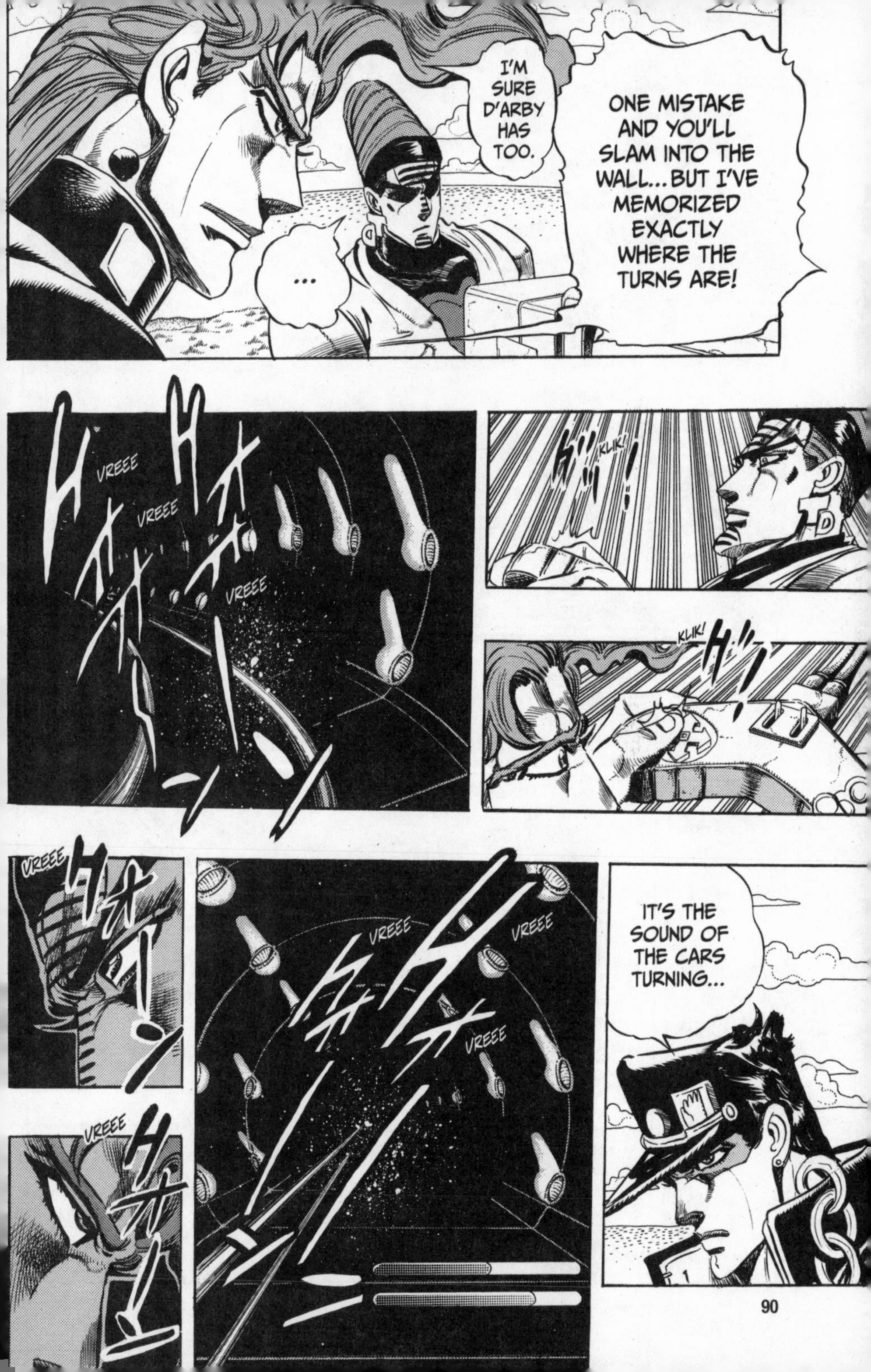

ONE MISTAKE AND YOU'LL SLAM INTO THE WALL...BUT I'VE MEMORIZED EXACTLY WHERE THE TURNS ARE!
I'M SURE D'ARBY HAS TOO.
...
KLIK!
KLIK!
VREEE
VREEE
VREEE
IT'S THE SOUND OF THE CARS TURNING...
VREEE
VREEE
VREEE
VREEE
VREEE

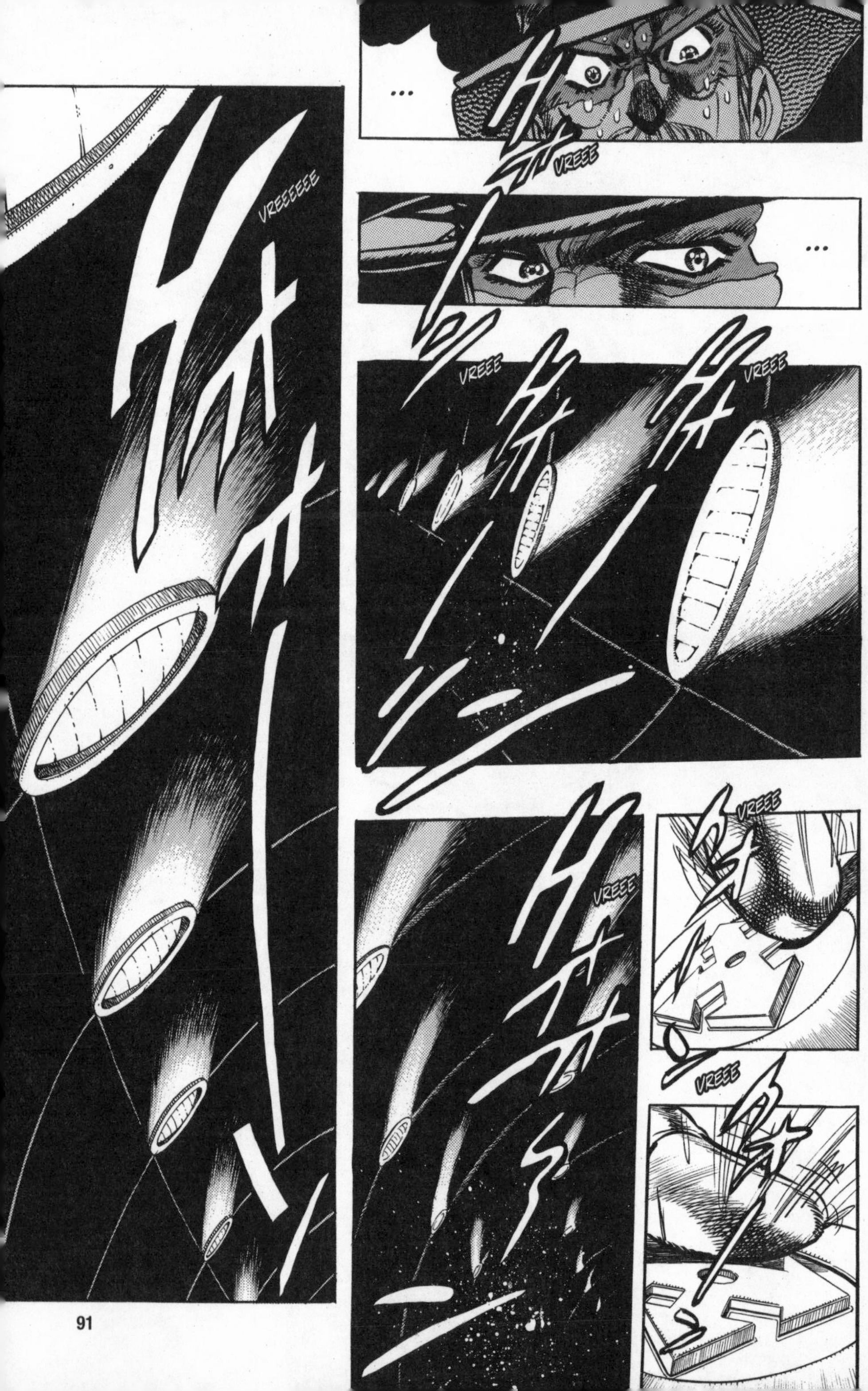
...
VREEE
...
VREEE
VREEE
VREEE
VREEE
VREEE
VREEEEEEE

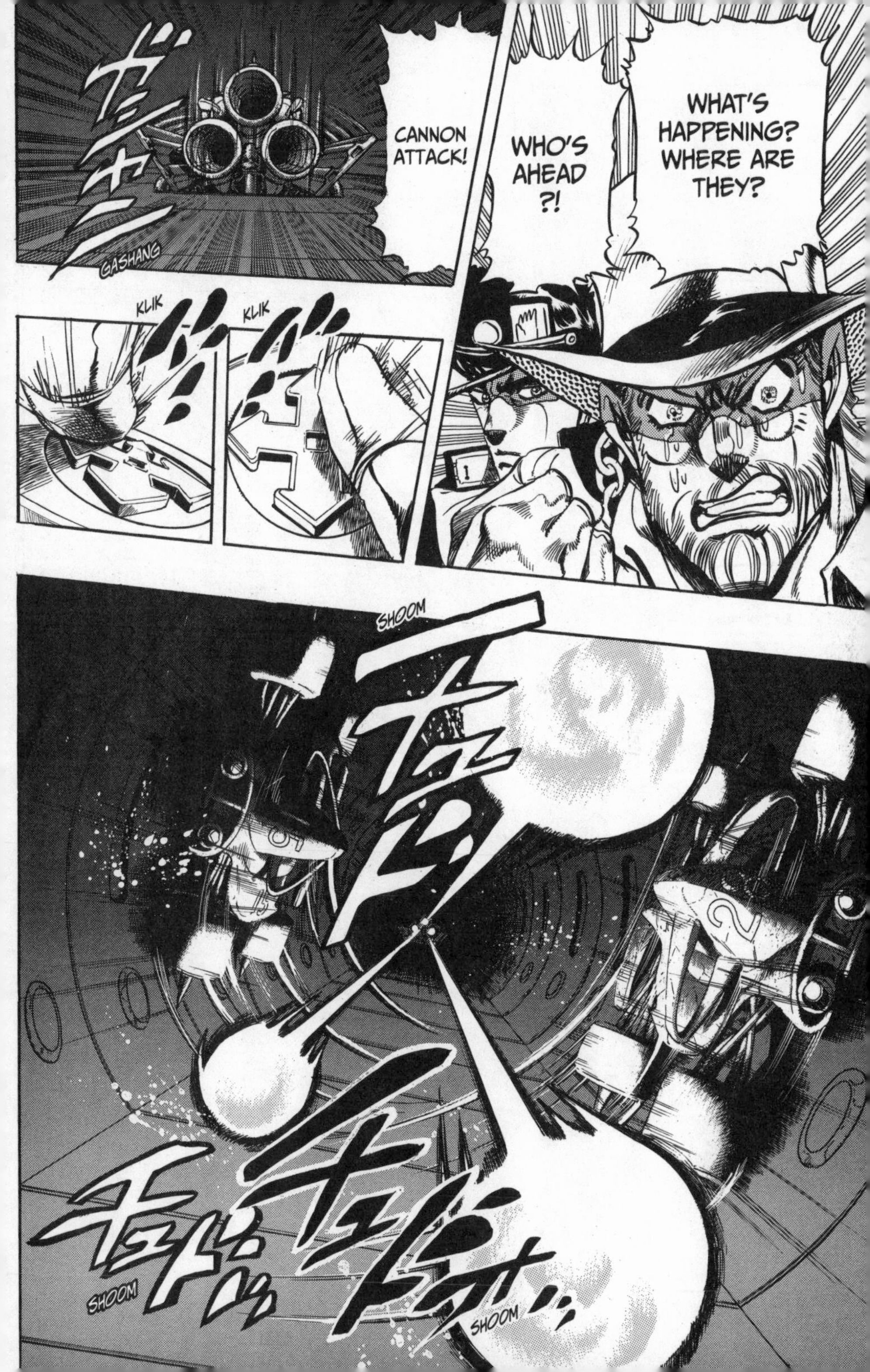
WHAT'S HAPPENING? WHERE ARE THEY?
WHO'S AHEAD ?!
CANNON ATTACK!
GASHANG
KLIK
KLIK
SHOOM
SHOOM
SHOOM

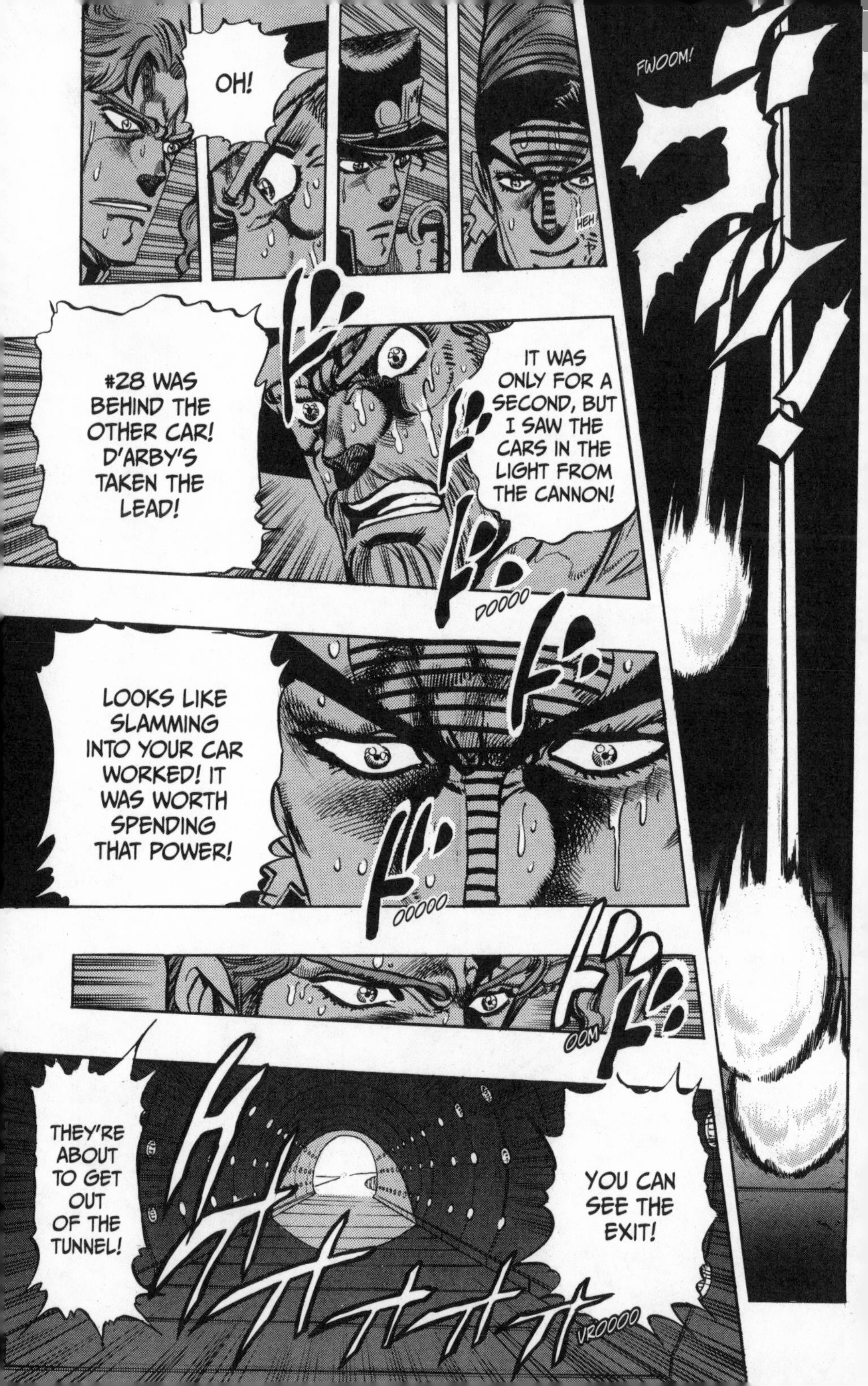
FWOOM!
OH!
HEH
IT WAS ONLY FOR A SECOND, BUT I SAW THE CARS IN THE LIGHT FROM THE CANNON!
#28 WAS BEHIND THE OTHER CAR! D'ARBY'S TAKEN THE LEAD!
DOOOO
LOOKS LIKE SLAMMING INTO YOUR CAR WORKED! IT WAS WORTH SPENDING THAT POWER!
OOOOO
OOM
YOU CAN SEE THE EXIT!
THEY'RE ABOUT TO GET OUT OF THE TUNNEL!
VROOOO

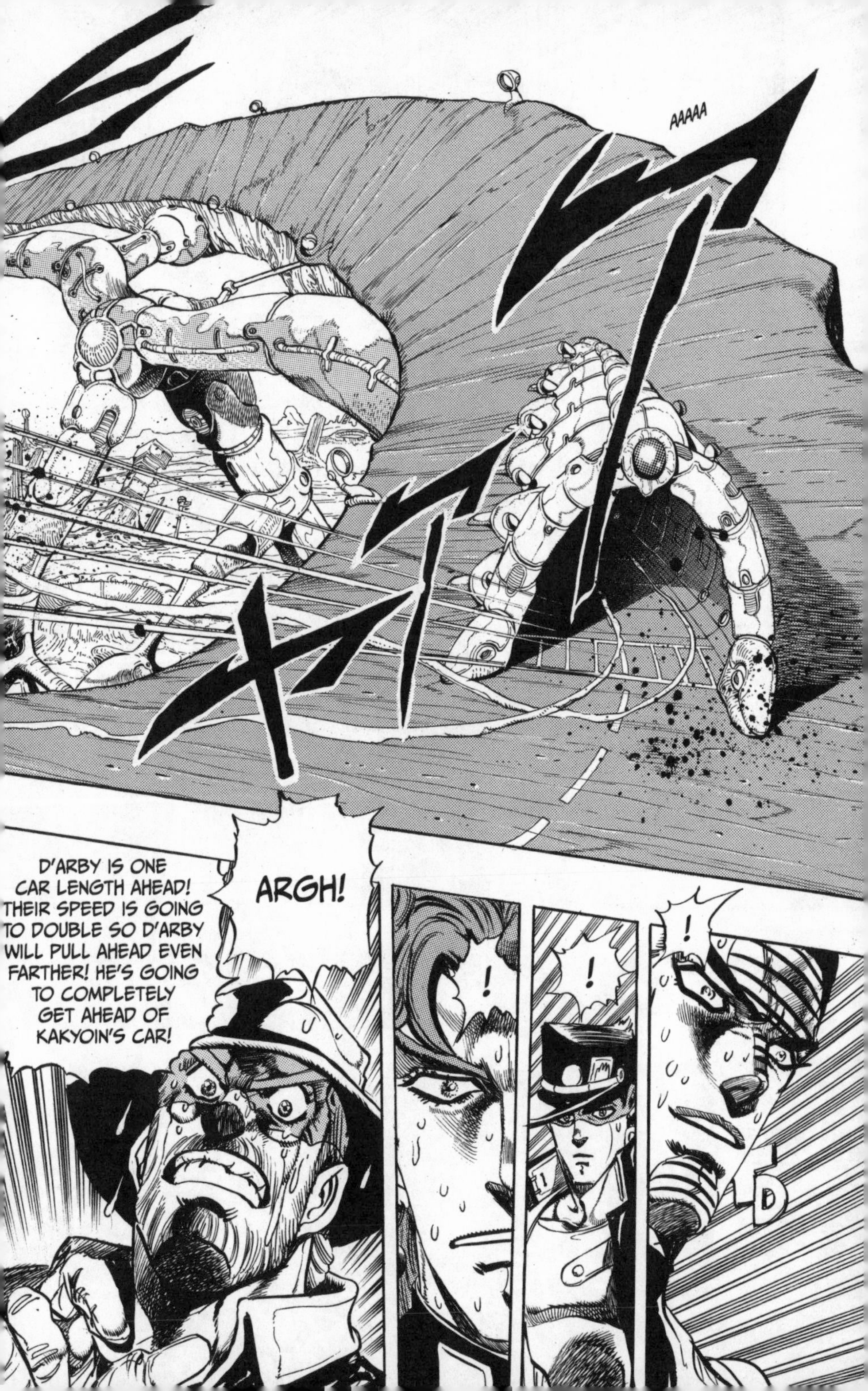
AAAAA
ARGH!
D'ARBY IS ONE CAR LENGTH AHEAD! THEIR SPEED IS GOING TO DOUBLE SO D'ARBY WILL PULL AHEAD EVEN FARTHER! HE'S GOING TO COMPLETELY GET AHEAD OF KAKYOIN'S CAR!
!
!
!

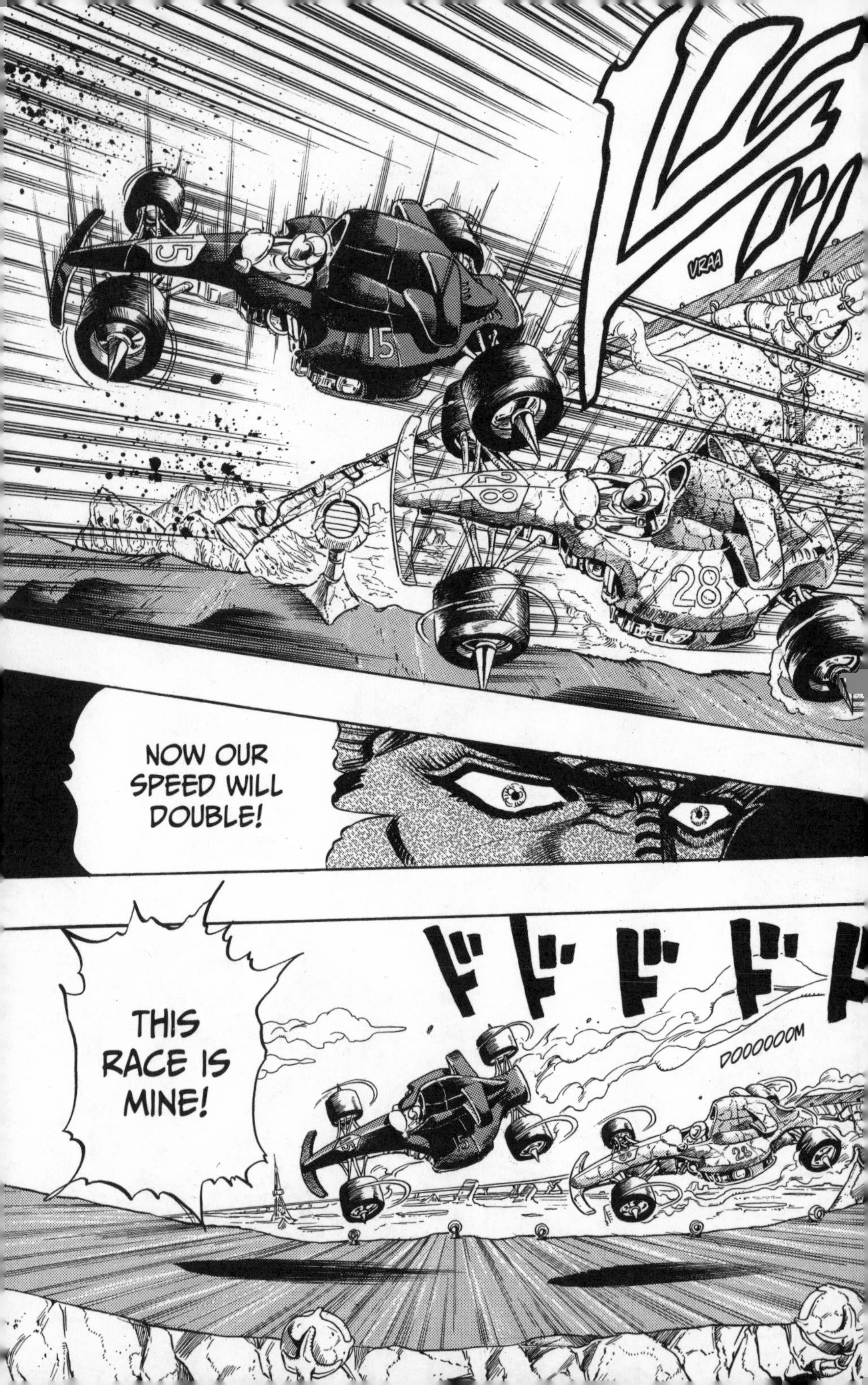
VRAA
NOW OUR SPEED WILL DOUBLE!
THIS RACE IS MINE!
DOOOOOOM

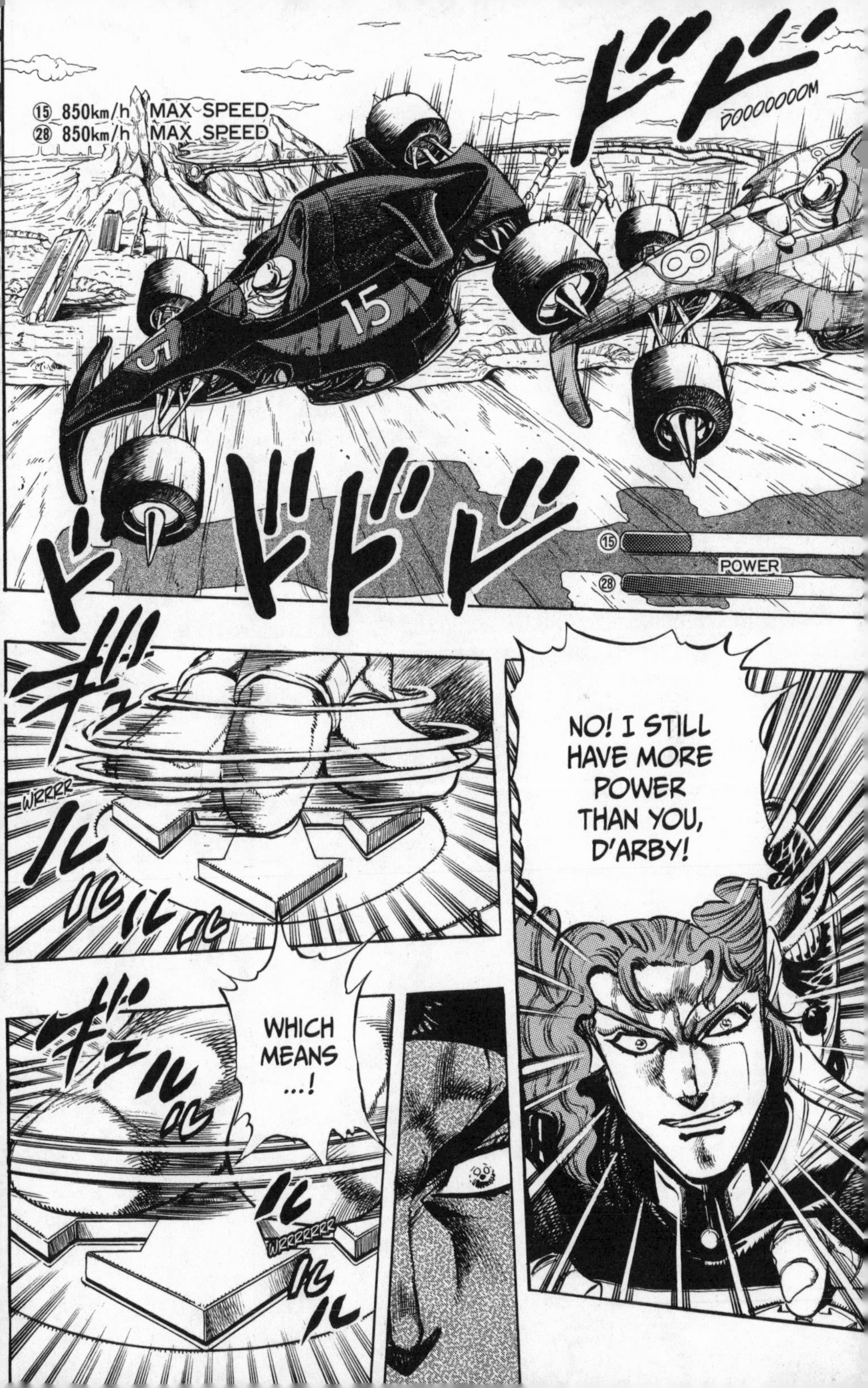
⑮ 850km/h MAX SPEED
㉘ 850km/h MAX SPEED
DOOOOOOOM
⑮
POWER
㉘
NO! I STILL HAVE MORE POWER THAN YOU, D'ARBY!
WRRRR
WHICH MEANS ...!
WRRRRRRR

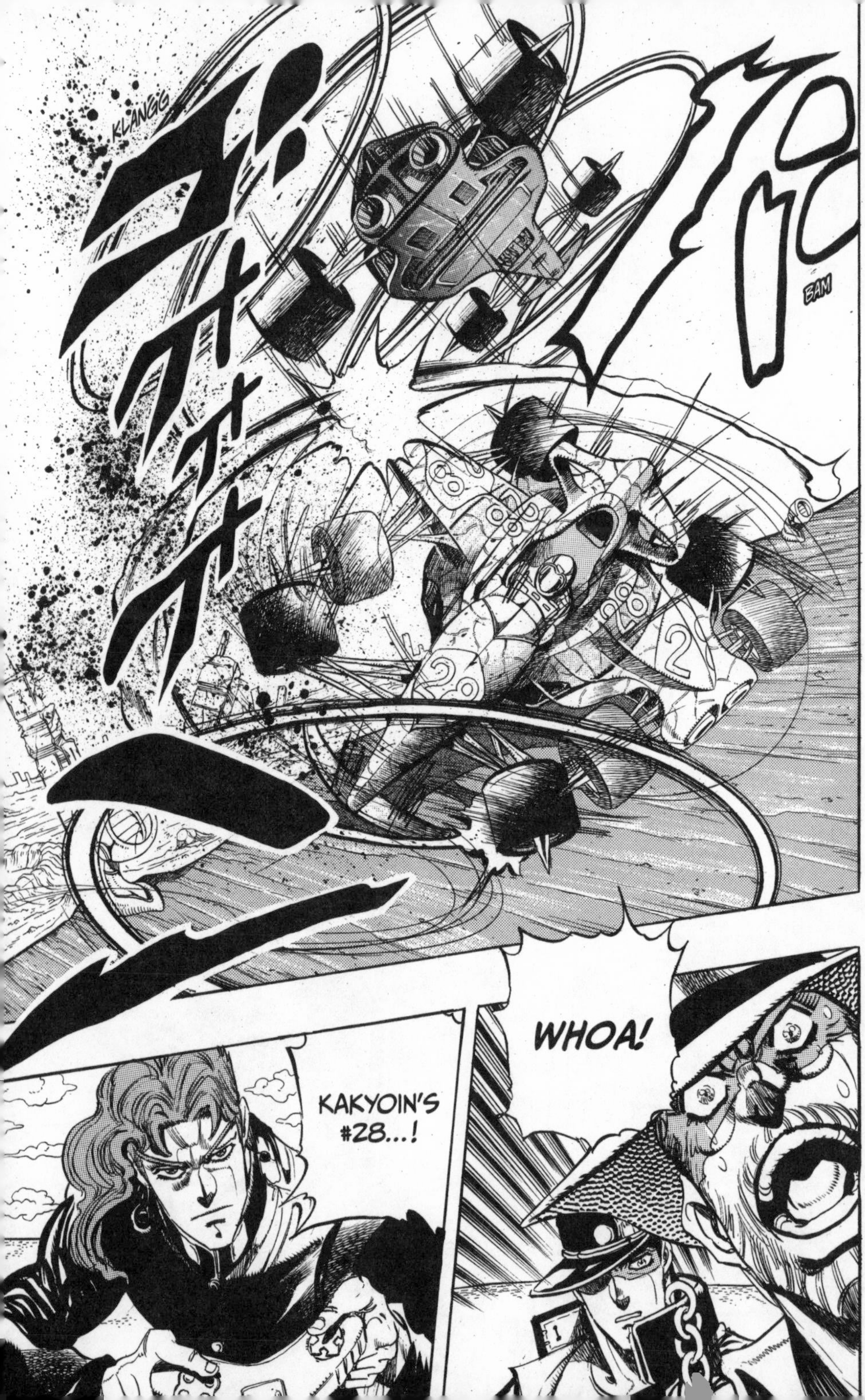
BAM
KLANGG
WHOA!
KAKYOIN'S
#28...!

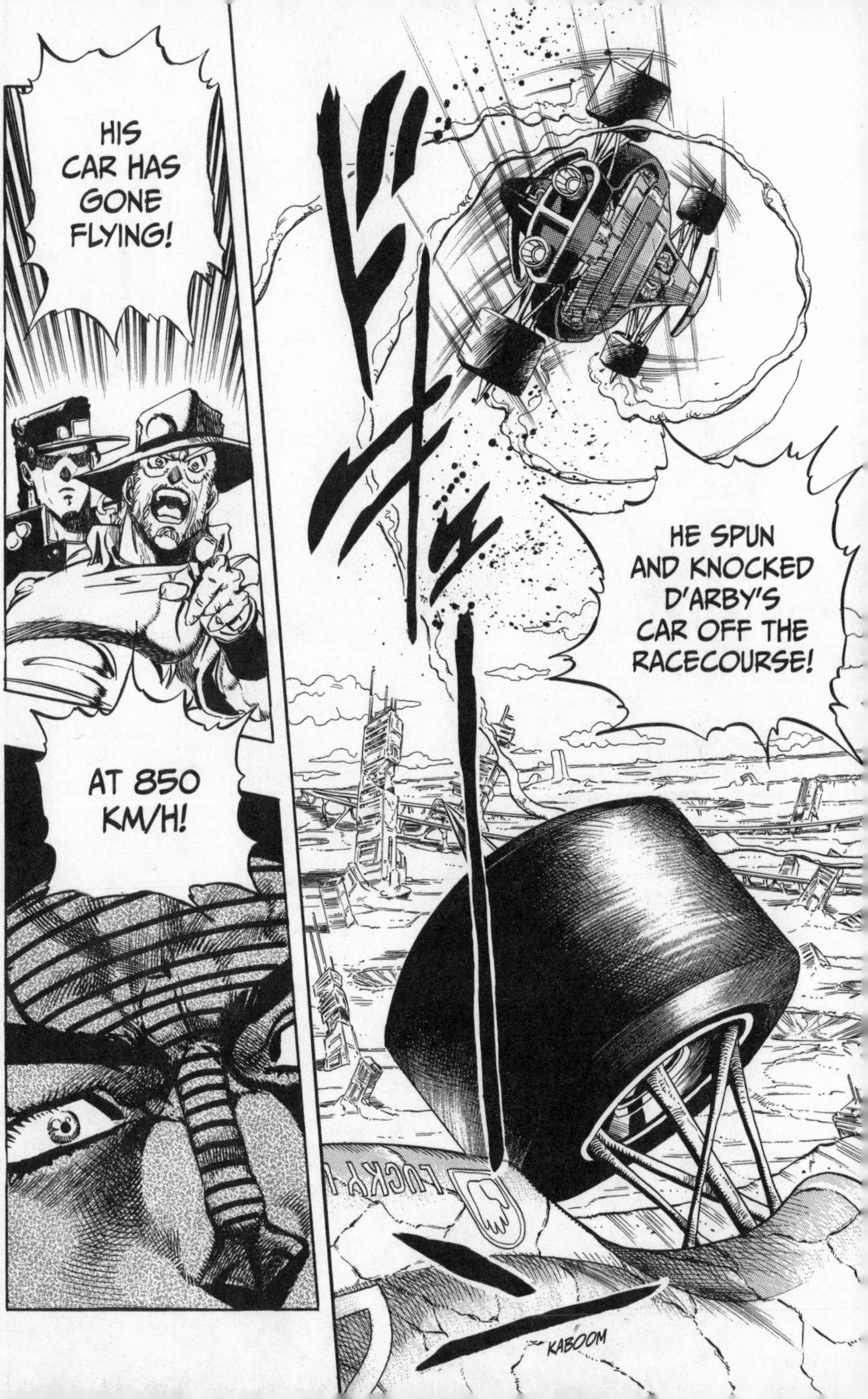
HE SPUN AND KNOCKED D'ARBY'S CAR OFF THE RACECOURSE!
KABOOM
HIS CAR HAS GONE FLYING!
AT 850 KM/H!

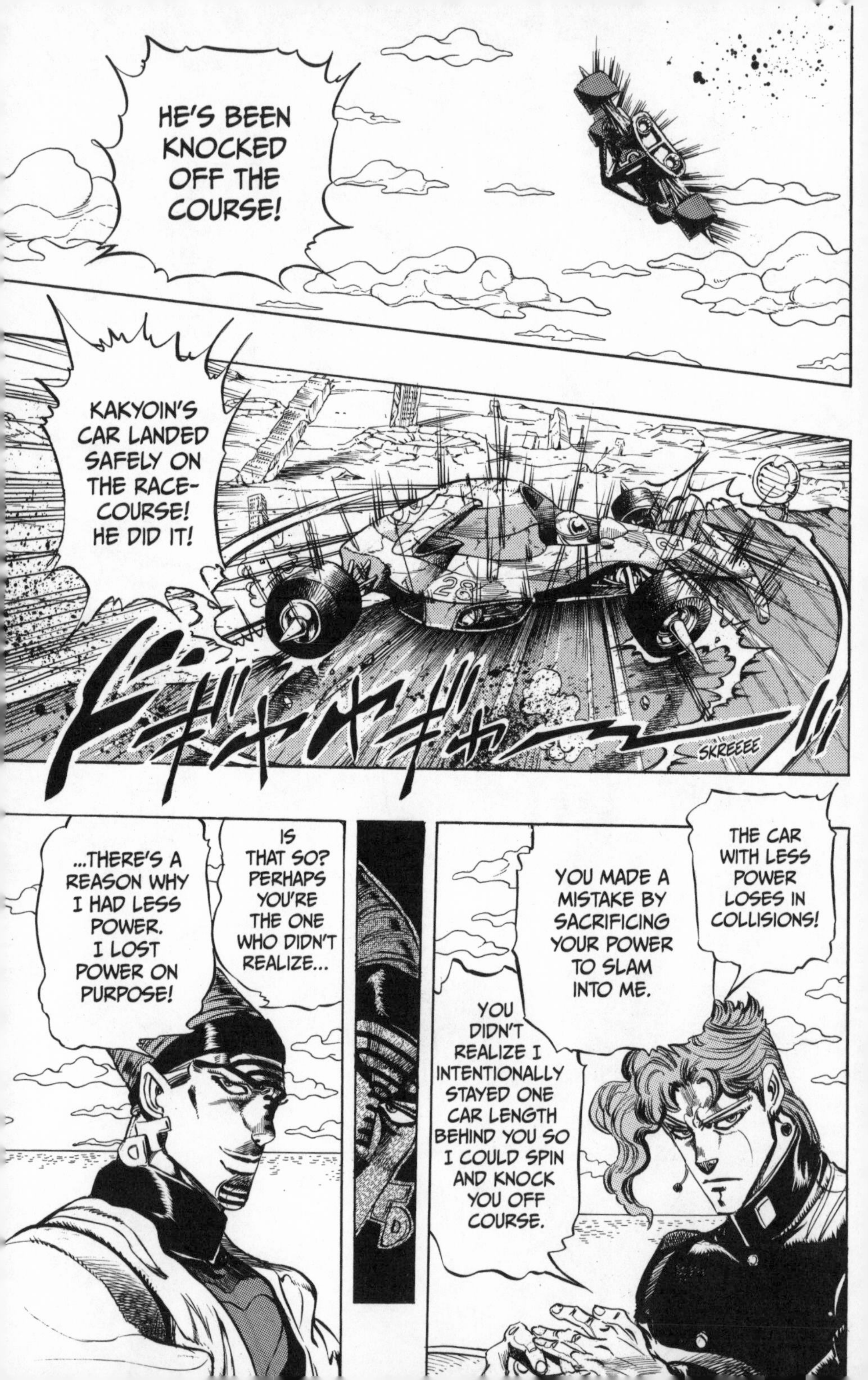

HE'S BEEN KNOCKED OFF THE COURSE!
KAKYOIN'S CAR LANDED SAFELY ON THE RACE-COURSE! HE DID IT!
SKREEEE
THE CAR WITH LESS POWER LOSES IN COLLISIONS!
YOU MADE A MISTAKE BY SACRIFICING YOUR POWER TO SLAM INTO ME.
YOU DIDN'T REALIZE I INTENTIONALLY STAYED ONE CAR LENGTH BEHIND YOU SO I COULD SPIN AND KNOCK YOU OFF COURSE.
IS THAT SO? PERHAPS YOU'RE THE ONE WHO DIDN'T REALIZE...
...THERE'S A REASON WHY I HAD LESS POWER. I LOST POWER ON PURPOSE!

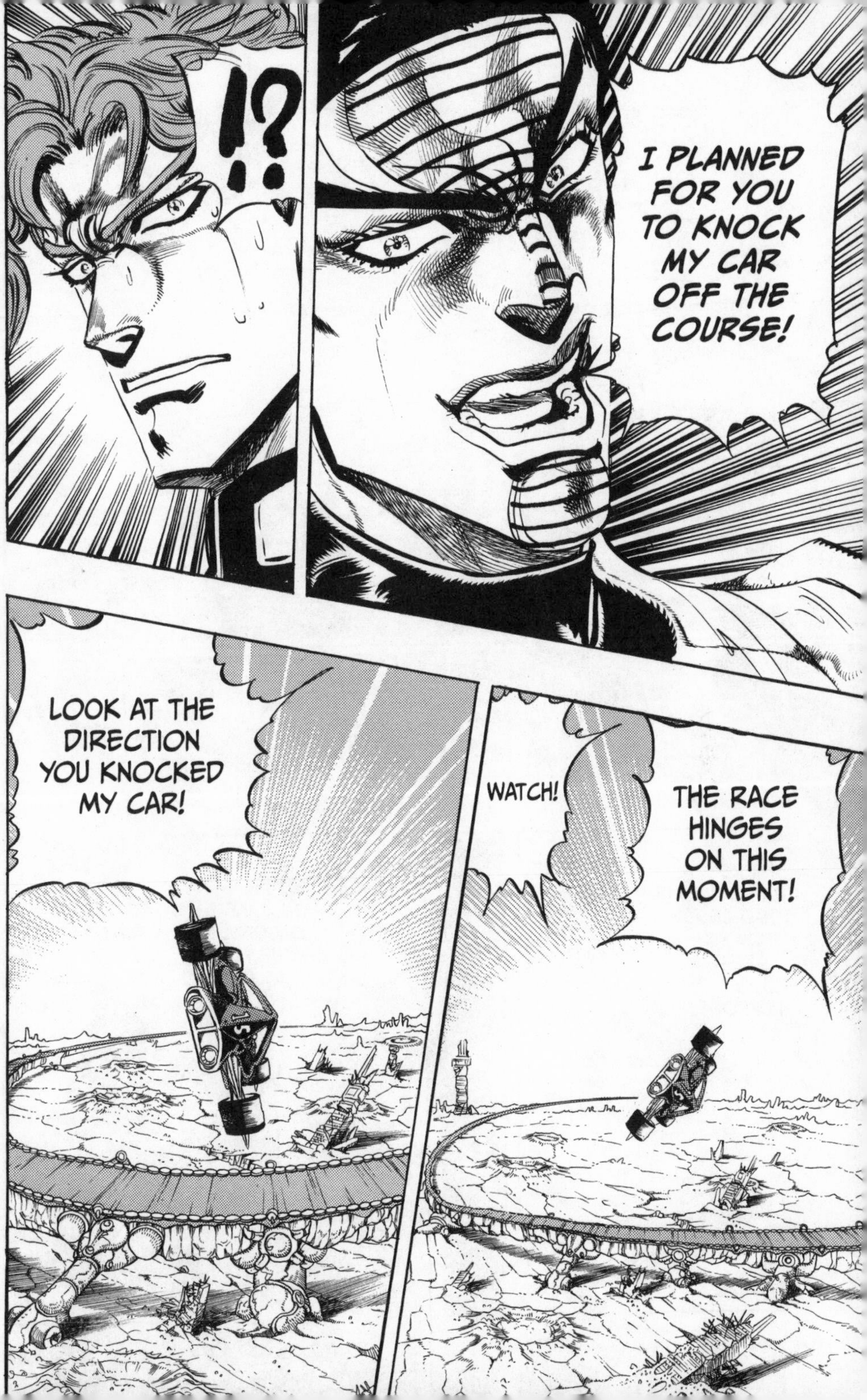
I PLANNED FOR YOU TO KNOCK MY CAR OFF THE COURSE!
!?
THE RACE HINGES ON THIS MOMENT!
WATCH!
LOOK AT THE DIRECTION YOU KNOCKED MY CAR!

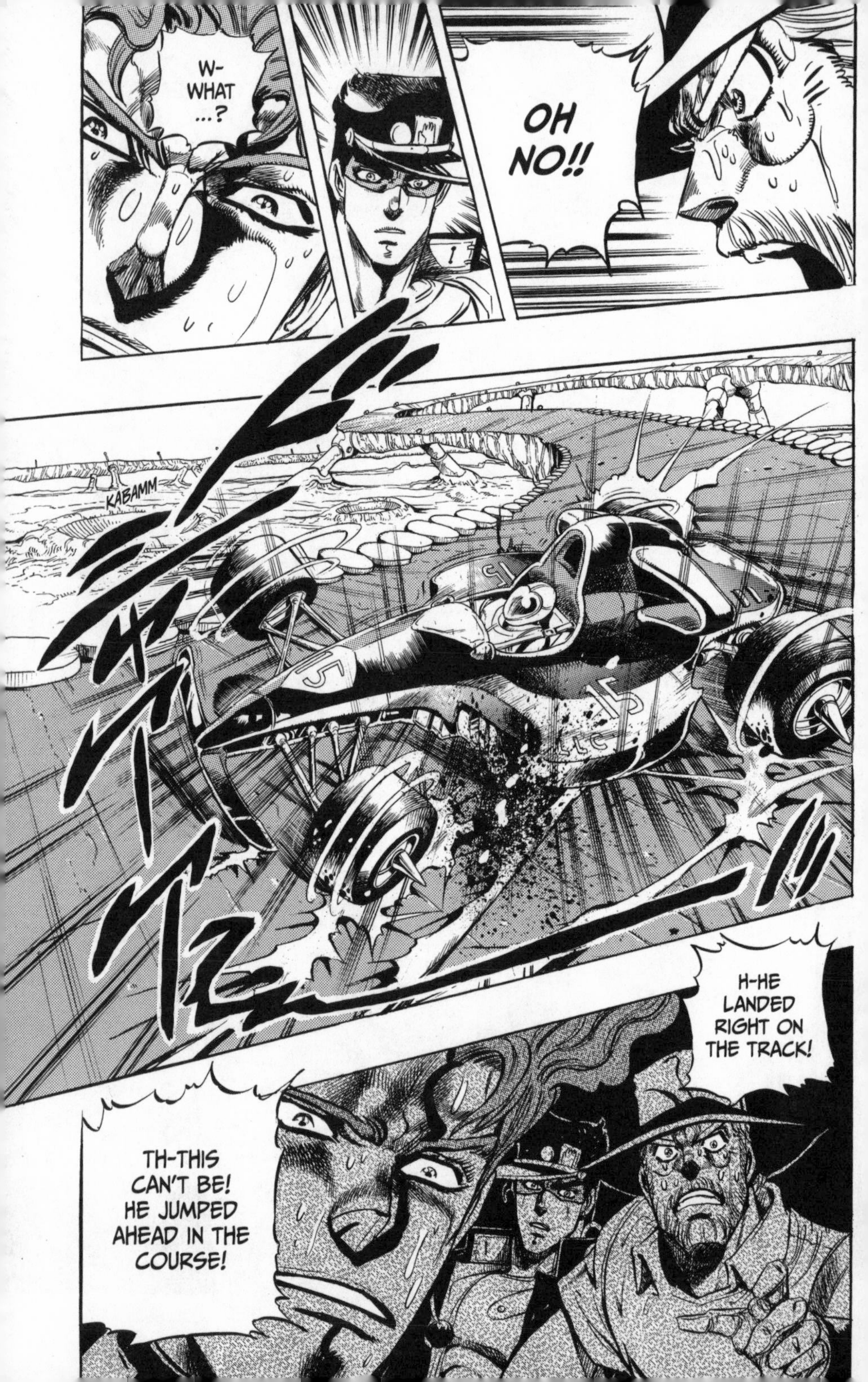
OH NO!!
W-WHAT ...?
KABAMM
H-HE LANDED RIGHT ON THE TRACK!
TH-THIS CAN'T BE! HE JUMPED AHEAD IN THE COURSE!

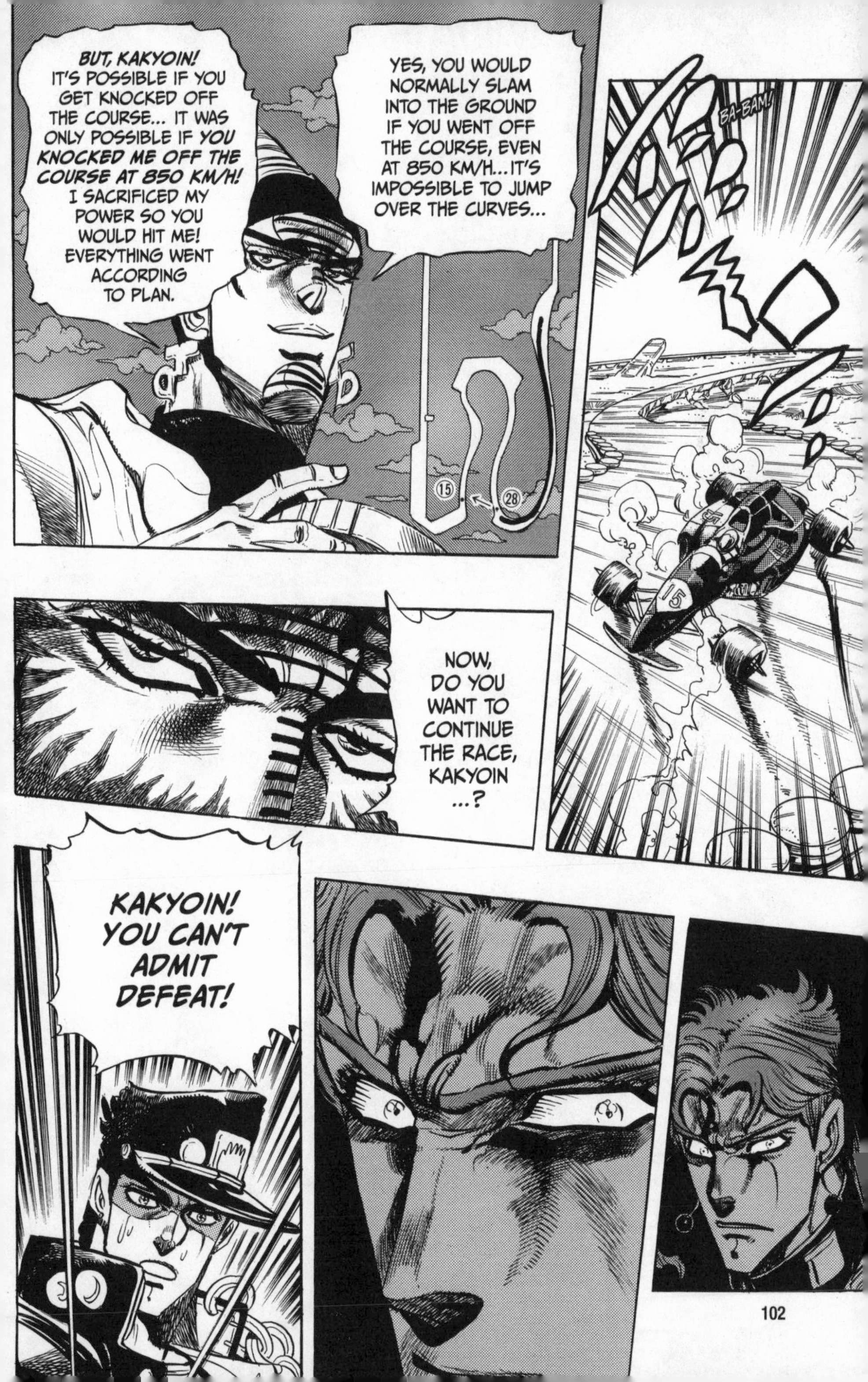
BA-BAM!
YES, YOU WOULD NORMALLY SLAM INTO THE GROUND IF YOU WENT OFF THE COURSE, EVEN AT 850 KM/H...IT'S IMPOSSIBLE TO JUMP OVER THE CURVES...
BUT, KAKYOIN! IT'S POSSIBLE IF YOU GET KNOCKED OFF THE COURSE... IT WAS ONLY POSSIBLE IF YOU KNOCKED ME OFF THE COURSE AT 850 KM/H! I SACRIFICED MY POWER SO YOU WOULD HIT ME! EVERYTHING WENT ACCORDING TO PLAN.
15
28
NOW, DO YOU WANT TO CONTINUE THE RACE, KAKYOIN ...?
KAKYOIN! YOU CAN'T ADMIT DEFEAT!

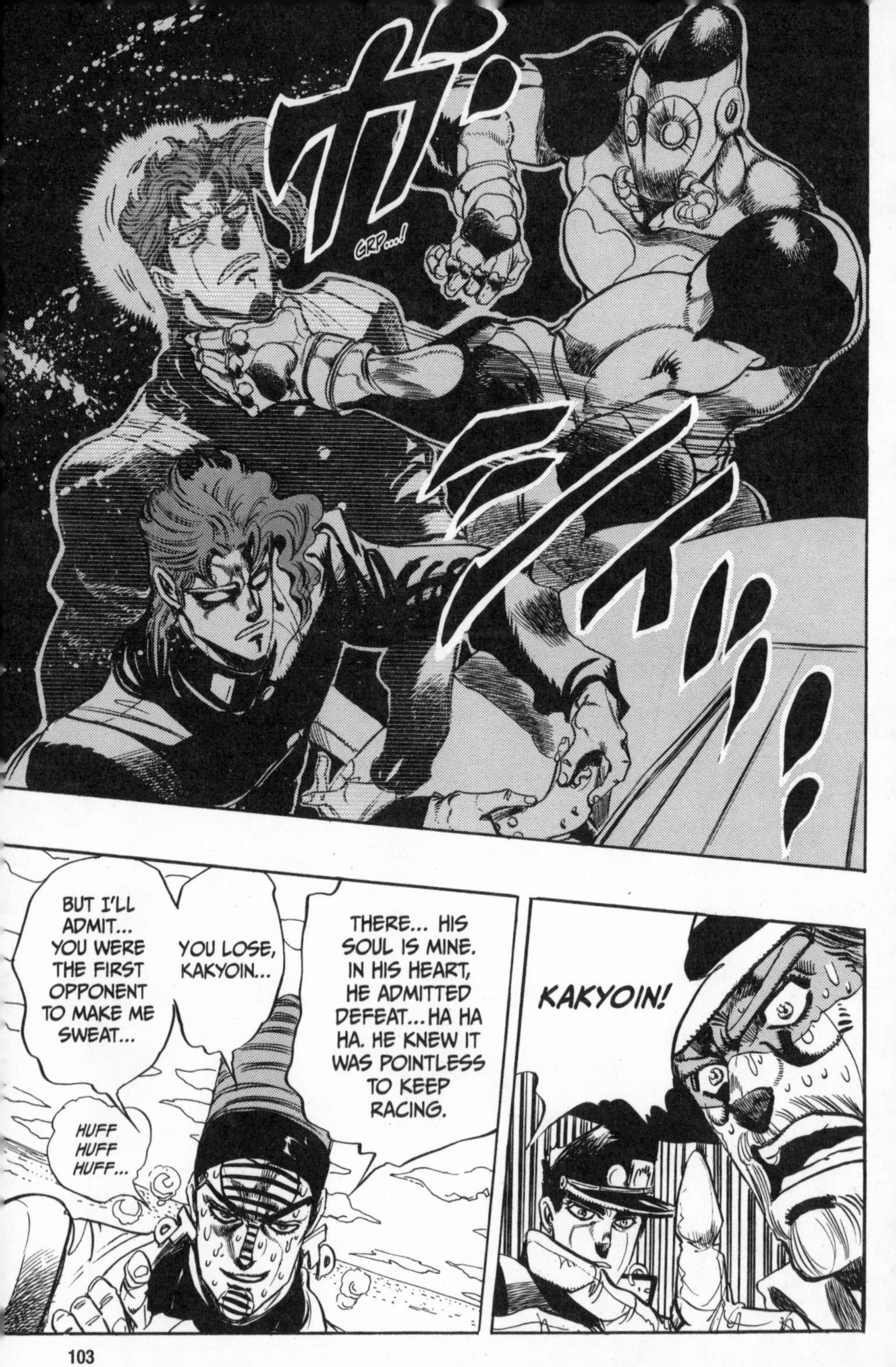
GRP...!
KAKYOIN!
THERE... HIS SOUL IS MINE. IN HIS HEART, HE ADMITTED DEFEAT... HA HA HA. HE KNEW IT WAS POINTLESS TO KEEP RACING.
YOU LOSE, KAKYOIN...
BUT I'LL ADMIT... YOU WERE THE FIRST OPPONENT TO MAKE ME SWEAT...
HUFF HUFF HUFF...

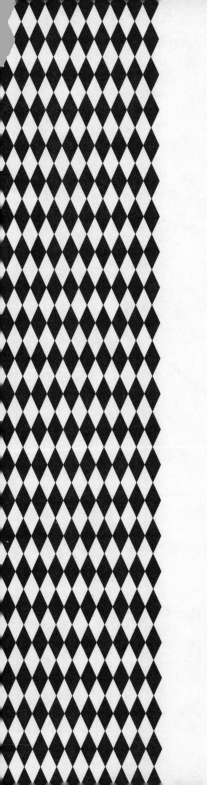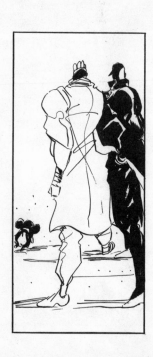

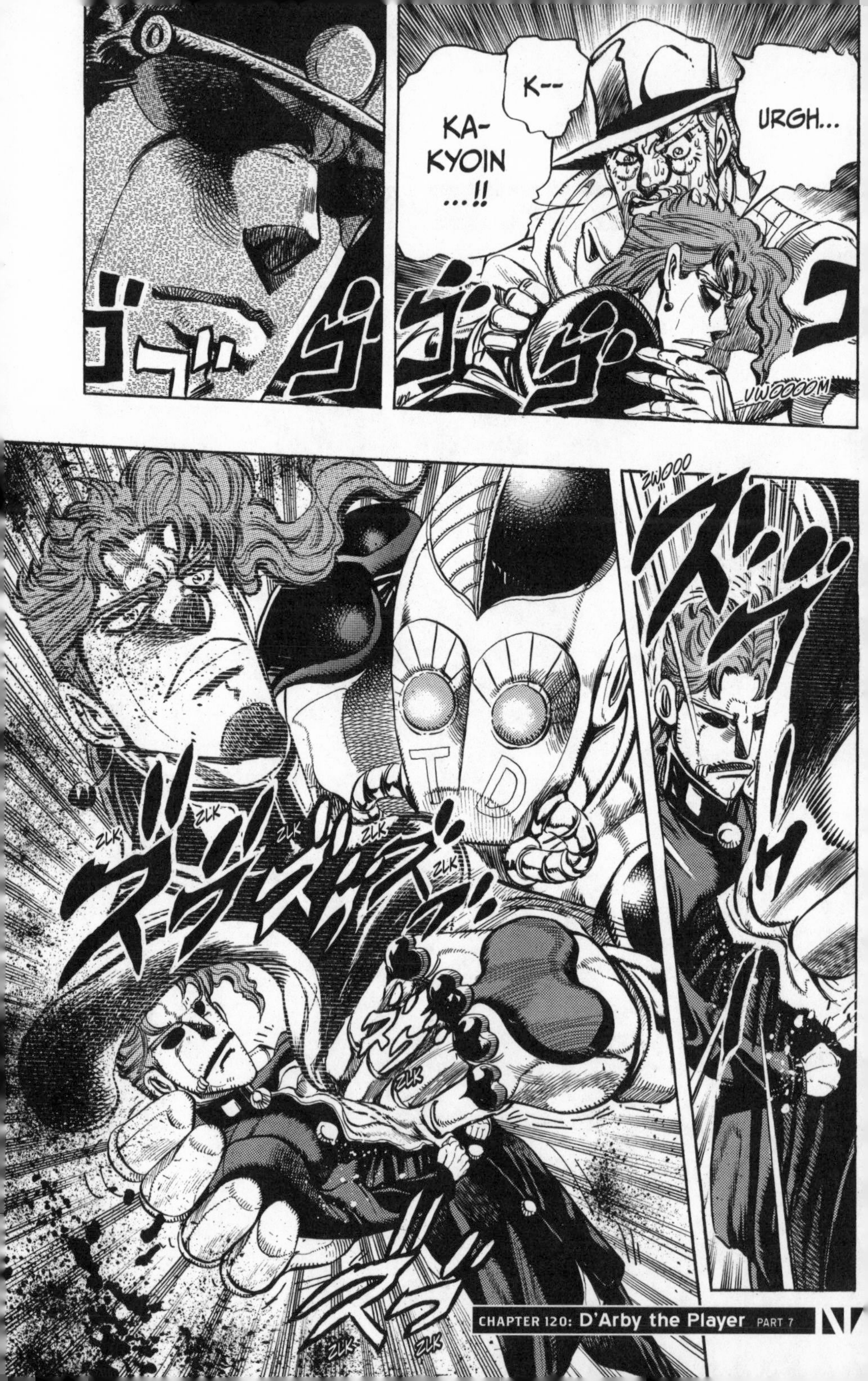
URGH...
K--
KA-KYOIN ...!!
VWOOOOM
ZWOOO
ZLK
ZLK
ZLK
ZLK
ZLK
ZLK
ZLK
ZLK
ZLK
CHAPTER 120: D'Arby the Player PART 7

CHAPTER 120: D'Arby the Player PART 7

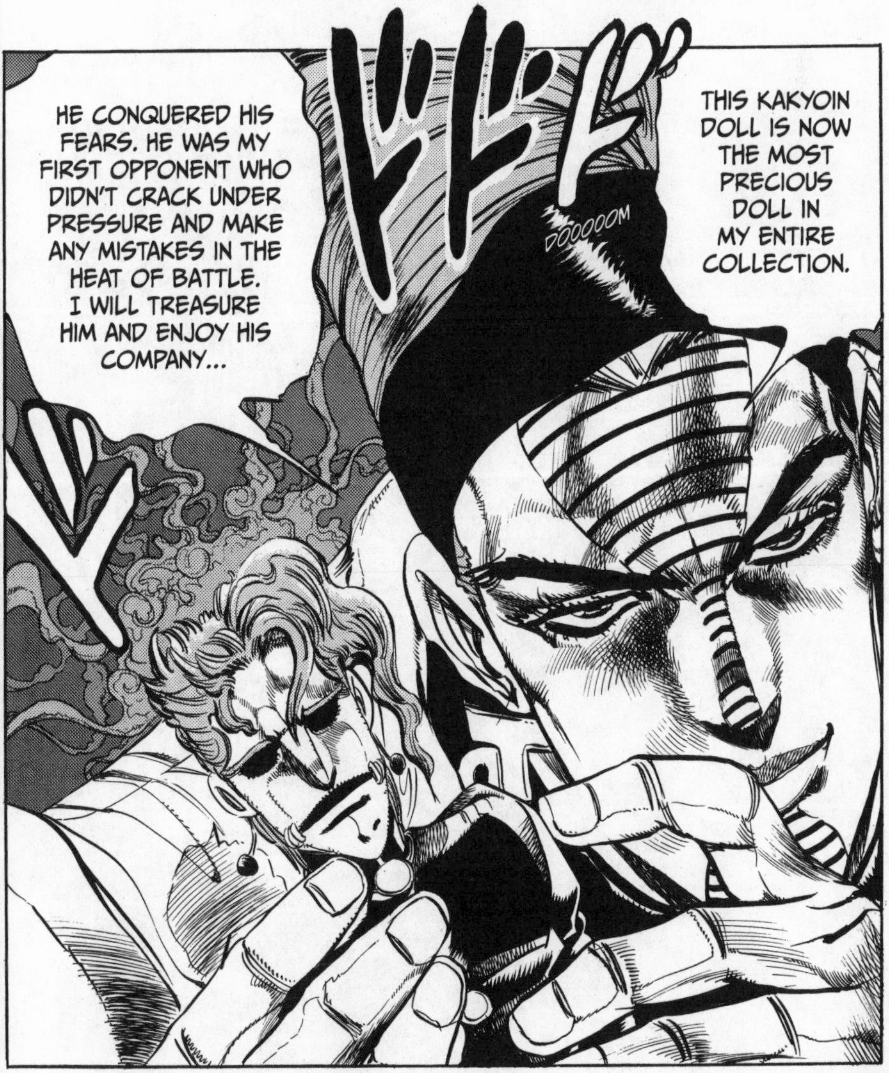
DOOOOOM
THIS KAKYOIN DOLL IS NOW THE MOST PRECIOUS DOLL IN MY ENTIRE COLLECTION.
HE CONQUERED HIS FEARS. HE WAS MY FIRST OPPONENT WHO DIDN'T CRACK UNDER PRESSURE AND MAKE ANY MISTAKES IN THE HEAT OF BATTLE. I WILL TREASURE HIM AND ENJOY HIS COMPANY...

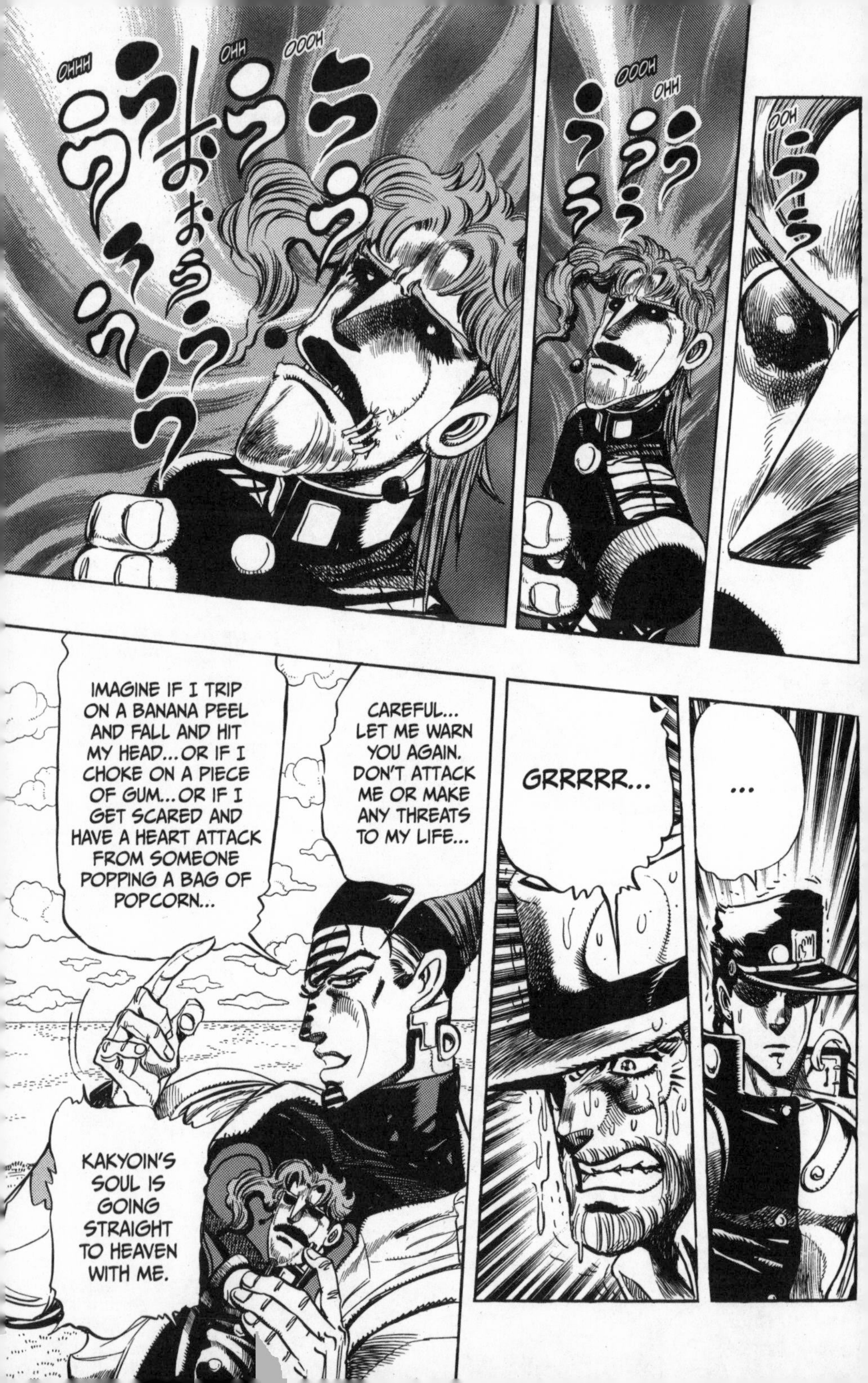
OOH
OOOH
OHH
OOOH
OHH
OHHH
...
GRRRRR...
CAREFUL... LET ME WARN YOU AGAIN. DON'T ATTACK ME OR MAKE ANY THREATS TO MY LIFE...
IMAGINE IF I TRIP ON A BANANA PEEL AND FALL AND HIT MY HEAD...OR IF I CHOKE ON A PIECE OF GUM...OR IF I GET SCARED AND HAVE A HEART ATTACK FROM SOMEONE POPPING A BAG OF POPCORN...
KAKYOIN'S SOUL IS GOING STRAIGHT TO HEAVEN WITH ME.

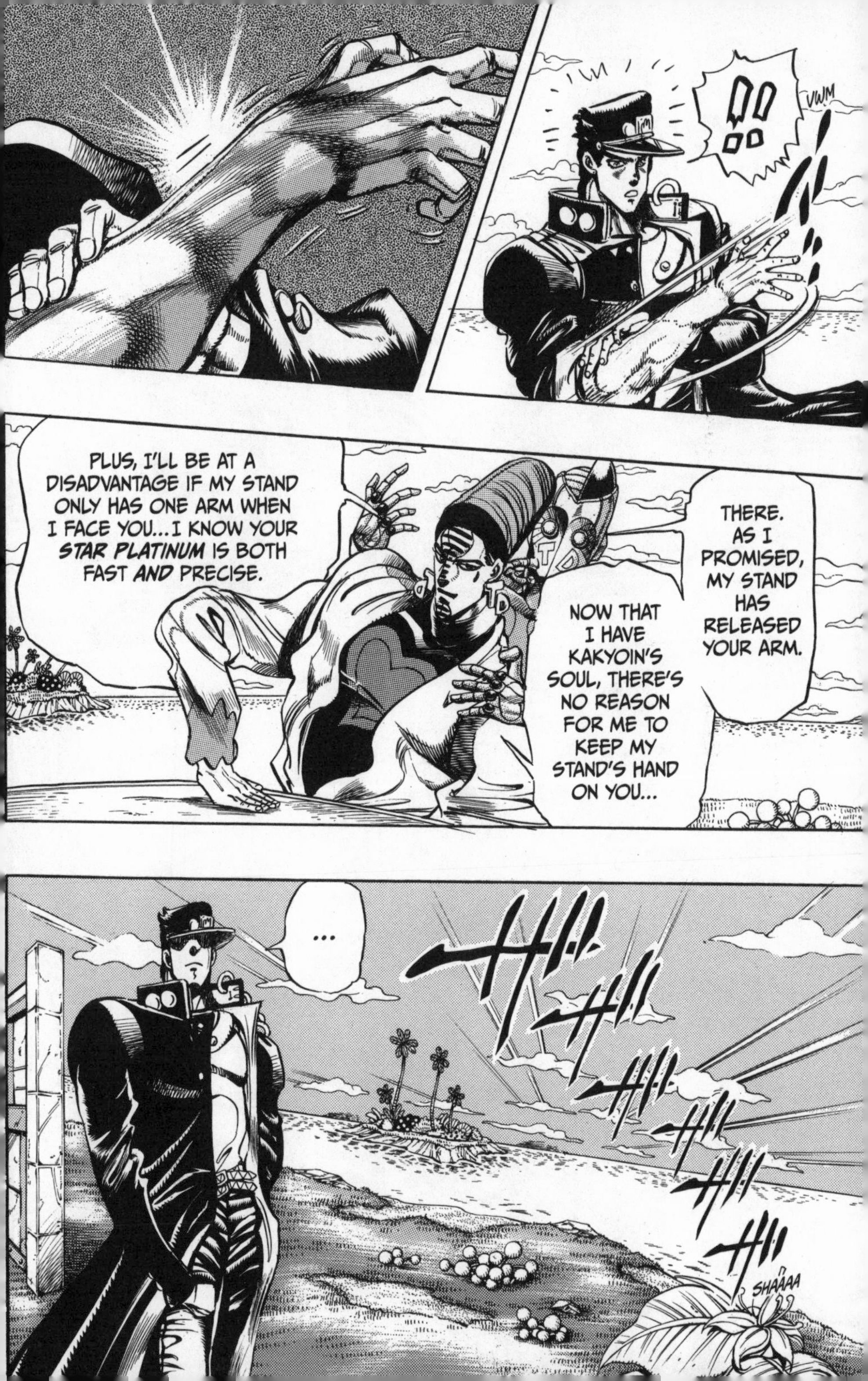
VWM
THERE. AS I PROMISED, MY STAND HAS RELEASED YOUR ARM.
NOW THAT I HAVE KAKYOIN'S SOUL, THERE'S NO REASON FOR ME TO KEEP MY STAND'S HAND ON YOU...
PLUS, I'LL BE AT A DISADVANTAGE IF MY STAND ONLY HAS ONE ARM WHEN I FACE YOU...I KNOW YOUR *STAR PLATINUM* IS BOTH FAST *AND* PRECISE.
...
SHAAAA

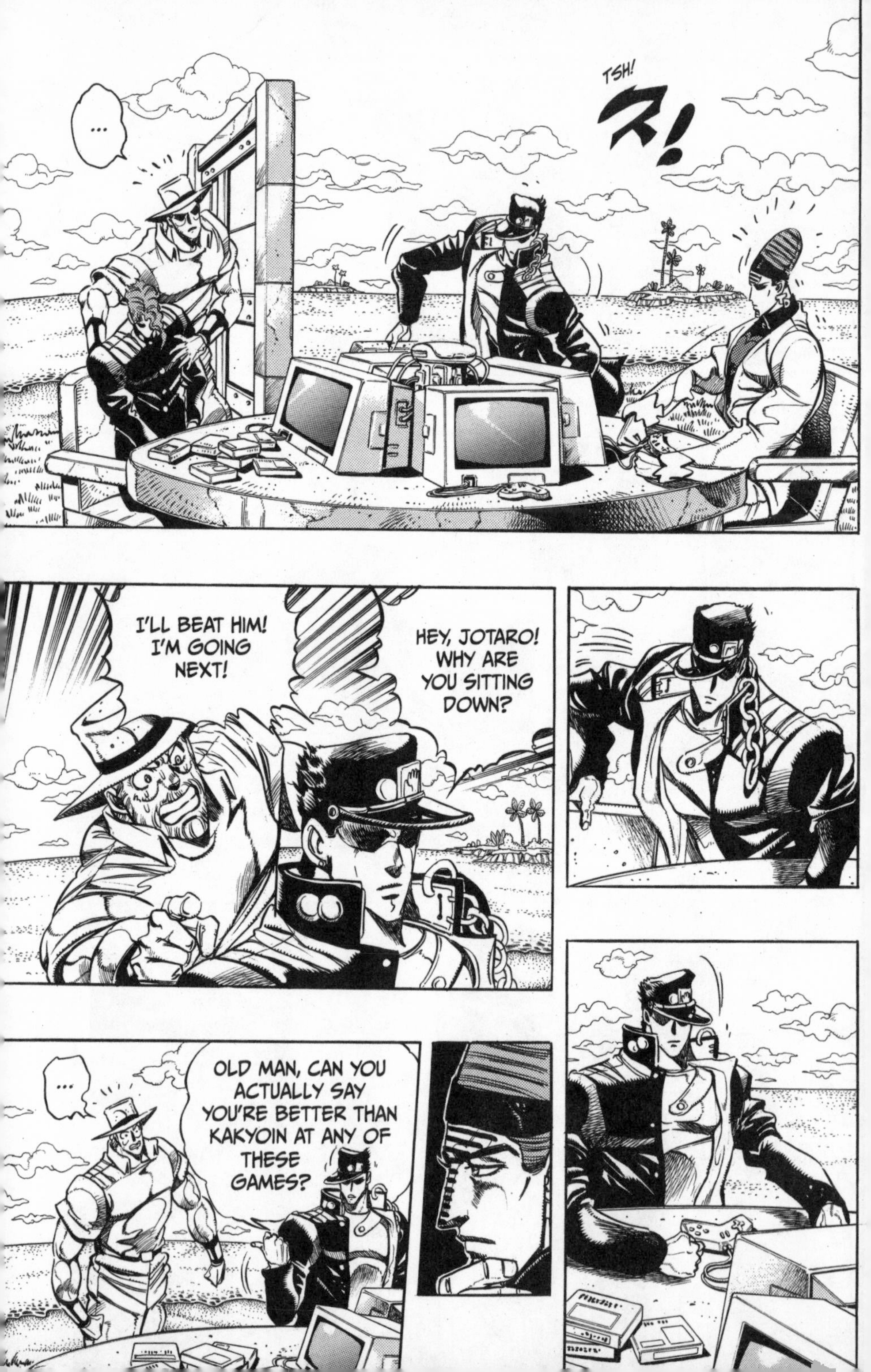
TSH!
ス!
...
HEY, JOTARO! WHY ARE YOU SITTING DOWN?
I'LL BEAT HIM! I'M GOING NEXT!
OLD MAN, CAN YOU ACTUALLY SAY YOU'RE BETTER THAN KAKYOIN AT ANY OF THESE GAMES?
...

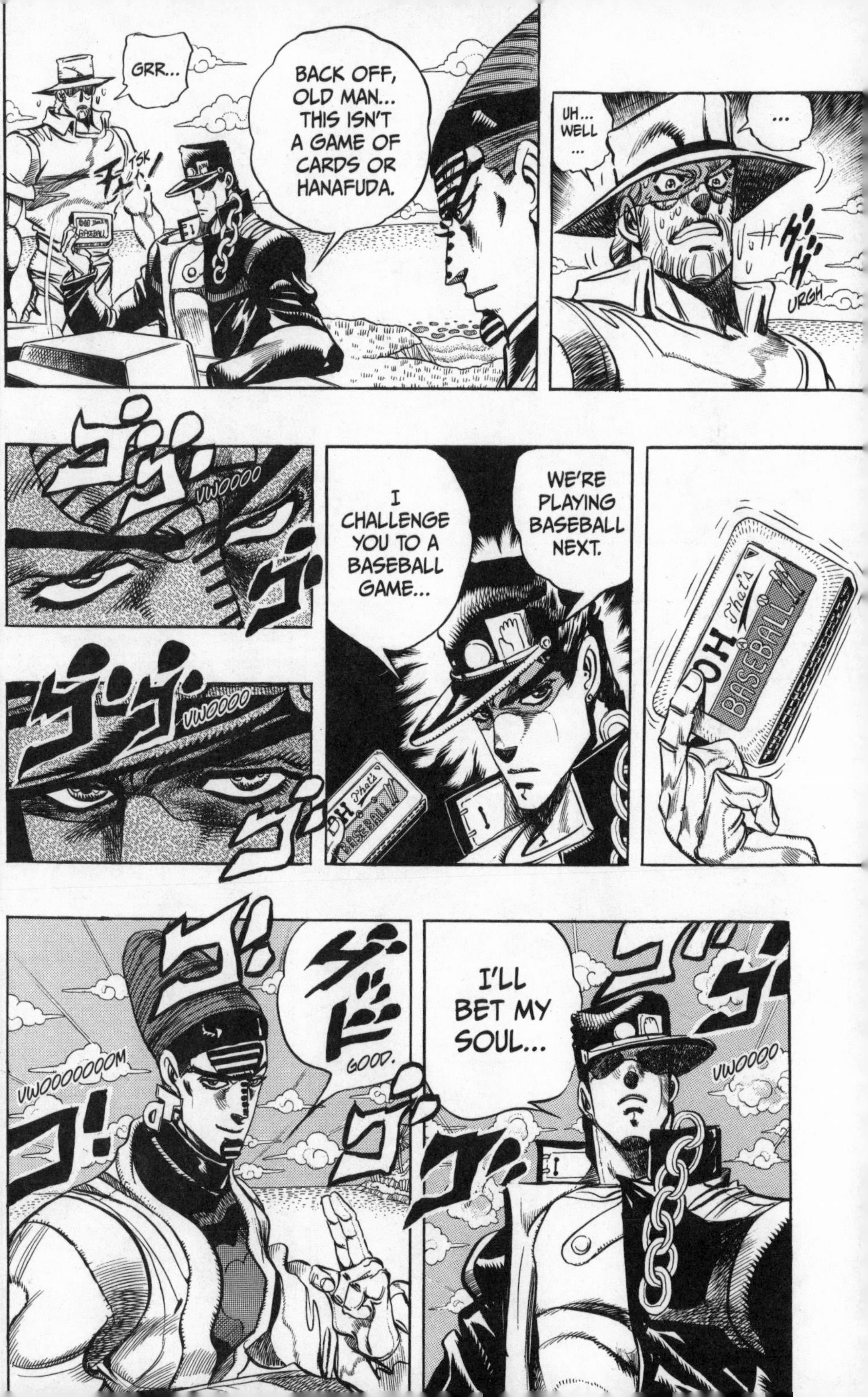
...
UH... WELL ...
URGH
BACK OFF, OLD MAN... THIS ISN'T A GAME OF CARDS OR HANAFUDA.
GRR...
TSK
WE'RE PLAYING BASEBALL NEXT.
I CHALLENGE YOU TO A BASEBALL GAME...
VWOOOO
VWOOOO
I'LL BET MY SOUL...
VWOOOO
GOOD.
VWOOOOOOOM

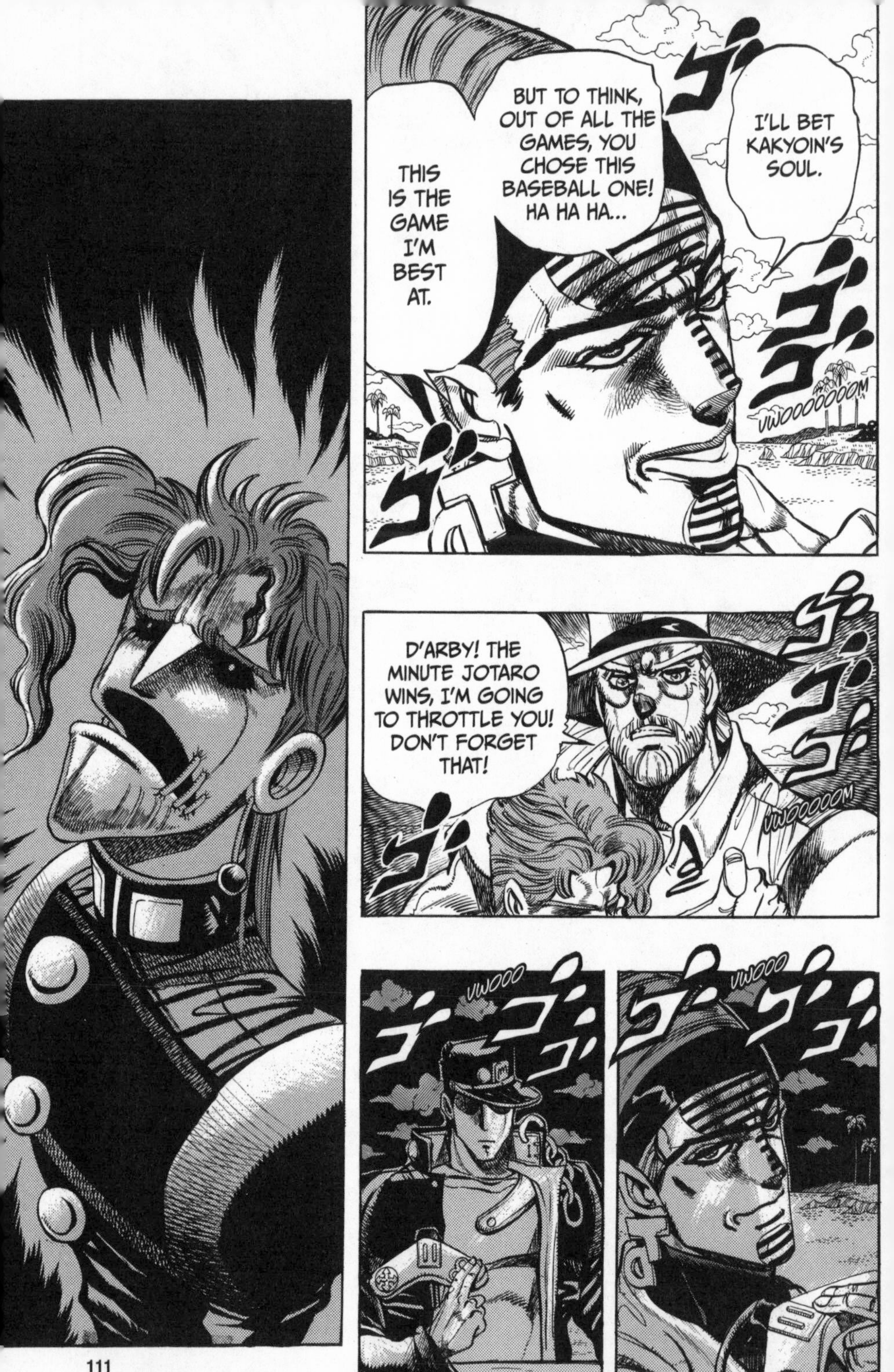
I'LL BET KAKYOIN'S SOUL.
BUT TO THINK, OUT OF ALL THE GAMES, YOU CHOSE THIS BASEBALL ONE! HA HA HA...
THIS IS THE GAME I'M BEST AT.
VWOOOOOOOM
D'ARBY! THE MINUTE JOTARO WINS, I'M GOING TO THROTTLE YOU! DON'T FORGET THAT!
VWOOOOOOM
VWOOO
VWOOO

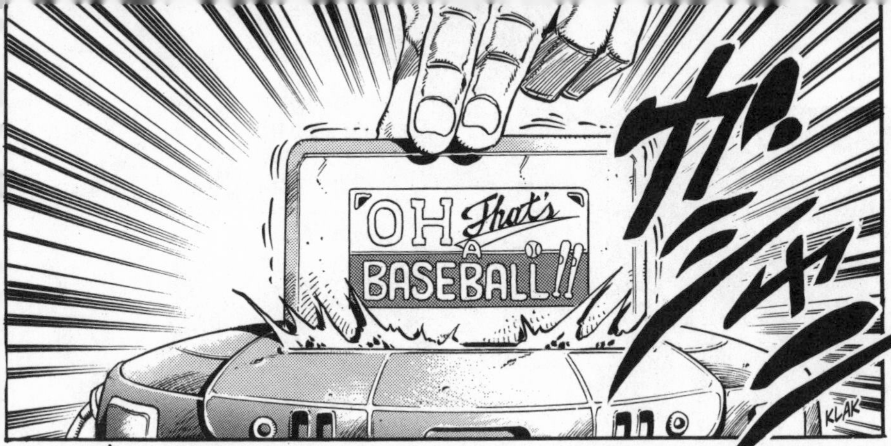
OH That's A BASEBALL!!
ガシャン
KLAK

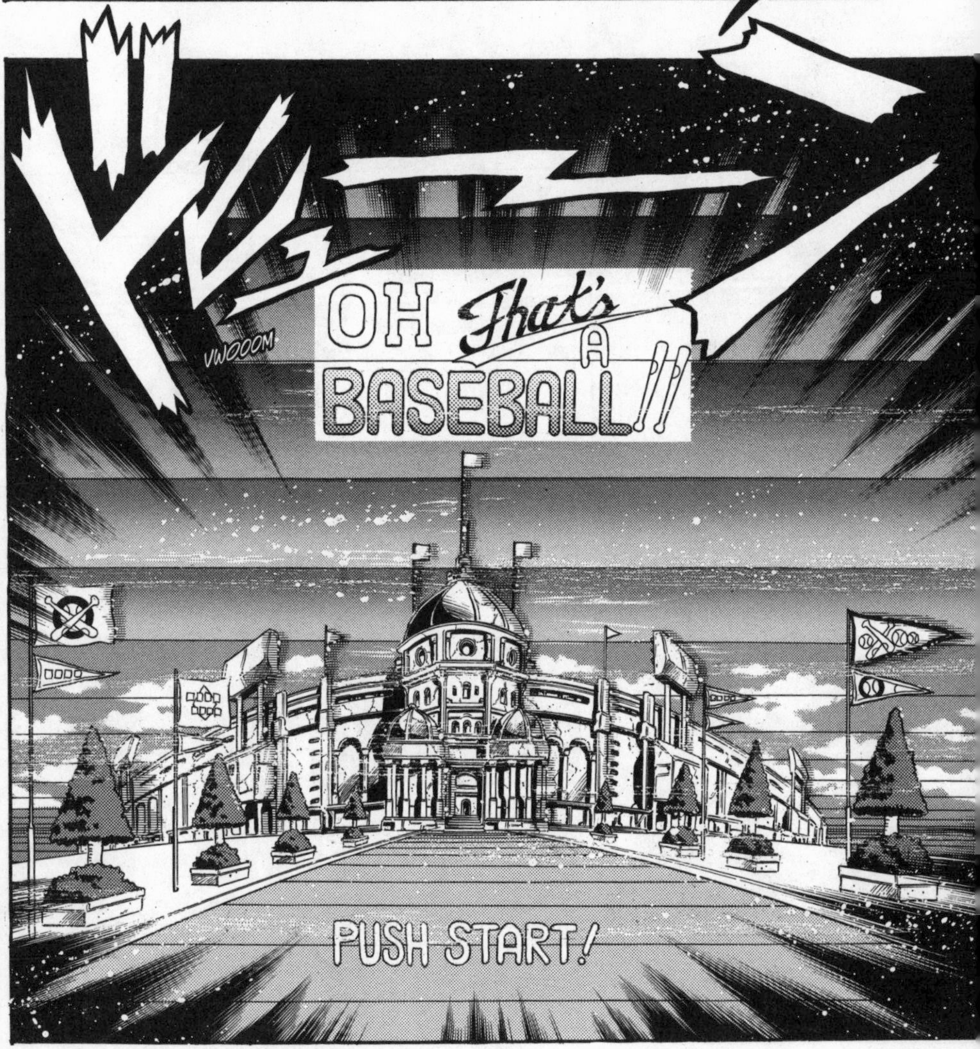
ドゥーン
VWOOOM
OH That's A BASEBALL!!
PUSH START!

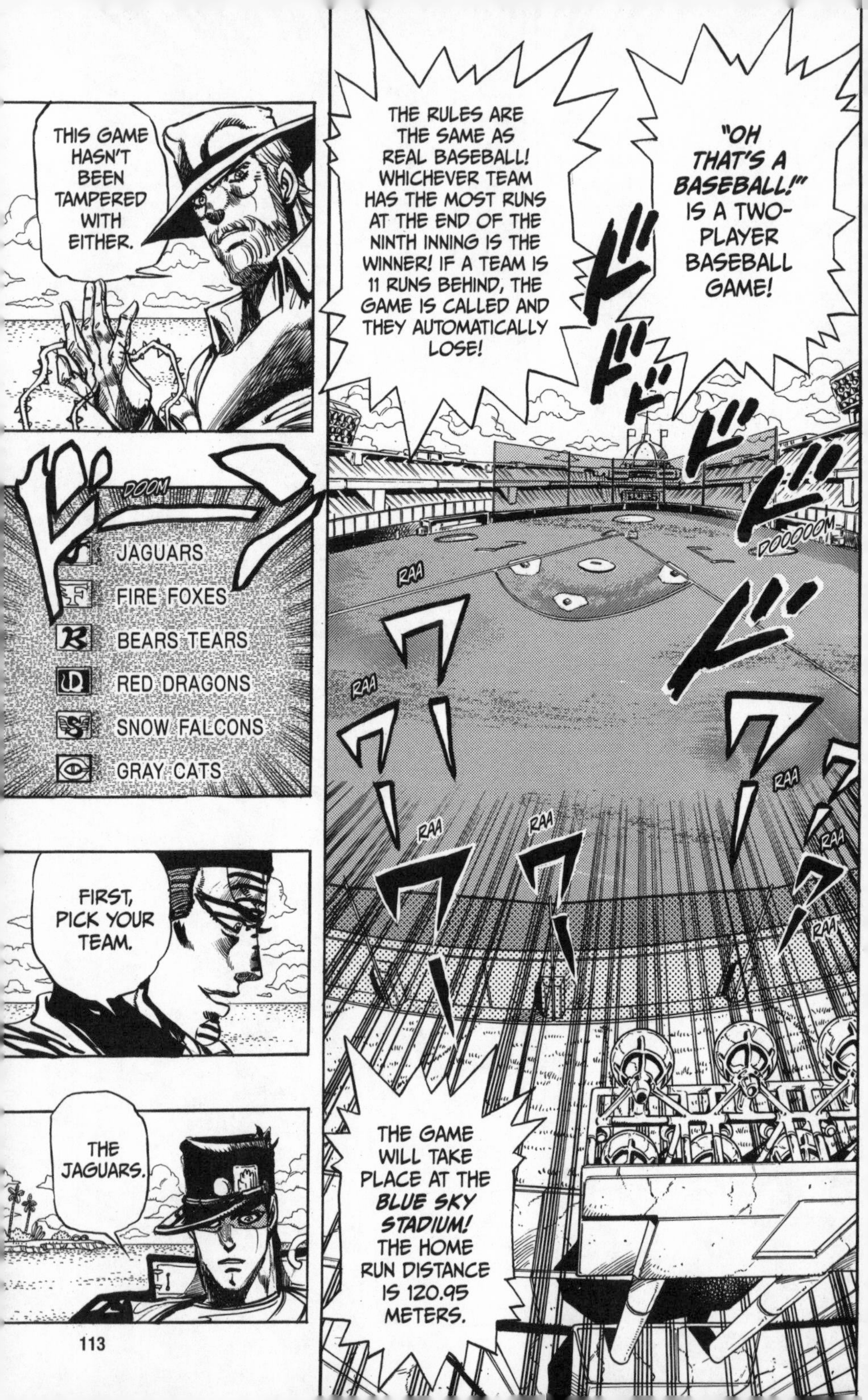
"OH THAT'S A BASEBALL!" IS A TWO-PLAYER BASEBALL GAME!
THE RULES ARE THE SAME AS REAL BASEBALL! WHICHEVER TEAM HAS THE MOST RUNS AT THE END OF THE NINTH INNING IS THE WINNER! IF A TEAM IS 11 RUNS BEHIND, THE GAME IS CALLED AND THEY AUTOMATICALLY LOSE!
DOOOOOM
RAA
RAA
RAA
RAA
RAA
RAA
RAA
THE GAME WILL TAKE PLACE AT THE BLUE SKY STADIUM! THE HOME RUN DISTANCE IS 120.95 METERS.
THIS GAME HASN'T BEEN TAMPERED WITH EITHER.
DOOM
JAGUARS
FIRE FOXES
BEARS TEARS
RED DRAGONS
SNOW FALCONS
GRAY CATS
FIRST, PICK YOUR TEAM.
THE JAGUARS.

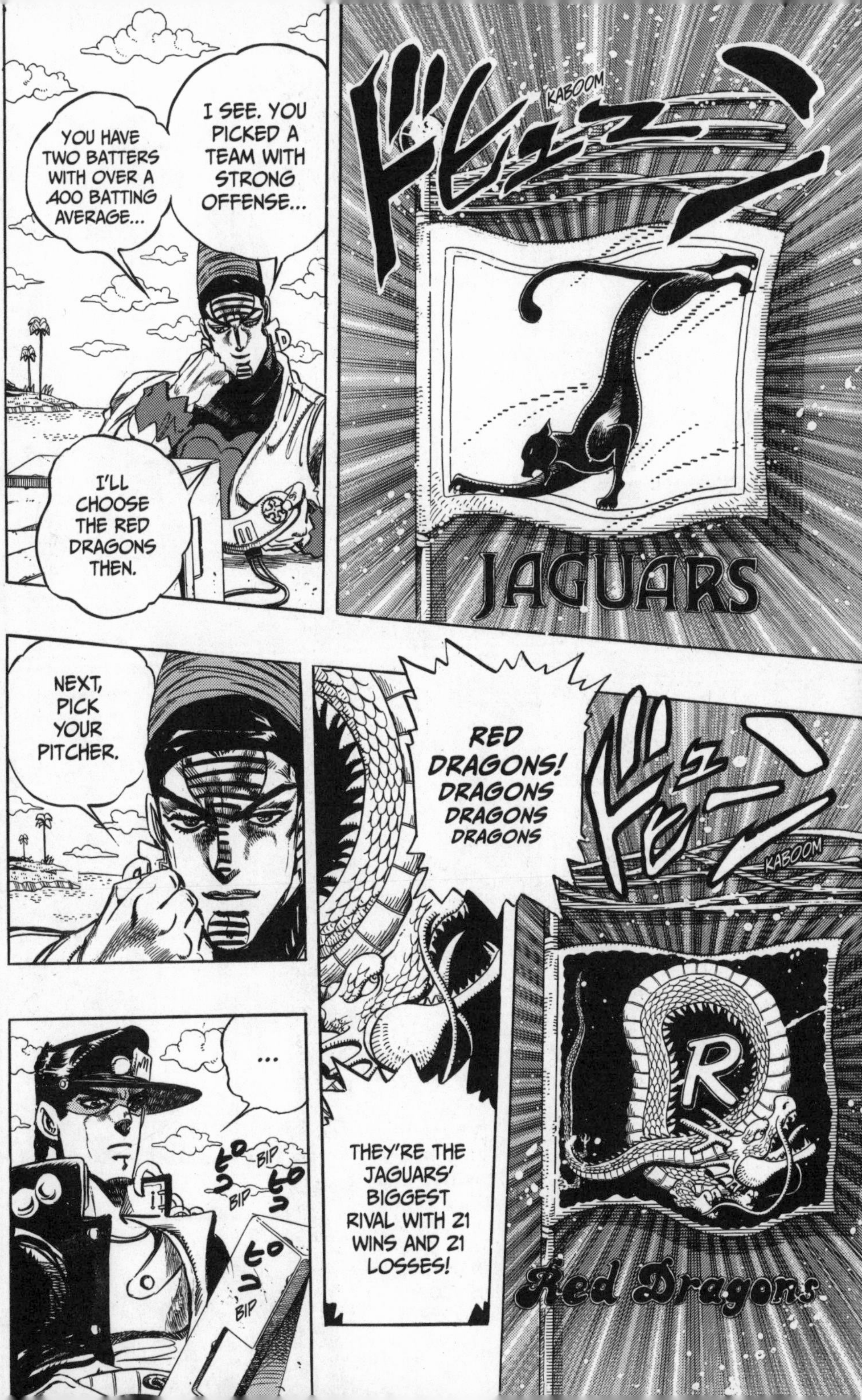
KABOOM
JAGUARS
I SEE. YOU PICKED A TEAM WITH STRONG OFFENSE...
YOU HAVE TWO BATTERS WITH OVER A .400 BATTING AVERAGE...
I'LL CHOOSE THE RED DRAGONS THEN.
KABOOM
RED DRAGONS! DRAGONS DRAGONS DRAGONS
R
Red Dragons
THEY'RE THE JAGUARS' BIGGEST RIVAL WITH 21 WINS AND 21 LOSSES!
NEXT, PICK YOUR PITCHER.
...
BIP
BIP
BIP

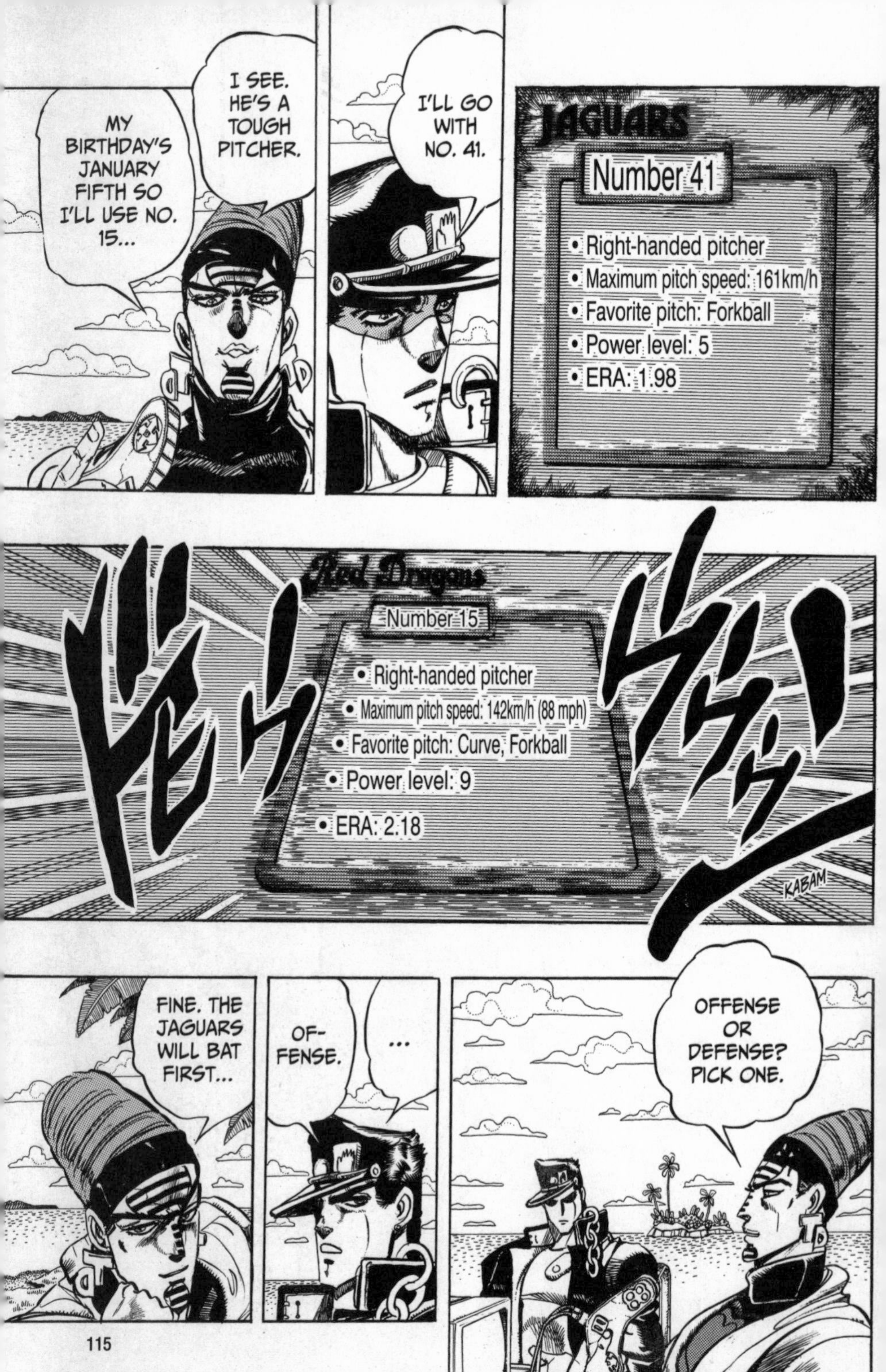
JAGUARS
Number 41
• Right-handed pitcher
• Maximum pitch speed: 161km/h
• Favorite pitch: Forkball
• Power level: 5
• ERA: 1.98
I'LL GO WITH NO. 41.
I SEE. HE'S A TOUGH PITCHER.
MY BIRTHDAY'S JANUARY FIFTH SO I'LL USE NO. 15...
Red Dragons
Number 15
• Right-handed pitcher
• Maximum pitch speed: 142km/h (88 mph)
• Favorite pitch: Curve, Forkball
• Power level: 9
• ERA: 2.18
KABAM
OFFENSE OR DEFENSE? PICK ONE.
...
OF-FENSE.
FINE. THE JAGUARS WILL BAT FIRST...

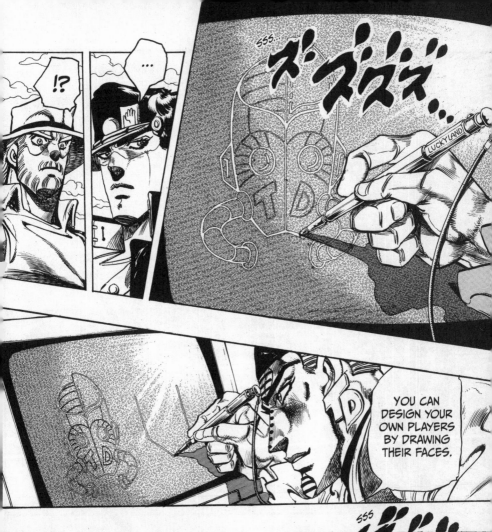

YOU CAN
DESIGN YOUR
OWN PLAYERS
BY DRAWING
THEIR FACES.

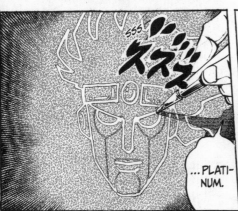

THIS IS
STAR...

...PLATI-
NUM.

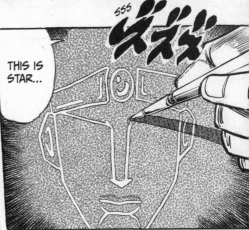

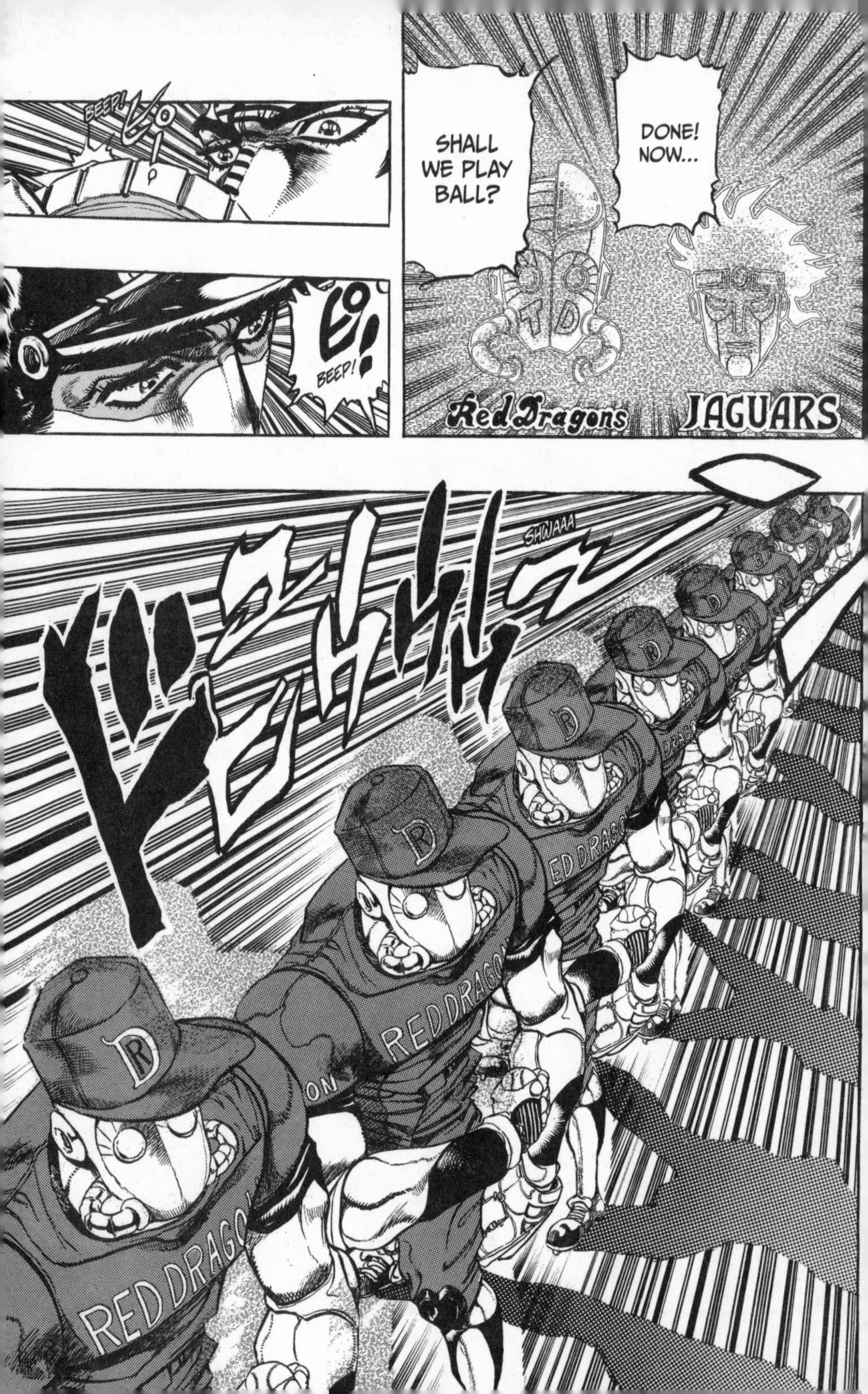
DONE! NOW...
SHALL WE PLAY BALL?
JAGUARS
Red Dragons
BEEP!
BEEP!
SHWAAA

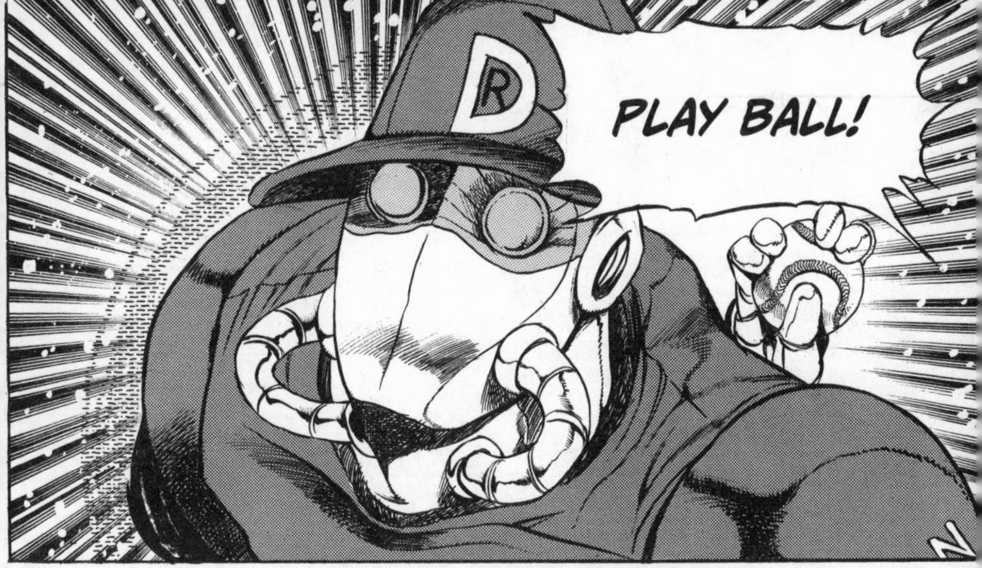
PLAY BALL!

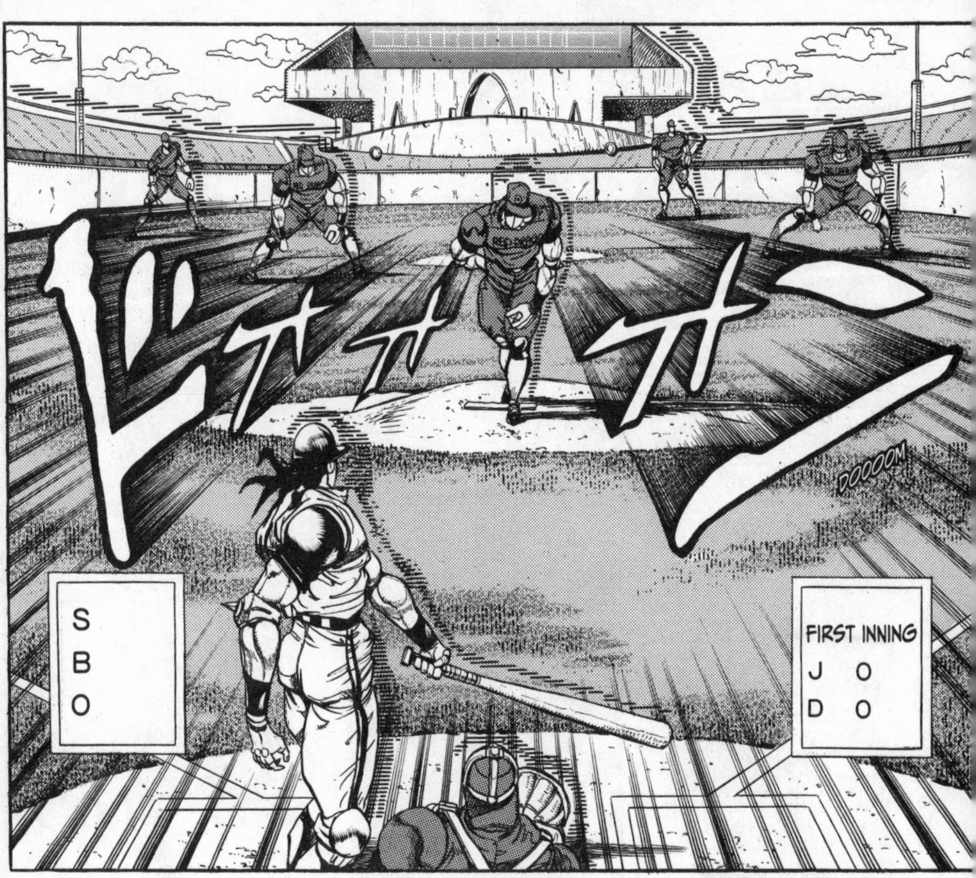
DOOOOM
S
B
O
FIRST INNING
J O
D O

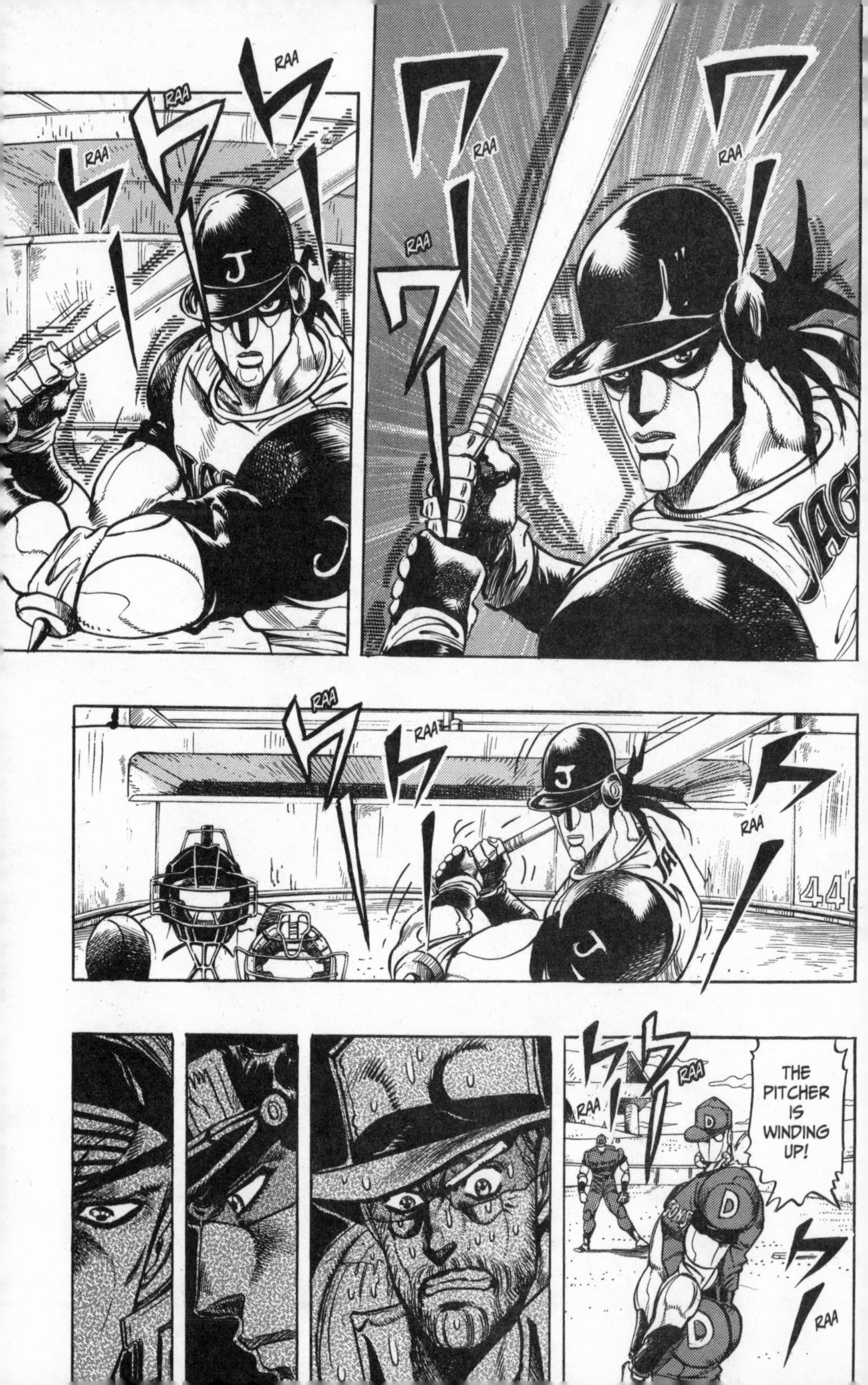
RAA
RAA
RAA
RAA
RAA
RAA
RAA
RAA
RAA
THE PITCHER IS WINDING UP!
RAA
RAA
RAA

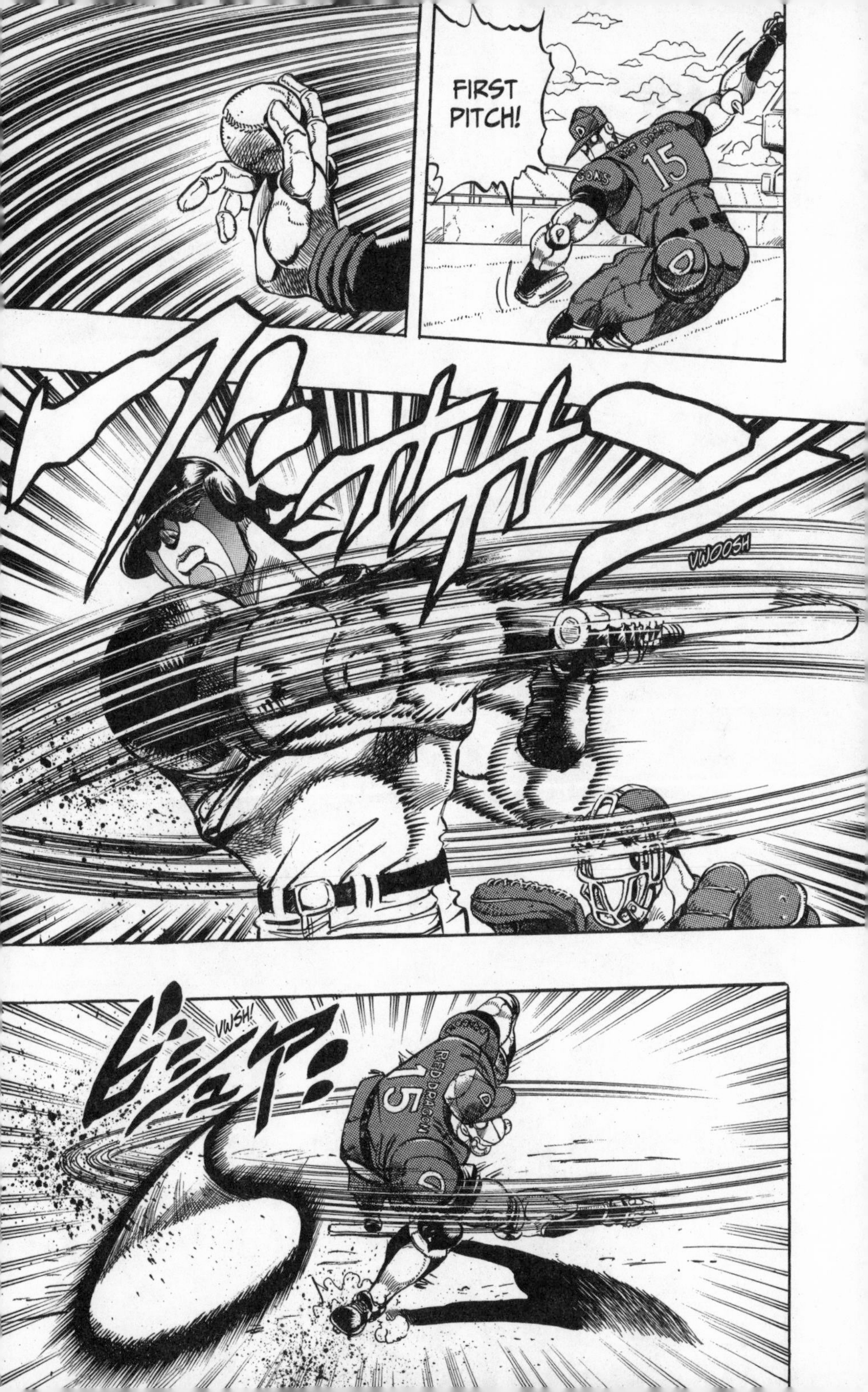
FIRST PITCH!
15
VWOOSH
VWSH!
RED DRAGON
15

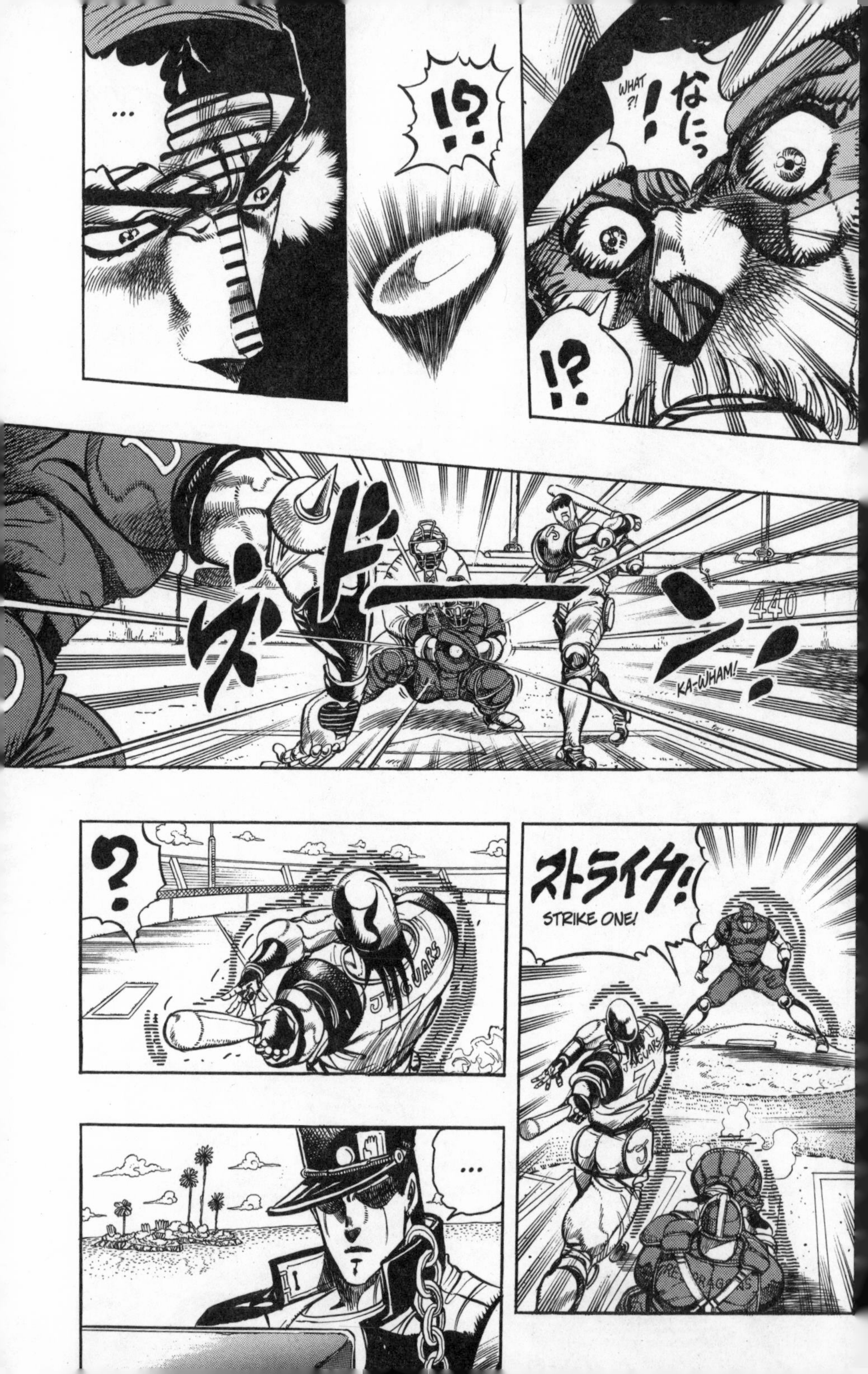

なにっ!
WHAT ?!
!?
!?
...
ズドーーン!?
KA-WHAM!
ストライク!
STRIKE ONE!
?
...

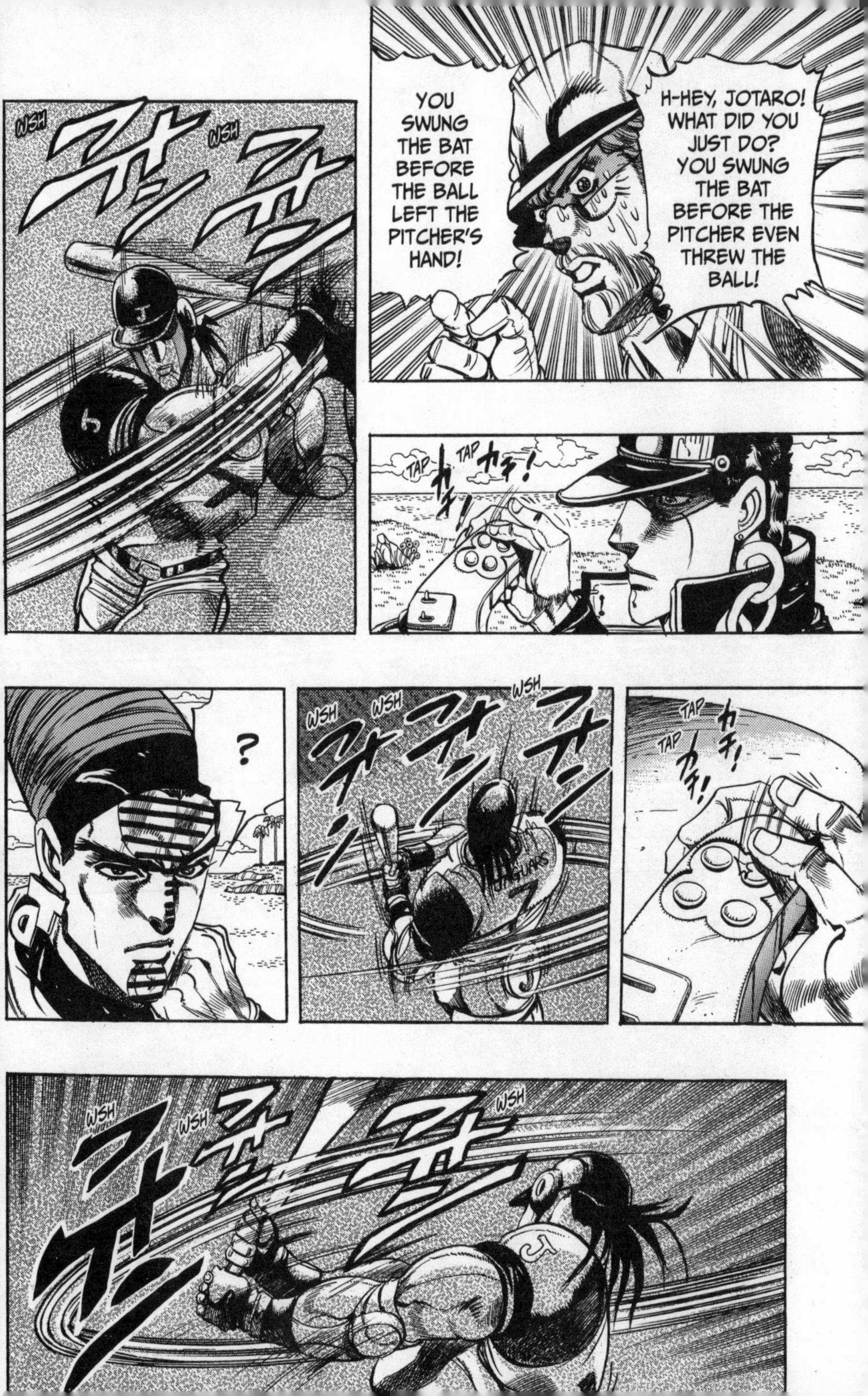
H-HEY, JOTARO! WHAT DID YOU JUST DO? YOU SWUNG THE BAT BEFORE THE PITCHER EVEN THREW THE BALL!
YOU SWUNG THE BAT BEFORE THE BALL LEFT THE PITCHER'S HAND!
TAP
TAP
WSH
WSH
TAP
TAP
WSH
WSH
WSH
?
WSH
WSH
WSH

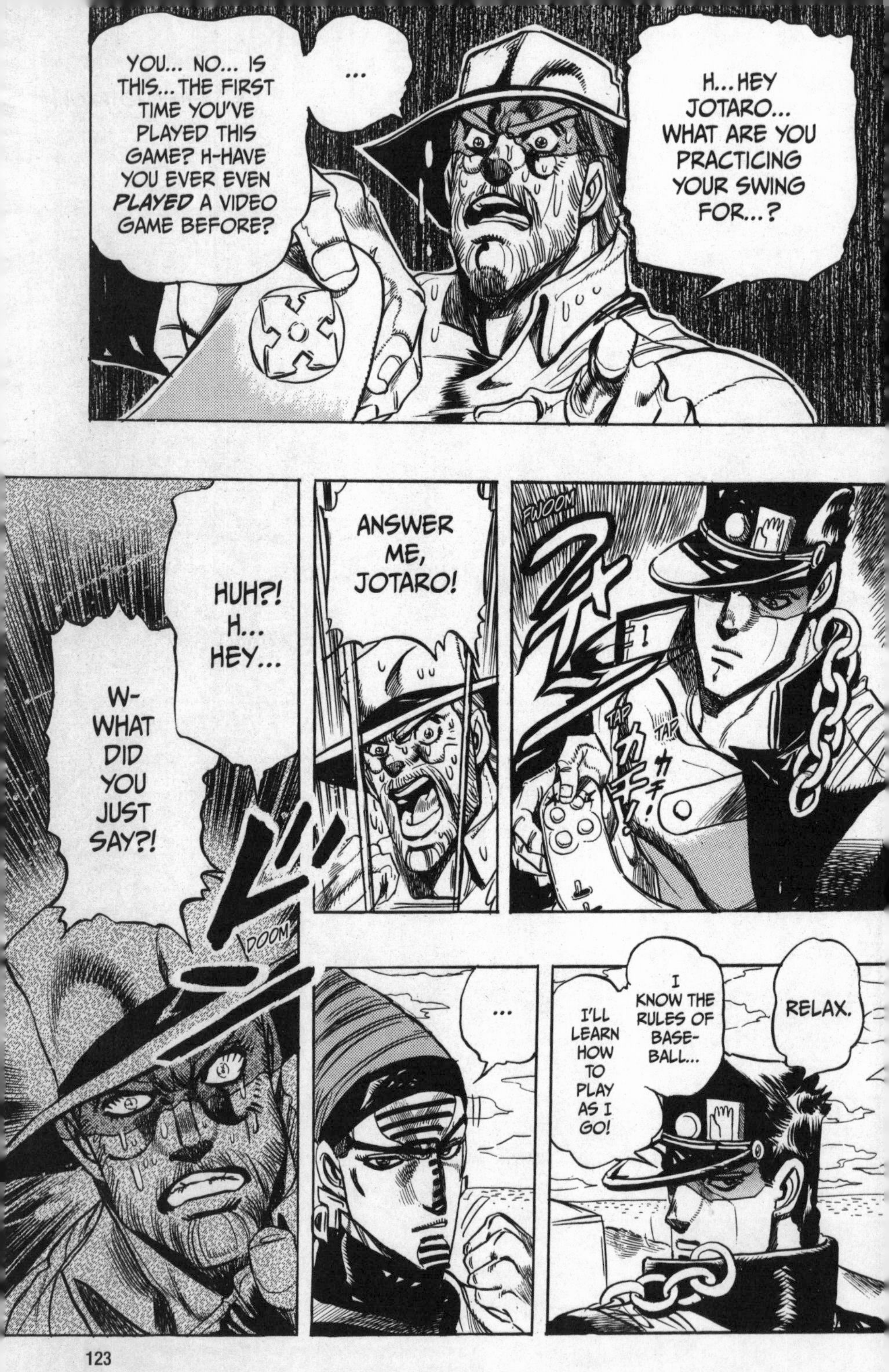

H...HEY JOTARO... WHAT ARE YOU PRACTICING YOUR SWING FOR...?
...
YOU... NO... IS THIS...THE FIRST TIME YOU'VE PLAYED THIS GAME? H-HAVE YOU EVER EVEN *PLAYED* A VIDEO GAME BEFORE?
FWOOM
TAP
TAP
ANSWER ME, JOTARO!
RELAX.
I KNOW THE RULES OF BASE-BALL...
I'LL LEARN HOW TO PLAY AS I GO!
...
HUH?! H... HEY...
W-WHAT DID YOU JUST SAY?!
DOOM

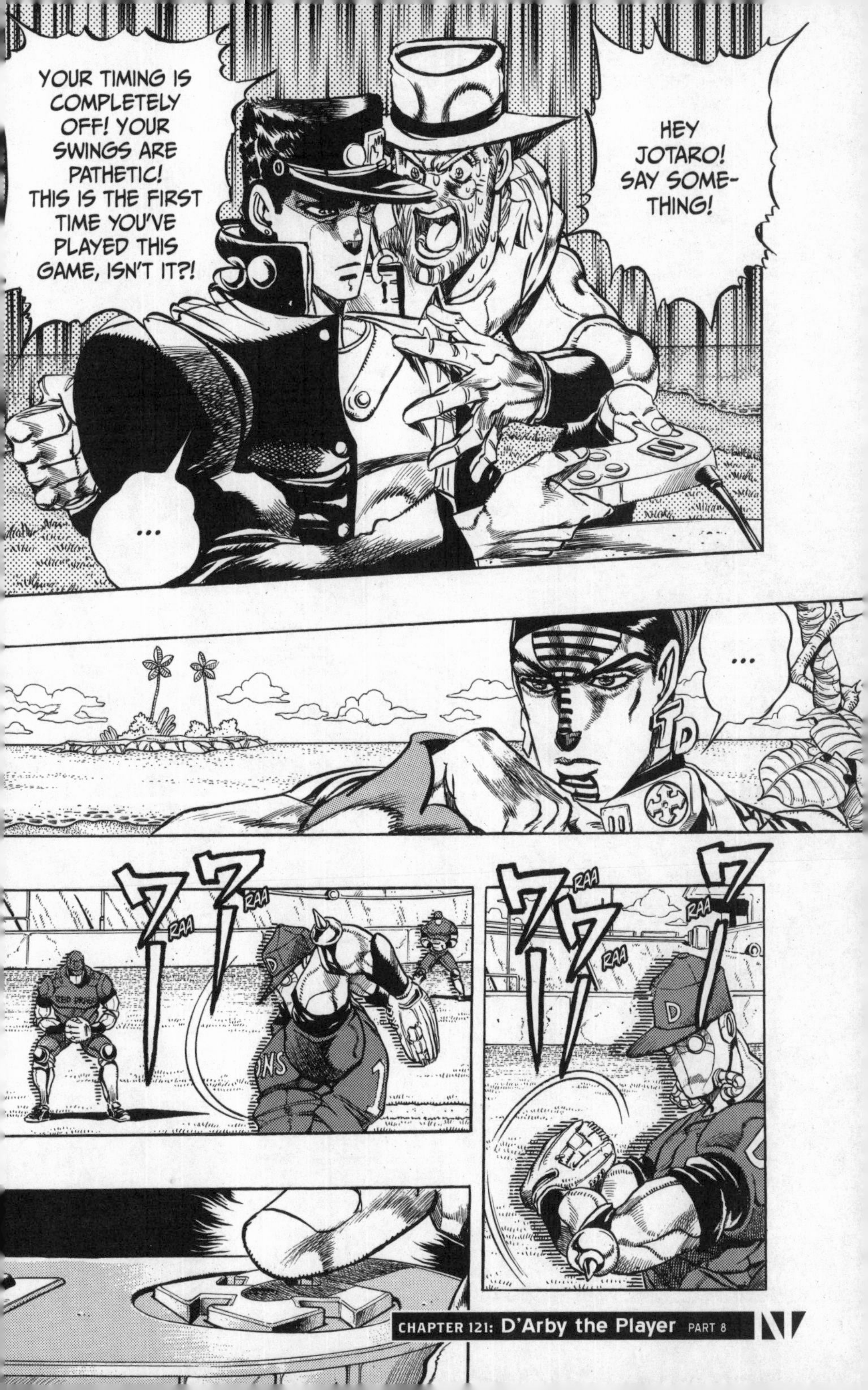
HEY JOTARO! SAY SOME-THING!
YOUR TIMING IS COMPLETELY OFF! YOUR SWINGS ARE PATHETIC! THIS IS THE FIRST TIME YOU'VE PLAYED THIS GAME, ISN'T IT?!
...
...
RAA
RAA
RAA
RAA
RAA
CHAPTER 121: D'Arby the Player PART 8

CHAPTER 121: D'Arby the Player PART 8

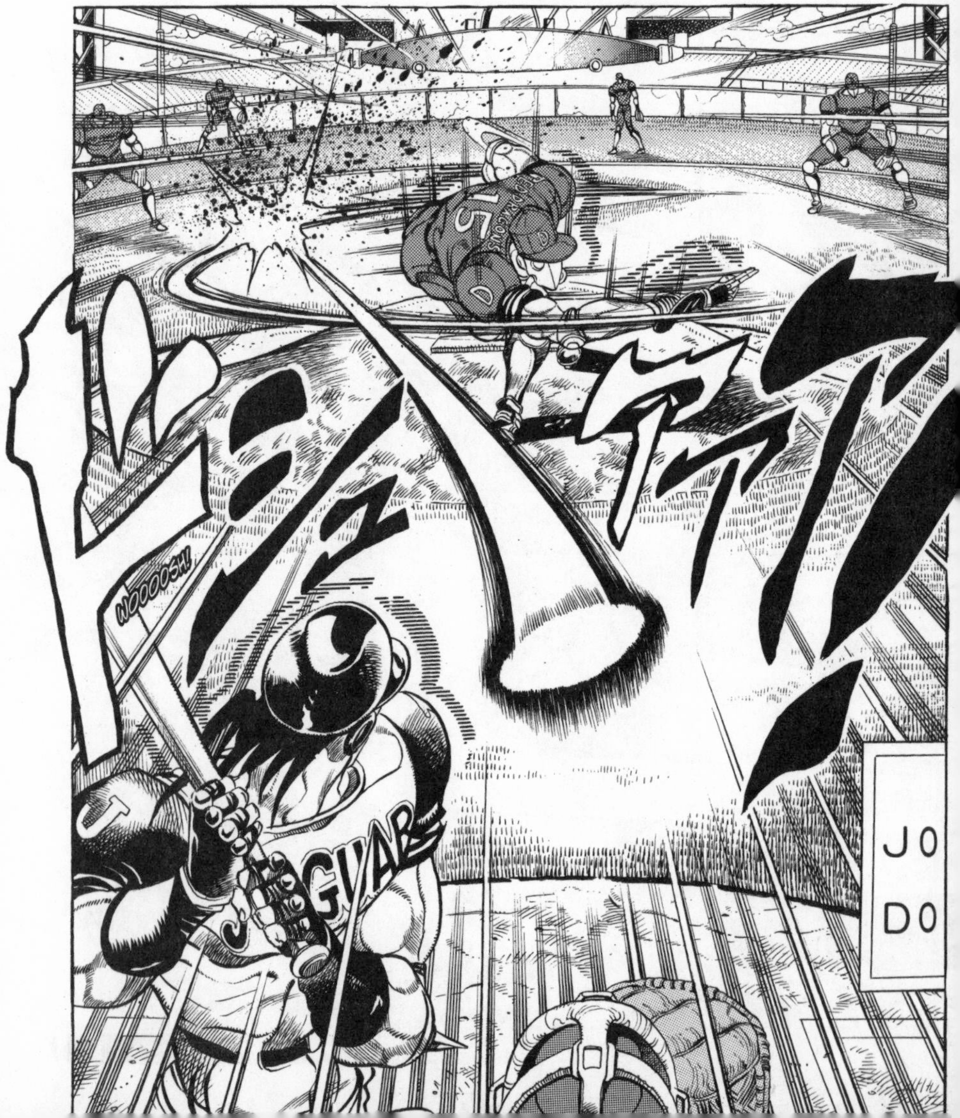
WOOOOSH!
JO
DO

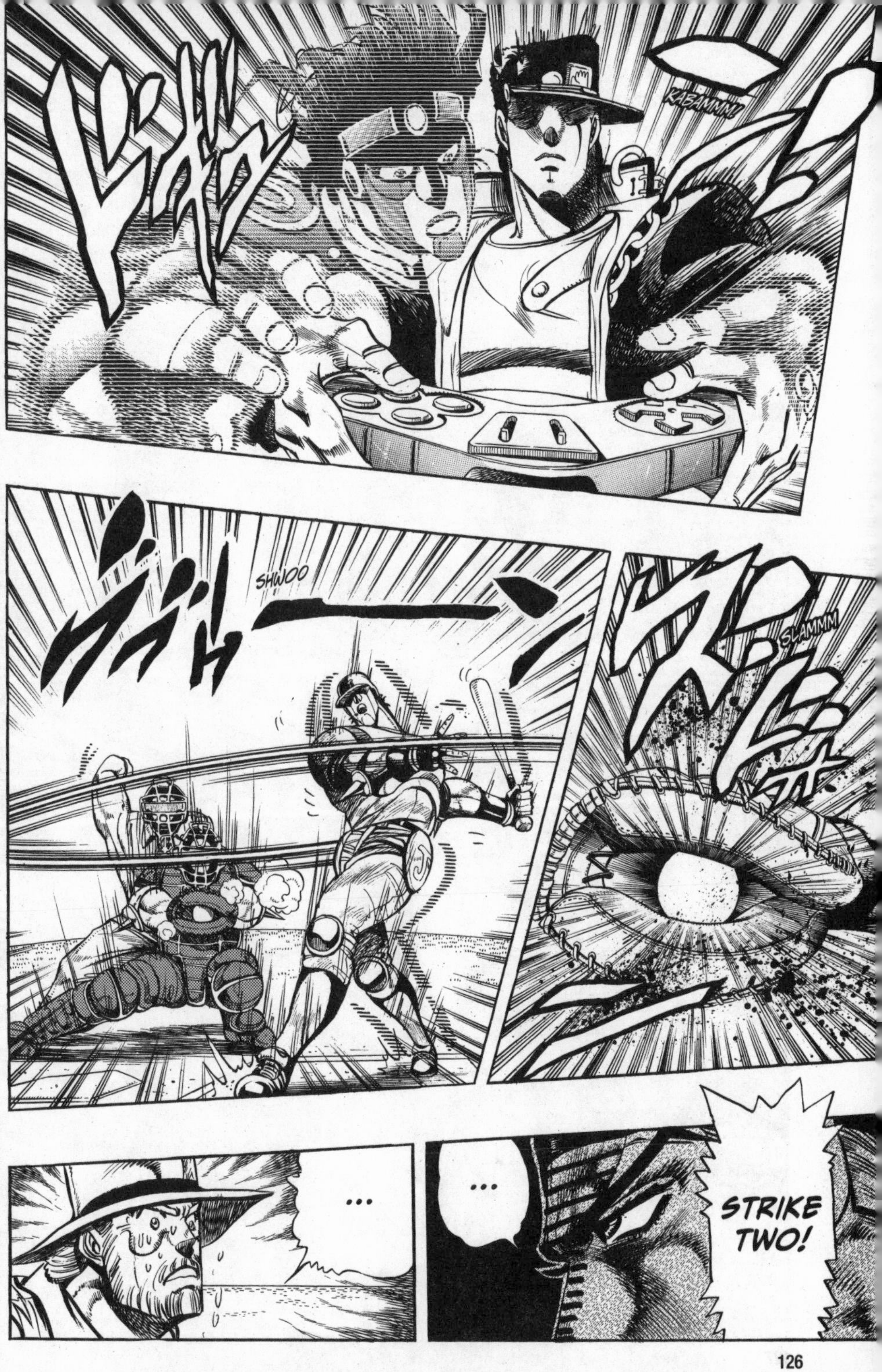
KABAMMN!
SLAMMM
SHWOO
STRIKE TWO!
...
...

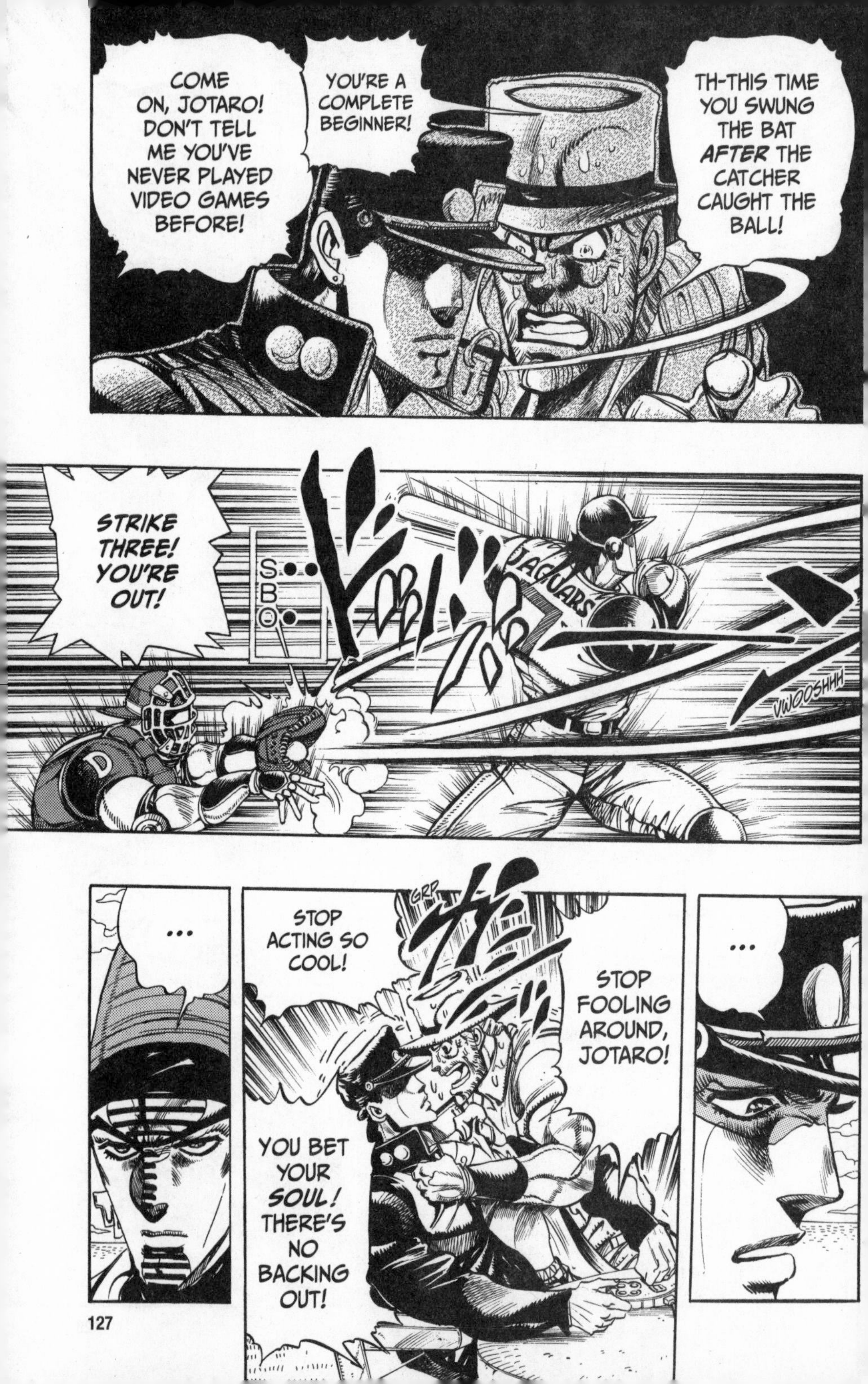
TH-THIS TIME YOU SWUNG THE BAT *AFTER* THE CATCHER CAUGHT THE BALL!
YOU'RE A COMPLETE BEGINNER!
COME ON, JOTARO! DON'T TELL ME YOU'VE NEVER PLAYED VIDEO GAMES BEFORE!
VWOOSHHH
JAGUARS
S
B
O
STRIKE THREE! YOU'RE OUT!
...
STOP FOOLING AROUND, JOTARO!
GRP
STOP ACTING SO COOL!
YOU BET YOUR *SOUL!* THERE'S NO BACKING OUT!
...

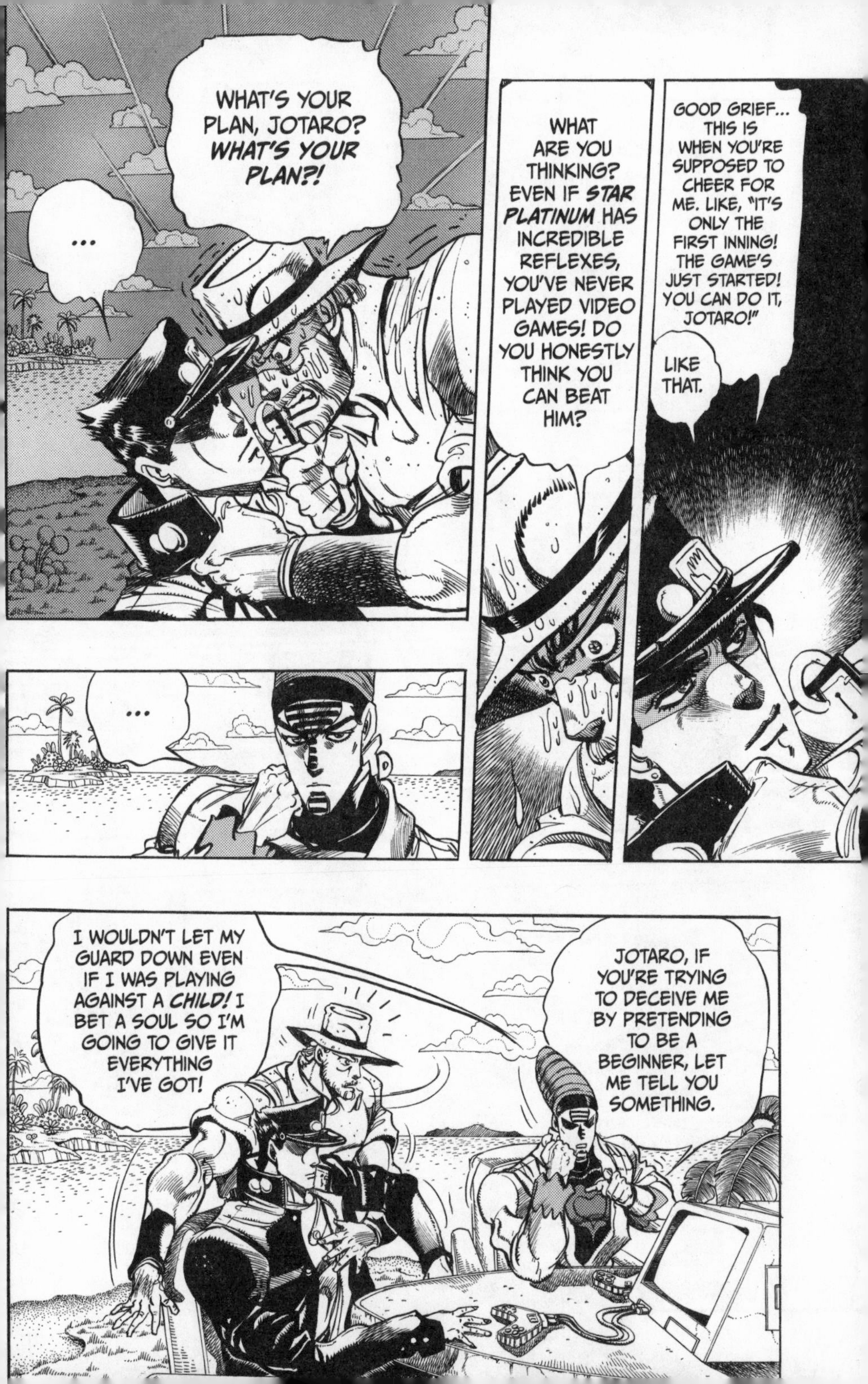
GOOD GRIEF... THIS IS WHEN YOU'RE SUPPOSED TO CHEER FOR ME. LIKE, "IT'S ONLY THE FIRST INNING! THE GAME'S JUST STARTED! YOU CAN DO IT, JOTARO!"
LIKE THAT.
WHAT ARE YOU THINKING? EVEN IF *STAR PLATINUM* HAS INCREDIBLE REFLEXES, YOU'VE NEVER PLAYED VIDEO GAMES! DO YOU HONESTLY THINK YOU CAN BEAT HIM?
WHAT'S YOUR PLAN, JOTARO? *WHAT'S YOUR PLAN?!*
...
...
JOTARO, IF YOU'RE TRYING TO DECEIVE ME BY PRETENDING TO BE A BEGINNER, LET ME TELL YOU SOMETHING.
I WOULDN'T LET MY GUARD DOWN EVEN IF I WAS PLAYING AGAINST A *CHILD!* I BET A SOUL SO I'M GOING TO GIVE IT EVERYTHING I'VE GOT!

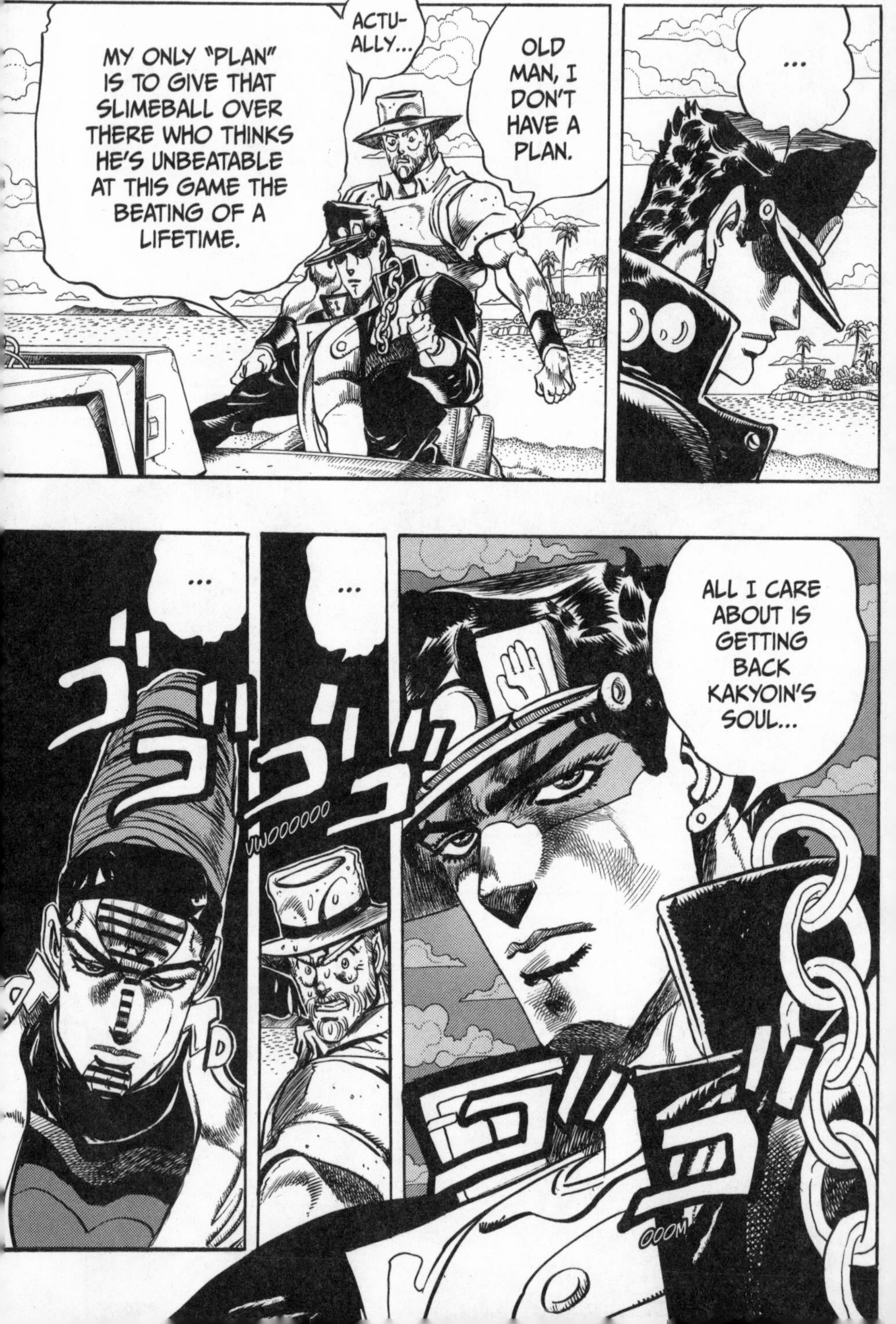
...
OLD MAN, I DON'T HAVE A PLAN.
ACTU-ALLY...
MY ONLY "PLAN" IS TO GIVE THAT SLIMEBALL OVER THERE WHO THINKS HE'S UNBEATABLE AT THIS GAME THE BEATING OF A LIFETIME.
ALL I CARE ABOUT IS GETTING BACK KAKYOIN'S SOUL...
OOOM
...
VWOOOOOO
...

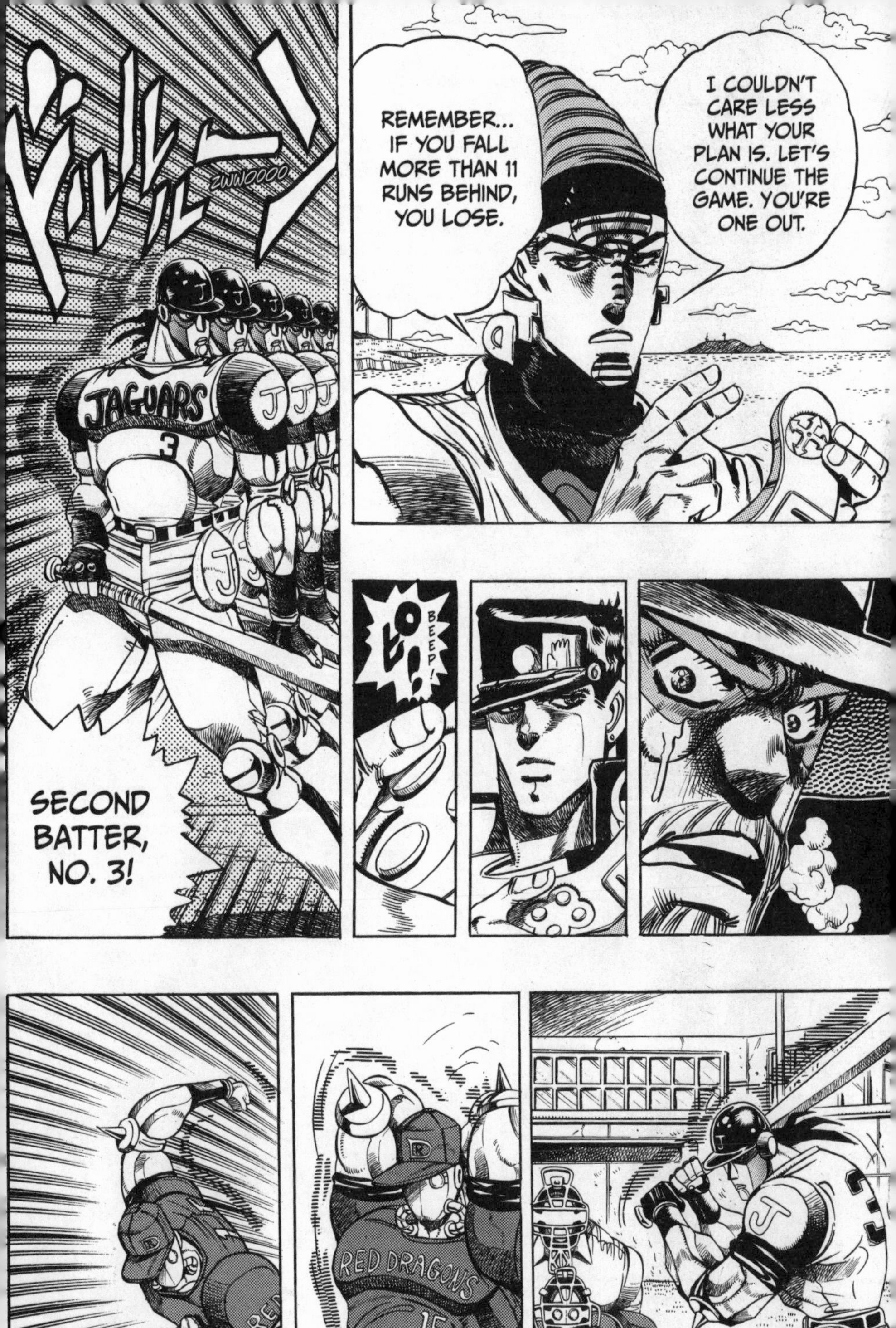
I COULDN'T CARE LESS WHAT YOUR PLAN IS. LET'S CONTINUE THE GAME. YOU'RE ONE OUT.
REMEMBER... IF YOU FALL MORE THAN 11 RUNS BEHIND, YOU LOSE.
BEEP!
ZWWOOOO
JAGUARS
SECOND BATTER, NO. 3!
RED DRAGONS
15

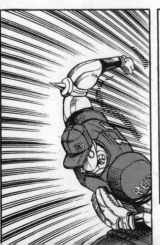

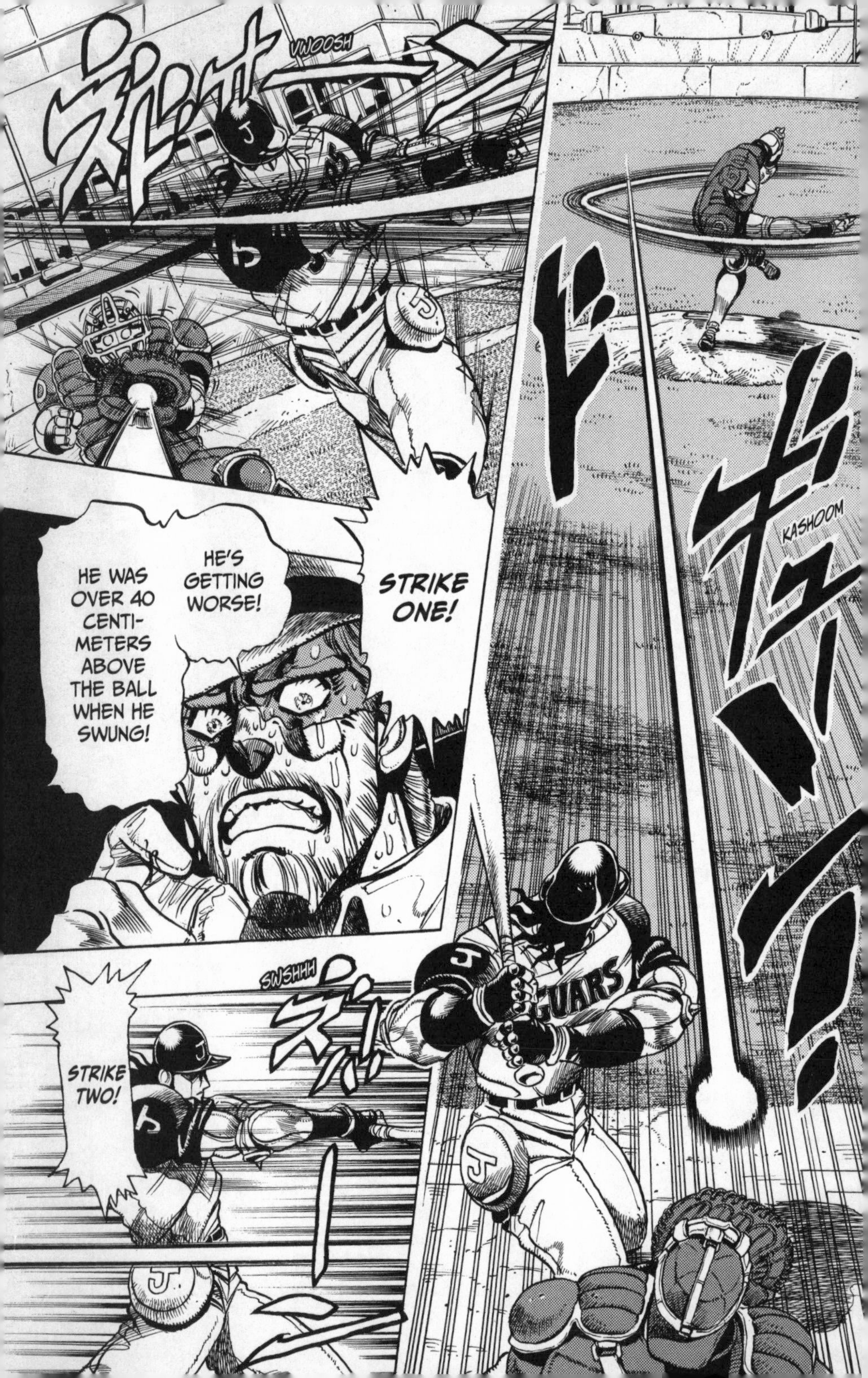
KASHOOM
VWOOSH
STRIKE ONE!
HE'S GETTING WORSE!
HE WAS OVER 40 CENTI-METERS ABOVE THE BALL WHEN HE SWUNG!
SWSHHH
STRIKE TWO!

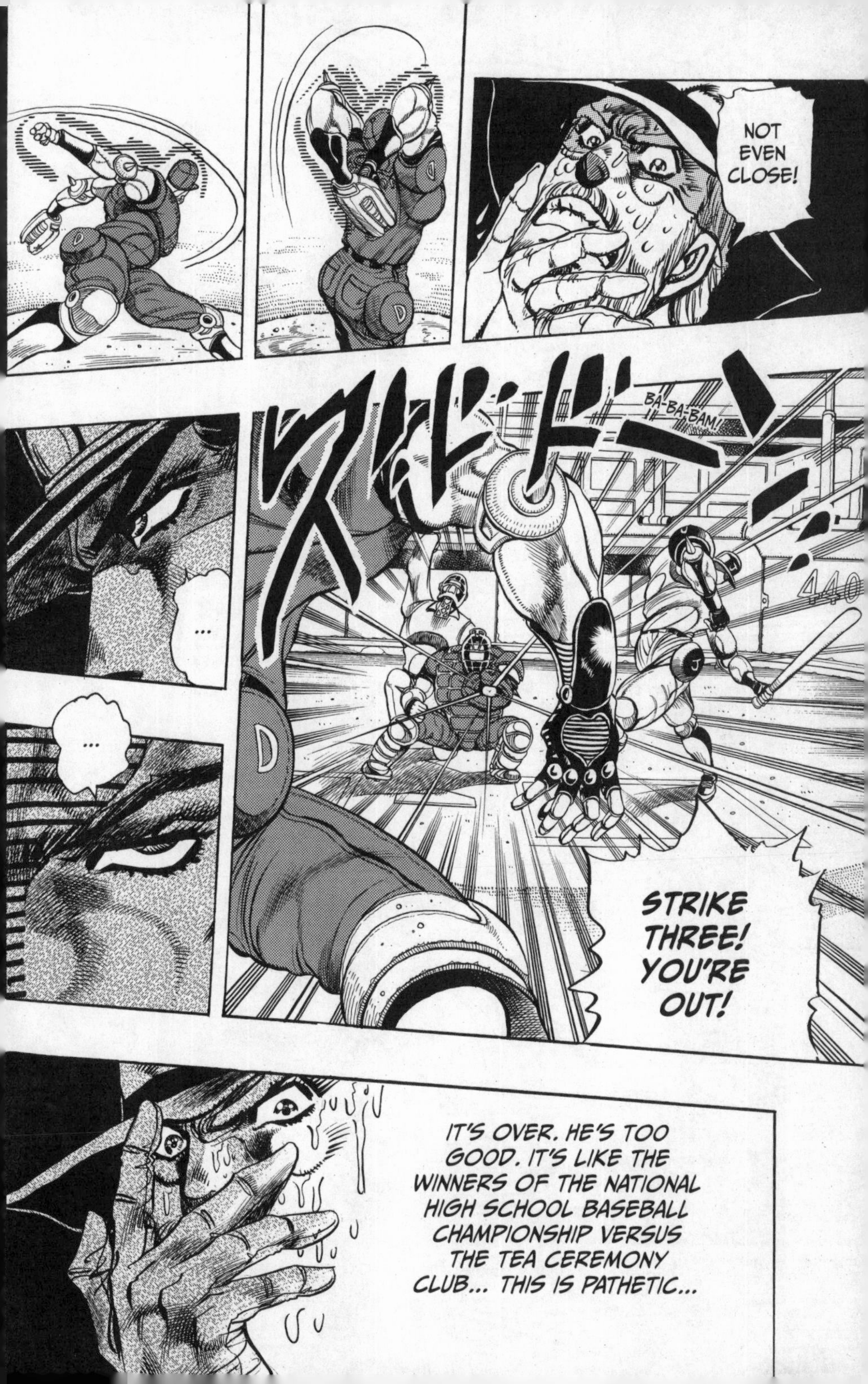
NOT EVEN CLOSE!
BA-BA-BAM!
STRIKE THREE! YOU'RE OUT!
...
...
IT'S OVER. HE'S TOO GOOD. IT'S LIKE THE WINNERS OF THE NATIONAL HIGH SCHOOL BASEBALL CHAMPIONSHIP VERSUS THE TEA CEREMONY CLUB... THIS IS PATHETIC...

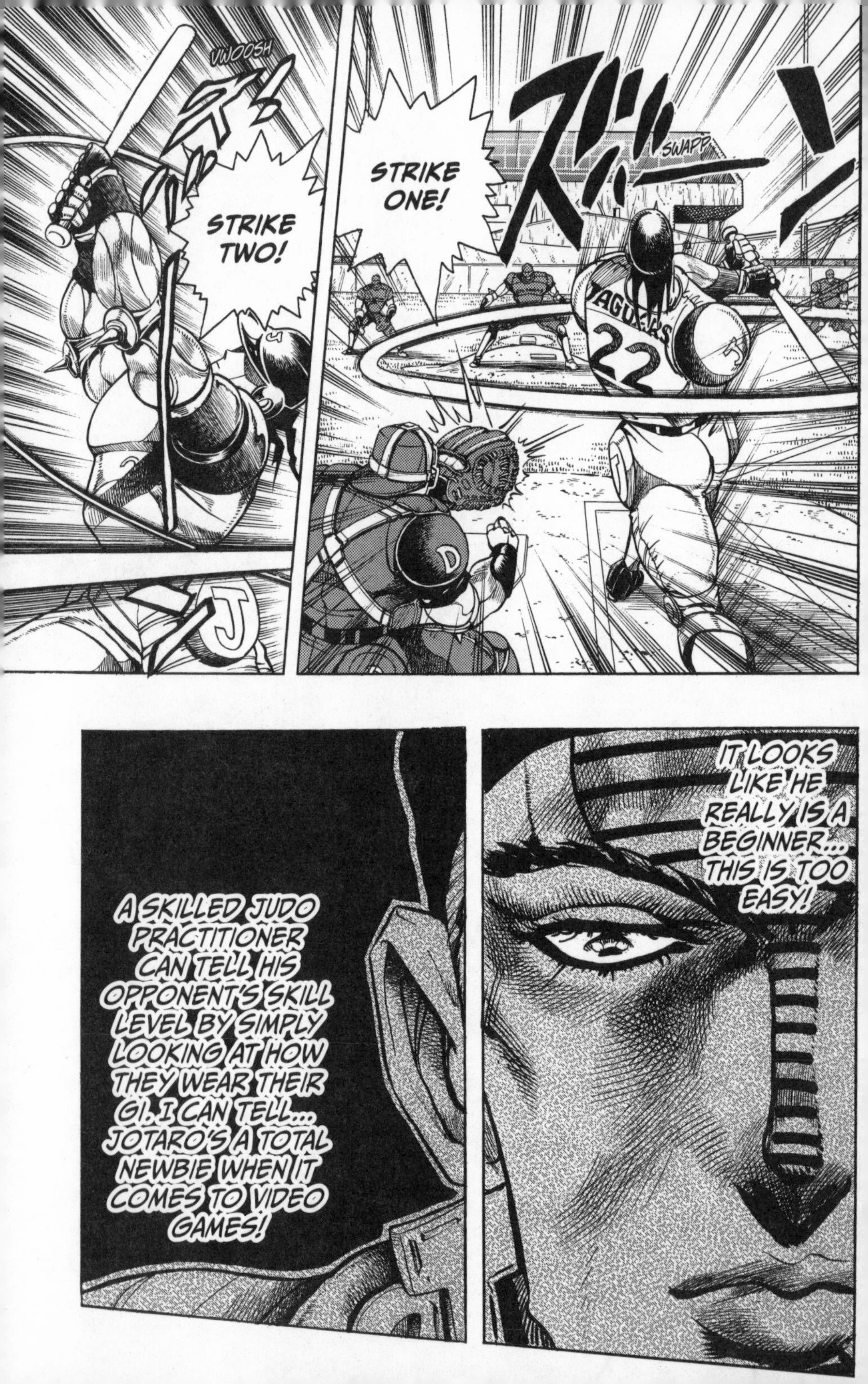
STRIKE ONE!
SWAPP
VWOOSH
STRIKE TWO!
IT LOOKS LIKE HE REALLY IS A BEGINNER... THIS IS TOO EASY!
A SKILLED JUDO PRACTITIONER CAN TELL HIS OPPONENT'S SKILL LEVEL BY SIMPLY LOOKING AT HOW THEY WEAR THEIR GI. I CAN TELL... JOTARO'S A TOTAL NEWBIE WHEN IT COMES TO VIDEO GAMES!

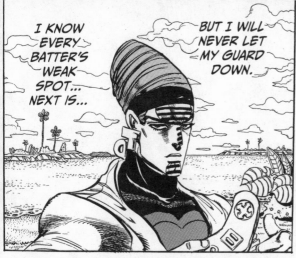

I KNOW EVERY BATTER'S WEAK SPOT... NEXT IS...

BUT I WILL NEVER LET MY GUARD DOWN.

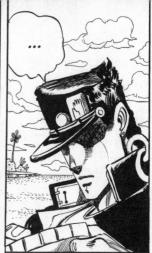

...

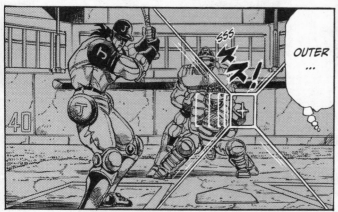

OUTER...

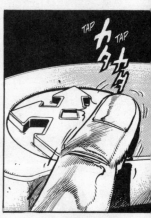

TAP
TAP

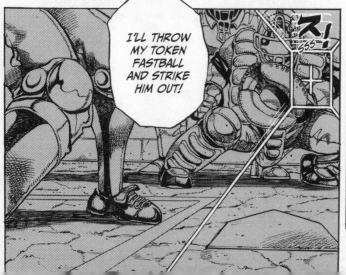

I'LL THROW MY TOKEN FASTBALL AND STRIKE HIM OUT!

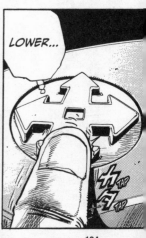

LOWER...

TAP
TAP

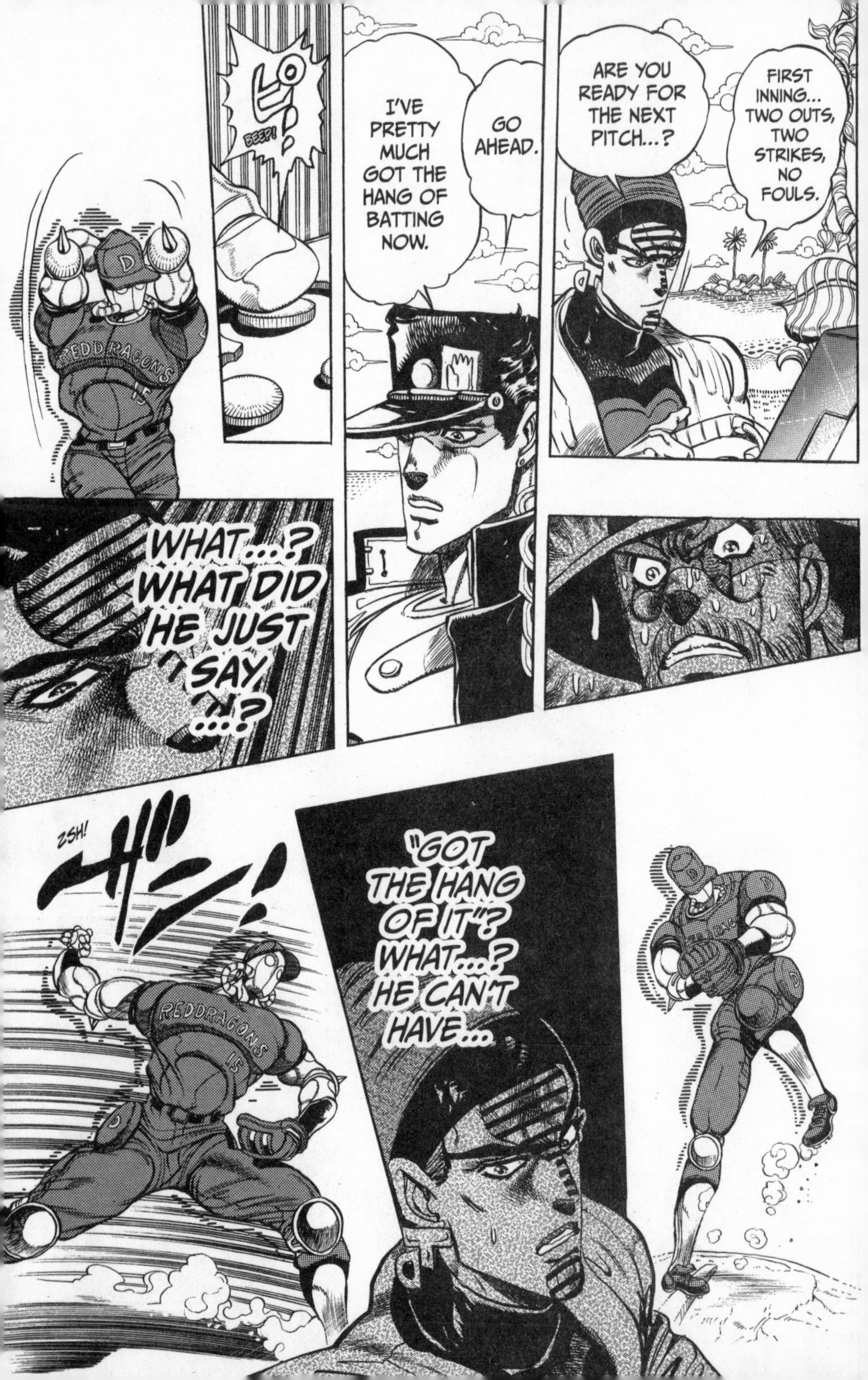
FIRST INNING... TWO OUTS, TWO STRIKES, NO FOULS.
ARE YOU READY FOR THE NEXT PITCH...?
GO AHEAD.
I'VE PRETTY MUCH GOT THE HANG OF BATTING NOW.
BEEP!
WHAT...? WHAT DID HE JUST SAY...?
"GOT THE HANG OF IT"? WHAT...? HE CAN'T HAVE...
ZSH!

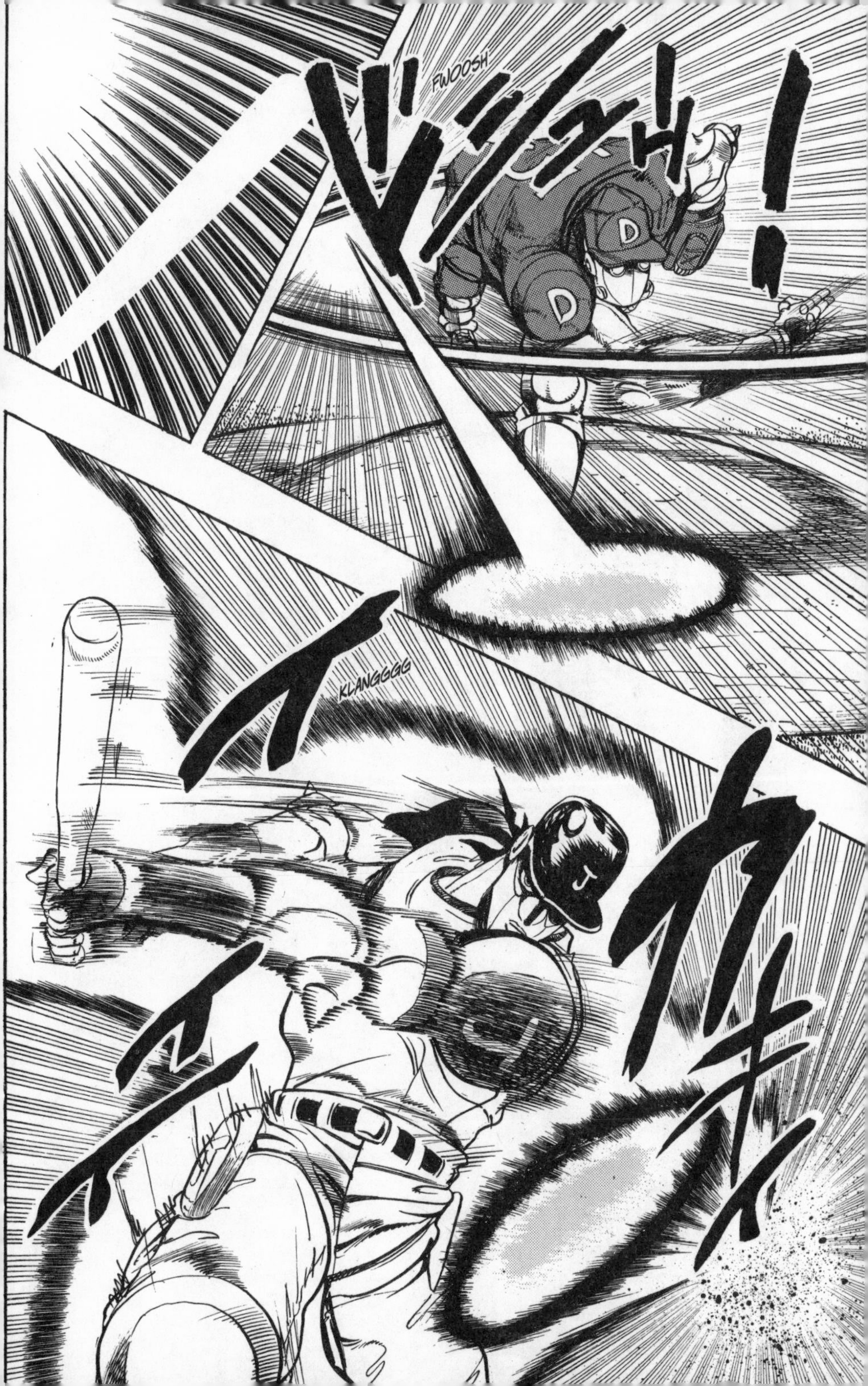
FWOOSH
KLANGGGG

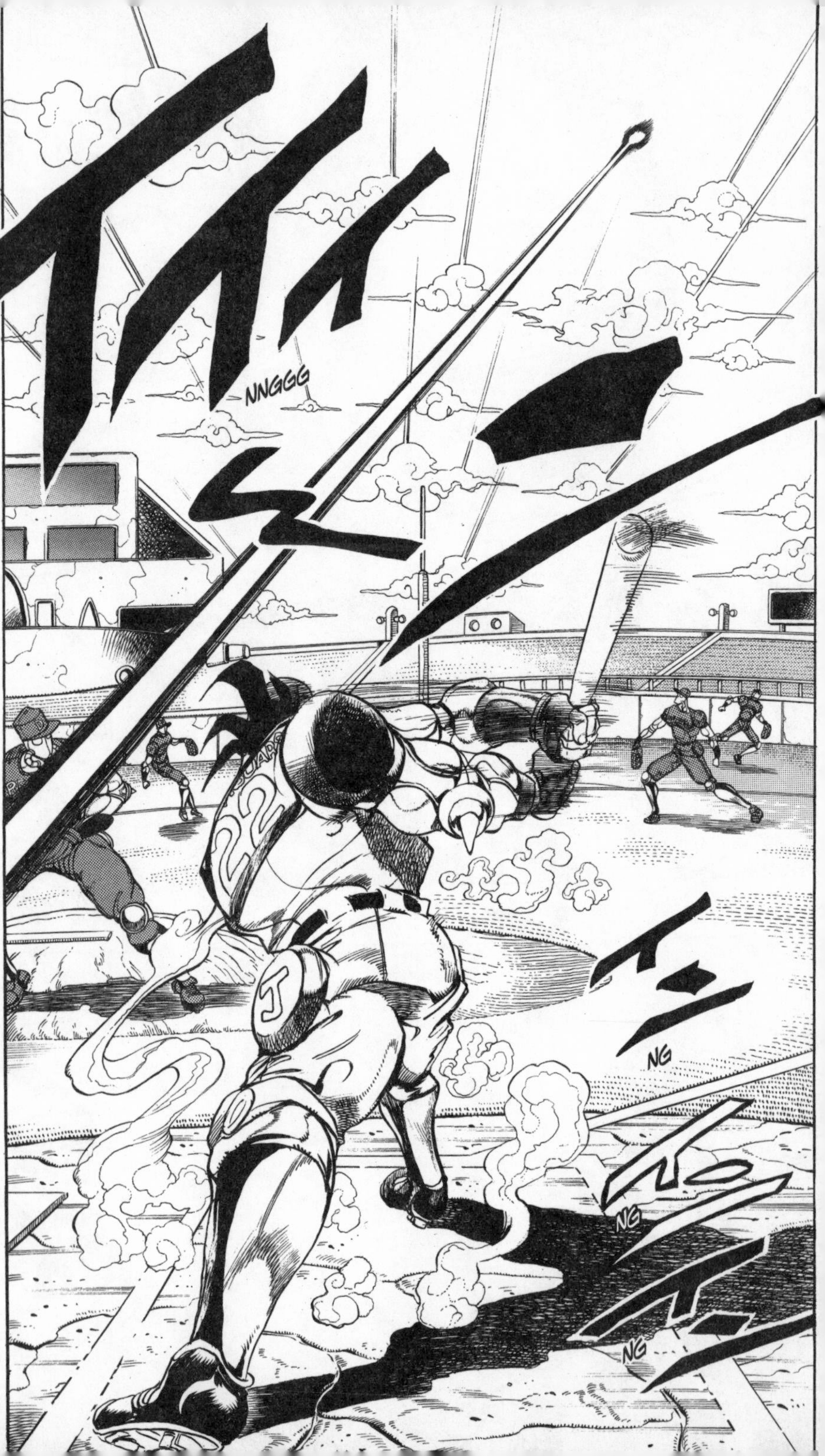
NNGGG
NG
NG
NG

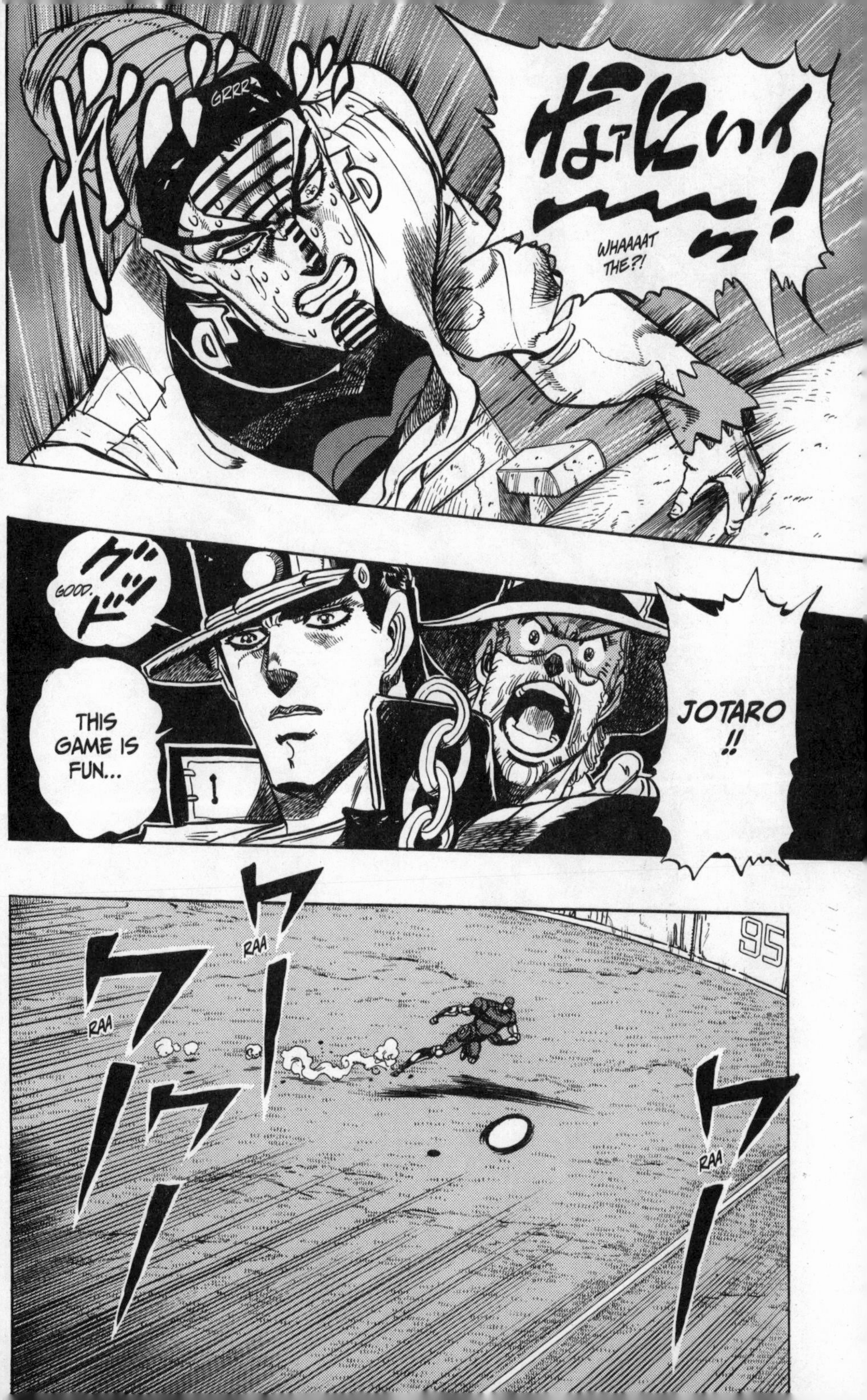
WHAAAAT THE?!
GRRR
JOTARO!!
GOOD.
THIS GAME IS FUN...
95
RAA
RAA
RAA

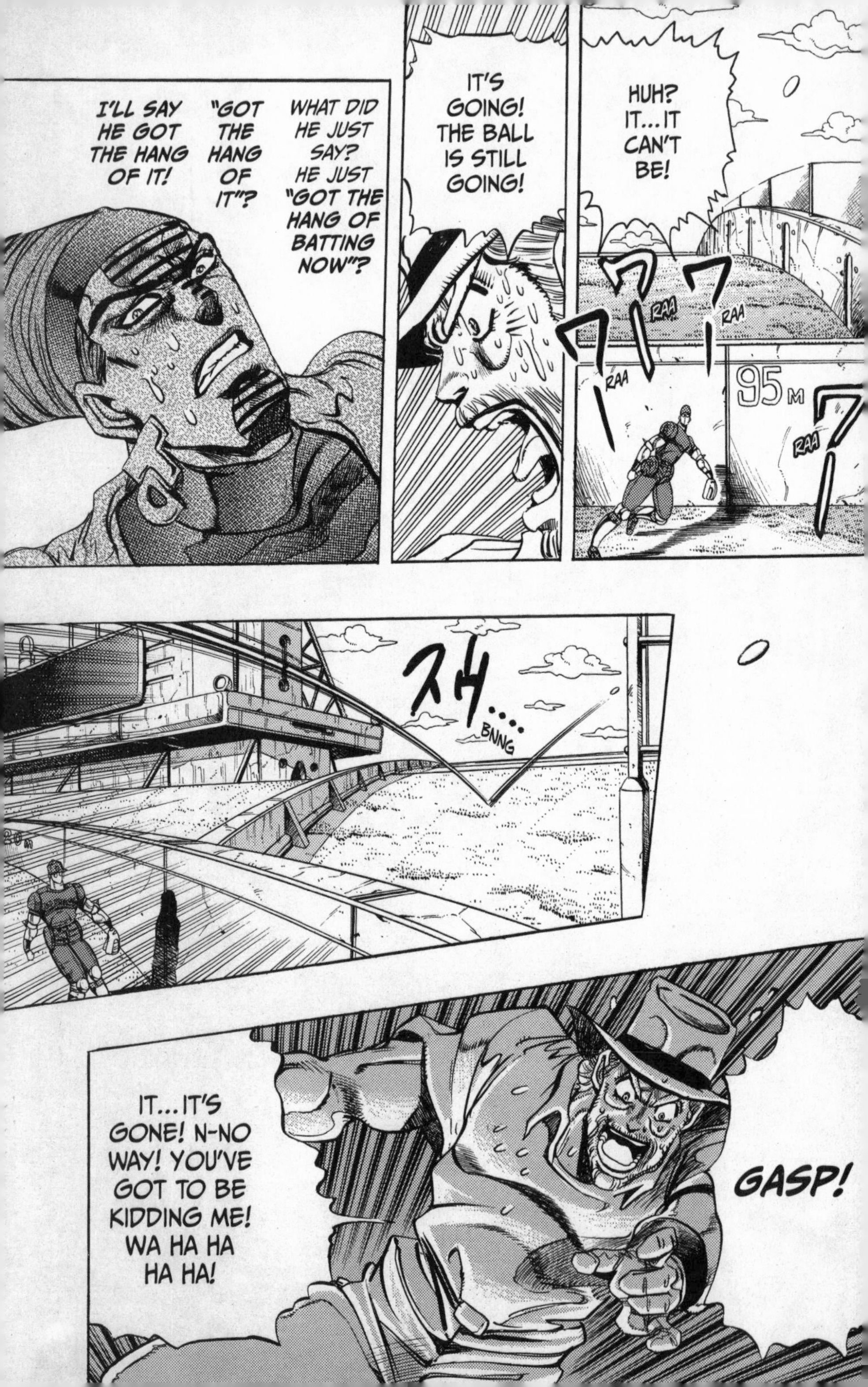
HUH? IT...IT CAN'T BE!
RAA
RAA
RAA
RAA
95 M
IT'S GOING! THE BALL IS STILL GOING!
WHAT DID HE JUST SAY? HE JUST "GOT THE HANG OF BATTING NOW"?
"GOT THE HANG OF IT"?
I'LL SAY HE GOT THE HANG OF IT!
재....
BNNG
IT...IT'S GONE! N-NO WAY! YOU'VE GOT TO BE KIDDING ME! WA HA HA HA HA!
GASP!

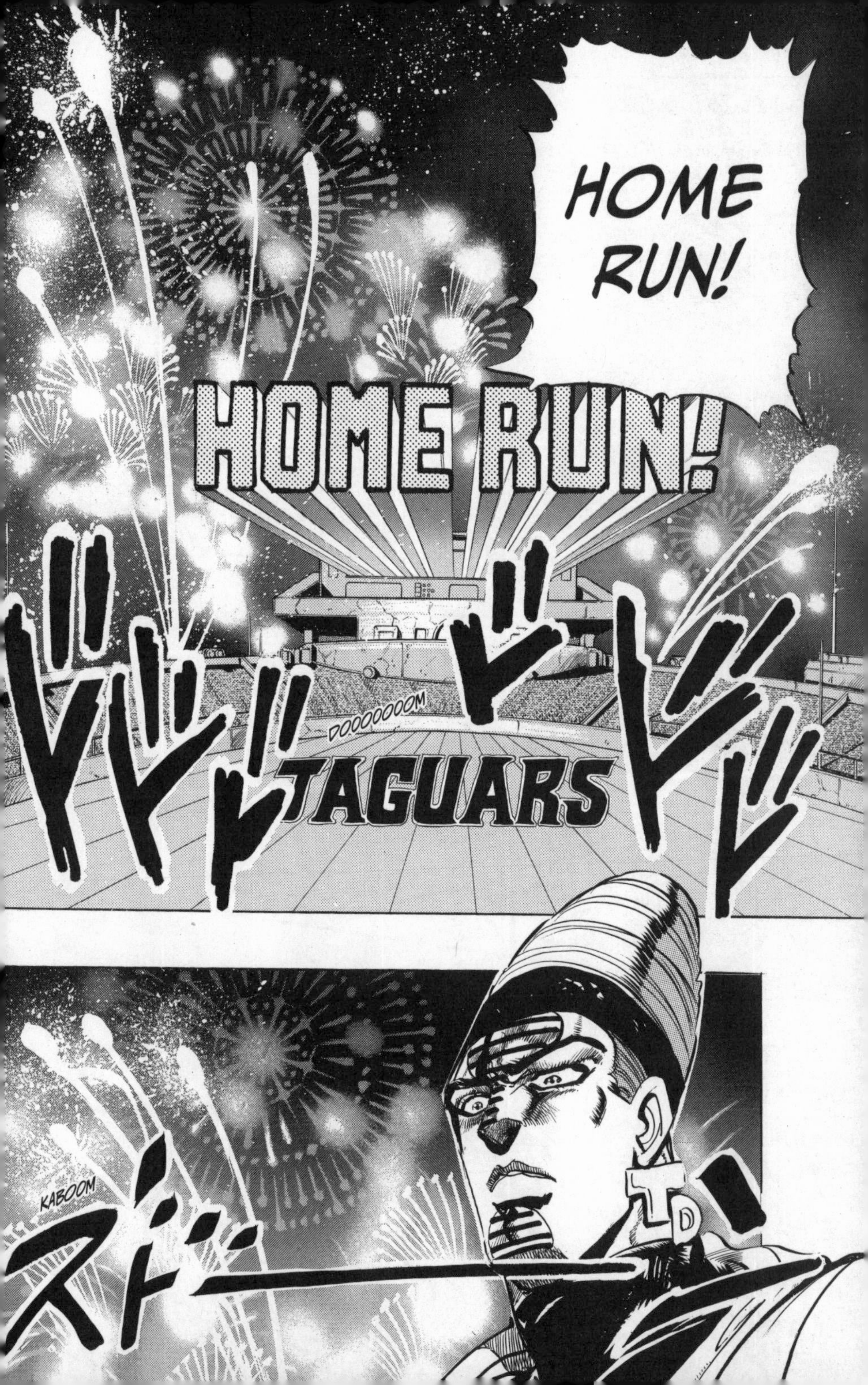
HOME RUN!
HOME RUN!
DOOOOOOOM
JAGUARS
KABOOM

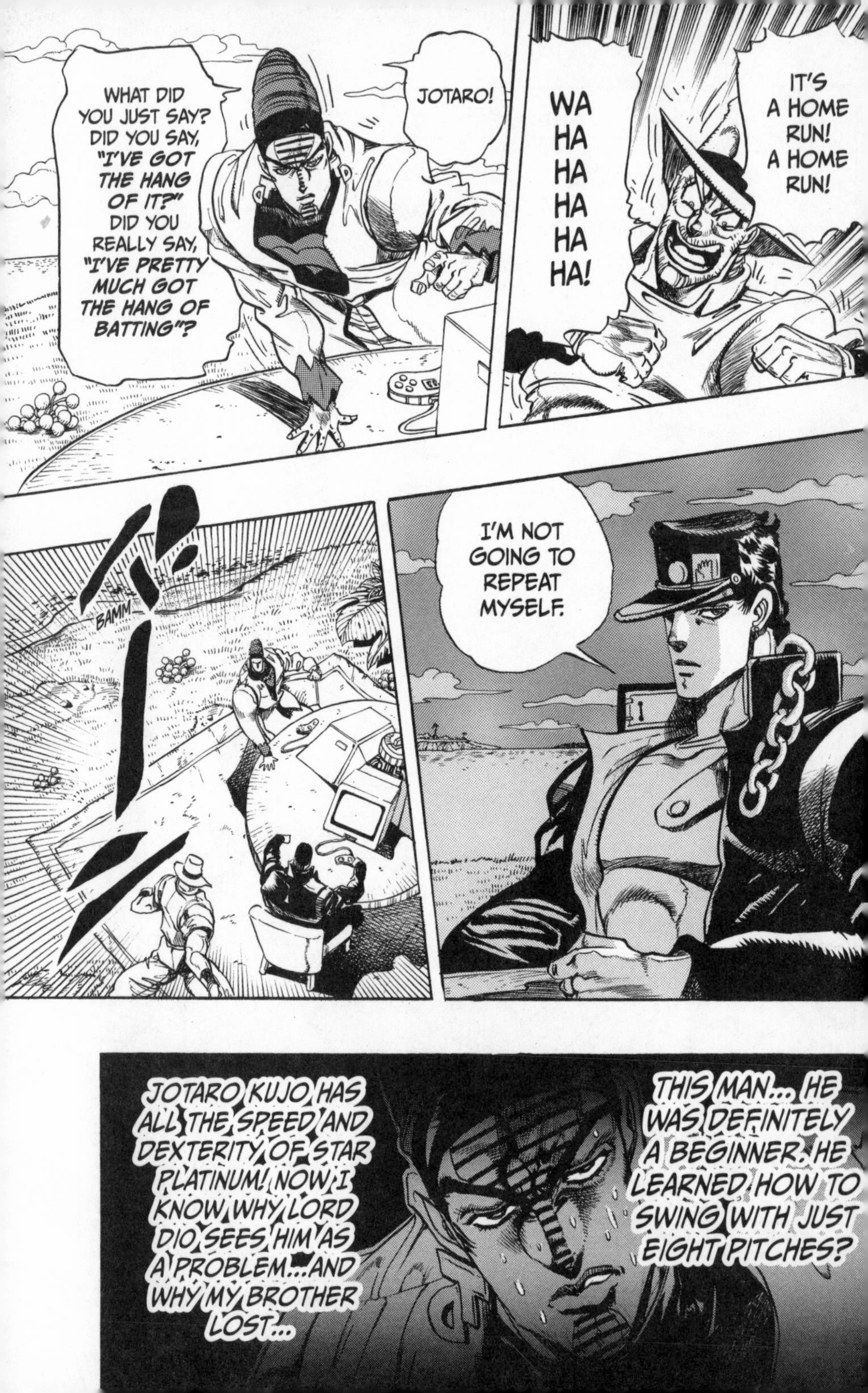
IT'S A HOME RUN! A HOME RUN!
WA HA HA HA HA HA HA!
JOTARO!
WHAT DID YOU JUST SAY? DID YOU SAY, "I'VE GOT THE HANG OF IT?" DID YOU REALLY SAY, "I'VE PRETTY MUCH GOT THE HANG OF BATTING"?
I'M NOT GOING TO REPEAT MYSELF.
BAMM
THIS MAN... HE WAS DEFINITELY A BEGINNER. HE LEARNED HOW TO SWING WITH JUST EIGHT PITCHES?
JOTARO KUJO HAS ALL THE SPEED AND DEXTERITY OF STAR PLATINUM! NOW I KNOW WHY LORD DIO SEES HIM AS A PROBLEM...AND WHY MY BROTHER LOST...

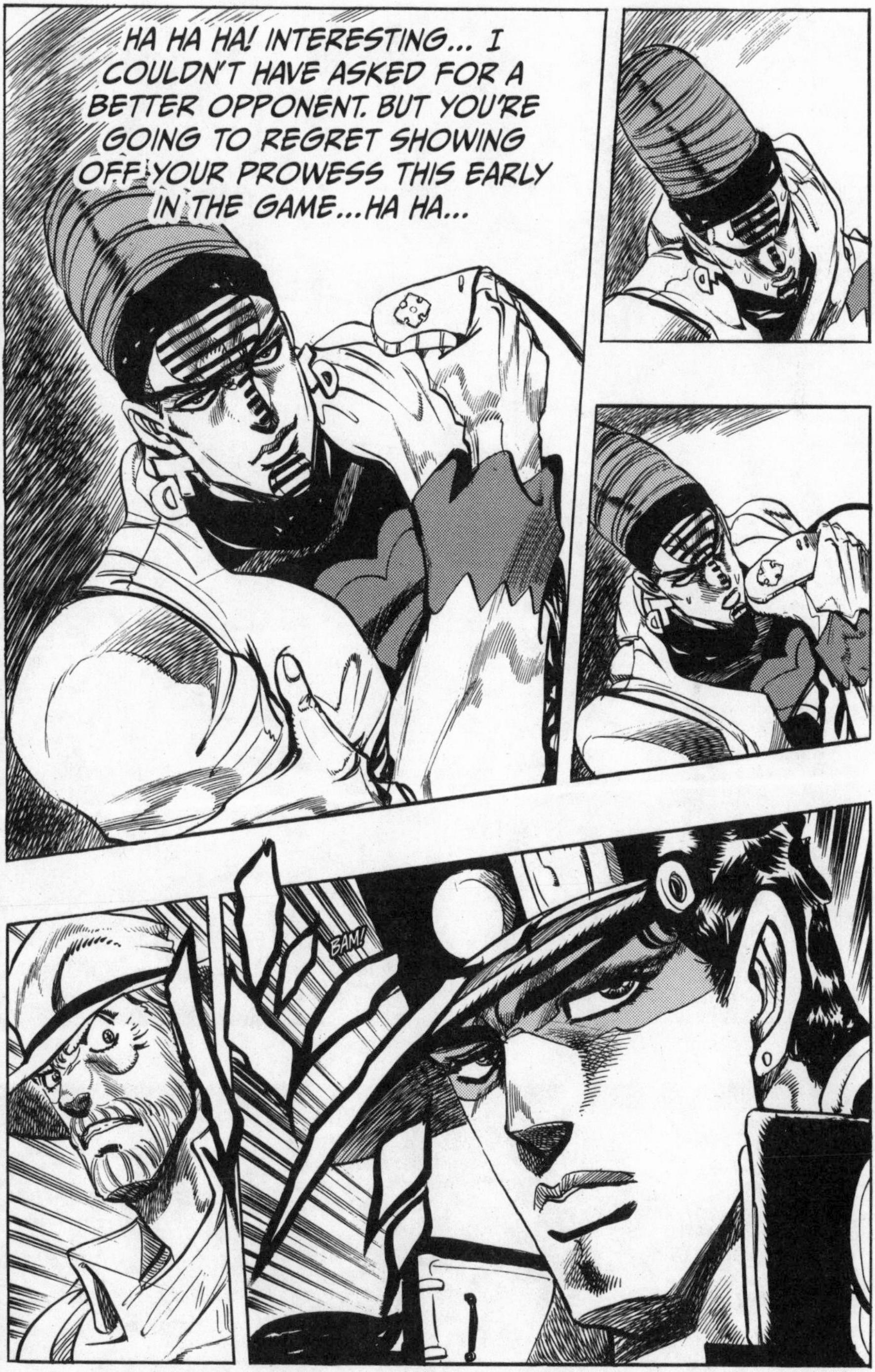
HA HA HA! INTERESTING... I COULDN'T HAVE ASKED FOR A BETTER OPPONENT. BUT YOU'RE GOING TO REGRET SHOWING OFF YOUR PROWESS THIS EARLY IN THE GAME...HA HA...
BAM!

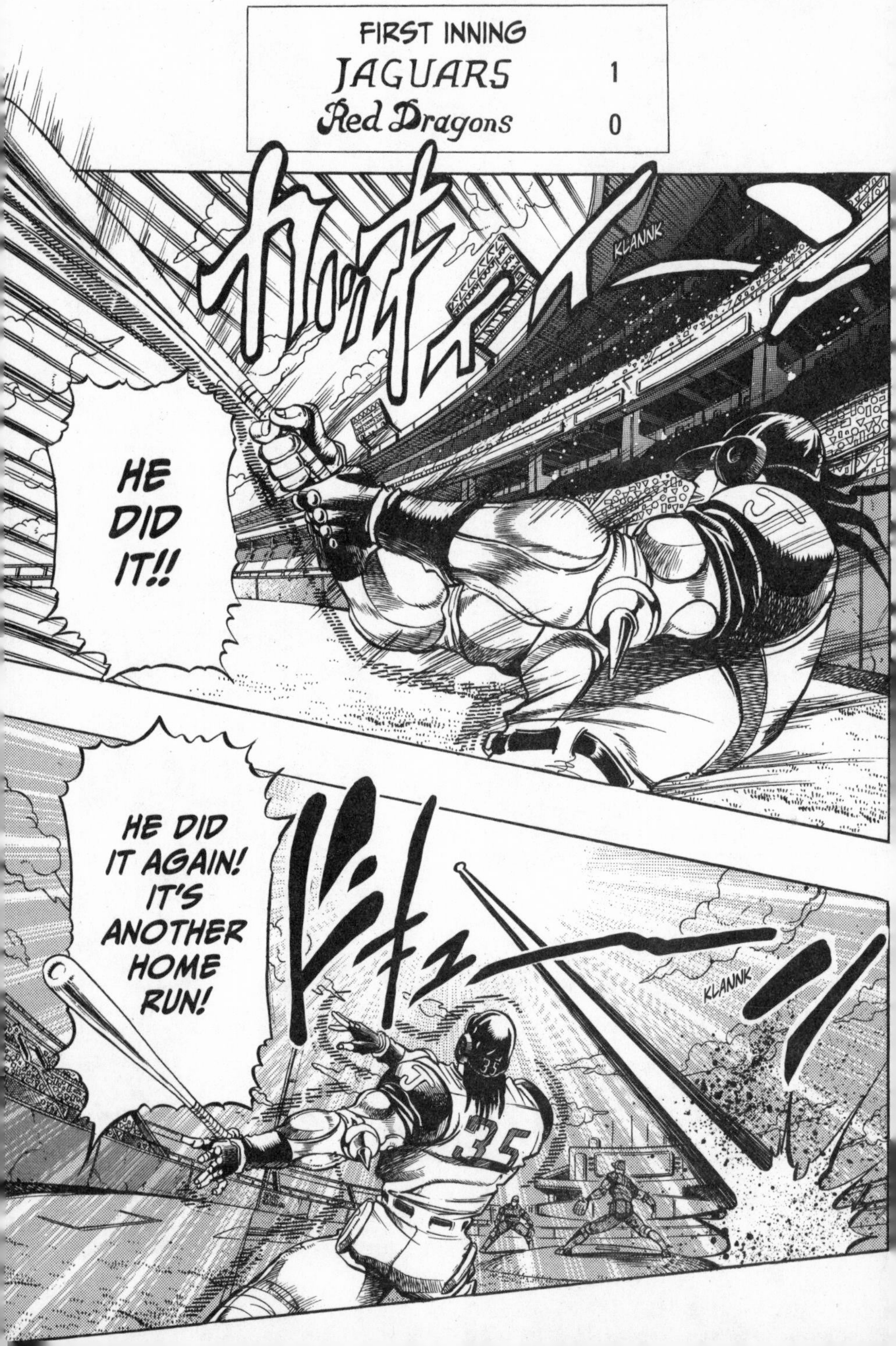
FIRST INNING
JAGUARS 1
Red Dragons 0
KLANNK
HE DID IT!!
HE DID IT AGAIN! IT'S ANOTHER HOME RUN!
KLANNK

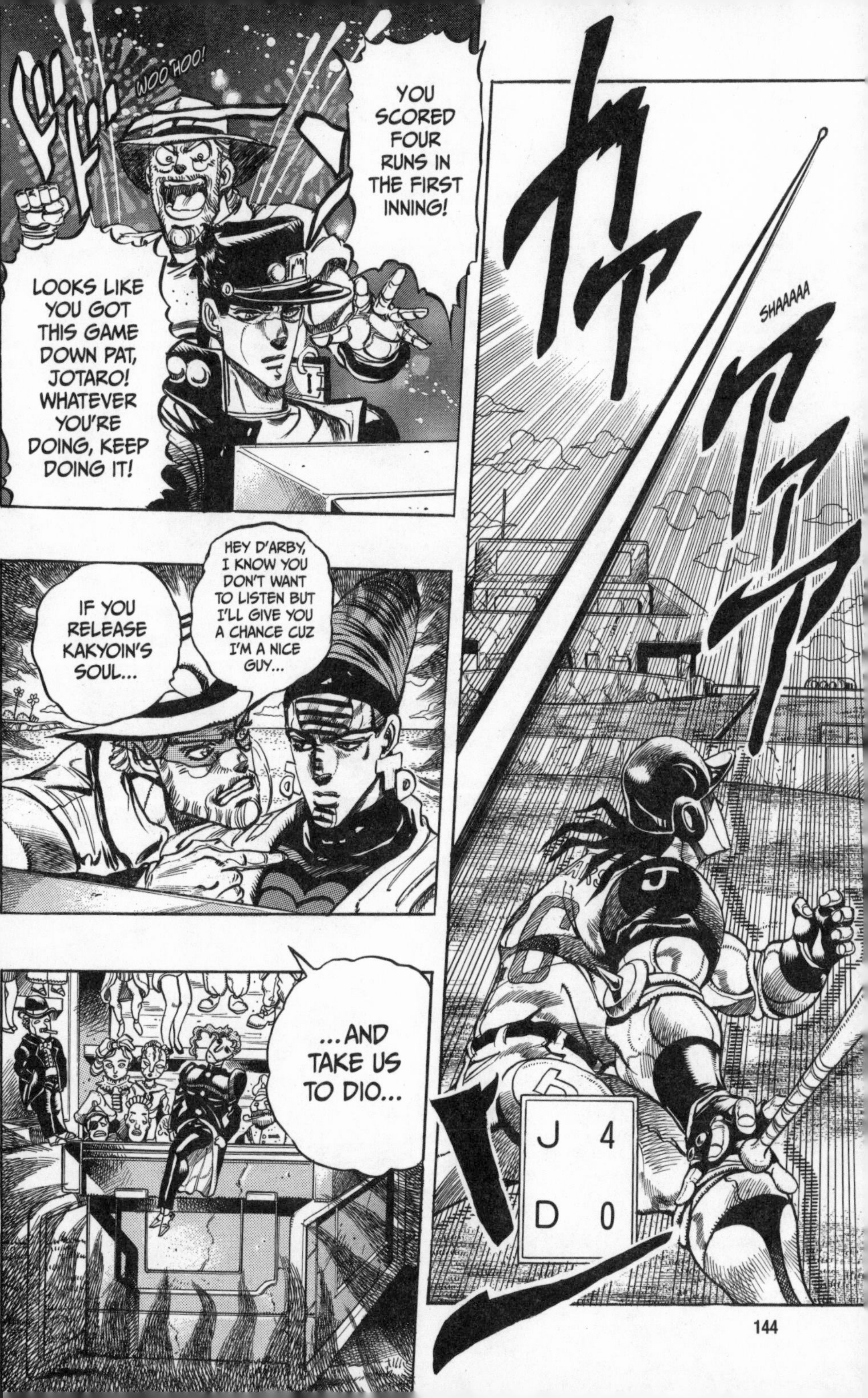

SHAAAAA
J 4
D 0
YOU SCORED FOUR RUNS IN THE FIRST INNING!
WOO HOO!
LOOKS LIKE YOU GOT THIS GAME DOWN PAT, JOTARO! WHATEVER YOU'RE DOING, KEEP DOING IT!
HEY D'ARBY, I KNOW YOU DON'T WANT TO LISTEN BUT I'LL GIVE YOU A CHANCE CUZ I'M A NICE GUY...
IF YOU RELEASE KAKYOIN'S SOUL...
...AND TAKE US TO DIO...

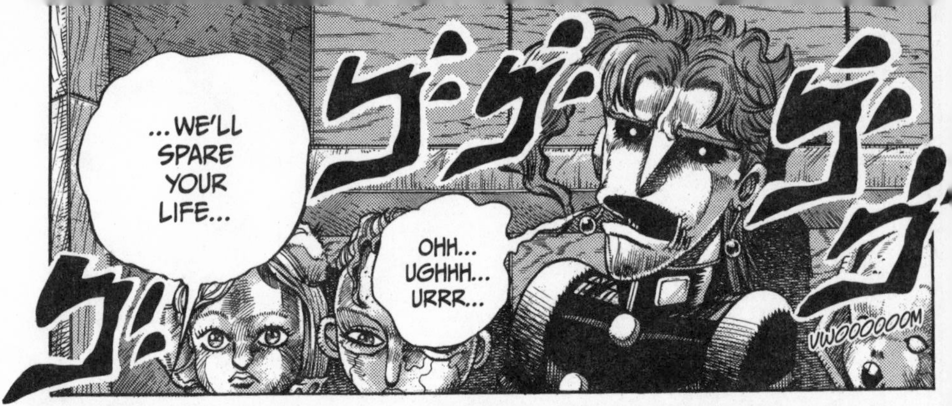
VWOOOOOOOM
OHH... UGHHH... URRR...
...WE'LL SPARE YOUR LIFE...

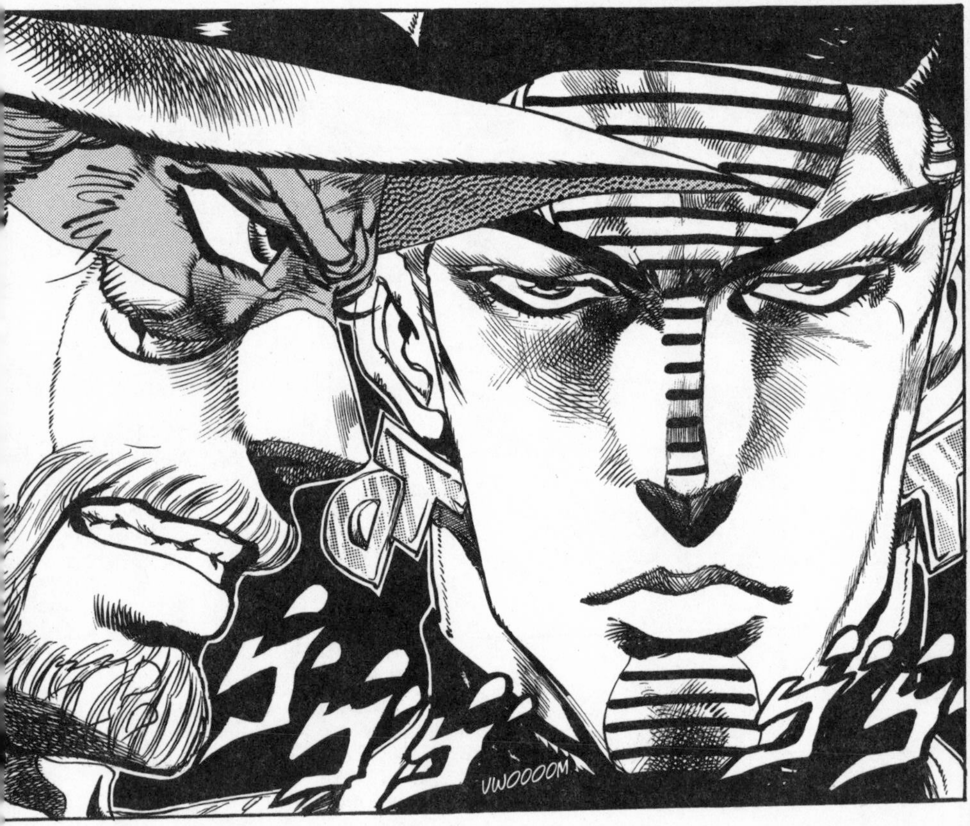
VWOOOOM

CHAPTER 122: D'Arby the Player PART 9

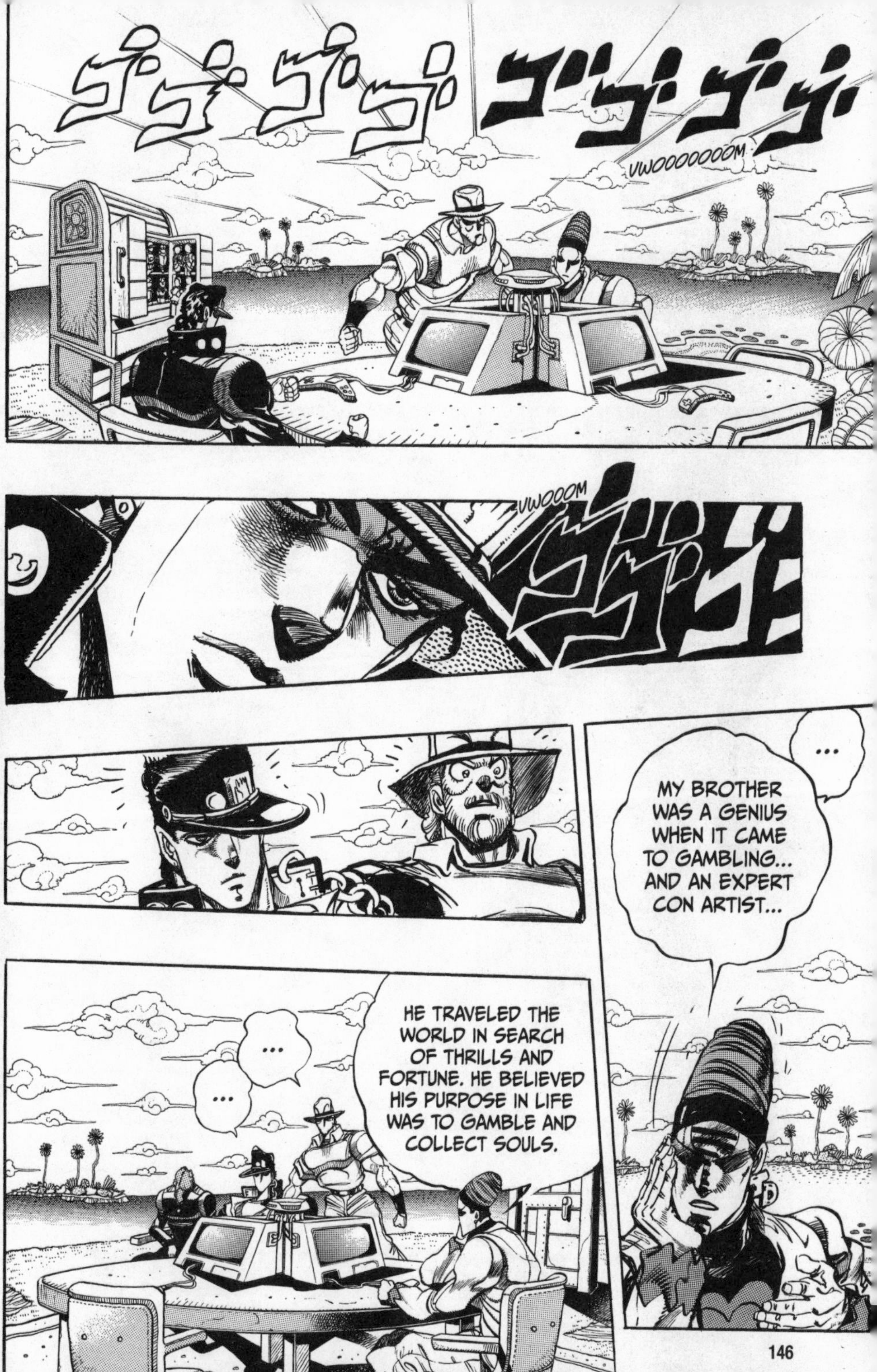
VWOOOOOOOM
VWOOOM
...
MY BROTHER WAS A GENIUS WHEN IT CAME TO GAMBLING... AND AN EXPERT CON ARTIST...
HE TRAVELED THE WORLD IN SEARCH OF THRILLS AND FORTUNE. HE BELIEVED HIS PURPOSE IN LIFE WAS TO GAMBLE AND COLLECT SOULS.
...
...

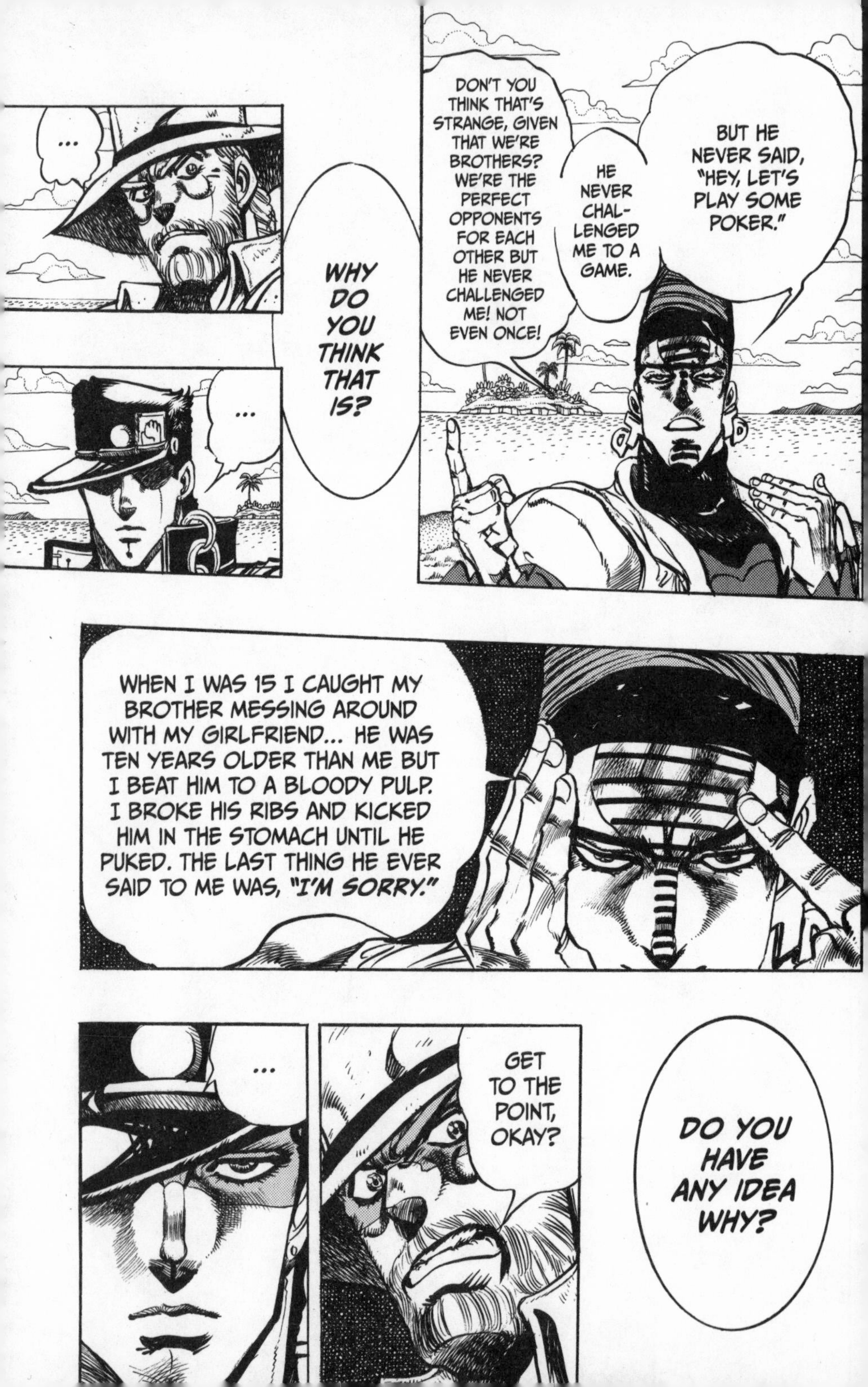
BUT HE NEVER SAID, "HEY, LET'S PLAY SOME POKER."
HE NEVER CHAL-LENGED ME TO A GAME.
DON'T YOU THINK THAT'S STRANGE, GIVEN THAT WE'RE BROTHERS? WE'RE THE PERFECT OPPONENTS FOR EACH OTHER BUT HE NEVER CHALLENGED ME! NOT EVEN ONCE!
WHY DO YOU THINK THAT IS?
...
...
WHEN I WAS 15 I CAUGHT MY BROTHER MESSING AROUND WITH MY GIRLFRIEND... HE WAS TEN YEARS OLDER THAN ME BUT I BEAT HIM TO A BLOODY PULP. I BROKE HIS RIBS AND KICKED HIM IN THE STOMACH UNTIL HE PUKED. THE LAST THING HE EVER SAID TO ME WAS, *"I'M SORRY."*
DO YOU HAVE ANY IDEA WHY?
GET TO THE POINT, OKAY?
...

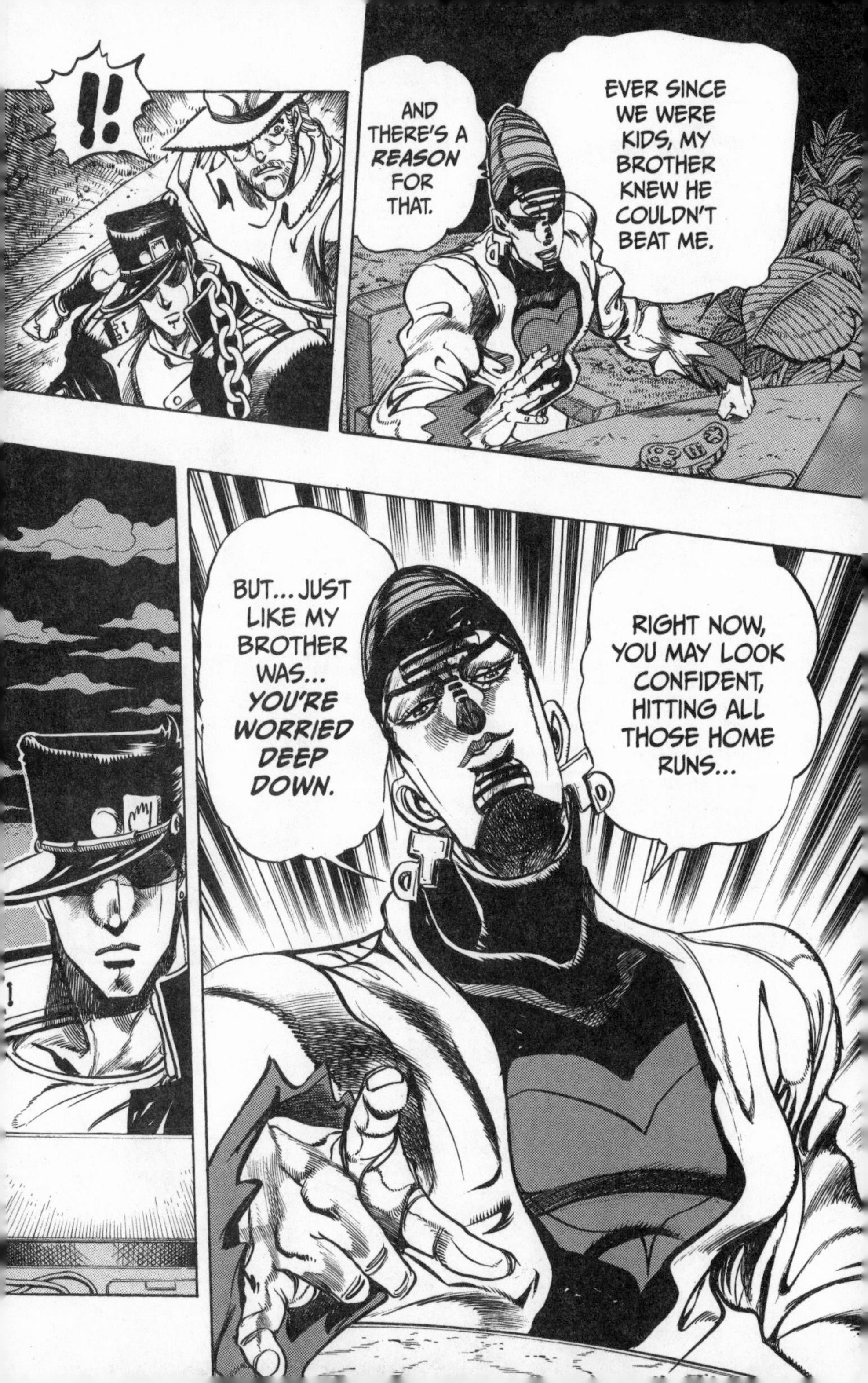
EVER SINCE WE WERE KIDS, MY BROTHER KNEW HE COULDN'T BEAT ME.
AND THERE'S A *REASON* FOR THAT.
!!
RIGHT NOW, YOU MAY LOOK CONFIDENT, HITTING ALL THOSE HOME RUNS...
BUT... JUST LIKE MY BROTHER WAS... *YOU'RE WORRIED DEEP DOWN.*

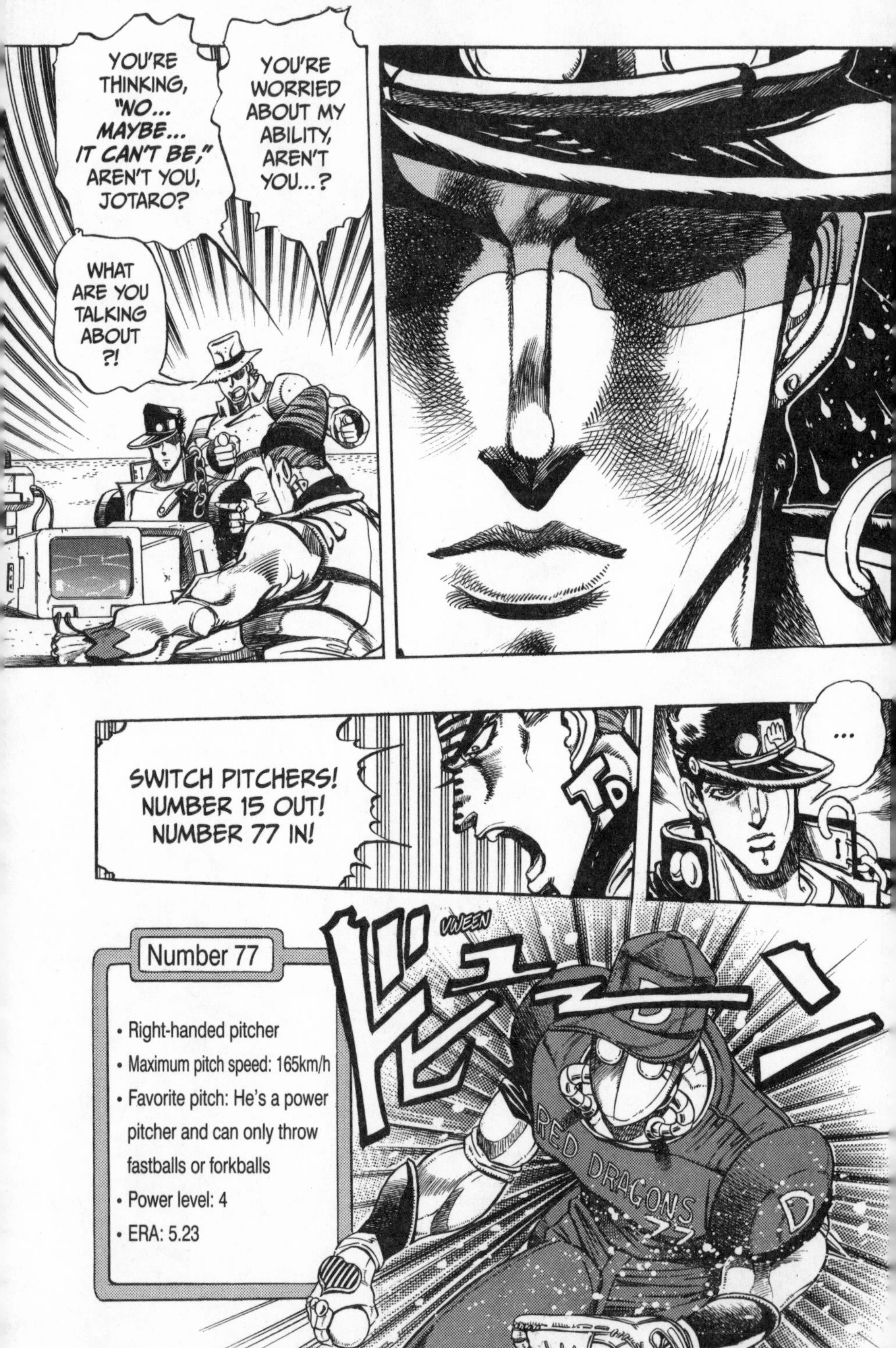
YOU'RE WORRIED ABOUT MY ABILITY, AREN'T YOU...?
YOU'RE THINKING, "NO... MAYBE... IT CAN'T BE," AREN'T YOU, JOTARO?
WHAT ARE YOU TALKING ABOUT ?!
...
SWITCH PITCHERS! NUMBER 15 OUT! NUMBER 77 IN!
VWEEN
Number 77
• Right-handed pitcher
• Maximum pitch speed: 165km/h
• Favorite pitch: He's a power pitcher and can only throw fastballs or forkballs
• Power level: 4
• ERA: 5.23
RED DRAGONS 77

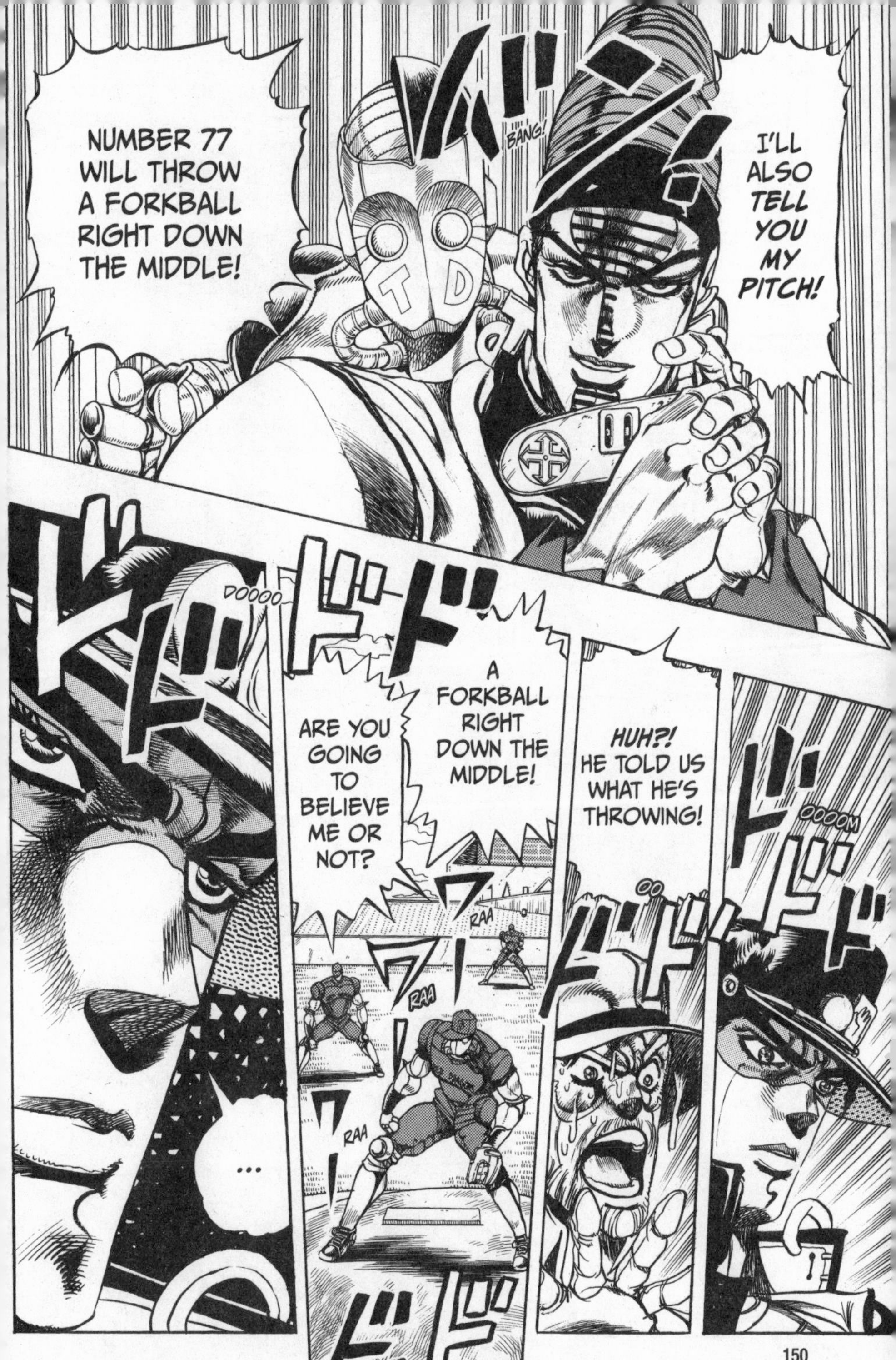
I'LL ALSO TELL YOU MY PITCH!
BANG!
NUMBER 77 WILL THROW A FORKBALL RIGHT DOWN THE MIDDLE!
OOOOM
HUH?! HE TOLD US WHAT HE'S THROWING!
A FORKBALL RIGHT DOWN THE MIDDLE!
ARE YOU GOING TO BELIEVE ME OR NOT?
RAA
RAA
RAA
DD
DOOOO
...

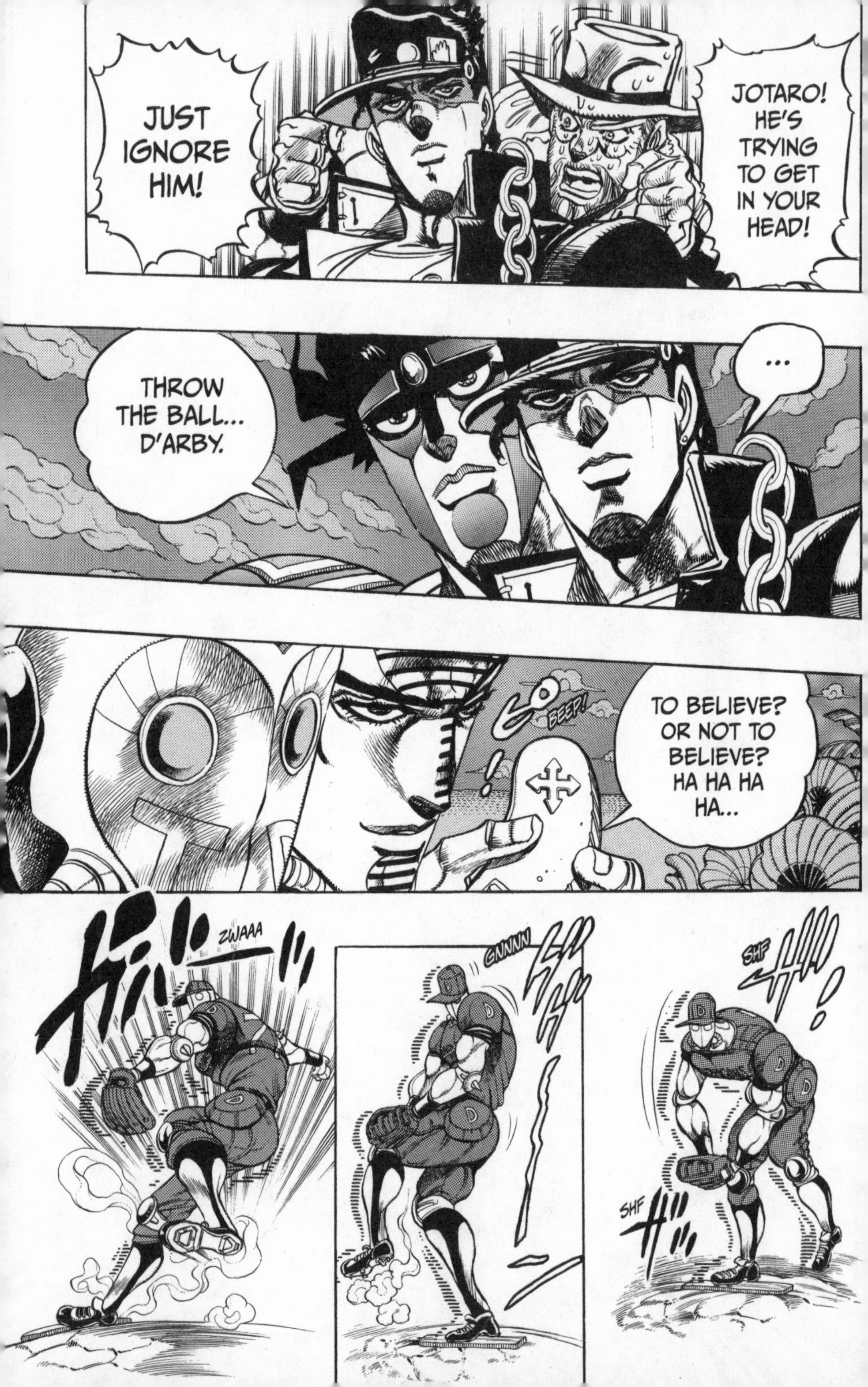
JOTARO! HE'S TRYING TO GET IN YOUR HEAD!
JUST IGNORE HIM!
...
THROW THE BALL... D'ARBY.
TO BELIEVE? OR NOT TO BELIEVE? HA HA HA HA...
BEEP!
SHF
SHF
GNNNN
ZWAAA

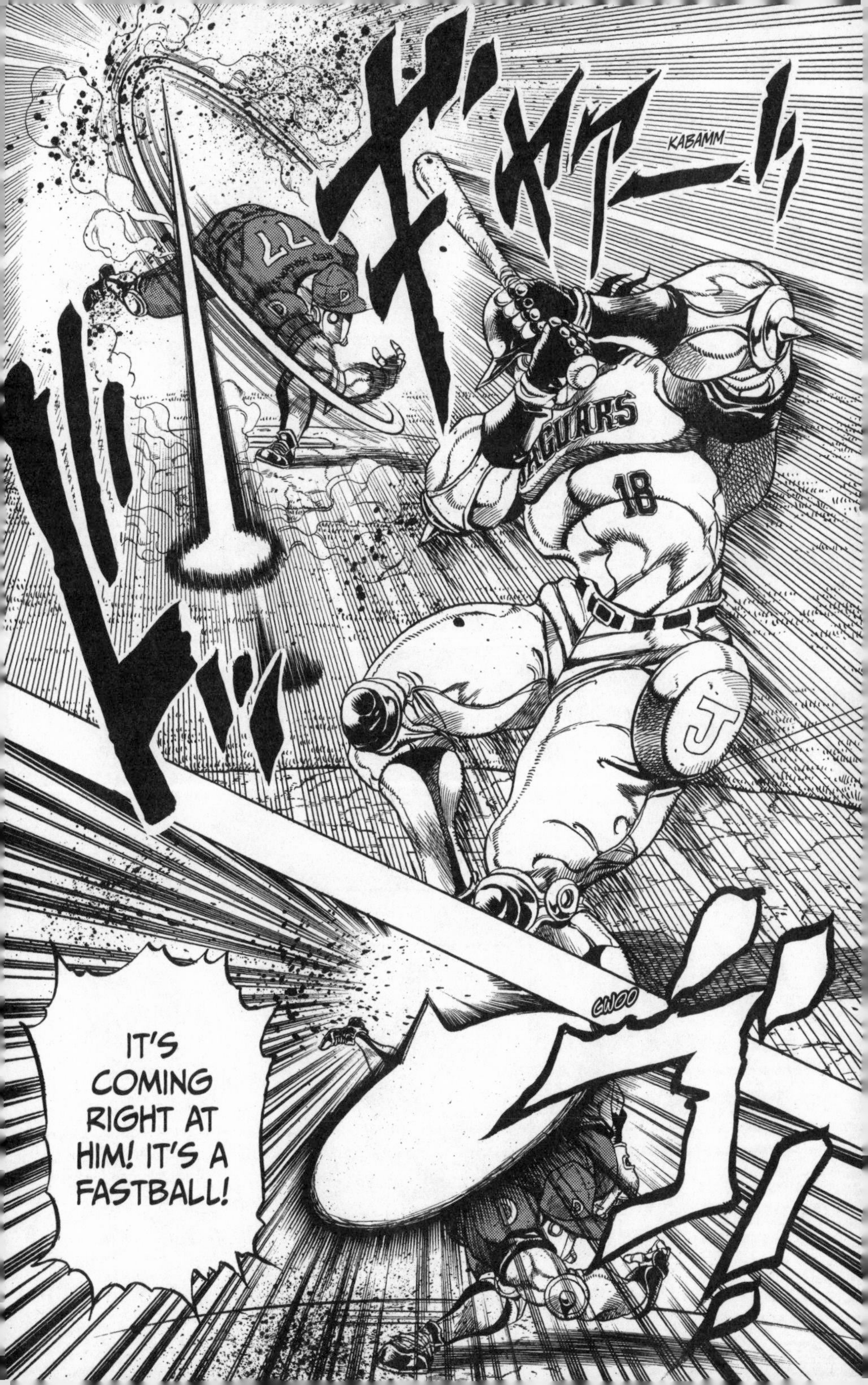
KABAMM
GWOO
IT'S COMING RIGHT AT HIM! IT'S A FASTBALL!

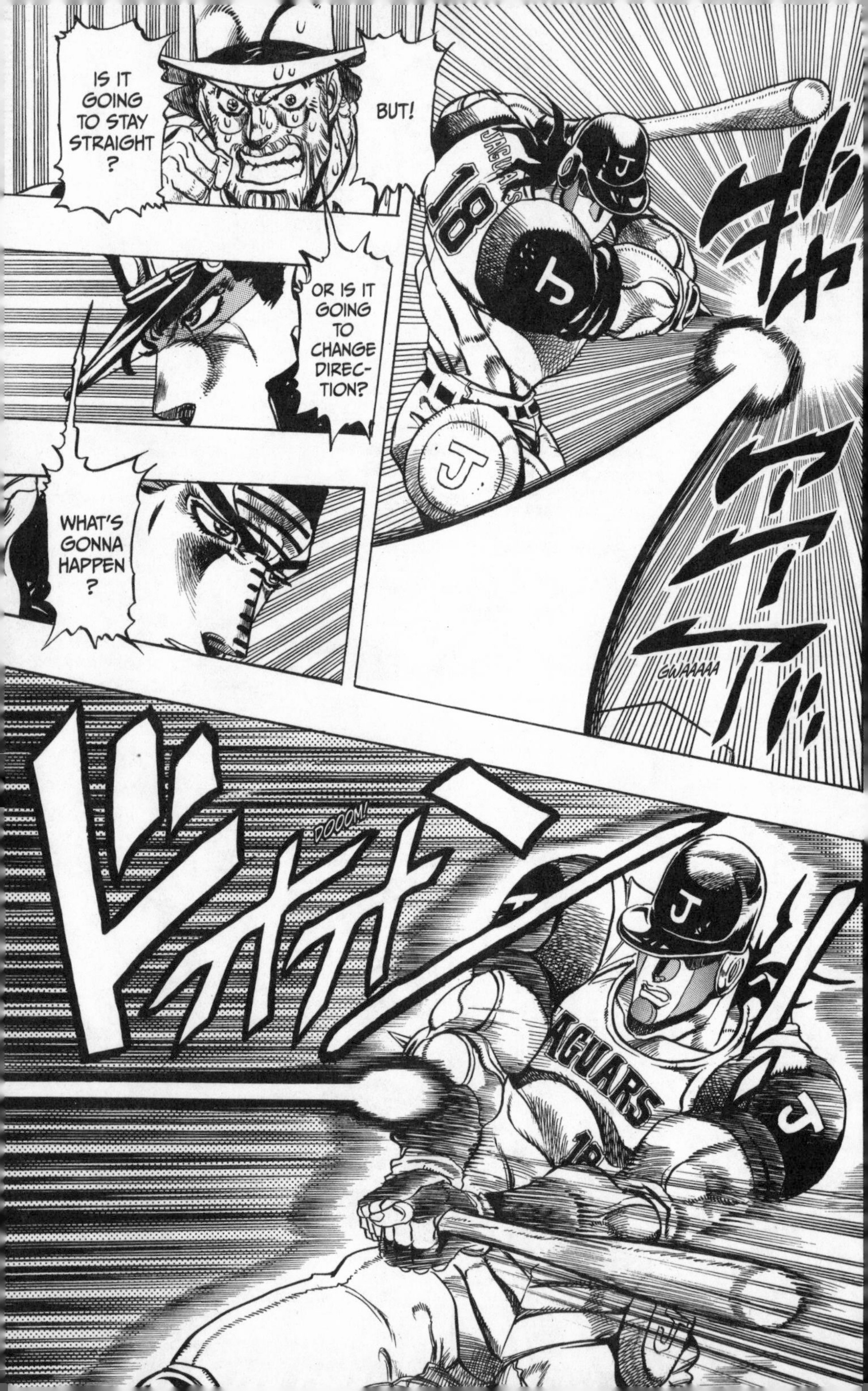
GWAAAAA
BUT!
IS IT GOING TO STAY STRAIGHT?
OR IS IT GOING TO CHANGE DIRECTION?
WHAT'S GONNA HAPPEN?
DOOOM!

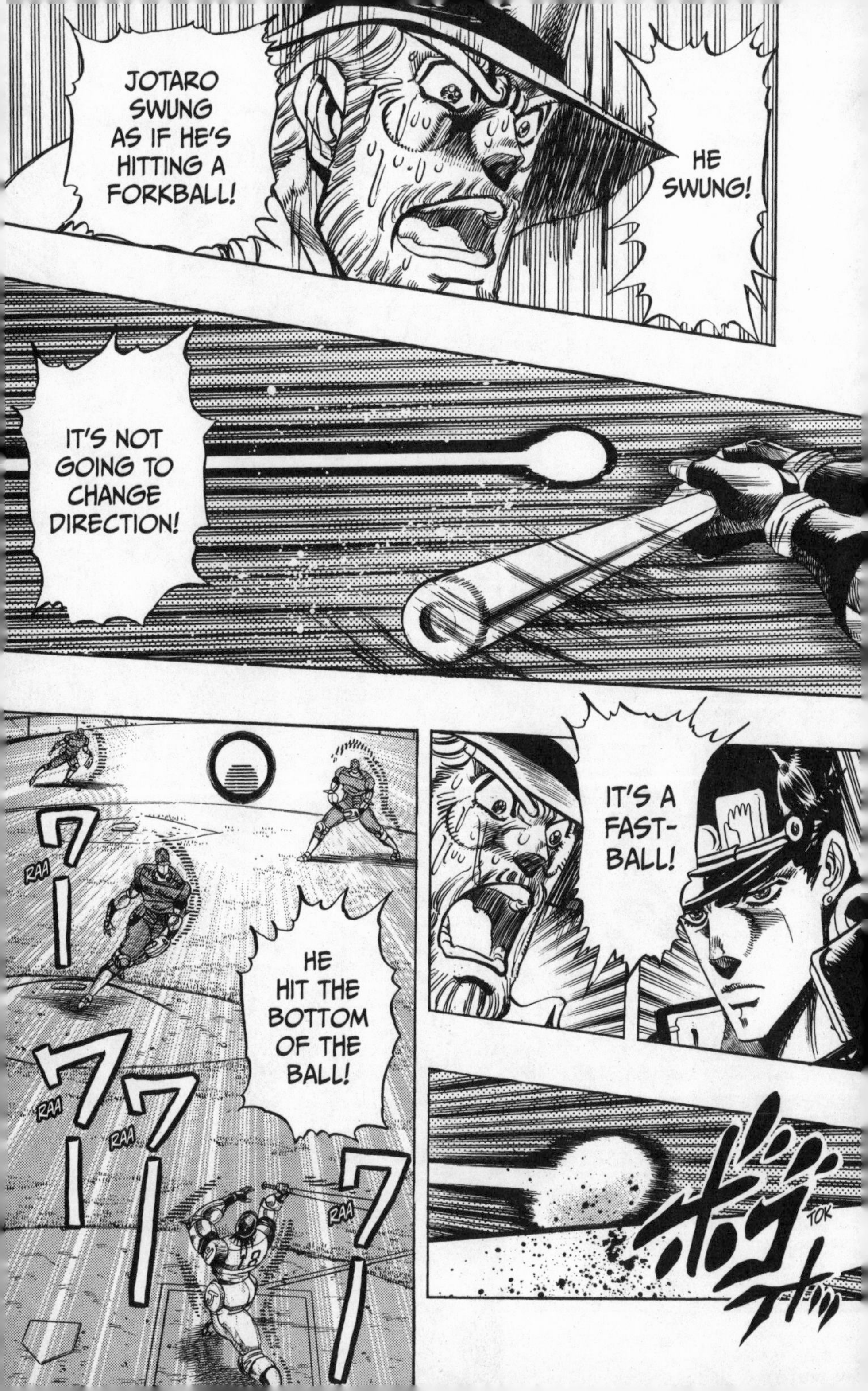
HE SWUNG!
JOTARO SWUNG AS IF HE'S HITTING A FORKBALL!
IT'S NOT GOING TO CHANGE DIRECTION!
IT'S A FAST-BALL!
TOK
HE HIT THE BOTTOM OF THE BALL!
RAA
RAA
RAA
RAA

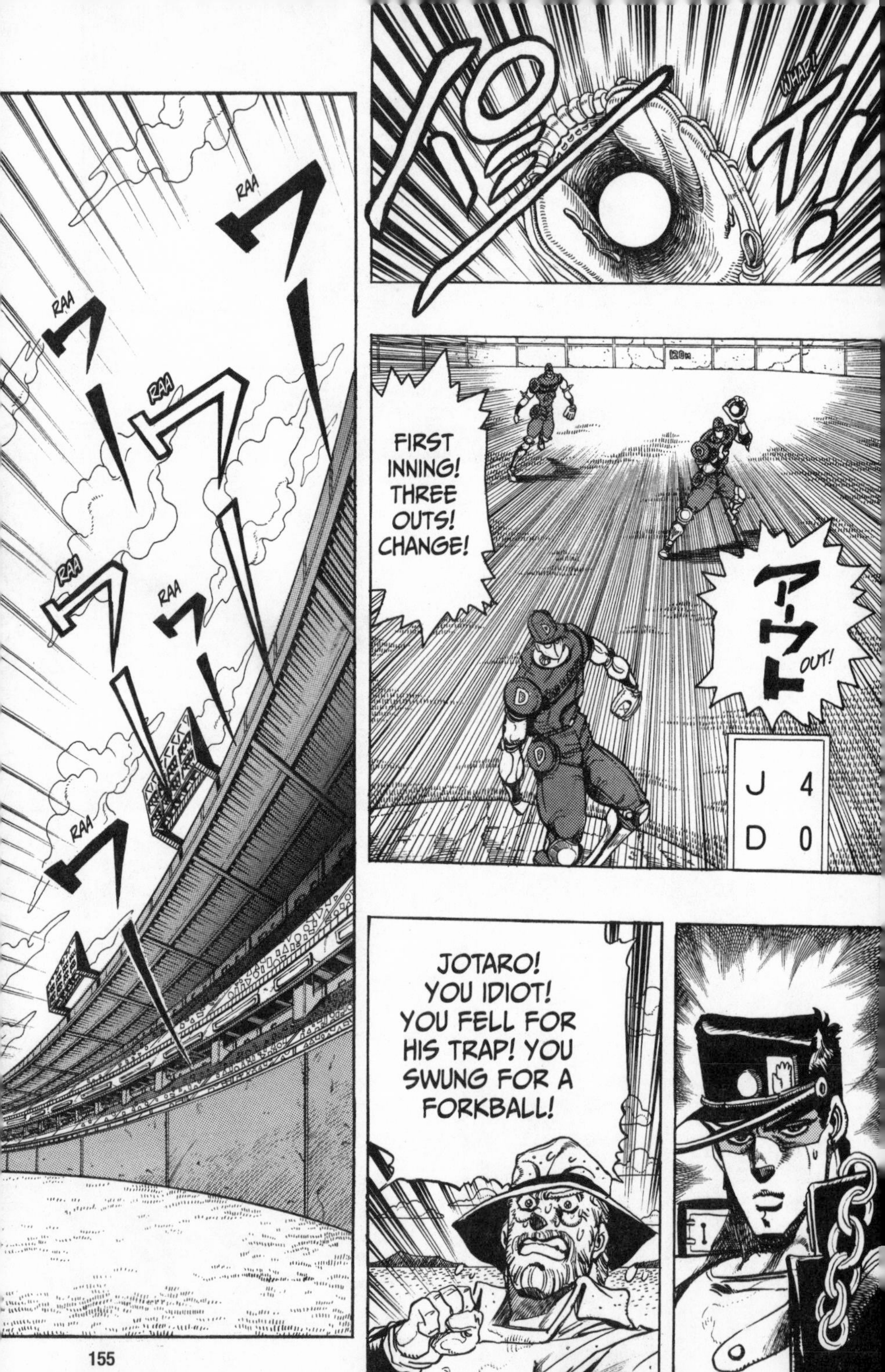
WHAP!
FIRST INNING! THREE OUTS! CHANGE!
120m
アウト
OUT!
J 4
D 0
JOTARO! YOU IDIOT! YOU FELL FOR HIS TRAP! YOU SWUNG FOR A FORKBALL!
RAA
RAA
RAA
RAA
RAA
RAA

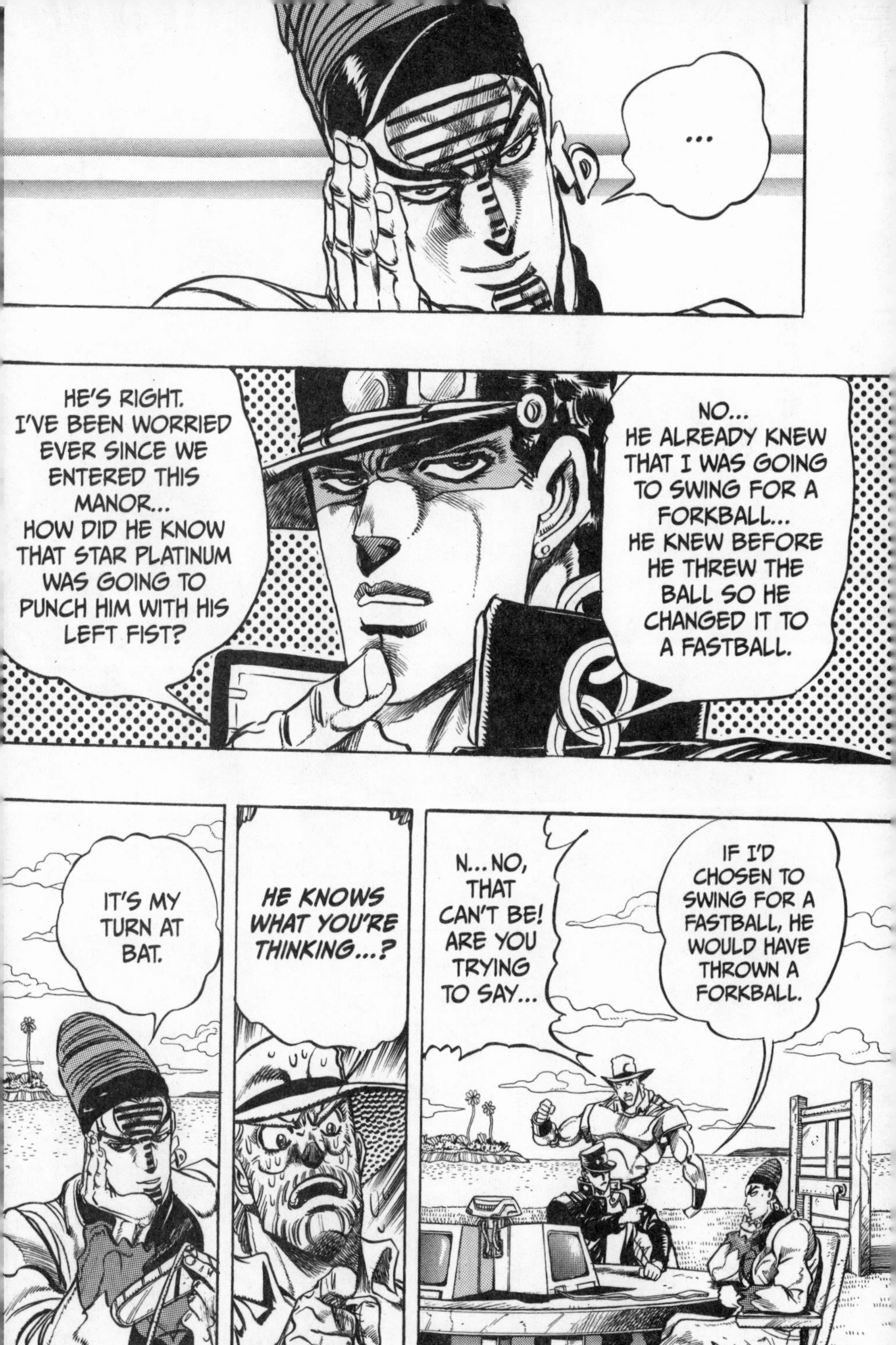
...
NO... HE ALREADY KNEW THAT I WAS GOING TO SWING FOR A FORKBALL... HE KNEW BEFORE HE THREW THE BALL SO HE CHANGED IT TO A FASTBALL.
HE'S RIGHT. I'VE BEEN WORRIED EVER SINCE WE ENTERED THIS MANOR... HOW DID HE KNOW THAT STAR PLATINUM WAS GOING TO PUNCH HIM WITH HIS LEFT FIST?
IF I'D CHOSEN TO SWING FOR A FASTBALL, HE WOULD HAVE THROWN A FORKBALL.
N... NO, THAT CAN'T BE! ARE YOU TRYING TO SAY...
HE KNOWS WHAT YOU'RE THINKING...?
IT'S MY TURN AT BAT.

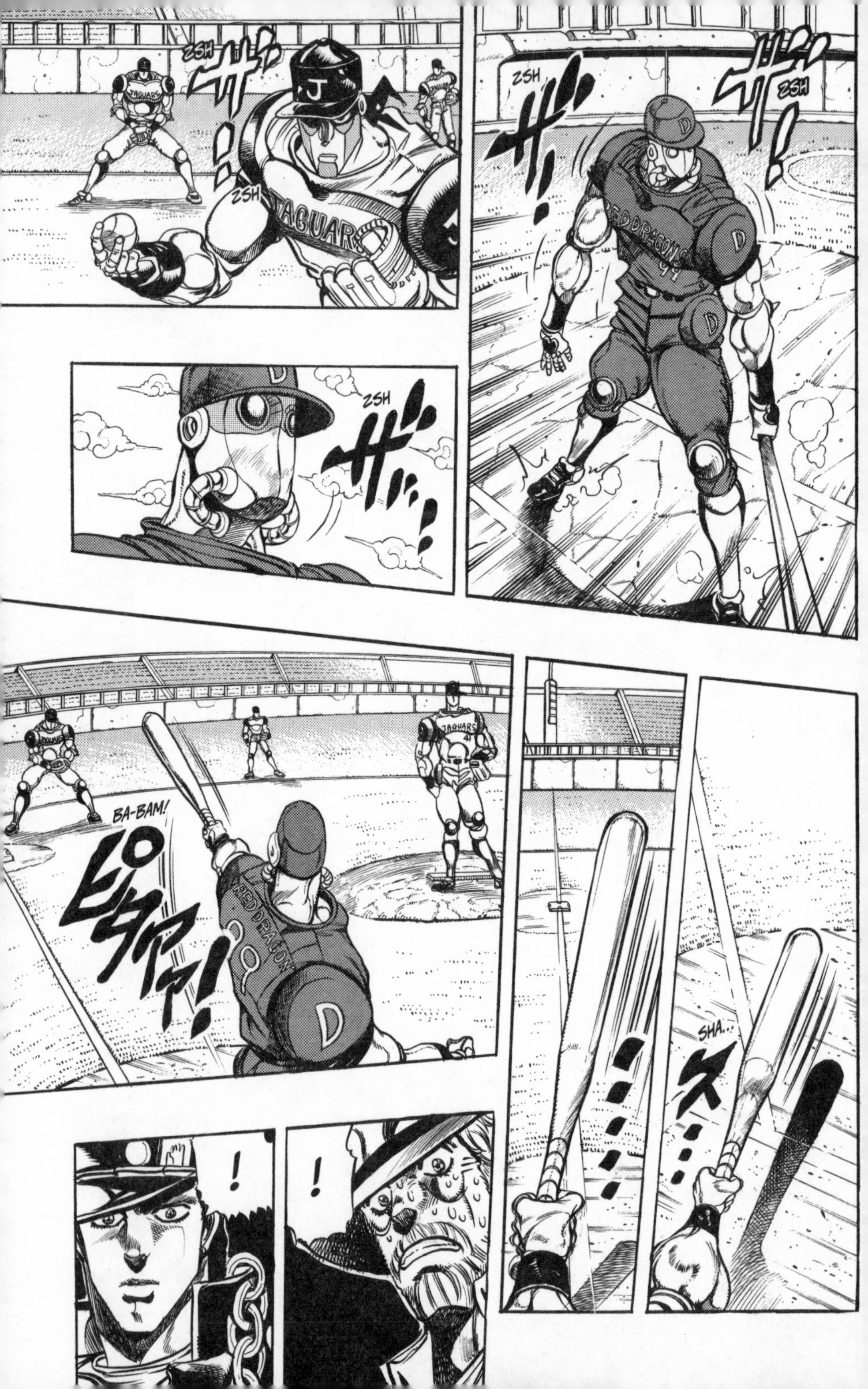
ZSH
ZSH
ZSH
ZSH
ZSH
SHA...
BA-BAM!
!
!

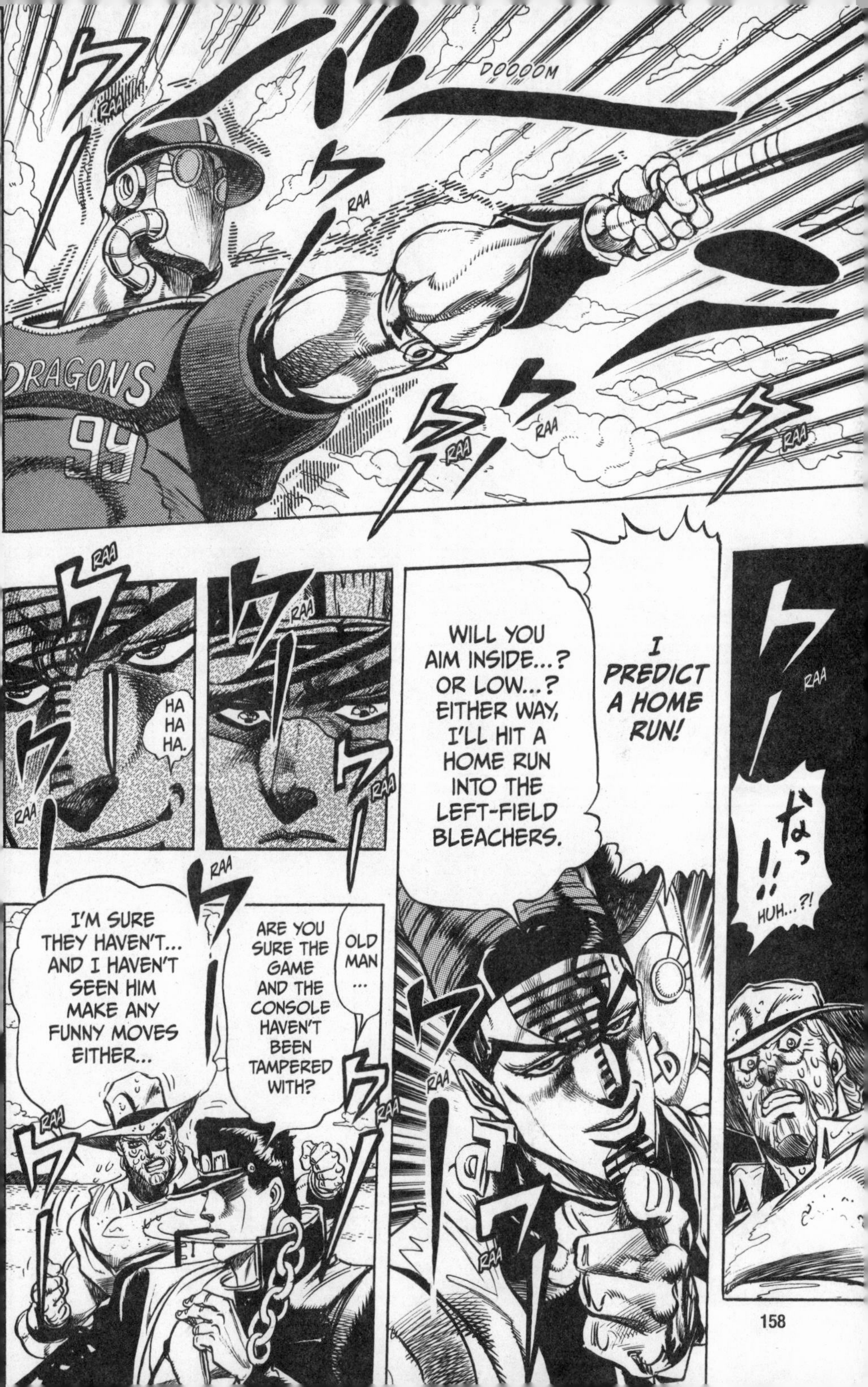
DOOOOM
RAA
RAA
RAA
RAA
RAA
RAA
なっ!!
HUH...?!
I PREDICT A HOME RUN!
WILL YOU AIM INSIDE...? OR LOW...? EITHER WAY, I'LL HIT A HOME RUN INTO THE LEFT-FIELD BLEACHERS.
RAA
RAA
RAA
HA HA HA.
RAA
RAA
RAA
RAA
OLD MAN...
ARE YOU SURE THE GAME AND THE CONSOLE HAVEN'T BEEN TAMPERED WITH?
I'M SURE THEY HAVEN'T... AND I HAVEN'T SEEN HIM MAKE ANY FUNNY MOVES EITHER...
RAA

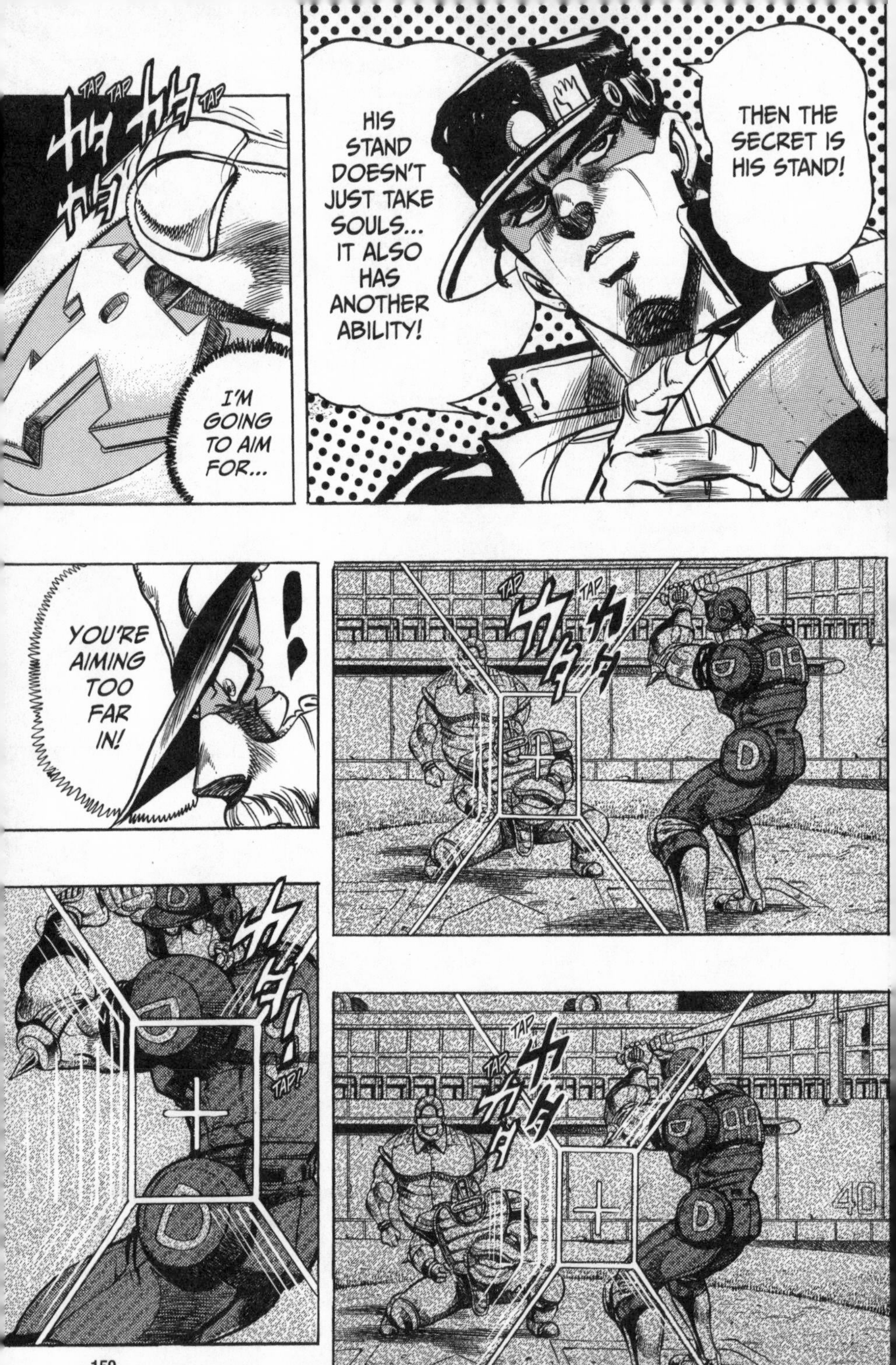
THEN THE SECRET IS HIS STAND!
HIS STAND DOESN'T JUST TAKE SOULS... IT ALSO HAS ANOTHER ABILITY!
TAP TAP TAP
I'M GOING TO AIM FOR...
TAP TAP
YOU'RE AIMING TOO FAR IN!
TAP TAP
TAP

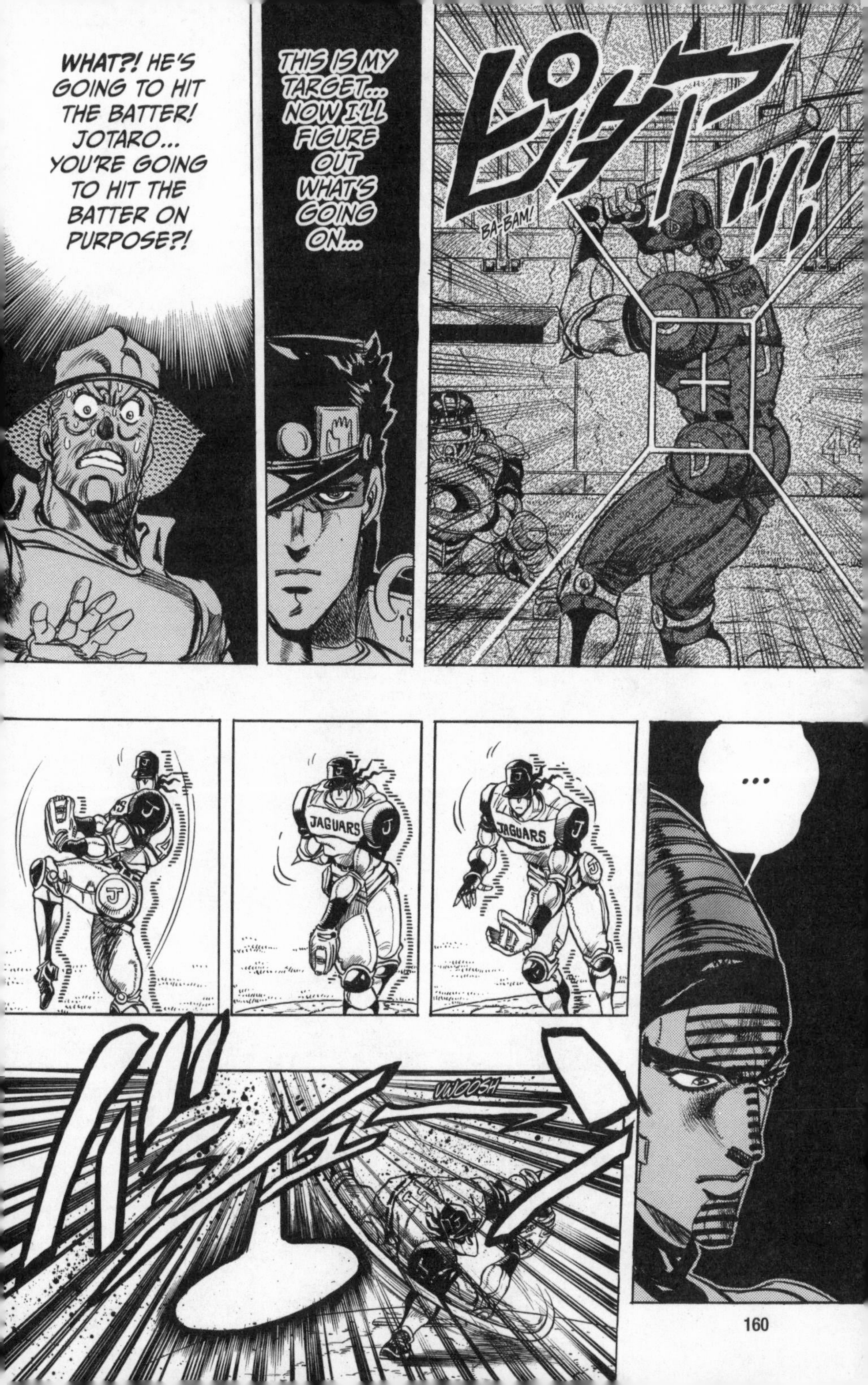
BA-BAM!
THIS IS MY TARGET... NOW I'LL FIGURE OUT WHAT'S GOING ON...
WHAT?! HE'S GOING TO HIT THE BATTER! JOTARO... YOU'RE GOING TO HIT THE BATTER ON PURPOSE?!
...
JAGUARS
JAGUARS
VWOOSH

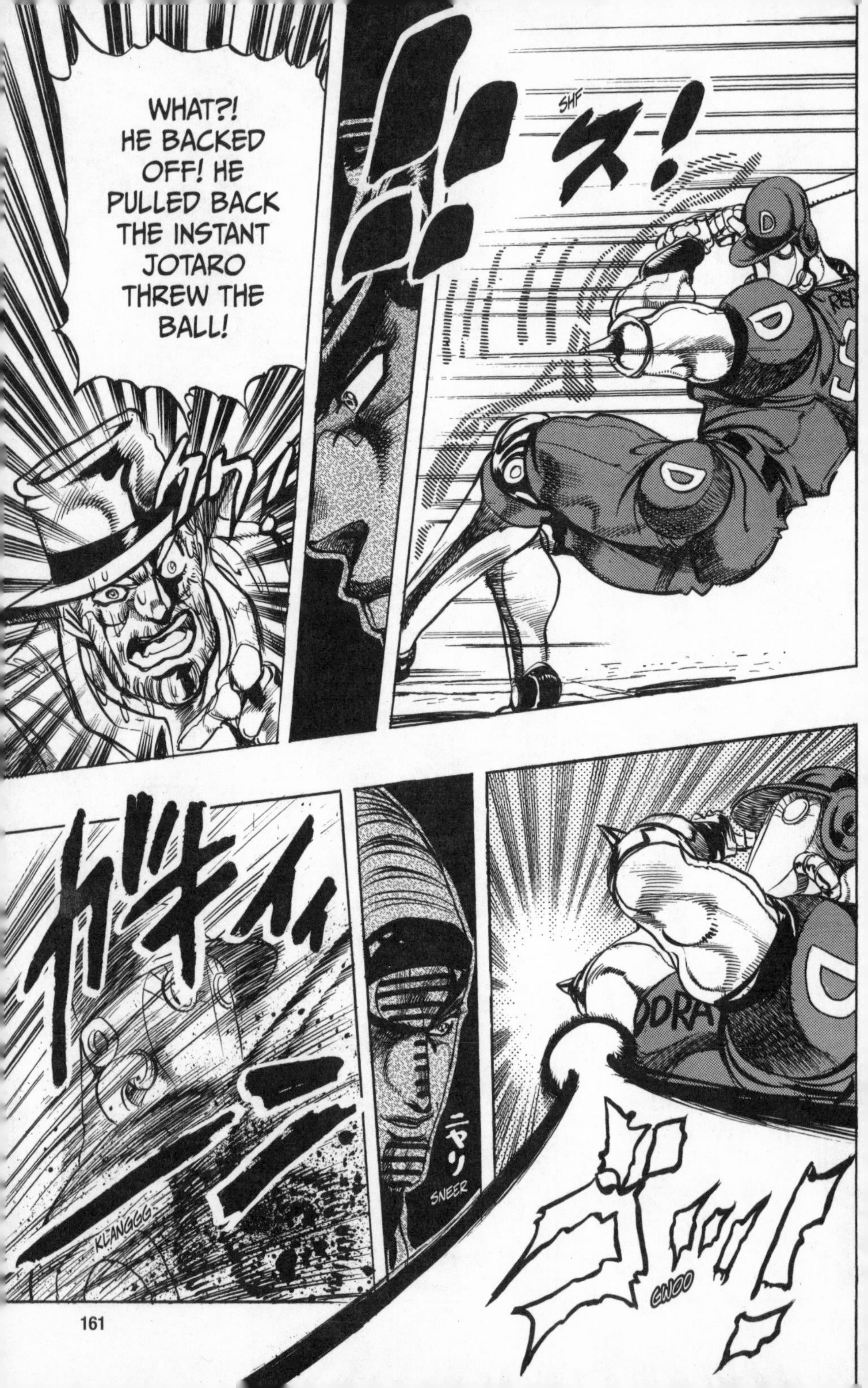
SHF
WHAT?! HE BACKED OFF! HE PULLED BACK THE INSTANT JOTARO THREW THE BALL!
GWOO
ニヤリ
SNEER
KLANGGG

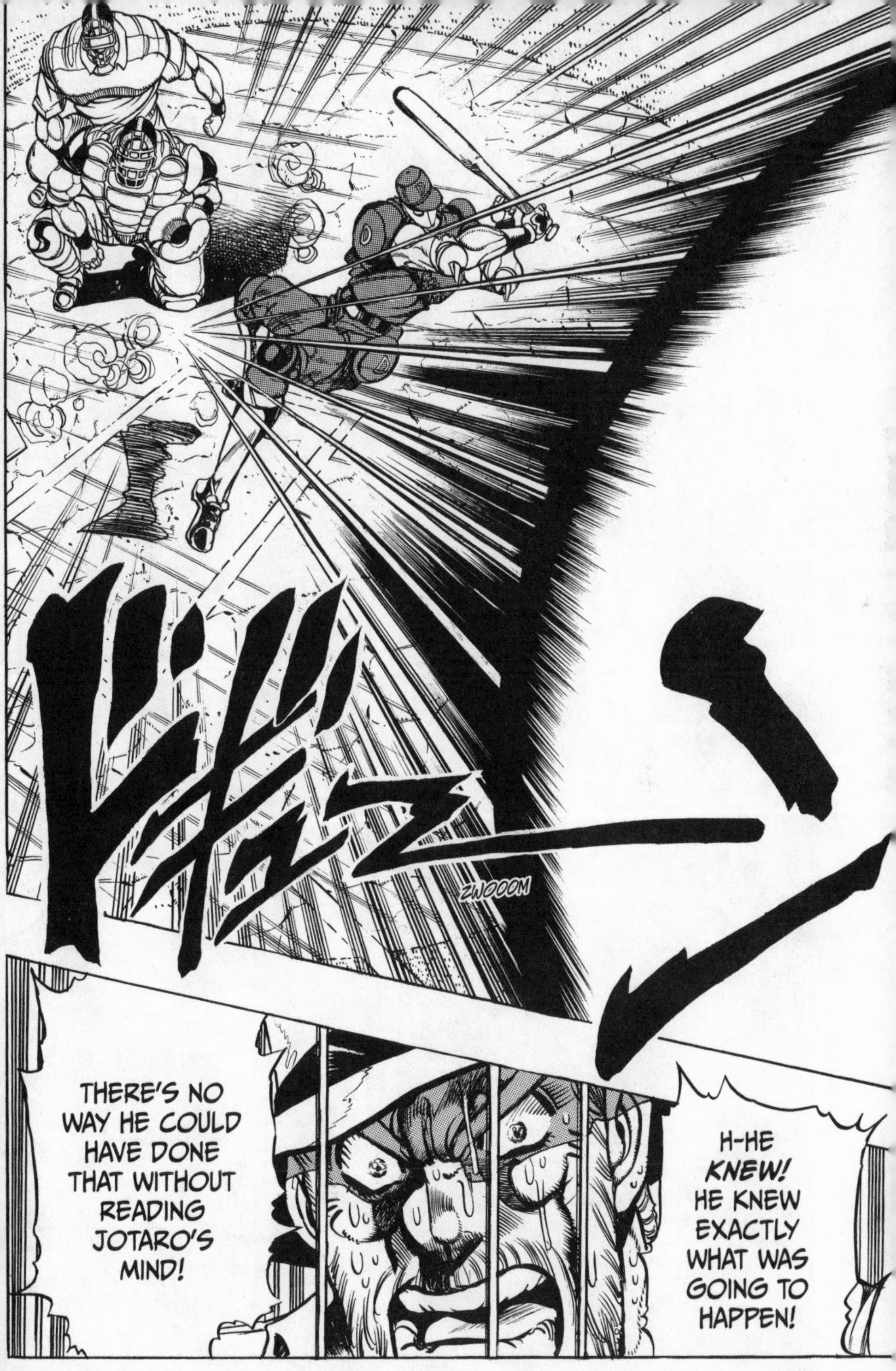
ZWOOOM
H-HE *KNEW!* HE KNEW EXACTLY WHAT WAS GOING TO HAPPEN!
THERE'S NO WAY HE COULD HAVE DONE THAT WITHOUT READING JOTARO'S MIND!

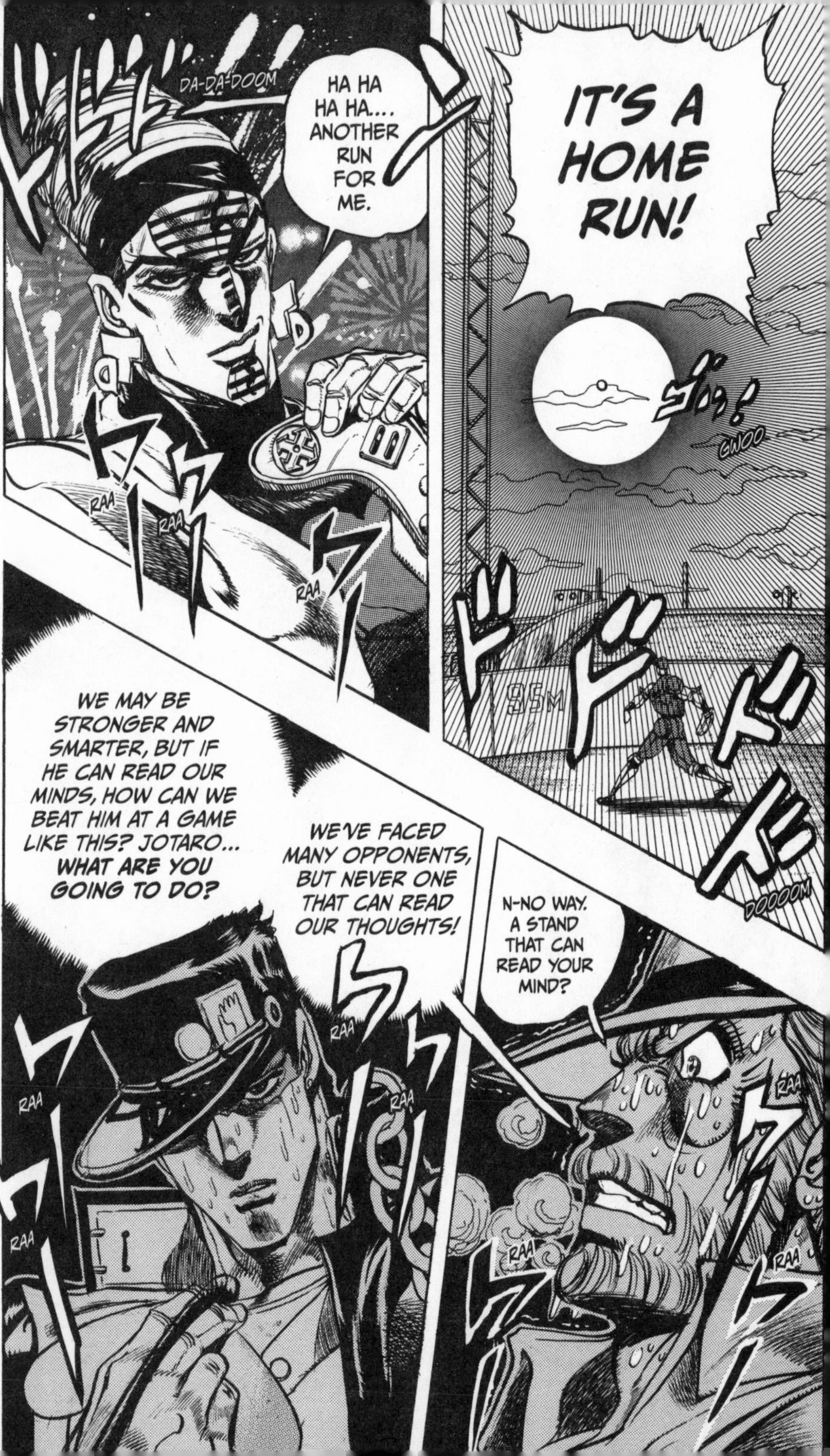

IT'S A HOME RUN!
GWOO
95M
DOOOOM
DA-DA-DOOM
HA HA HA HA.... ANOTHER RUN FOR ME.
RAA
RAA
RAA
N-NO WAY. A STAND THAT CAN READ YOUR MIND?
RAA
RAA
RAA
WE'VE FACED MANY OPPONENTS, BUT NEVER ONE THAT CAN READ OUR THOUGHTS!
WE MAY BE STRONGER AND SMARTER, BUT IF HE CAN READ OUR MINDS, HOW CAN WE BEAT HIM AT A GAME LIKE THIS? JOTARO... WHAT ARE YOU GOING TO DO?
RAA
RAA
RAA
RAA

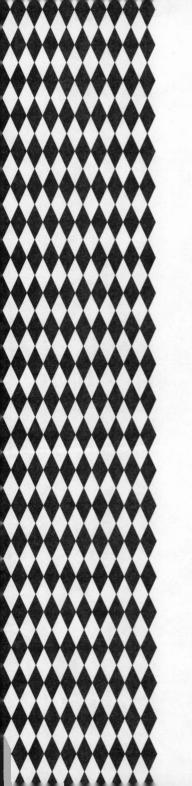
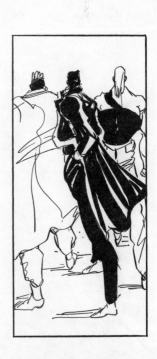

CHAPTER 123: D'Arby the Player PART 10

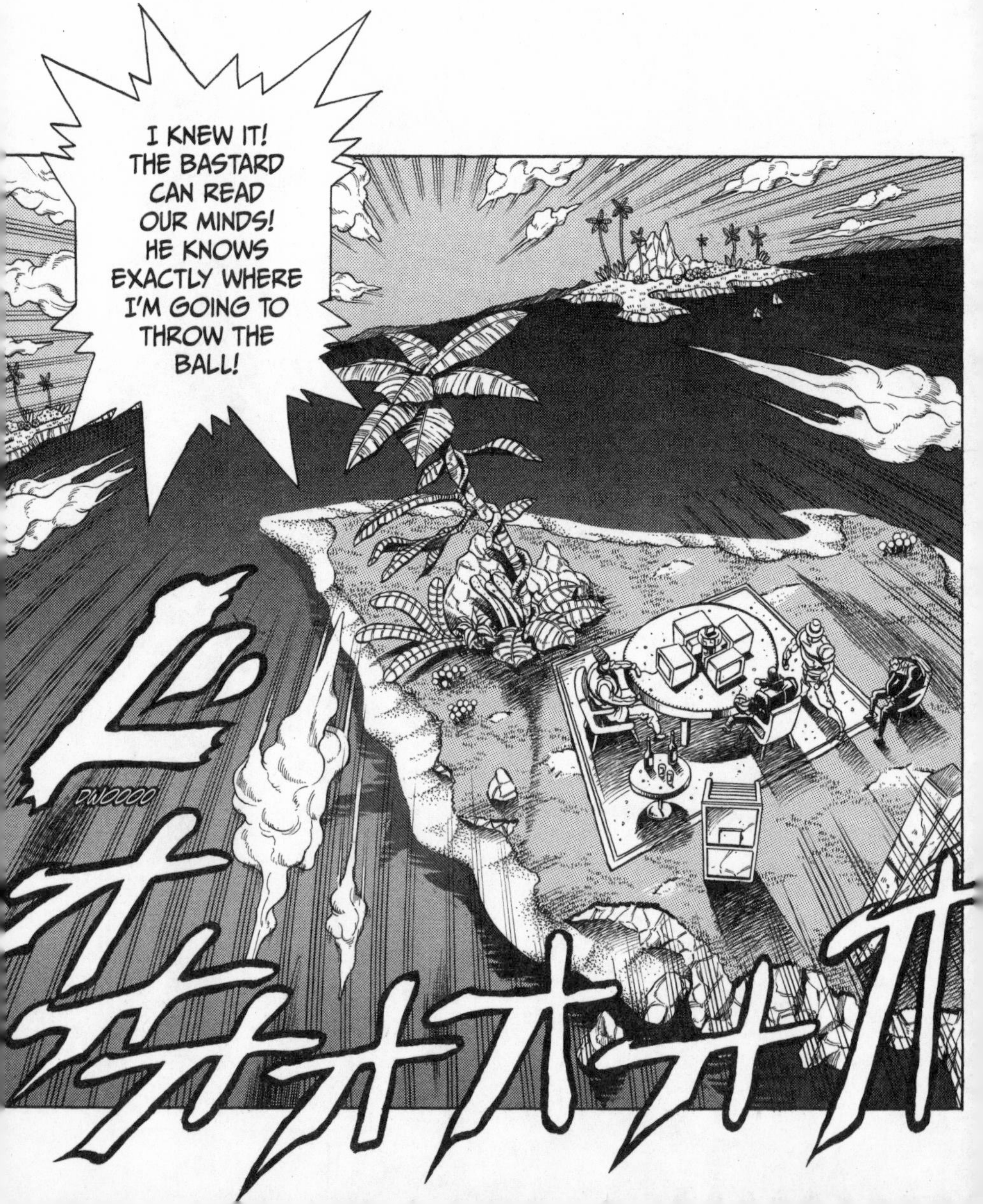
I KNEW IT! THE BASTARD CAN READ OUR MINDS! HE KNOWS EXACTLY WHERE I'M GOING TO THROW THE BALL!
DWOOOO

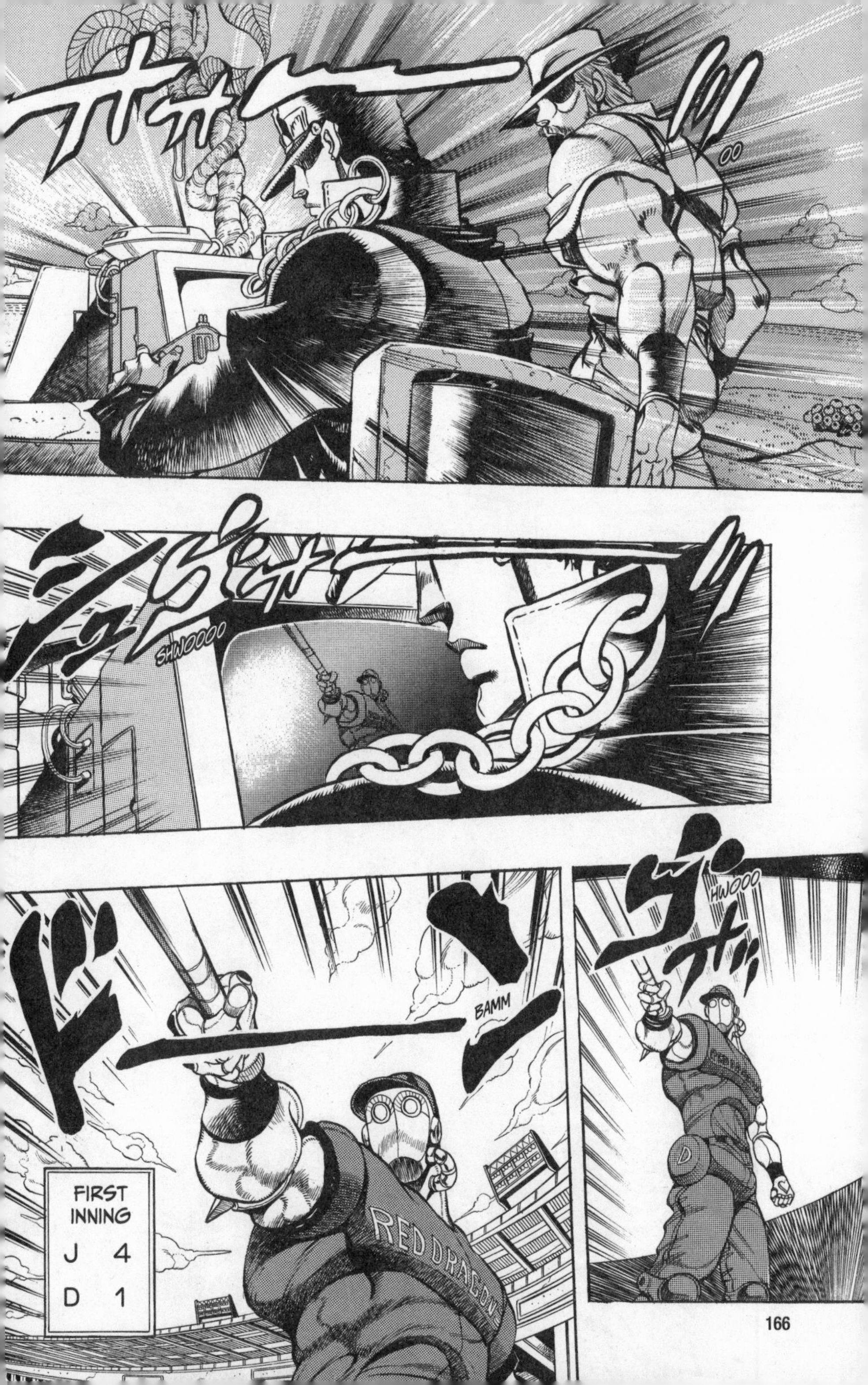
SHWOOOO
HWOOO
BAMM
FIRST INNING
J 4
D 1

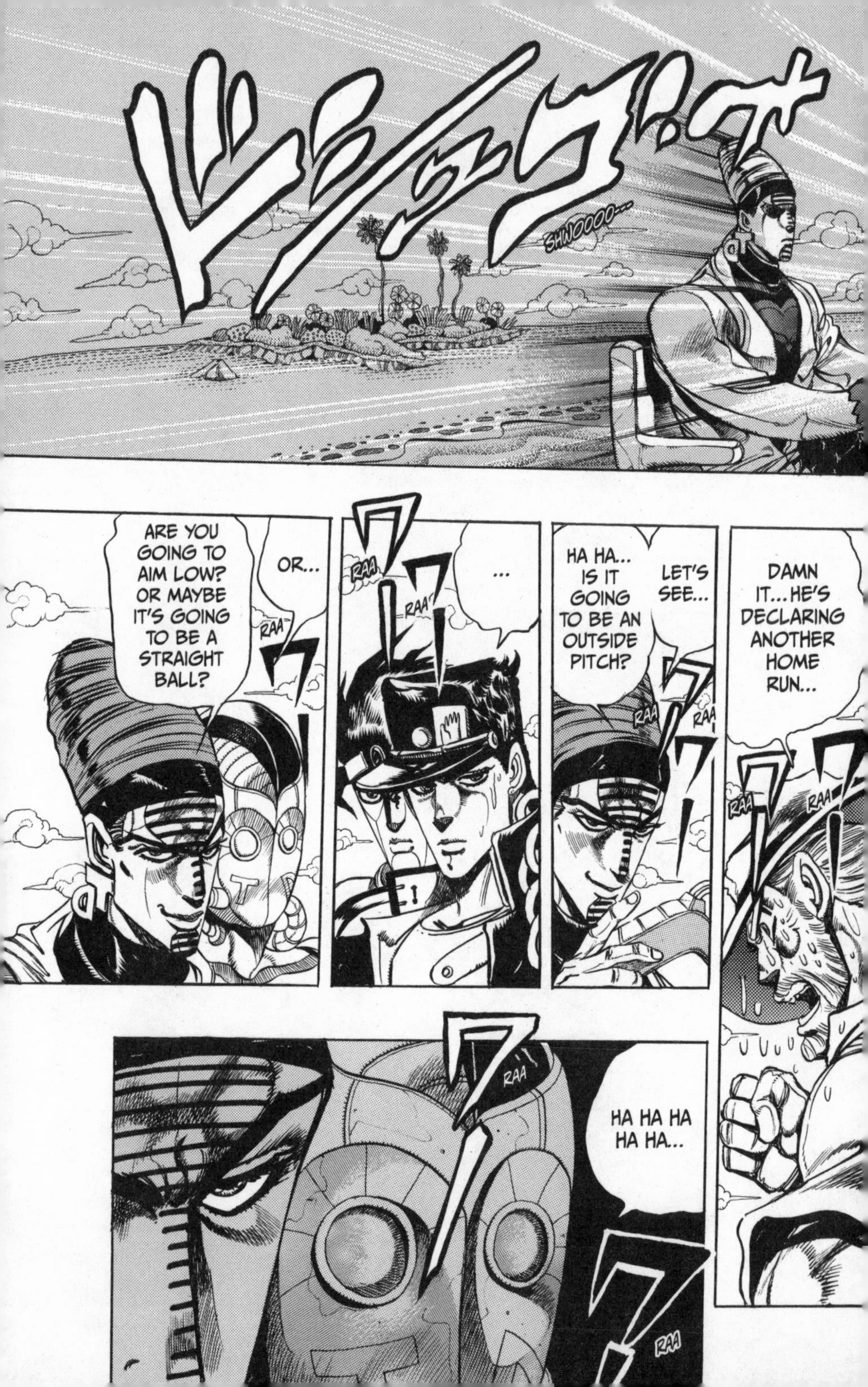
SHWOOOO---
DAMN IT... HE'S DECLARING ANOTHER HOME RUN...
RAA
RAA
LET'S SEE...
HA HA... IS IT GOING TO BE AN OUTSIDE PITCH?
RAA
RAA
...
RAA
RAA
OR...
ARE YOU GOING TO AIM LOW? OR MAYBE IT'S GOING TO BE A STRAIGHT BALL?
RAA
HA HA HA HA HA...
RAA
RAA

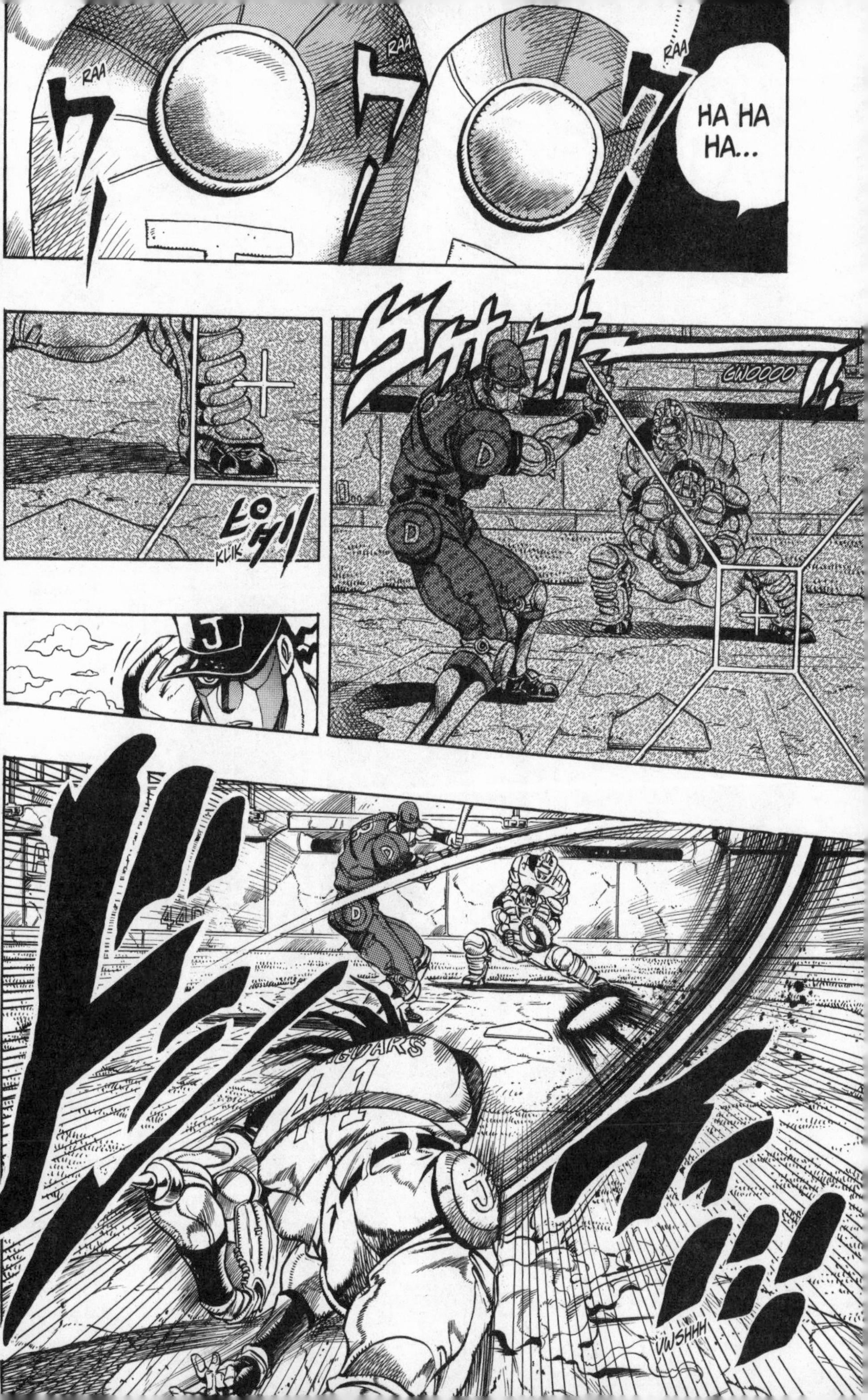
RAA
HA HA HA...
RAA
RAA
GWOOOO
KLIK
VWSHHH

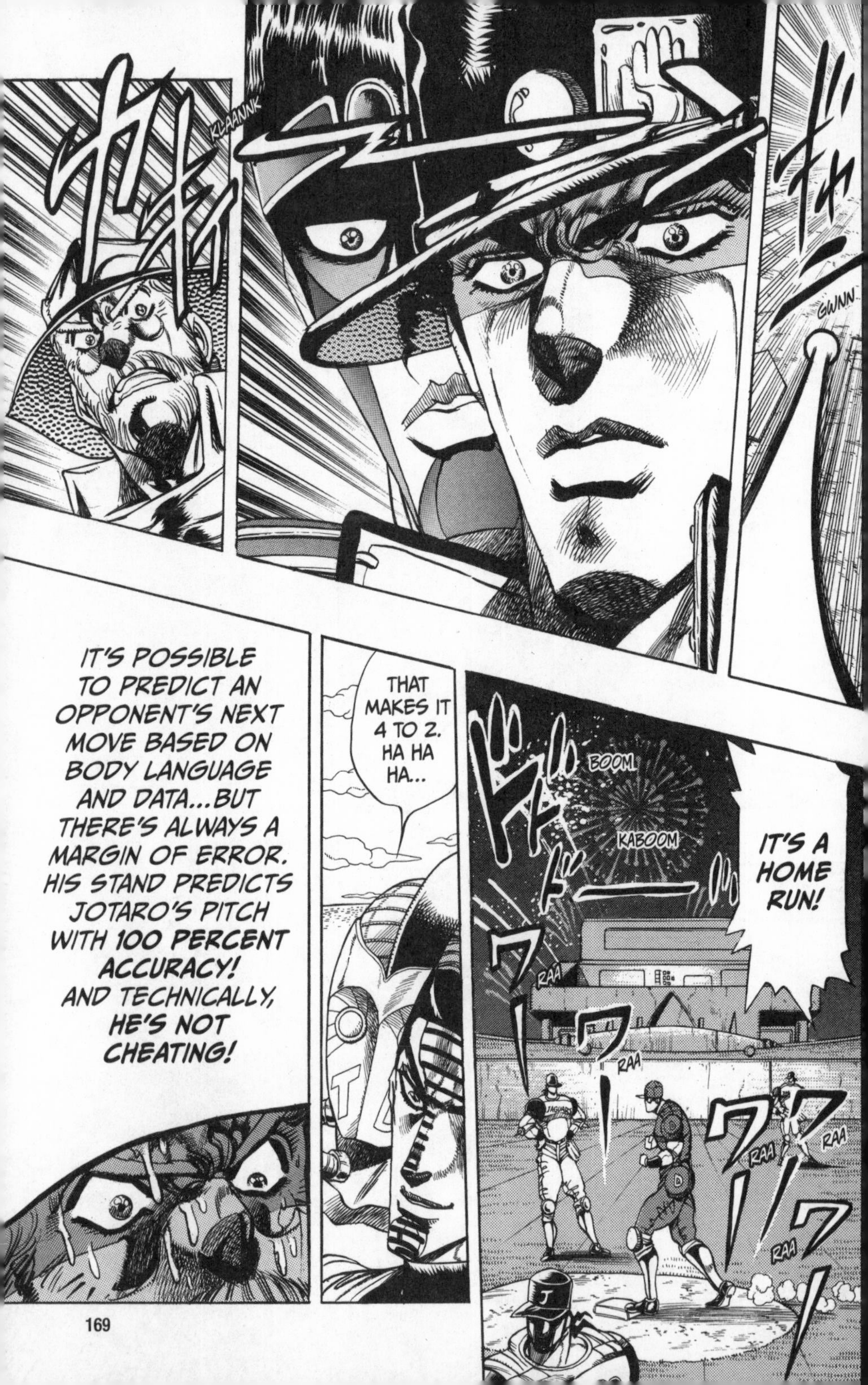

GWNN
KLAANNK
BOOM
KABOOM
IT'S A HOME RUN!
RAA
RAA
RAA
RAA
RAA
THAT MAKES IT 4 TO 2. HA HA HA...
IT'S POSSIBLE TO PREDICT AN OPPONENT'S NEXT MOVE BASED ON BODY LANGUAGE AND DATA...BUT THERE'S ALWAYS A MARGIN OF ERROR. HIS STAND PREDICTS JOTARO'S PITCH WITH 100 PERCENT ACCURACY! AND TECHNICALLY, HE'S NOT CHEATING!

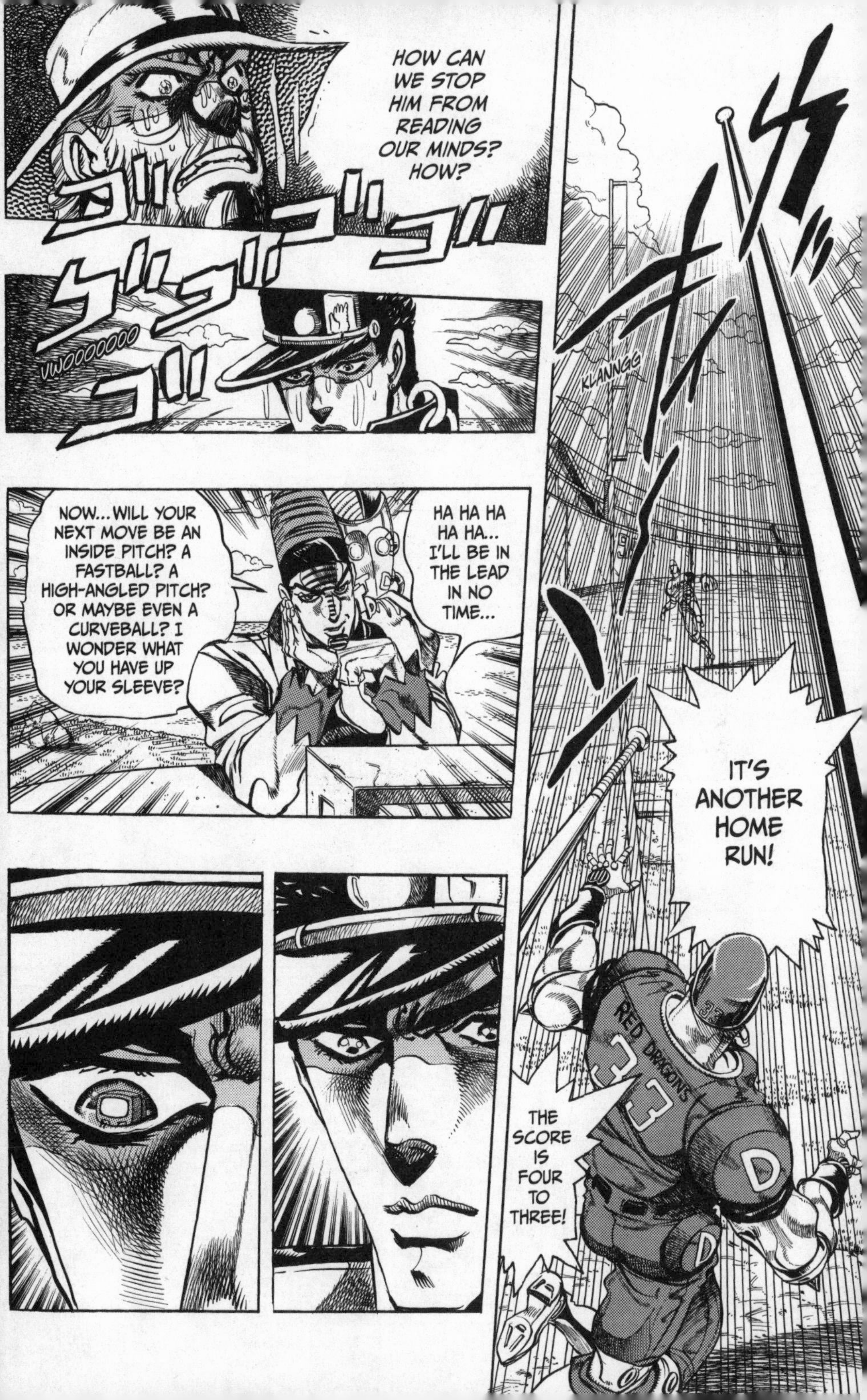
KLANNGG
IT'S ANOTHER HOME RUN!
THE SCORE IS FOUR TO THREE!
RED DRAGONS
HOW CAN WE STOP HIM FROM READING OUR MINDS? HOW?
VWOOOOOOO
HA HA HA HA HA... I'LL BE IN THE LEAD IN NO TIME...
NOW...WILL YOUR NEXT MOVE BE AN INSIDE PITCH? A FASTBALL? A HIGH-ANGLED PITCH? OR MAYBE EVEN A CURVEBALL? I WONDER WHAT YOU HAVE UP YOUR SLEEVE?

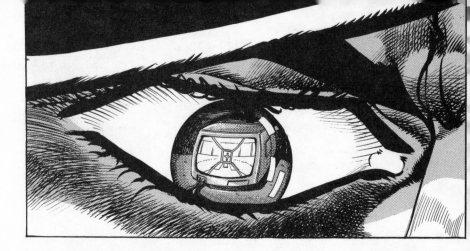

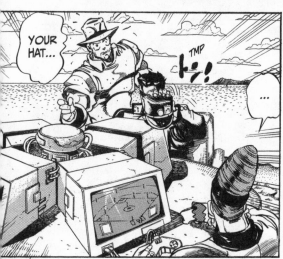

YOUR HAT...
TMP
トン!
...
YOU FOOL ...
DO YOU HONESTLY THINK I WOULD CHEAT LIKE MY BROTHER?
JOTARO! THAT WON'T WORK!
HIDING YOUR FACE WITH YOUR HAT IS USELESS.
HE'S NOT WATCHING THE REFLECTION OF THE TV IN YOUR EYES. EVEN IF HE WAS, THERE'S NO WAY HE CAN SEE WHAT YOU'RE PRESSING OR WHAT PITCH YOU'RE CHOOSING. I'VE BEEN WATCHING HIM. HE'S NOT CHEATING...

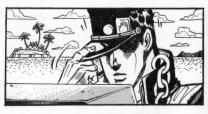

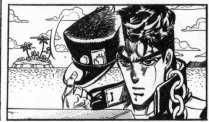

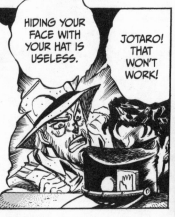

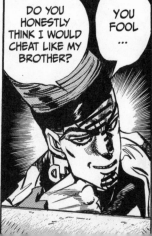

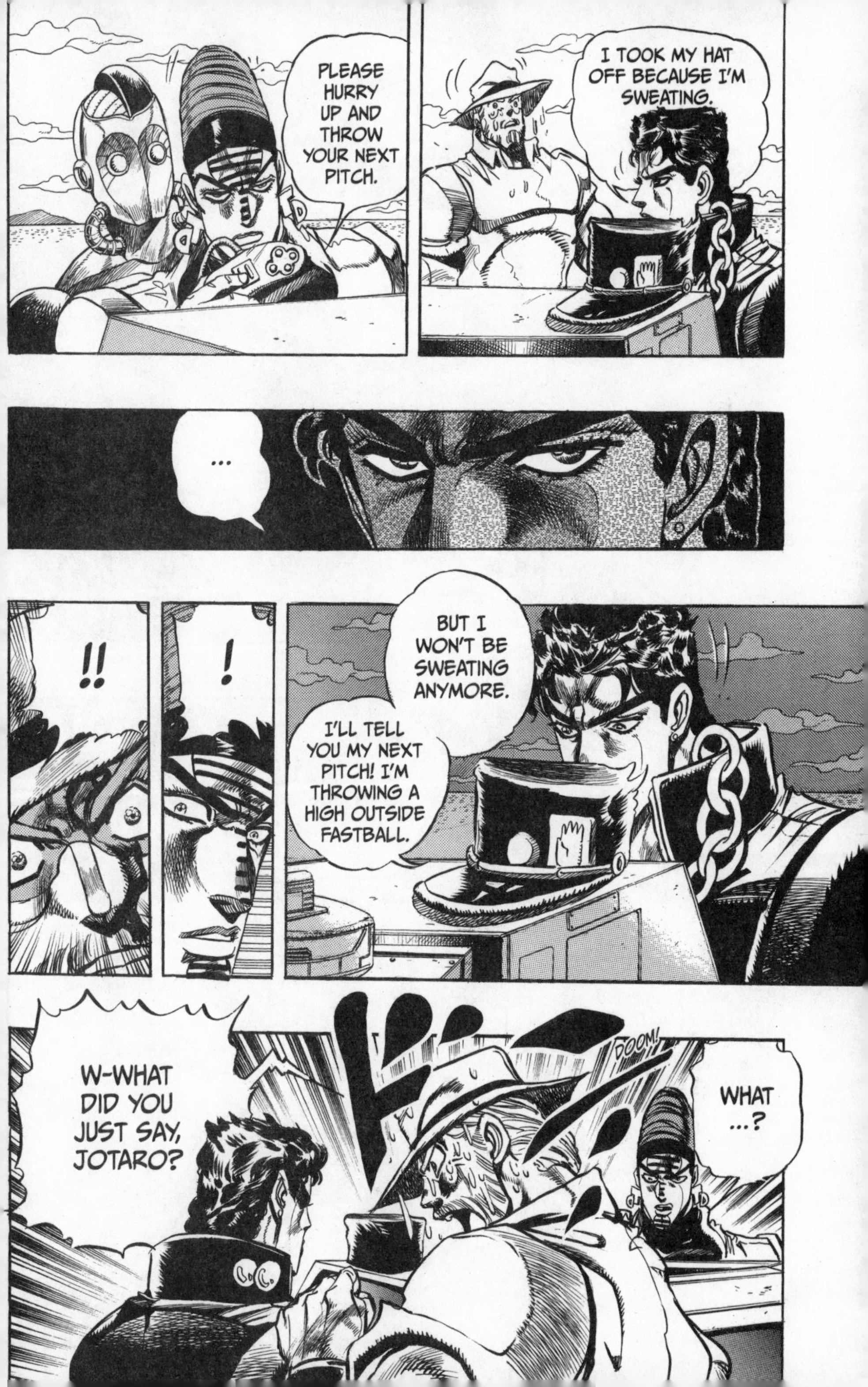
I TOOK MY HAT OFF BECAUSE I'M SWEATING.
PLEASE HURRY UP AND THROW YOUR NEXT PITCH.
...
BUT I WON'T BE SWEATING ANYMORE.
I'LL TELL YOU MY NEXT PITCH! I'M THROWING A HIGH OUTSIDE FASTBALL.
!
!!
DOOM!
WHAT ...?
W-WHAT DID YOU JUST SAY, JOTARO?

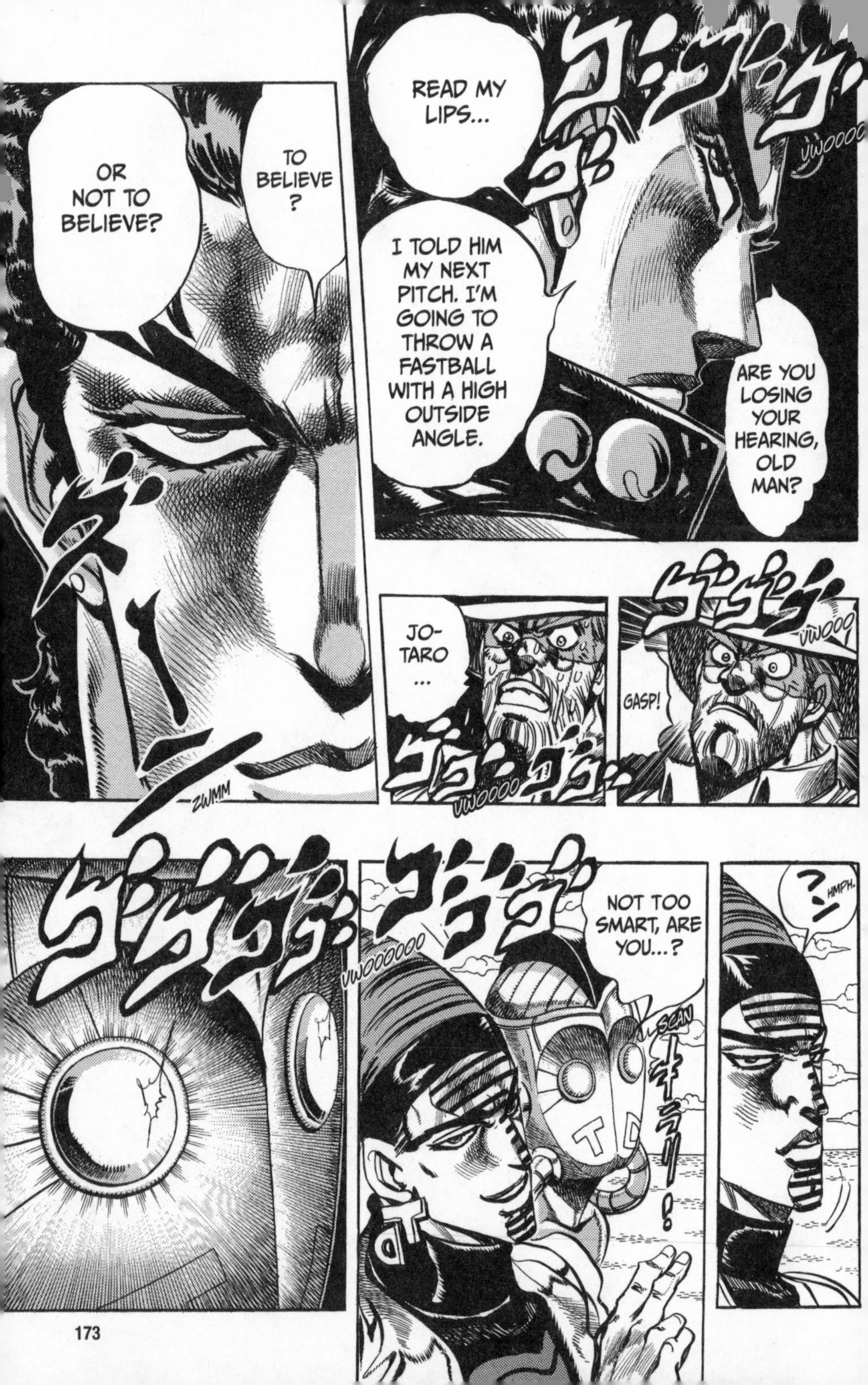
VWOOOO
READ MY LIPS...
I TOLD HIM MY NEXT PITCH. I'M GOING TO THROW A FASTBALL WITH A HIGH OUTSIDE ANGLE.
ARE YOU LOSING YOUR HEARING, OLD MAN?
VWOOOO
GASP!
JO-TARO ...
VWOOOO
TO BELIEVE ?
OR NOT TO BELIEVE?
ZWMM
HMPH.
NOT TOO SMART, ARE YOU...?
SCAN
VWOOOOOOO

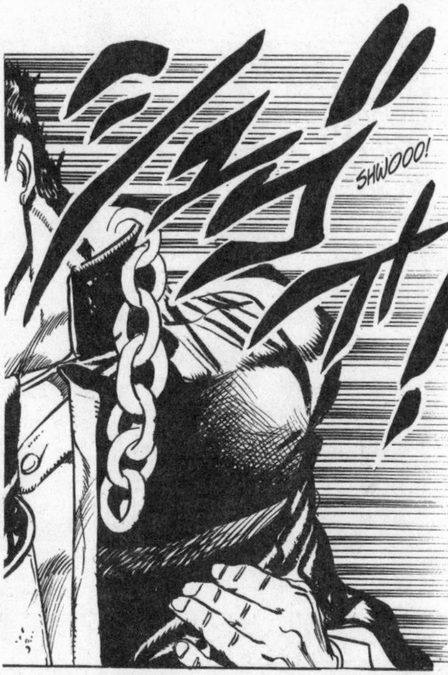
SHWOOO!
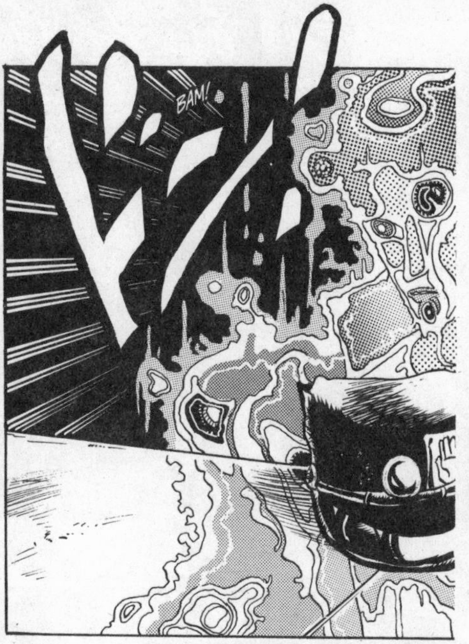
BAM!
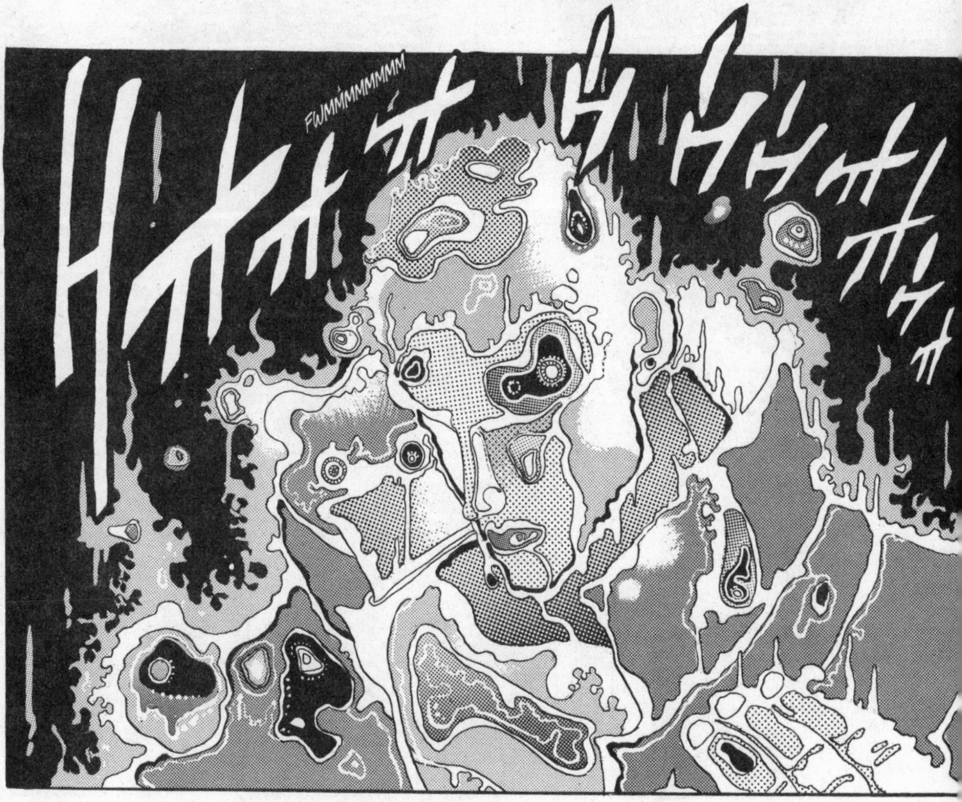
FWMMMMMMMM

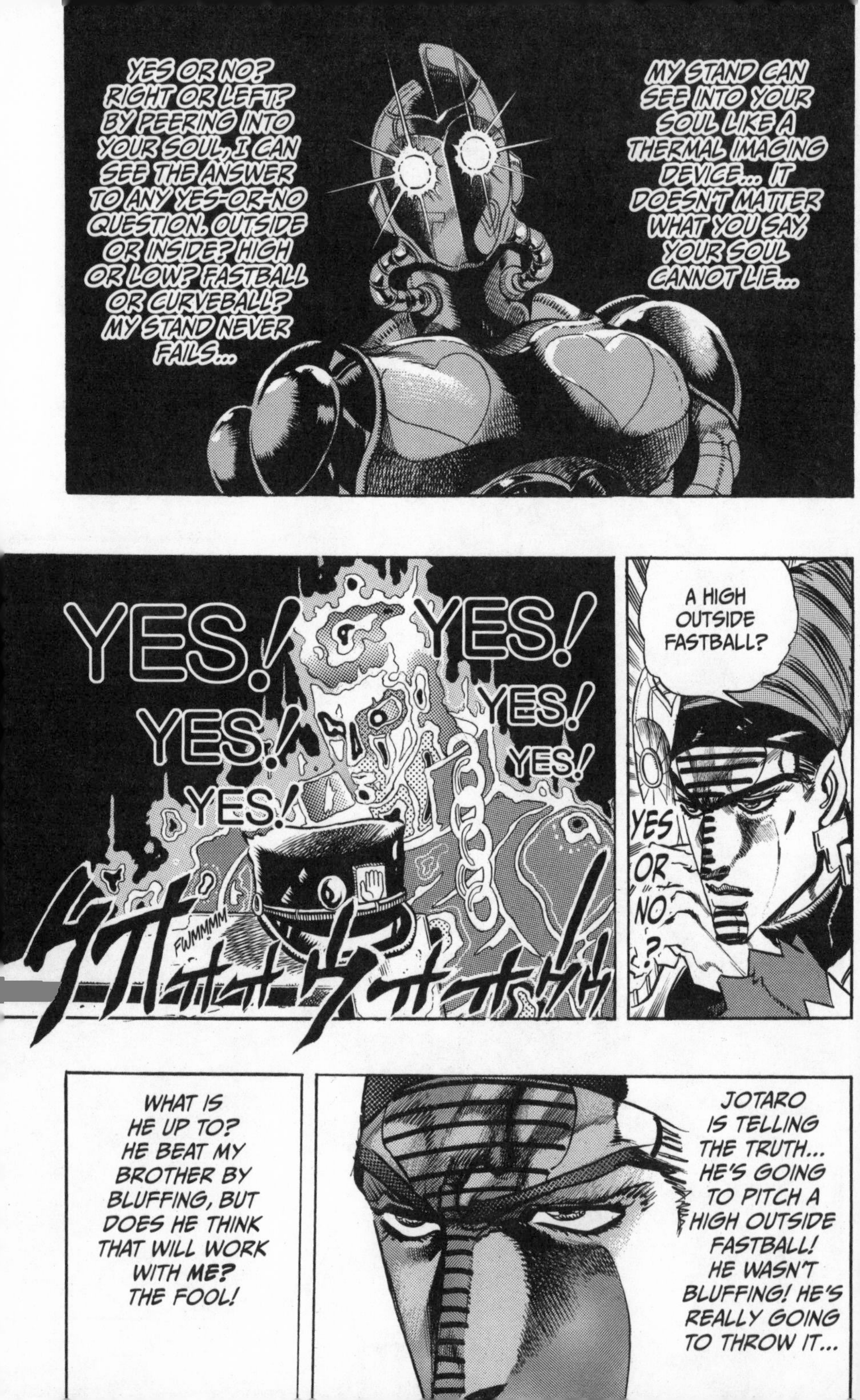
MY STAND CAN SEE INTO YOUR SOUL LIKE A THERMAL IMAGING DEVICE... IT DOESN'T MATTER WHAT YOU SAY, YOUR SOUL CANNOT LIE...
YES OR NO? RIGHT OR LEFT? BY PEERING INTO YOUR SOUL, I CAN SEE THE ANSWER TO ANY YES-OR-NO QUESTION. OUTSIDE OR INSIDE? HIGH OR LOW? FASTBALL OR CURVEBALL? MY STAND NEVER FAILS...
A HIGH OUTSIDE FASTBALL?
YES OR NO ?
YES! YES!
YES!
YES!
YES!
YES!
FWUMMMM
JOTARO IS TELLING THE TRUTH... HE'S GOING TO PITCH A HIGH OUTSIDE FASTBALL! HE WASN'T BLUFFING! HE'S REALLY GOING TO THROW IT...
WHAT IS HE UP TO? HE BEAT MY BROTHER BY BLUFFING, BUT DOES HE THINK THAT WILL WORK WITH ME? THE FOOL!

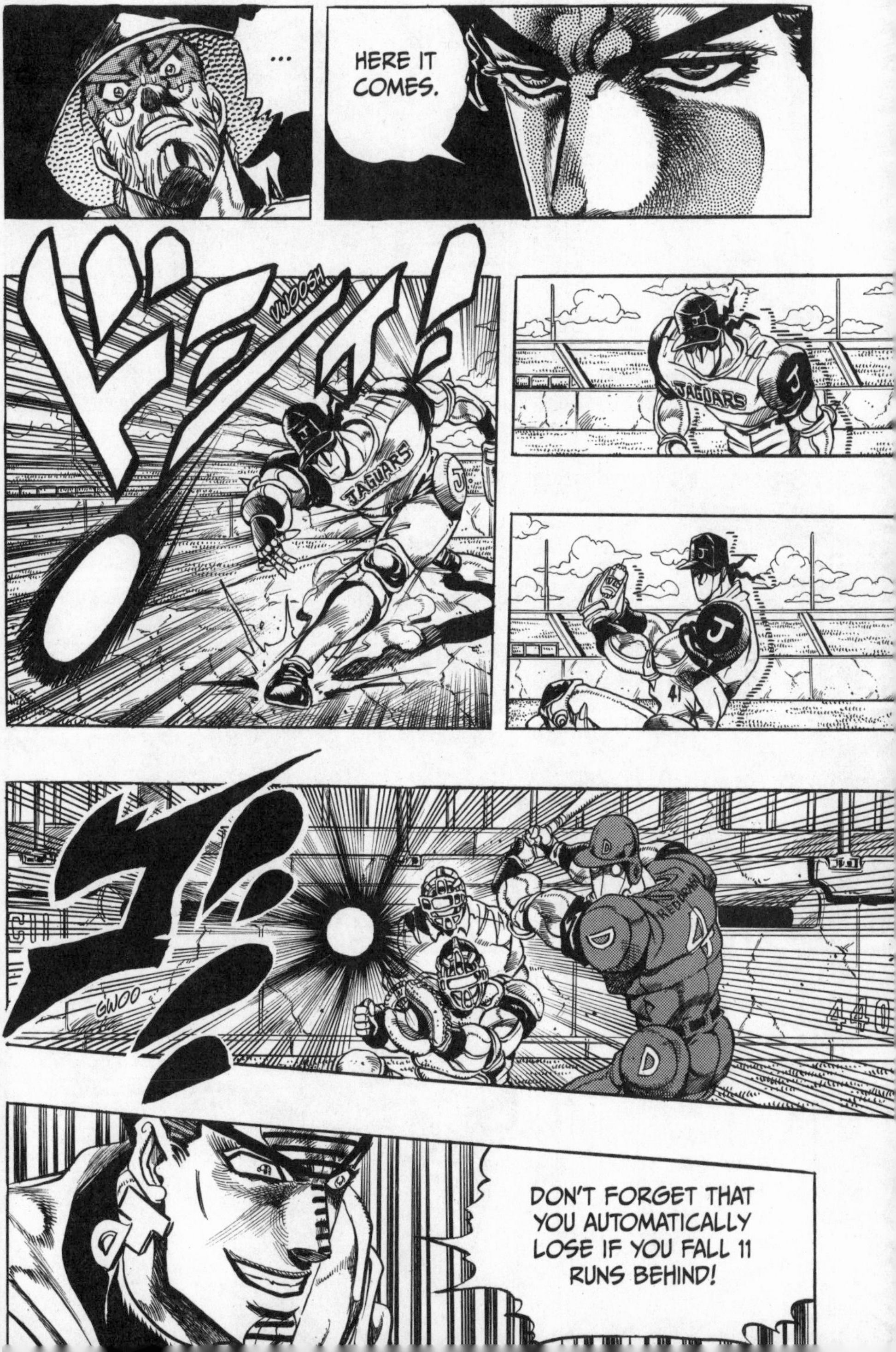
HERE IT COMES.
...
WHOOSH
GWOO
440
DON'T FORGET THAT YOU AUTOMATICALLY LOSE IF YOU FALL 11 RUNS BEHIND!

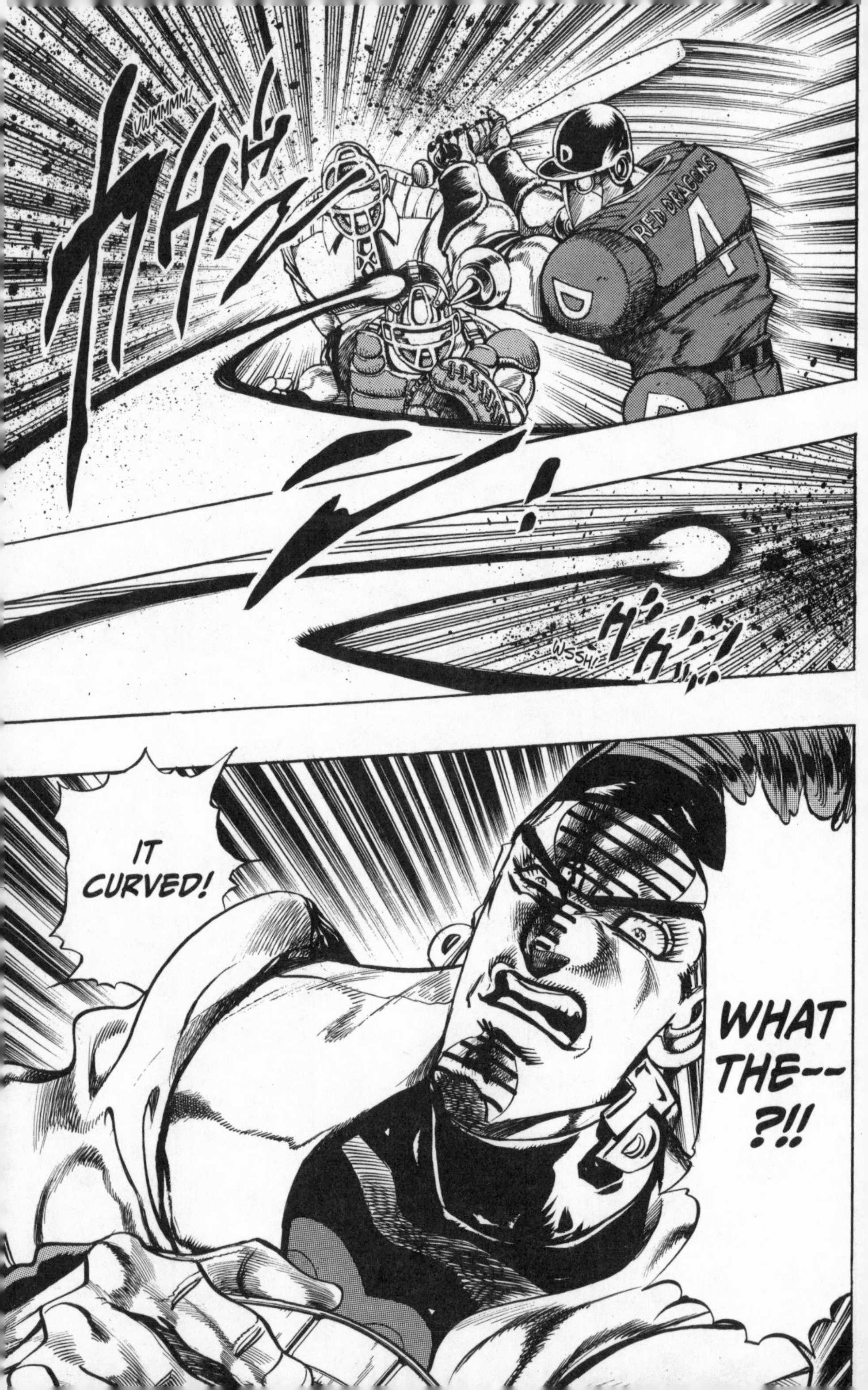
VWMMMM!
WSSH!
IT CURVED!
WHAT THE-- ?!!

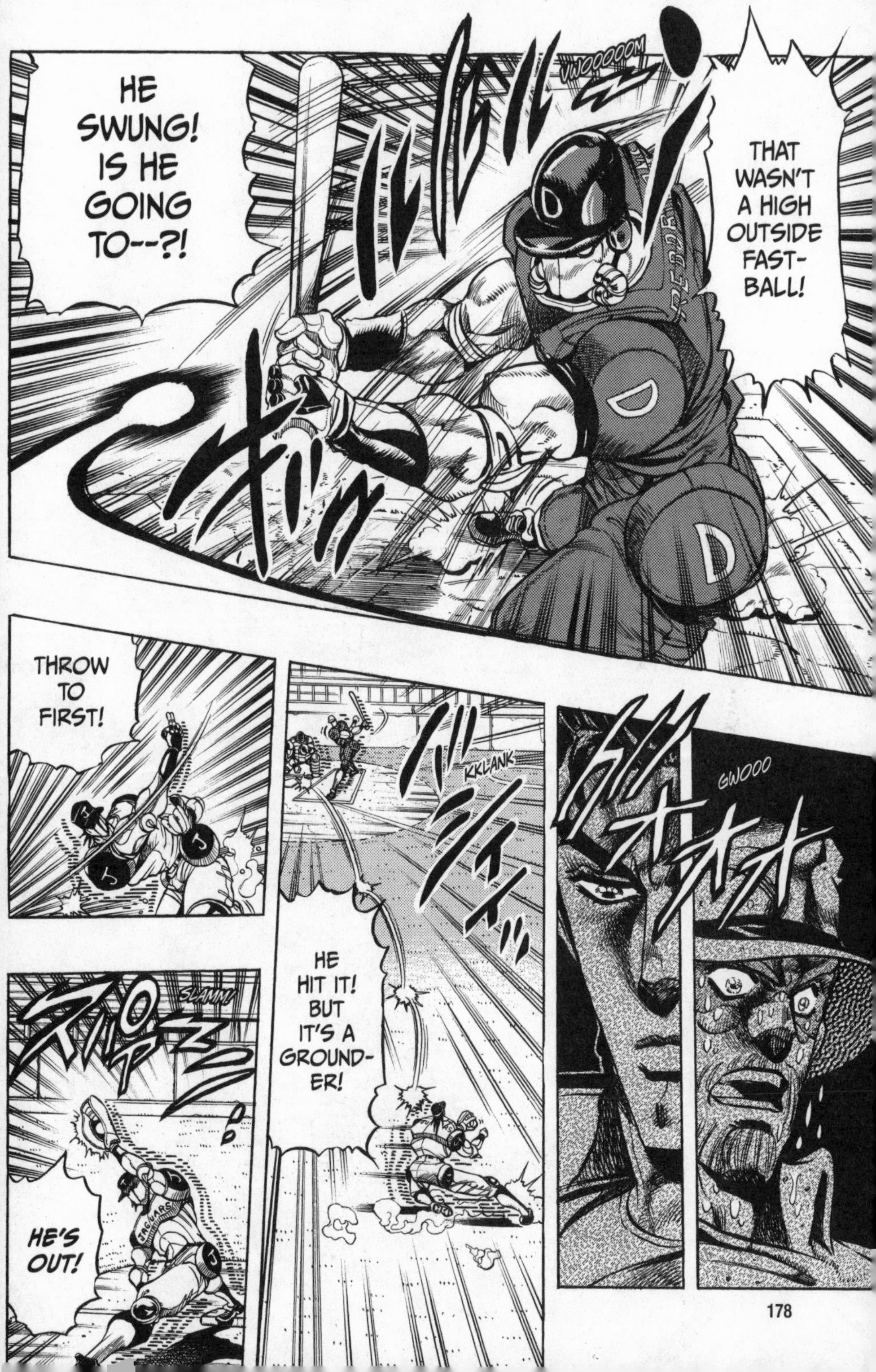
THAT WASN'T A HIGH OUTSIDE FAST-BALL!
VWOOOOOM
HE SWUNG! IS HE GOING TO--?!
GWOOO
KKLANK
HE HIT IT! BUT IT'S A GROUND-ER!
THROW TO FIRST!
SLAMM!
HE'S OUT!

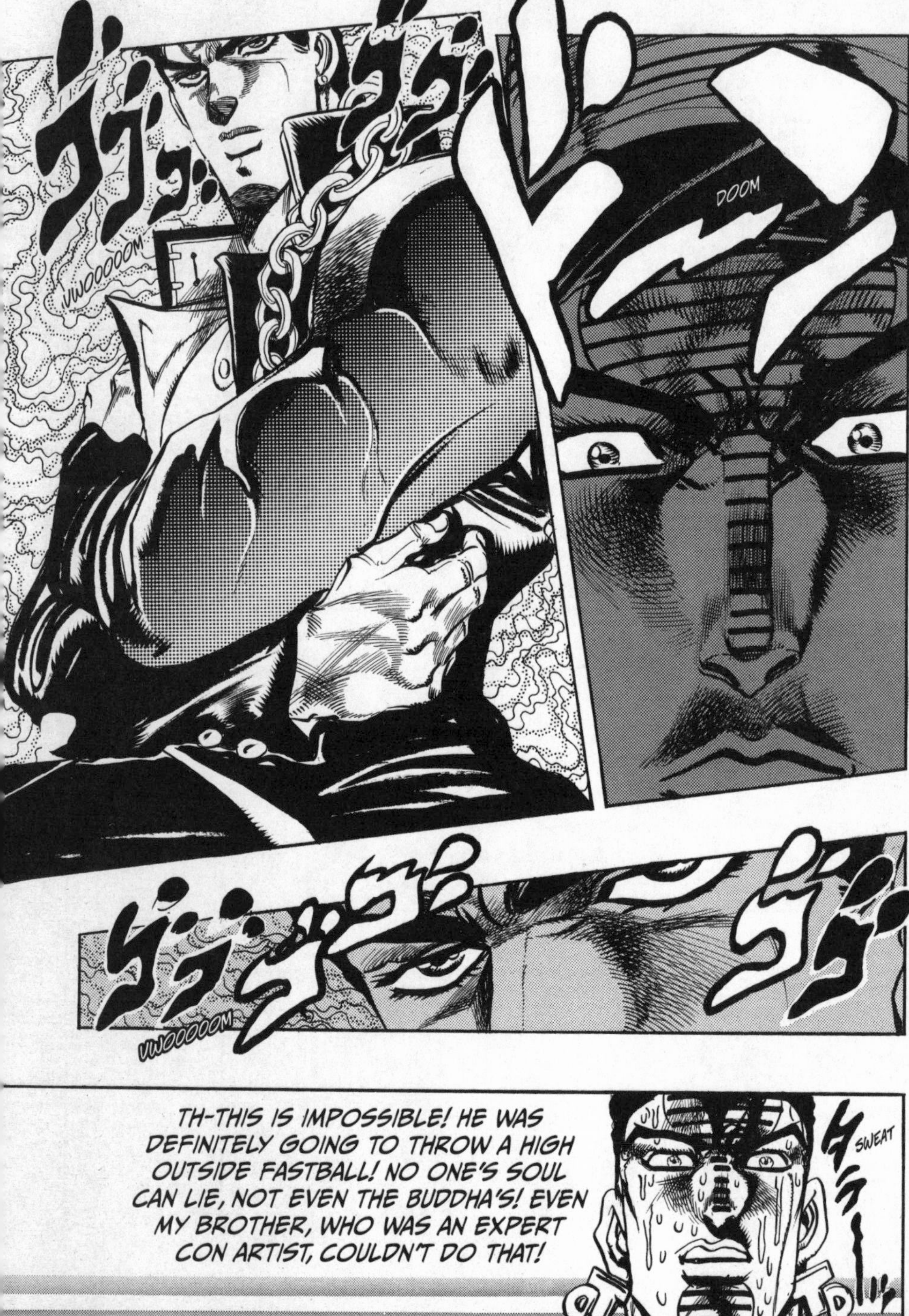
DOOM
VWOOOOOM
VWOOOOOM
TH-THIS IS IMPOSSIBLE! HE WAS DEFINITELY GOING TO THROW A HIGH OUTSIDE FASTBALL! NO ONE'S SOUL CAN LIE, NOT EVEN THE BUDDHA'S! EVEN MY BROTHER, WHO WAS AN EXPERT CON ARTIST, COULDN'T DO THAT!
SWEAT

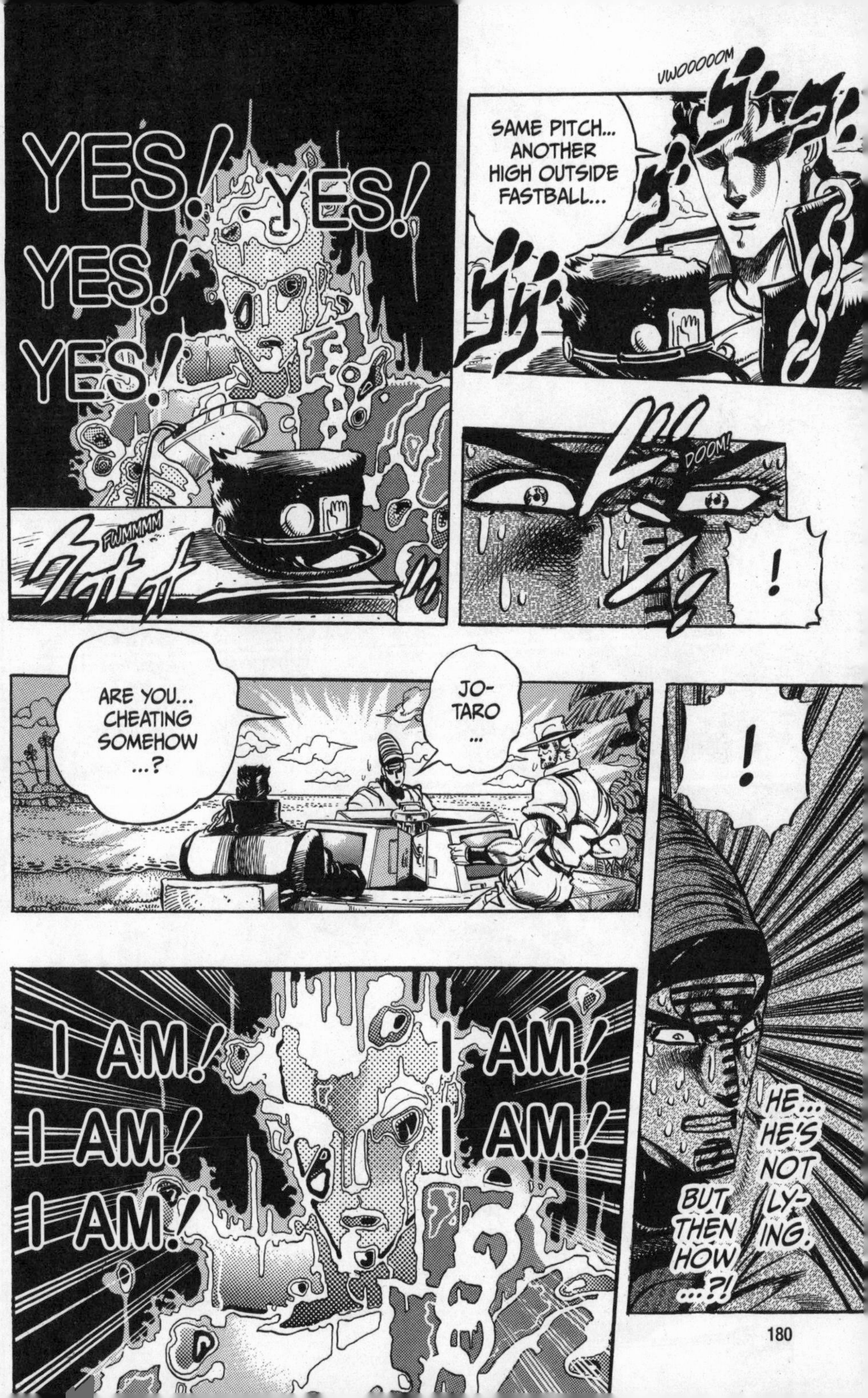
VWOOOOOM
SAME PITCH... ANOTHER HIGH OUTSIDE FASTBALL...
DOOM!
!
YES! YES! YES! YES!
FWMMMM
!
HE... HE'S NOT LYING.
BUT THEN HOW...?!
JO-TARO...
ARE YOU... CHEATING SOMEHOW...?
I AM! I AM! I AM! I AM! I AM!

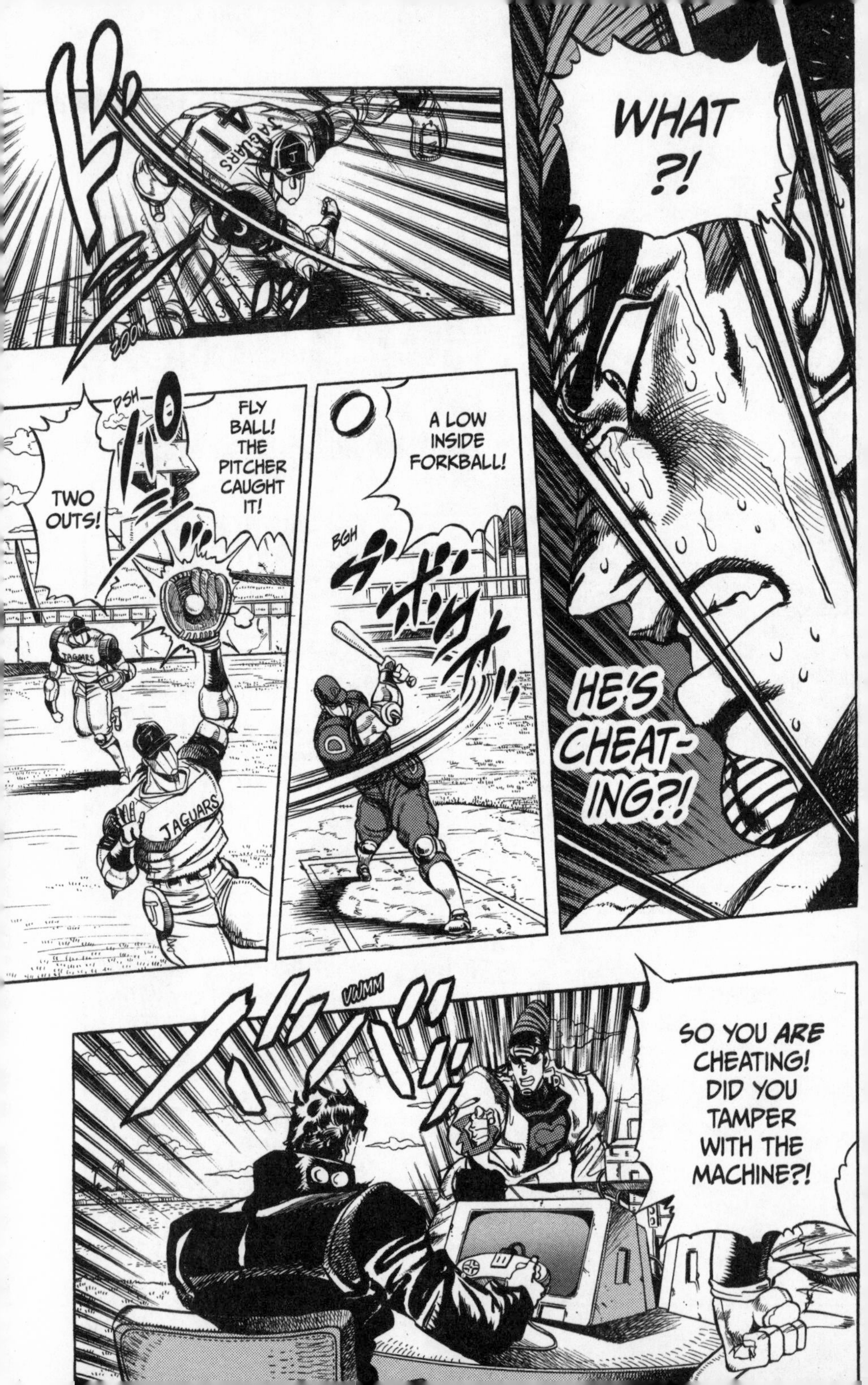
WHAT ?!
HE'S CHEAT-ING?!
ZOOM
A LOW INSIDE FORKBALL!
BGH
FLY BALL! THE PITCHER CAUGHT IT!
PSH
TWO OUTS!
SO YOU ARE CHEATING! DID YOU TAMPER WITH THE MACHINE?!
VWMM

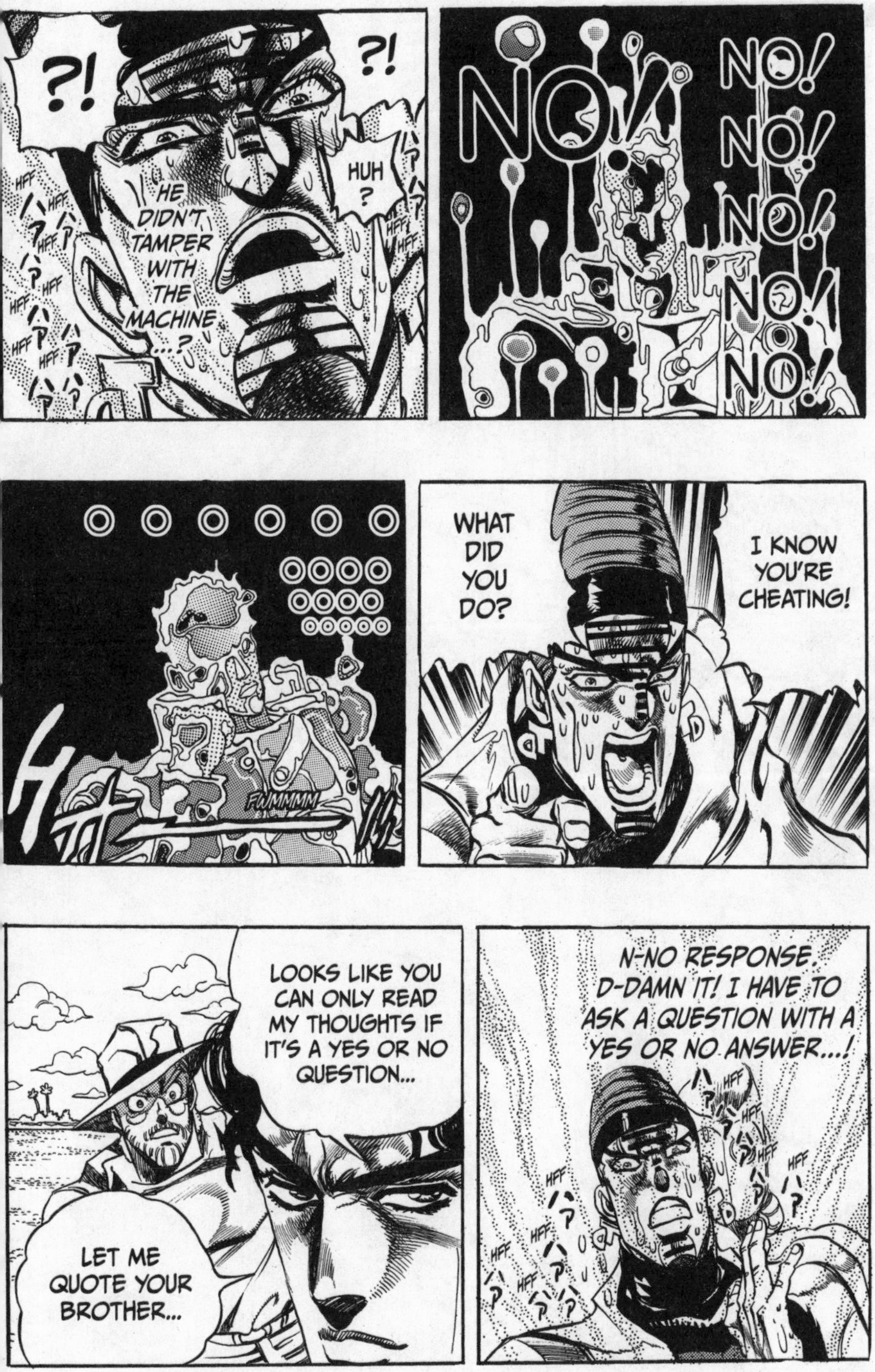
NO!
NO!
NO!
NO!
NO!
NO!
?!
?!
HUH?
HE DIDN'T TAMPER WITH THE MACHINE...?
I KNOW YOU'RE CHEATING!
WHAT DID YOU DO?
FWMMMM
N-NO RESPONSE. D-DAMN IT! I HAVE TO ASK A QUESTION WITH A YES OR NO ANSWER...!
LOOKS LIKE YOU CAN ONLY READ MY THOUGHTS IF IT'S A YES OR NO QUESTION...
LET ME QUOTE YOUR BROTHER...

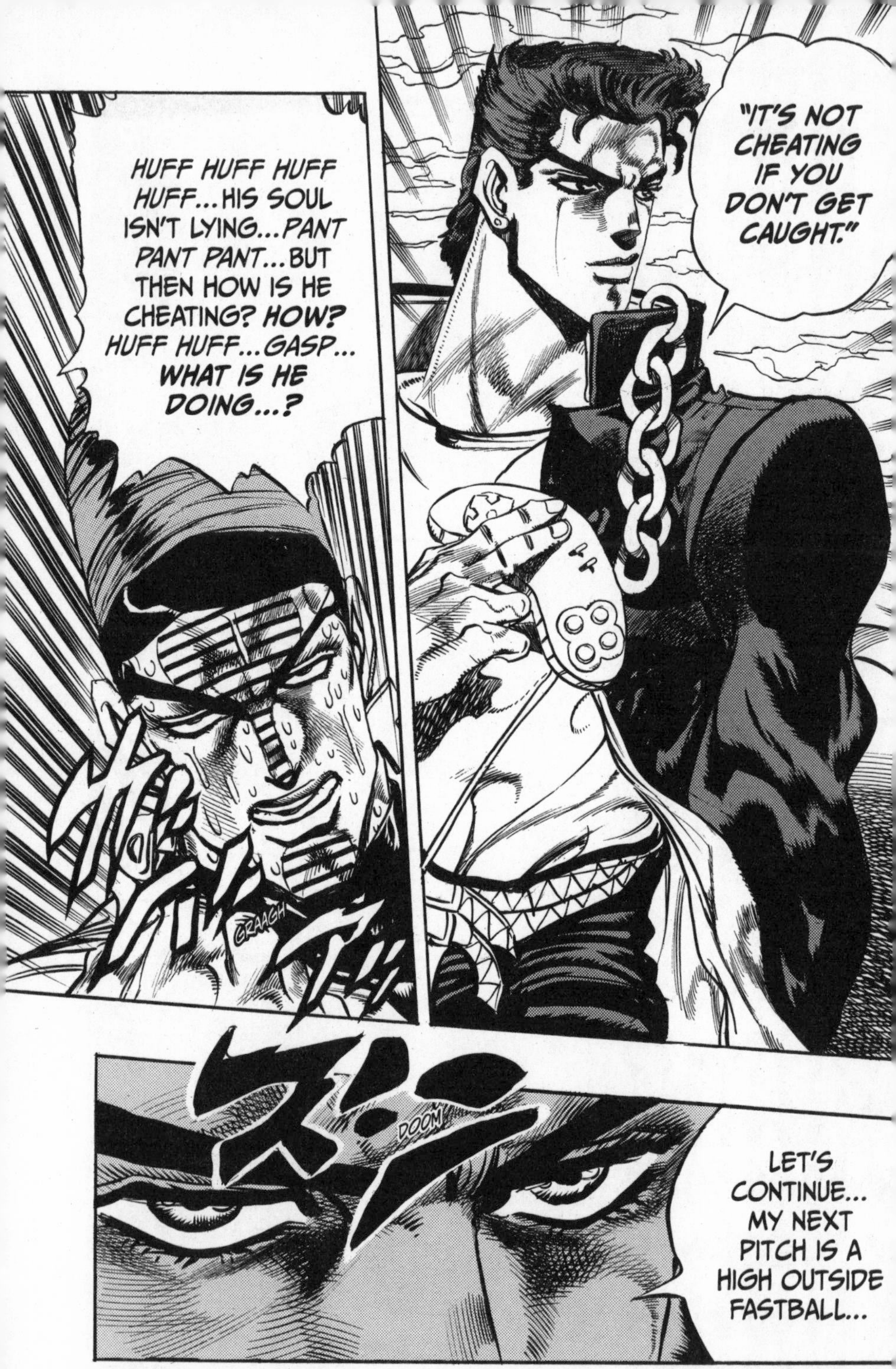
"IT'S NOT CHEATING IF YOU DON'T GET CAUGHT."
HUFF HUFF HUFF HUFF... HIS SOUL ISN'T LYING... PANT PANT PANT... BUT THEN HOW IS HE CHEATING? HOW? HUFF HUFF... GASP... WHAT IS HE DOING...?
GRAAGH
DOOM
LET'S CONTINUE... MY NEXT PITCH IS A HIGH OUTSIDE FASTBALL...

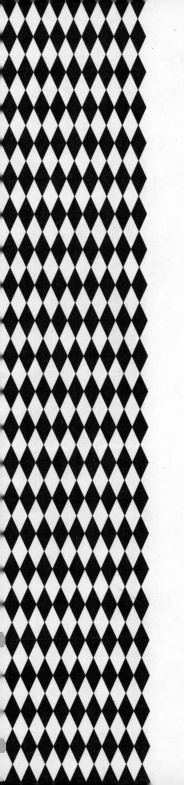
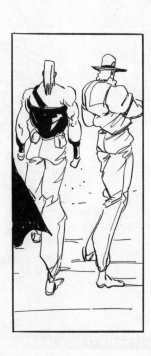

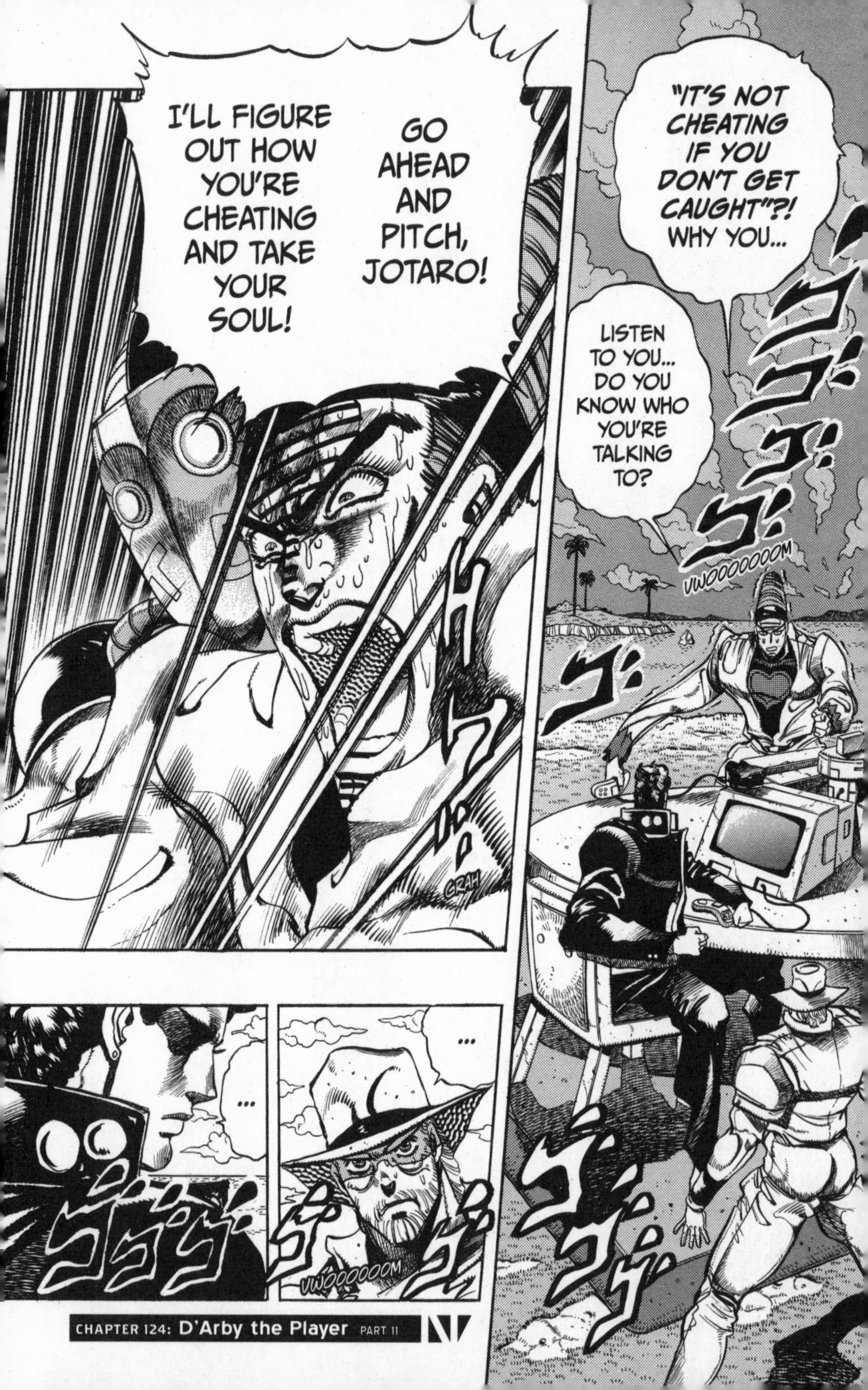
"IT'S NOT CHEATING IF YOU DON'T GET CAUGHT"?! WHY YOU...
LISTEN TO YOU... DO YOU KNOW WHO YOU'RE TALKING TO?
VWOOOOOOOM
GO AHEAD AND PITCH, JOTARO!
I'LL FIGURE OUT HOW YOU'RE CHEATING AND TAKE YOUR SOUL!
GRAH
...
VWOOOOOOOM
...

CHAPTER 124: D'Arby the Player PART 11

CHAPTER 124: D'Arby the Player PART 11

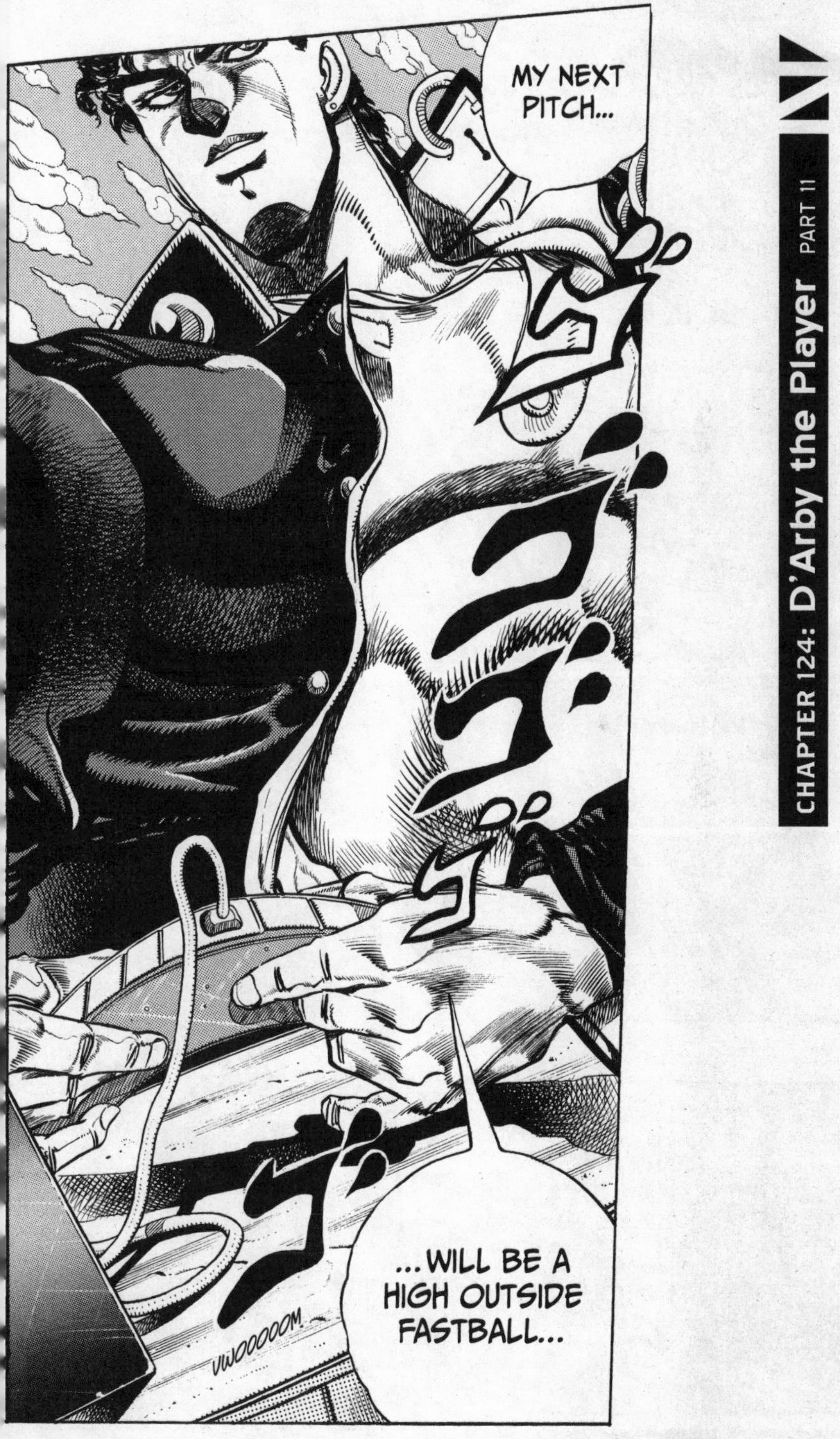
MY NEXT PITCH...
...WILL BE A HIGH OUTSIDE FASTBALL...
VWOOOOOM

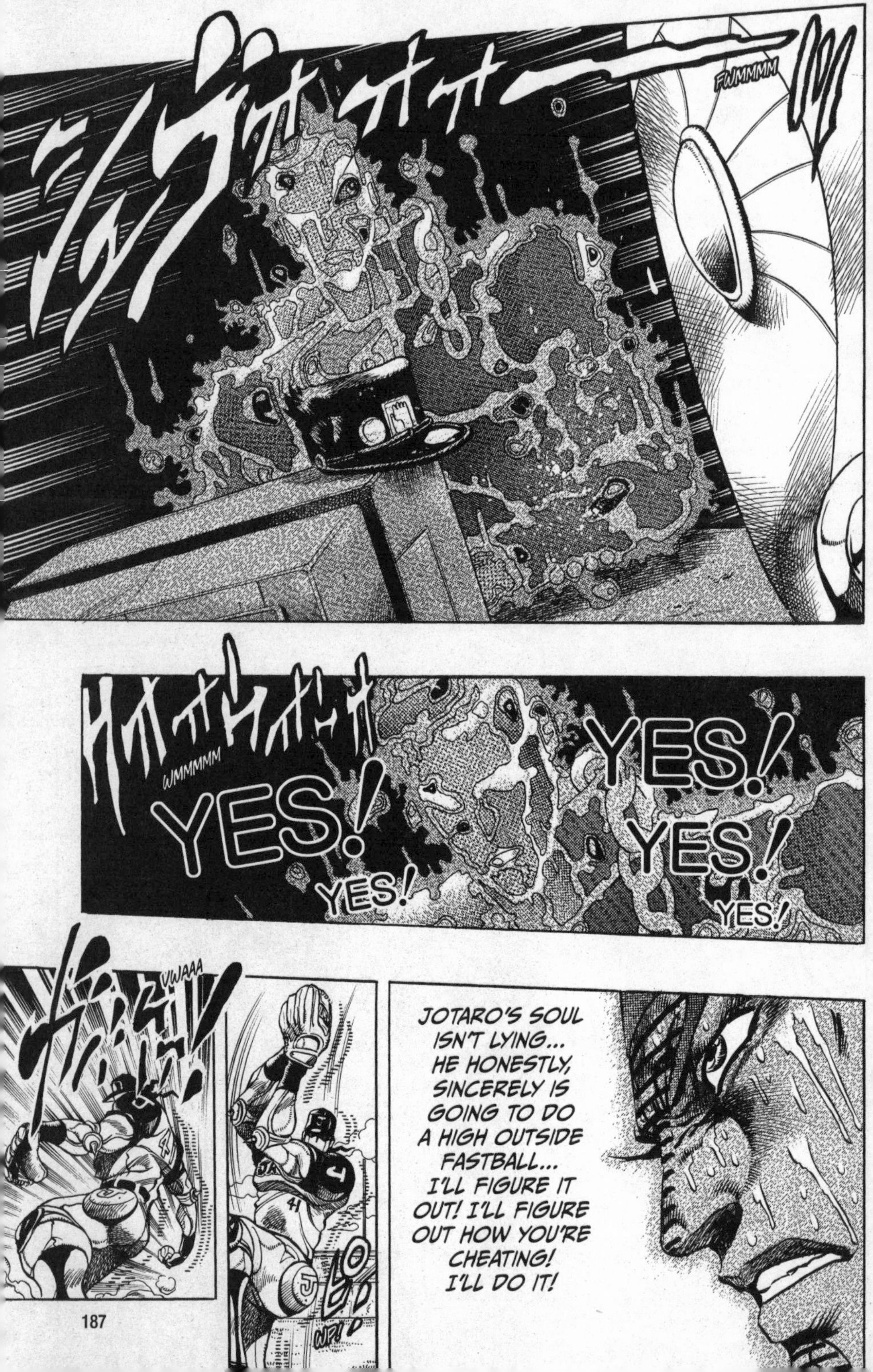
FWUMMMM
YES!
YES!
YES!
WMMMMM
YES!
YES!
JOTARO'S SOUL ISN'T LYING... HE HONESTLY, SINCERELY IS GOING TO DO A HIGH OUTSIDE FASTBALL... I'LL FIGURE IT OUT! I'LL FIGURE OUT HOW YOU'RE CHEATING! I'LL DO IT!
WP!
VWAAA

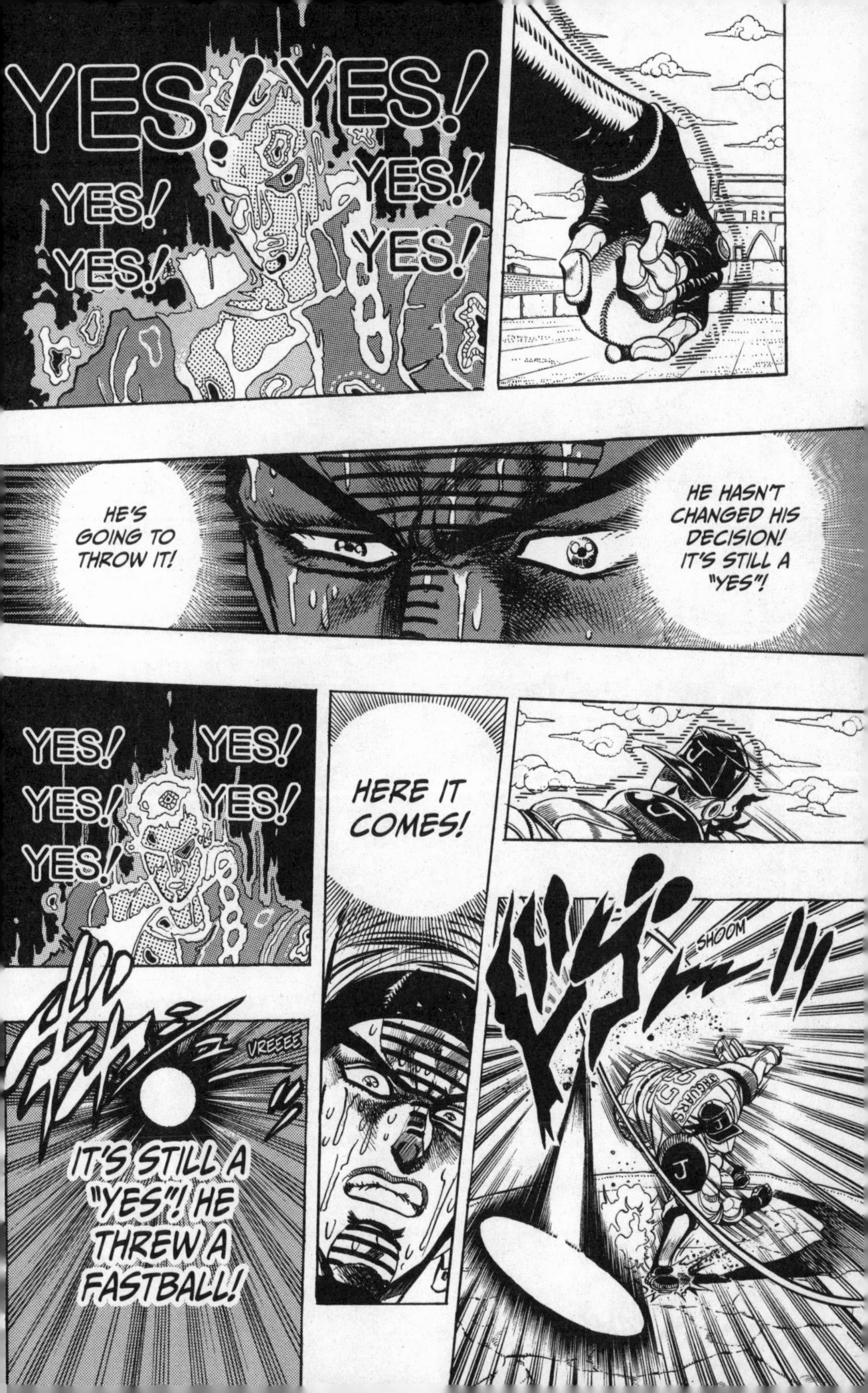
YES! YES!
YES!
YES!
YES!
YES!
HE HASN'T CHANGED HIS DECISION! IT'S STILL A "YES"!
HE'S GOING TO THROW IT!
SHOOM
HERE IT COMES!
YES! YES!
YES! YES!
YES!
VREEEE
IT'S STILL A "YES"! HE THREW A FASTBALL!

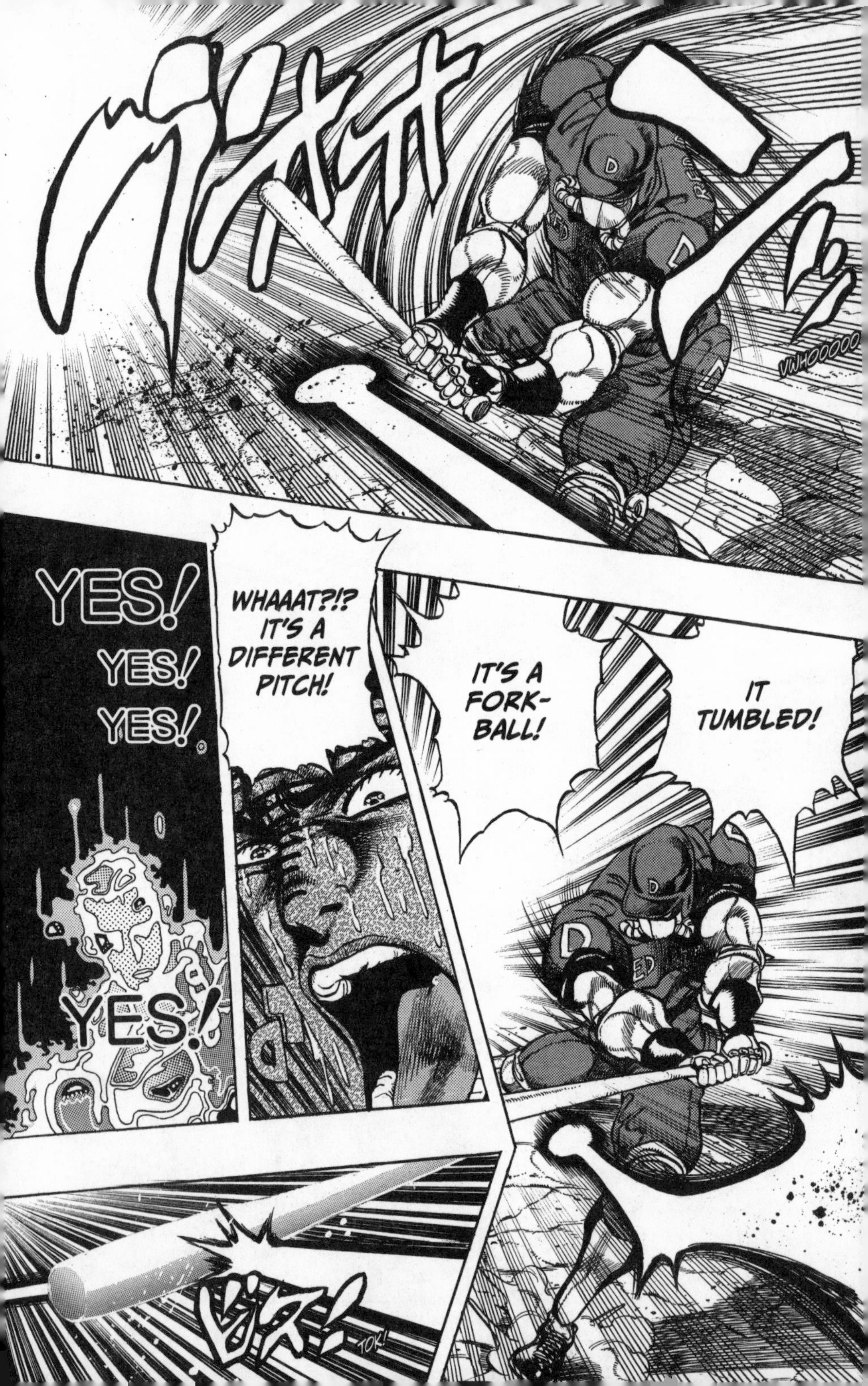
VWHOOOOO
IT TUMBLED!
IT'S A FORK-BALL!
WHAAAT?!? IT'S A DIFFERENT PITCH!
YES!
YES!
YES!
YES!
TOK!

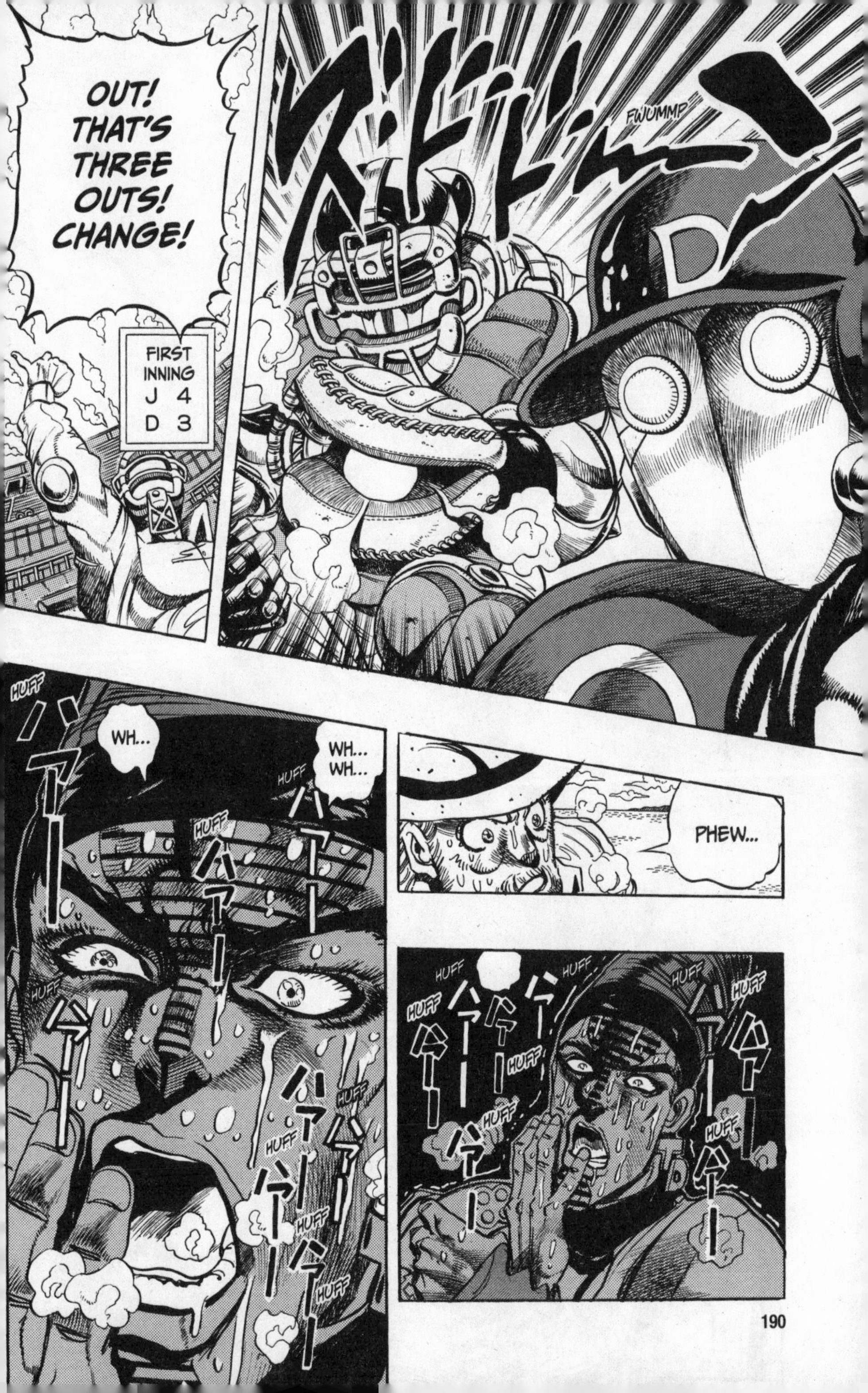
FWUMMP
OUT! THAT'S THREE OUTS! CHANGE!
FIRST INNING
J 4
D 3
PHEW...
HUFF
HUFF
HUFF
HUFF
HUFF
HUFF
HUFF
HUFF
WH... WH...
WH...
HUFF
HUFF
HUFF
HUFF
HUFF
HUFF
HUFF
HUFF

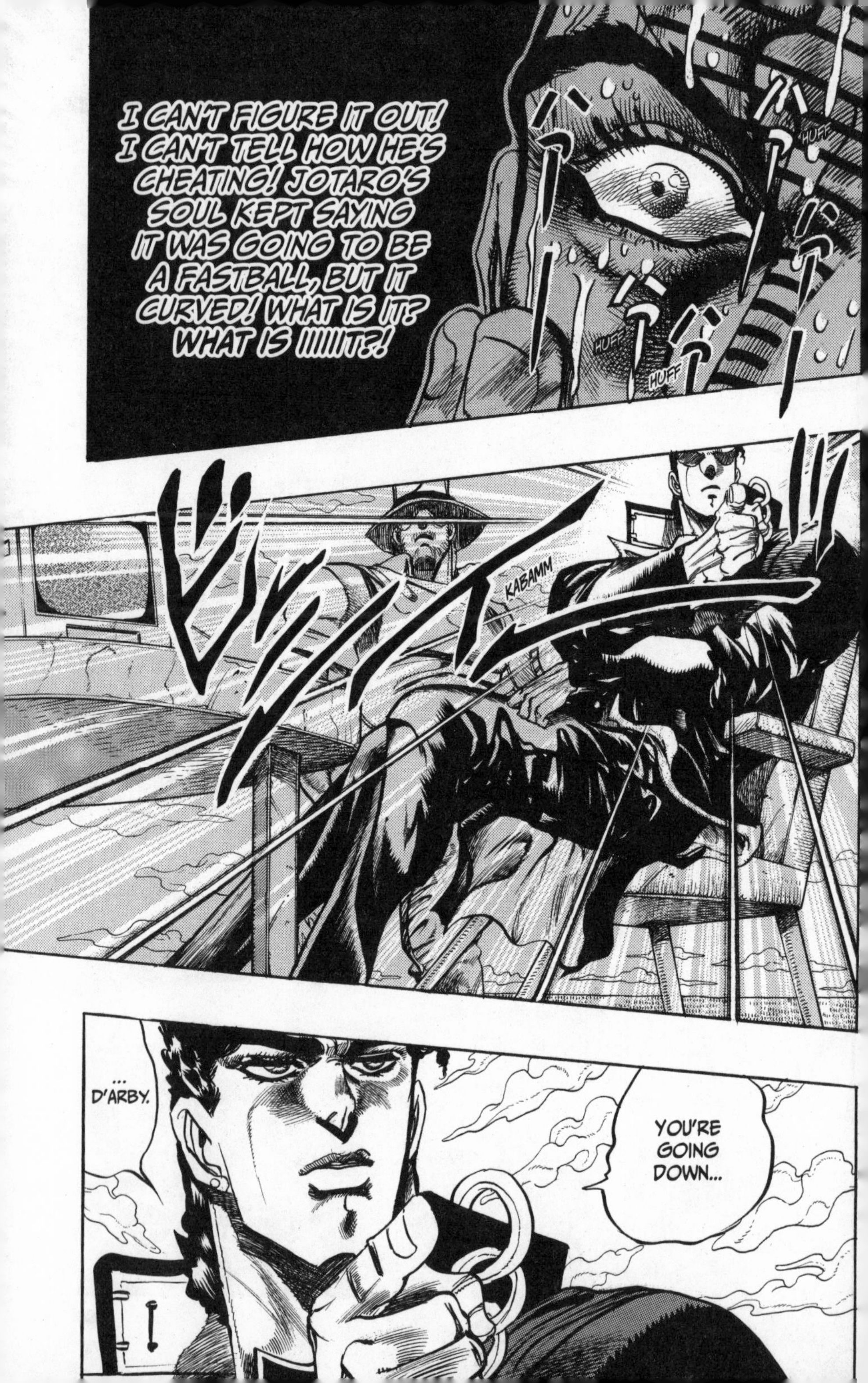
I CAN'T FIGURE IT OUT! I CAN'T TELL HOW HE'S CHEATING! JOTARO'S SOUL KEPT SAYING IT WAS GOING TO BE A FASTBALL, BUT IT CURVED! WHAT IS IT? WHAT IS IIIIIIT?!
HUFF
HUFF
HUFF
KABAMM
YOU'RE GOING DOWN...
... D'ARBY.

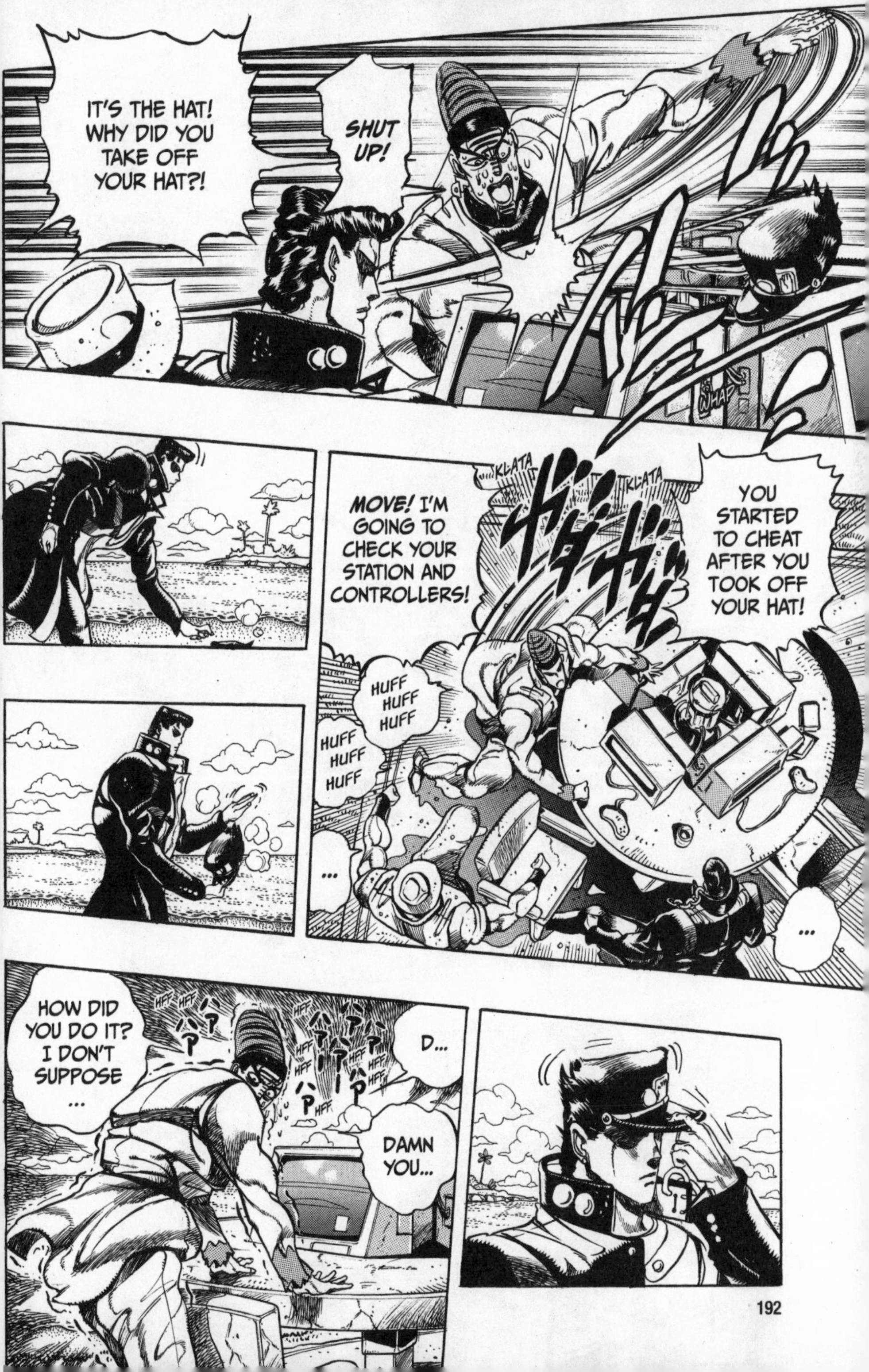
IT'S THE HAT! WHY DID YOU TAKE OFF YOUR HAT?!
SHUT UP!
WHAP
YOU STARTED TO CHEAT AFTER YOU TOOK OFF YOUR HAT!
KLATA
KLATA
MOVE! I'M GOING TO CHECK YOUR STATION AND CONTROLLERS!
HUFF HUFF HUFF
HUFF HUFF HUFF
...
...
HOW DID YOU DO IT? I DON'T SUPPOSE ...
HFF HFF
D...
DAMN YOU...

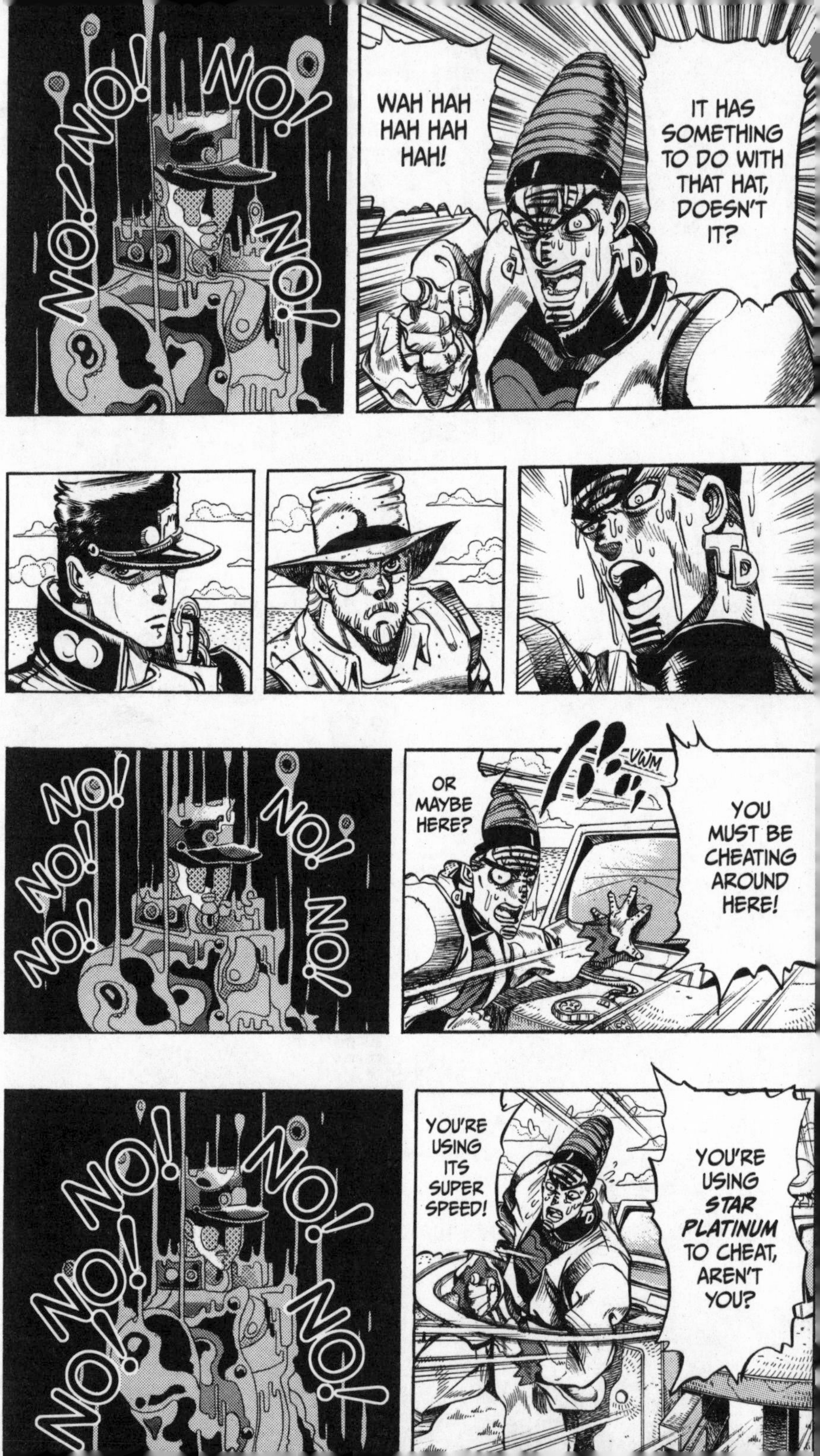
IT HAS SOMETHING TO DO WITH THAT HAT, DOESN'T IT?
WAH HAH HAH HAH HAH!
NO! NO! NO! NO!
VWM
YOU MUST BE CHEATING AROUND HERE!
OR MAYBE HERE?
NO! NO! NO! NO! NO!
YOU'RE USING *STAR PLATINUM* TO CHEAT, AREN'T YOU?
YOU'RE USING ITS SUPER SPEED!
NO! NO! NO! NO! NO!

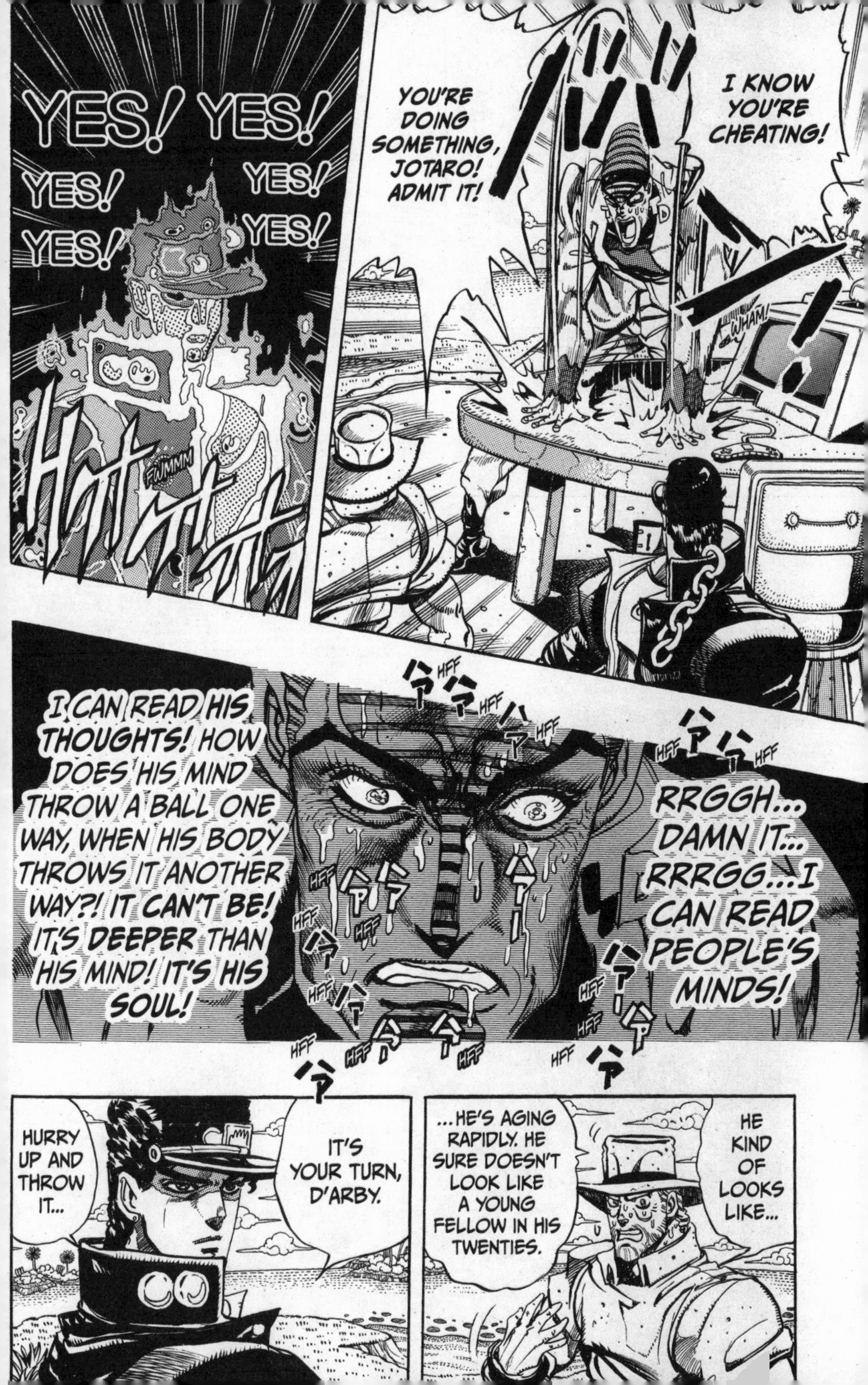
I KNOW YOU'RE CHEATING!
YOU'RE DOING SOMETHING, JOTARO! ADMIT IT!
WHAM!
YES! YES!
YES!
YES!
YES!
YES!
FWUMMM
RRGGH... DAMN IT... RRRGG...I CAN READ PEOPLE'S MINDS!
I CAN READ HIS THOUGHTS! HOW DOES HIS MIND THROW A BALL ONE WAY, WHEN HIS BODY THROWS IT ANOTHER WAY?! IT CAN'T BE! IT'S DEEPER THAN HIS MIND! IT'S HIS SOUL!
HFF HFF HFF
HE KIND OF LOOKS LIKE...
...HE'S AGING RAPIDLY. HE SURE DOESN'T LOOK LIKE A YOUNG FELLOW IN HIS TWENTIES.
IT'S YOUR TURN, D'ARBY.
HURRY UP AND THROW IT...

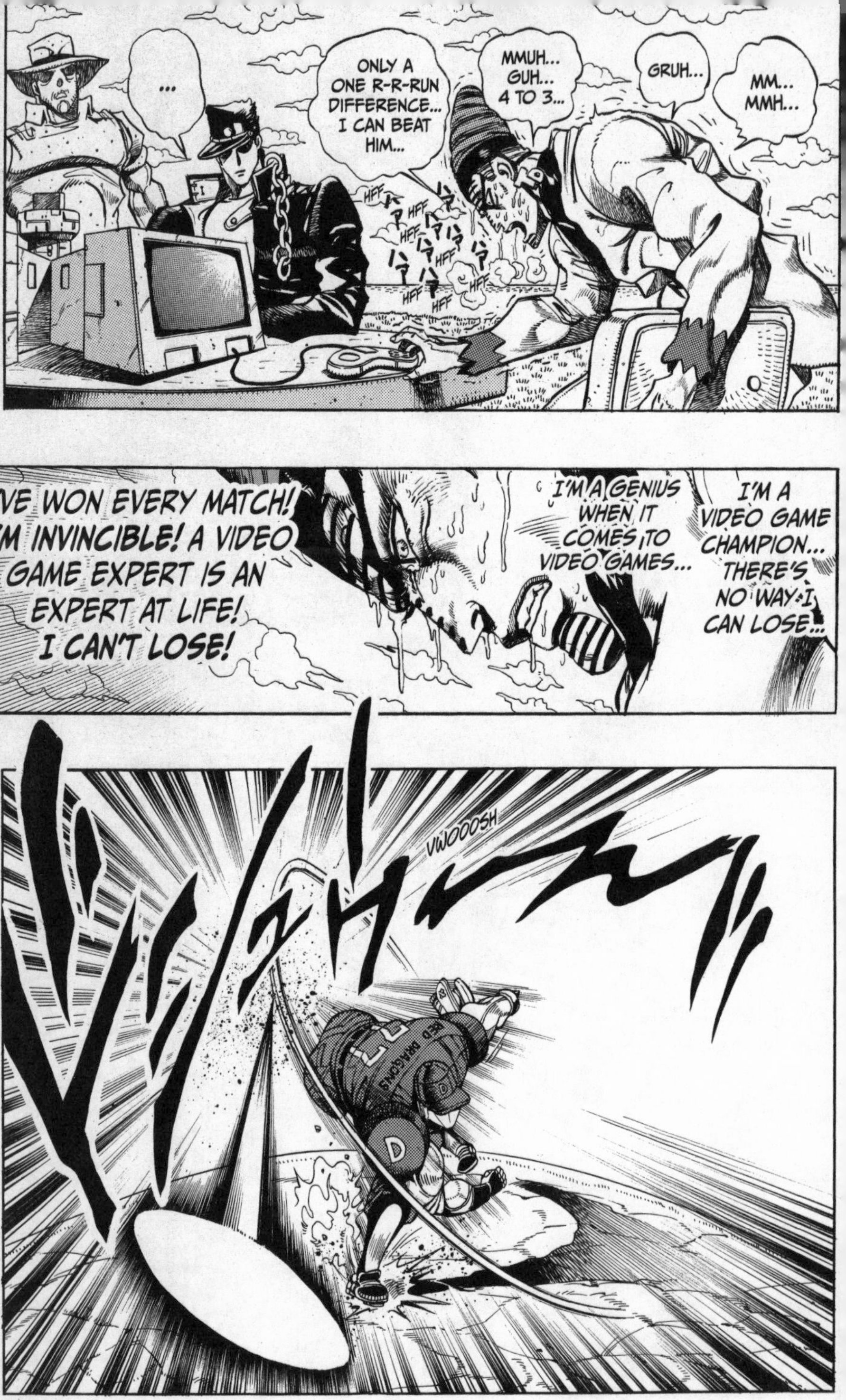
MM... MMH...
GRUH...
MMUH... GUH... 4 TO 3...
ONLY A ONE R-R-RUN DIFFERENCE... I CAN BEAT HIM...
...
I'M A VIDEO GAME CHAMPION... THERE'S NO WAY I CAN LOSE...
I'M A GENIUS WHEN IT COMES TO VIDEO GAMES...
I'VE WON EVERY MATCH! I'M INVINCIBLE! A VIDEO GAME EXPERT IS AN EXPERT AT LIFE! I CAN'T LOSE!
VWOOOSH

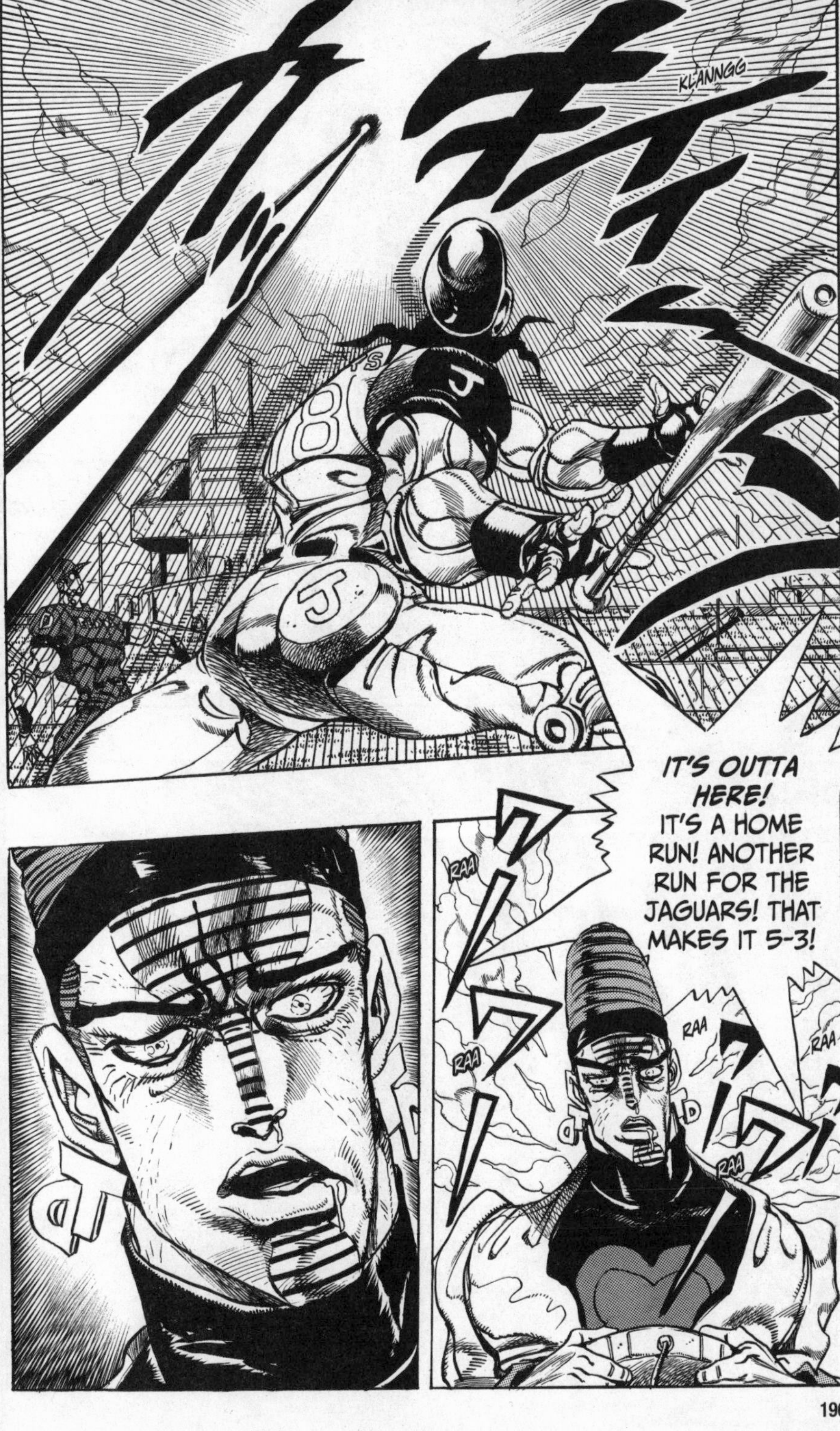
KLANNGG
IT'S OUTTA HERE!
IT'S A HOME RUN! ANOTHER RUN FOR THE JAGUARS! THAT MAKES IT 5-3!
RAA
RAA
RAA
RAA
RAA

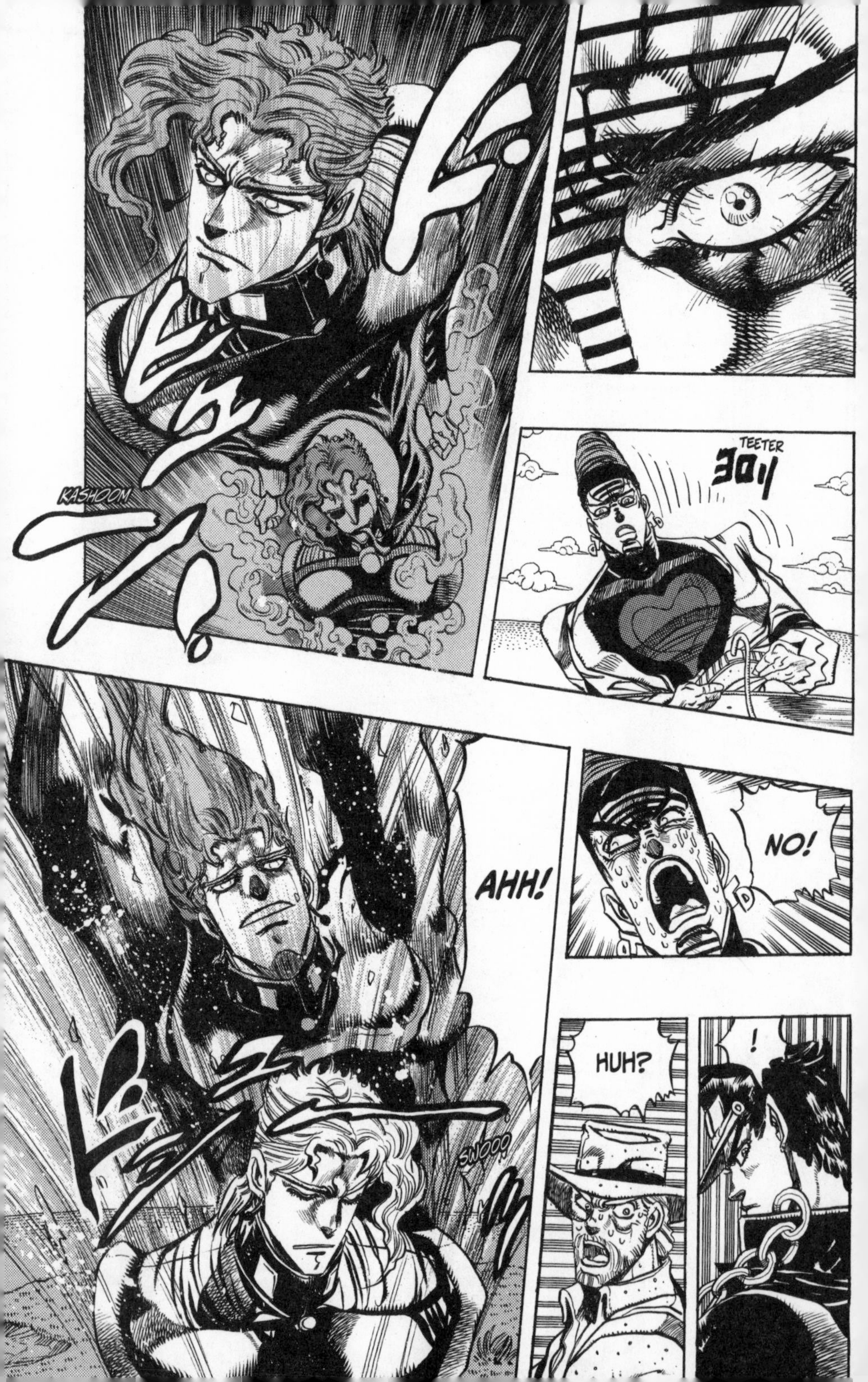
TEETER
KASHOOM
NO!
AHH!
!
HUH?
SWOOO

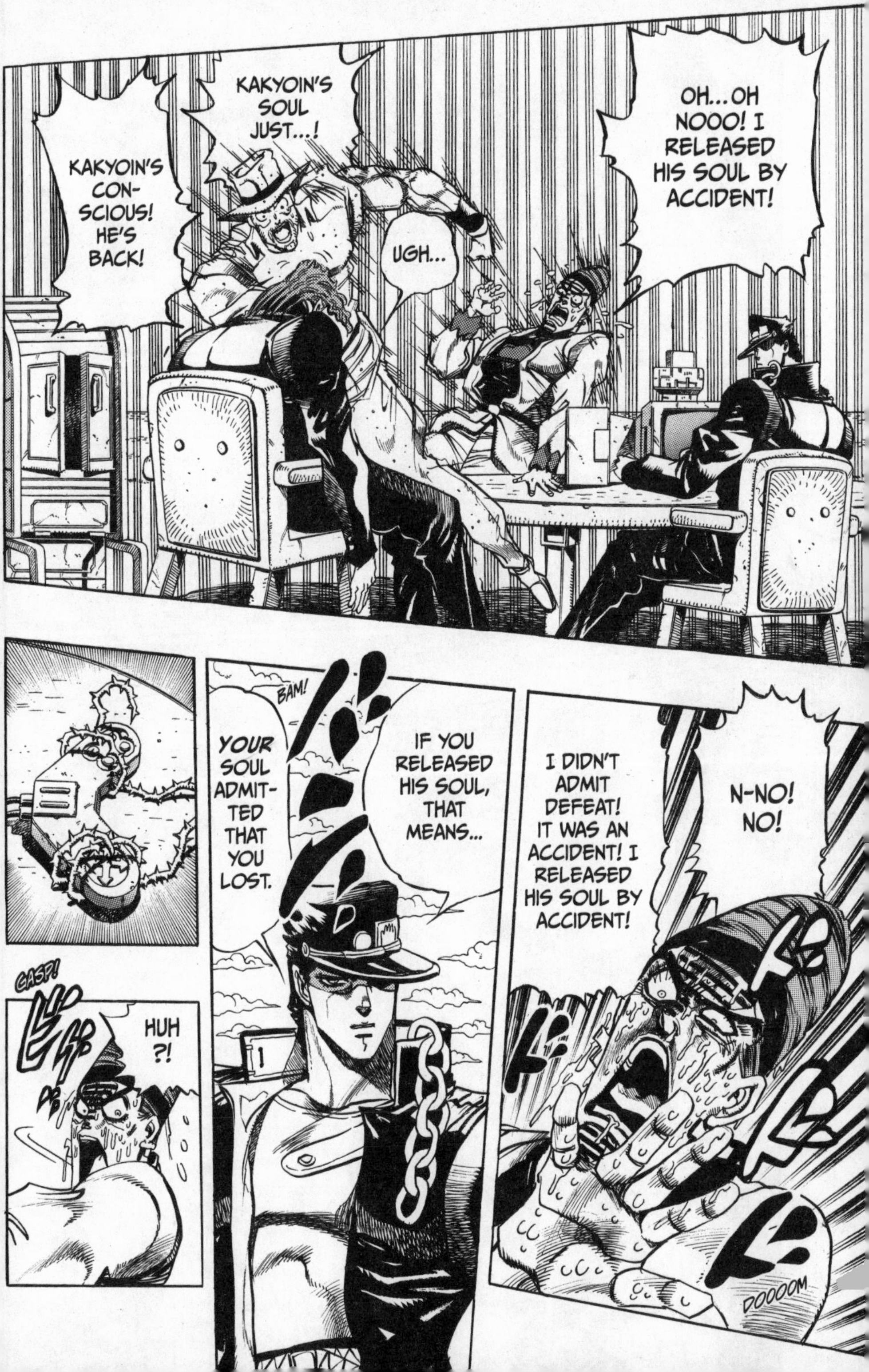
OH...OH NOOO! I RELEASED HIS SOUL BY ACCIDENT!
KAKYOIN'S SOUL JUST...!
UGH...
KAKYOIN'S CON-SCIOUS! HE'S BACK!
N-NO! NO!
I DIDN'T ADMIT DEFEAT! IT WAS AN ACCIDENT! I RELEASED HIS SOUL BY ACCIDENT!
DOOOOM
BAM!
IF YOU RELEASED HIS SOUL, THAT MEANS...
YOUR SOUL ADMIT-TED THAT YOU LOST.
GASP!
HUH ?!

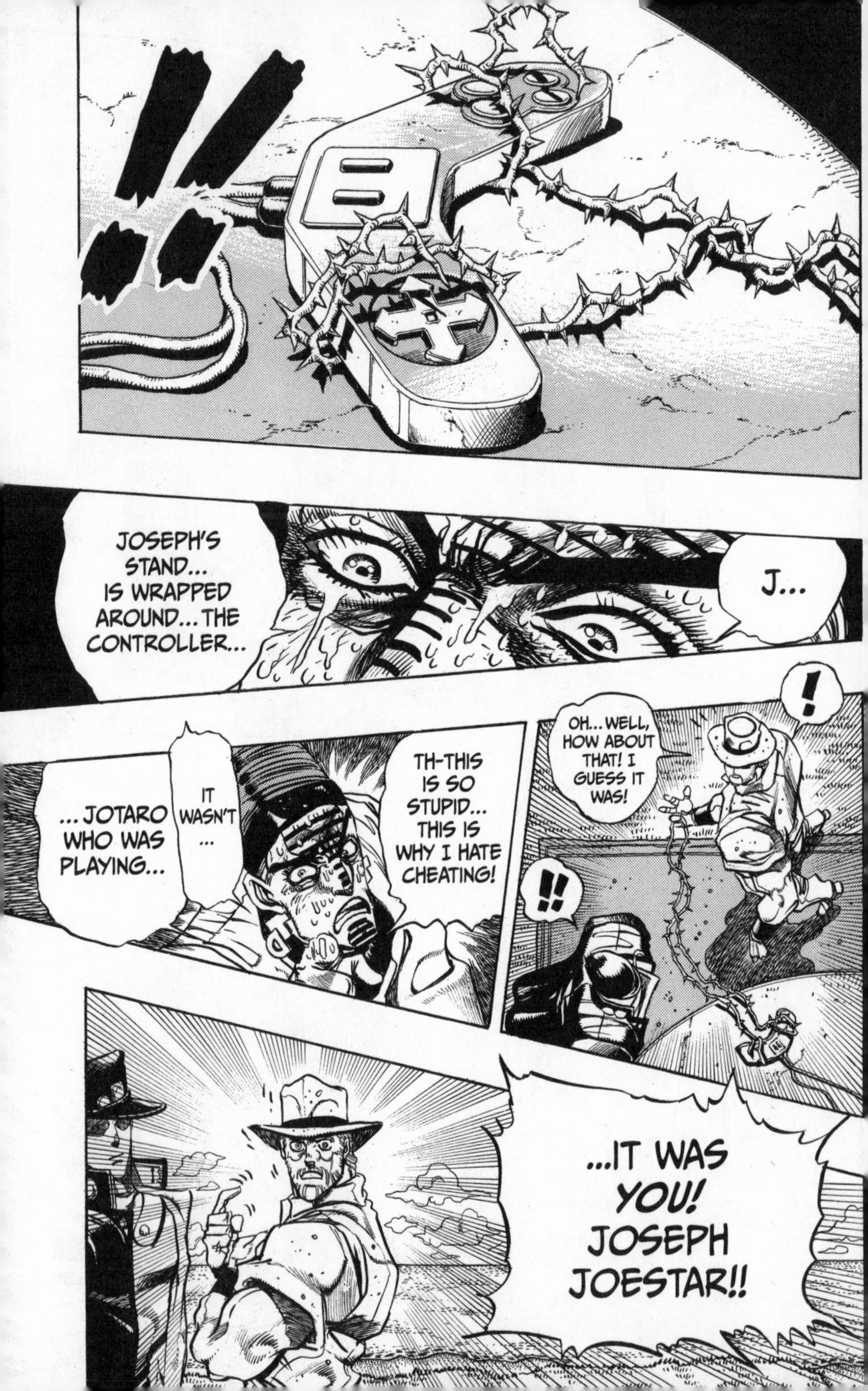
!!
J...
JOSEPH'S STAND... IS WRAPPED AROUND... THE CONTROLLER...
!
OH... WELL, HOW ABOUT THAT! I GUESS IT WAS!
!!
TH-THIS IS SO STUPID... THIS IS WHY I HATE CHEATING!
IT WASN'T ...
... JOTARO WHO WAS PLAYING...
...IT WAS YOU! JOSEPH JOESTAR!!

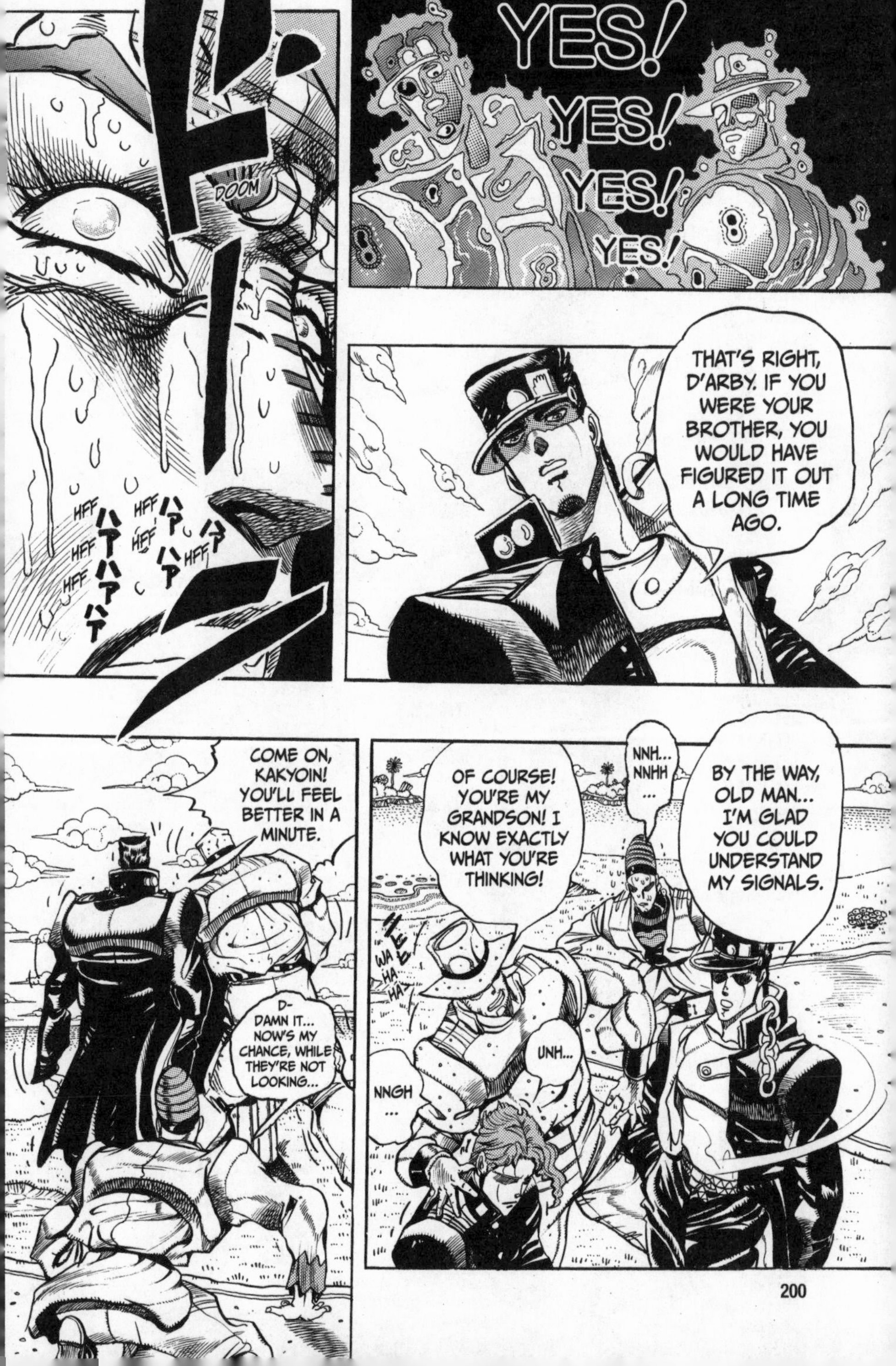
YES! YES! YES! YES!
THAT'S RIGHT, D'ARBY. IF YOU WERE YOUR BROTHER, YOU WOULD HAVE FIGURED IT OUT A LONG TIME AGO.
DOOM
HFF HFF HFF HFF HFF HFF
ハァハァハァ ハァハァ ハァ
BY THE WAY, OLD MAN... I'M GLAD YOU COULD UNDERSTAND MY SIGNALS.
NNH... NNHH ...
OF COURSE! YOU'RE MY GRANDSON! I KNOW EXACTLY WHAT YOU'RE THINKING!
WA HA HA
UNH...
NNGH ...
COME ON, KAKYOIN! YOU'LL FEEL BETTER IN A MINUTE.
D- DAMN IT... NOW'S MY CHANCE, WHILE THEY'RE NOT LOOKING...

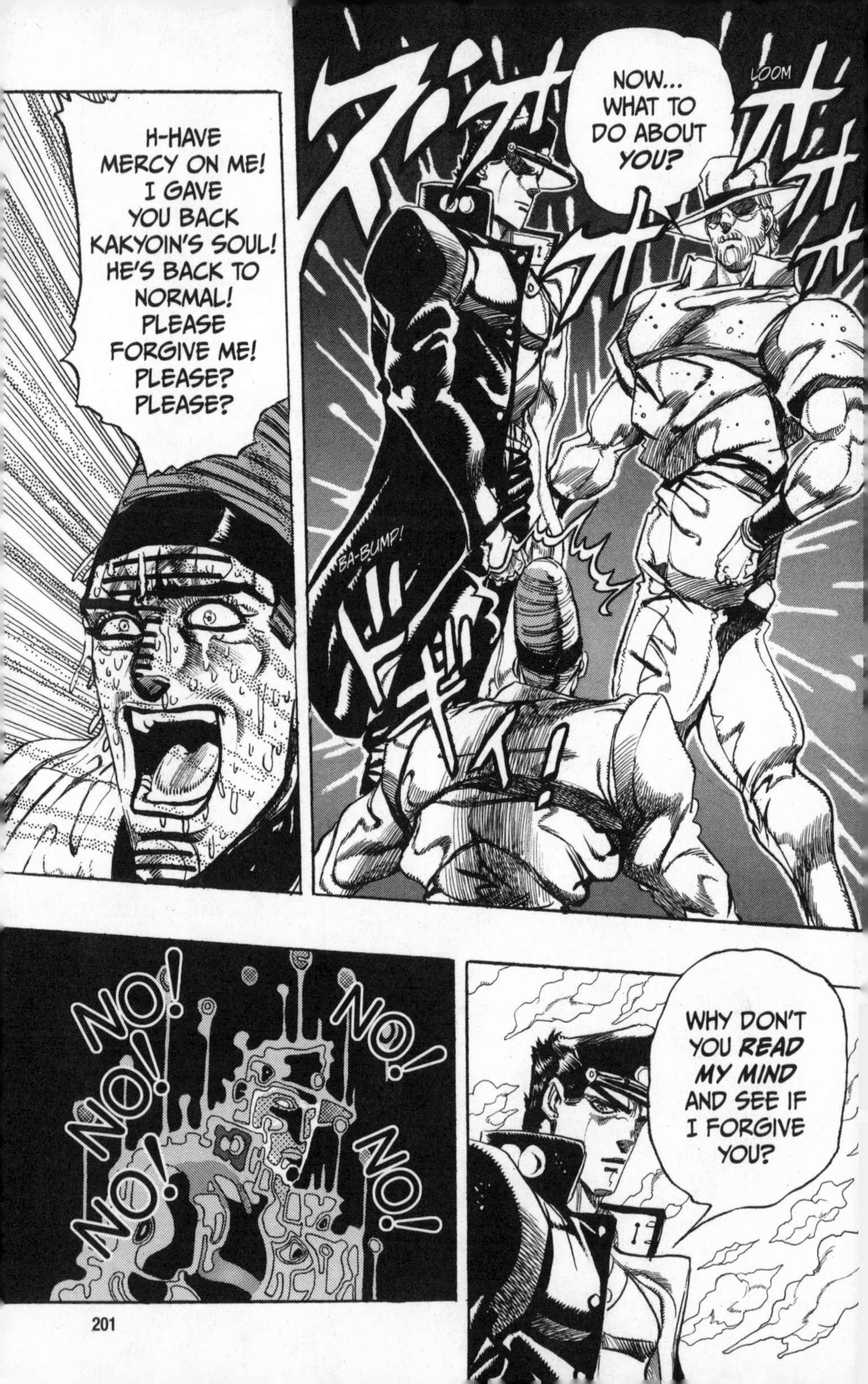
LOOM
NOW... WHAT TO DO ABOUT YOU?
BA-BUMP!
H-HAVE MERCY ON ME! I GAVE YOU BACK KAKYOIN'S SOUL! HE'S BACK TO NORMAL! PLEASE FORGIVE ME! PLEASE? PLEASE?
WHY DON'T YOU READ MY MIND AND SEE IF I FORGIVE YOU?
NO! NO! NO! NO! NO! NO!

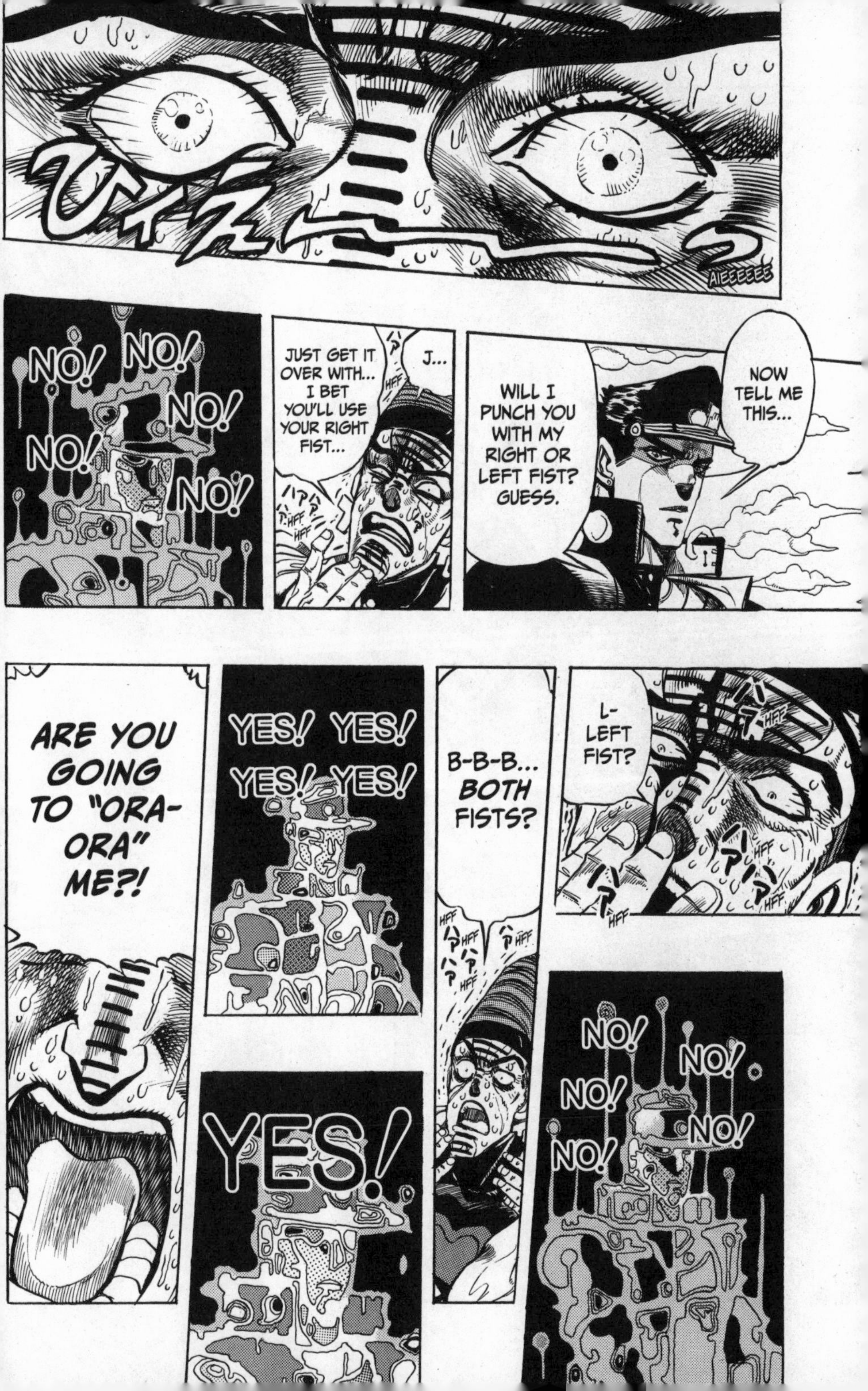
AIEEEEEE
NOW TELL ME THIS...
WILL I PUNCH YOU WITH MY RIGHT OR LEFT FIST? GUESS.
J...
JUST GET IT OVER WITH... I BET YOU'LL USE YOUR RIGHT FIST...
HFF HFF HFF
NO! NO! NO! NO! NO!
HFF HFF HFF HFF
L- LEFT FIST?
B-B-B... BOTH FISTS?
HFF HFF HFF HFF
YES! YES! YES! YES!
ARE YOU GOING TO "ORA-ORA" ME?!
NO! NO! NO! NO! NO!
YES!

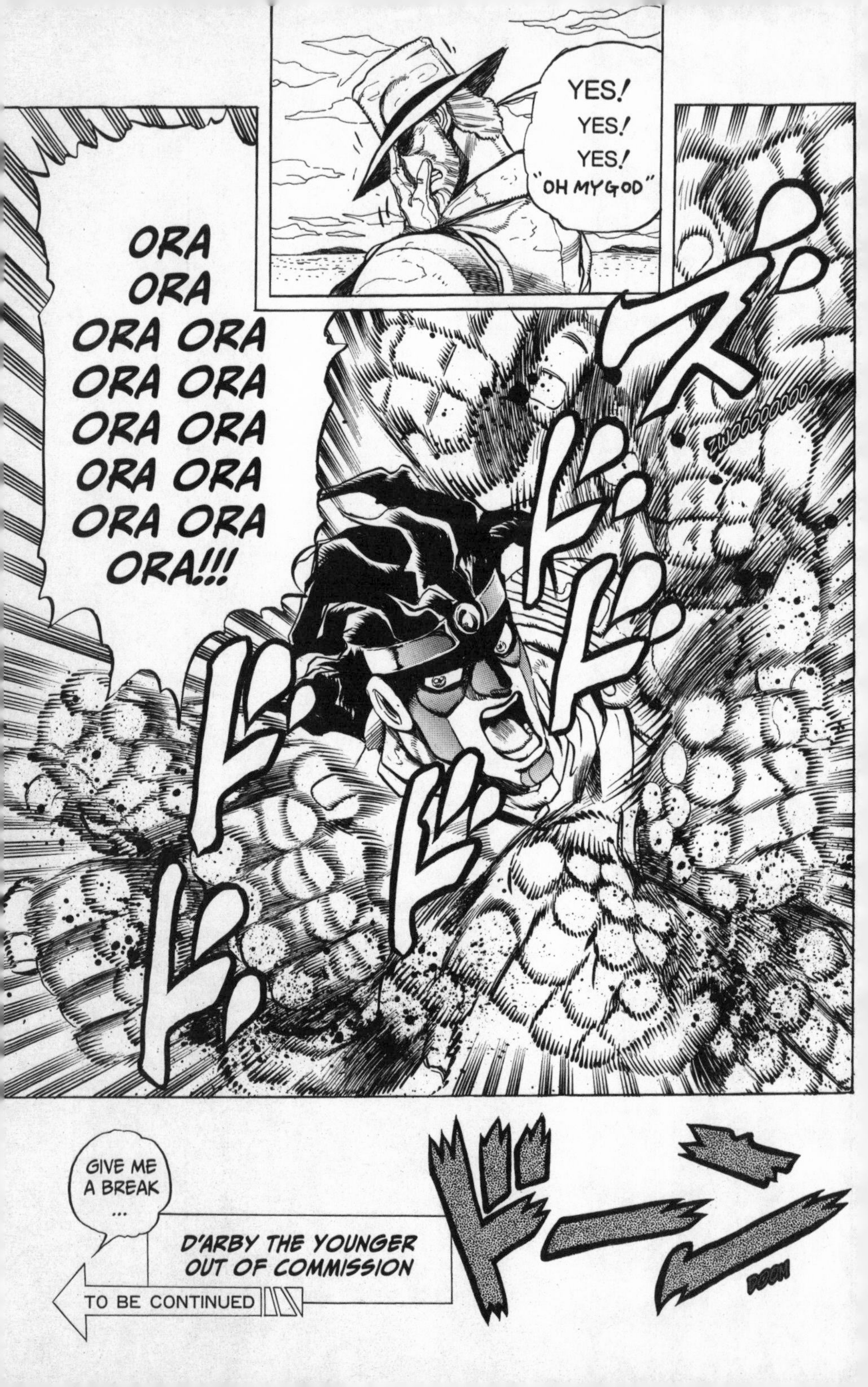
YES! YES! YES! "OH MY GOD"
ORA ORA ORA ORA ORA ORA ORA ORA ORA ORA ORA ORA ORA ORA ORA ORA ORA!!!
ZWOOOOOOOOO
GIVE ME A BREAK ...
D'ARBY THE YOUNGER OUT OF COMMISSION
DOOM
TO BE CONTINUED

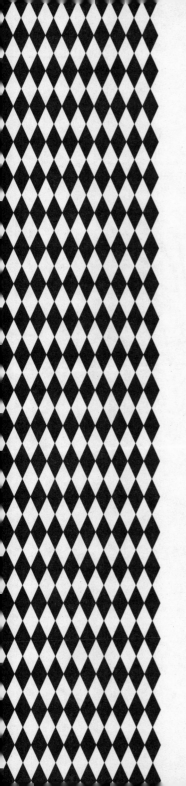

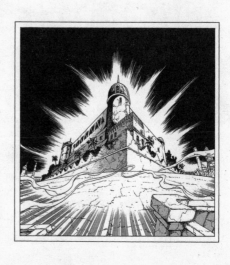

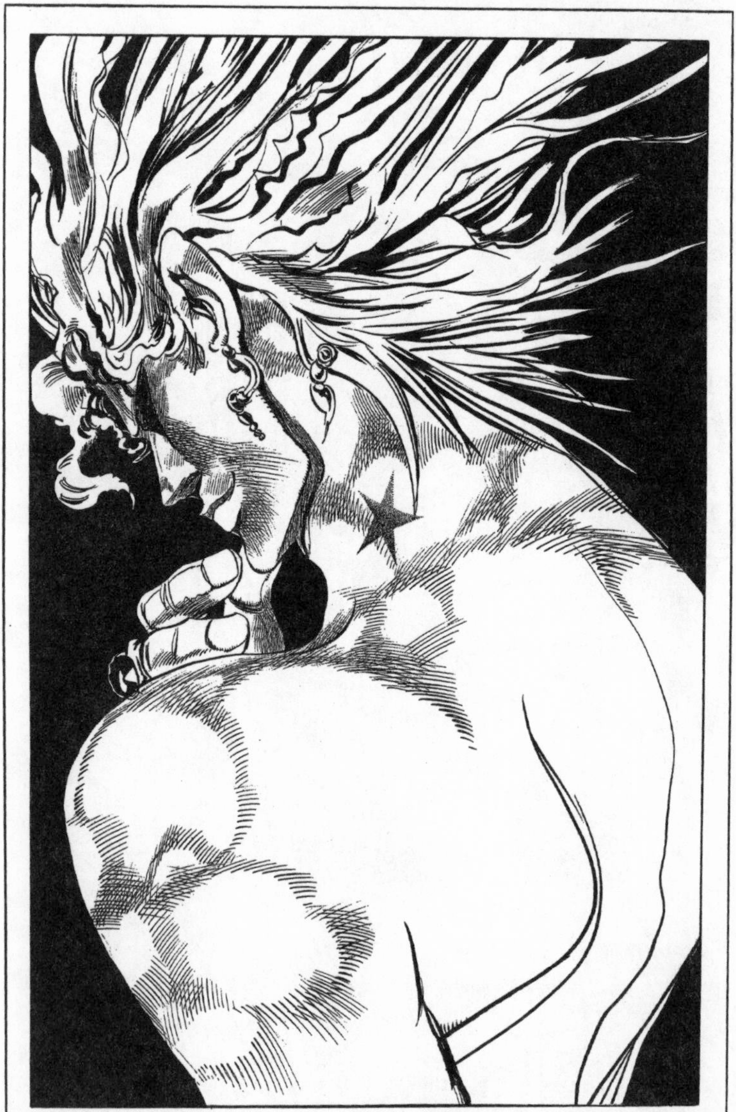

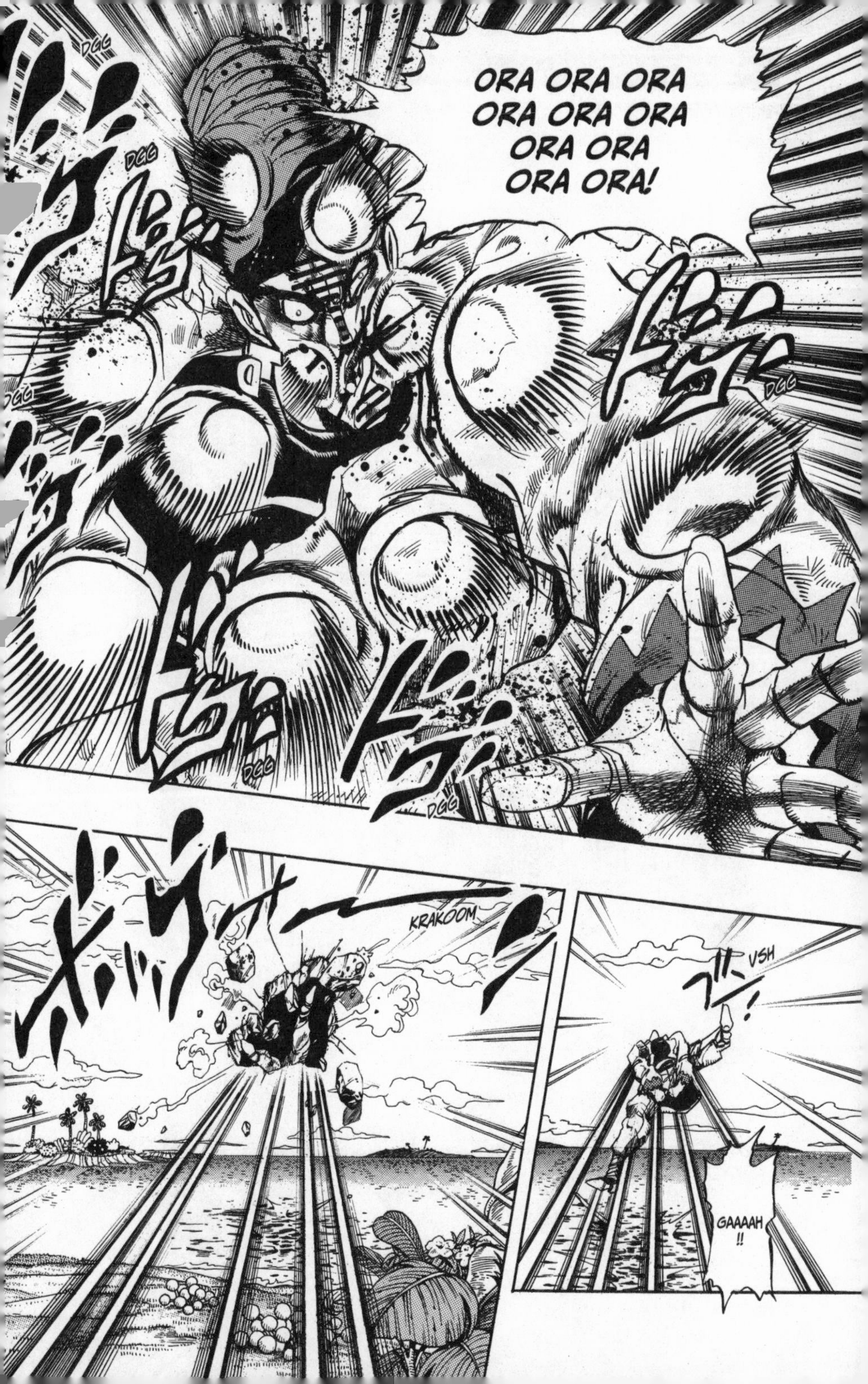
ORA ORA ORA
ORA ORA ORA
ORA ORA
ORA ORA!
DGG
DGG
DGG
DGG
DGG
DGG
VSH
GAAAAH
!!
KRAKOOM

CHAPTER 125:
The Dark Void of Cool Ice PART 1

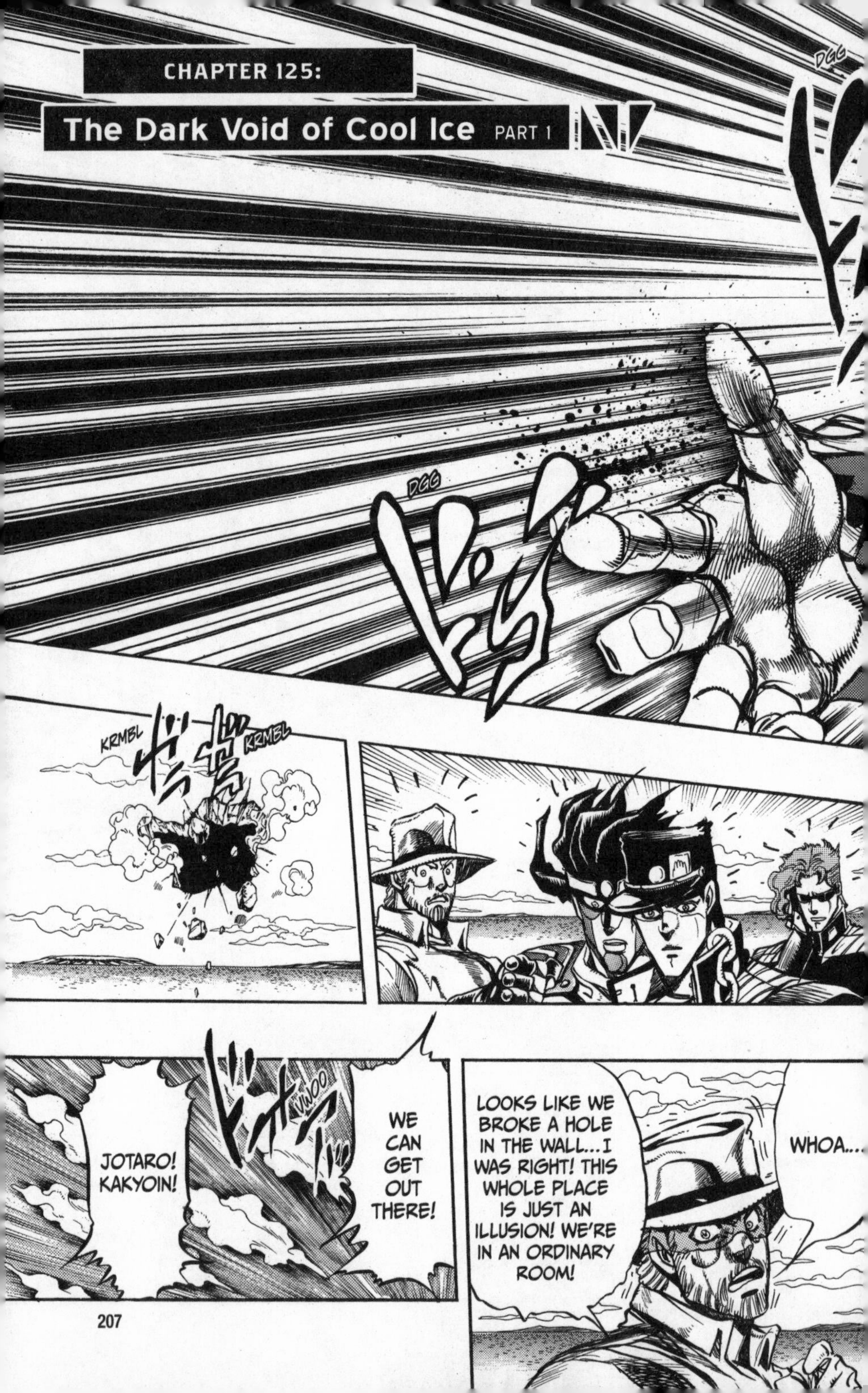
DGG
DGG
KRMBL
KRMBL
WHOA....
LOOKS LIKE WE BROKE A HOLE IN THE WALL...I WAS RIGHT! THIS WHOLE PLACE IS JUST AN ILLUSION! WE'RE IN AN ORDINARY ROOM!
WE CAN GET OUT THERE!
VWOO
JOTARO! KAKYOIN!

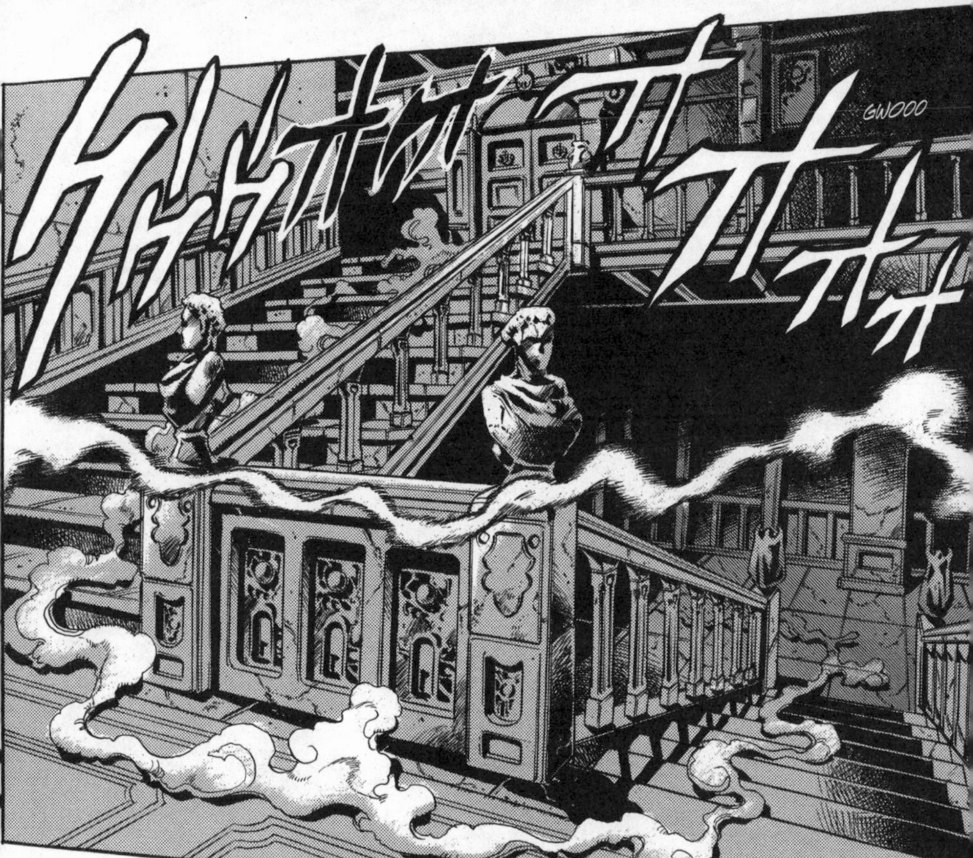
GWOOO
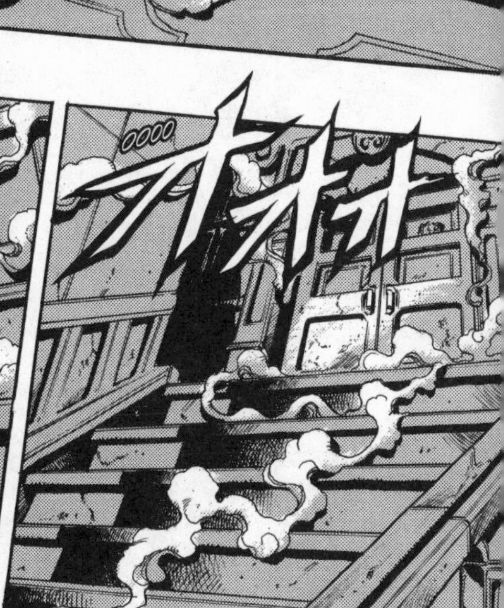
OOOO
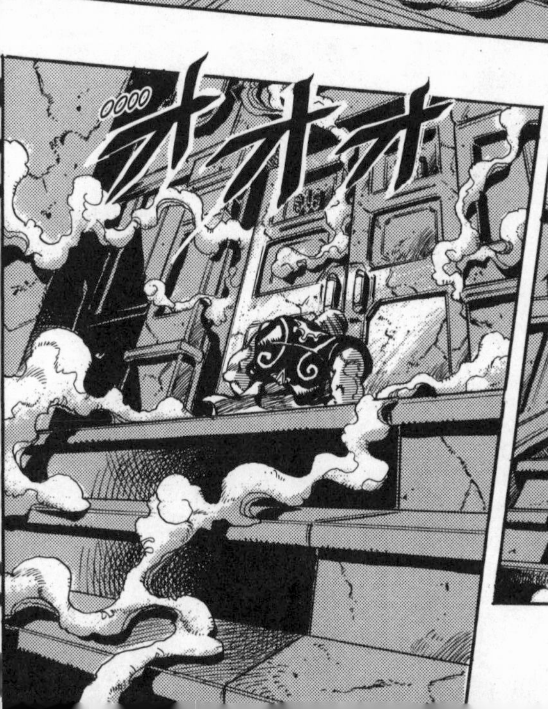
OOOO

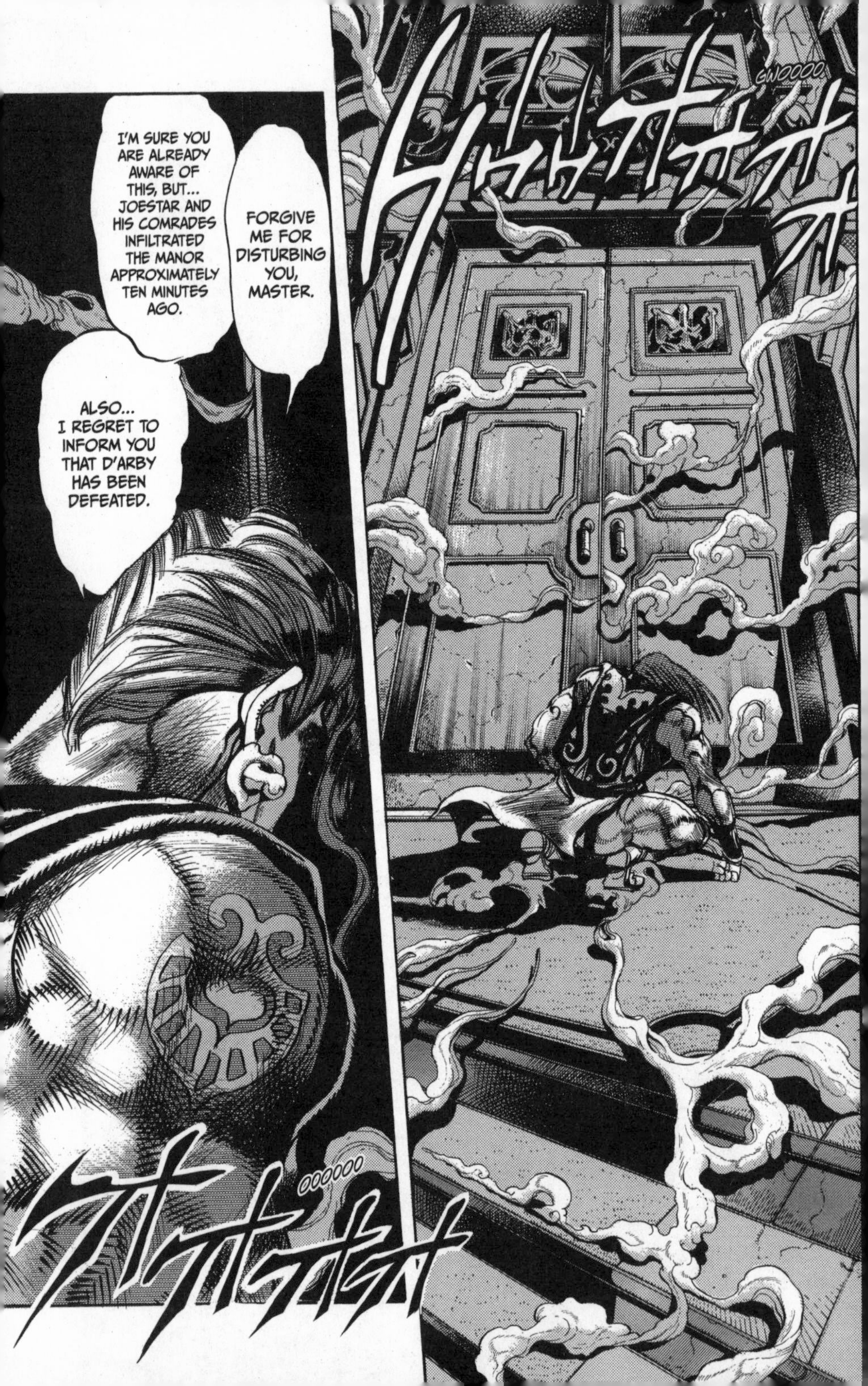
GWOOOO
FORGIVE ME FOR DISTURBING YOU, MASTER.
I'M SURE YOU ARE ALREADY AWARE OF THIS, BUT... JOESTAR AND HIS COMRADES INFILTRATED THE MANOR APPROXIMATELY TEN MINUTES AGO.
ALSO... I REGRET TO INFORM YOU THAT D'ARBY HAS BEEN DEFEATED.
OOOOOO

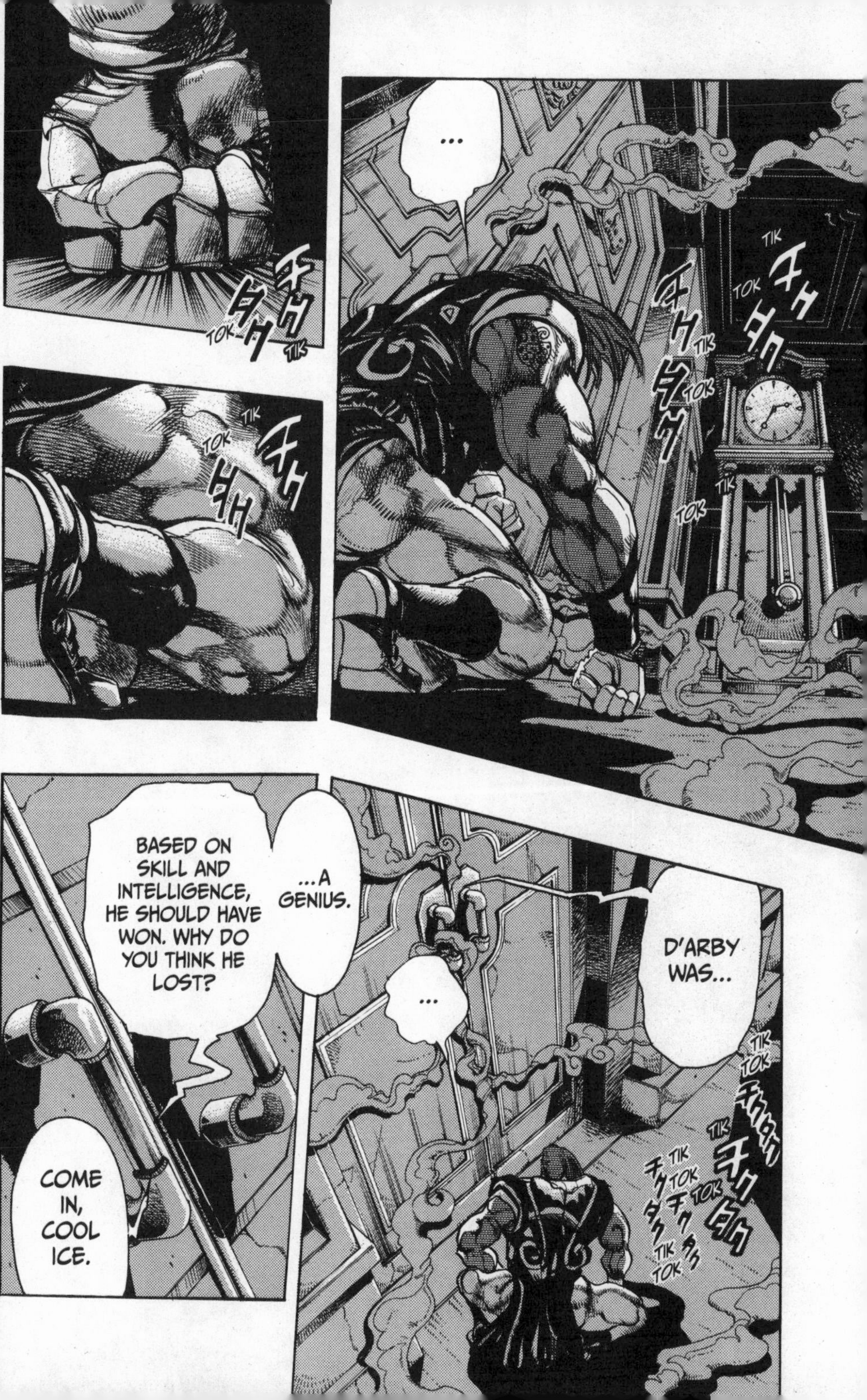

...
TIK TOK
TIK TOK
TIK TOK
TOK TIK
TIK TOK
D'ARBY WAS...
...
...A GENIUS.
TIK TOK
TIK TOK
TIK TOK
TIK TOK
BASED ON SKILL AND INTELLIGENCE, HE SHOULD HAVE WON. WHY DO YOU THINK HE LOST?
COME IN, COOL ICE.

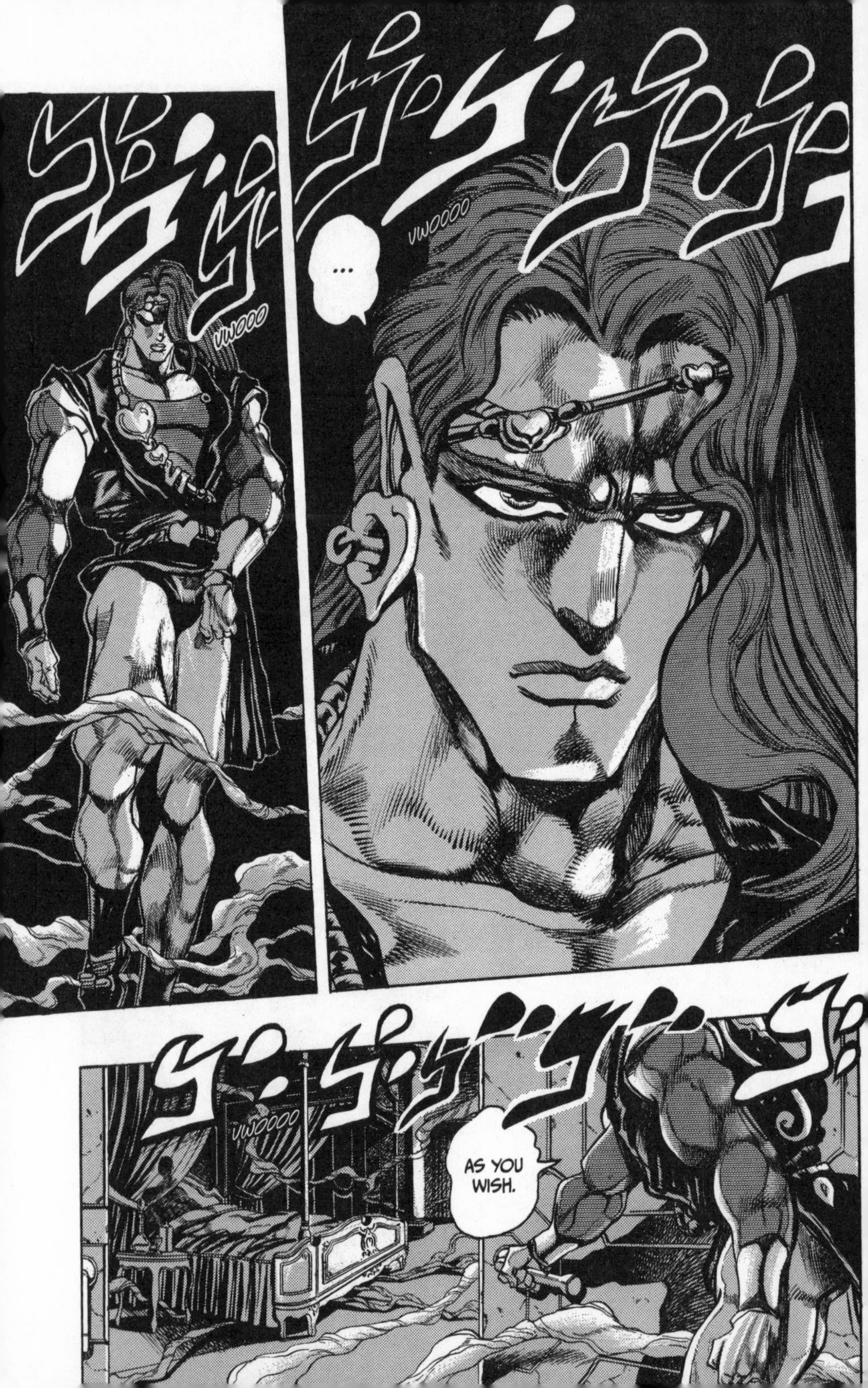
VWOOOO
...
VWOOO
VWOOOO
AS YOU WISH.

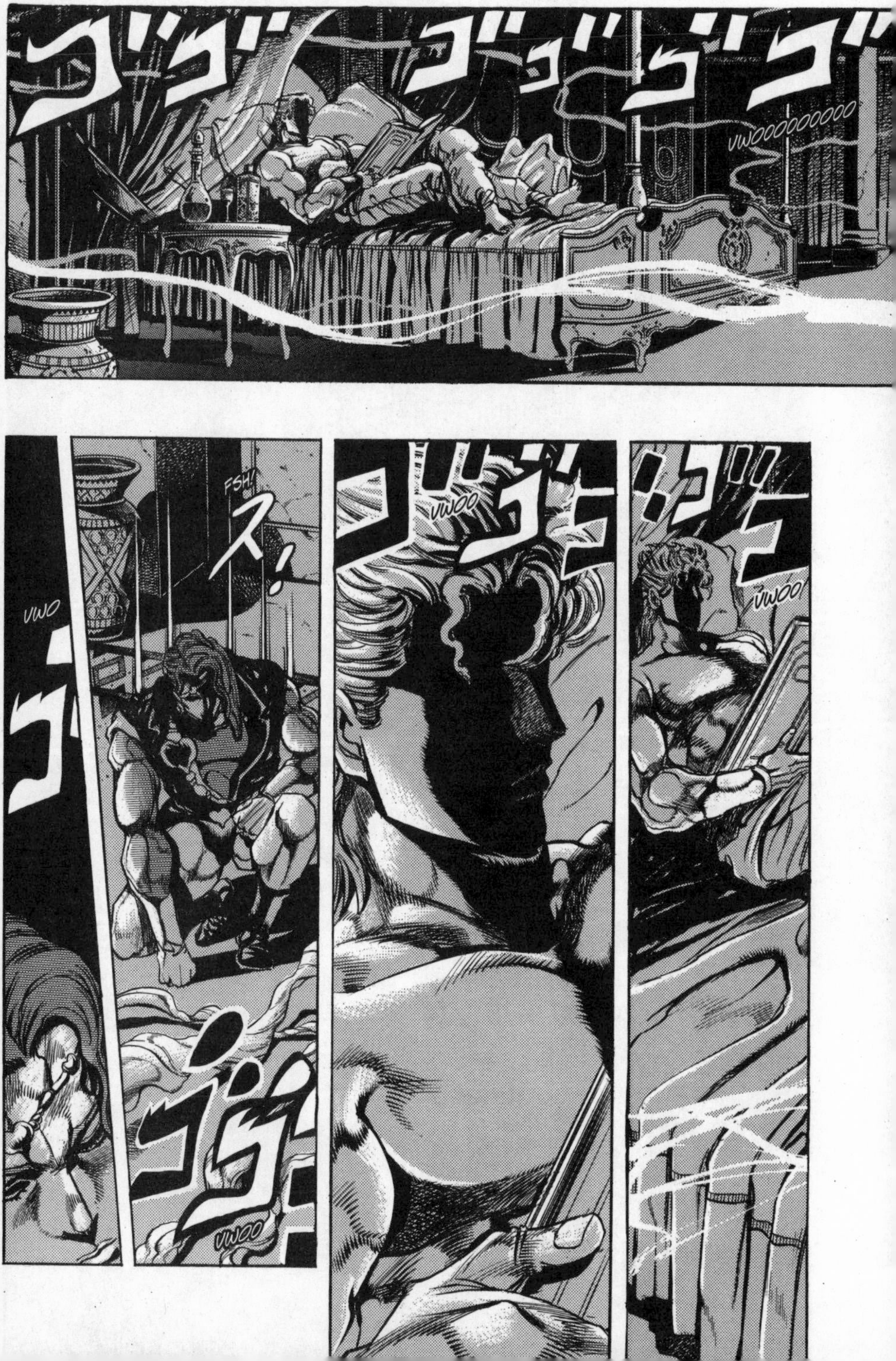
VWOOOOOOOOOO
VWOO
VWOO
FSH!
ス!
VWOO
VWO

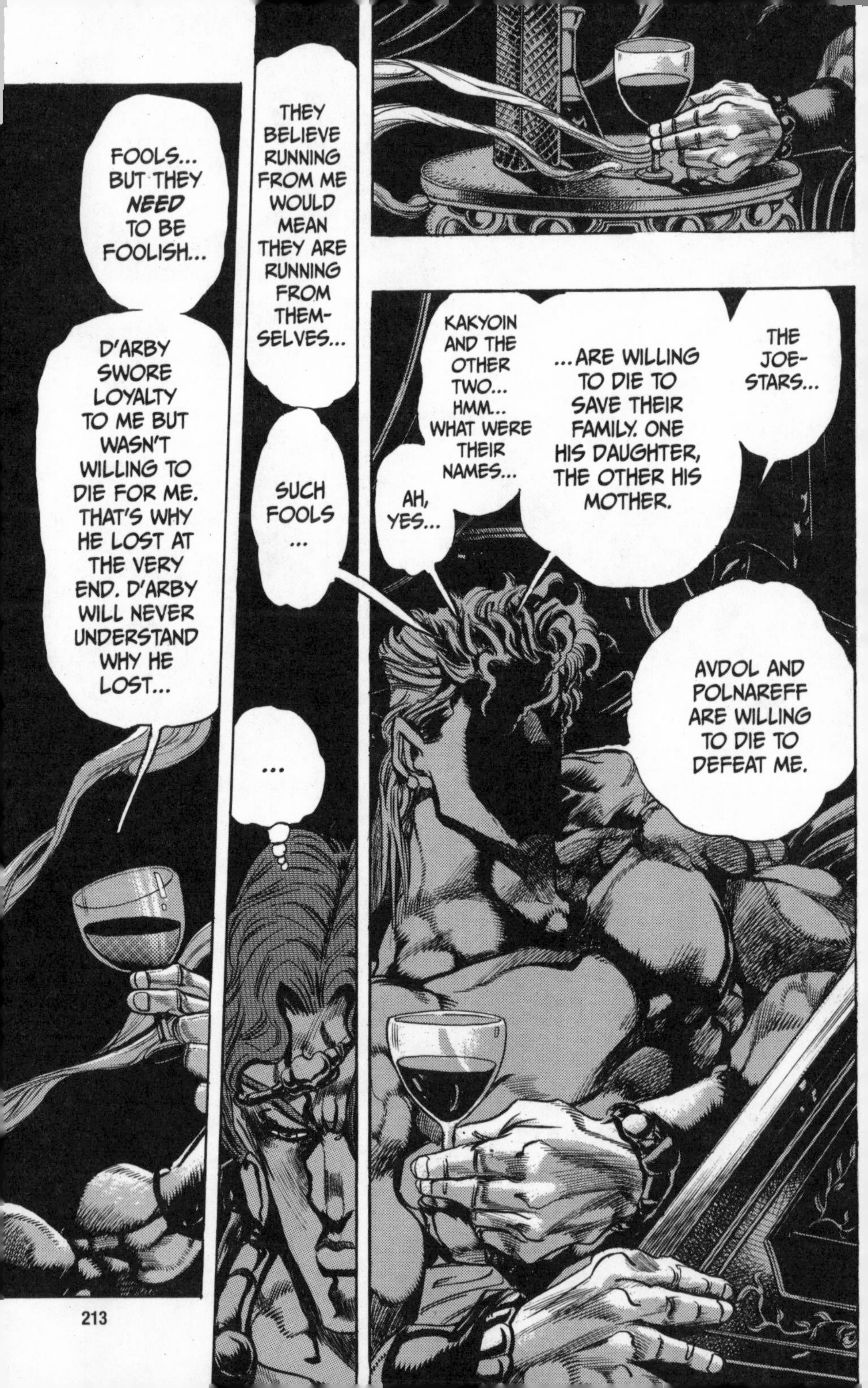
THE JOE-STARS...
...ARE WILLING TO DIE TO SAVE THEIR FAMILY. ONE HIS DAUGHTER, THE OTHER HIS MOTHER.
KAKYOIN AND THE OTHER TWO... HMM... WHAT WERE THEIR NAMES...
AH, YES...
AVDOL AND POLNAREFF ARE WILLING TO DIE TO DEFEAT ME.
THEY BELIEVE RUNNING FROM ME WOULD MEAN THEY ARE RUNNING FROM THEM-SELVES...
SUCH FOOLS ...
...
FOOLS... BUT THEY *NEED* TO BE FOOLISH...
D'ARBY SWORE LOYALTY TO ME BUT WASN'T WILLING TO DIE FOR ME. THAT'S WHY HE LOST AT THE VERY END. D'ARBY WILL NEVER UNDERSTAND WHY HE LOST...

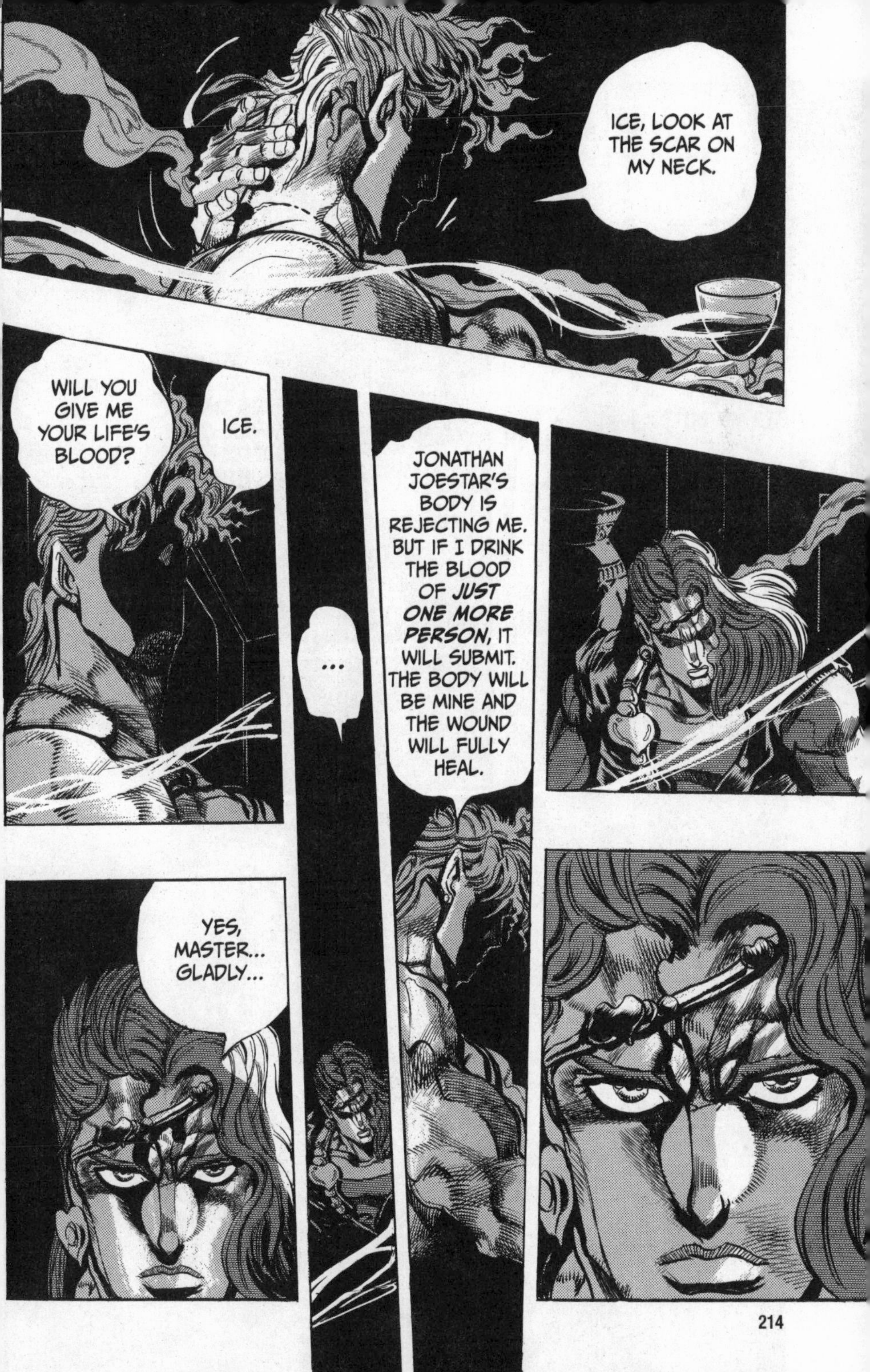
ICE, LOOK AT THE SCAR ON MY NECK.
JONATHAN JOESTAR'S BODY IS REJECTING ME. BUT IF I DRINK THE BLOOD OF *JUST ONE MORE PERSON*, IT WILL SUBMIT. THE BODY WILL BE MINE AND THE WOUND WILL FULLY HEAL.
...
ICE.
WILL YOU GIVE ME YOUR LIFE'S BLOOD?
YES, MASTER... GLADLY...

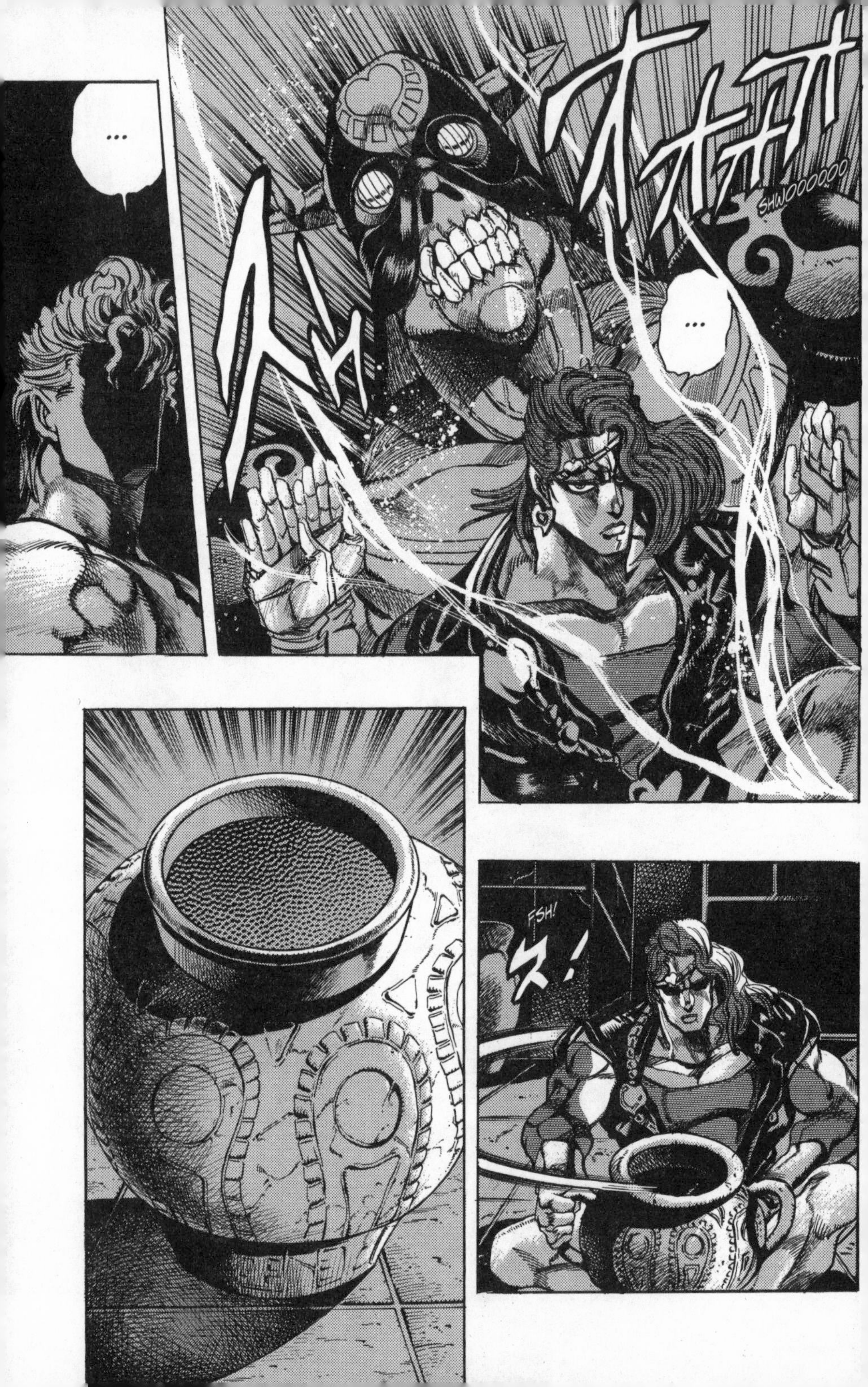
SHWOOOOOO
...
...
FSH!

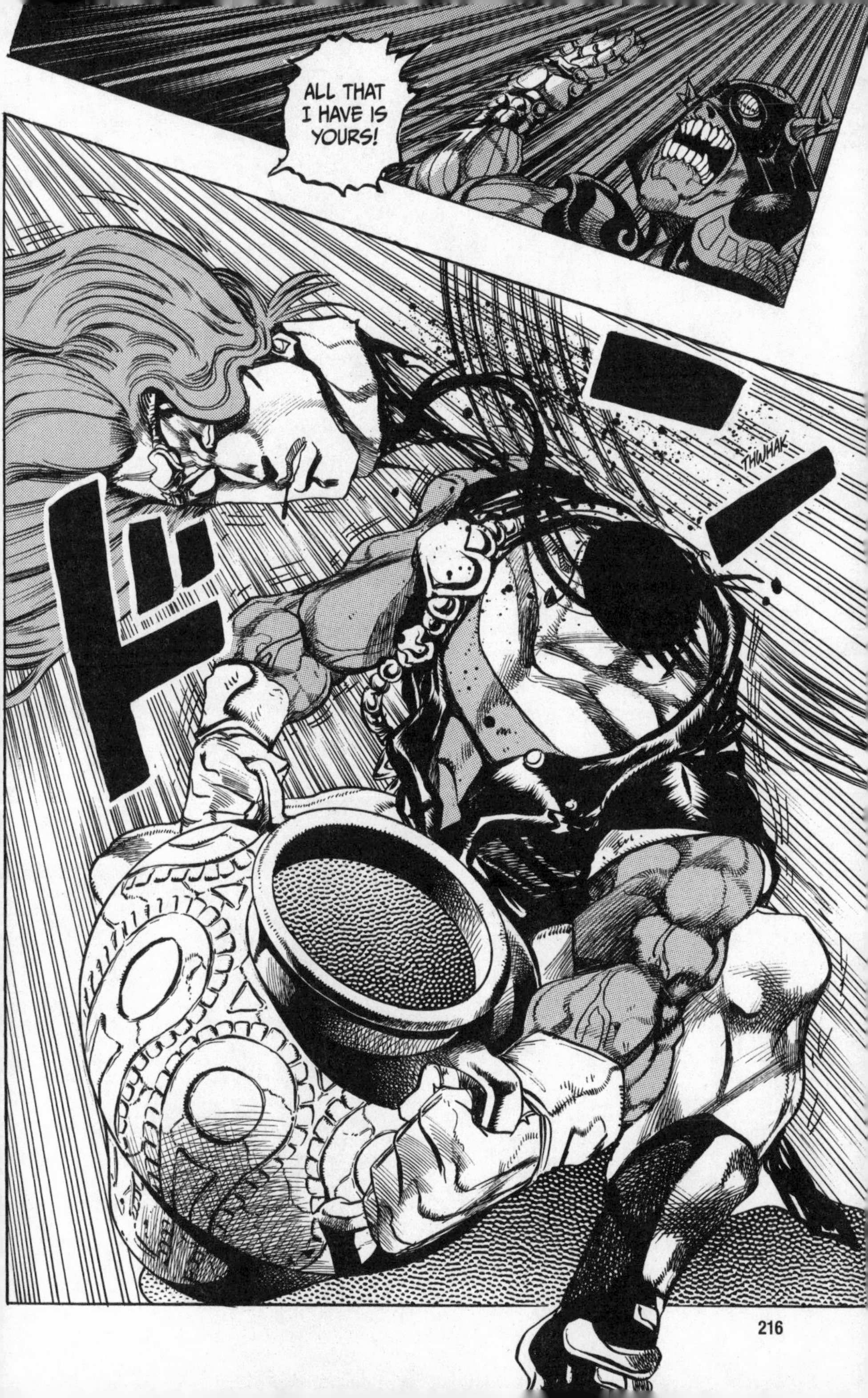
ALL THAT I HAVE IS YOURS!
THWHAK

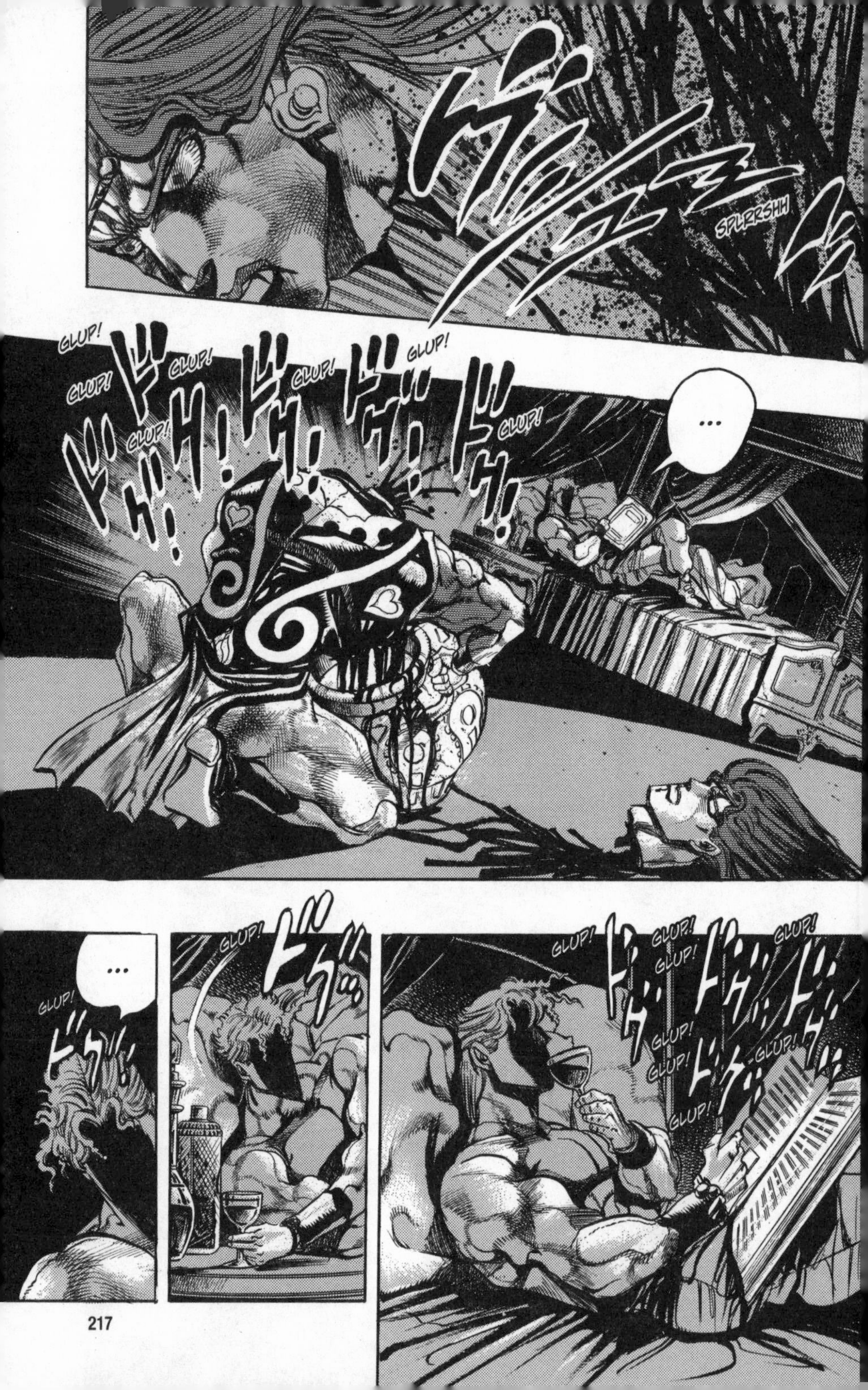
SPLRRSHH
...
GLUP!
GLUP!
GLUP!
GLUP!
GLUP!
GLUP!
GLUP!
GLUP!
GLUP!
GLUP!
GLUP!
GLUP!
GLUP!
GLUP!
GLUP!
...
GLUP!

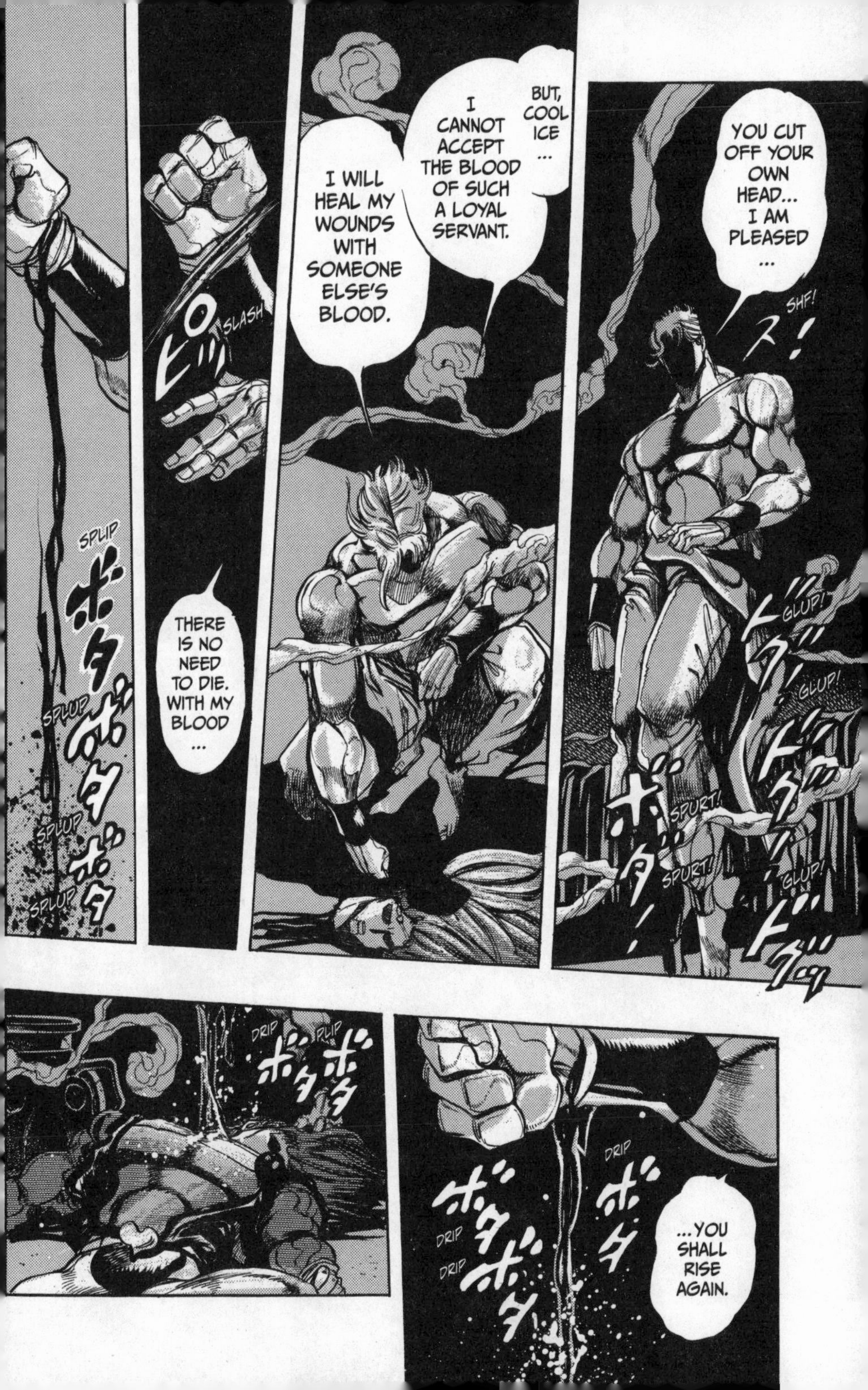
YOU CUT OFF YOUR OWN HEAD... I AM PLEASED ...
SHF!
GLUP!
GLUP!
GLUP!
SPURT!
SPURT!
BUT, COOL ICE ...
I CANNOT ACCEPT THE BLOOD OF SUCH A LOYAL SERVANT.
I WILL HEAL MY WOUNDS WITH SOMEONE ELSE'S BLOOD.
SLASH
THERE IS NO NEED TO DIE. WITH MY BLOOD ...
SPLIP
SPLUP
SPLUP
SPLUP
DRIP
DRIP
DRIP
...YOU SHALL RISE AGAIN.
DRIP
SPLIP

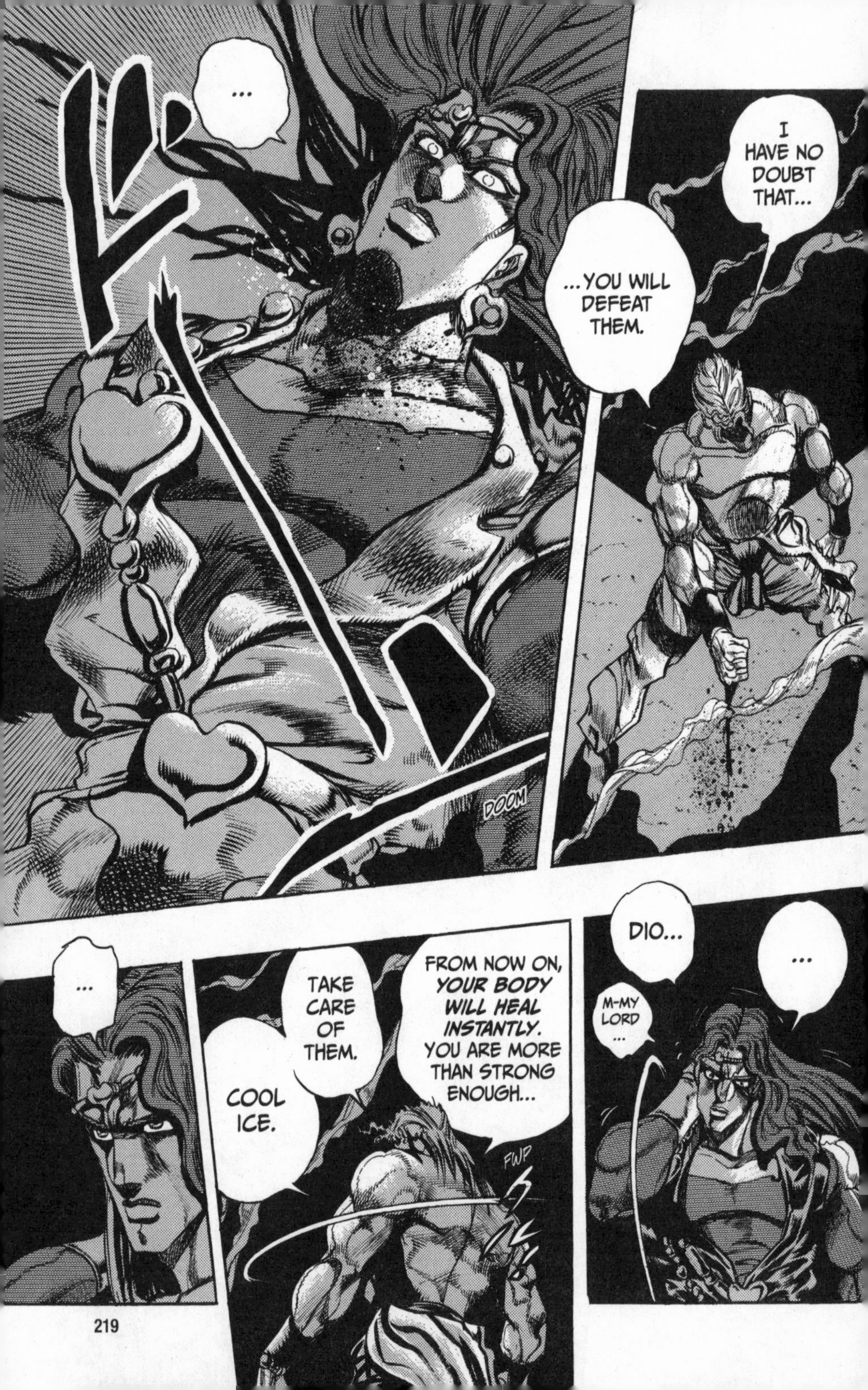
I HAVE NO DOUBT THAT...
...YOU WILL DEFEAT THEM.
...
DOOM
DIO...
...
M-MY LORD ...
FROM NOW ON, *YOUR BODY WILL HEAL INSTANTLY.* YOU ARE MORE THAN STRONG ENOUGH...
TAKE CARE OF THEM.
COOL ICE.
FWP
...

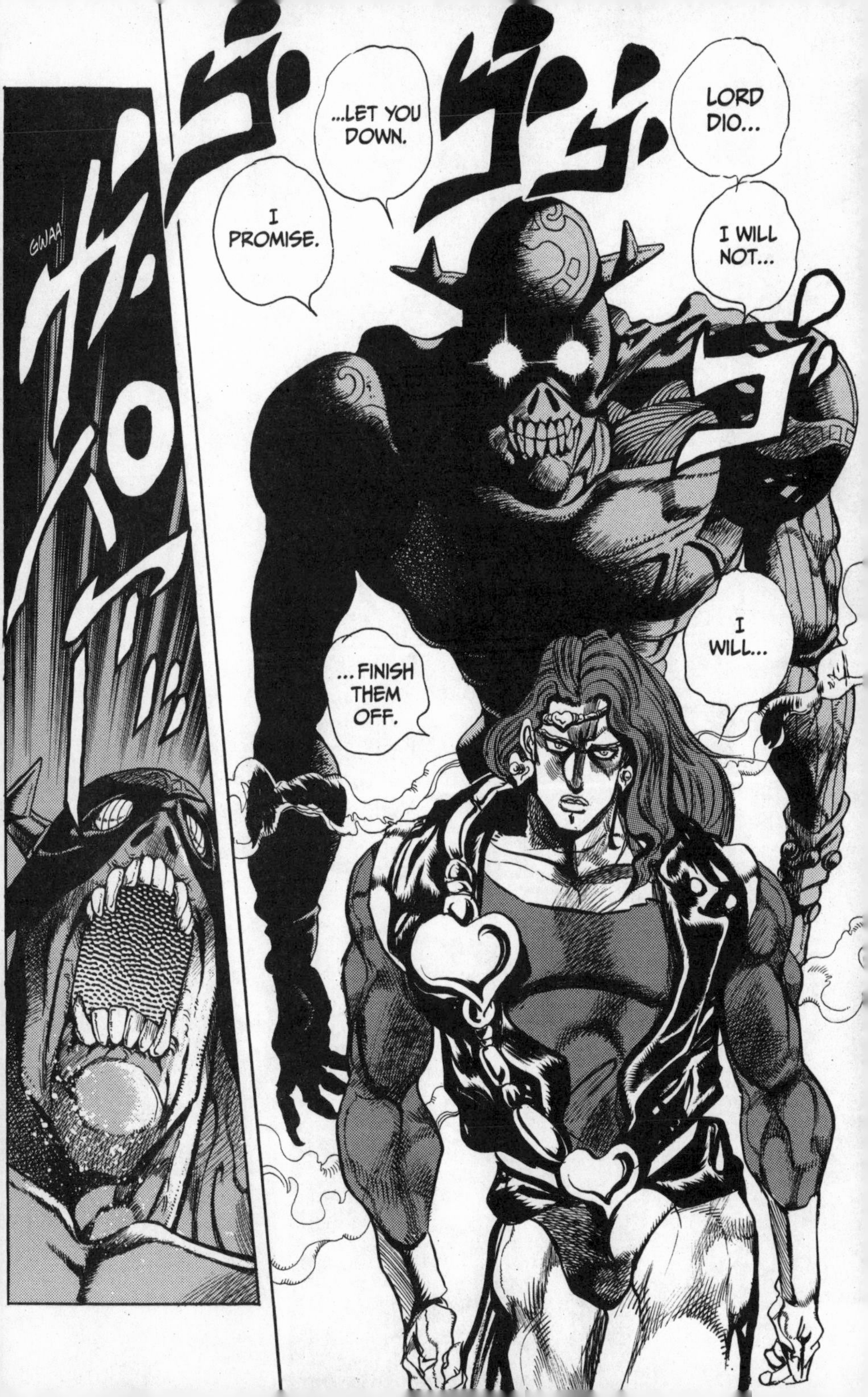
LORD DIO...
I WILL NOT...
...LET YOU DOWN.
I PROMISE.
I WILL...
...FINISH THEM OFF.
GWAA

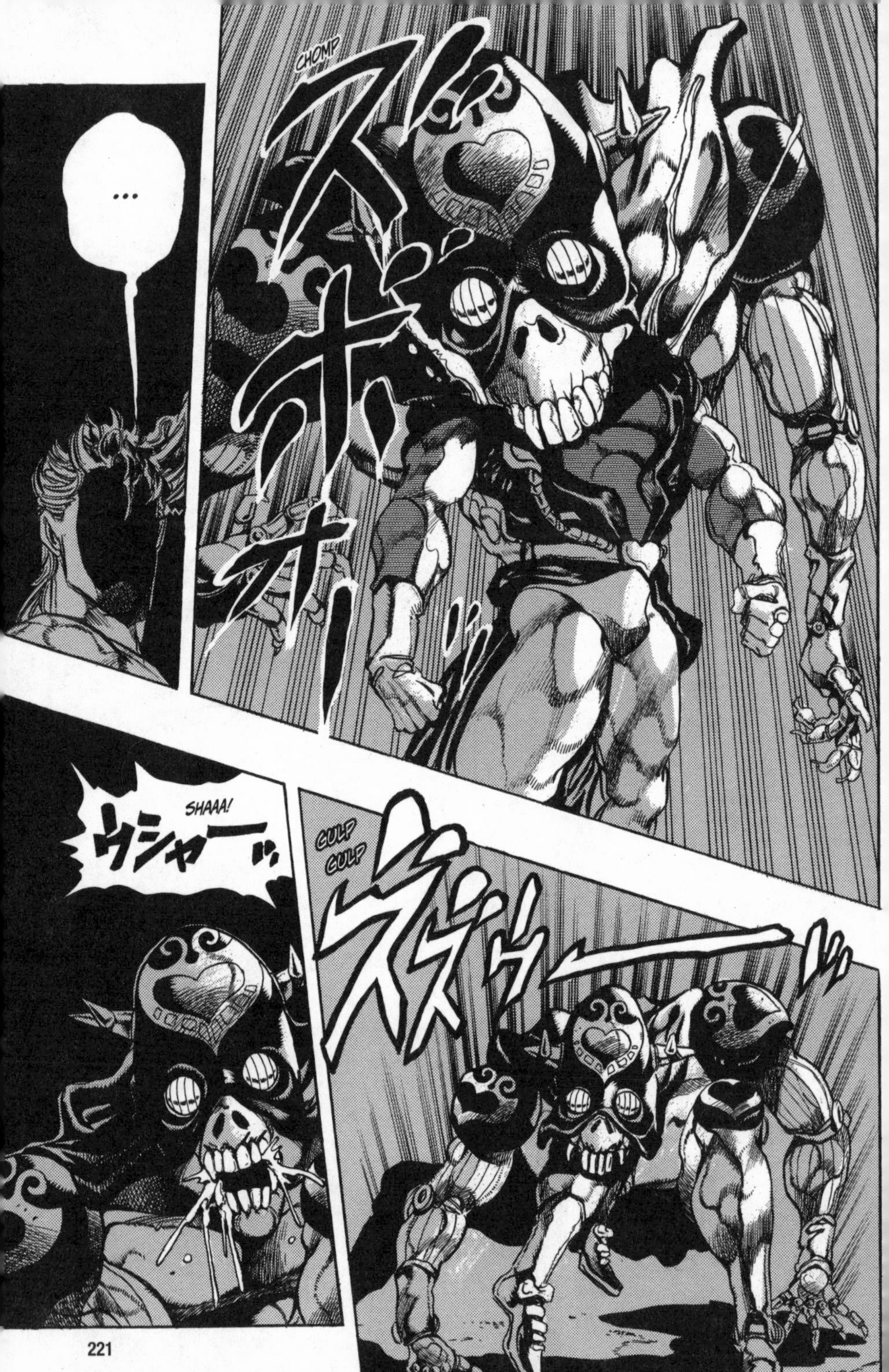
CHOMP
...
GULP GULP
SHAAA!
ウシャーッ

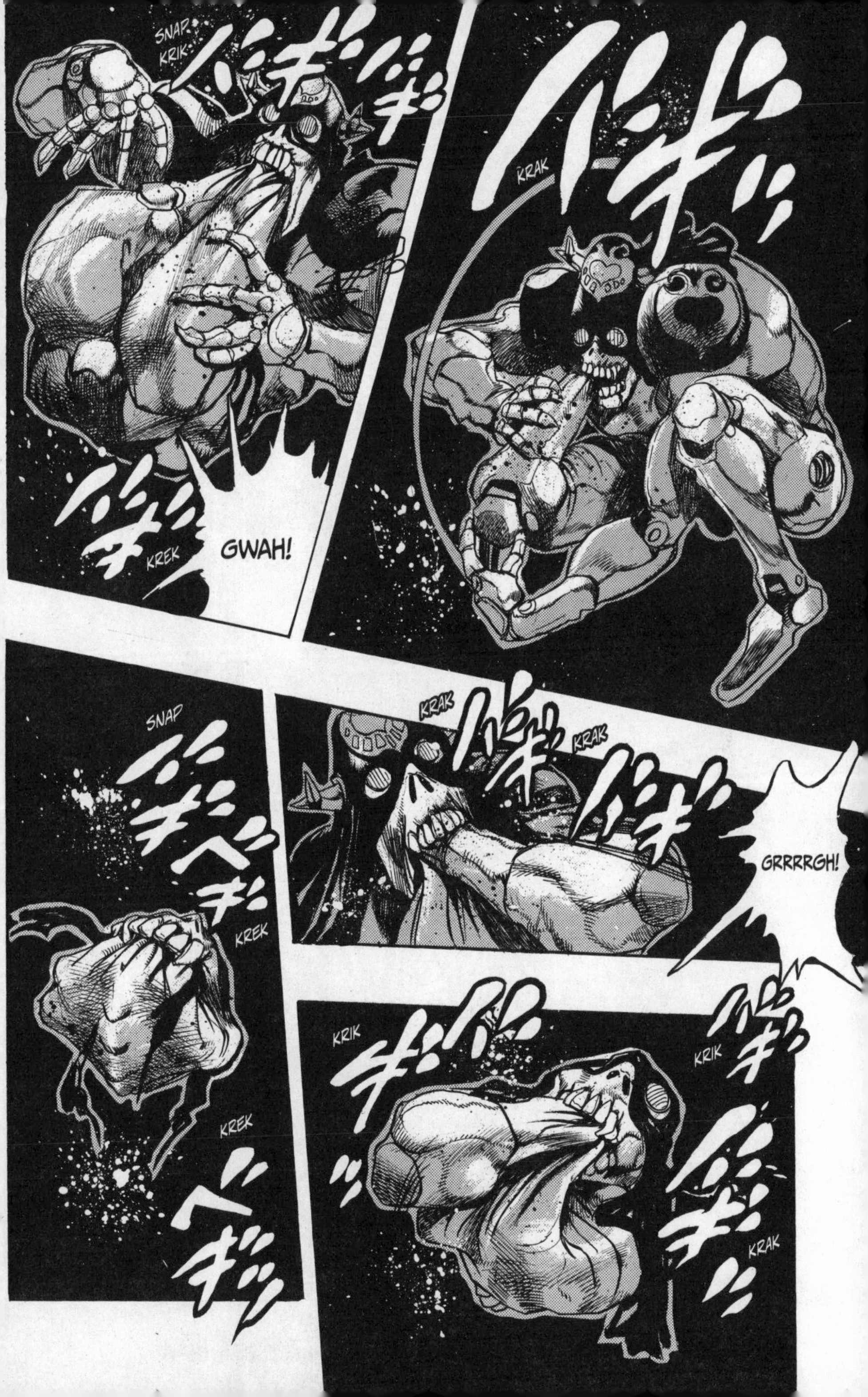
KRAK
SNAP
KRIK
KREK
GWAH!
KRAK
KRAK
GRRRRGH!
KRIK
KRIK
KRAK
SNAP
KREK
KREK

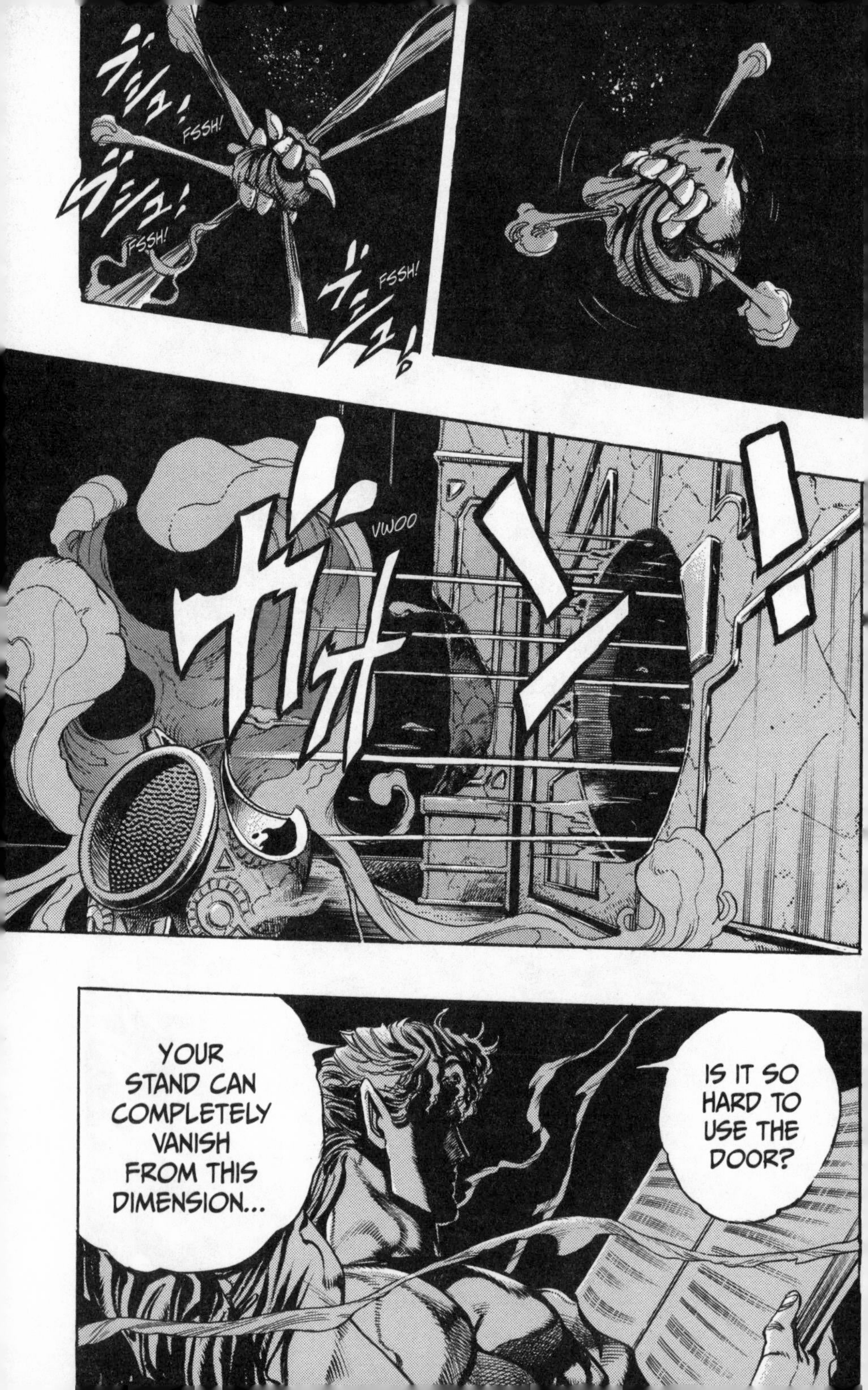
FSSH!
FSSH!
FSSH!
VWOO
IS IT SO HARD TO USE THE DOOR?
YOUR STAND CAN COMPLETELY VANISH FROM THIS DIMENSION...

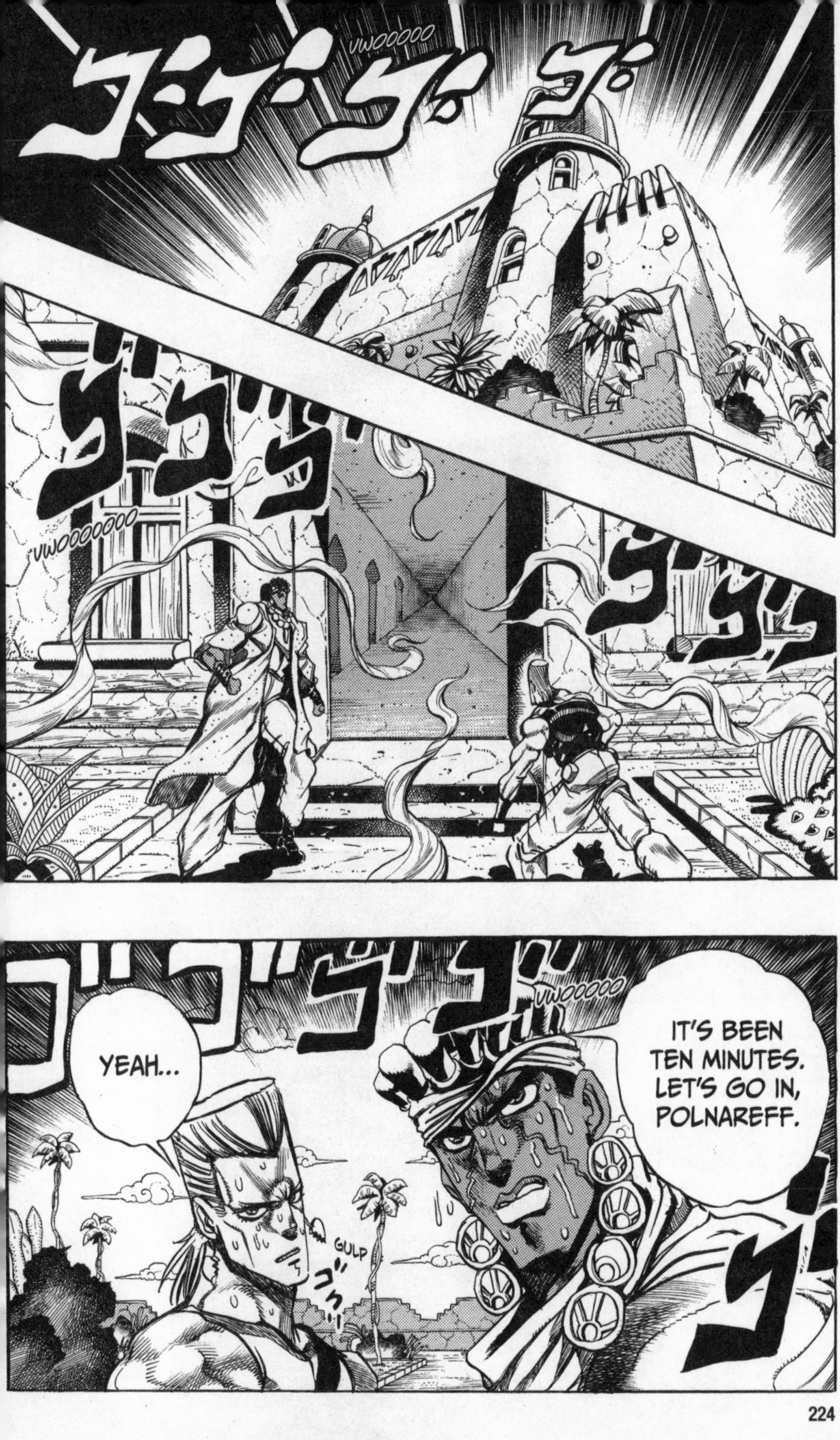
VWOOOOO
VWOOOOOOOO
VWOOOOO
IT'S BEEN TEN MINUTES. LET'S GO IN, POLNAREFF.
GULP
YEAH...

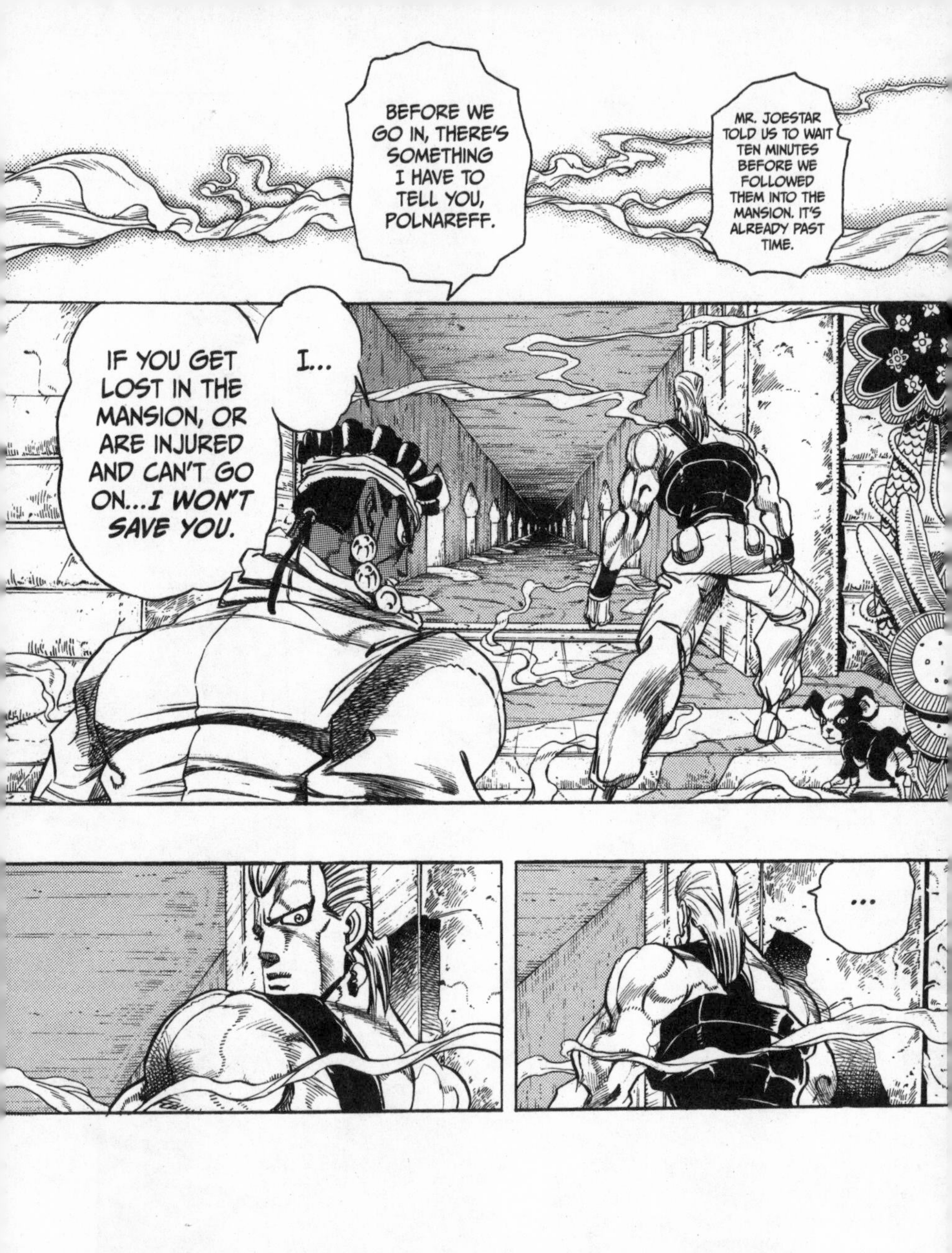
MR. JOESTAR TOLD US TO WAIT TEN MINUTES BEFORE WE FOLLOWED THEM INTO THE MANSION. IT'S ALREADY PAST TIME.
BEFORE WE GO IN, THERE'S SOMETHING I HAVE TO TELL YOU, POLNAREFF.
I...
IF YOU GET LOST IN THE MANSION, OR ARE INJURED AND CAN'T GO ON...I WON'T SAVE YOU.
...

CHAPTER 126: The Dark Void of Cool Ice PART 2

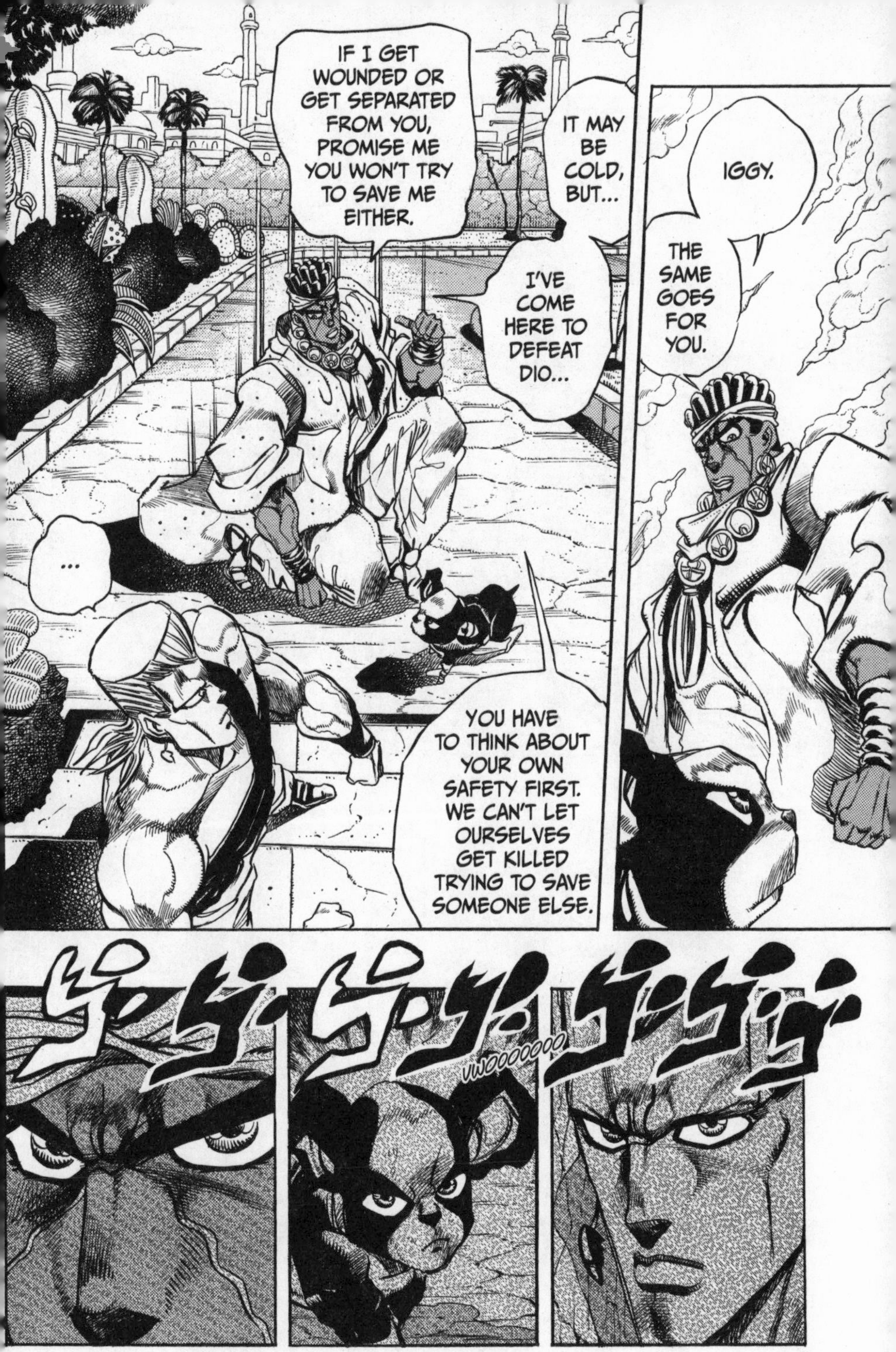
IGGY.
THE SAME GOES FOR YOU.
IT MAY BE COLD, BUT...
I'VE COME HERE TO DEFEAT DIO...
YOU HAVE TO THINK ABOUT YOUR OWN SAFETY FIRST. WE CAN'T LET OURSELVES GET KILLED TRYING TO SAVE SOMEONE ELSE.
IF I GET WOUNDED OR GET SEPARATED FROM YOU, PROMISE ME YOU WON'T TRY TO SAVE ME EITHER.
...
VWOOOOOOO

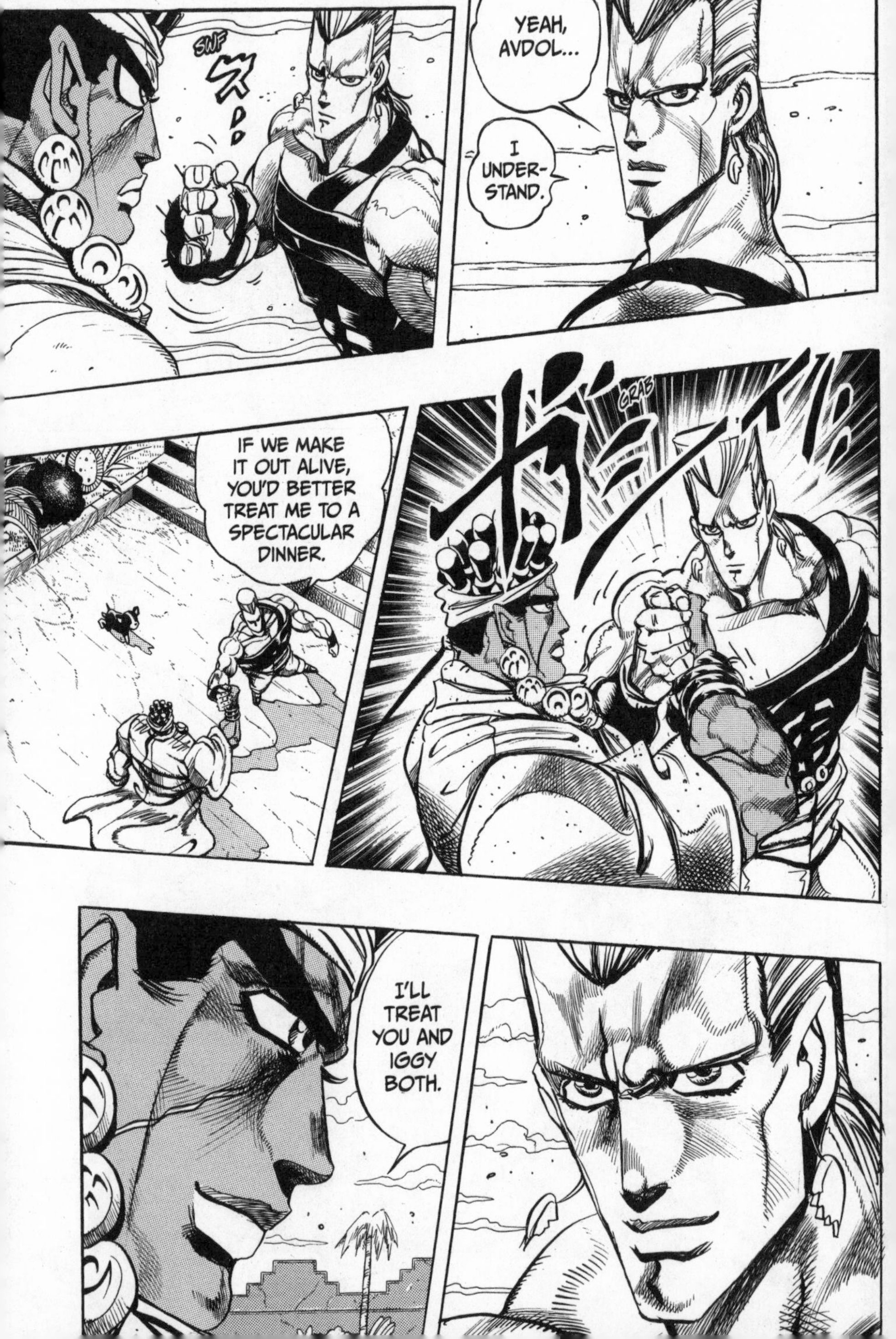
YEAH, AVDOL...
I UNDER-STAND.
SWF
IF WE MAKE IT OUT ALIVE, YOU'D BETTER TREAT ME TO A SPECTACULAR DINNER.
GRAB
I'LL TREAT YOU AND IGGY BOTH.

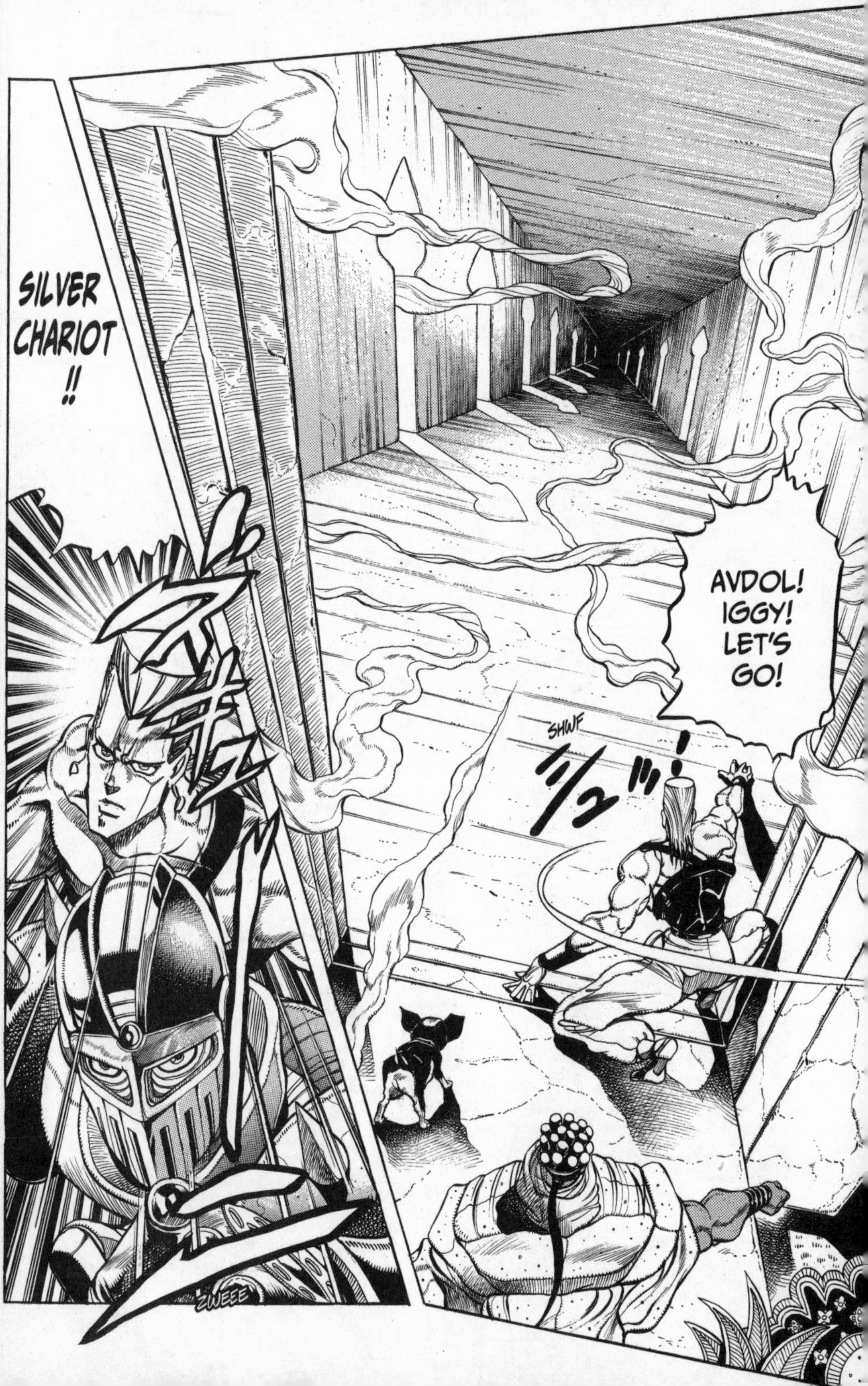
AVDOL! IGGY! LET'S GO!
SHWF
SILVER CHARIOT !!
ZWEEE

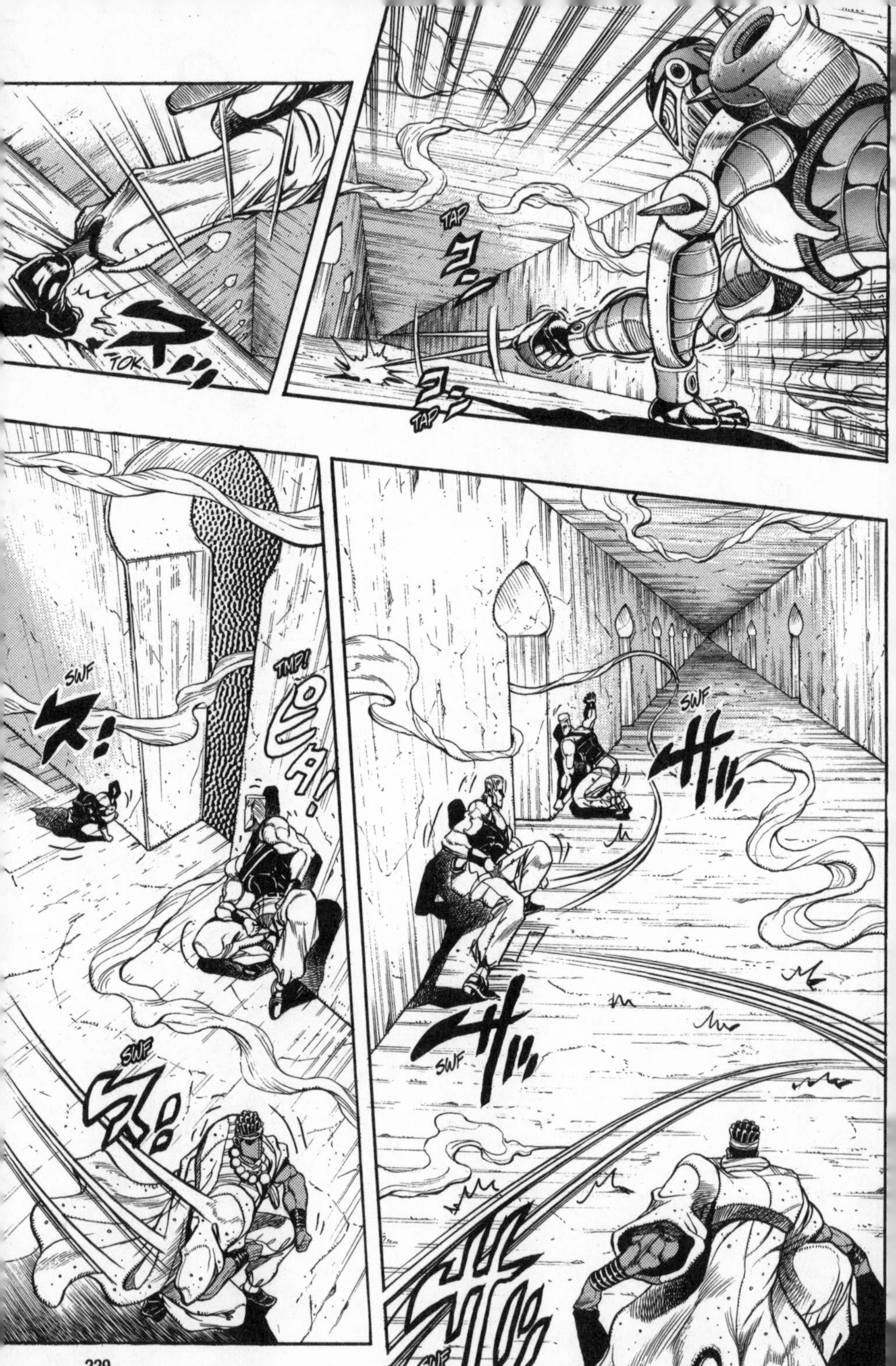
TAP
TAP
TOK
SWF
SWF
SWF
TMP!
SWF
SWF

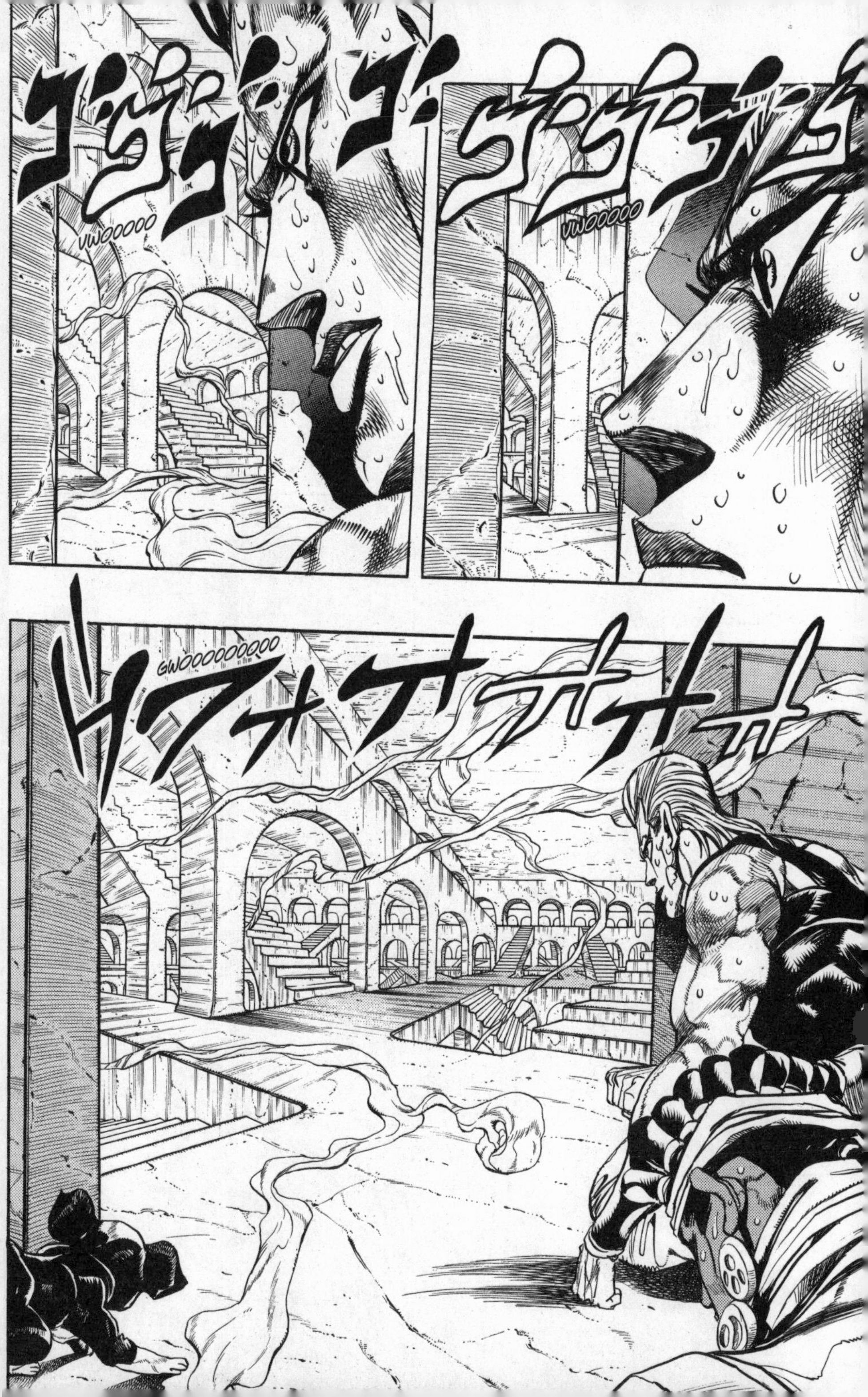
VWOOOOOO
VWOOOOO
GWOOOOOOOOO

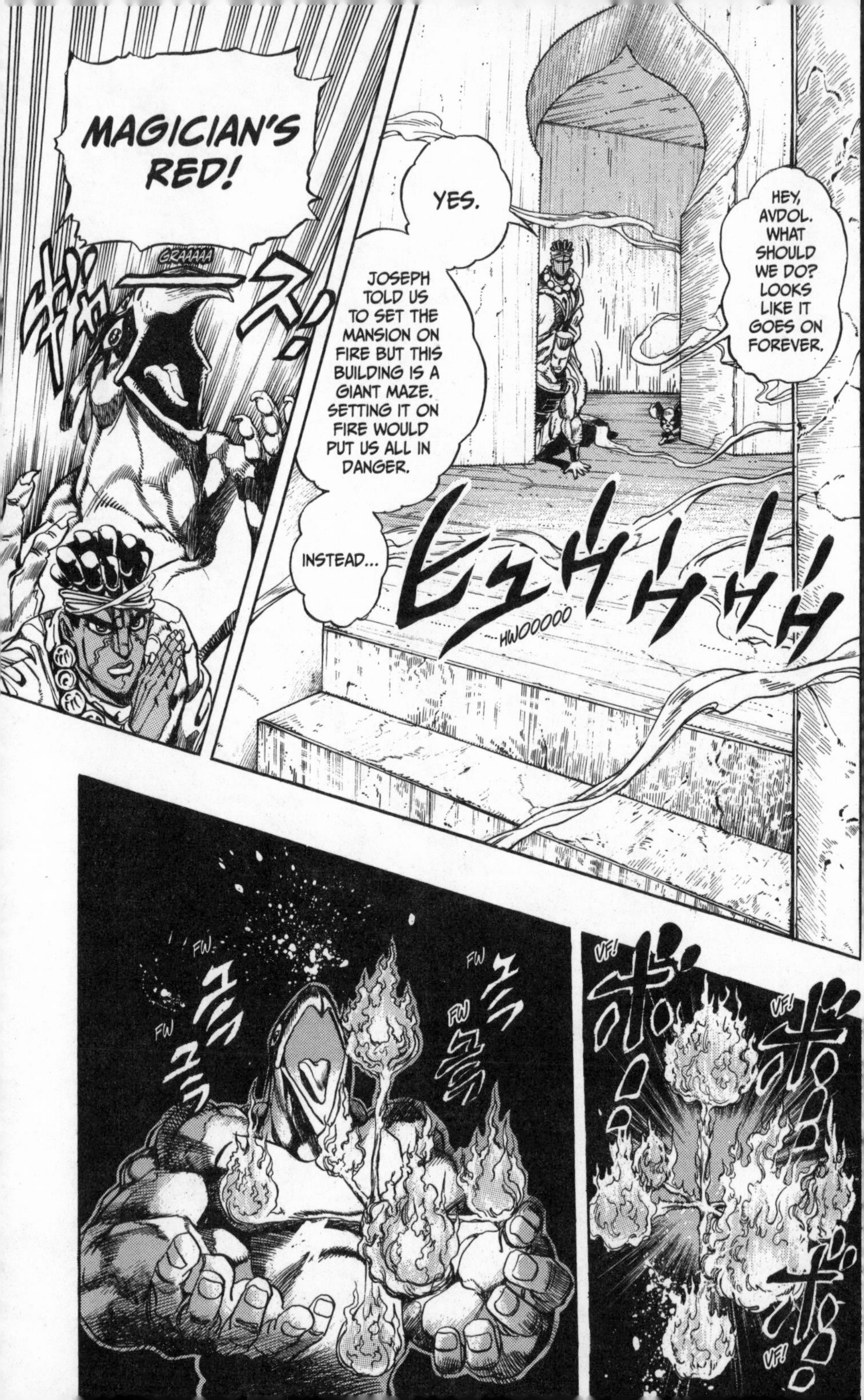
HEY, AVDOL. WHAT SHOULD WE DO? LOOKS LIKE IT GOES ON FOREVER.
YES.
JOSEPH TOLD US TO SET THE MANSION ON FIRE BUT THIS BUILDING IS A GIANT MAZE. SETTING IT ON FIRE WOULD PUT US ALL IN DANGER.
INSTEAD...
HWOOOOO
MAGICIAN'S RED!
GRAAAAA
VF!
VF!
VF!
FW
FW
FW
FW

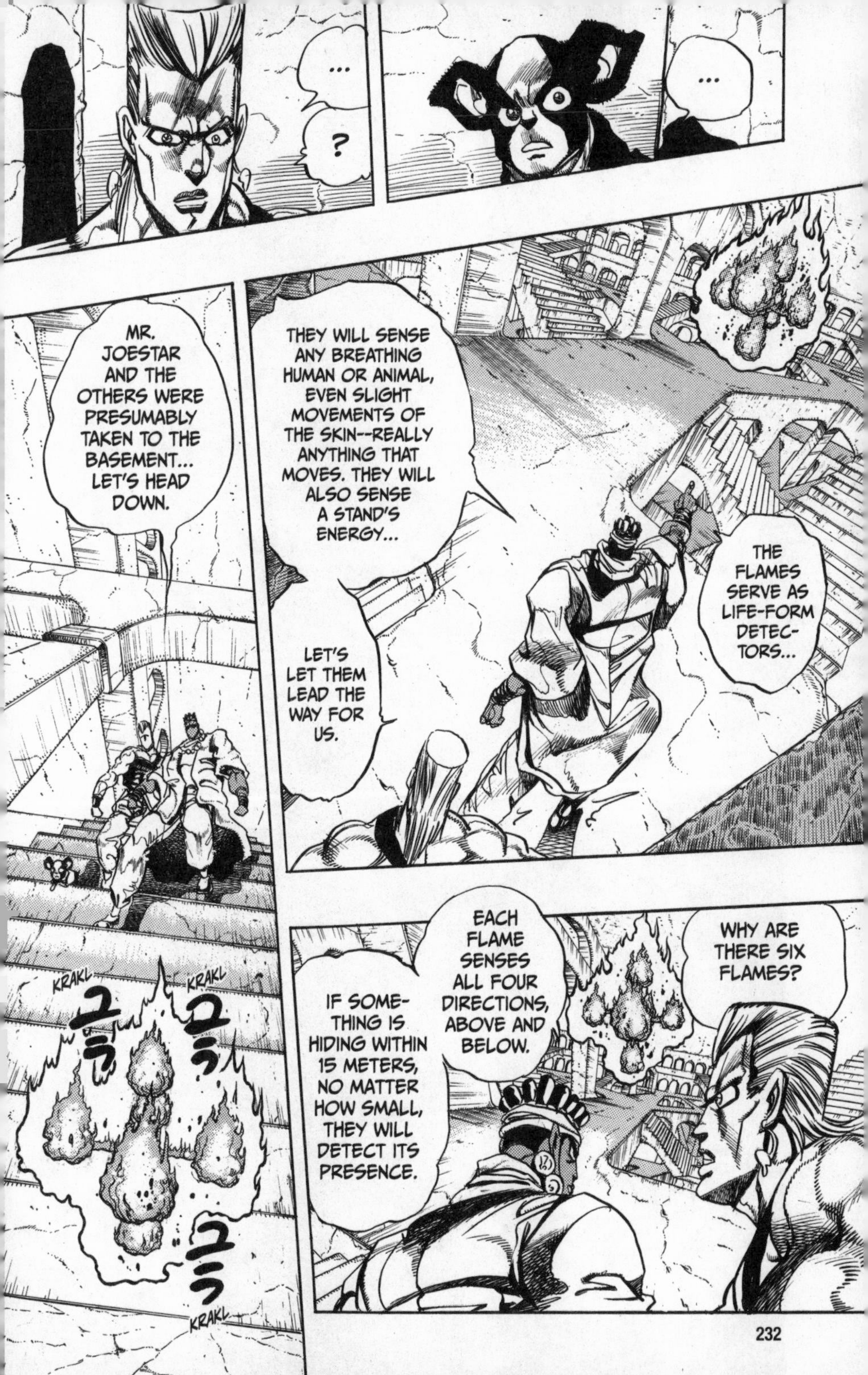
...
...
?
THE FLAMES SERVE AS LIFE-FORM DETECTORS...
THEY WILL SENSE ANY BREATHING HUMAN OR ANIMAL, EVEN SLIGHT MOVEMENTS OF THE SKIN--REALLY ANYTHING THAT MOVES. THEY WILL ALSO SENSE A STAND'S ENERGY...
LET'S LET THEM LEAD THE WAY FOR US.
MR. JOESTAR AND THE OTHERS WERE PRESUMABLY TAKEN TO THE BASEMENT... LET'S HEAD DOWN.
WHY ARE THERE SIX FLAMES?
EACH FLAME SENSES ALL FOUR DIRECTIONS, ABOVE AND BELOW.
IF SOMETHING IS HIDING WITHIN 15 METERS, NO MATTER HOW SMALL, THEY WILL DETECT ITS PRESENCE.
KRAKL ユラ
KRAKL ユラ
ユラ KRAKL

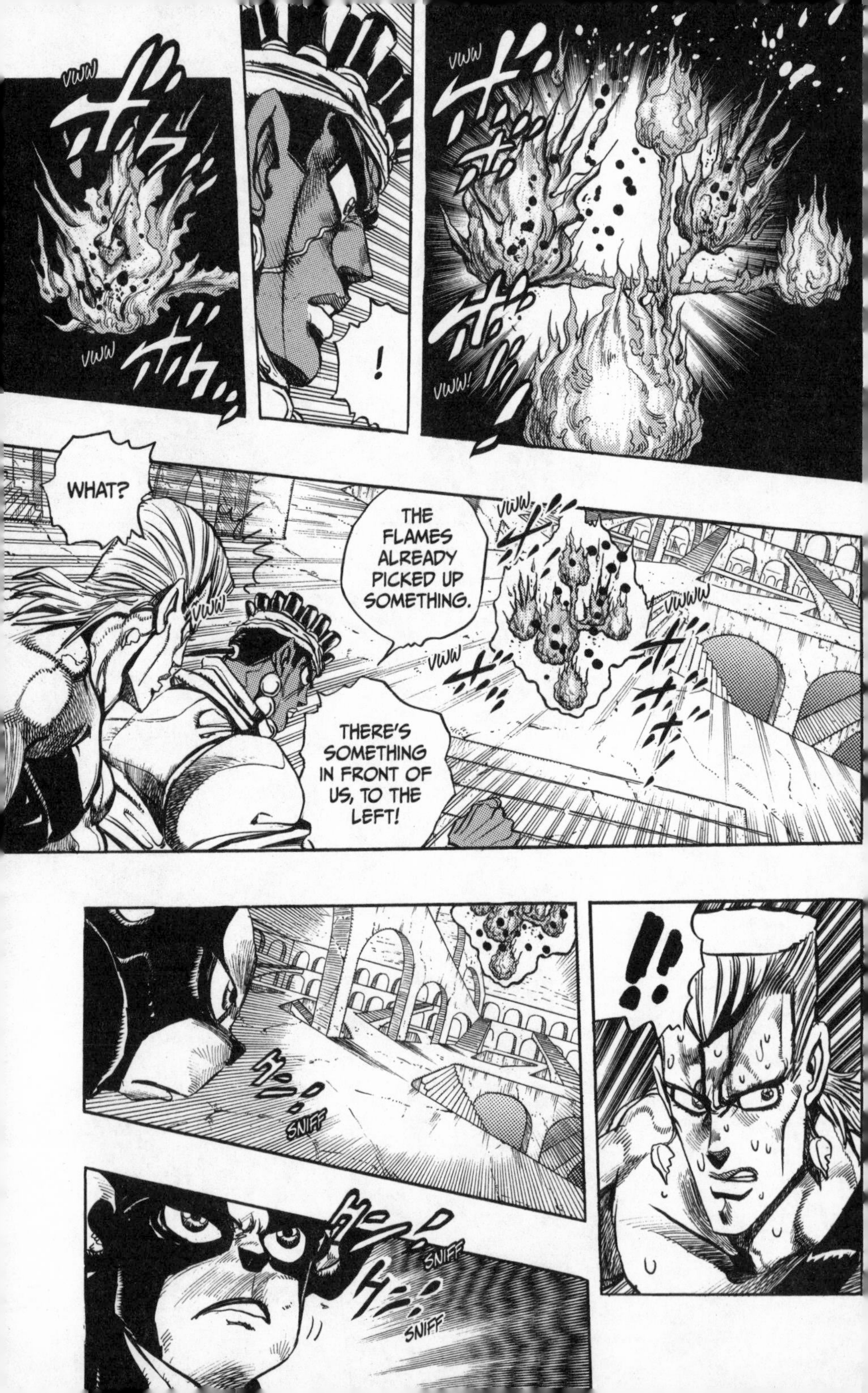
VWW
VWW!
!
VWW
VWW
VWWW
VWW
THE FLAMES ALREADY PICKED UP SOMETHING.
VWW
WHAT?
THERE'S SOMETHING IN FRONT OF US, TO THE LEFT!
!!
SNIFF
SNIFF
SNIFF

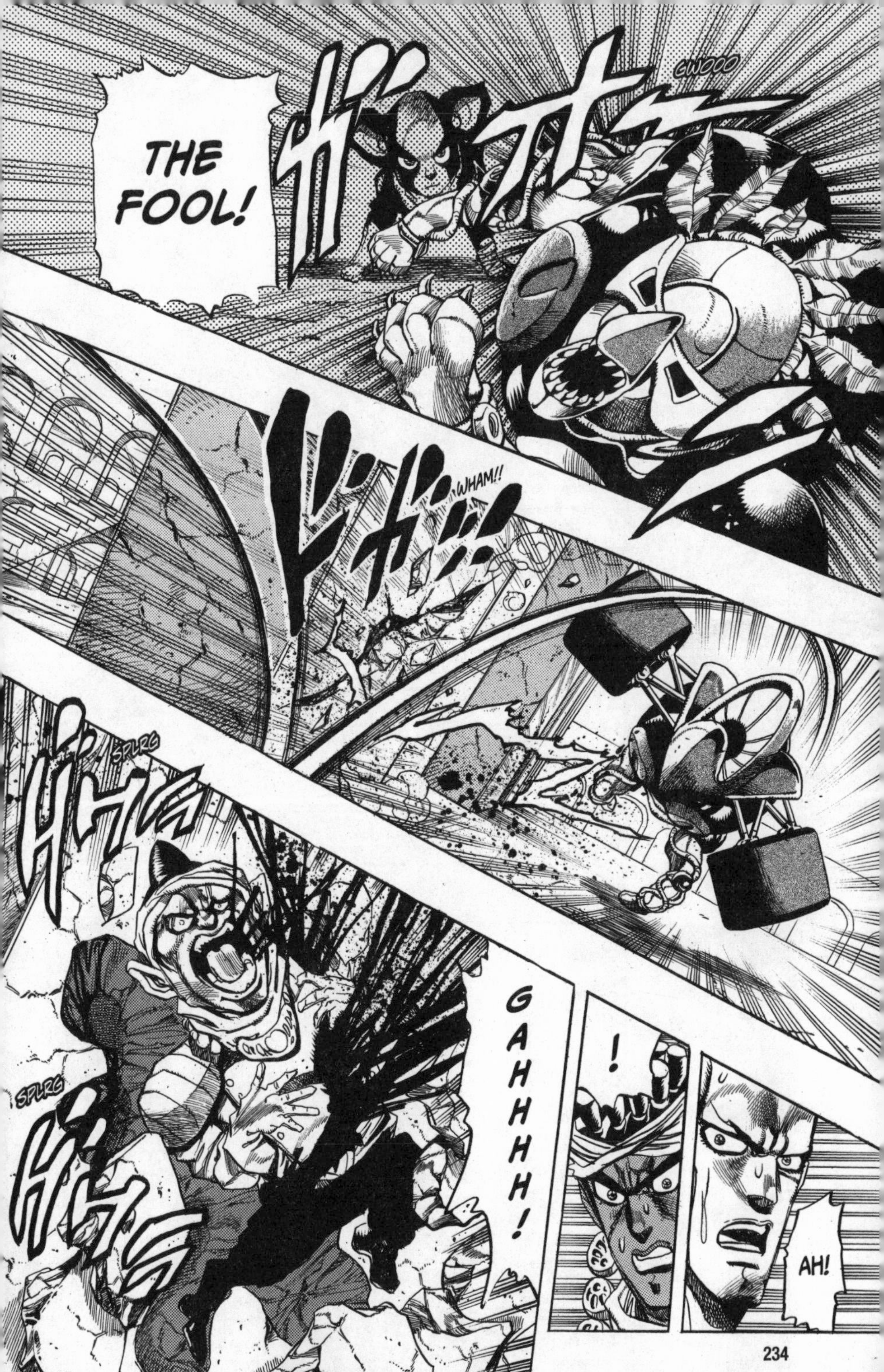
THE FOOL!
GWOOO
WHAM!!
AH!
!
GAHHHHH!
SPLRG
SPLRG

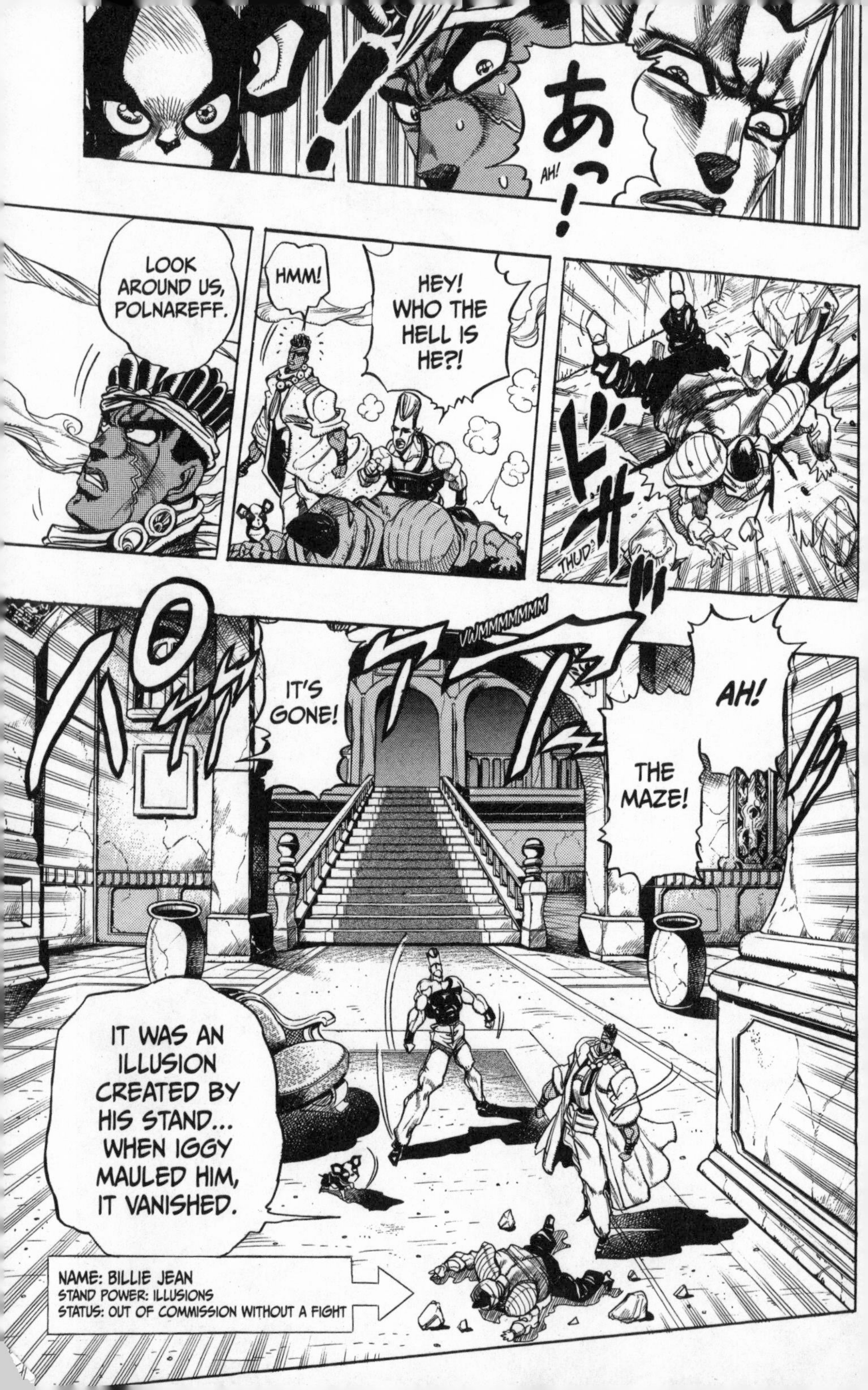

あっ!
AH!
ドサッ
THUD
HEY! WHO THE HELL IS HE?!
HMM!
LOOK AROUND US, POLNAREFF.
AH!
THE MAZE!
VWMMMMMMMM
IT'S GONE!
IT WAS AN ILLUSION CREATED BY HIS STAND... WHEN IGGY MAULED HIM, IT VANISHED.
NAME: BILLIE JEAN
STAND POWER: ILLUSIONS
STATUS: OUT OF COMMISSION WITHOUT A FIGHT

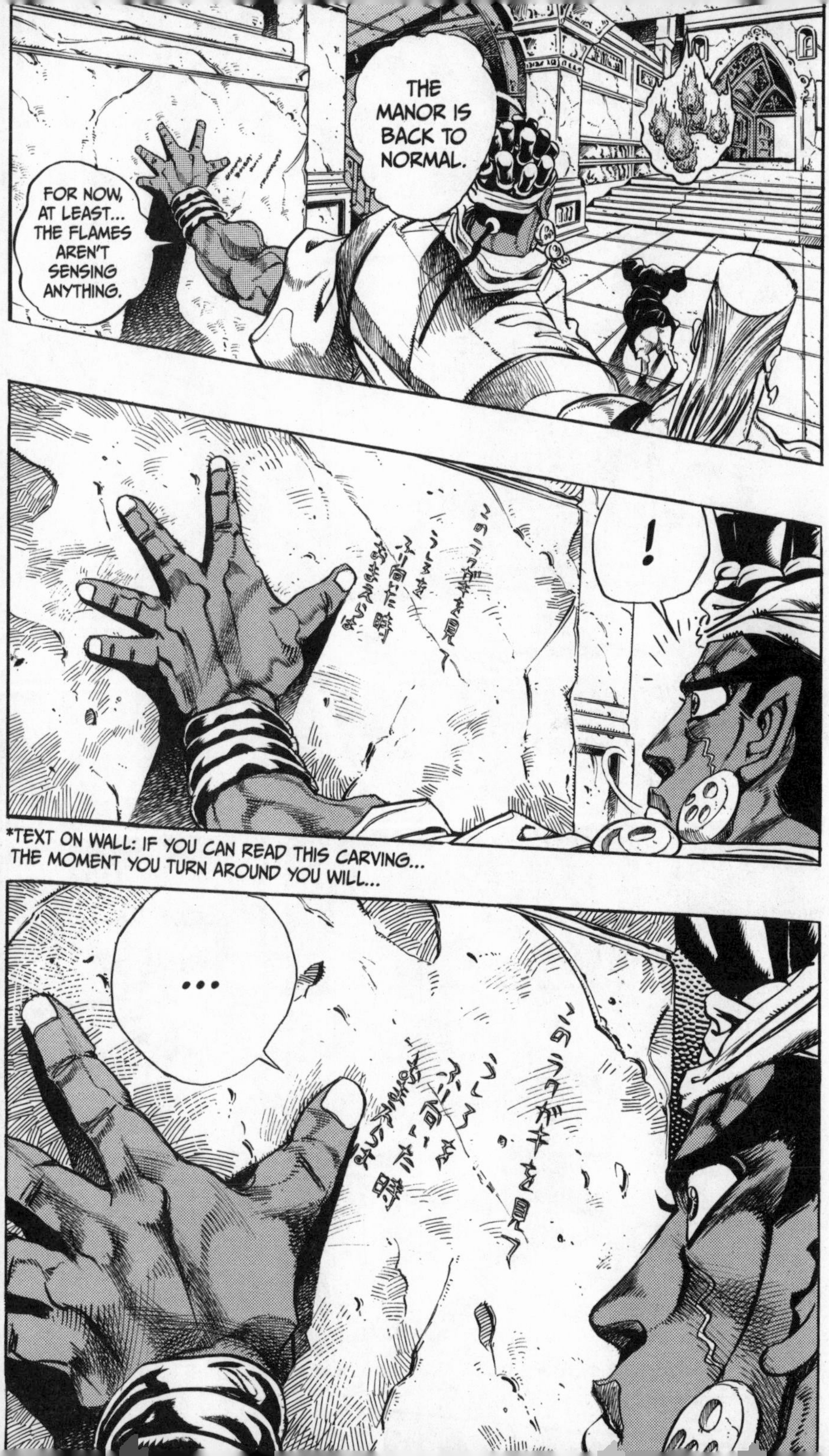
THE MANOR IS BACK TO NORMAL.
FOR NOW, AT LEAST... THE FLAMES AREN'T SENSING ANYTHING.
!
*TEXT ON WALL: IF YOU CAN READ THIS CARVING... THE MOMENT YOU TURN AROUND YOU WILL...
...

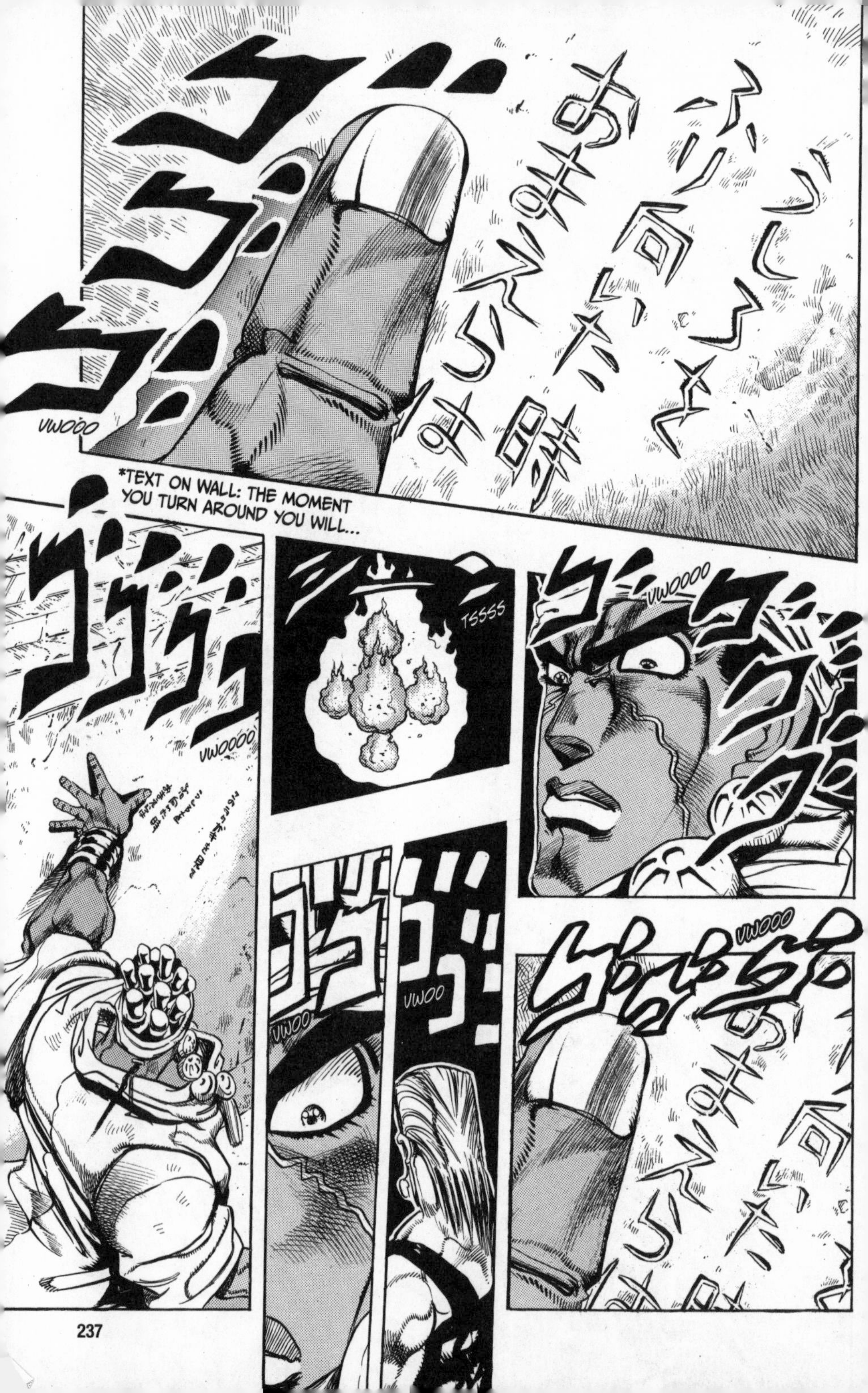

ふり向いた時
おまえらは
VWOOO
*TEXT ON WALL: THE MOMENT YOU TURN AROUND YOU WILL...
VWOOOO
TSSSS
VWOOOO
VWOOO
VWOO
VWOO

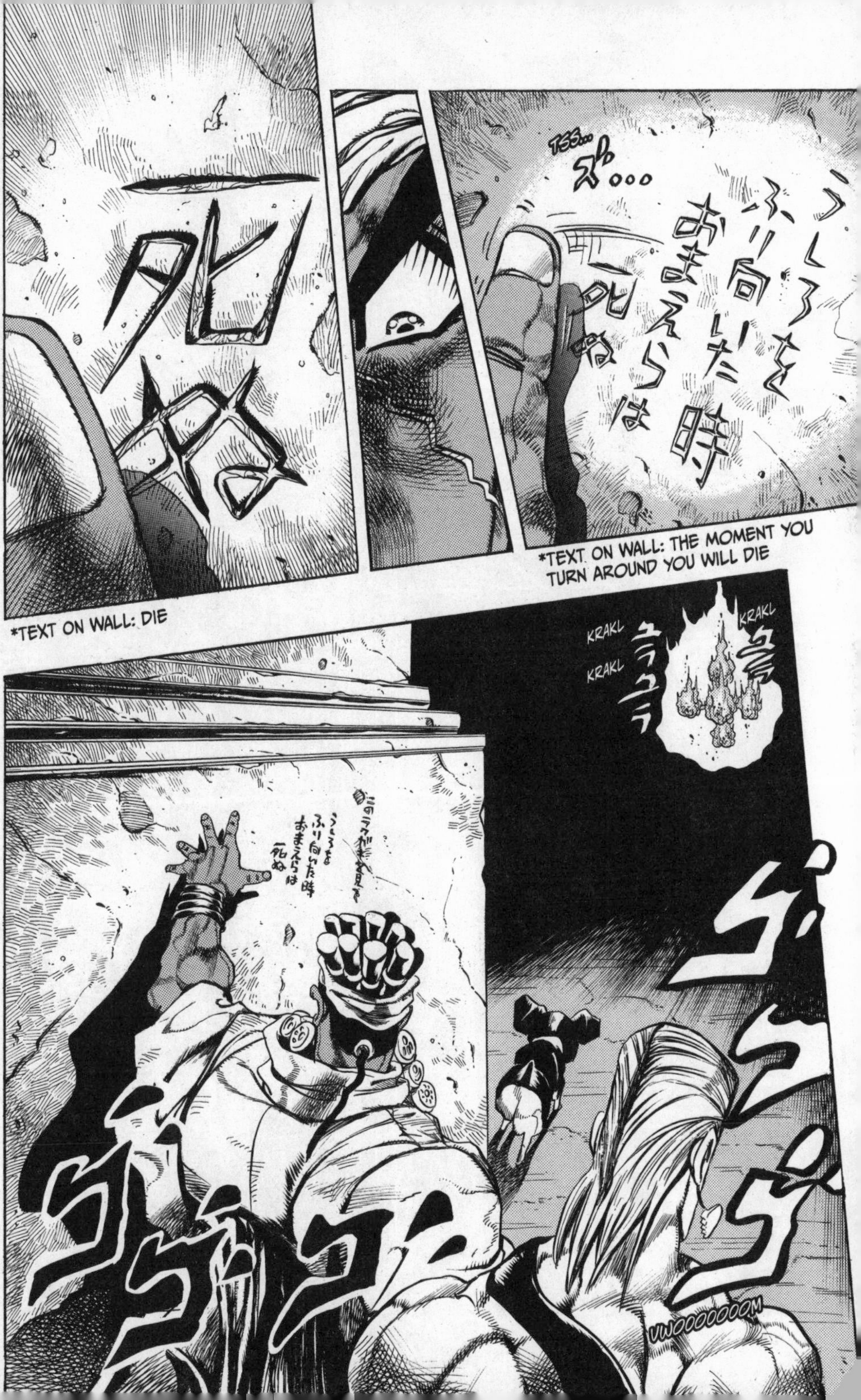
TSS...
うしろを
ふり向いた時
おまえらは
死ぬ
*TEXT ON WALL: THE MOMENT YOU TURN AROUND YOU WILL DIE
死ね
*TEXT ON WALL: DIE
KRAKL
KRAKL
KRAKL
このラクガキを見て
うしろをふり向いた時
おまえらは
死ぬ
UWOOOOOOOOM

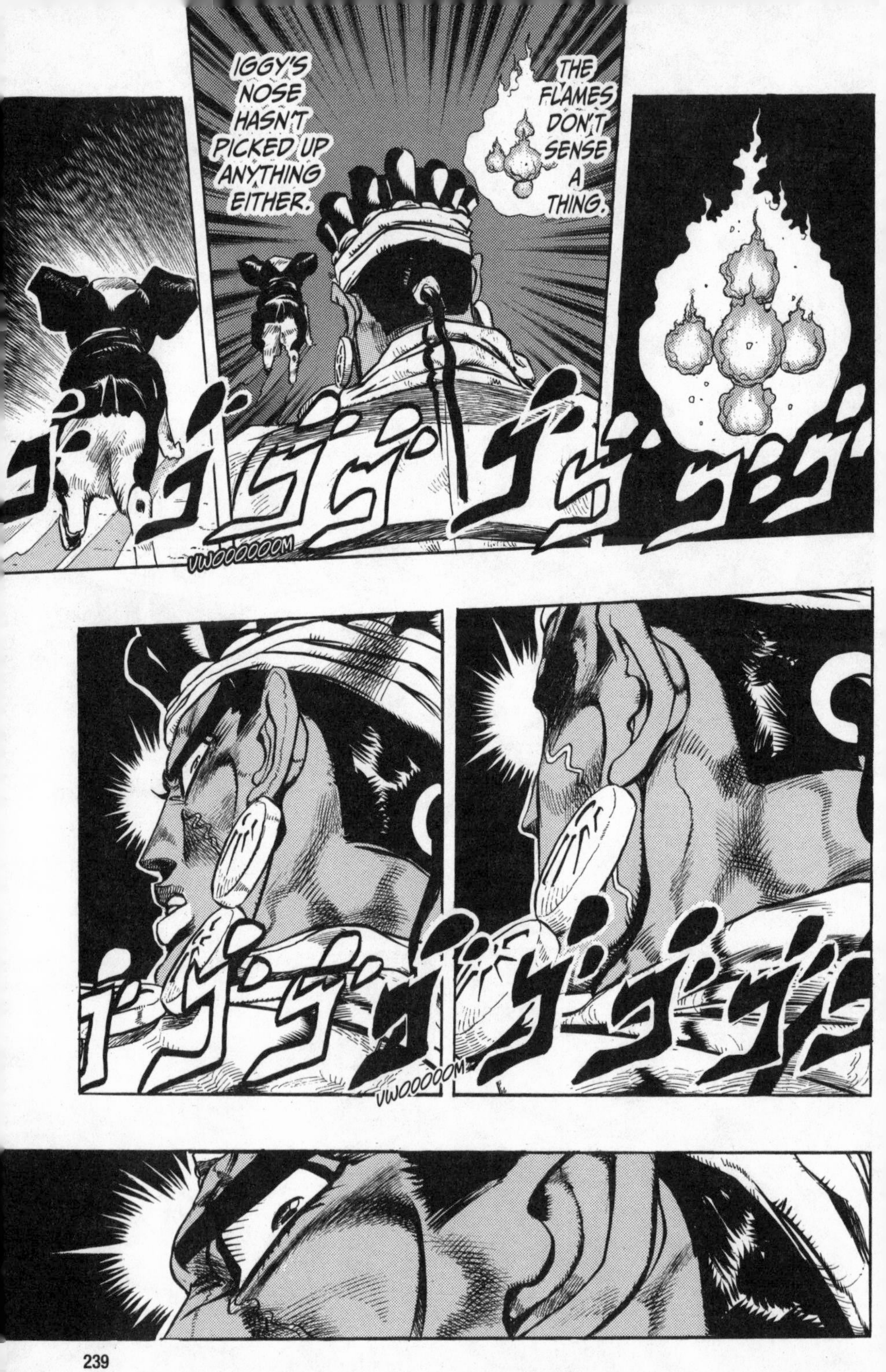
THE FLAMES DON'T SENSE A THING.
IGGY'S NOSE HASN'T PICKED UP ANYTHING EITHER.
VWOOOOOOM
VWOOOOOM

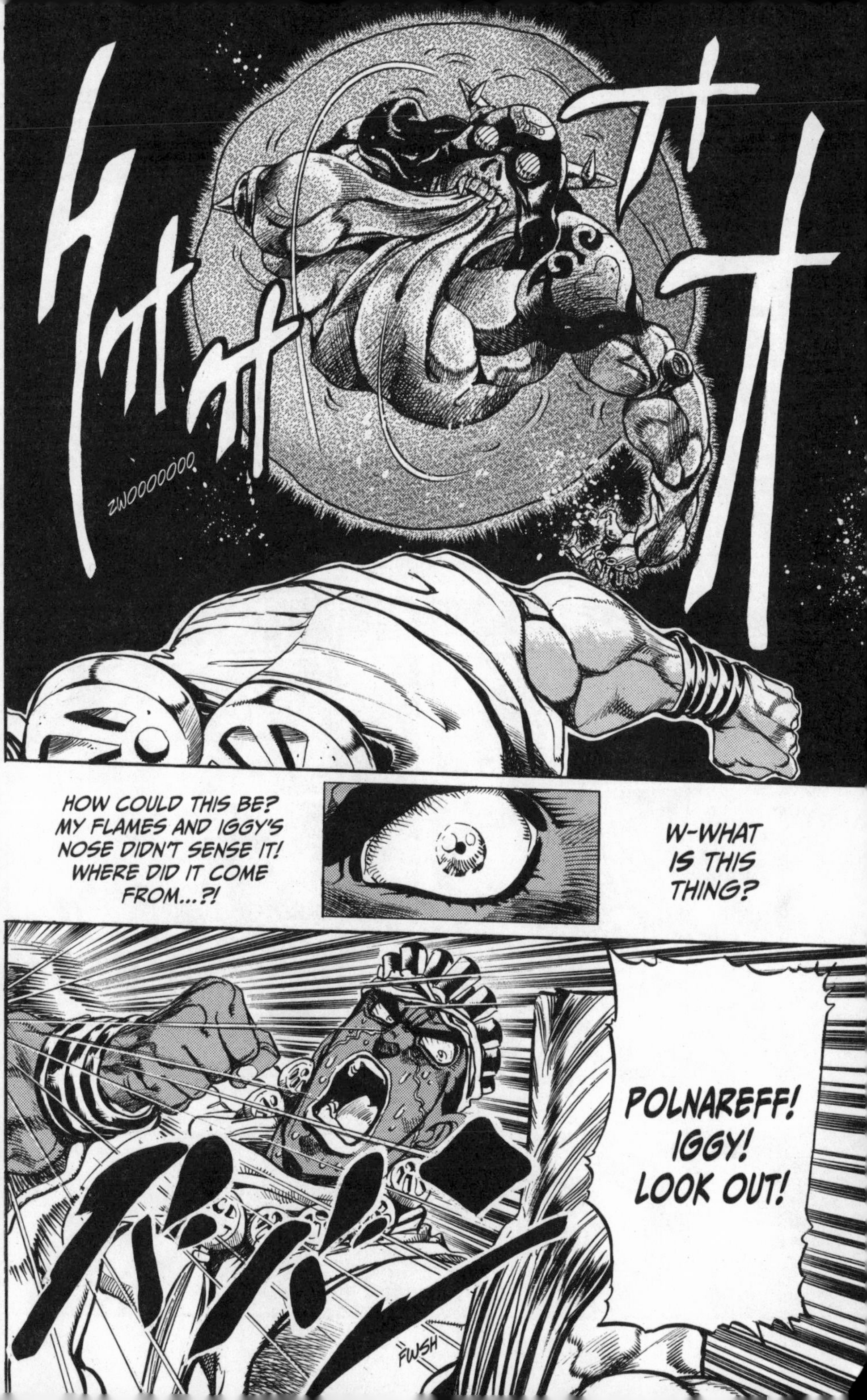
ZWOOOOOOO
W-WHAT IS THIS THING?
HOW COULD THIS BE? MY FLAMES AND IGGY'S NOSE DIDN'T SENSE IT! WHERE DID IT COME FROM...?!
POLNAREFF! IGGY! LOOK OUT!
FWSH

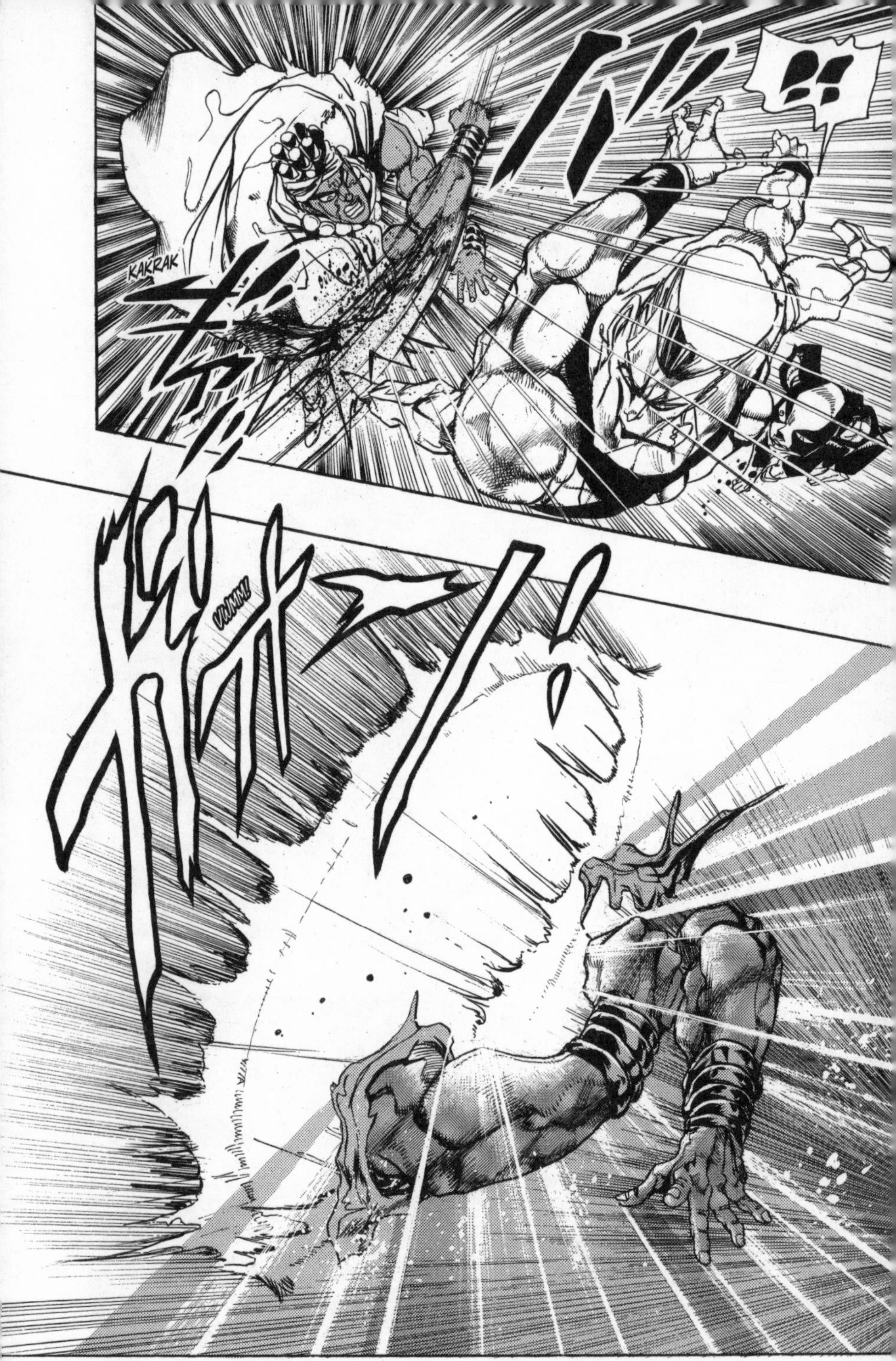
KAKRAK
VWMM!

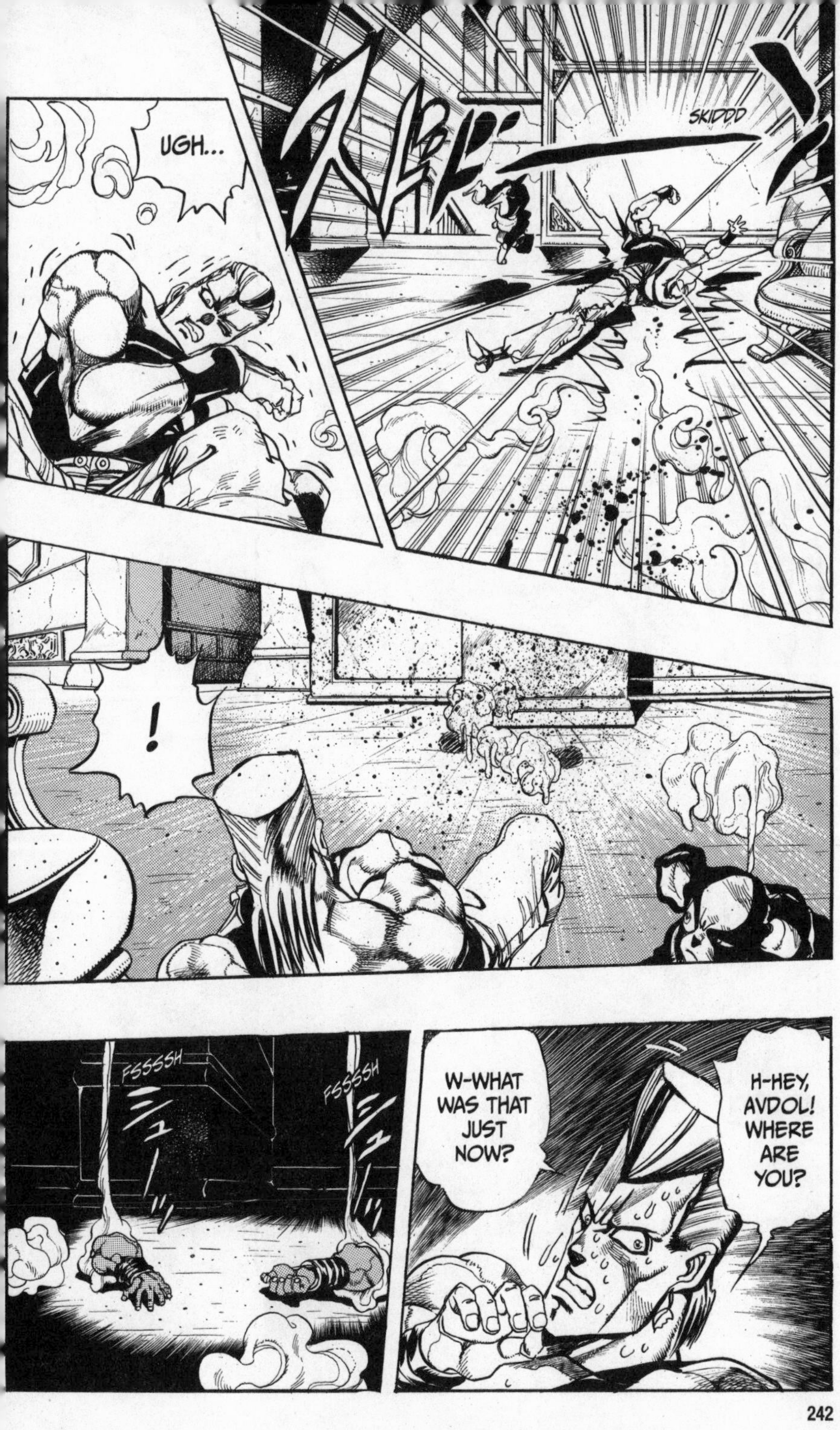
SKIDDD
UGH...
!
H-HEY, AVDOL! WHERE ARE YOU?
W-WHAT WAS THAT JUST NOW?
FSSSSH
FSSSSH

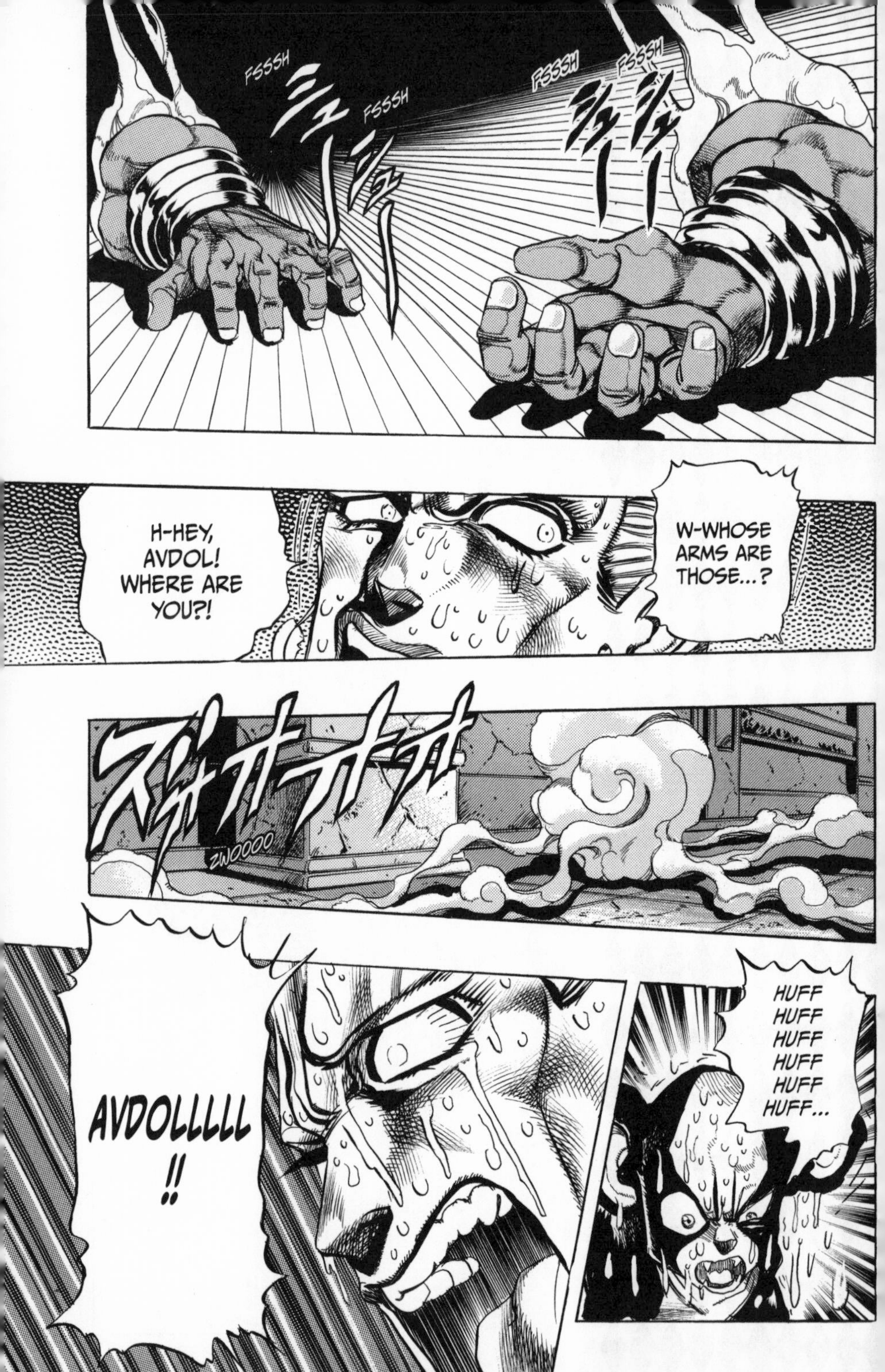
FSSSH
FSSSH
FSSSH
FSSSH
W-WHOSE ARMS ARE THOSE...?
H-HEY, AVDOL! WHERE ARE YOU?!
ZWOOOO
HUFF HUFF HUFF HUFF HUFF HUFF...
AVDOLLLLL !!

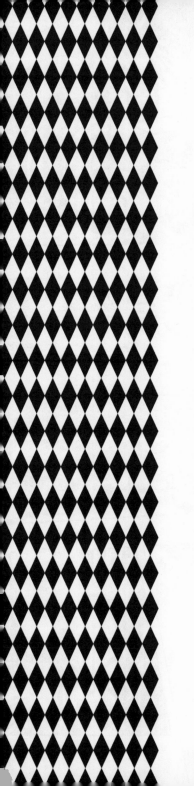
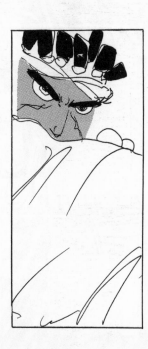

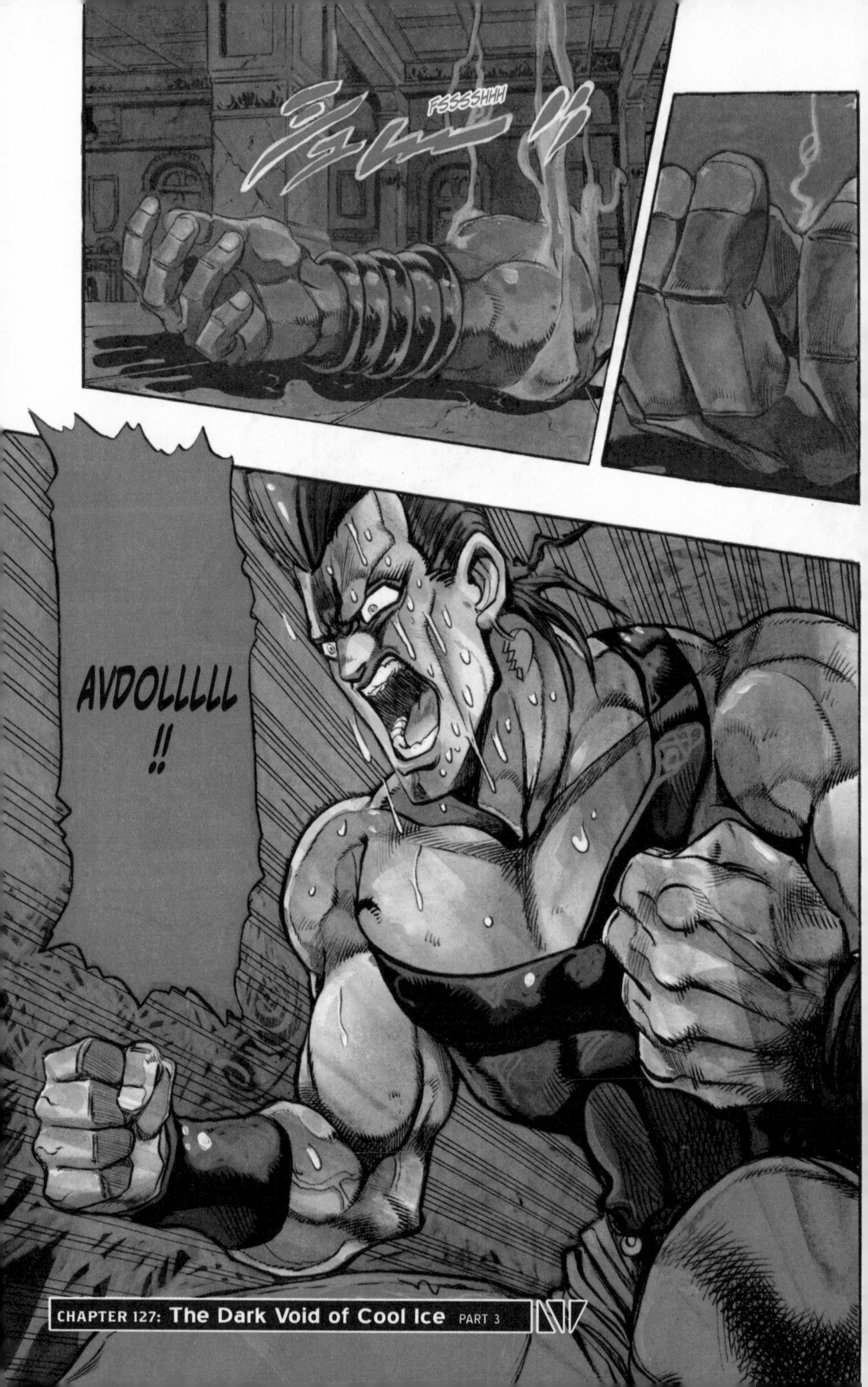
FSSSSHHH
AVDOLLLLL!!

CHAPTER 127: The Dark Void of Cool Ice PART 3

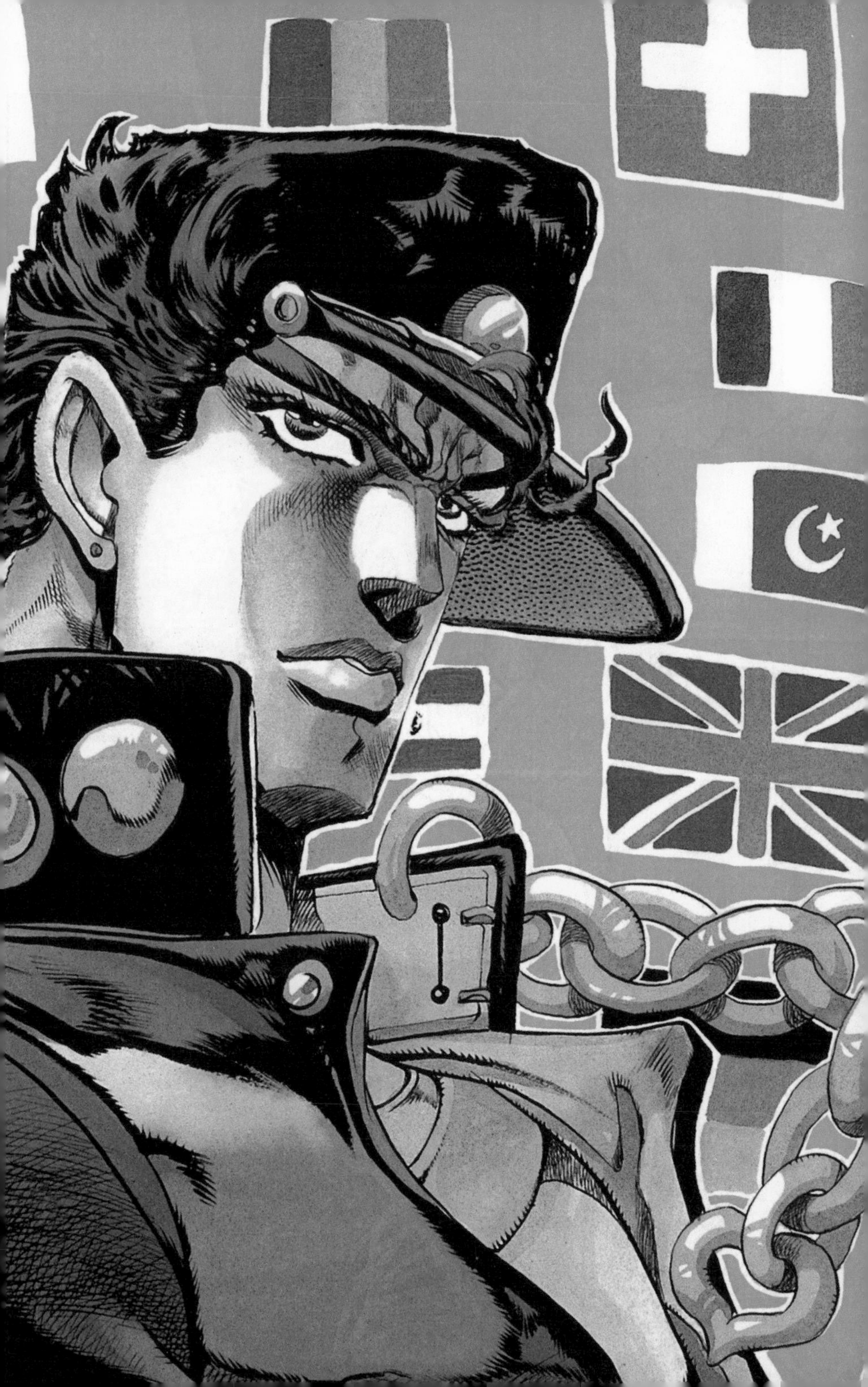

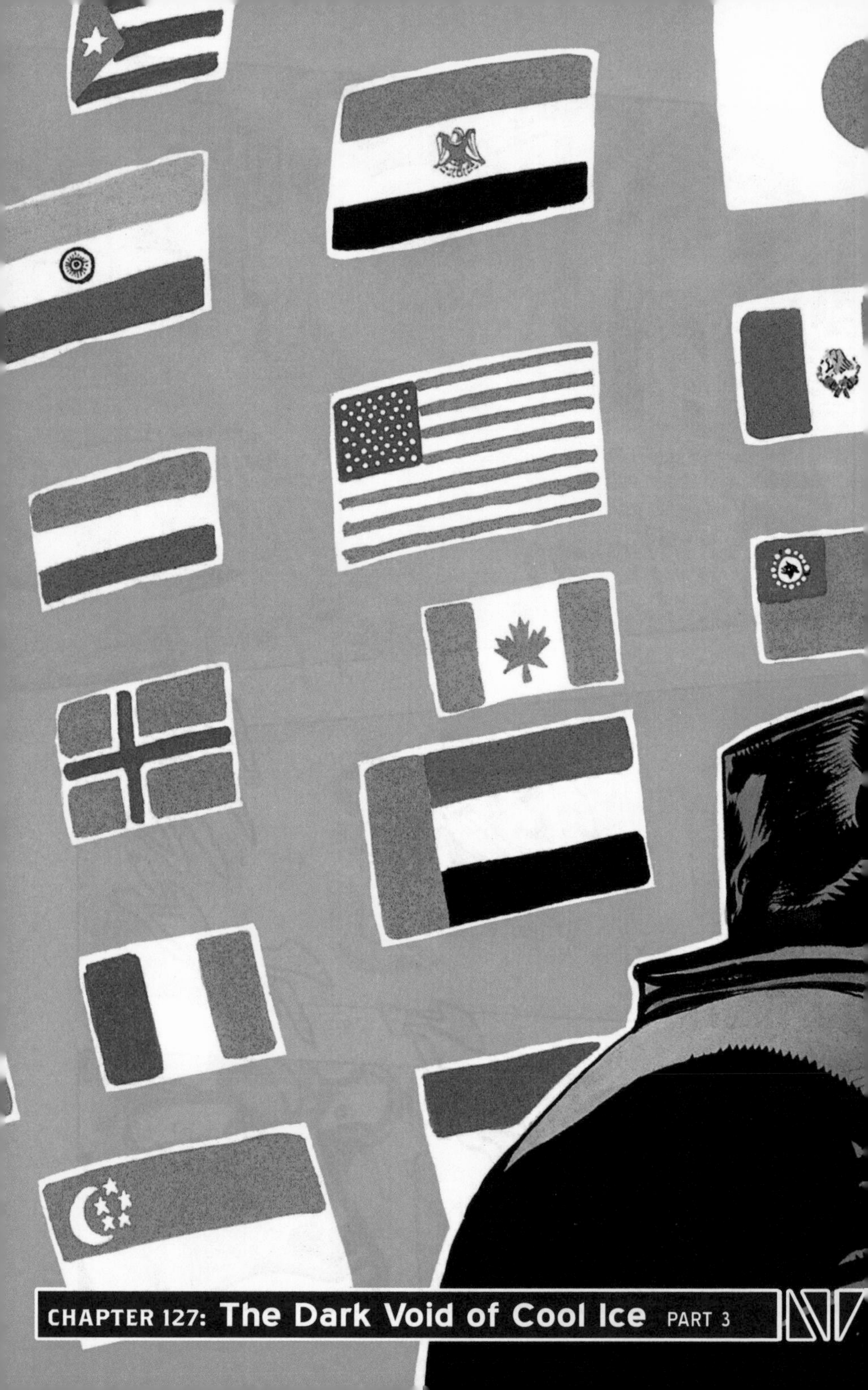

CHAPTER 127: The Dark Void of Cool Ice PART 3

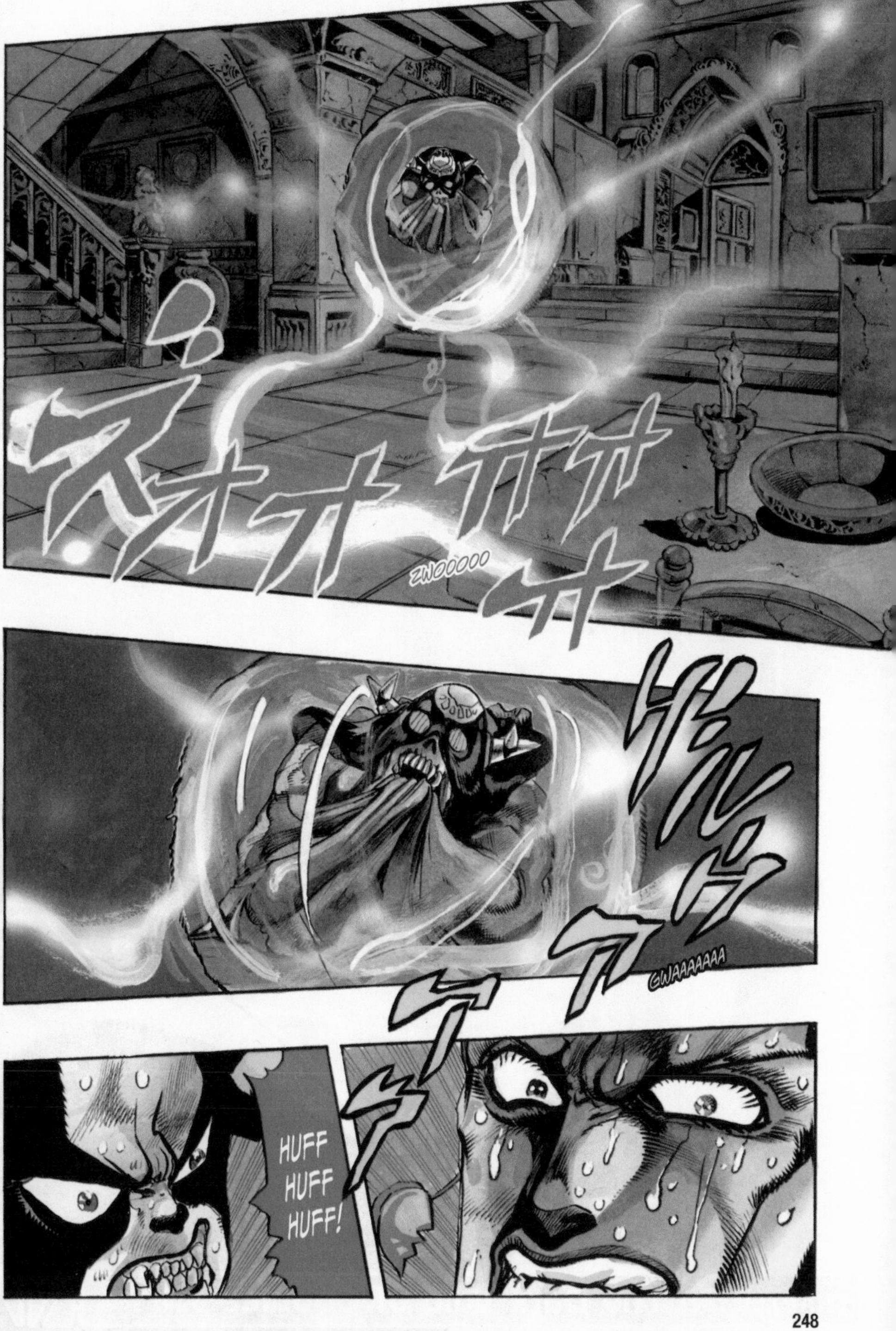
ZWOOOOO
GWAAAAAAA
HUFF
HUFF
HUFF!

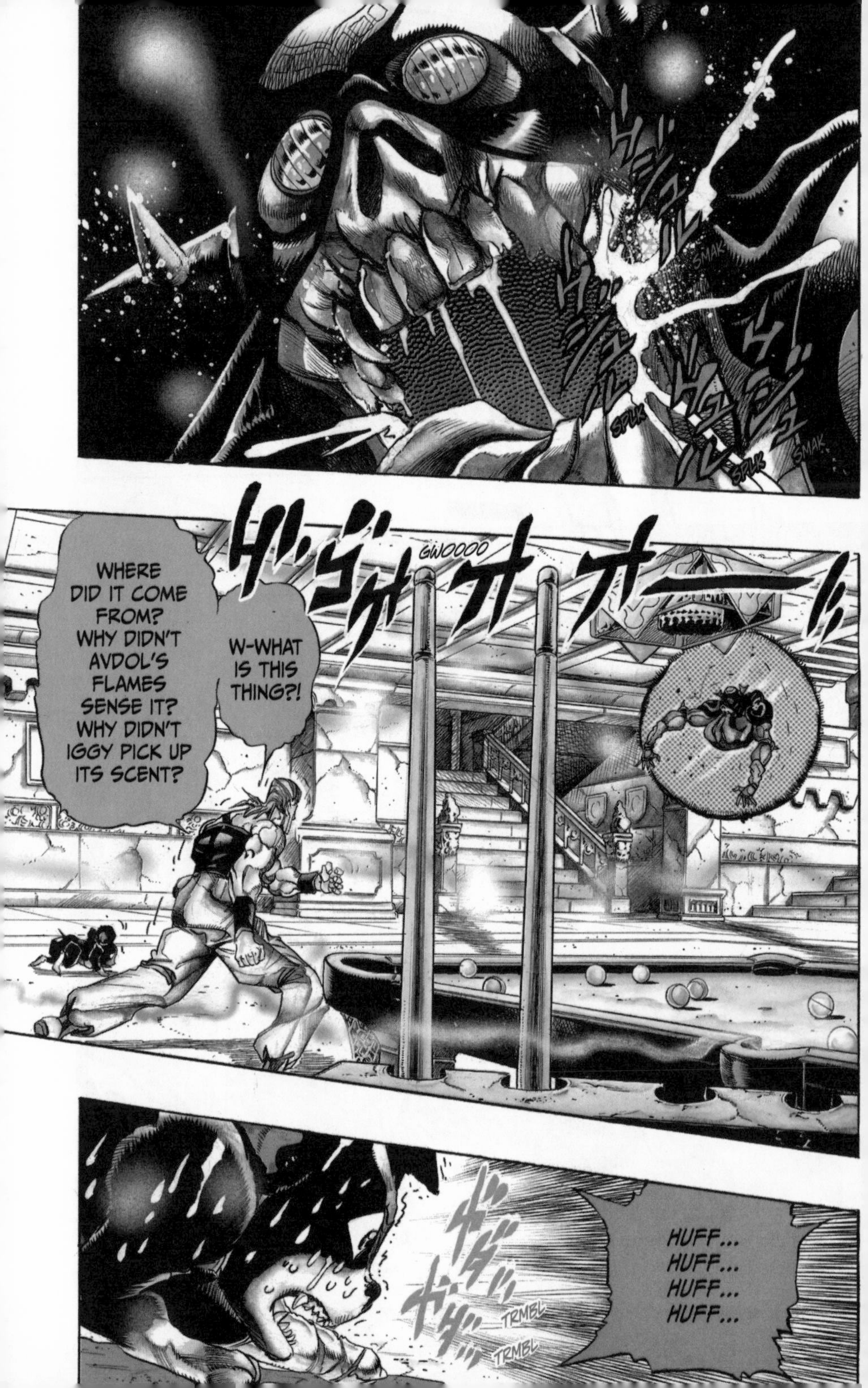
SMAK
SMAK
SPLK
SPLK
GWOOOO
W-WHAT IS THIS THING?!
WHERE DID IT COME FROM? WHY DIDN'T AVDOL'S FLAMES SENSE IT? WHY DIDN'T IGGY PICK UP ITS SCENT?
HUFF... HUFF... HUFF... HUFF...
TRMBL
TRMBL

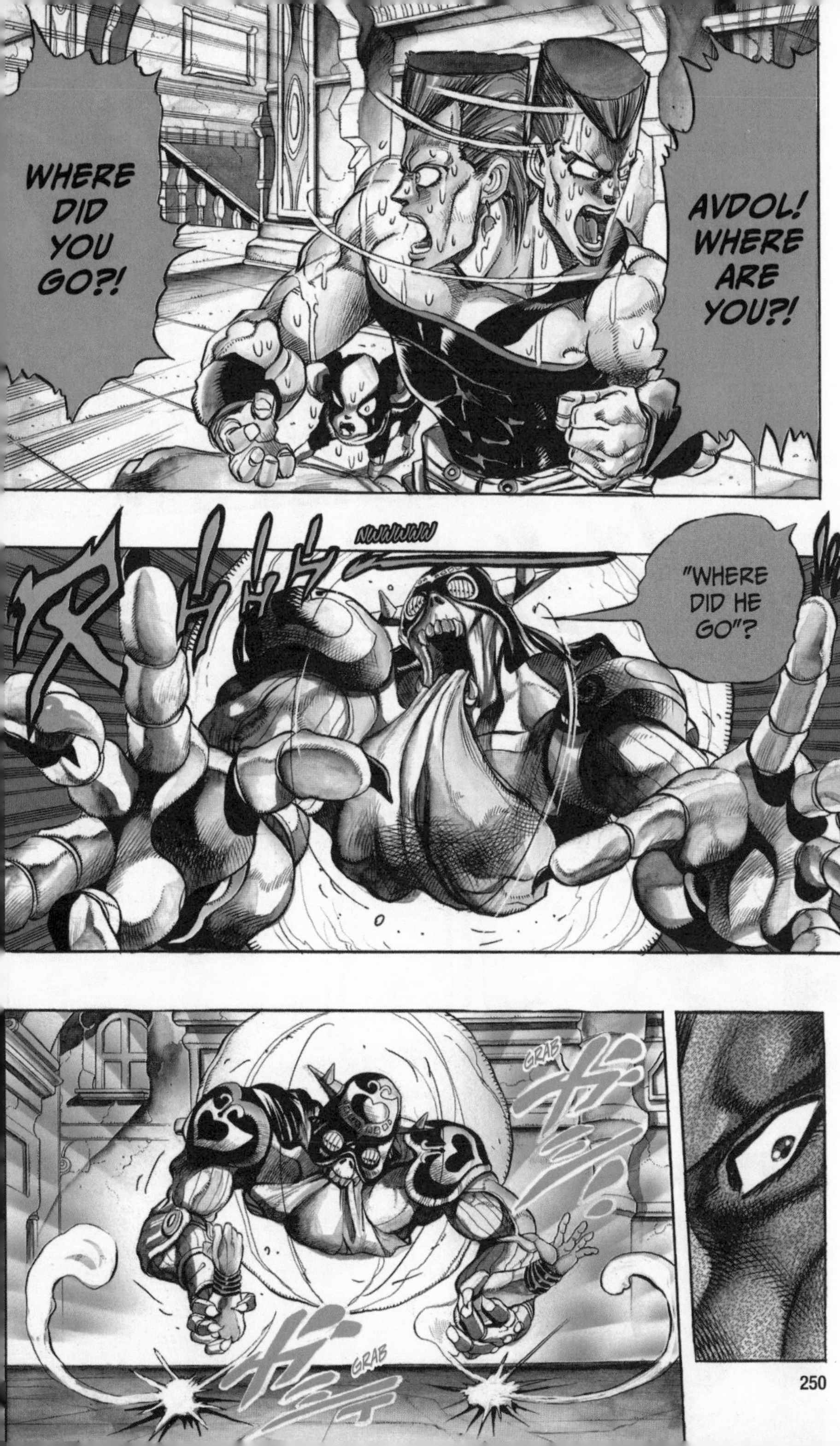
AVDOL! WHERE ARE YOU?!
WHERE DID YOU GO?!
NWWWWW
"WHERE DID HE GO"?
GRAB
GRAB

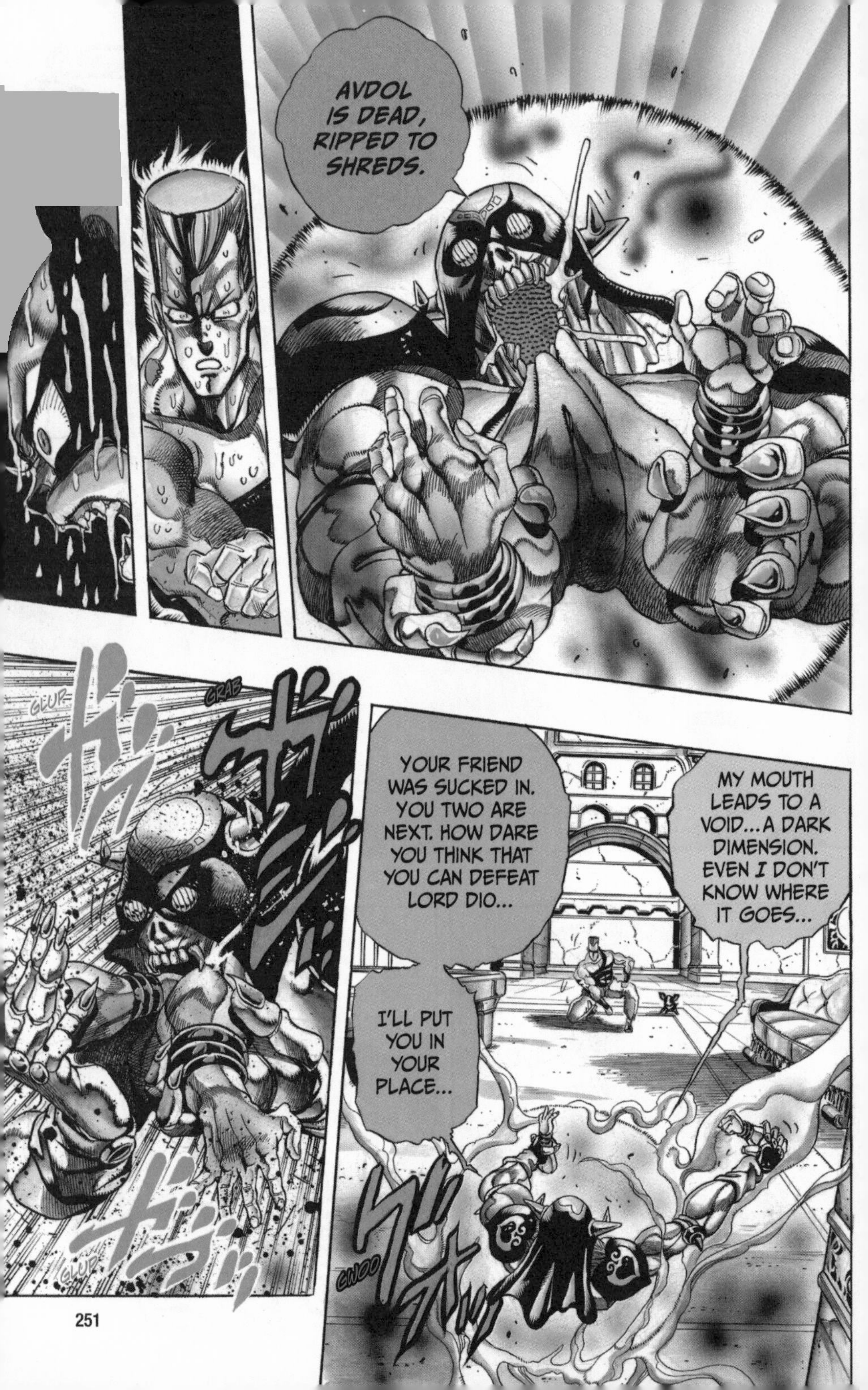
AVDOL IS DEAD, RIPPED TO SHREDS.
MY MOUTH LEADS TO A VOID...A DARK DIMENSION. EVEN I DON'T KNOW WHERE IT GOES...
YOUR FRIEND WAS SUCKED IN. YOU TWO ARE NEXT. HOW DARE YOU THINK THAT YOU CAN DEFEAT LORD DIO...
I'LL PUT YOU IN YOUR PLACE...
GWOO
GRAB
GLUP
GLUP

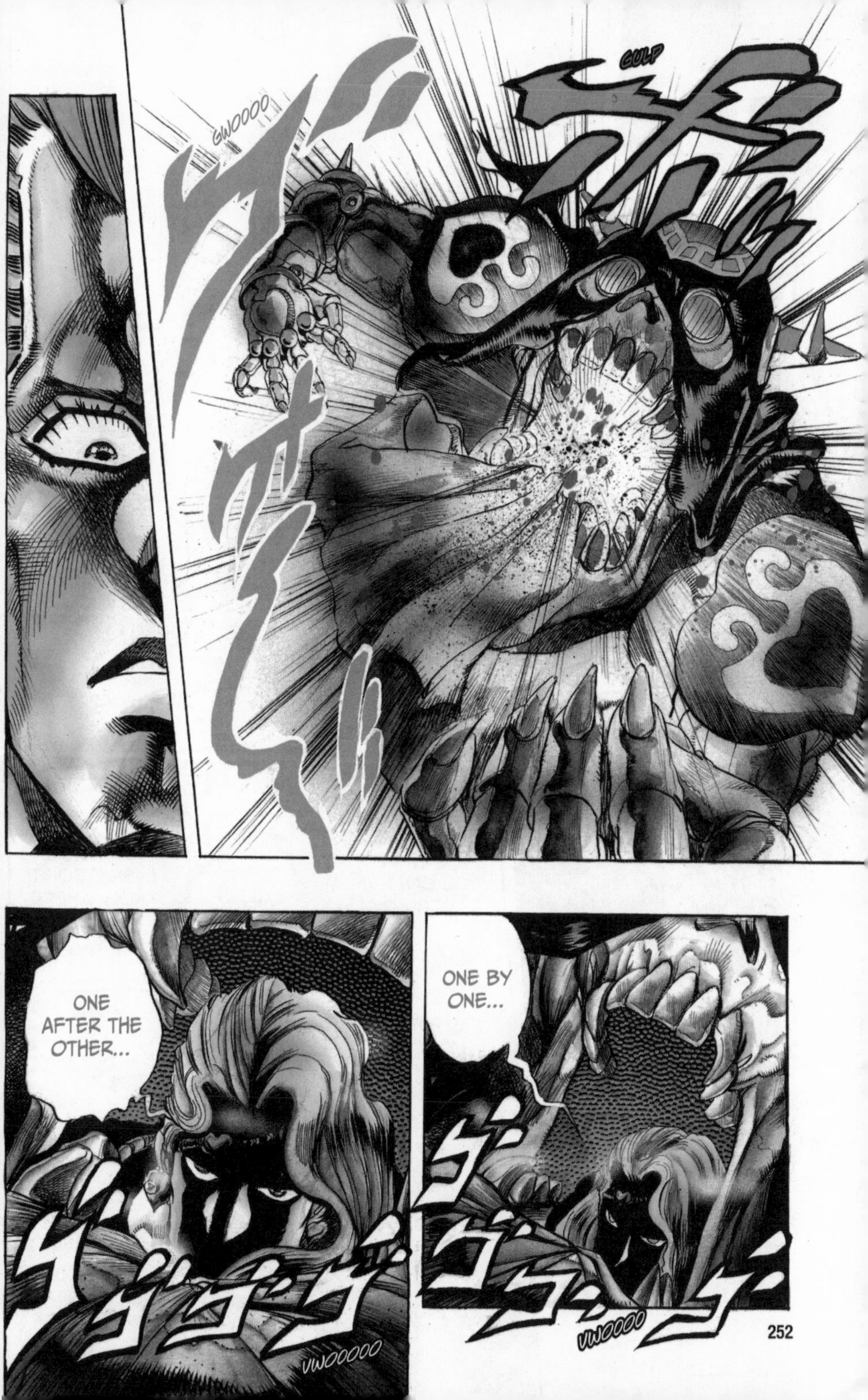
GULP
GWOOOO
ONE BY ONE...
VWOOOO
ONE AFTER THE OTHER...
VWOOOOO

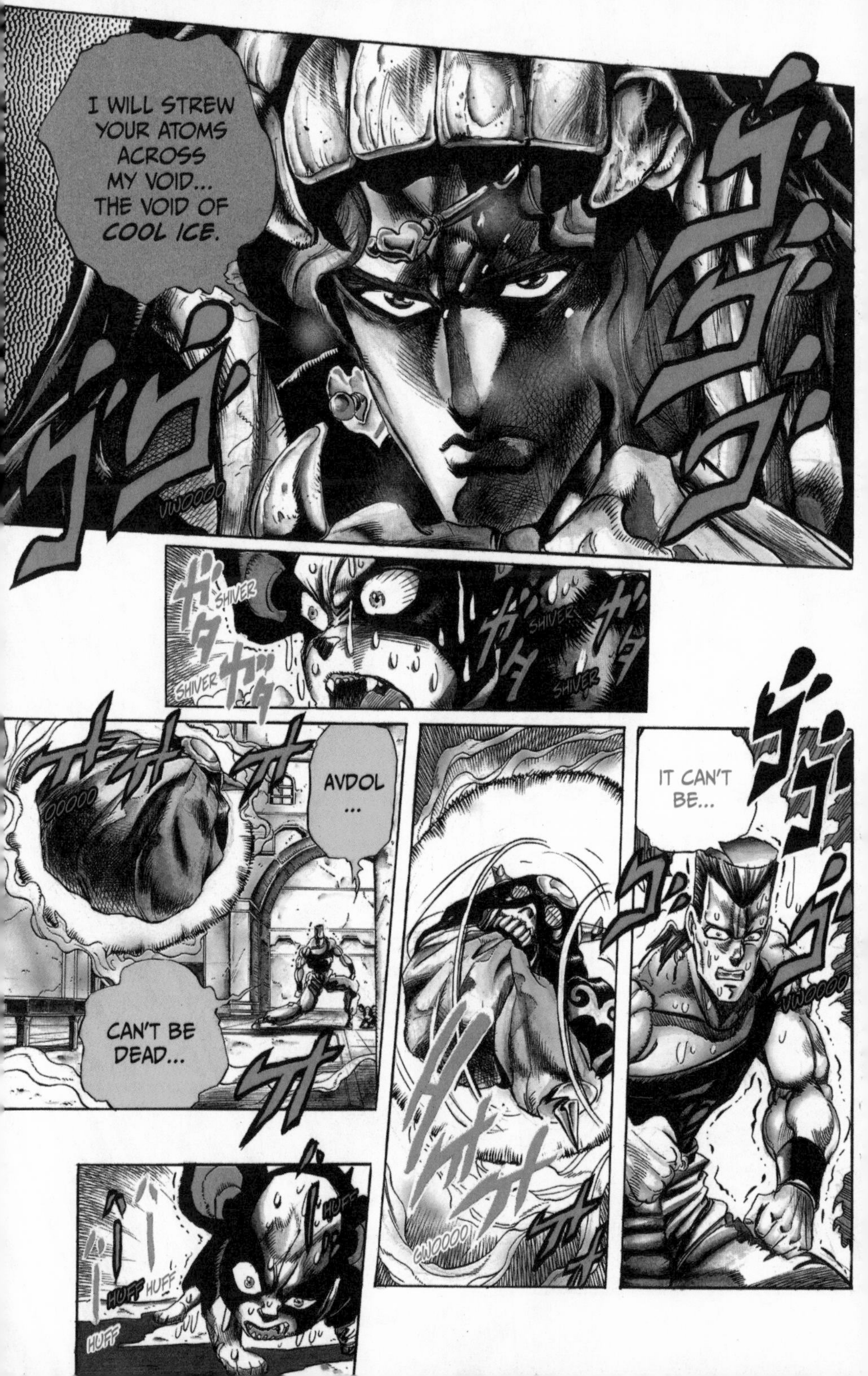
I WILL STREW YOUR ATOMS ACROSS MY VOID... THE VOID OF COOL ICE.
VWOOOO
SHIVER
SHIVER
SHIVER
SHIVER
IT CAN'T BE...
VWOOOO
GWOOOO
AVDOL ...
CAN'T BE DEAD...
HUFF
HUFF
HUFF
HUFF

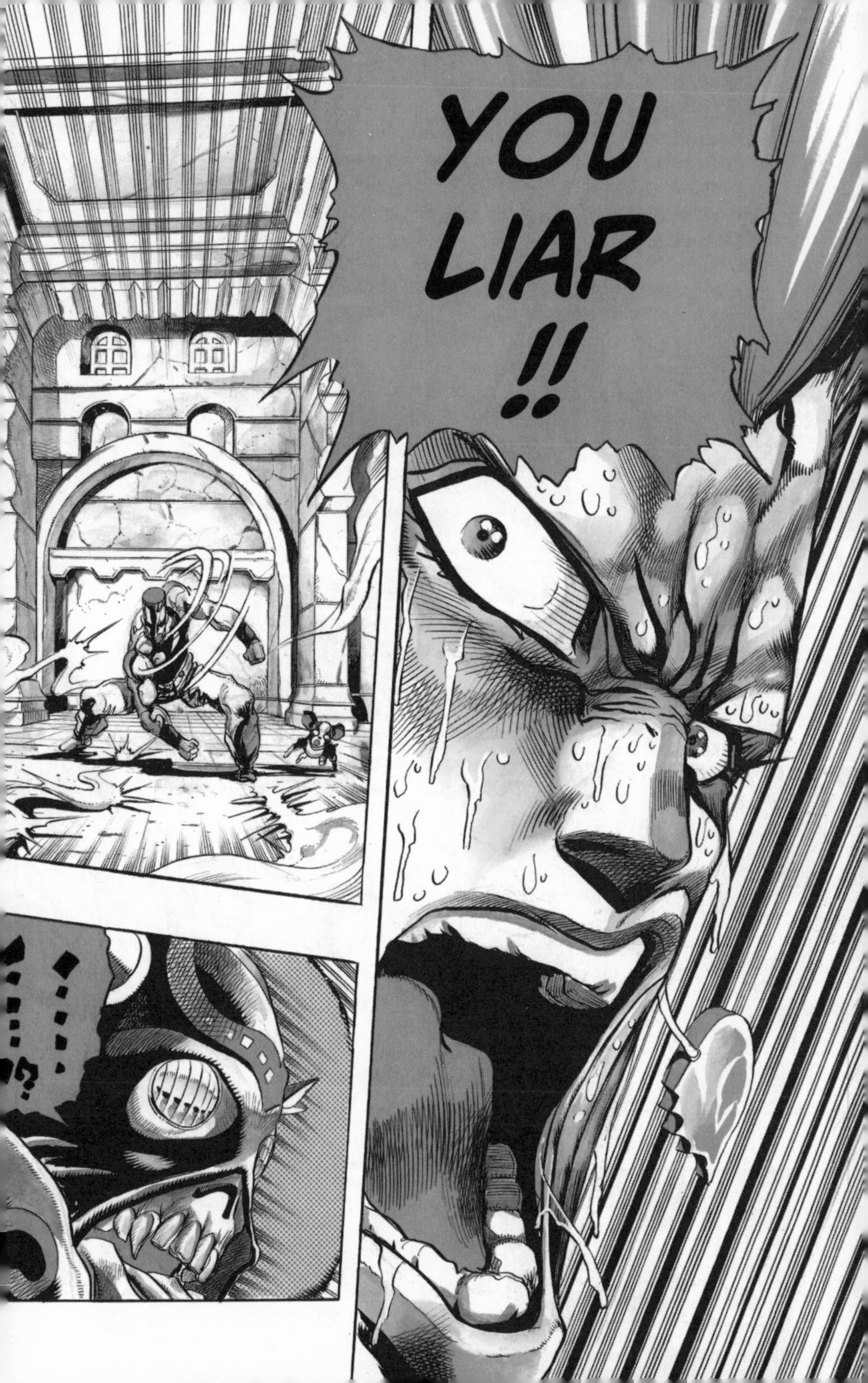
YOU LIAR!!
......!?

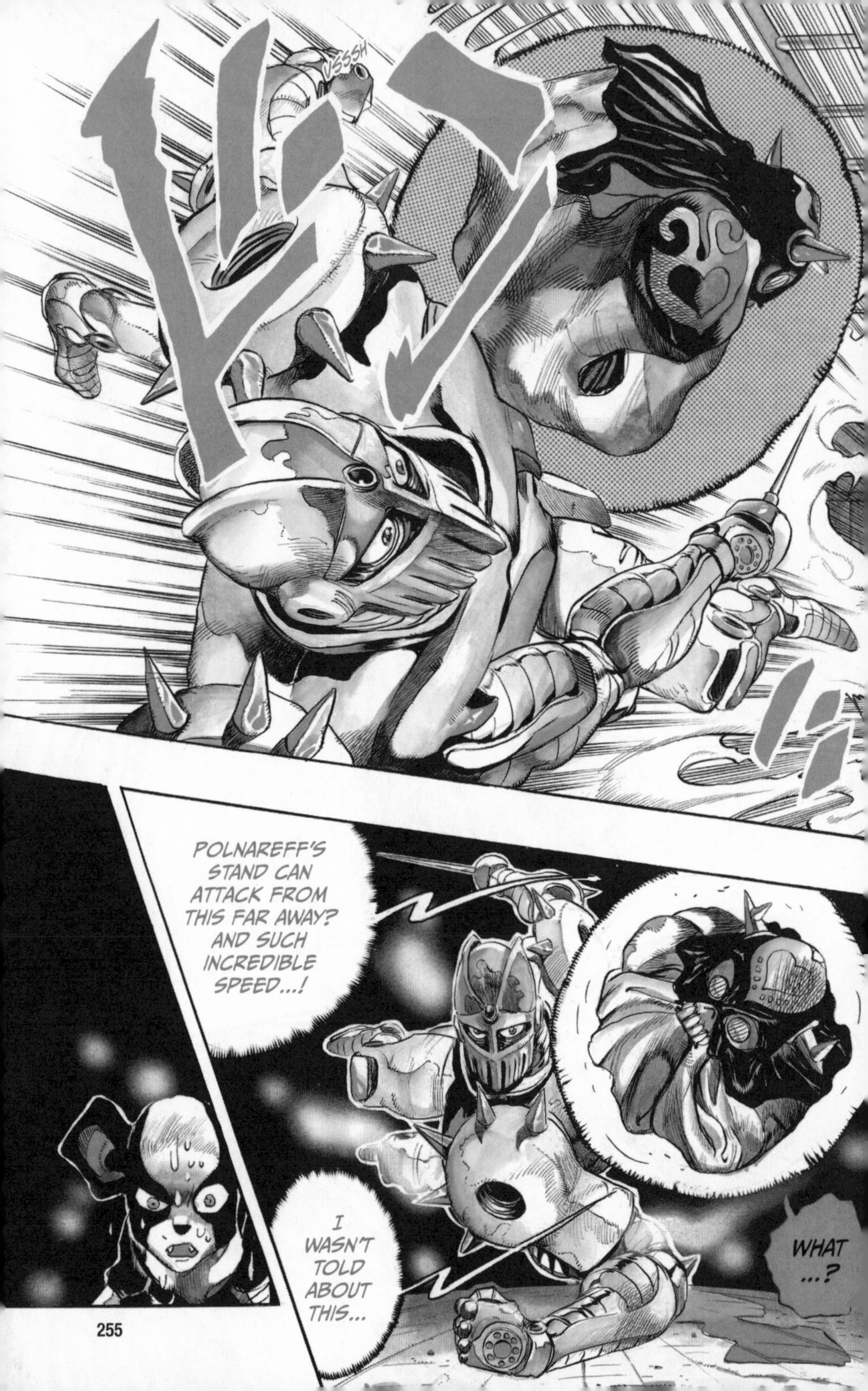
VSSSH
POLNAREFF'S STAND CAN ATTACK FROM THIS FAR AWAY? AND SUCH INCREDIBLE SPEED...!
WHAT ...?
I WASN'T TOLD ABOUT THIS...

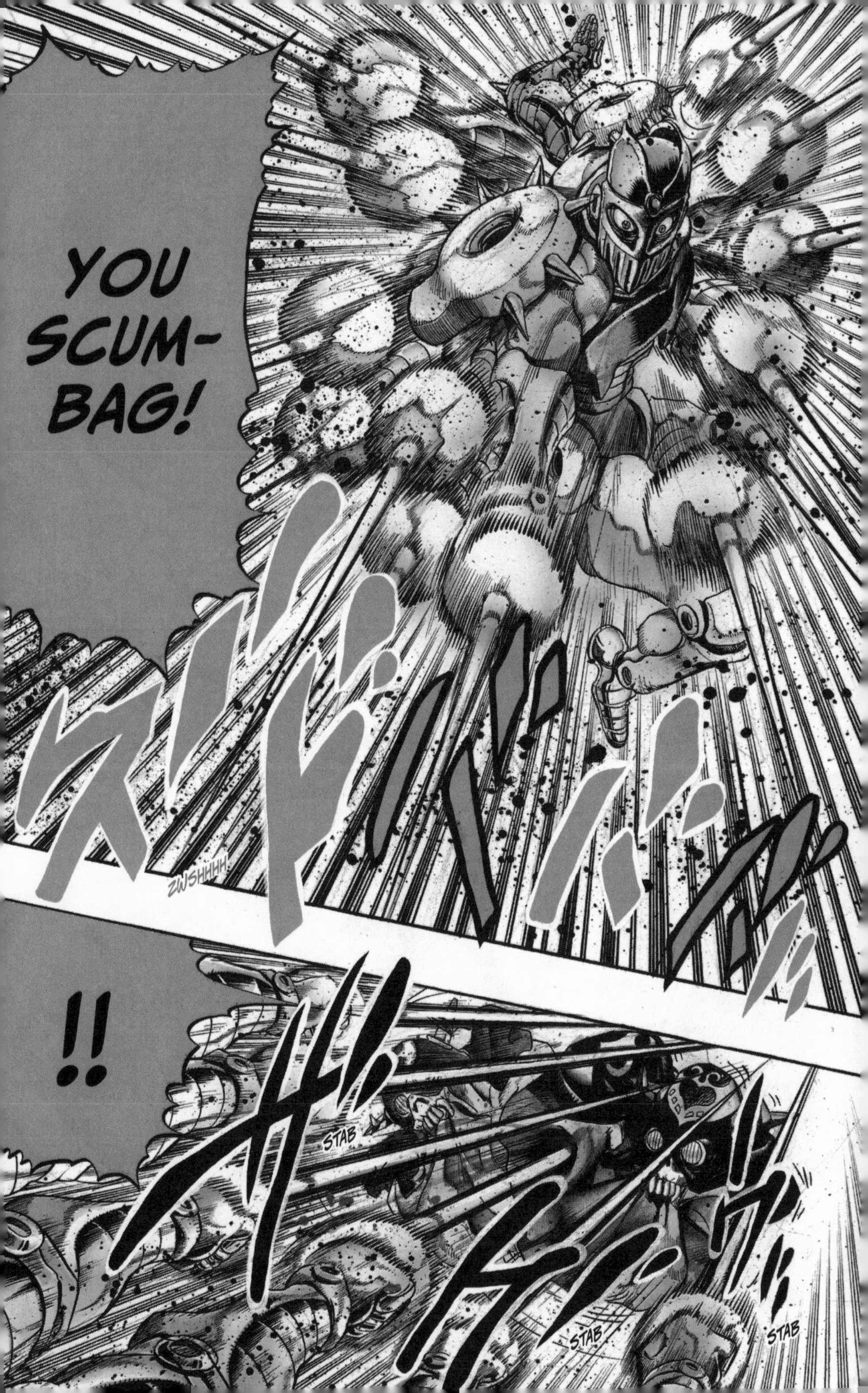
YOU SCUM-BAG!
ZWSHHHH
!!
STAB
STAB
STAB

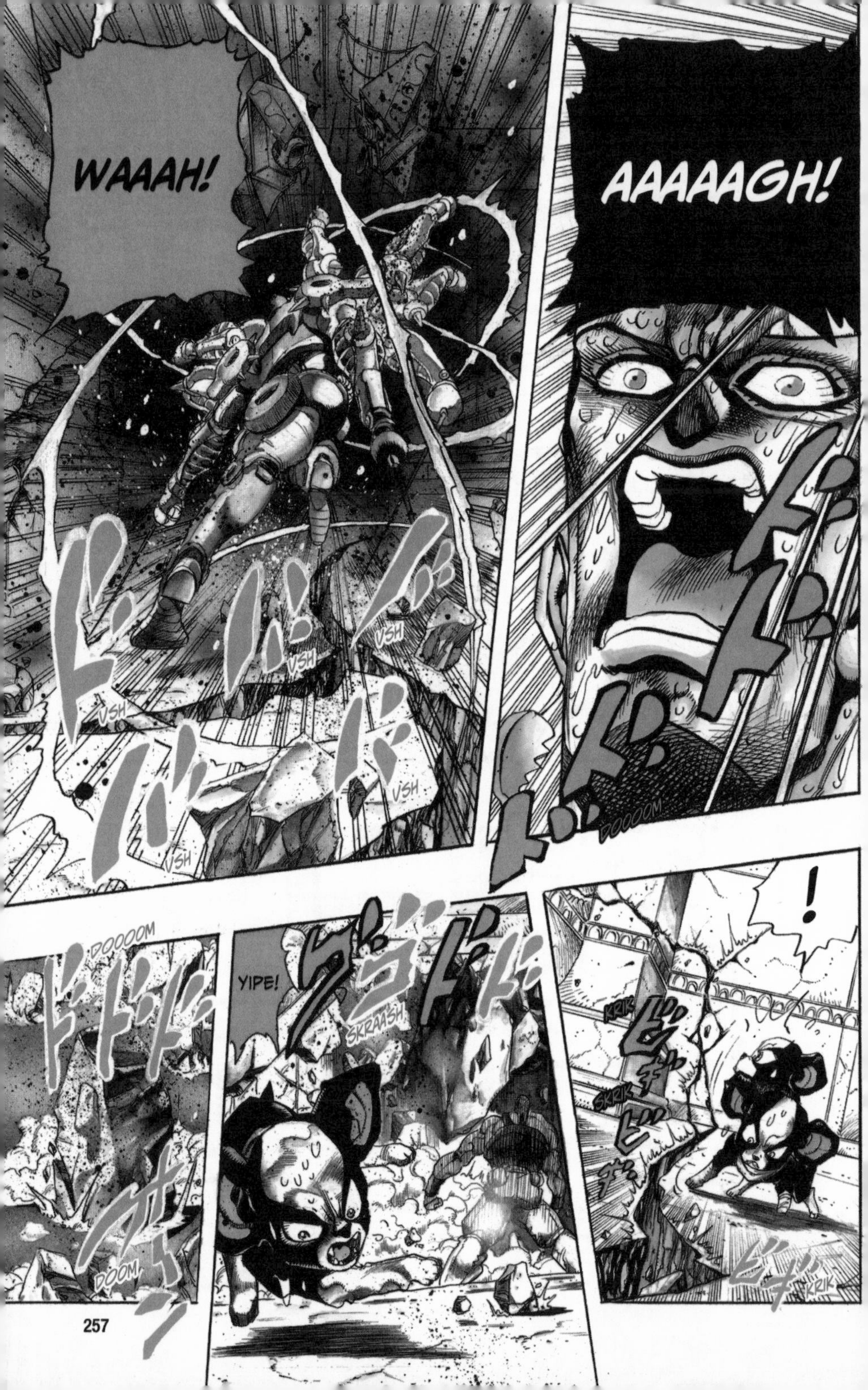
AAAAAGH!
DOOOOM
WAAAH!
VSH
VSH
VSH
VSH
VSH
!
KRIK
SKRIK
KRIK
YIPE!
SKRAASH
DOOOOM
DOOM

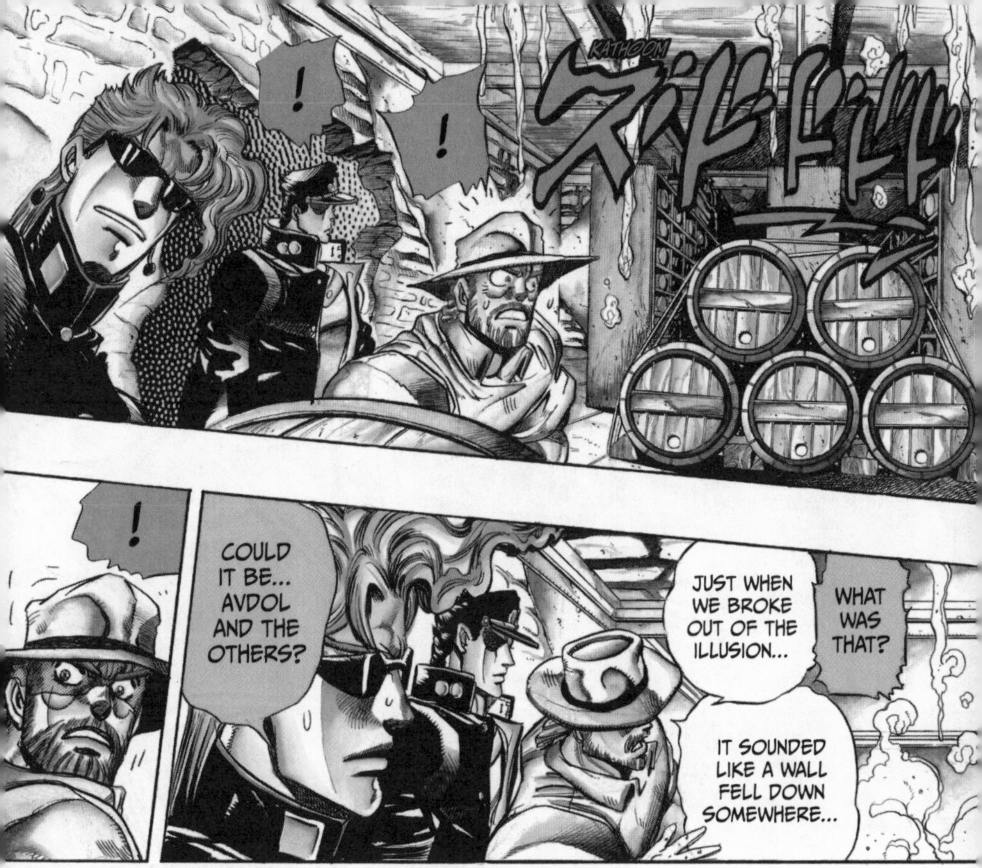
KATHOOM
!
!
WHAT WAS THAT?
JUST WHEN WE BROKE OUT OF THE ILLUSION...
IT SOUNDED LIKE A WALL FELL DOWN SOMEWHERE...
COULD IT BE... AVDOL AND THE OTHERS?
!

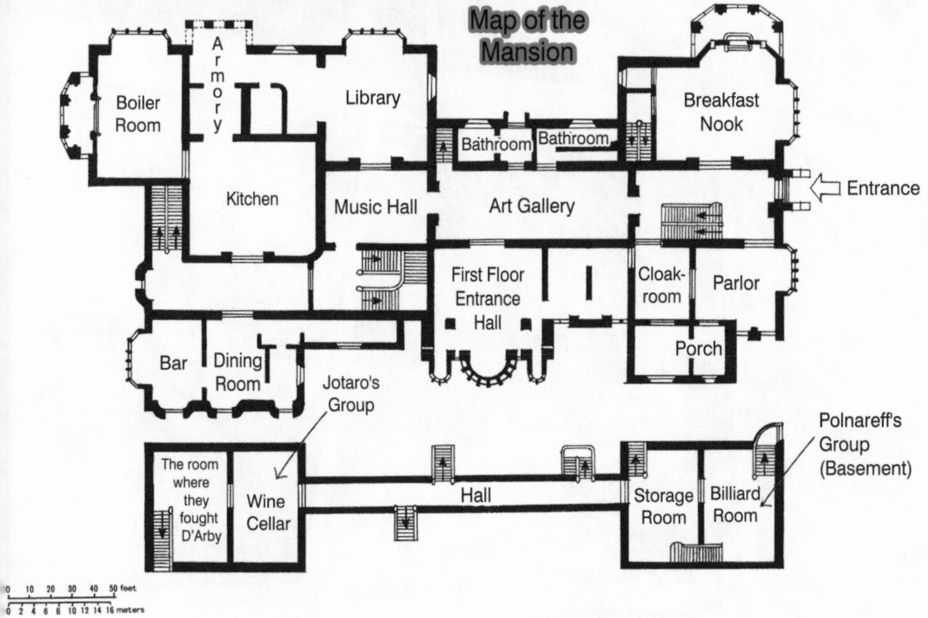
Map of the Mansion
Armory
Boiler Room
Library
Breakfast Nook
Bathroom
Bathroom
Entrance
Kitchen
Music Hall
Art Gallery
First Floor Entrance Hall
Cloak-room
Parlor
Porch
Bar
Dining Room
Jotaro's Group
Polnareff's Group (Basement)
The room where they fought D'Arby
Wine Cellar
Hall
Storage Room
Billiard Room
0 10 20 30 40 50 feet
0 2 4 6 8 10 12 14 16 meters

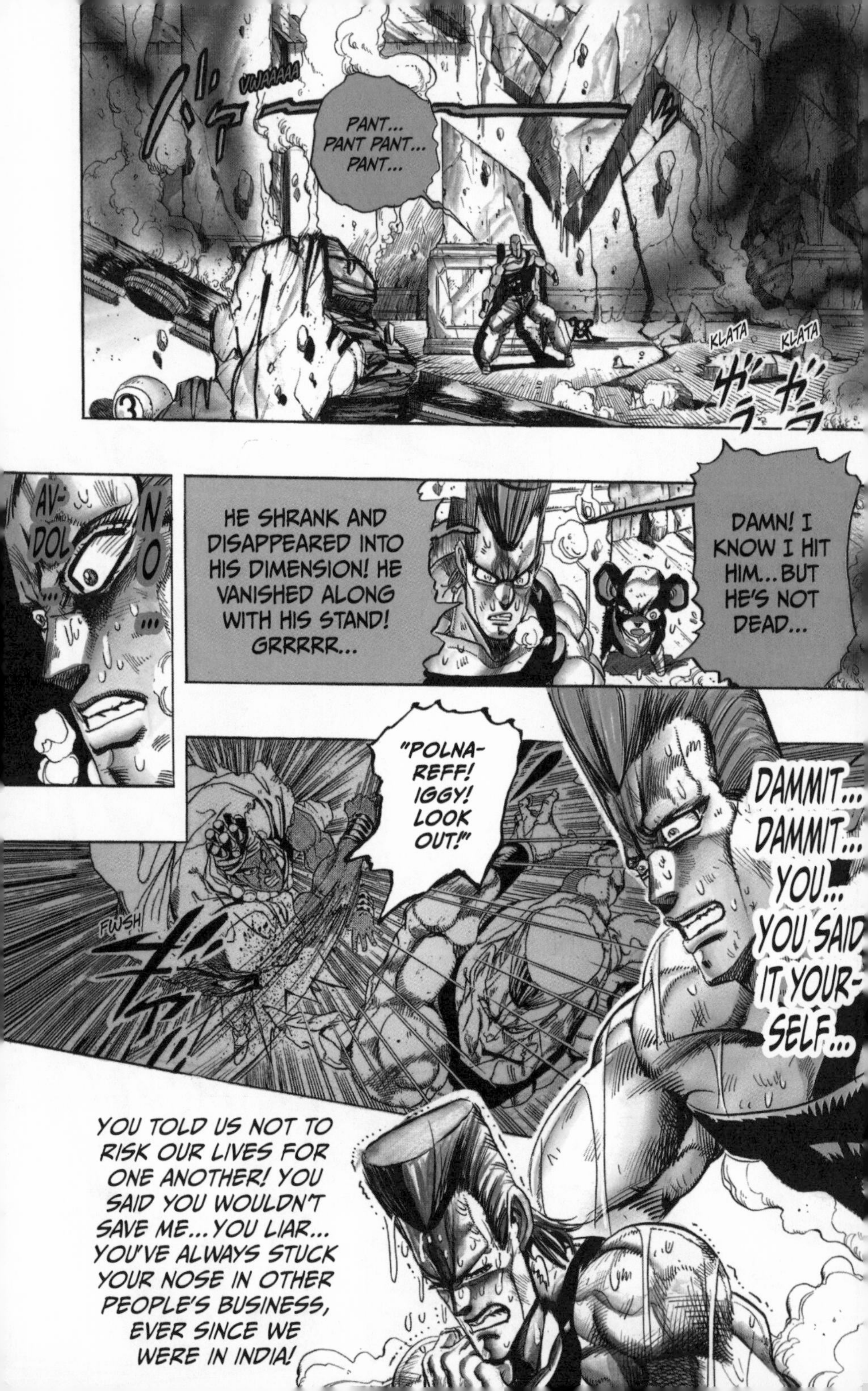
PANT... PANT PANT... PANT...
VWAAAAA
KLATA KLATA
DAMN! I KNOW I HIT HIM...BUT HE'S NOT DEAD...
HE SHRANK AND DISAPPEARED INTO HIS DIMENSION! HE VANISHED ALONG WITH HIS STAND! GRRRRR...
NO
AV-DOL
...
...
DAMMIT... DAMMIT... YOU... YOU SAID IT YOURSELF...
"POLNAREFF! IGGY! LOOK OUT!"
FWSH
YOU TOLD US NOT TO RISK OUR LIVES FOR ONE ANOTHER! YOU SAID YOU WOULDN'T SAVE ME...YOU LIAR... YOU'VE ALWAYS STUCK YOUR NOSE IN OTHER PEOPLE'S BUSINESS, EVER SINCE WE WERE IN INDIA!

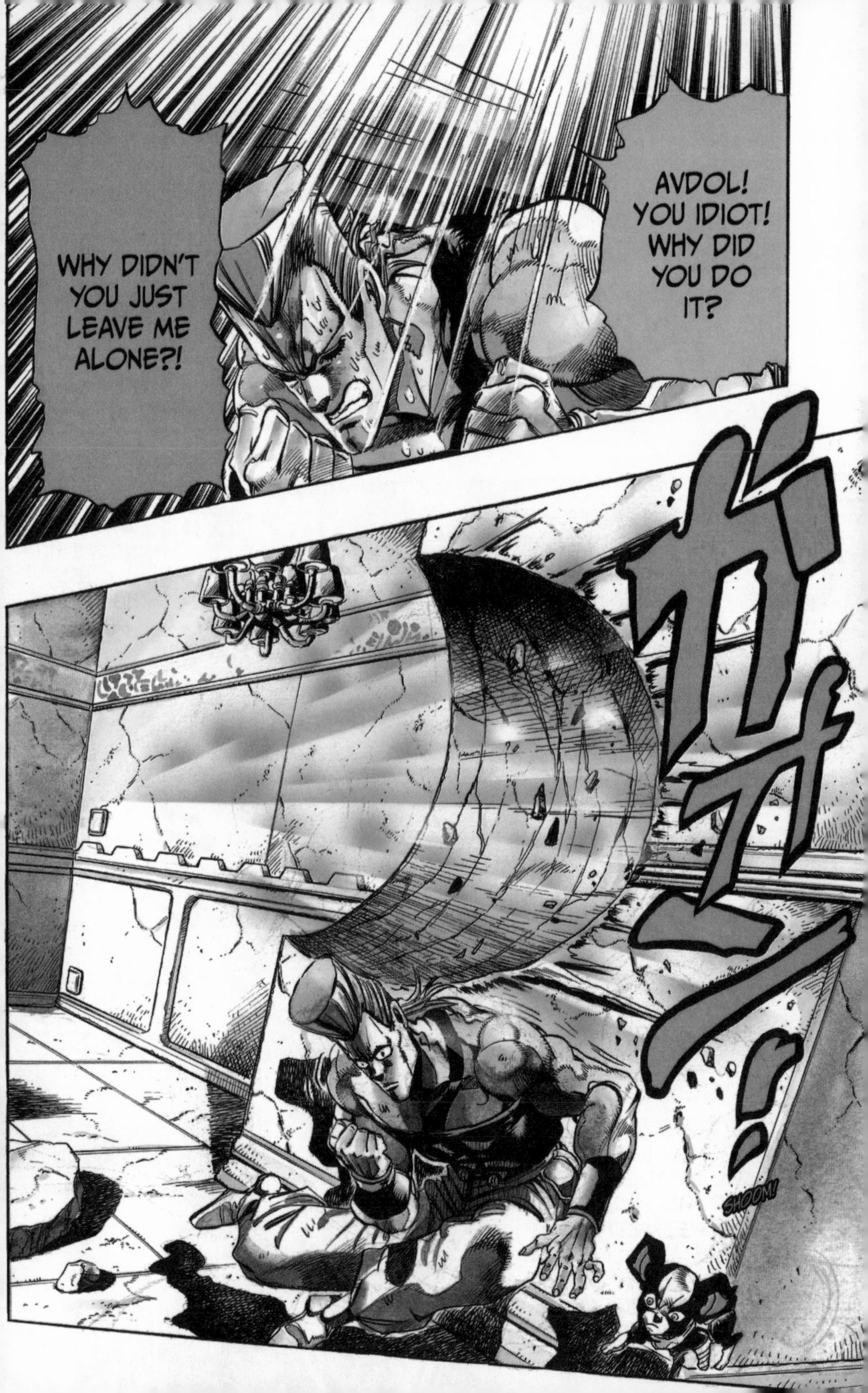
AVDOL! YOU IDIOT! WHY DID YOU DO IT?
WHY DIDN'T YOU JUST LEAVE ME ALONE?!
ガオン
SHOOM!

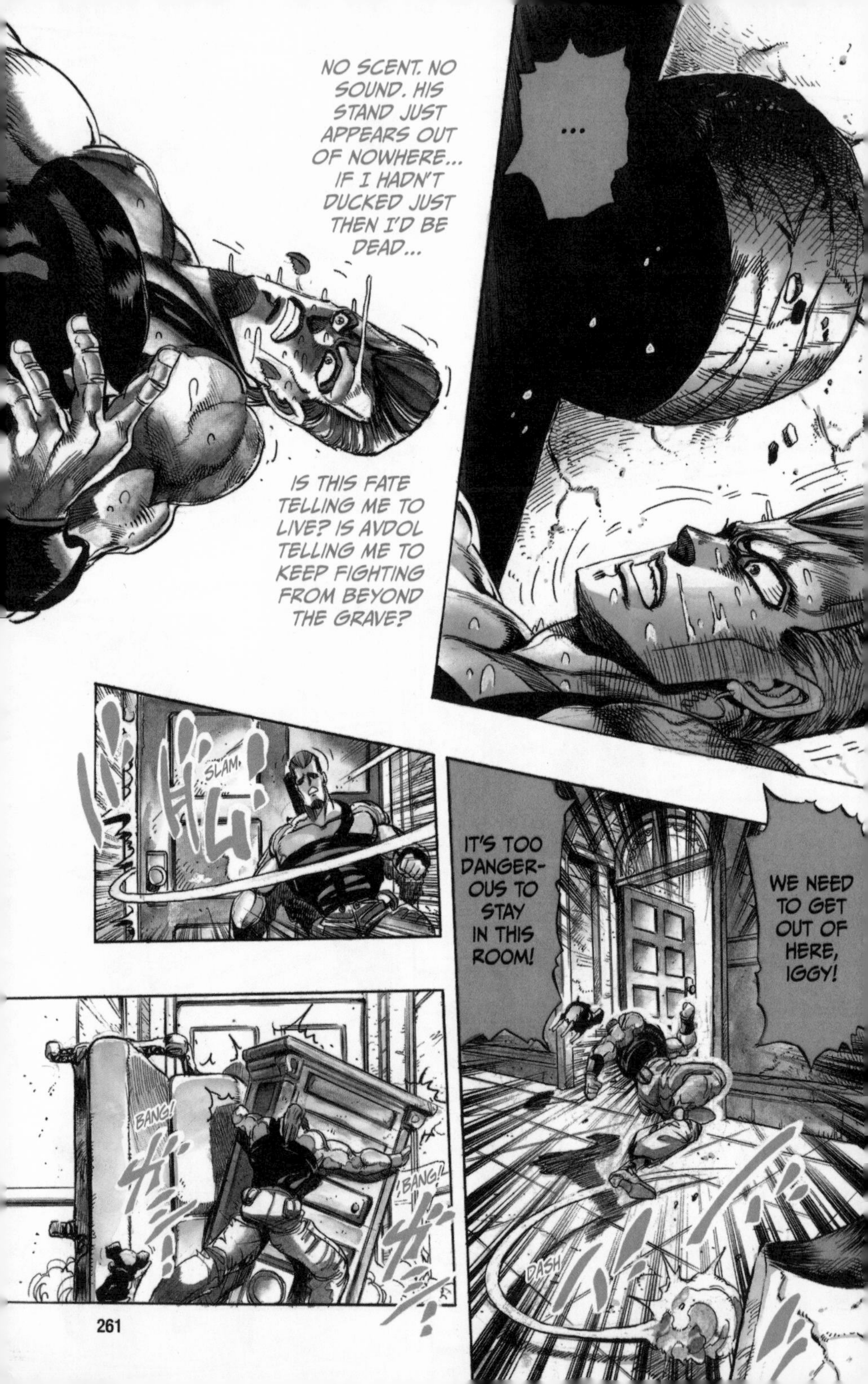
...
NO SCENT. NO SOUND. HIS STAND JUST APPEARS OUT OF NOWHERE... IF I HADN'T DUCKED JUST THEN I'D BE DEAD...
IS THIS FATE TELLING ME TO LIVE? IS AVDOL TELLING ME TO KEEP FIGHTING FROM BEYOND THE GRAVE?
WE NEED TO GET OUT OF HERE, IGGY!
IT'S TOO DANGER-OUS TO STAY IN THIS ROOM!
DASH
SLAM
BANG!
BANG!

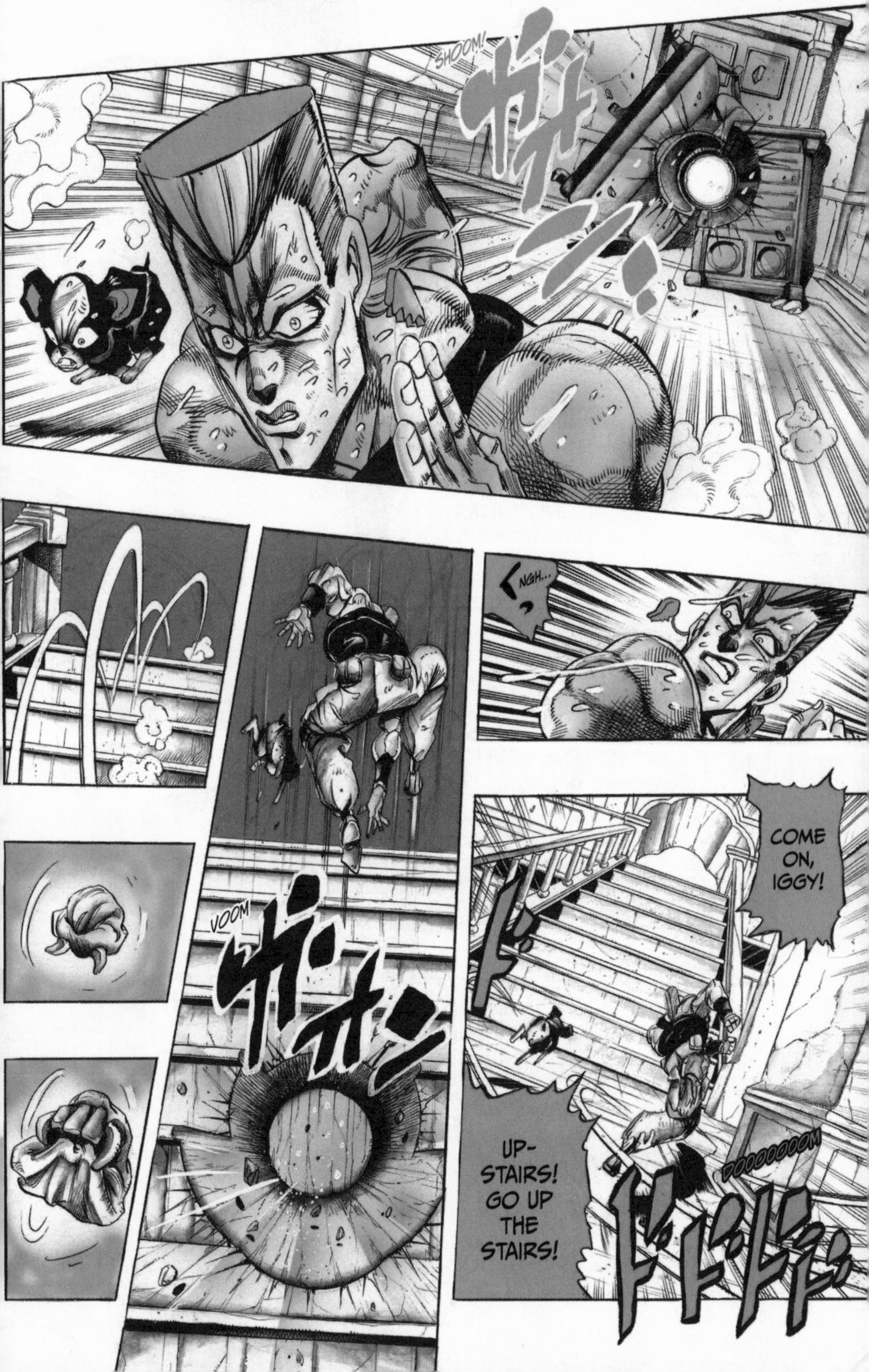
SHOOM!
NGH...
COME ON, IGGY!
UP-STAIRS! GO UP THE STAIRS!
DOOOOOOOOM
VOOM

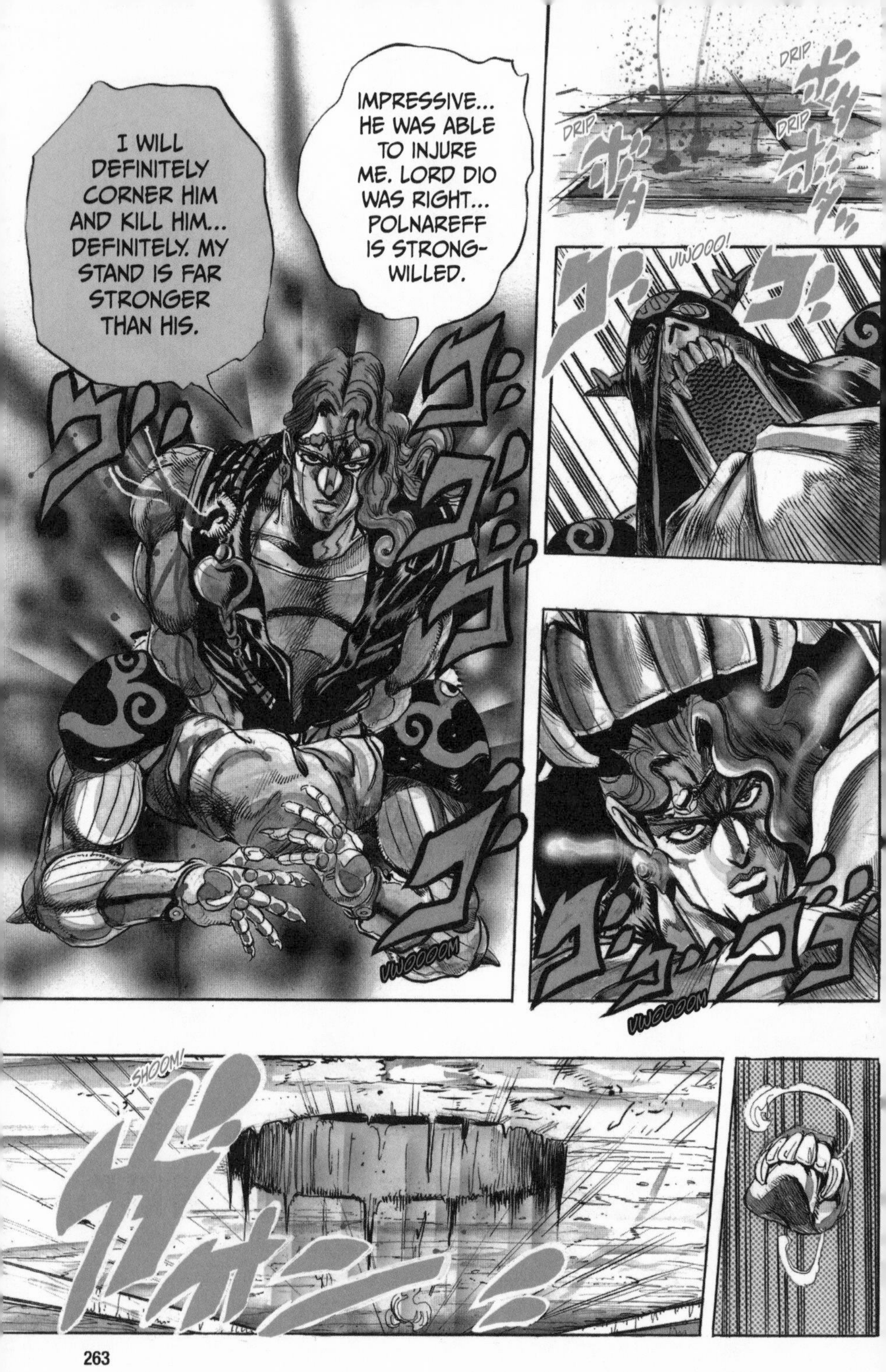
DRIP
DRIP
DRIP
VWOOO!
VWOOOOM
IMPRESSIVE... HE WAS ABLE TO INJURE ME. LORD DIO WAS RIGHT... POLNAREFF IS STRONG-WILLED.
I WILL DEFINITELY CORNER HIM AND KILL HIM... DEFINITELY. MY STAND IS FAR STRONGER THAN HIS.
VWOOOOM
SHOOM!

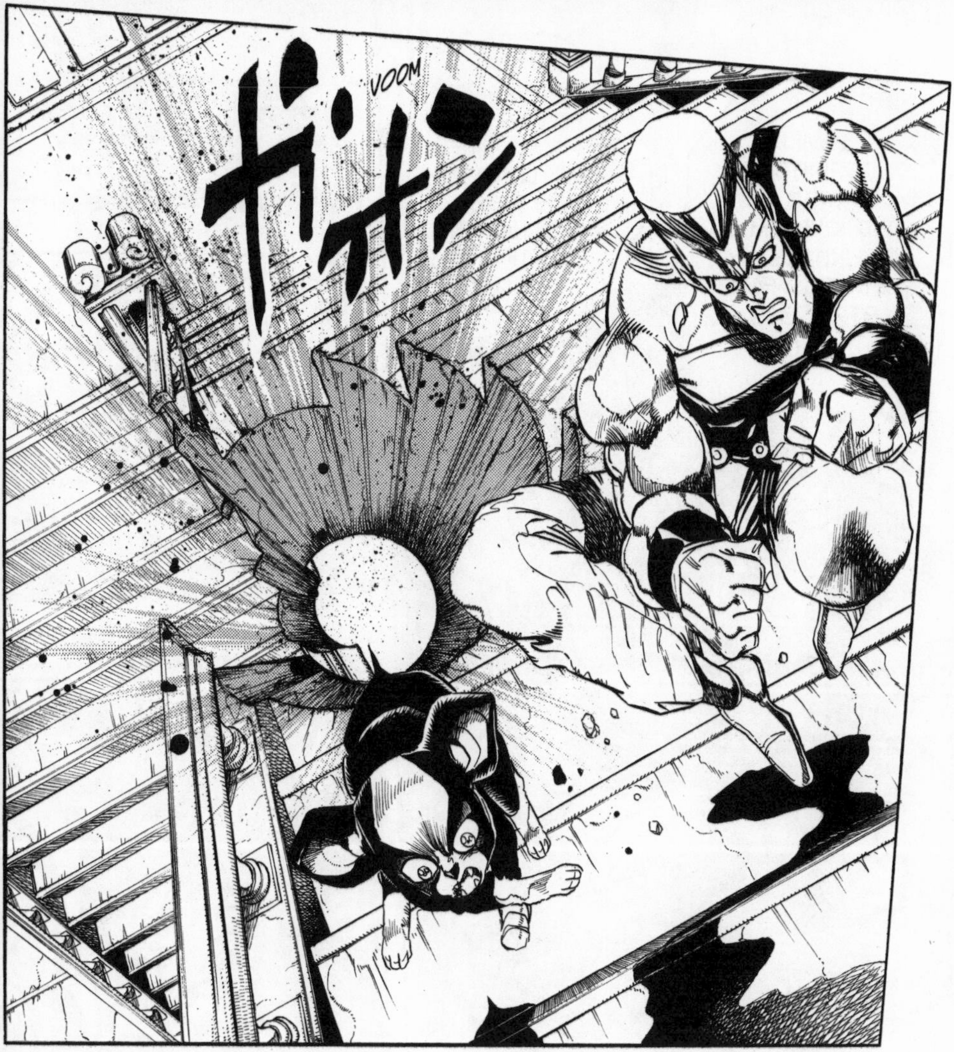
ガオン
VOOM

CHAPTER 128: The Dark Void of Cool Ice PART 4

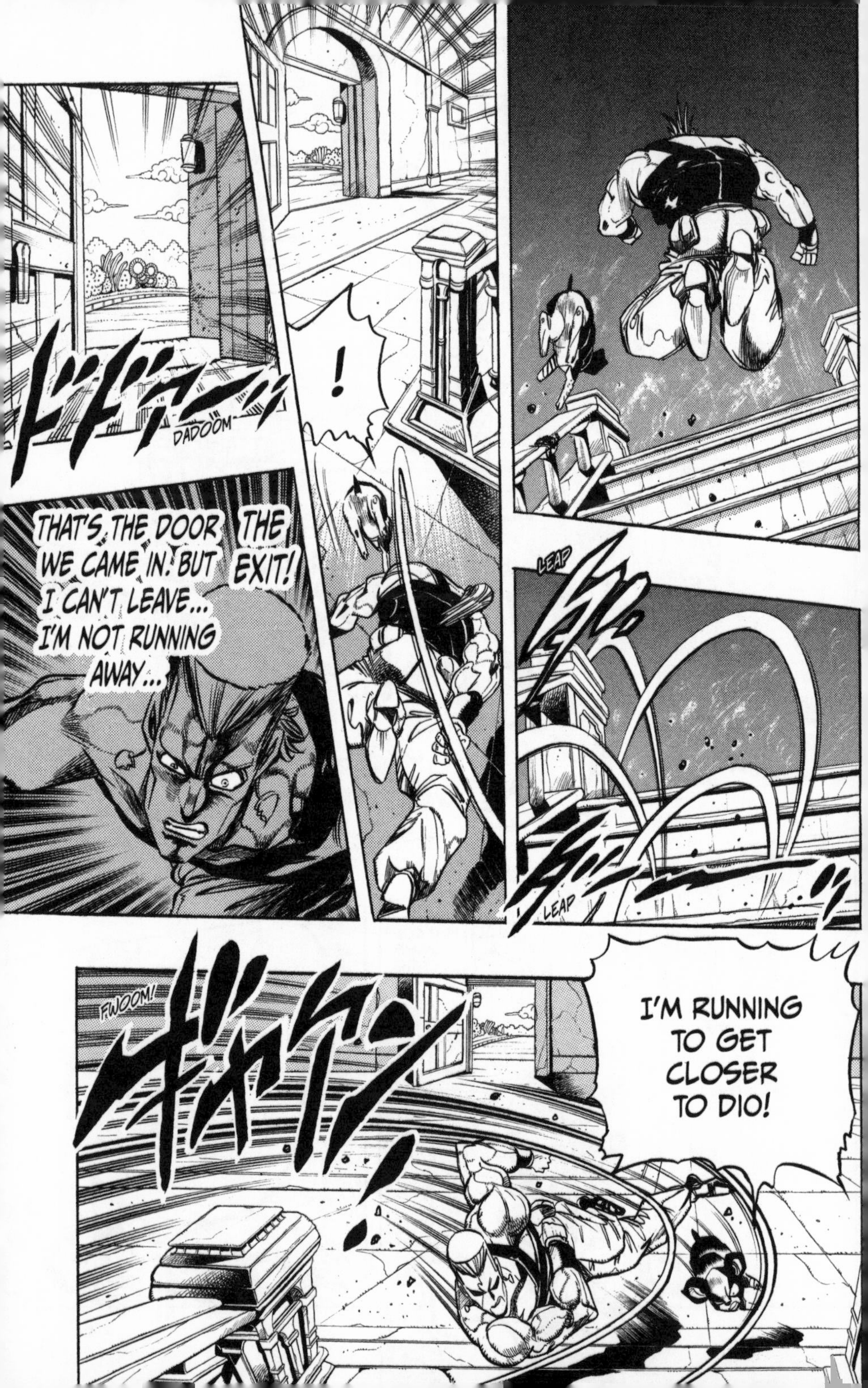
LEAP
LEAP
!
DADOOM
THE EXIT!
THAT'S THE DOOR WE CAME IN. BUT I CAN'T LEAVE... I'M NOT RUNNING AWAY...
I'M RUNNING TO GET CLOSER TO DIO!
FWOOM!

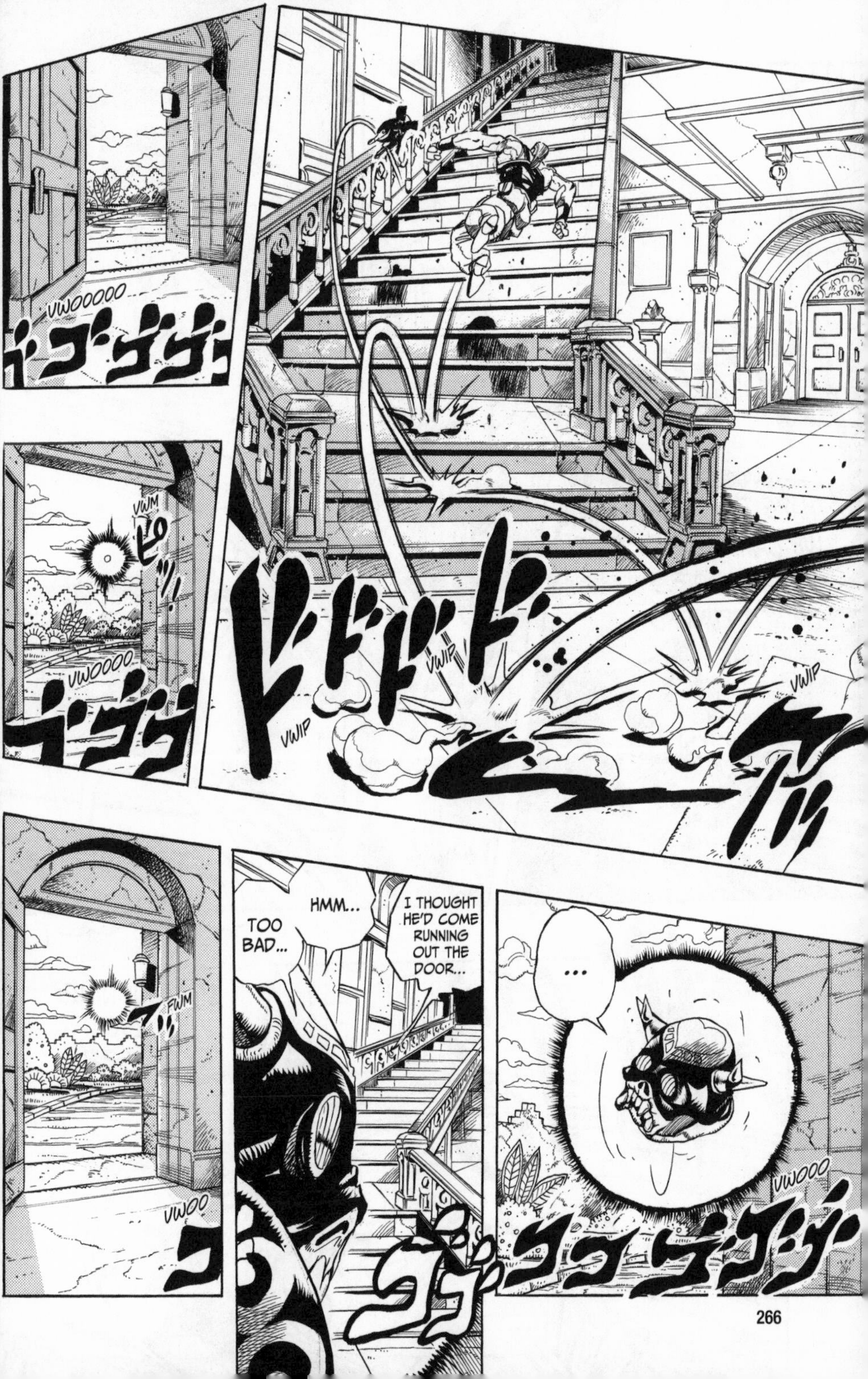
VWIP
VWIP
VWIP
VWOOOOO
VWM
VWOOOO
...
VWOOO
I THOUGHT HE'D COME RUNNING OUT THE DOOR...
HMM...
TOO BAD...
FWM
VWOO

Second Floor Map

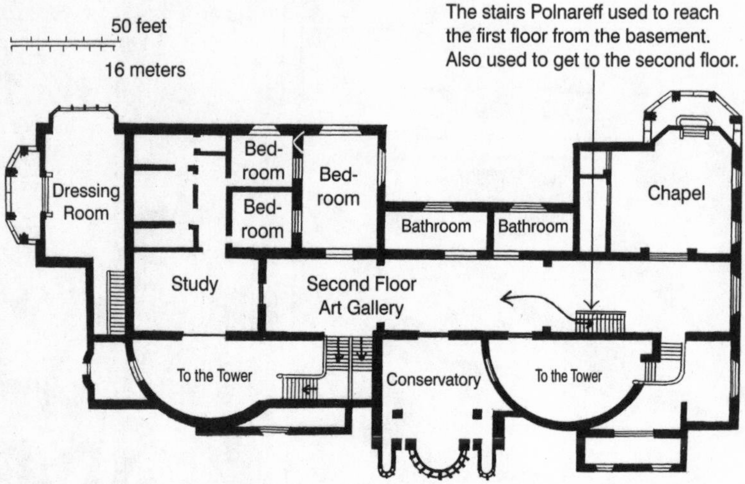
50 feet
16 meters
The stairs Polnareff used to reach the first floor from the basement. Also used to get to the second floor.
Dressing Room
Bed-room
Bed-room
Bed-room
Bathroom
Bathroom
Chapel
Study
Second Floor Art Gallery
To the Tower
Conservatory
To the Tower

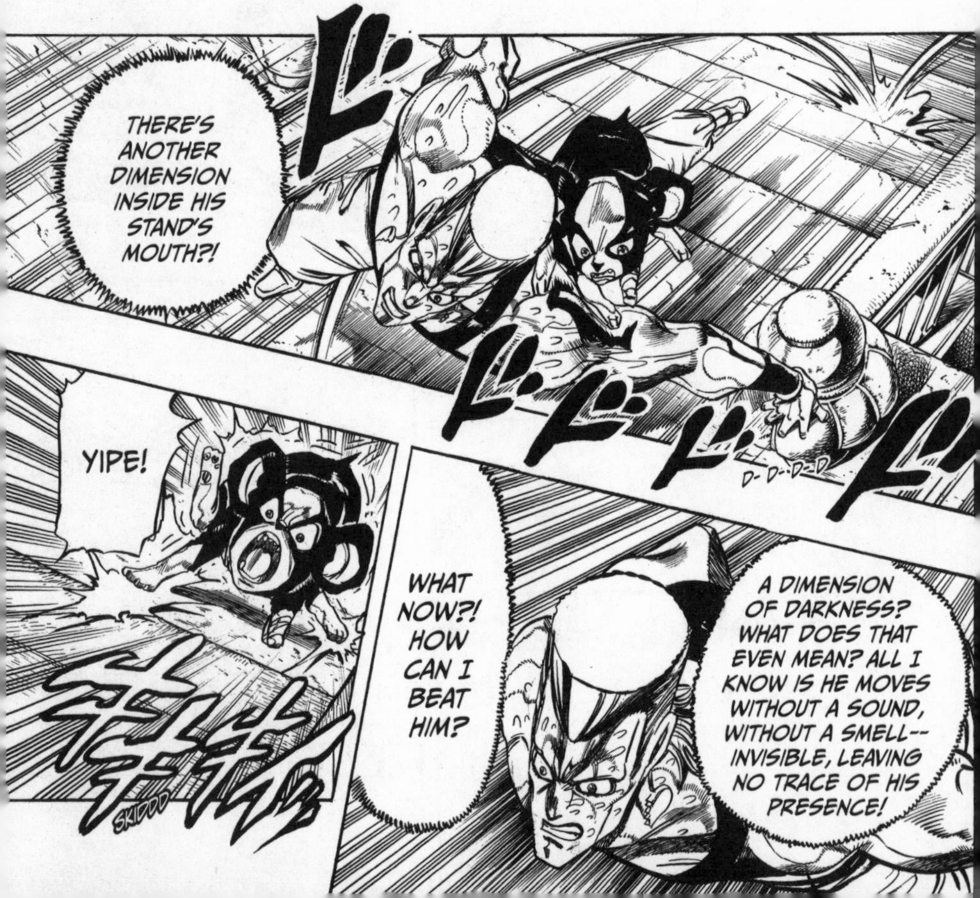
THERE'S ANOTHER DIMENSION INSIDE HIS STAND'S MOUTH?!
D-D-D-D
A DIMENSION OF DARKNESS? WHAT DOES THAT EVEN MEAN? ALL I KNOW IS HE MOVES WITHOUT A SOUND, WITHOUT A SMELL--INVISIBLE, LEAVING NO TRACE OF HIS PRESENCE!
WHAT NOW?! HOW CAN I BEAT HIM?
YIPE!
SKIDDD

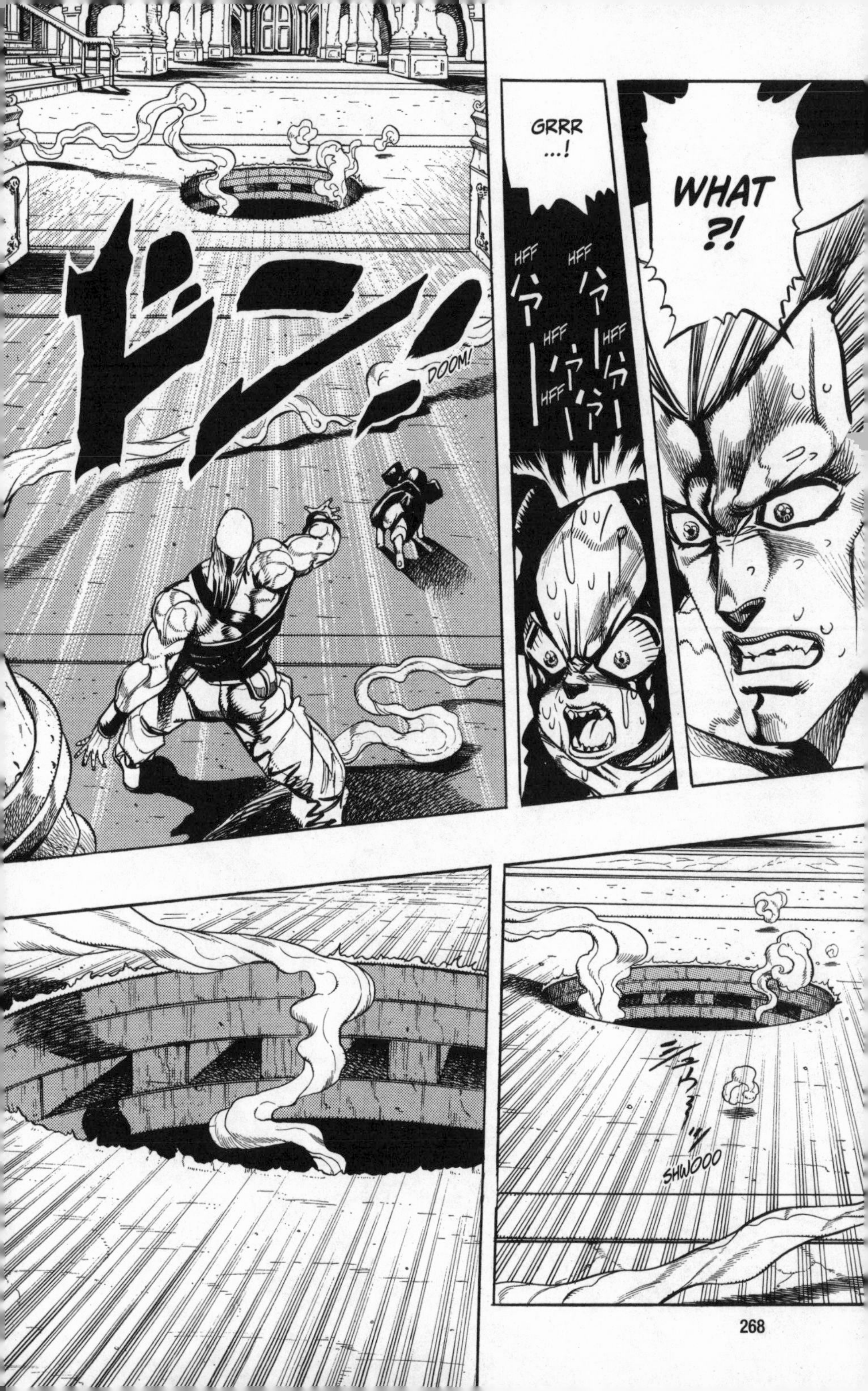
WHAT ?!
GRRR ...!
HFF HFF HFF HFF HFF HFF
DOOM!
SHWOOO

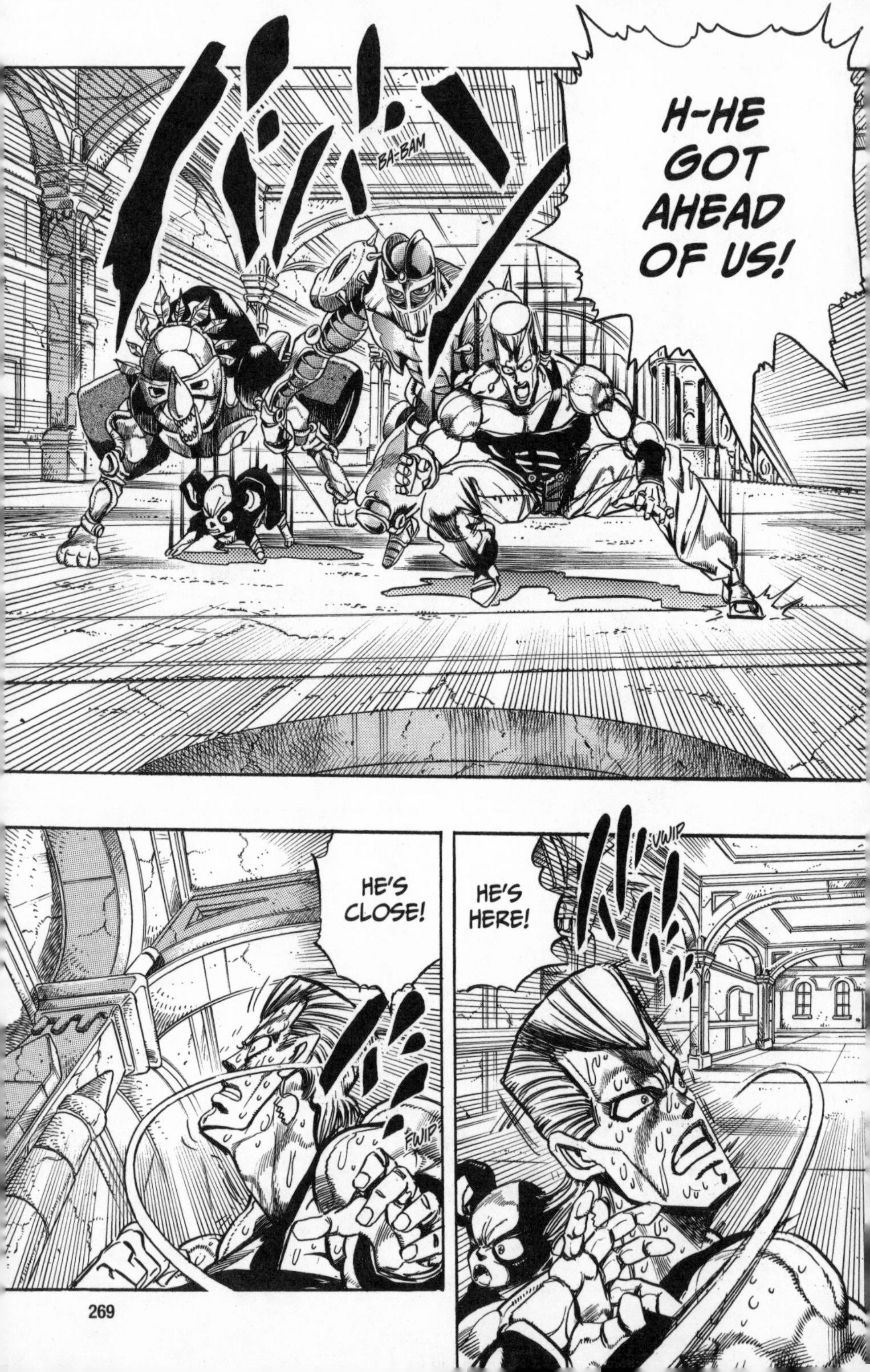
H-HE GOT AHEAD OF US!
BA-BAM
VWIP
HE'S HERE!
HE'S CLOSE!
FWIP

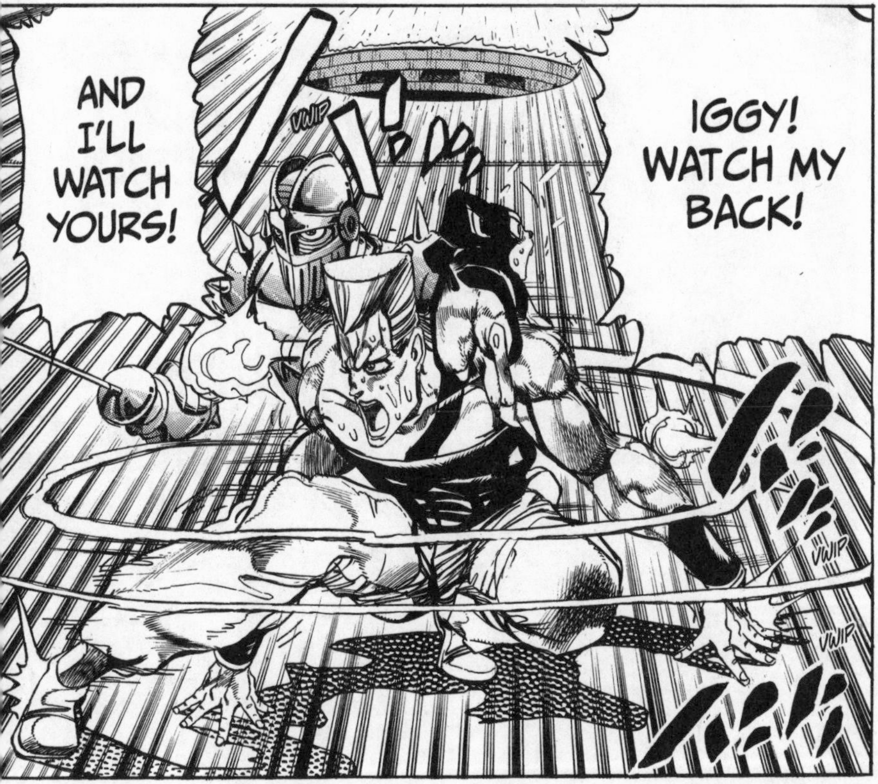
IGGY! WATCH MY BACK!
AND I'LL WATCH YOURS!
VWIP
VWIP
VWIP

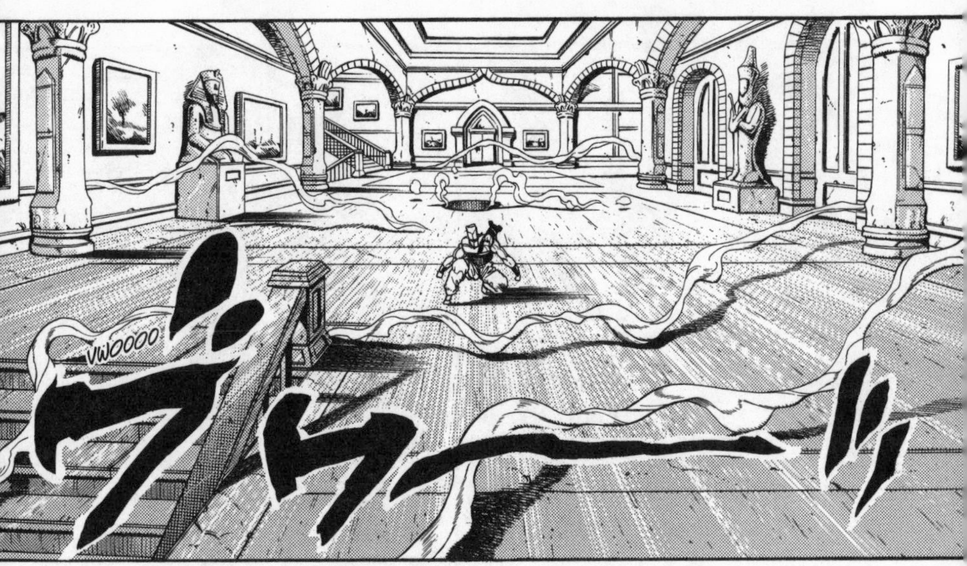
VWOOOO

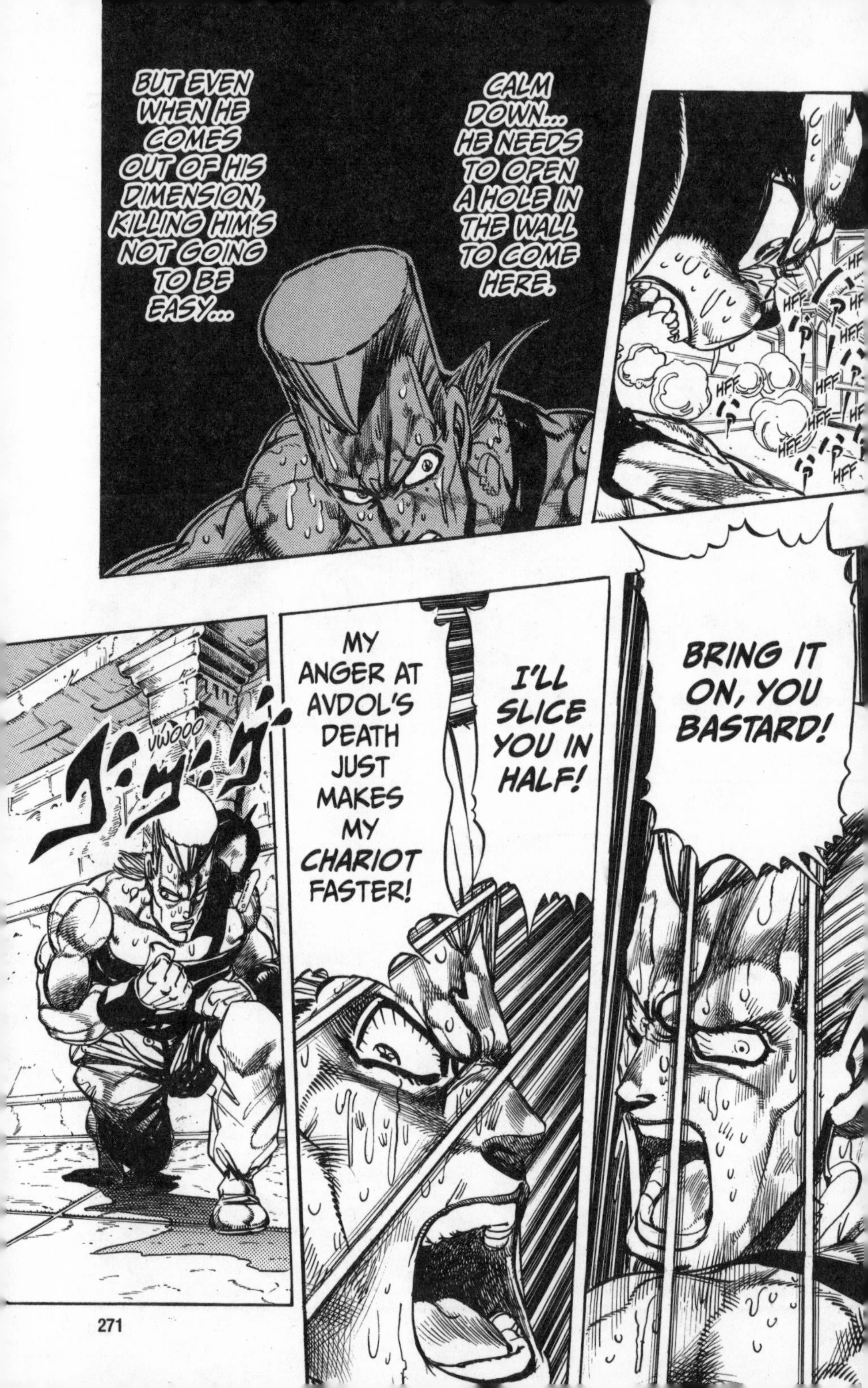
HFF
HFF
HFF
HFF
HFF
CALM DOWN... HE NEEDS TO OPEN A HOLE IN THE WALL TO COME HERE.
BUT EVEN WHEN HE COMES OUT OF HIS DIMENSION, KILLING HIM'S NOT GOING TO BE EASY...
BRING IT ON, YOU BASTARD!
I'LL SLICE YOU IN HALF!
MY ANGER AT AVDOL'S DEATH JUST MAKES MY CHARIOT FASTER!
VWOOO

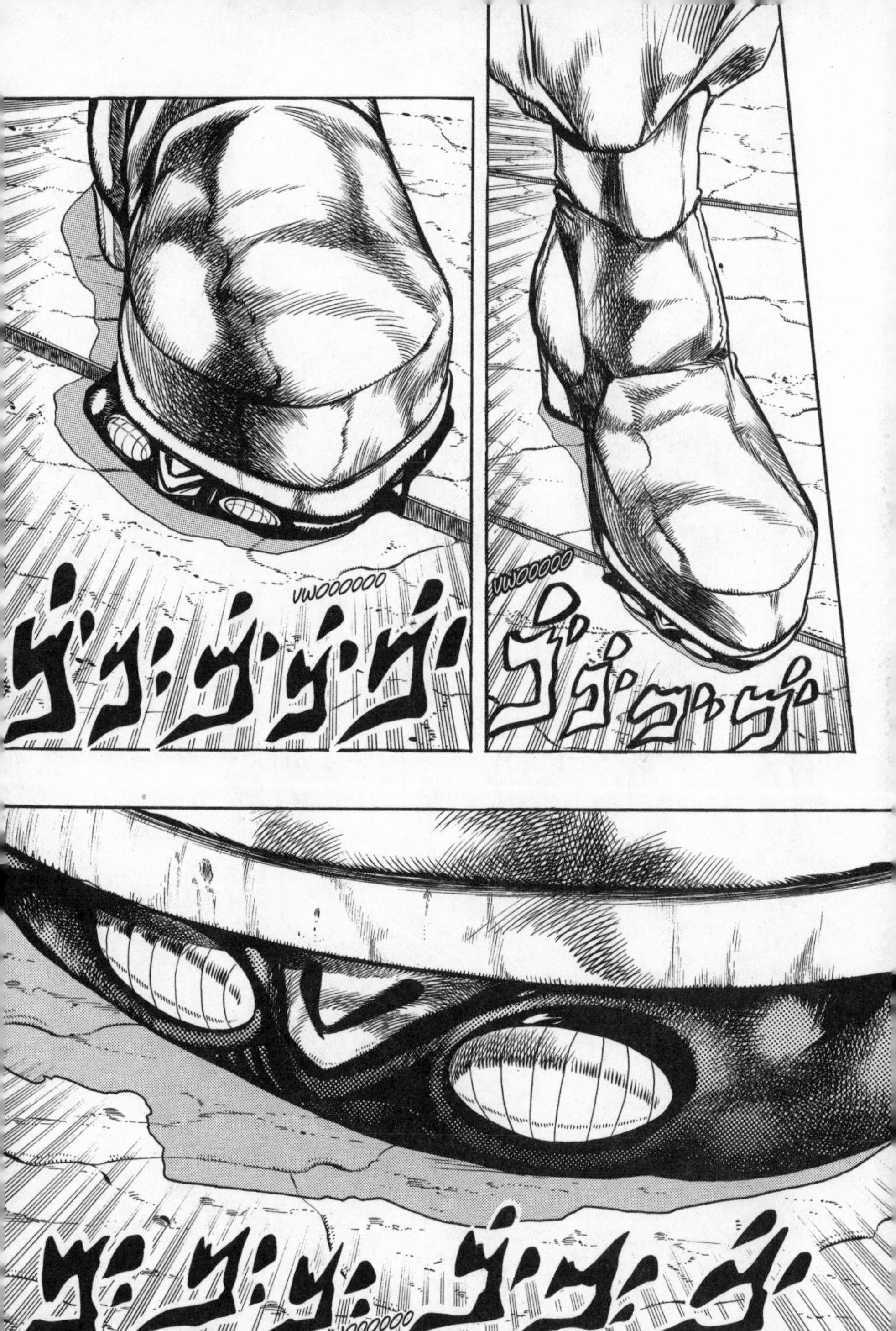
VWOOOOOO
VWOOOOOO
VWOOOOOOO

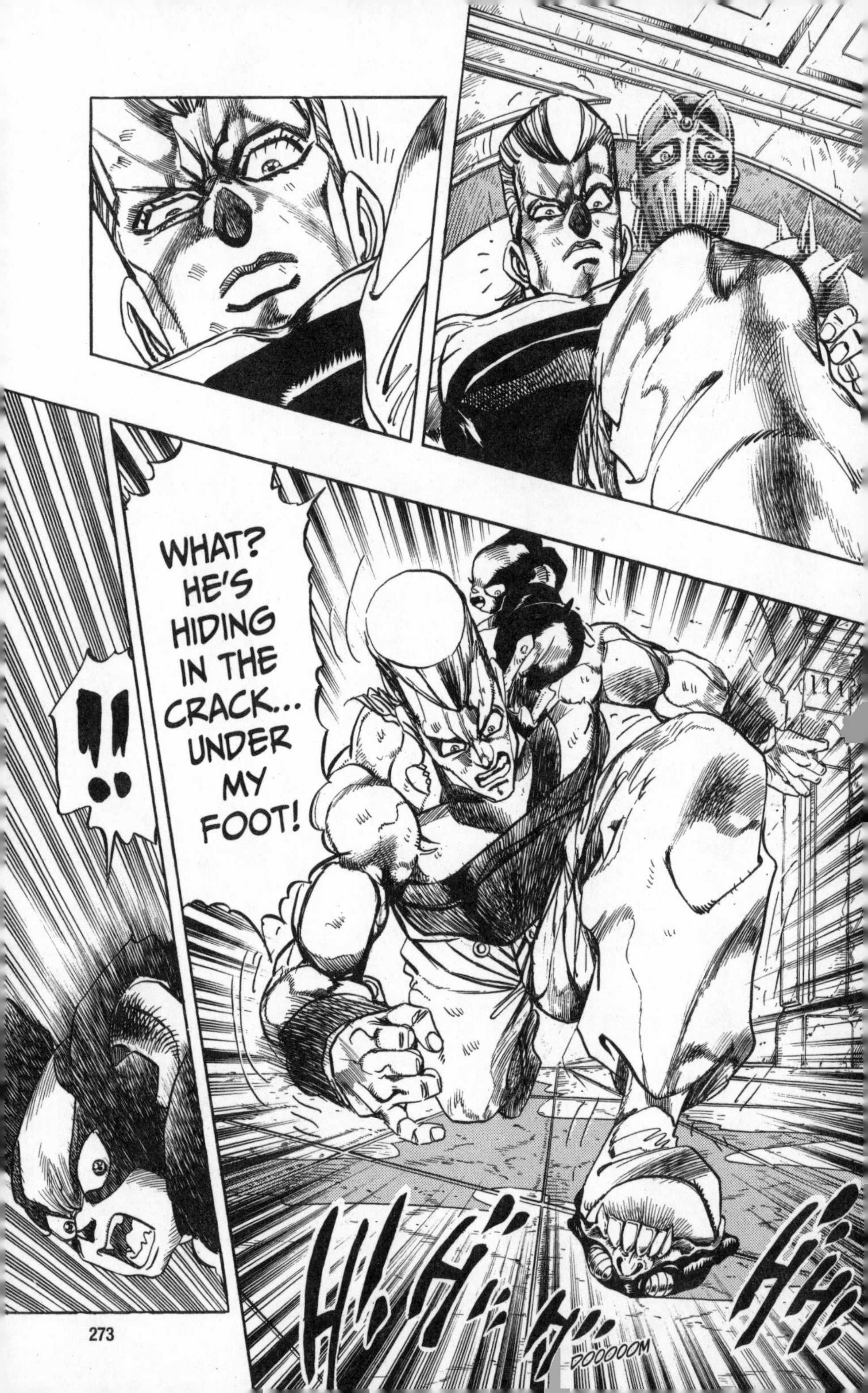
WHAT? HE'S HIDING IN THE CRACK... UNDER MY FOOT!
!!
DOOOOOM

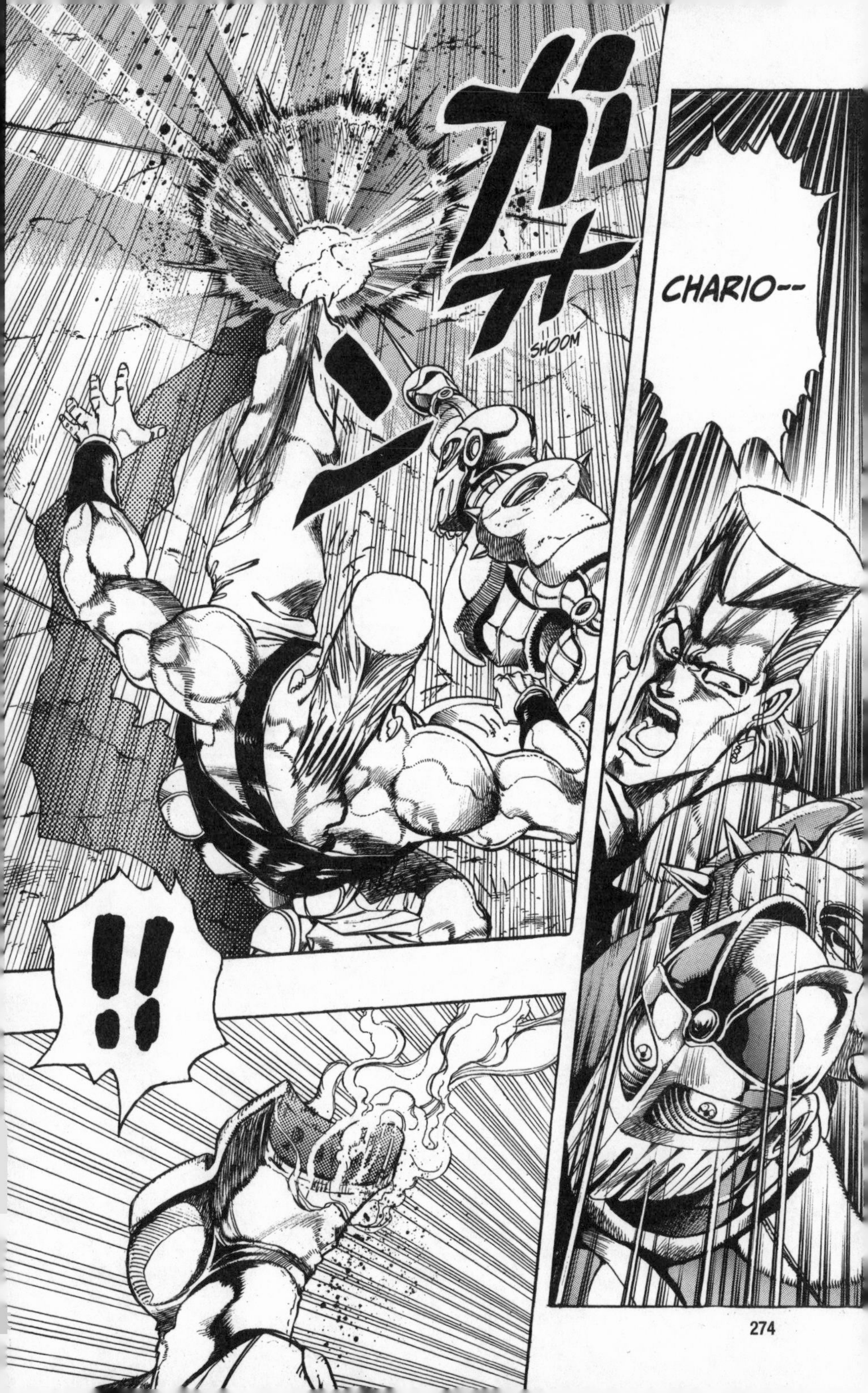
CHARIO--
ガオ
SHOOM
!!

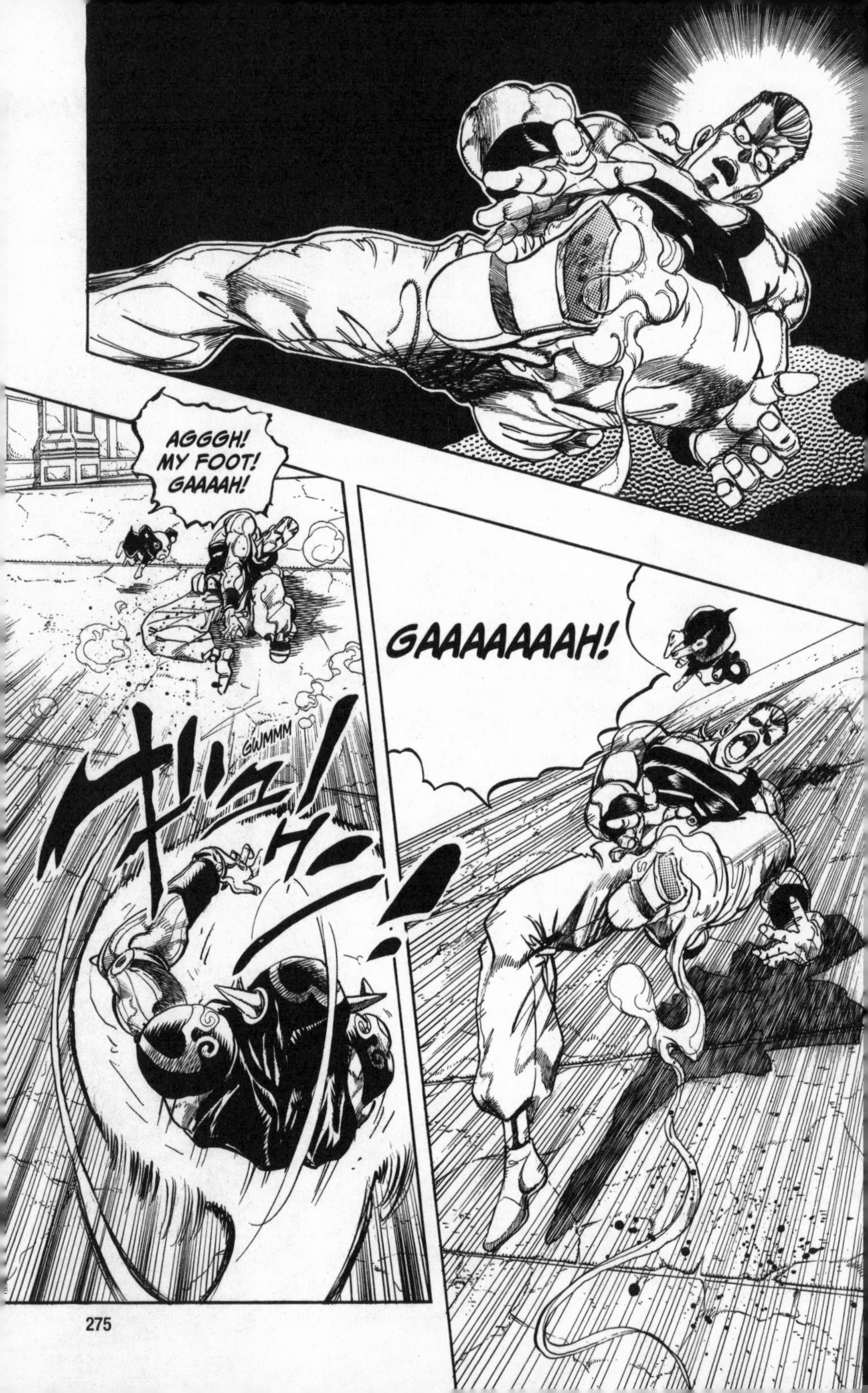
GAAAAAAAH!
AGGGH! MY FOOT! GAAAAH!
GWMMM

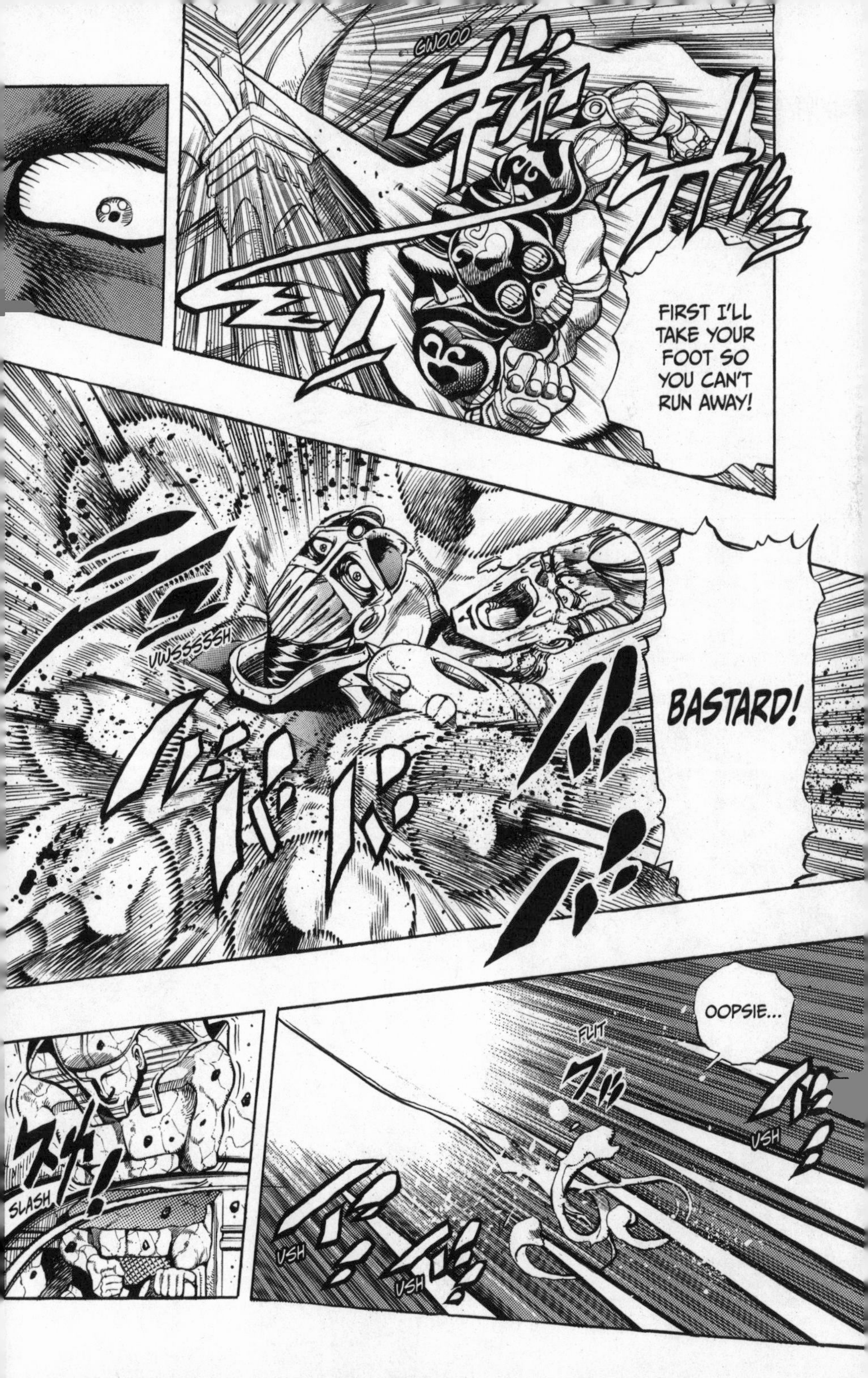
GWOOO
FIRST I'LL TAKE YOUR FOOT SO YOU CAN'T RUN AWAY!
BASTARD!
VWSSSSSH
OOPSIE...
FLIT
USH
USH
USH
SLASH

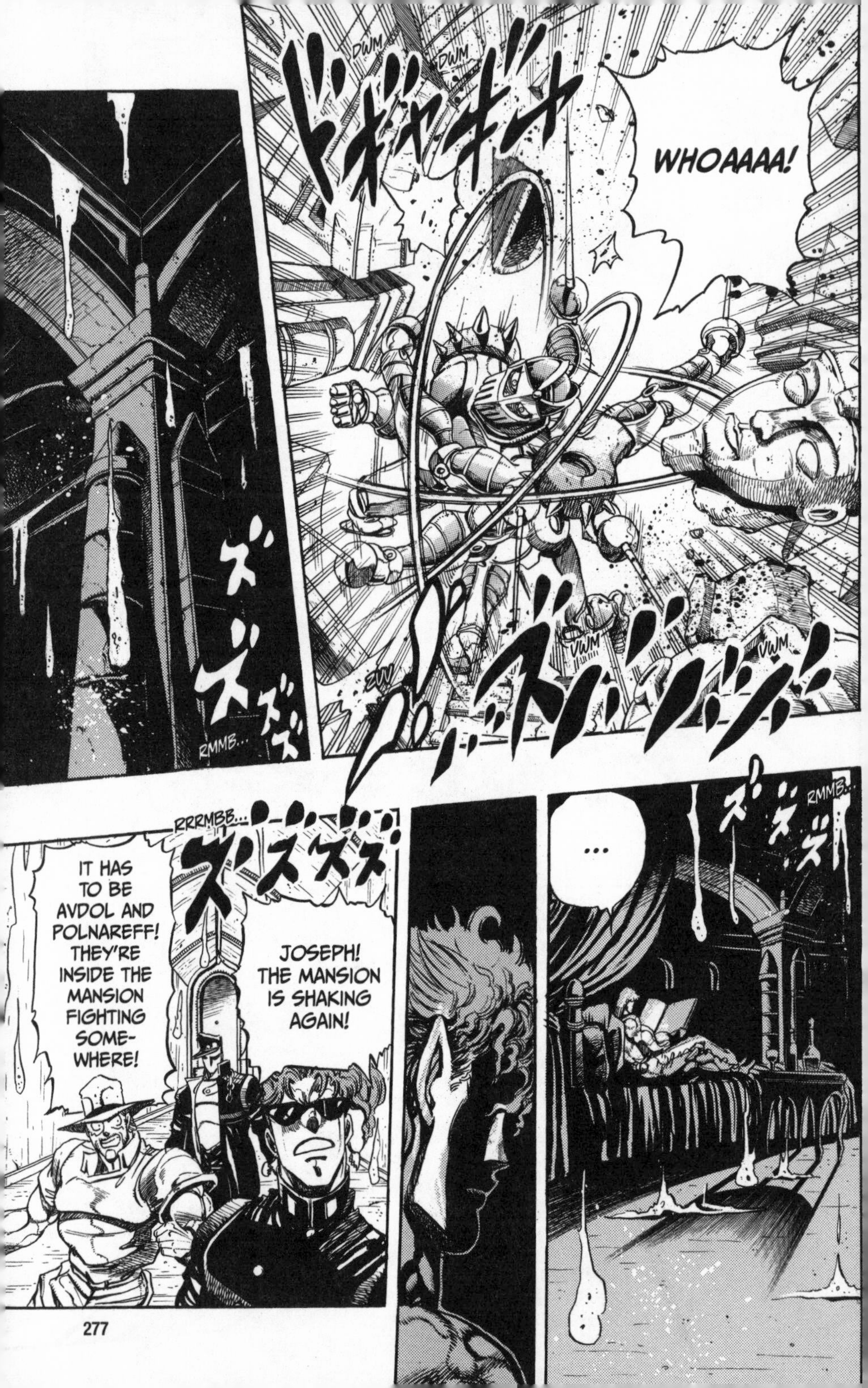
DWM
DWM
WHOAAAA!
VWM
VWM
ZUV
RMMB...
...
RMMB...
RRRMBB...
JOSEPH! THE MANSION IS SHAKING AGAIN!
IT HAS TO BE AVDOL AND POLNAREFF! THEY'RE INSIDE THE MANSION FIGHTING SOME-WHERE!

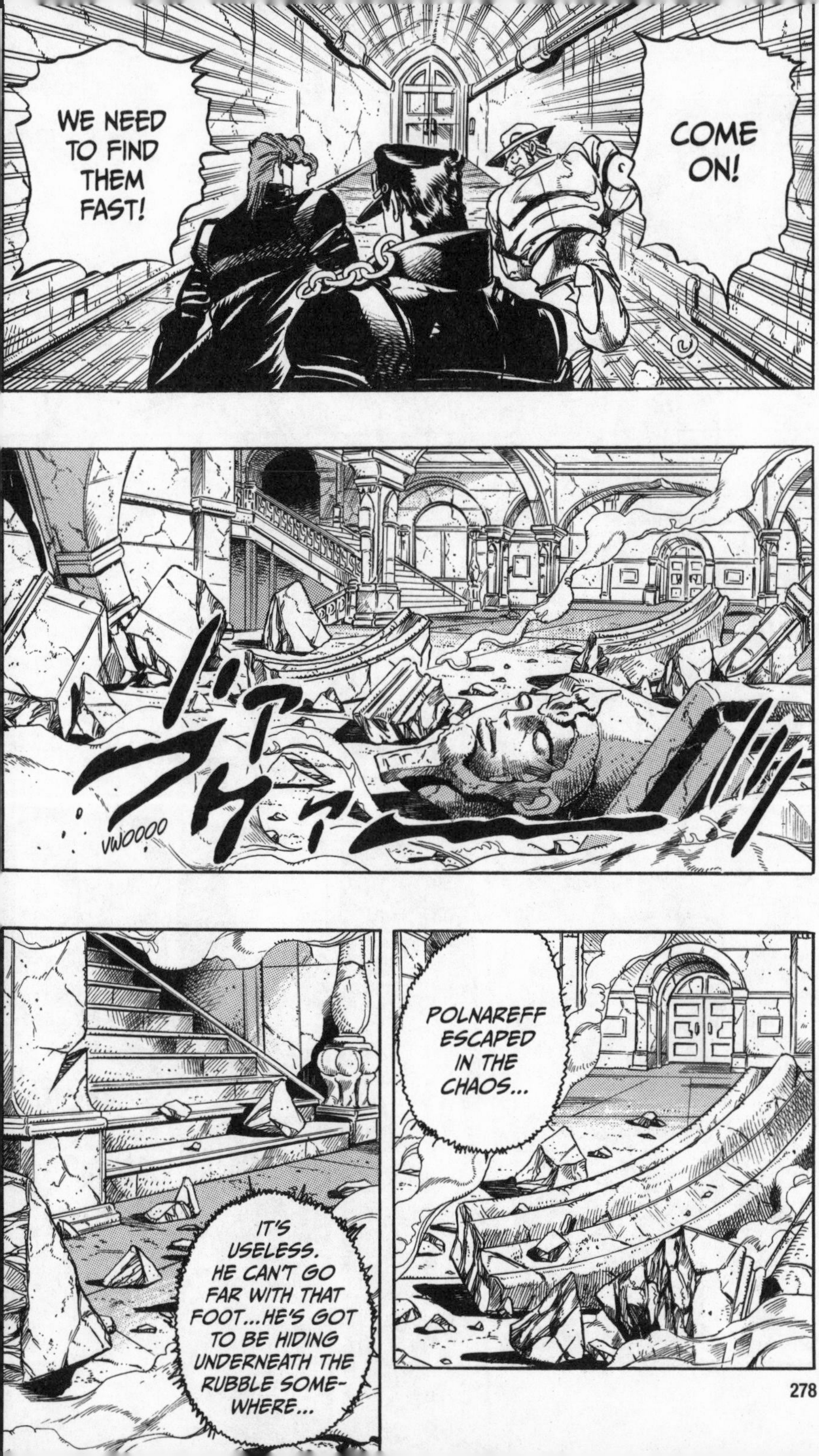
COME ON!
WE NEED TO FIND THEM FAST!
VWOOOO
POLNAREFF ESCAPED IN THE CHAOS...
IT'S USELESS. HE CAN'T GO FAR WITH THAT FOOT...HE'S GOT TO BE HIDING UNDERNEATH THE RUBBLE SOME-WHERE...

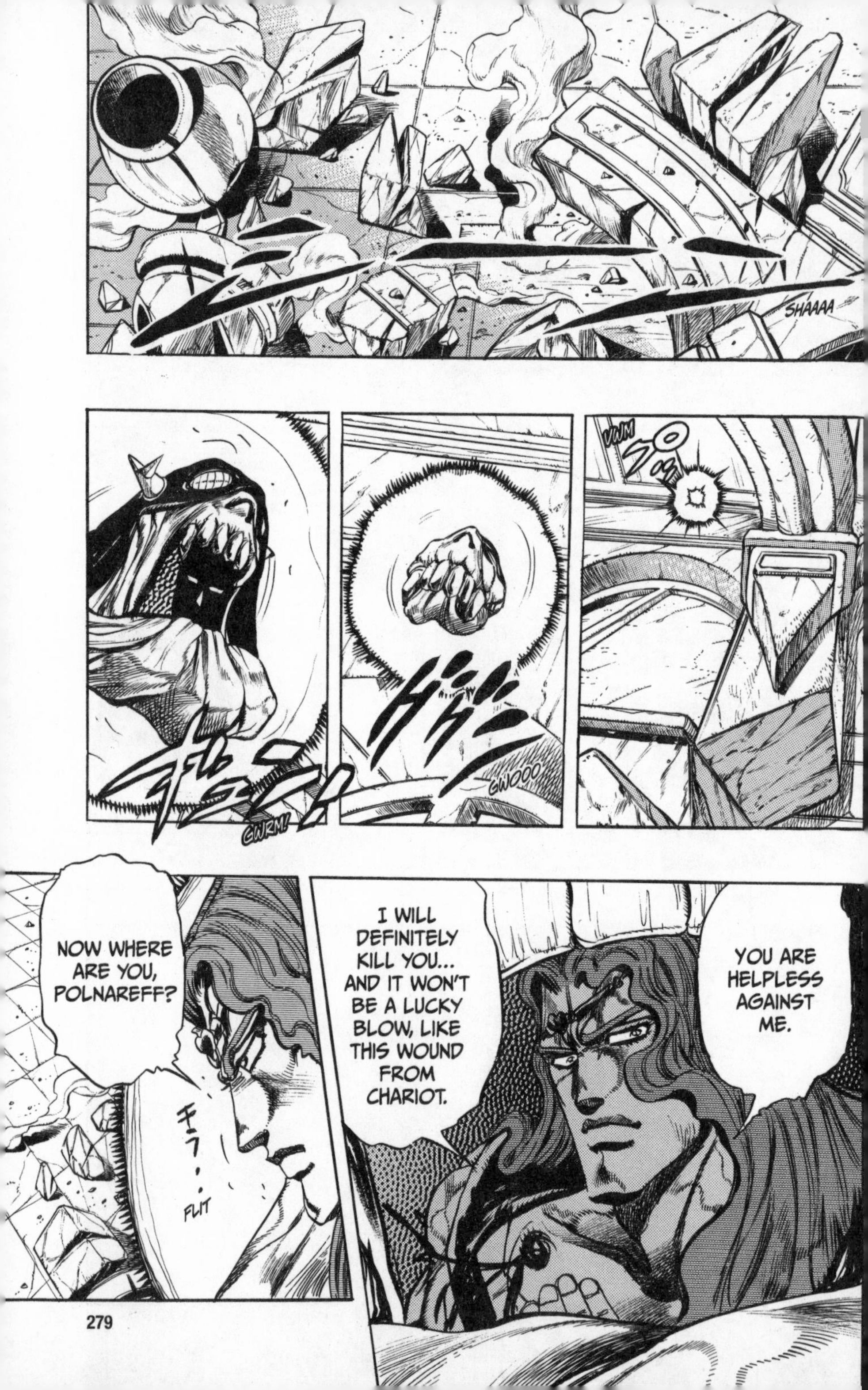
SHAAAA
VWM
GWOOO
GWRM!
YOU ARE HELPLESS AGAINST ME.
I WILL DEFINITELY KILL YOU... AND IT WON'T BE A LUCKY BLOW, LIKE THIS WOUND FROM CHARIOT.
NOW WHERE ARE YOU, POLNAREFF?
FLIT

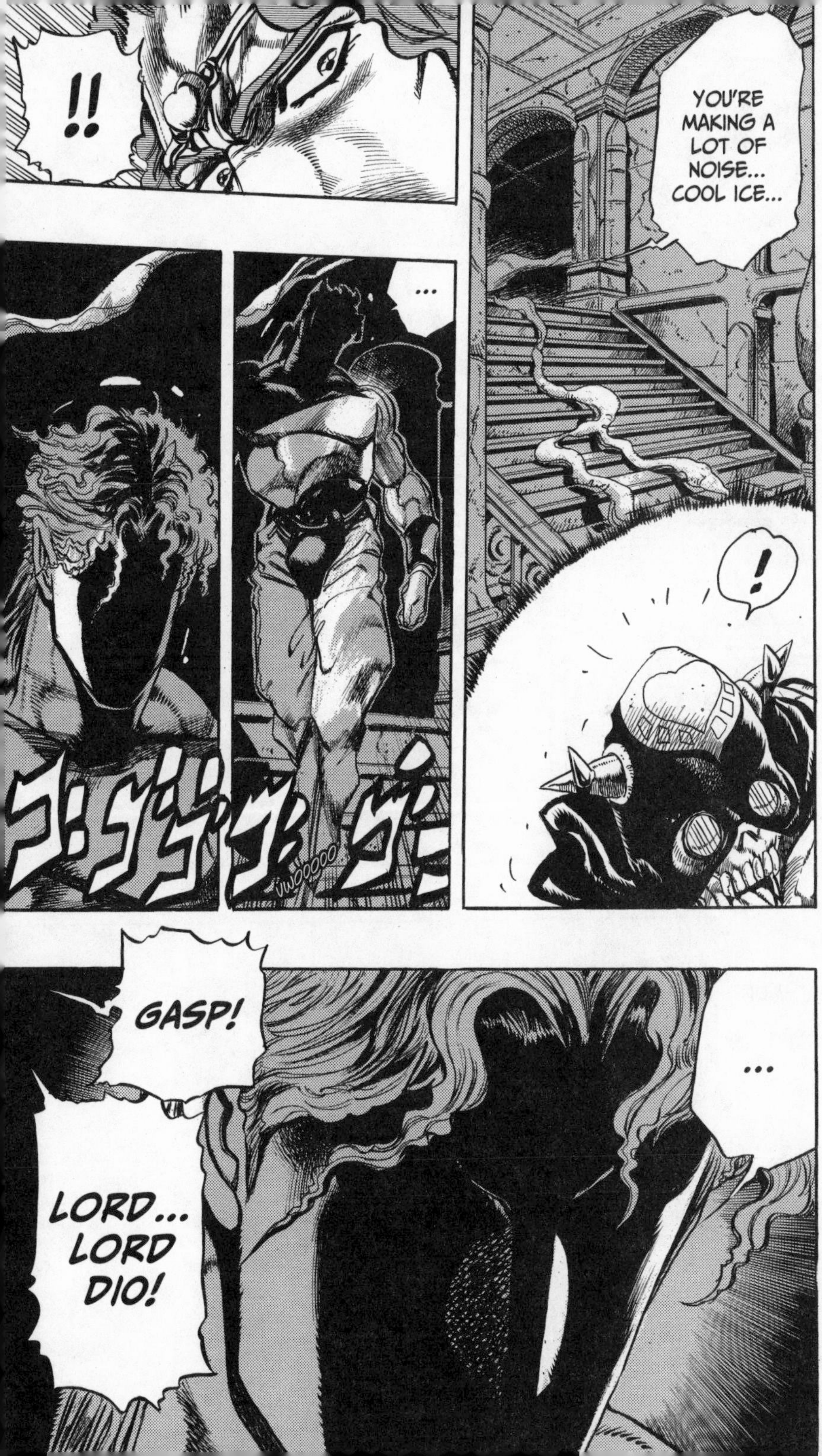
YOU'RE MAKING A LOT OF NOISE... COOL ICE...
!
!!
...
VWOOOOO
...
GASP!
LORD... LORD DIO!

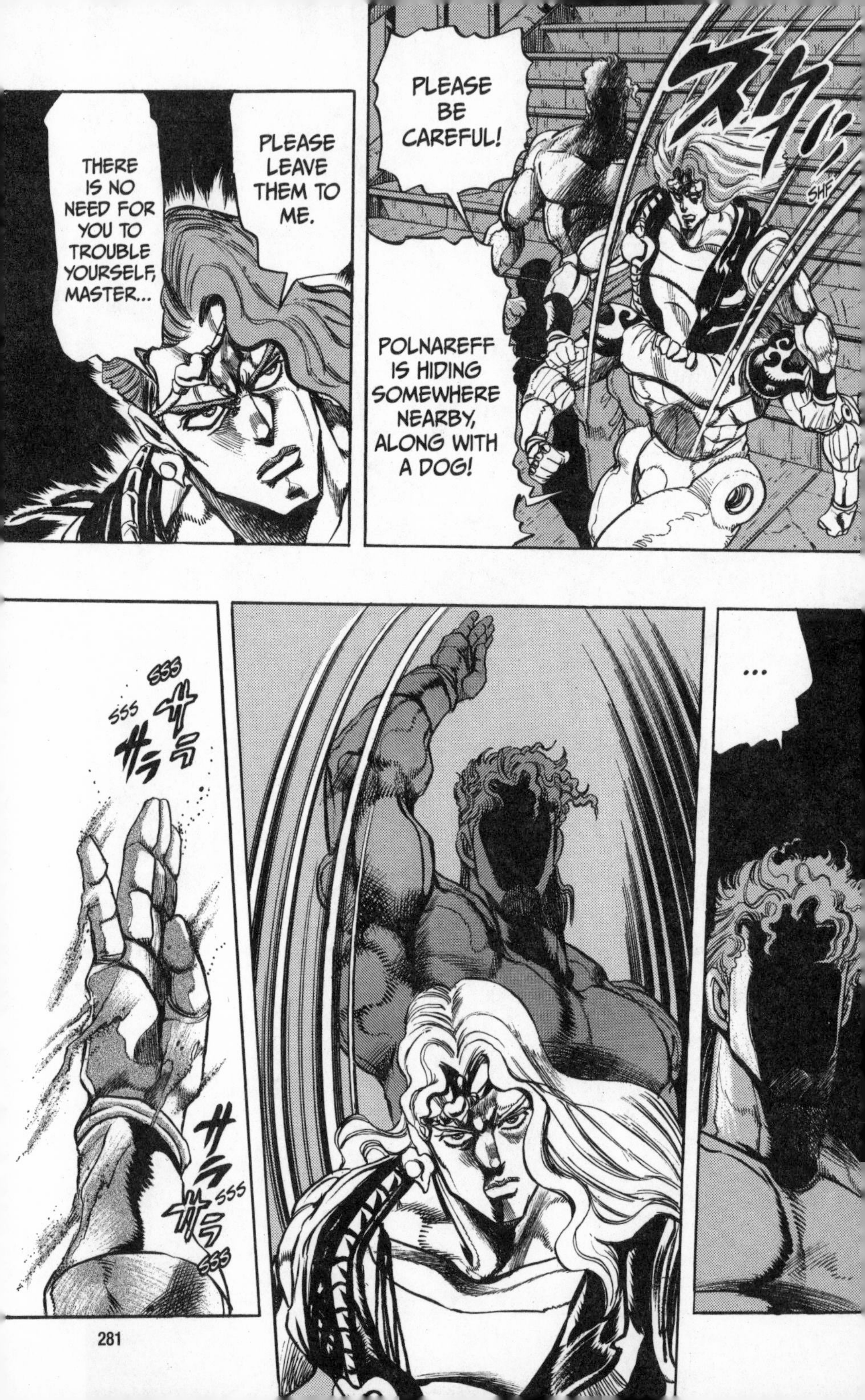
SHF
PLEASE BE CAREFUL!
POLNAREFF IS HIDING SOMEWHERE NEARBY, ALONG WITH A DOG!
PLEASE LEAVE THEM TO ME.
THERE IS NO NEED FOR YOU TO TROUBLE YOURSELF, MASTER...
...
SSS
SSS
SSS
SSS

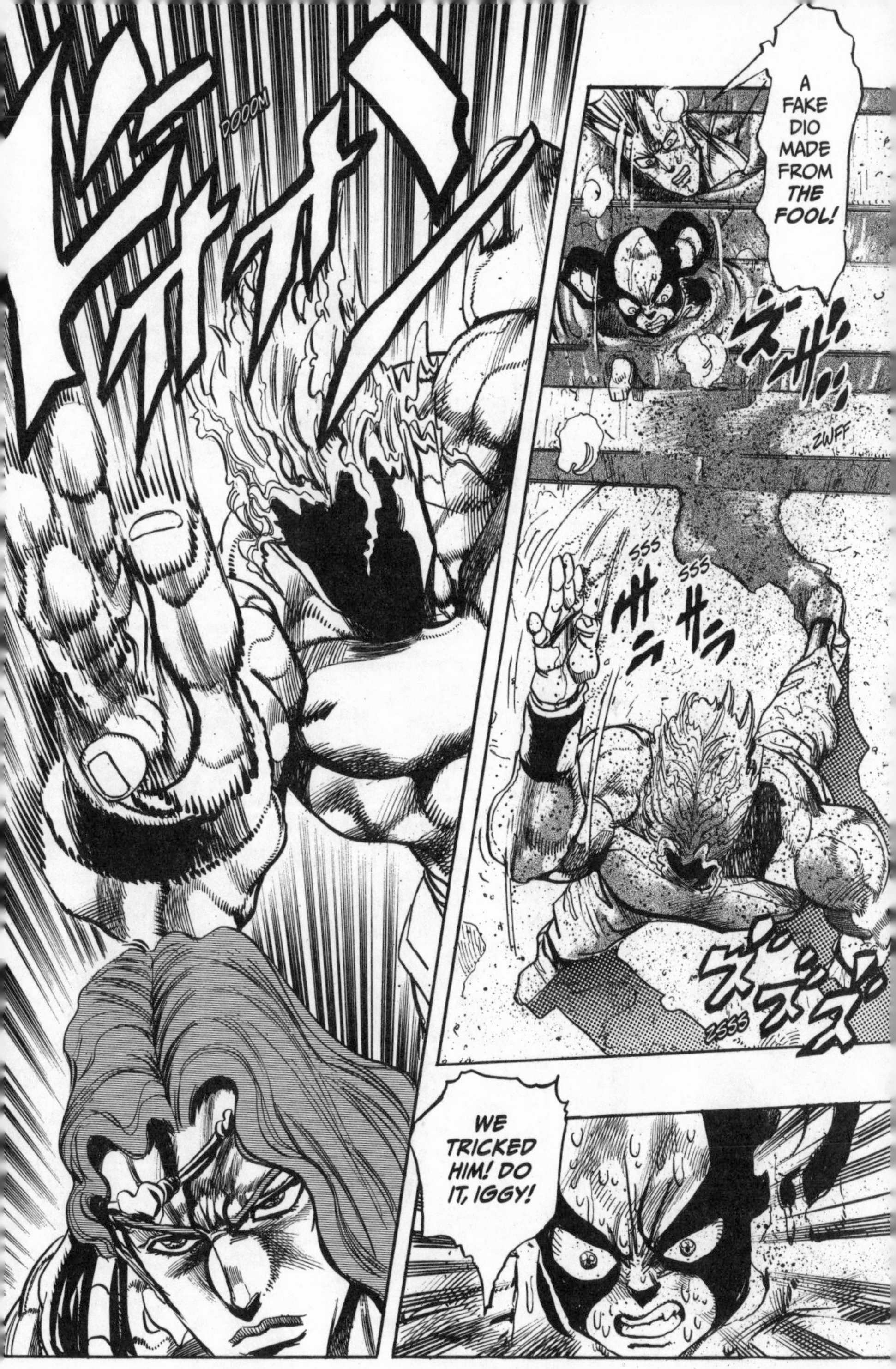
A FAKE DIO MADE FROM THE FOOL!
ZWFF
SSS
SSS
ZSSS
WE TRICKED HIM! DO IT, IGGY!
DOOOM

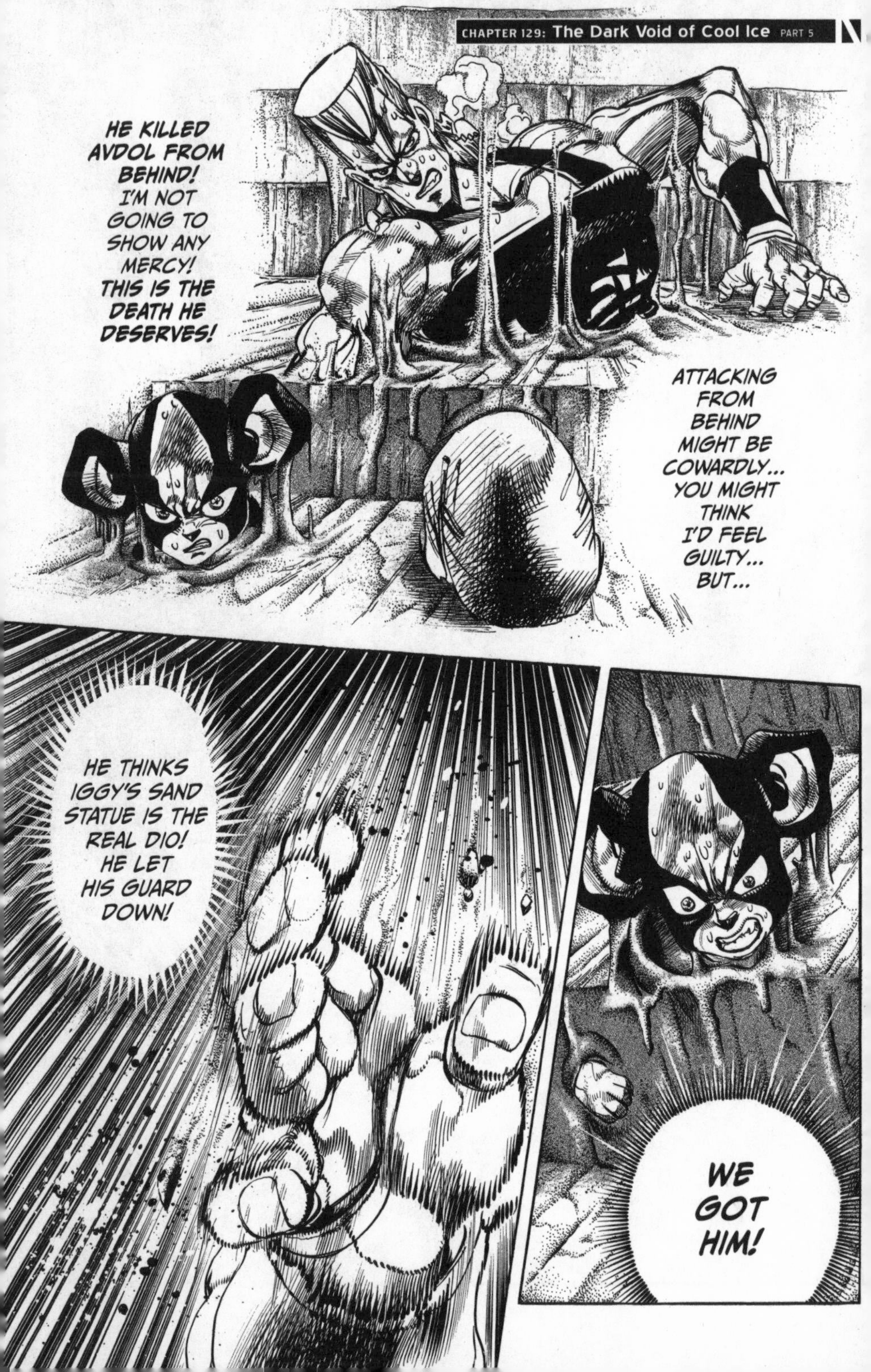
ATTACKING FROM BEHIND MIGHT BE COWARDLY... YOU MIGHT THINK I'D FEEL GUILTY... BUT...
HE KILLED AVDOL FROM BEHIND! I'M NOT GOING TO SHOW ANY MERCY! THIS IS THE DEATH HE DESERVES!
WE GOT HIM!
HE THINKS IGGY'S SAND STATUE IS THE REAL DIO! HE LET HIS GUARD DOWN!

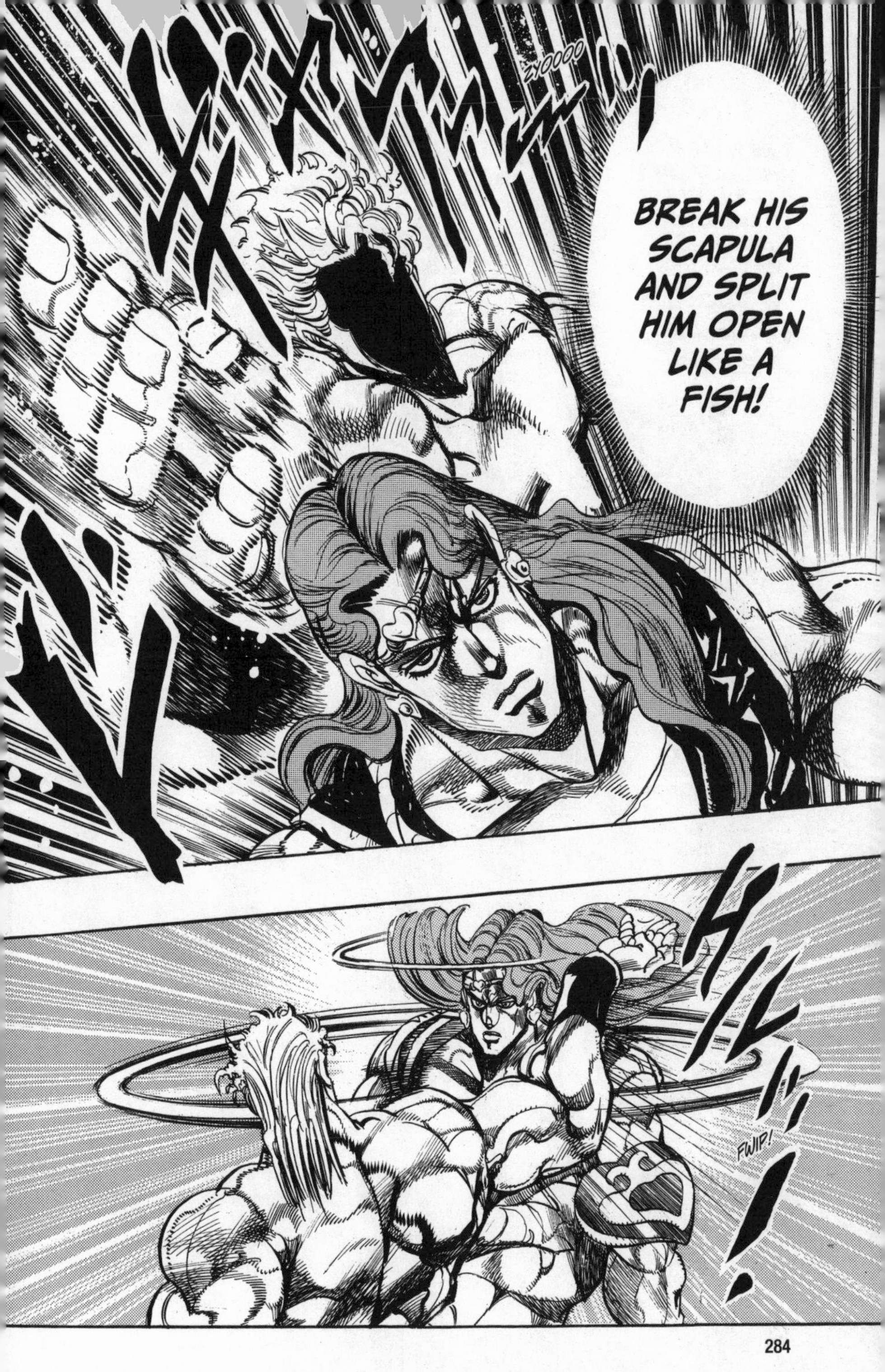
ZYOOOO
BREAK HIS SCAPULA AND SPLIT HIM OPEN LIKE A FISH!
FWIP!

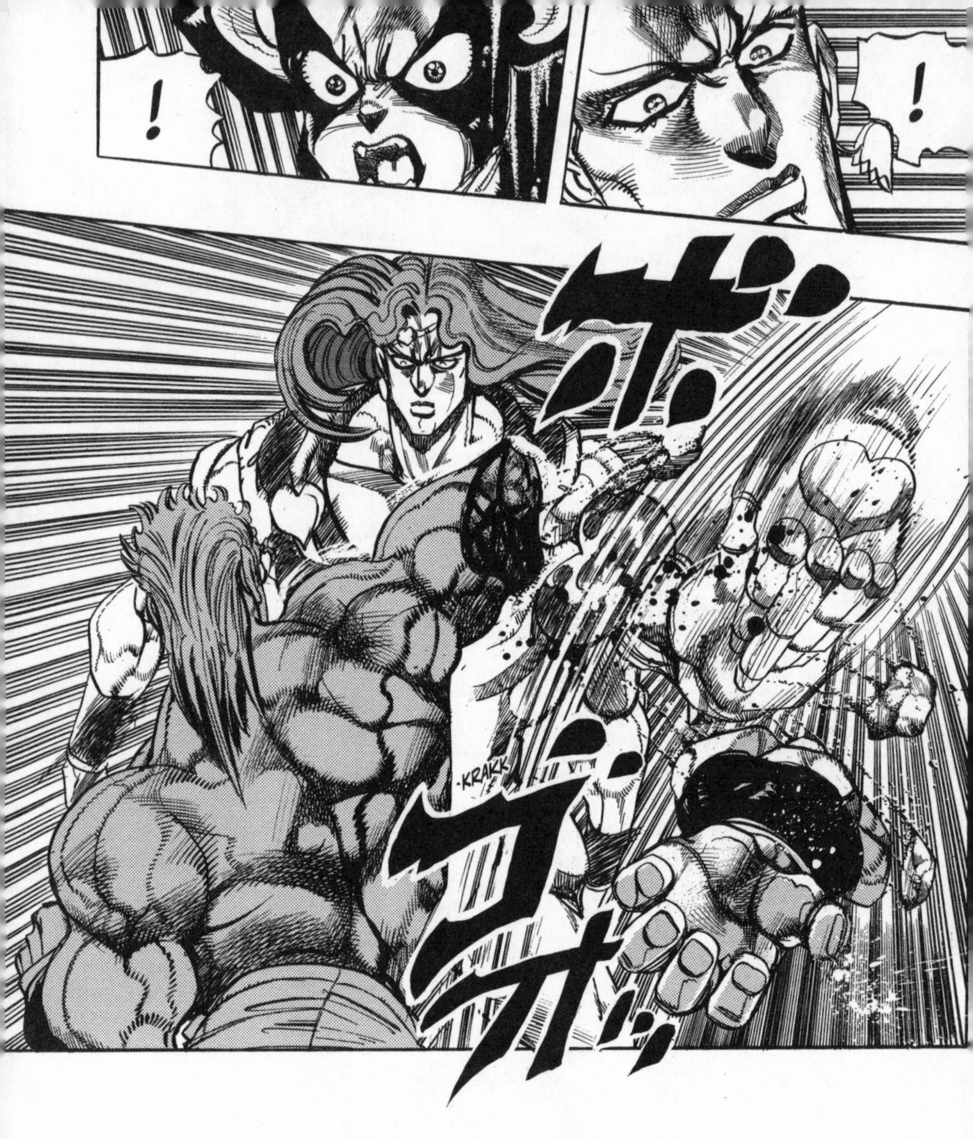
!
!
KRAKK

CHAPTER 129: The Dark Void of Cool Ice PART 5

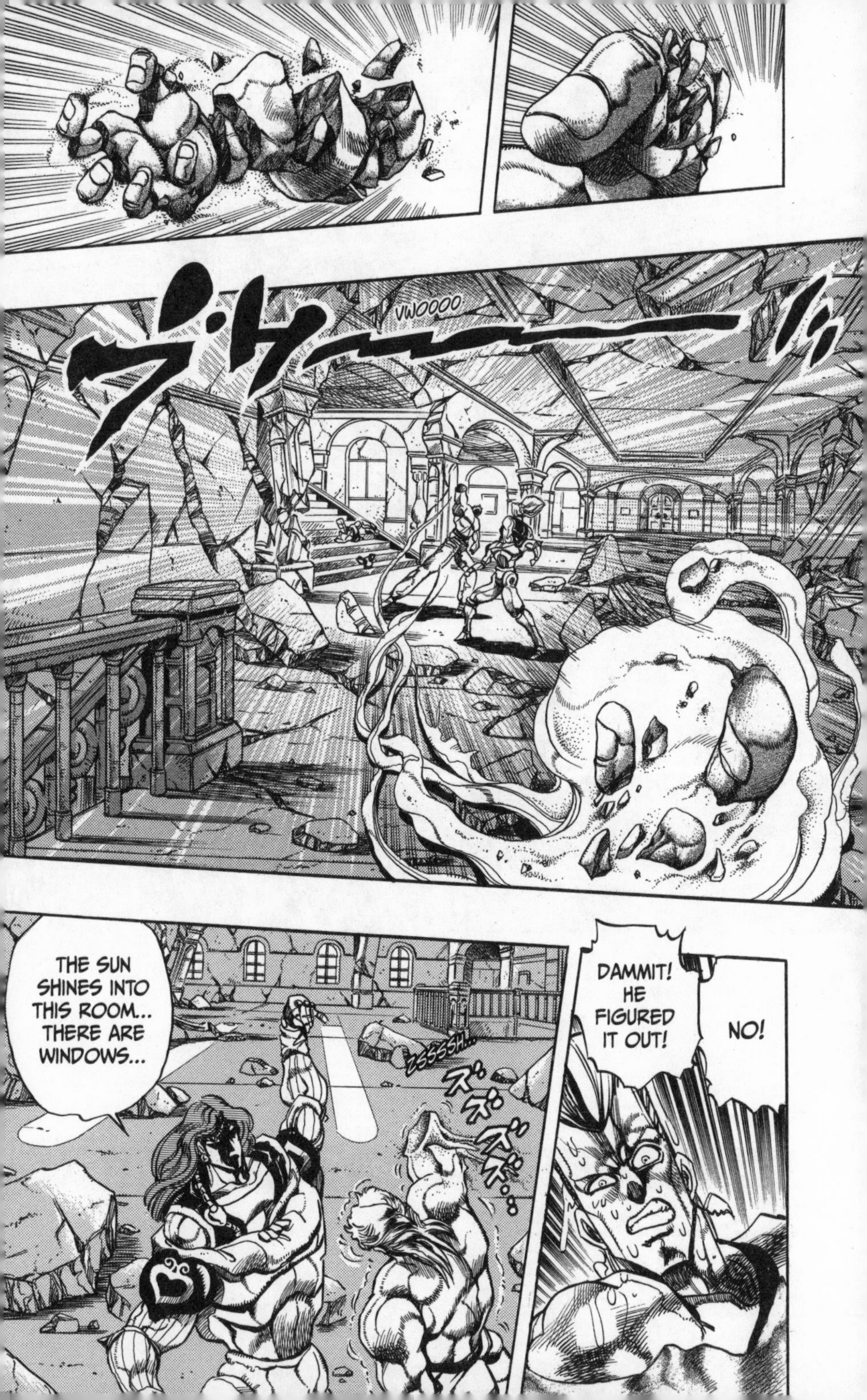
VWOOOO
NO!
DAMMIT! HE FIGURED IT OUT!
THE SUN SHINES INTO THIS ROOM... THERE ARE WINDOWS...
ZSSSSH...

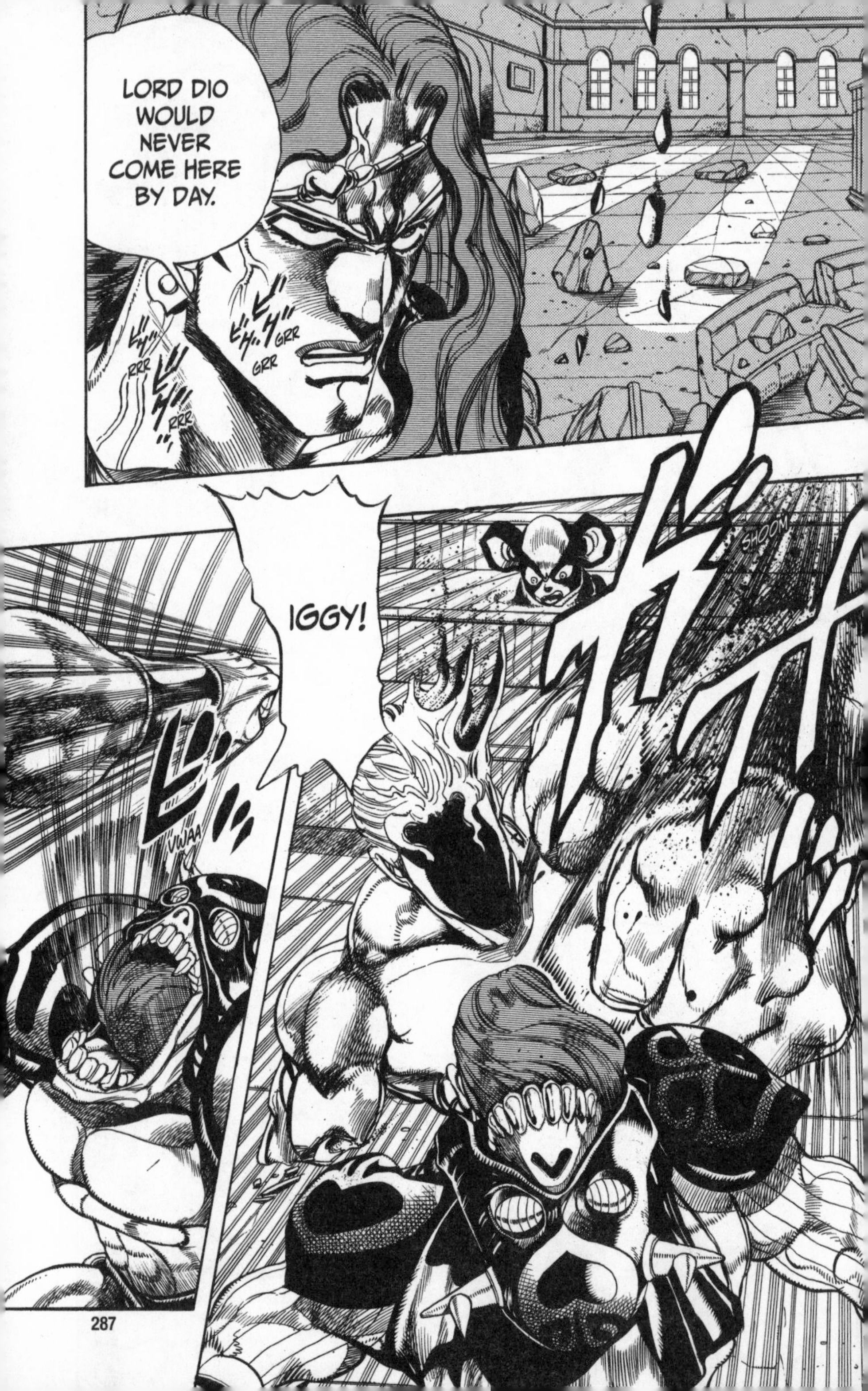
LORD DIO WOULD NEVER COME HERE BY DAY.
GRR
GRR
RRR
RRR
SHOOM
IGGY!
VWAA

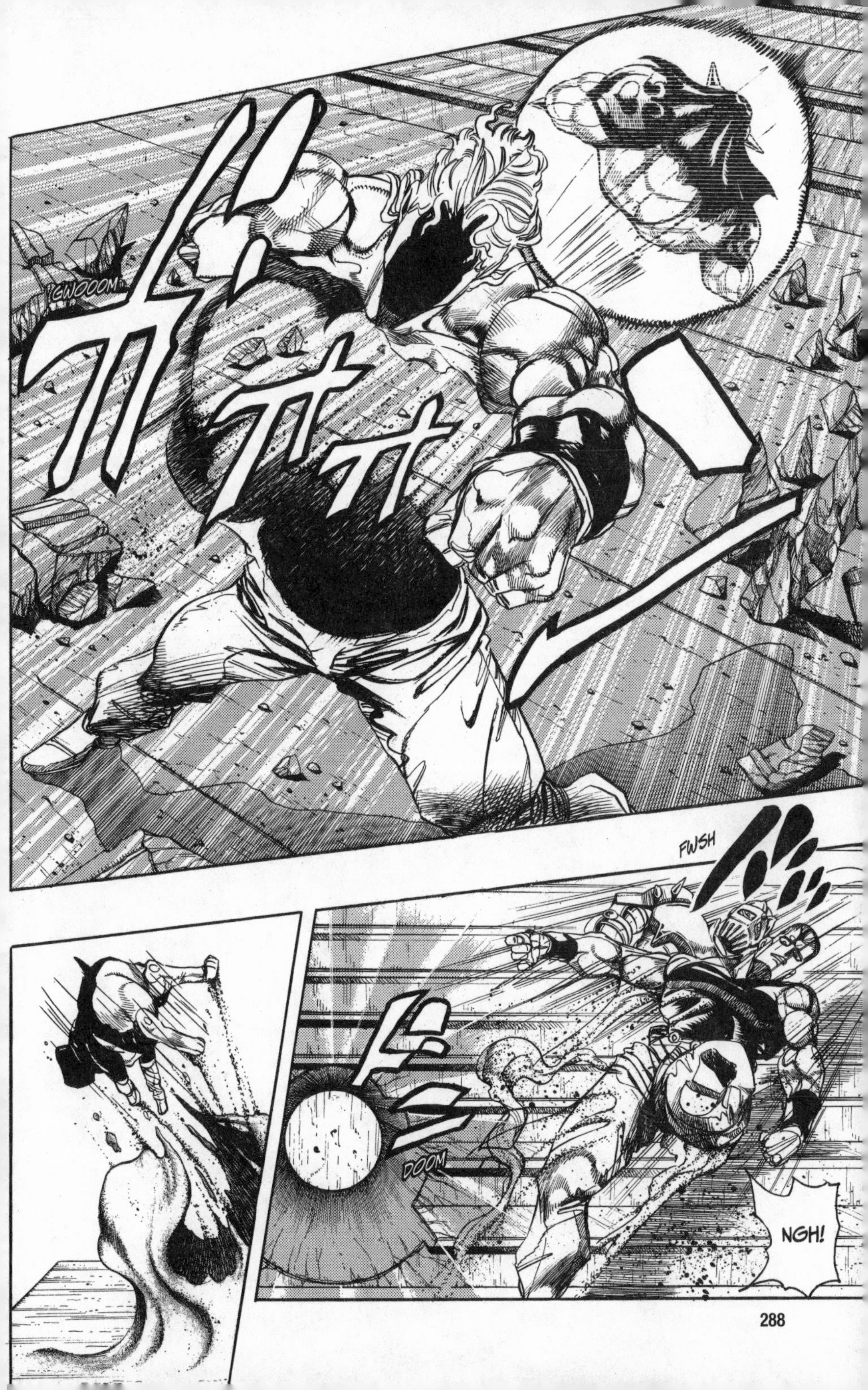
GWOOOM
FWSH
DOOM
NGH!

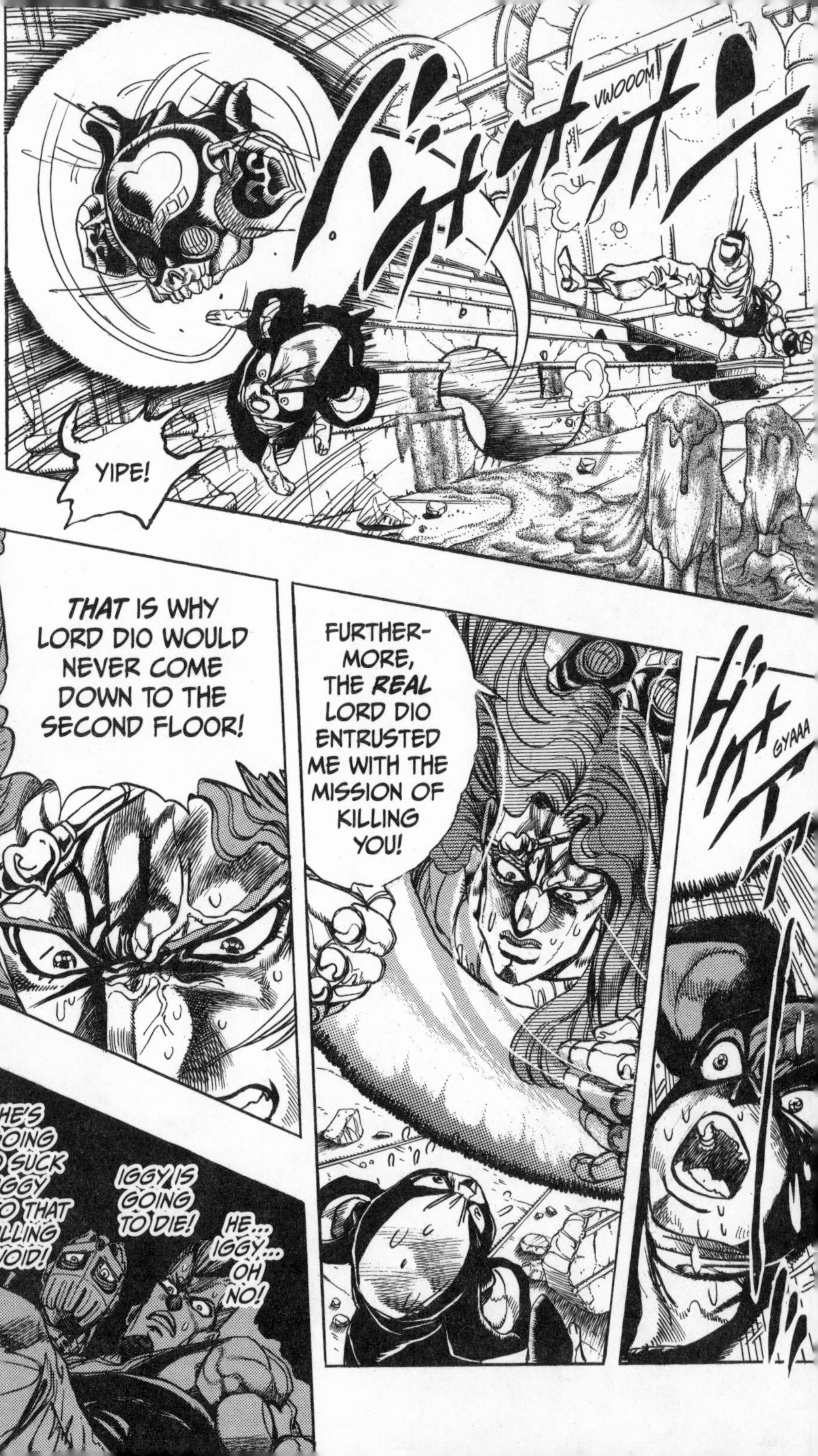
VWOOOM!
YIPE!
GYAAA
FURTHER-MORE, THE REAL LORD DIO ENTRUSTED ME WITH THE MISSION OF KILLING YOU!
THAT IS WHY LORD DIO WOULD NEVER COME DOWN TO THE SECOND FLOOR!
HE'S GOING TO SUCK IGGY INTO THAT KILLING VOID!
IGGY IS GOING TO DIE!
HE... IGGY... OH NO!

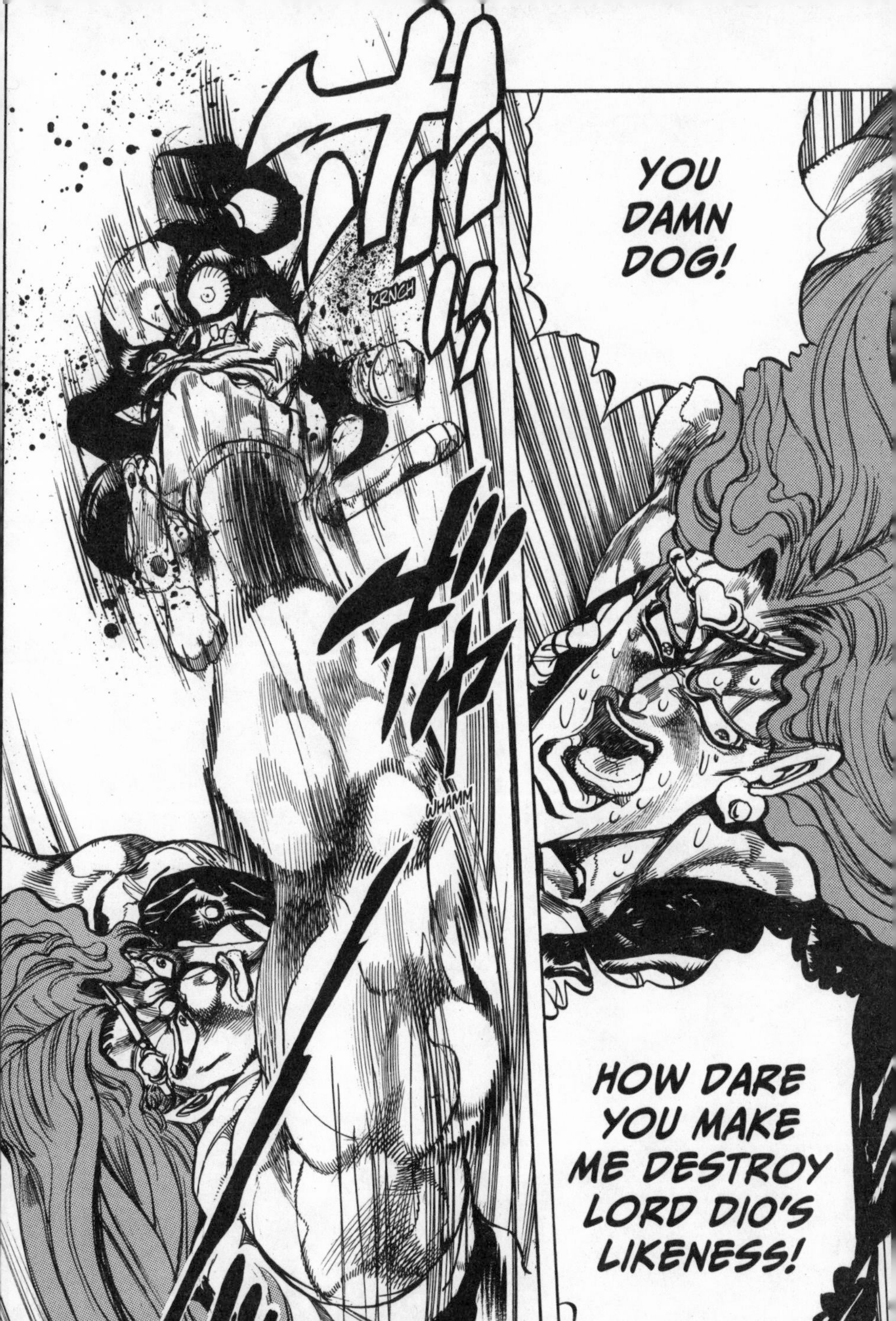

YOU DAMN DOG!
HOW DARE YOU MAKE ME DESTROY LORD DIO'S LIKENESS!
KRNCH
WHAMM

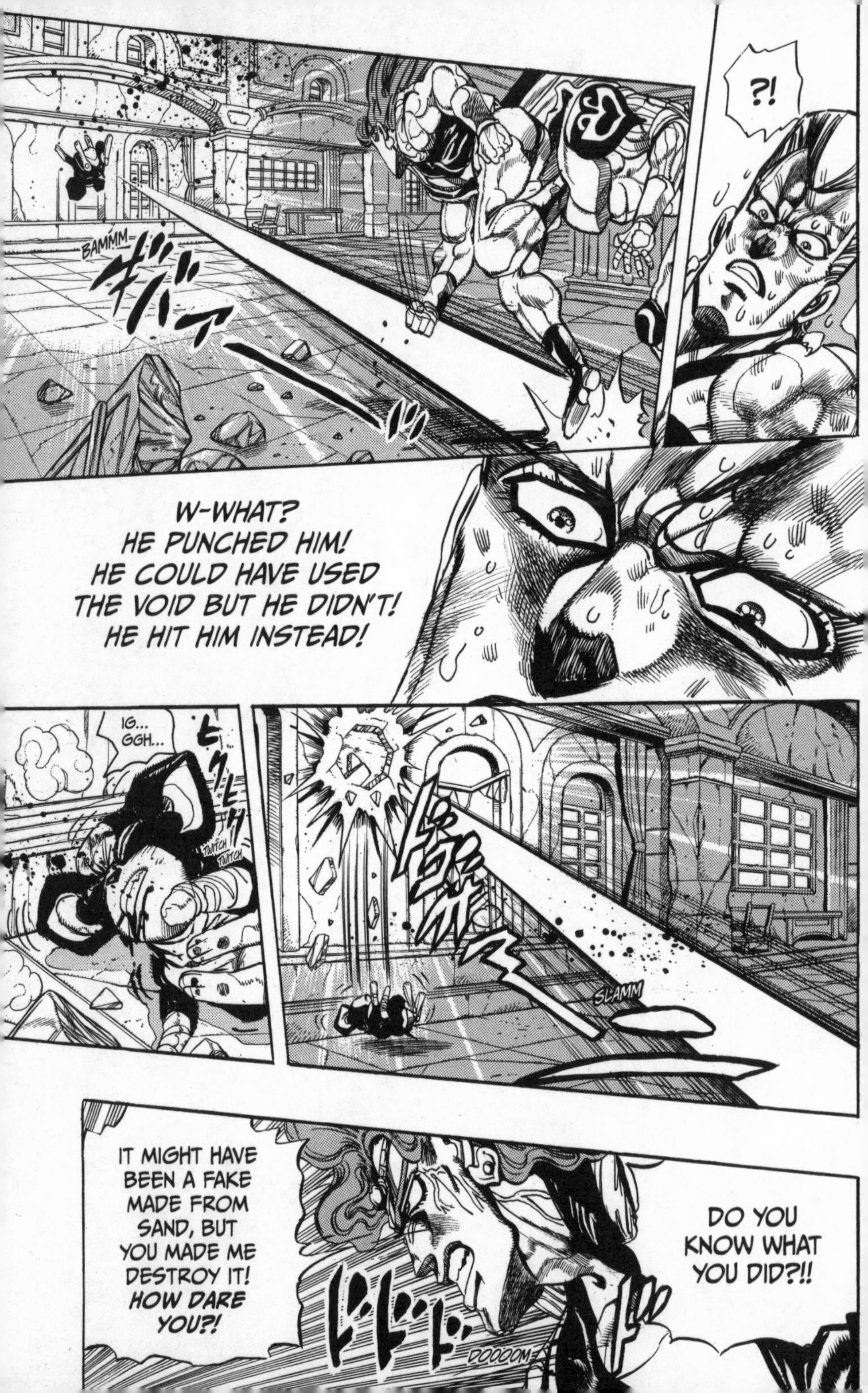
?!
BAMMM
W-WHAT? HE PUNCHED HIM! HE COULD HAVE USED THE VOID BUT HE DIDN'T! HE HIT HIM INSTEAD!
SLAMM
IG... GGH...
TWITCH TWITCH
DO YOU KNOW WHAT YOU DID?!!
IT MIGHT HAVE BEEN A FAKE MADE FROM SAND, BUT YOU MADE ME DESTROY IT! HOW DARE YOU?!
DOOOOM

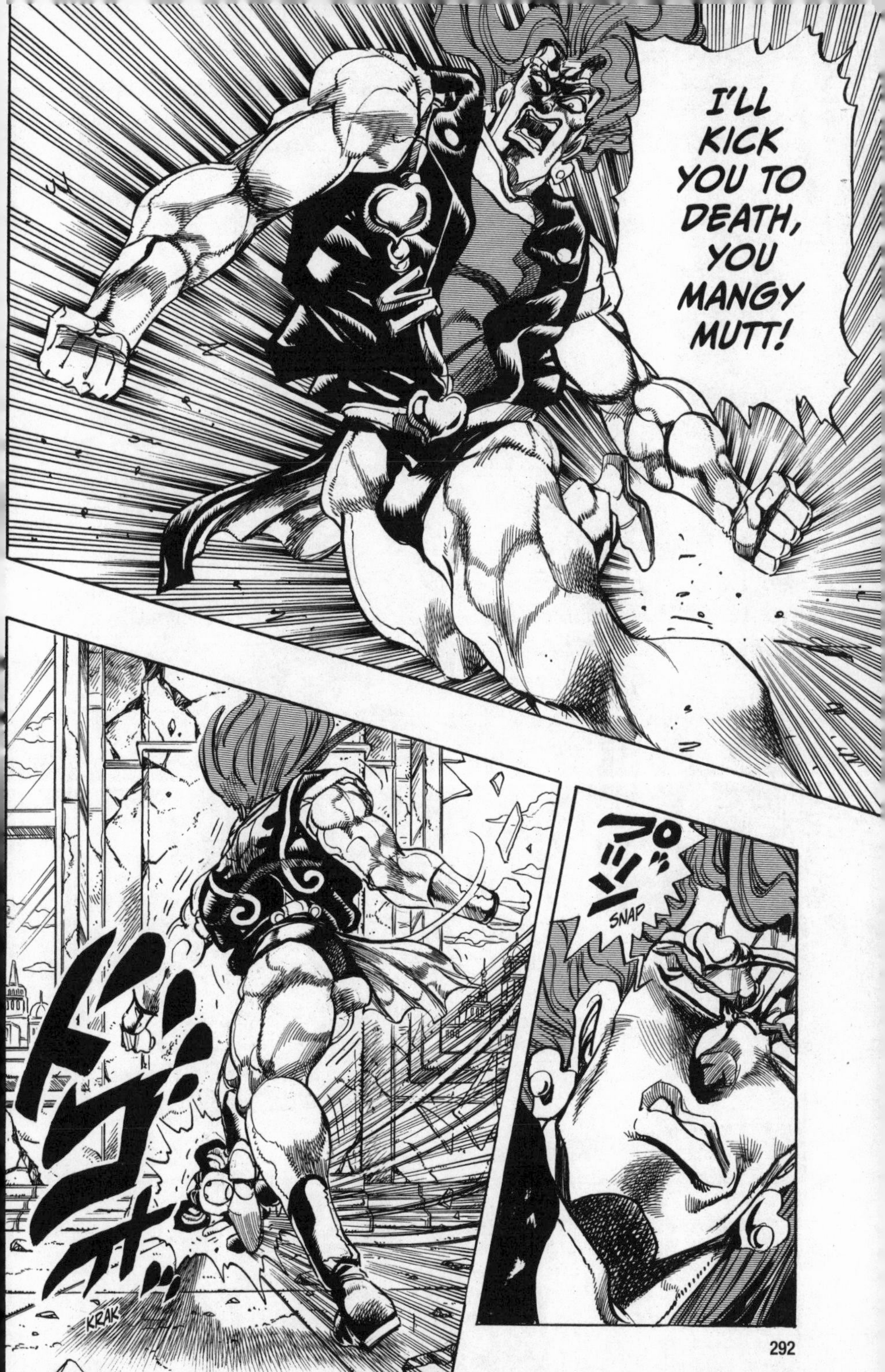
I'LL KICK YOU TO DEATH, YOU MANGY MUTT!
プッ
SNAP
ドグオッ
KRAK

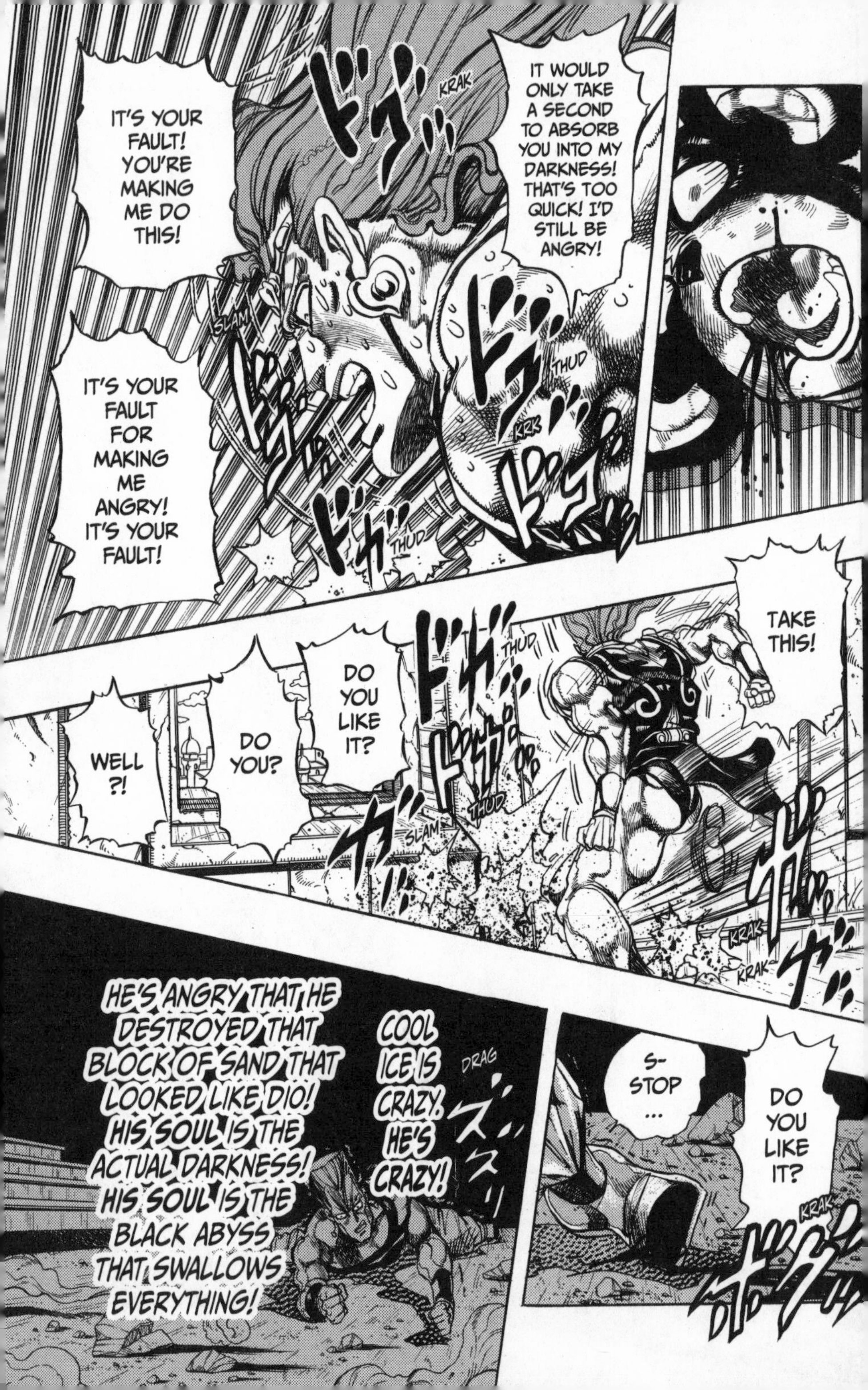
KRAK
IT WOULD ONLY TAKE A SECOND TO ABSORB YOU INTO MY DARKNESS! THAT'S TOO QUICK! I'D STILL BE ANGRY!
IT'S YOUR FAULT! YOU'RE MAKING ME DO THIS!
THUD
KRK
SLAM
IT'S YOUR FAULT FOR MAKING ME ANGRY! IT'S YOUR FAULT!
THUD
TAKE THIS!
THUD
DO YOU LIKE IT?
THUD
SLAM
DO YOU?
WELL?!
KRAK
KRAK
DO YOU LIKE IT?
S-STOP...
KRAK
DRAG
COOL ICE IS CRAZY. HE'S CRAZY!
HE'S ANGRY THAT HE DESTROYED THAT BLOCK OF SAND THAT LOOKED LIKE DIO! HIS SOUL IS THE ACTUAL DARKNESS! HIS SOUL IS THE BLACK ABYSS THAT SWALLOWS EVERYTHING!

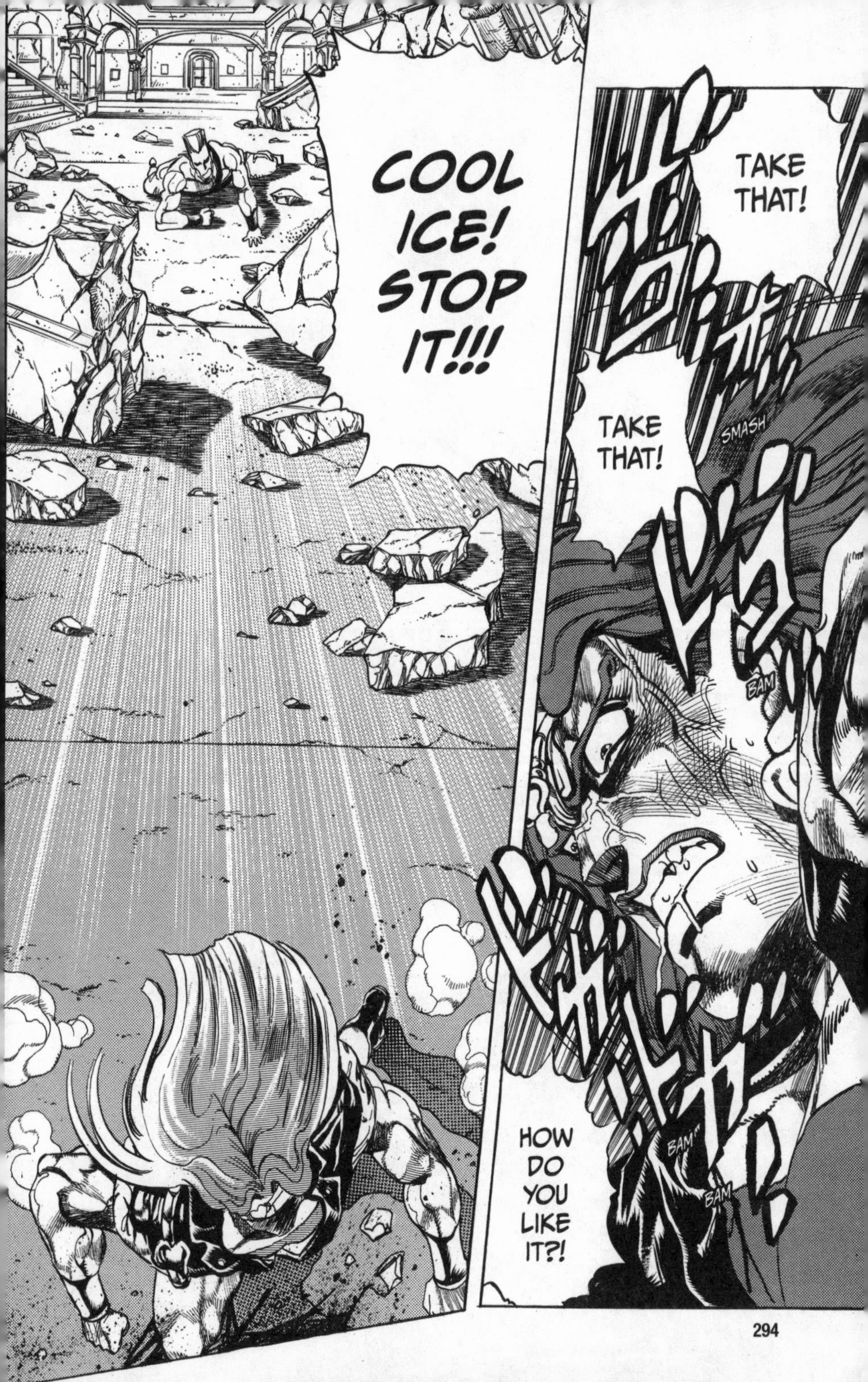
TAKE THAT!
SMASH
TAKE THAT!
BAM
BAM
BAM
HOW DO YOU LIKE IT?!
COOL ICE! STOP IT!!!

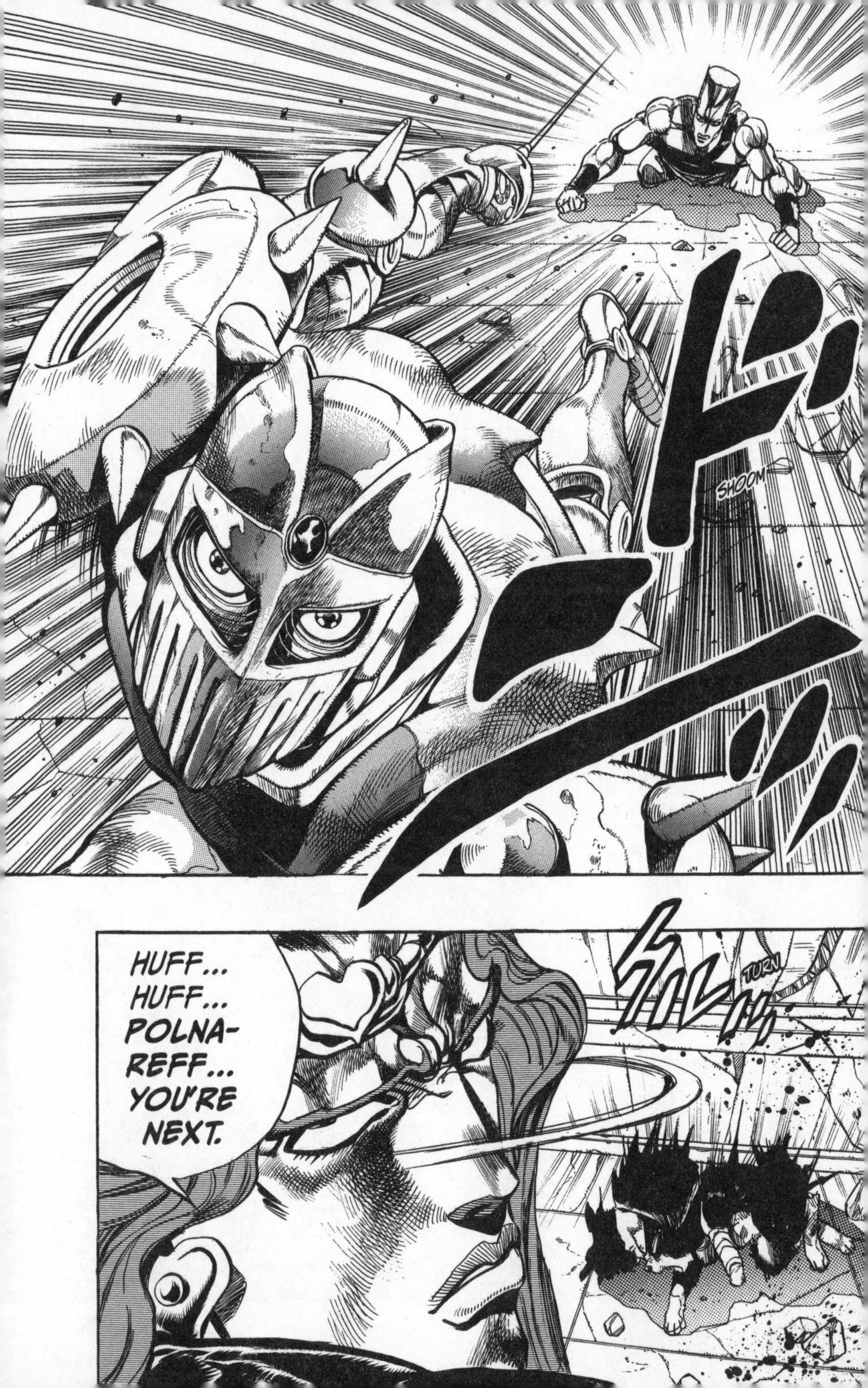
SHOOM
TURN
HUFF... HUFF... POLNAREFF... YOU'RE NEXT.

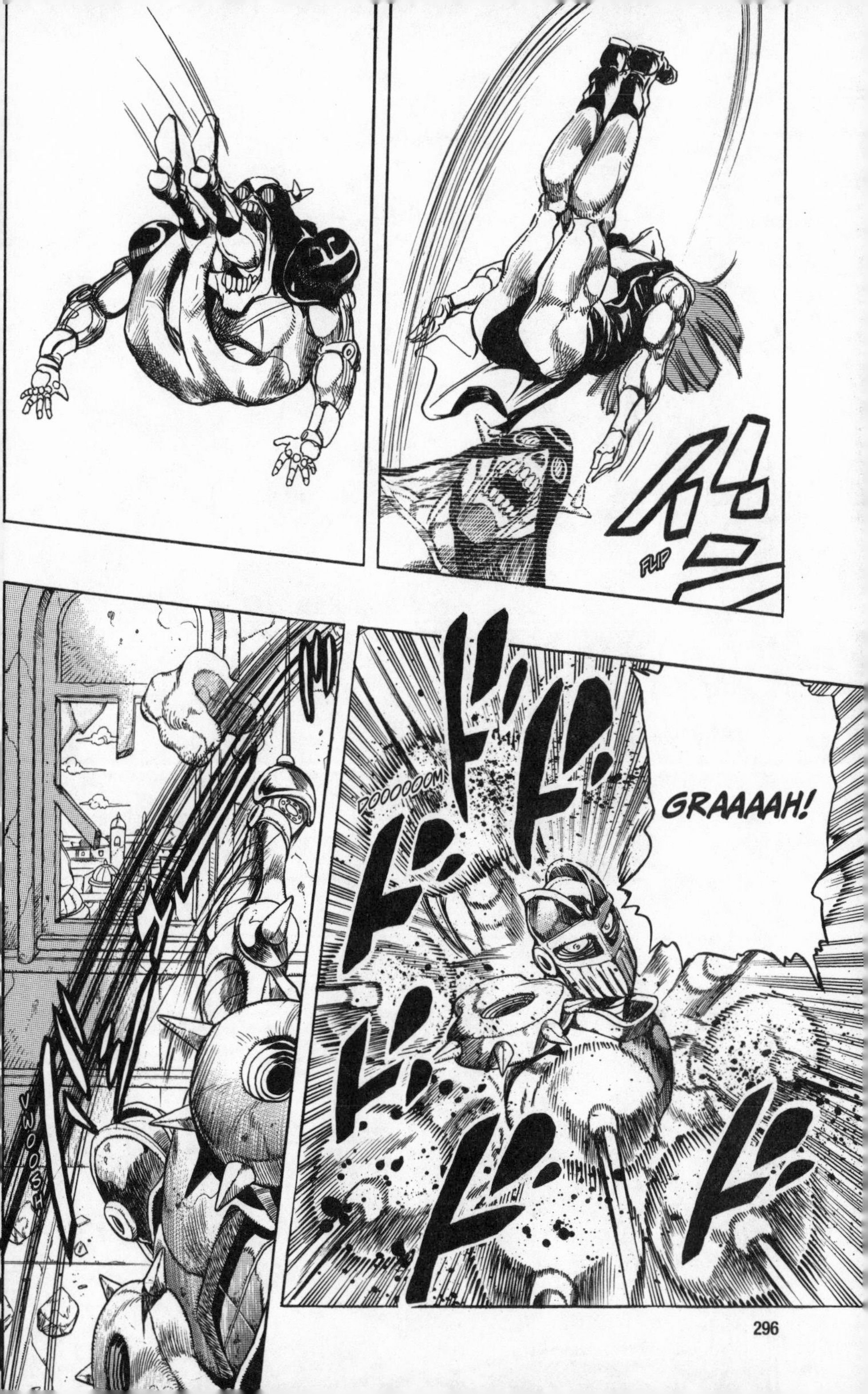
FLIP
DOOOOOOM
GRAAAAH!
VWOOSH

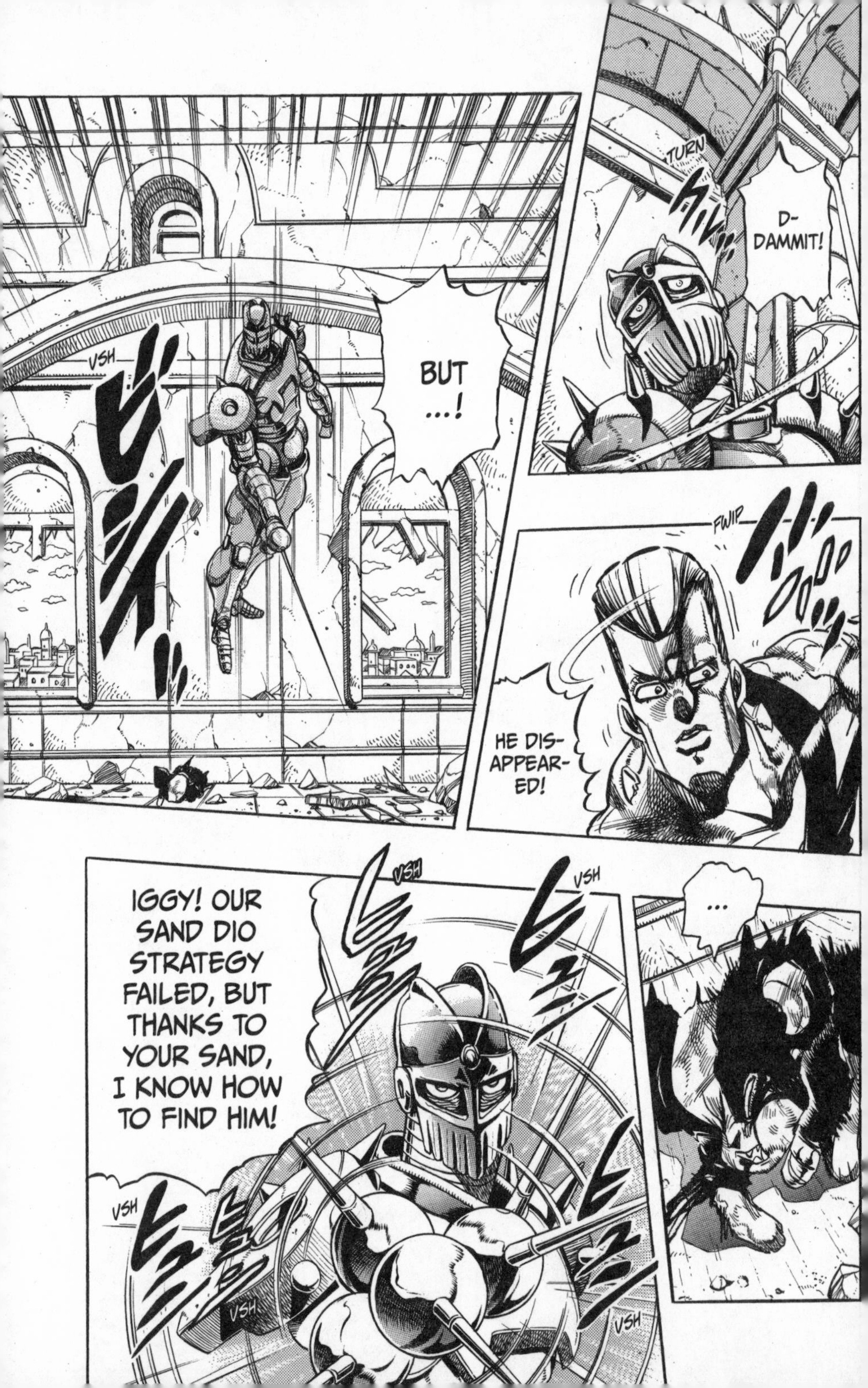
TURN
D-DAMMIT!
FWIP
HE DISAPPEARED!
VSH
BUT ...!
...
IGGY! OUR SAND DIO STRATEGY FAILED, BUT THANKS TO YOUR SAND, I KNOW HOW TO FIND HIM!
VSH
VSH
VSH
VSH
VSH

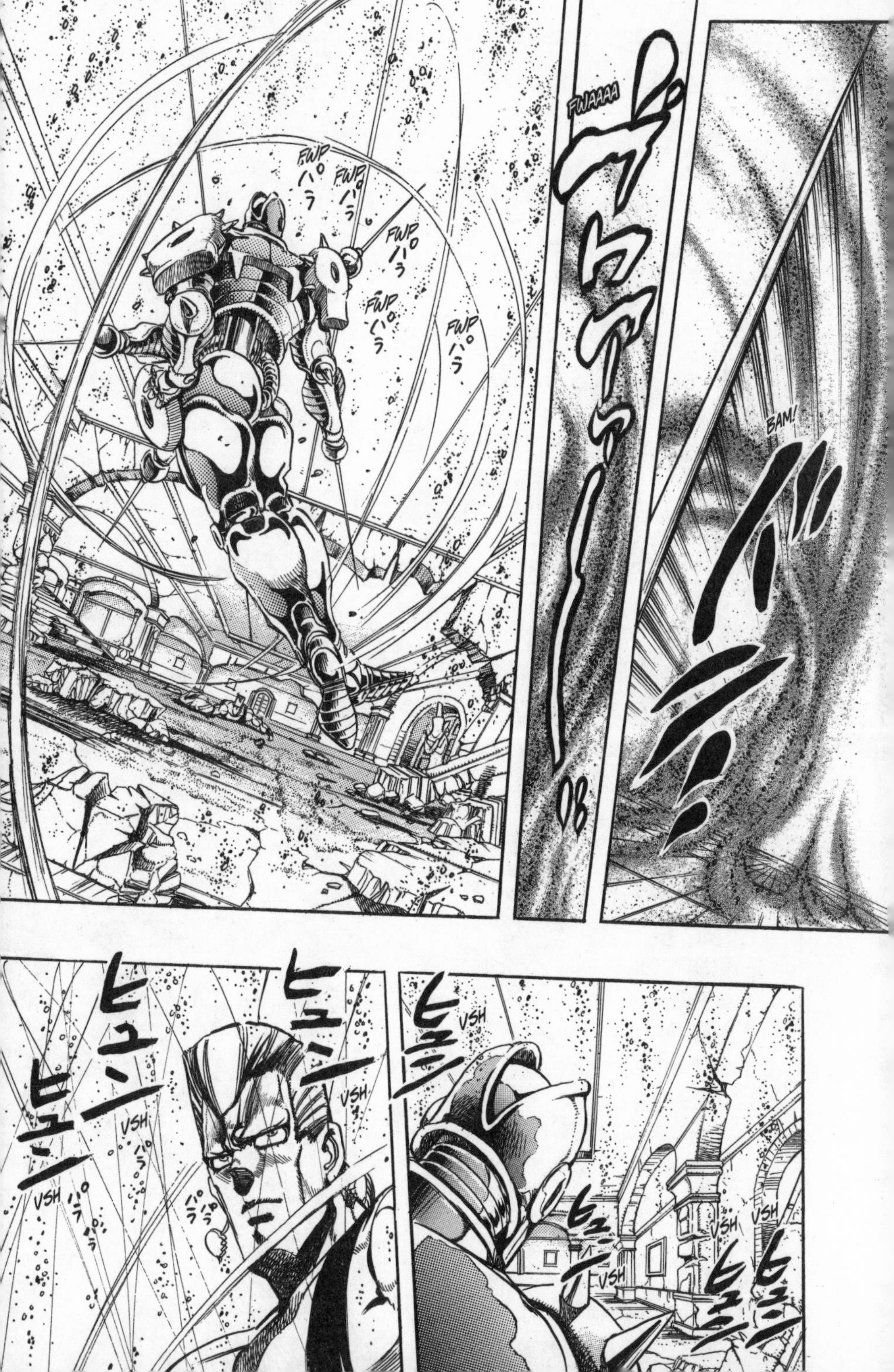
BAM!
FWAAAA
FWP
パラ
FWP
パラ
FWP
パラ
FWP
パラ
FWP
パラ
VSH
ヒュン
VSH
VSH
ヒュン
VSH
ヒュン
VSH
ヒュン
VSH
パラ
ヒュン
VSH
パラ

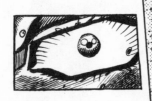

I CAN SEE HIM! I CAN SEE HIM MOVING! TAKE THAT! WE DID IT, DAMMIT!

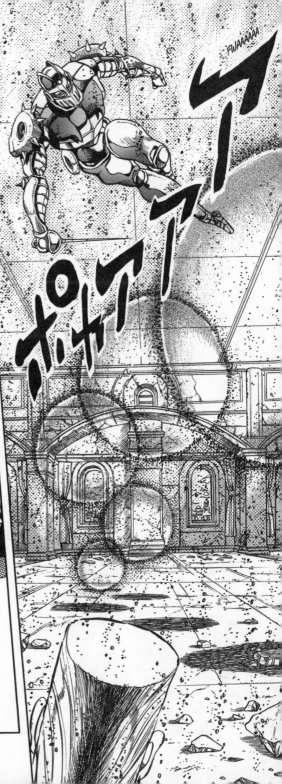

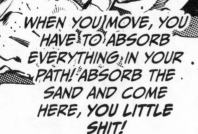

WHEN YOU MOVE, YOU HAVE TO ABSORB EVERYTHING IN YOUR PATH! ABSORB THE SAND AND COME HERE, YOU LITTLE SHIT!

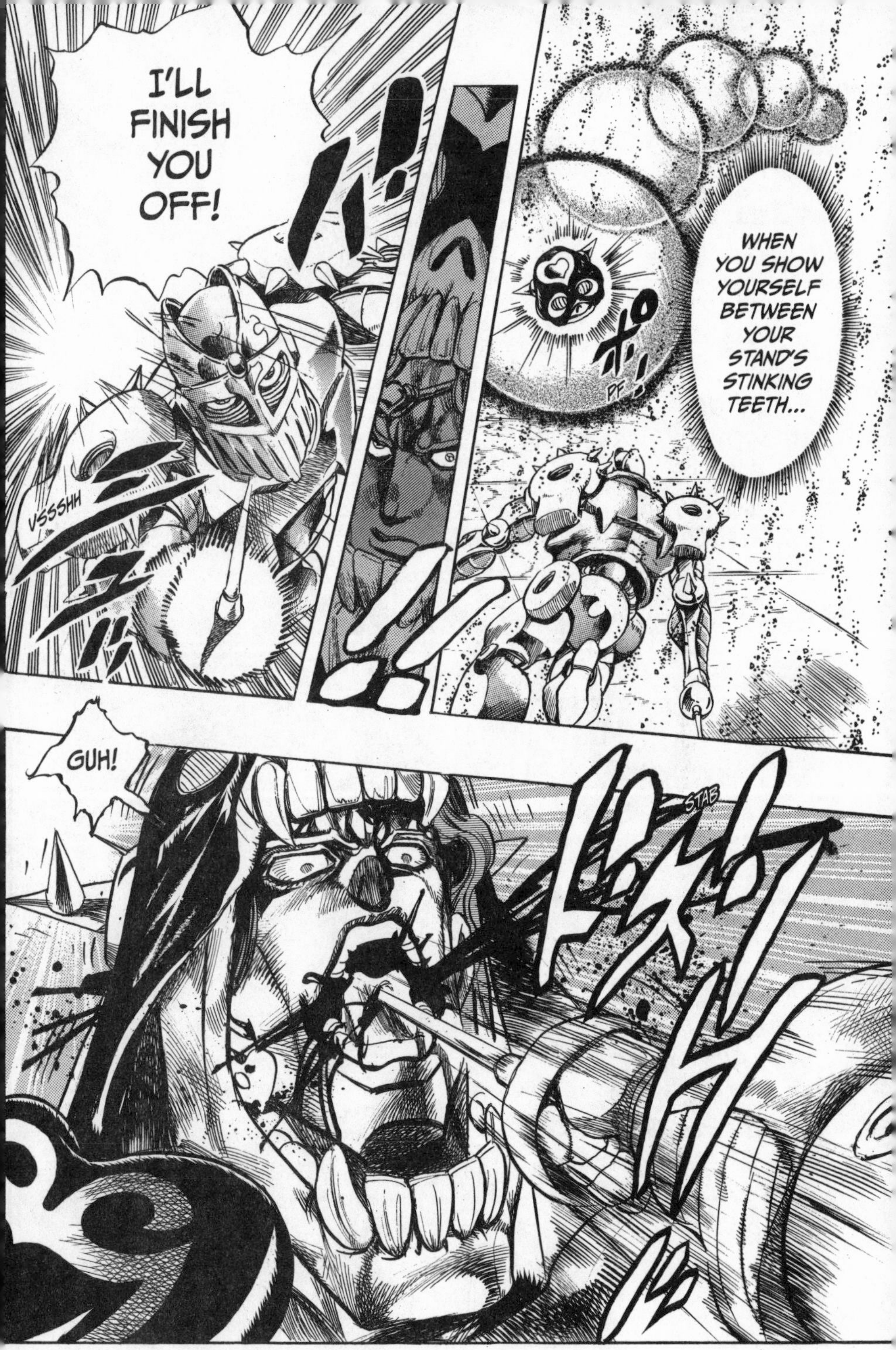
WHEN YOU SHOW YOURSELF BETWEEN YOUR STAND'S STINKING TEETH...
PF
I'LL FINISH YOU OFF!
VSSSHH
STAB
GUH!

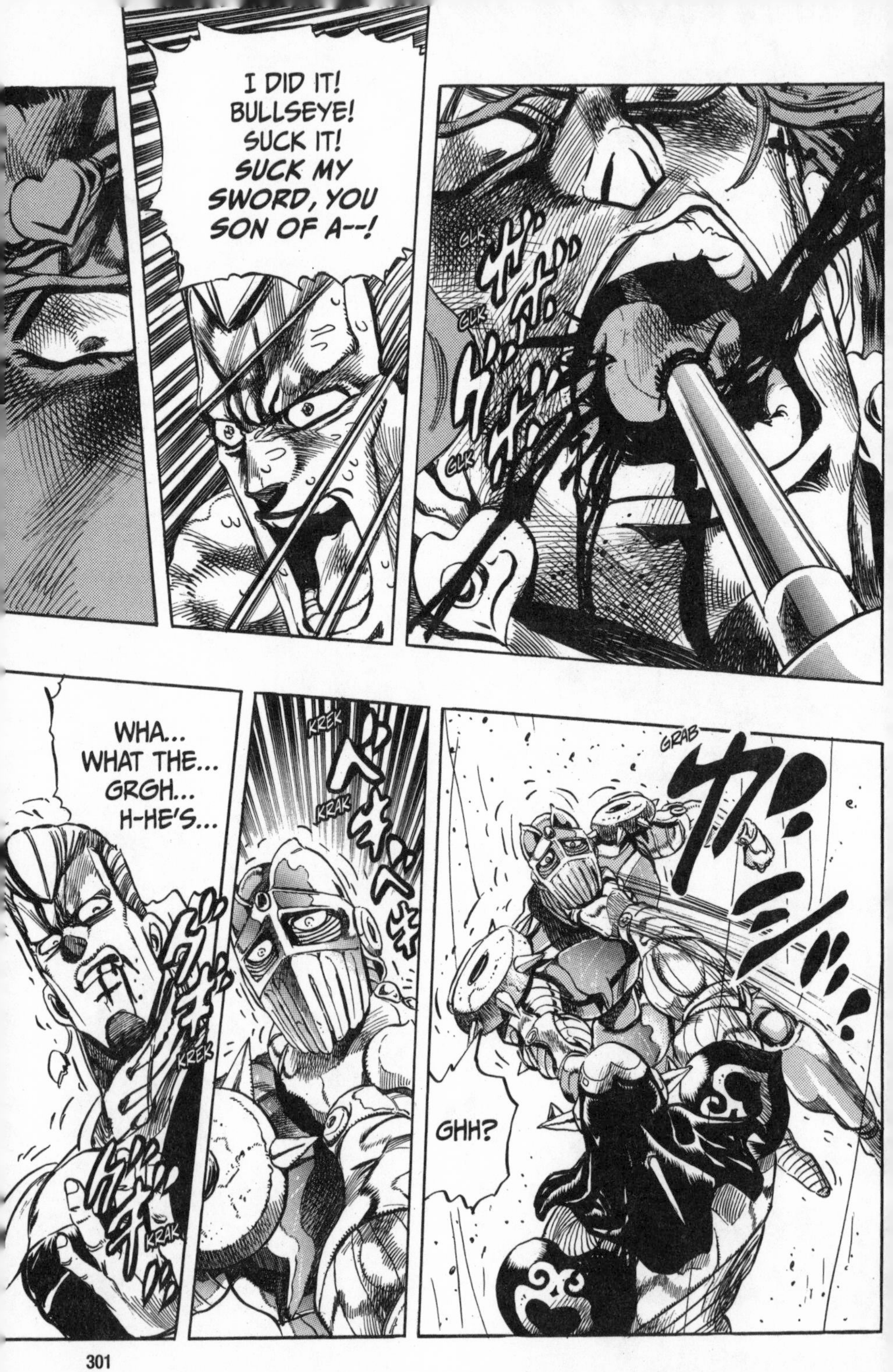
GLK
GLK
GLK
I DID IT! BULLSEYE! SUCK IT! SUCK MY SWORD, YOU SON OF A--!
GRAB
GHH?
KREK
KRAK
WHA... WHAT THE... GRGH... H-HE'S...
KREK
KRAK

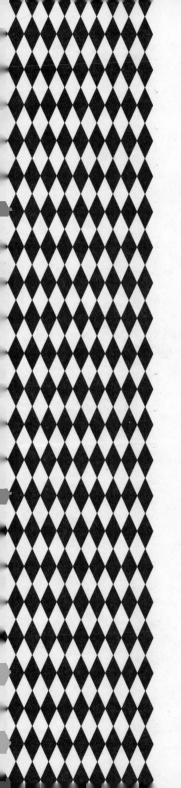

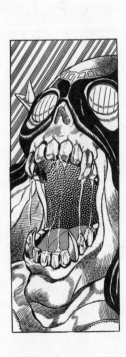

CHAPTER 130: The Dark Void of Cool Ice PART 6

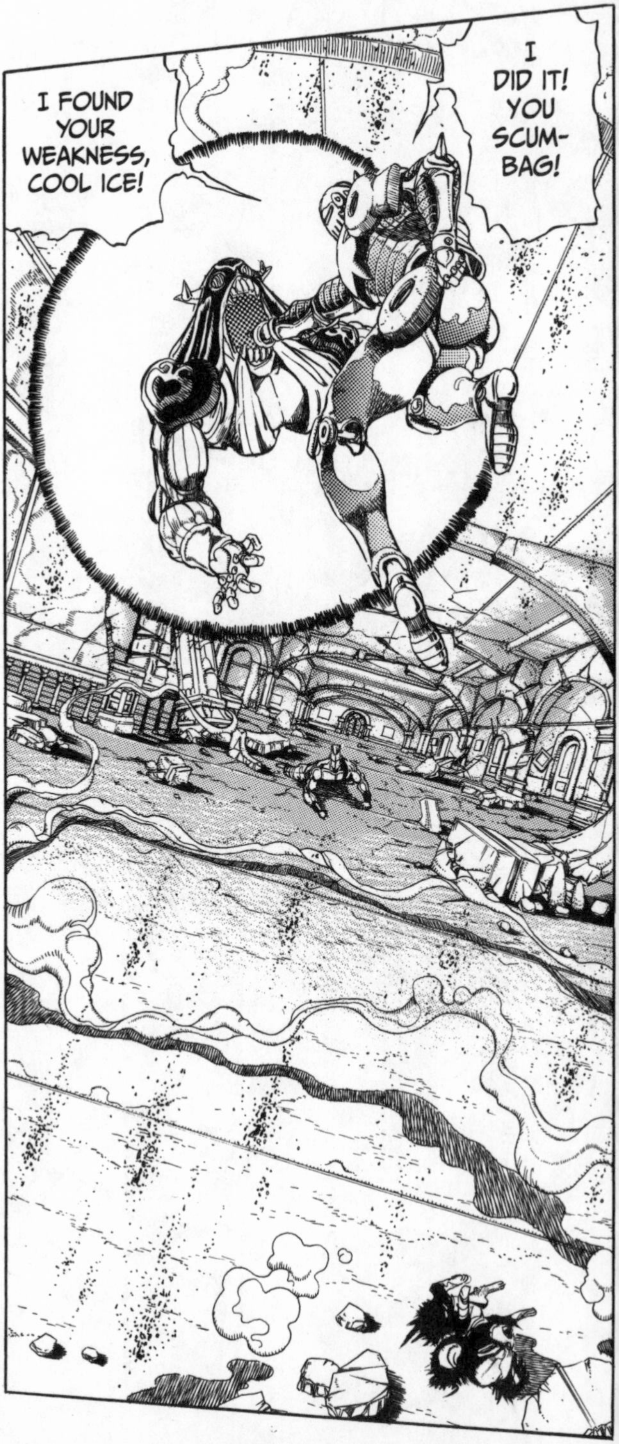
I DID IT! YOU SCUM-BAG!
I FOUND YOUR WEAKNESS, COOL ICE!

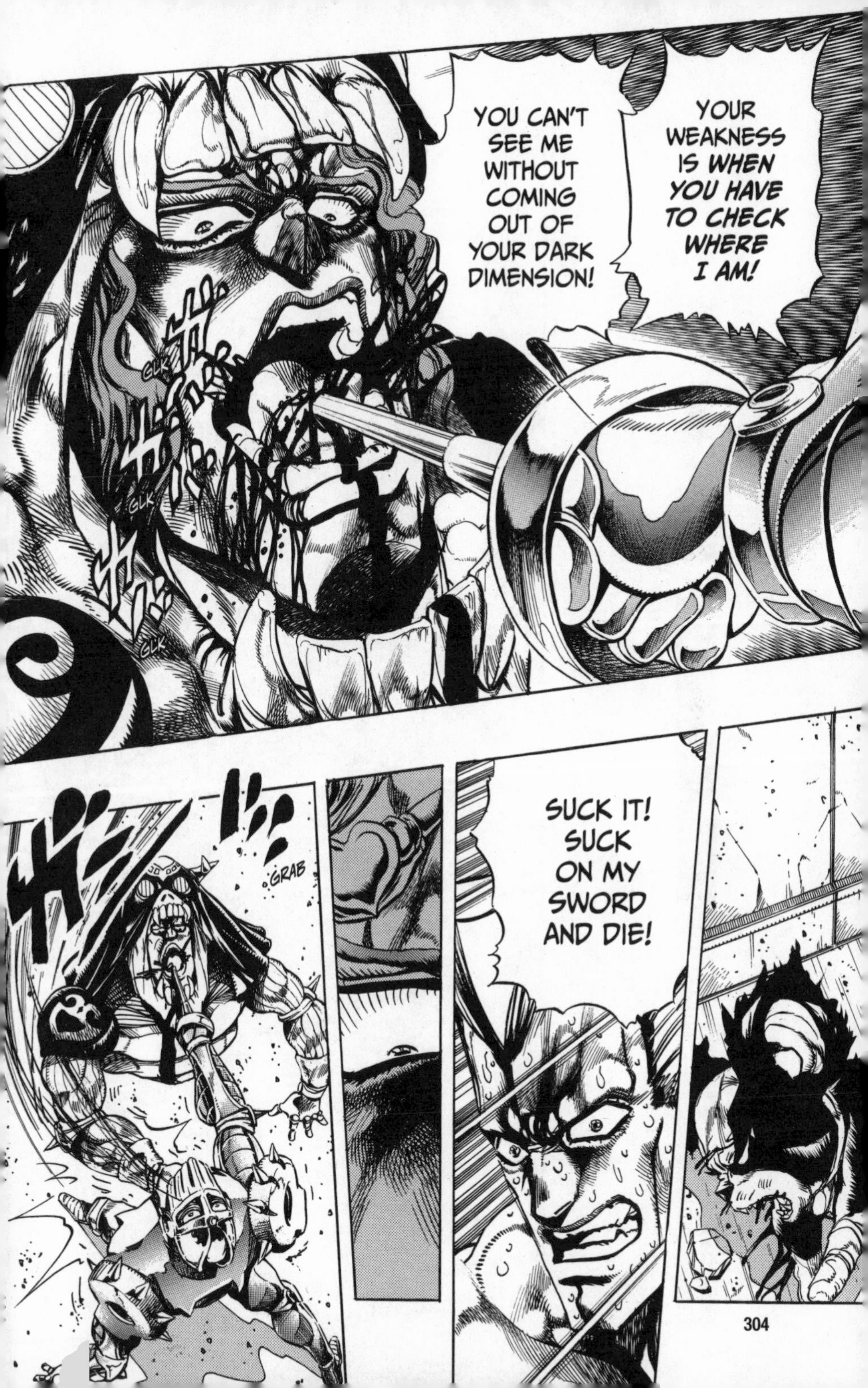
YOUR WEAKNESS IS WHEN YOU HAVE TO CHECK WHERE I AM!
YOU CAN'T SEE ME WITHOUT COMING OUT OF YOUR DARK DIMENSION!
GLK
GLK
GLK
SUCK IT! SUCK ON MY SWORD AND DIE!
GRAB

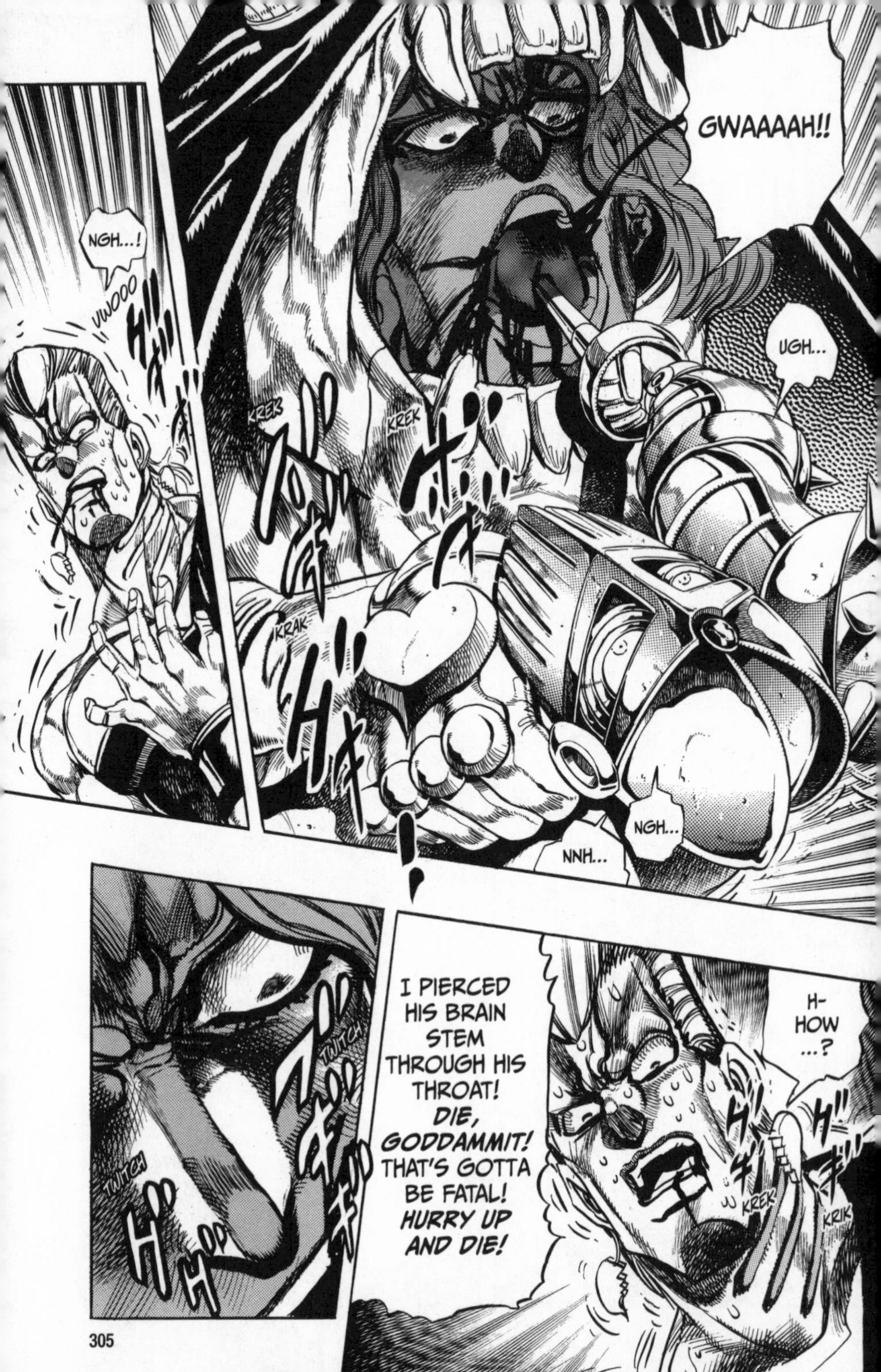
GWAAAAH!!
UGH...
KREK
KREK
KRAK
NGH...
NNH...
NGH...!
VWOOO
H-HOW...?
I PIERCED HIS BRAIN STEM THROUGH HIS THROAT! DIE, GODDAMMIT! THAT'S GOTTA BE FATAL! HURRY UP AND DIE!
KRIK
KREK
TWITCH
TWITCH

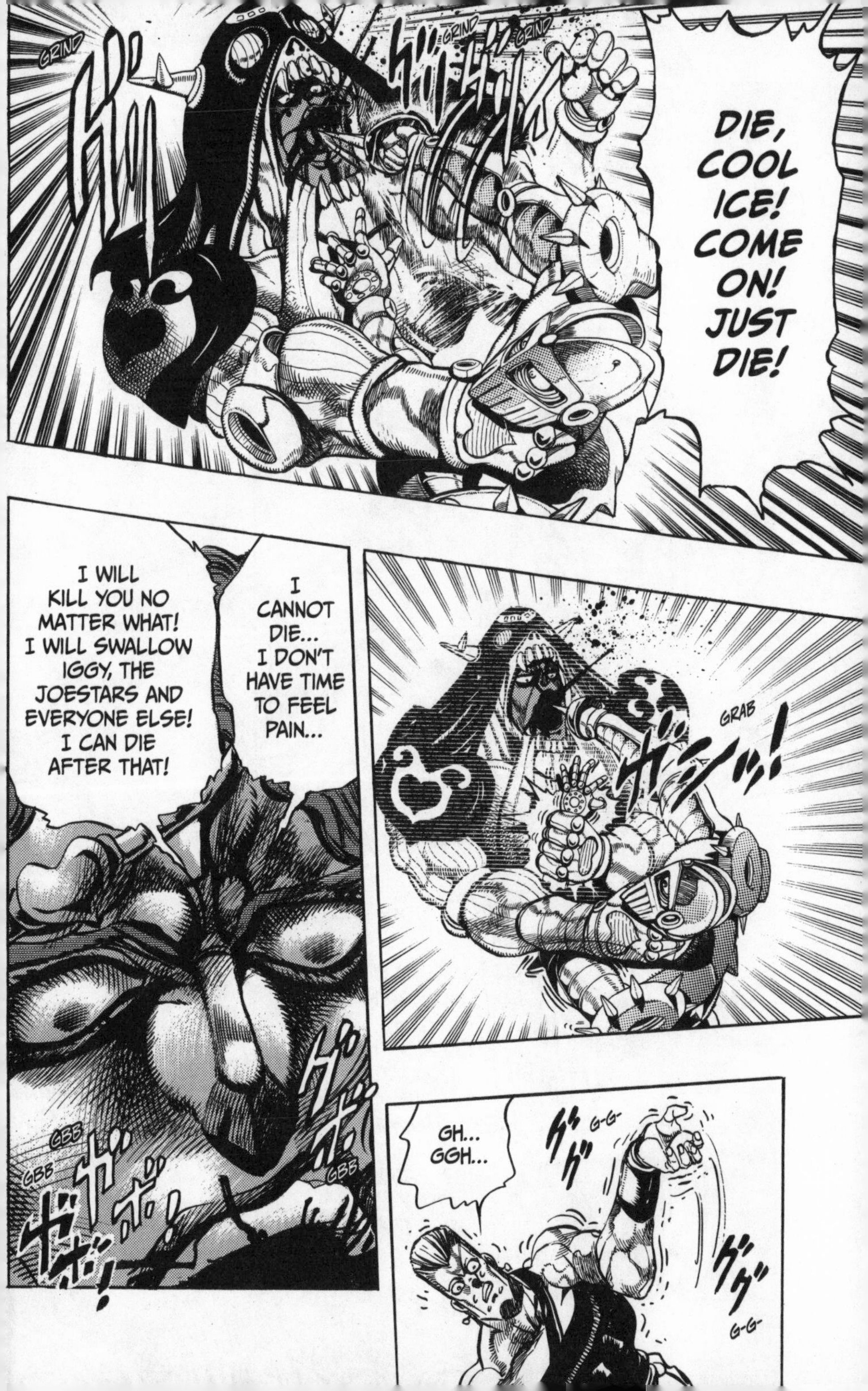
GRIND
GRIND
GRIND
DIE, COOL ICE! COME ON! JUST DIE!
GRAB
GH... GGH...
G-G-
G-G-
I CANNOT DIE... I DON'T HAVE TIME TO FEEL PAIN...
I WILL KILL YOU NO MATTER WHAT! I WILL SWALLOW IGGY, THE JOESTARS AND EVERYONE ELSE! I CAN DIE AFTER THAT!
GBB
GBB
GBB

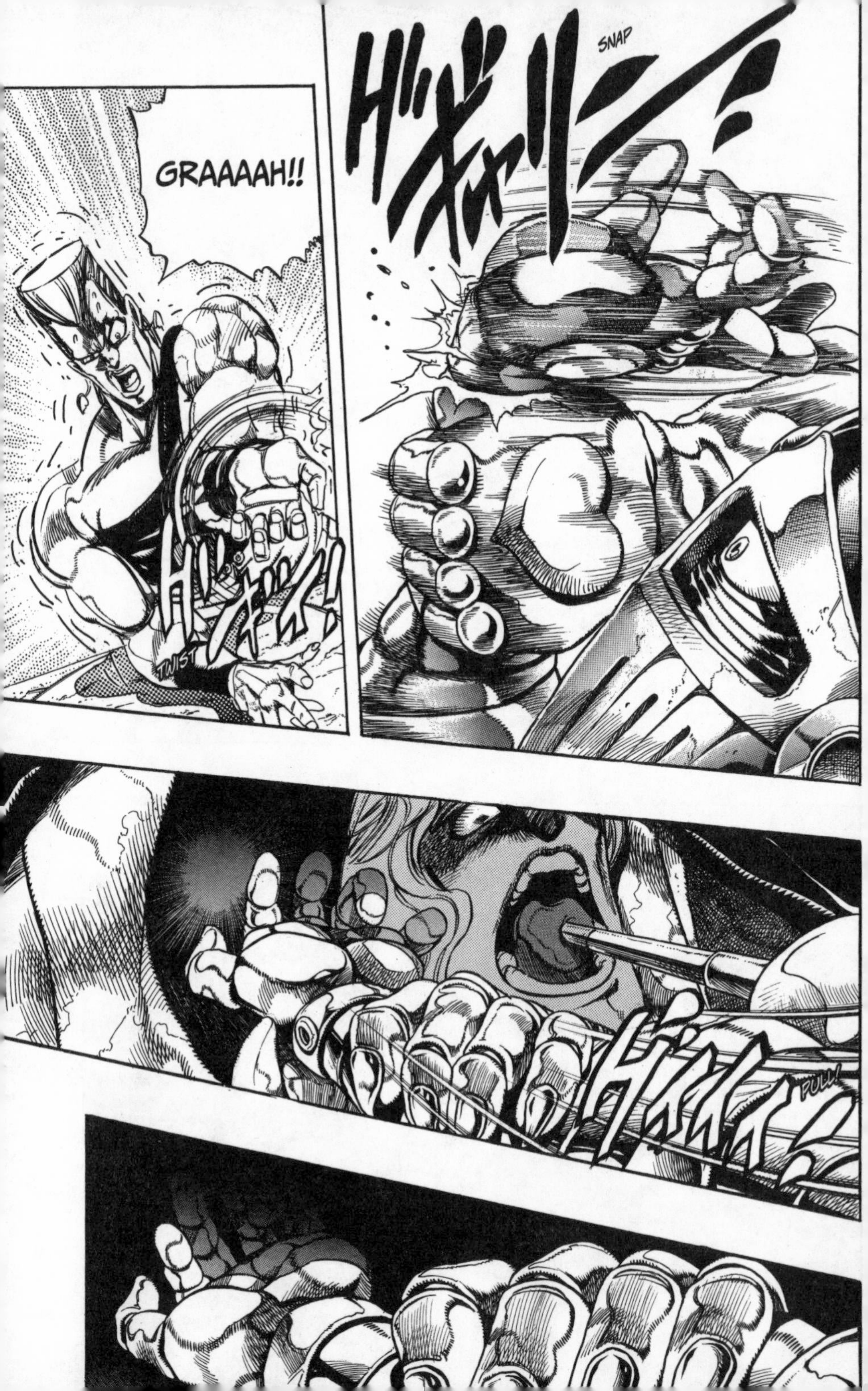
SNAP
GRAAAAH!!
TWIST
PULL

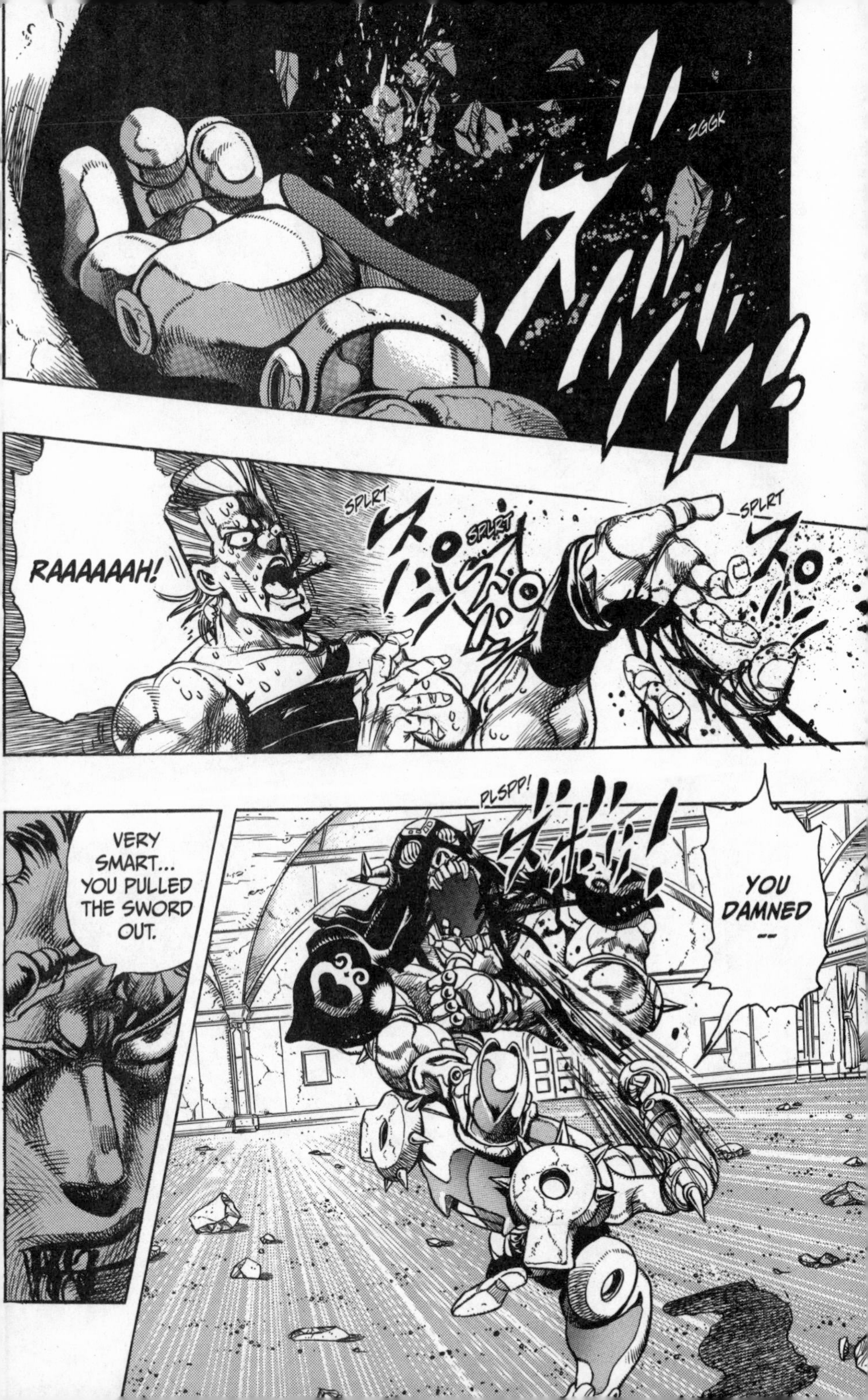
ZGGK
SPLRT
SPLRT
SPLRT
RAAAAAAH!
YOU DAMNED --
PLSPP!
VERY SMART... YOU PULLED THE SWORD OUT.

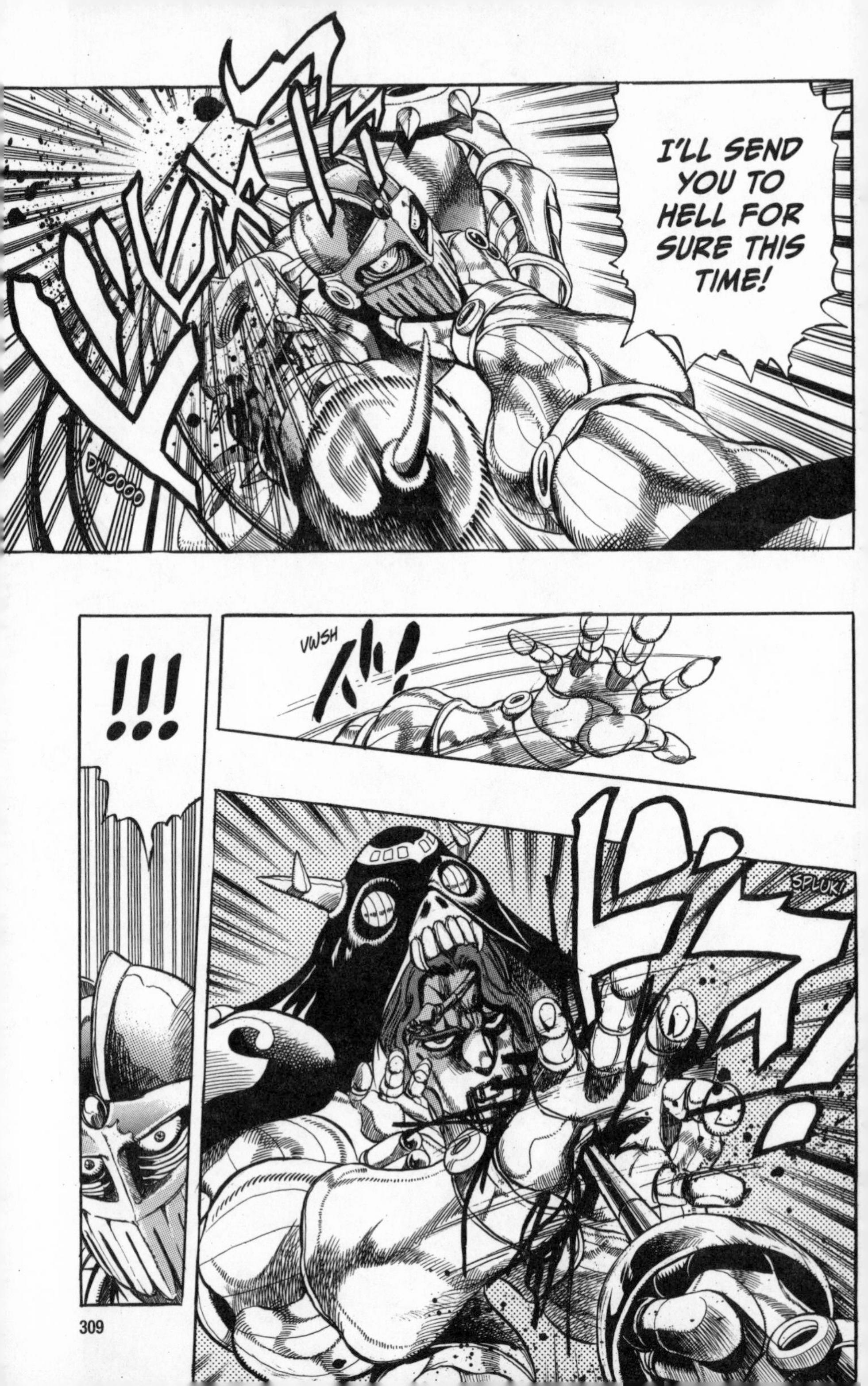

I'LL SEND YOU TO HELL FOR SURE THIS TIME!
DNOOOO
VWSH
!!!
SPLUK!

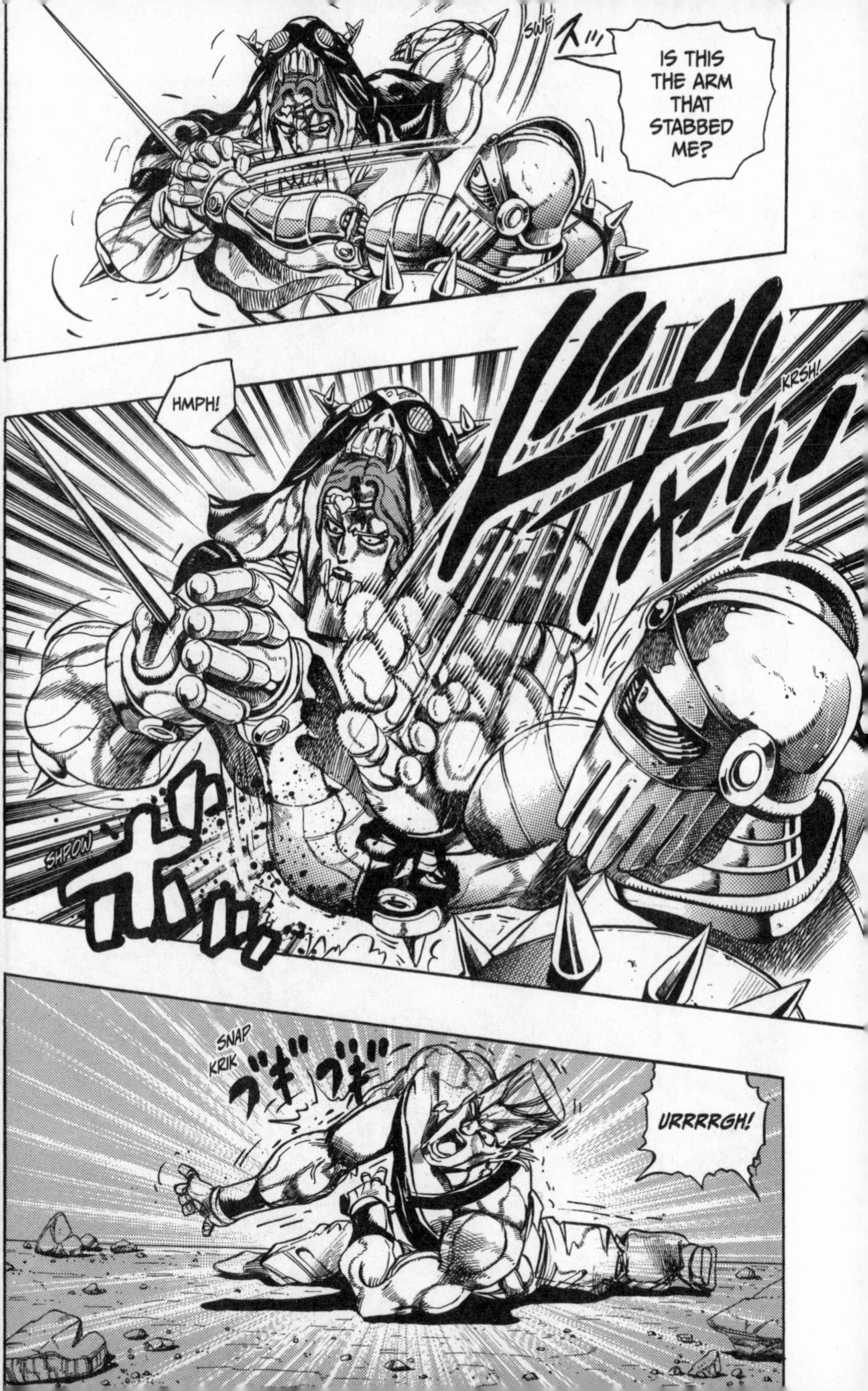
IS THIS THE ARM THAT STABBED ME?
SWF
ス…
KRSH!
HMPH!
SHPOW
SNAP
KRIK
ブギブギ
URRRRGH!

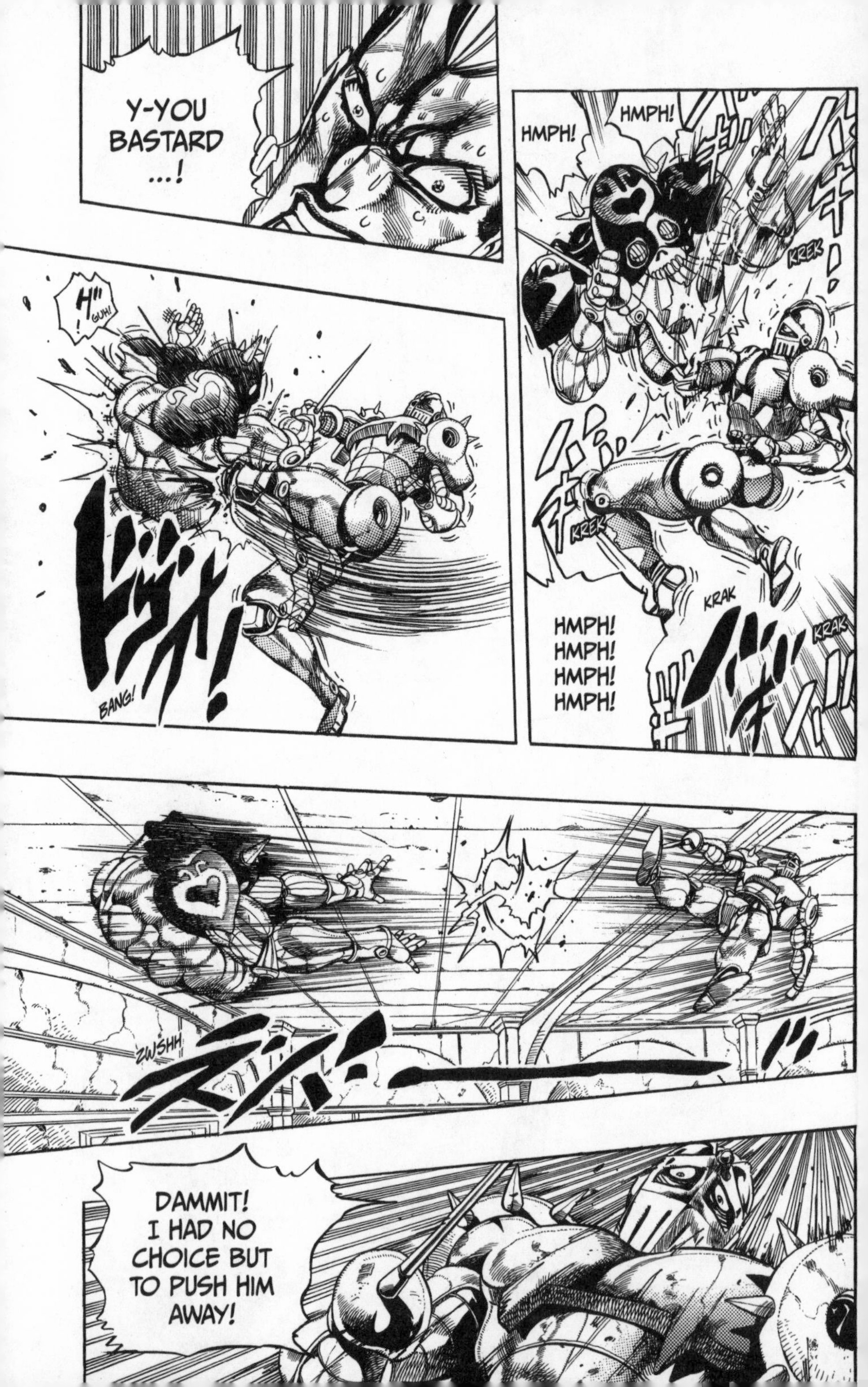
HMPH!
HMPH!
KREK
KREK
KRAK
KRAK
HMPH! HMPH! HMPH! HMPH!
Y-YOU BASTARD ...!
H"
GUH!
BANG!
ZWSHH
DAMMIT! I HAD NO CHOICE BUT TO PUSH HIM AWAY!

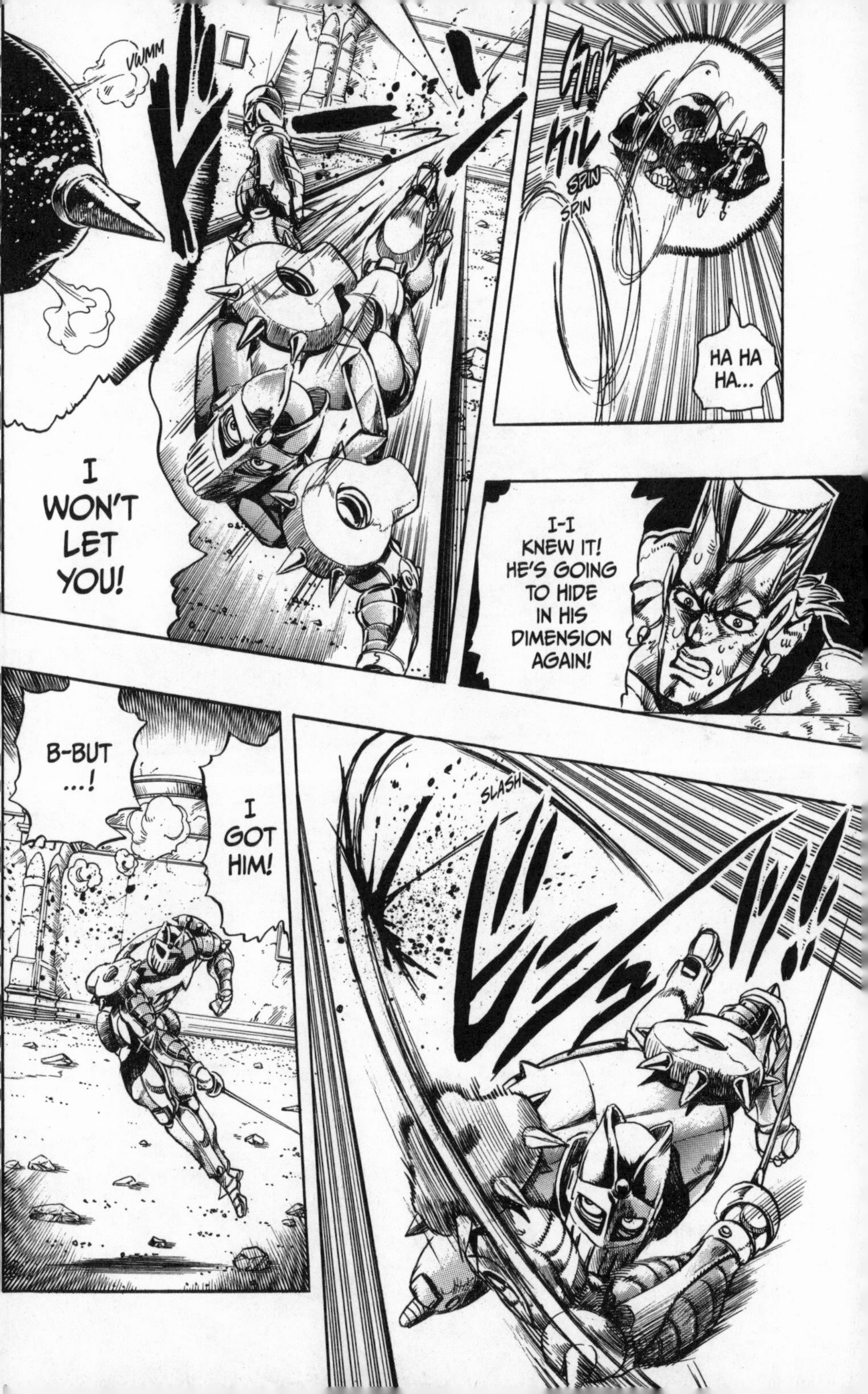
SPIN
SPIN
HA HA HA...
I-I KNEW IT! HE'S GOING TO HIDE IN HIS DIMENSION AGAIN!
VWMM
I WON'T LET YOU!
SLASH
I GOT HIM!
B-BUT ...!

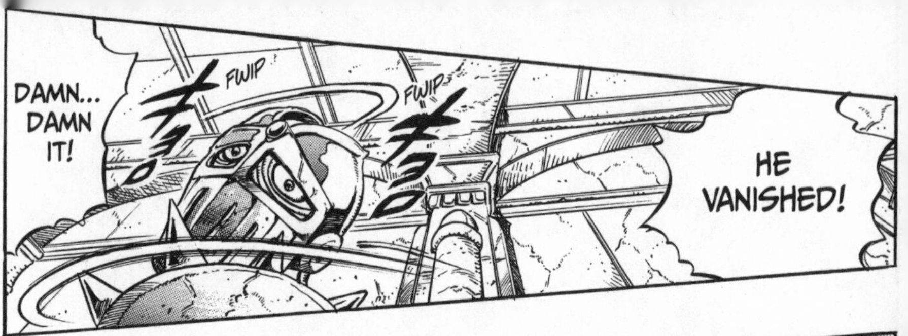
HE VANISHED!
FWIP
FWIP
DAMN... DAMN IT!
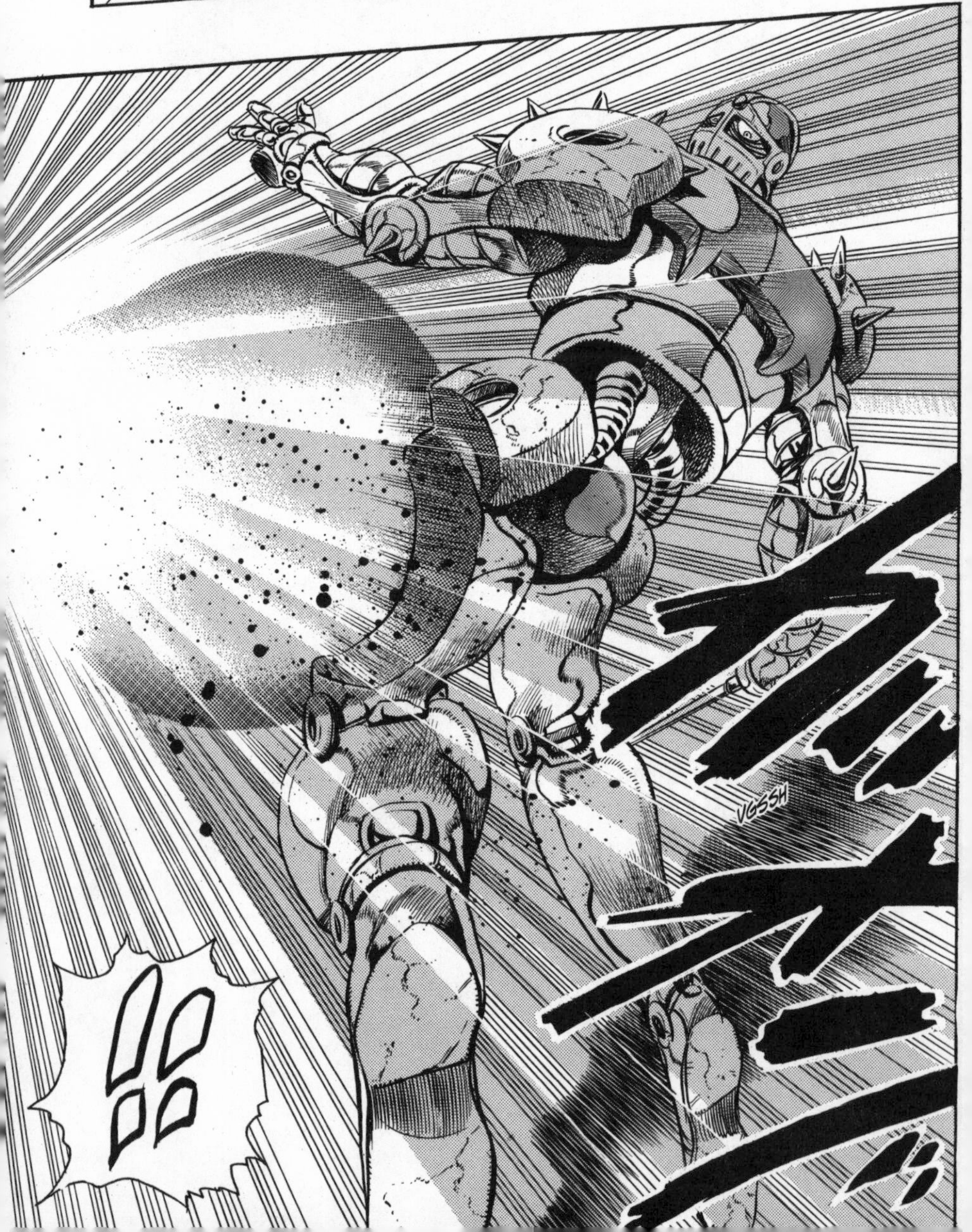
VGSSH
!!

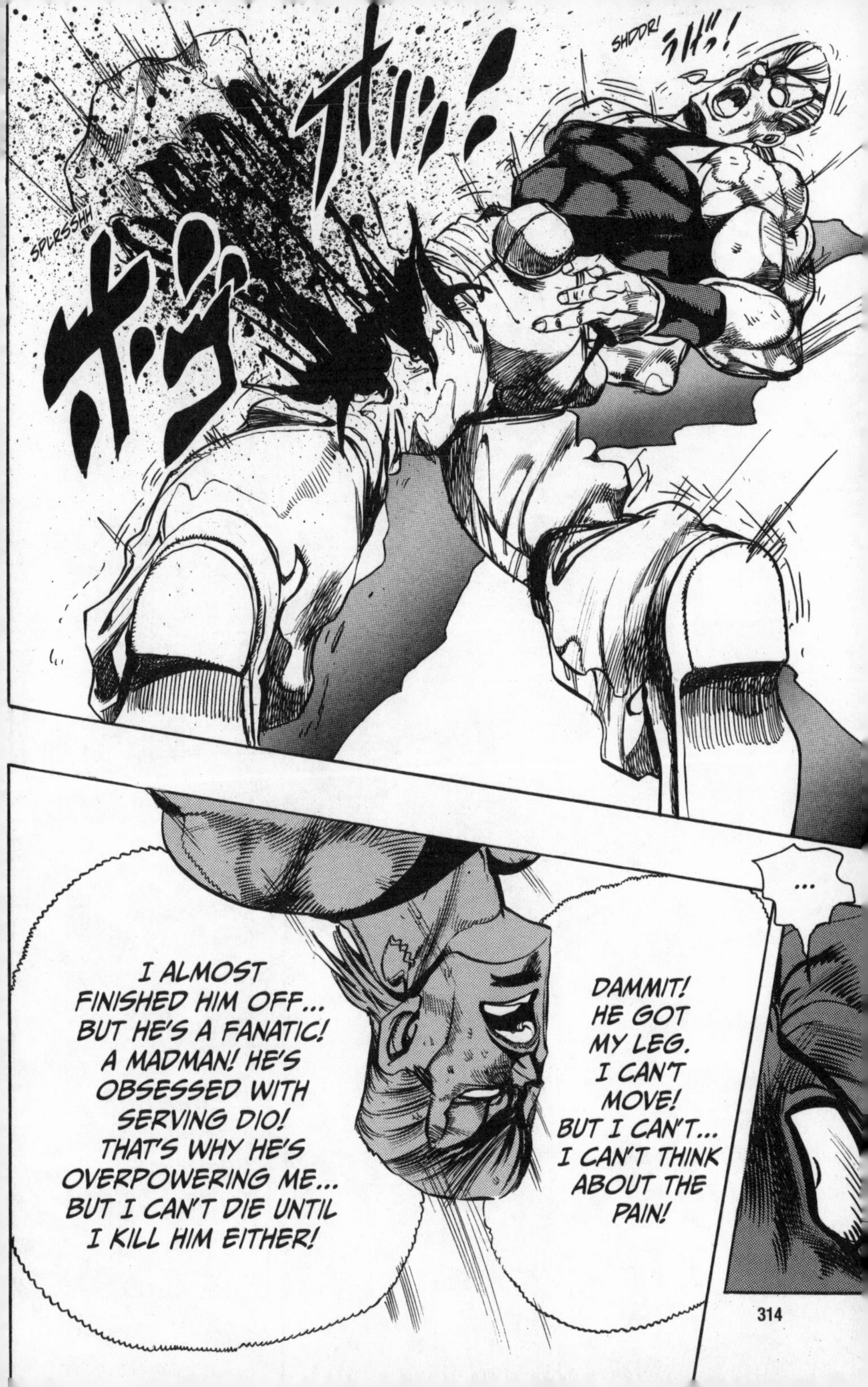
SHDDR!
SPLRSSHH
...
DAMMIT! HE GOT MY LEG. I CAN'T MOVE! BUT I CAN'T... I CAN'T THINK ABOUT THE PAIN!
I ALMOST FINISHED HIM OFF... BUT HE'S A FANATIC! A MADMAN! HE'S OBSESSED WITH SERVING DIO! THAT'S WHY HE'S OVERPOWERING ME... BUT I CAN'T DIE UNTIL I KILL HIM EITHER!

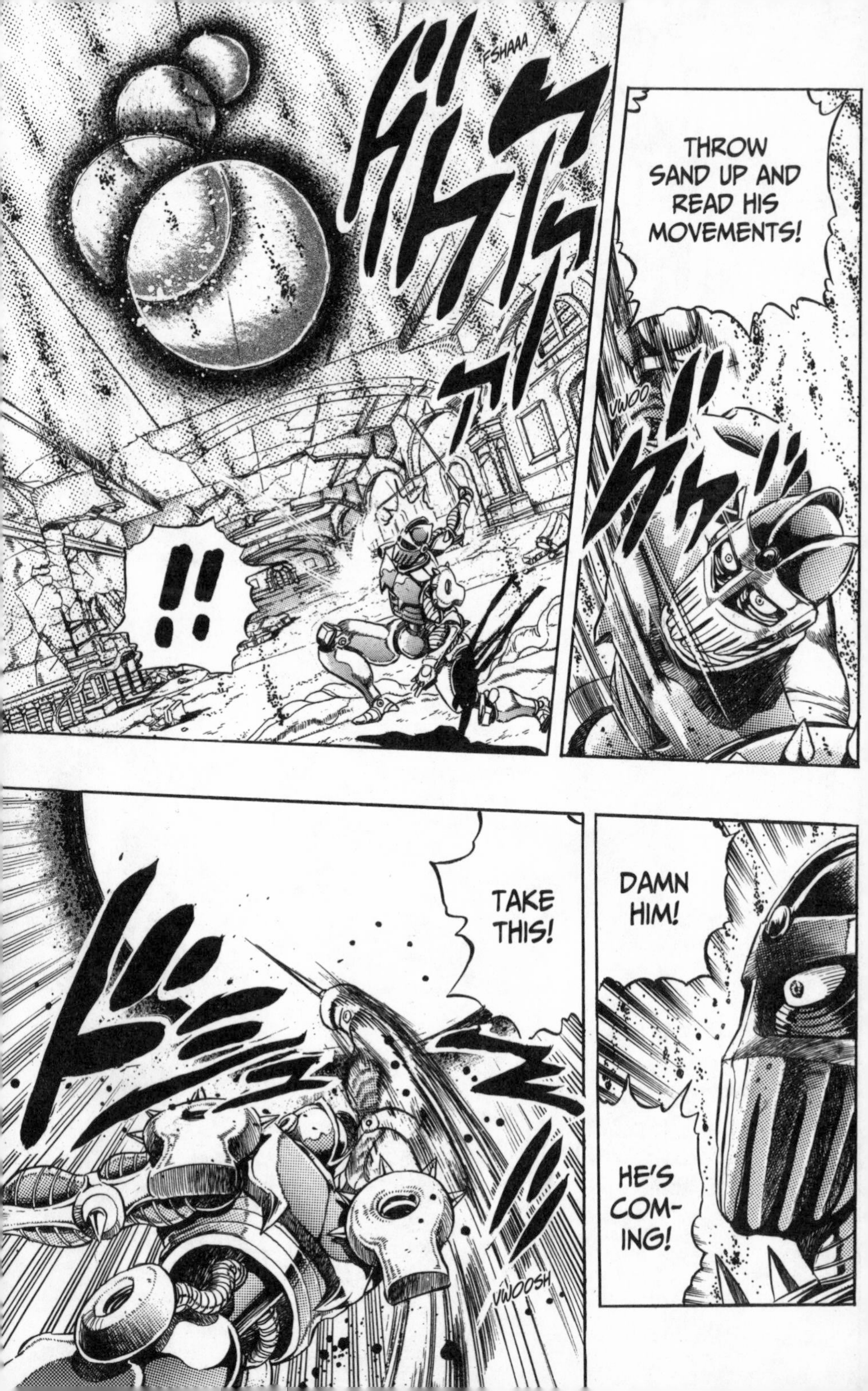
THROW SAND UP AND READ HIS MOVEMENTS!
VWOO
FSHAAA
!!
DAMN HIM!
HE'S COM-ING!
TAKE THIS!
VWOOSH

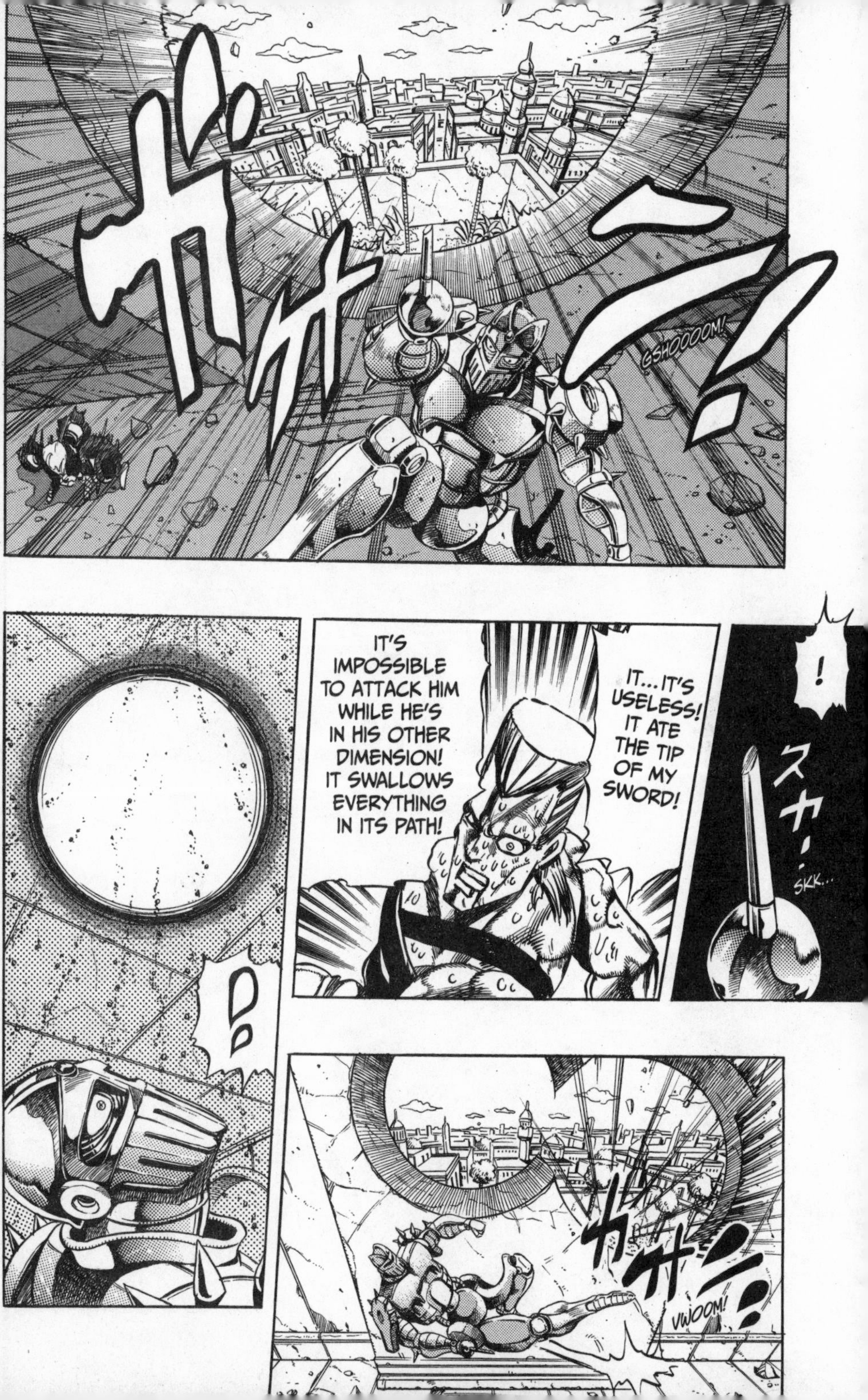
GSHOOOOM!
!
スカ
SKK...
IT... IT'S USELESS! IT ATE THE TIP OF MY SWORD!
IT'S IMPOSSIBLE TO ATTACK HIM WHILE HE'S IN HIS OTHER DIMENSION! IT SWALLOWS EVERYTHING IN ITS PATH!
VWOOM!
!?

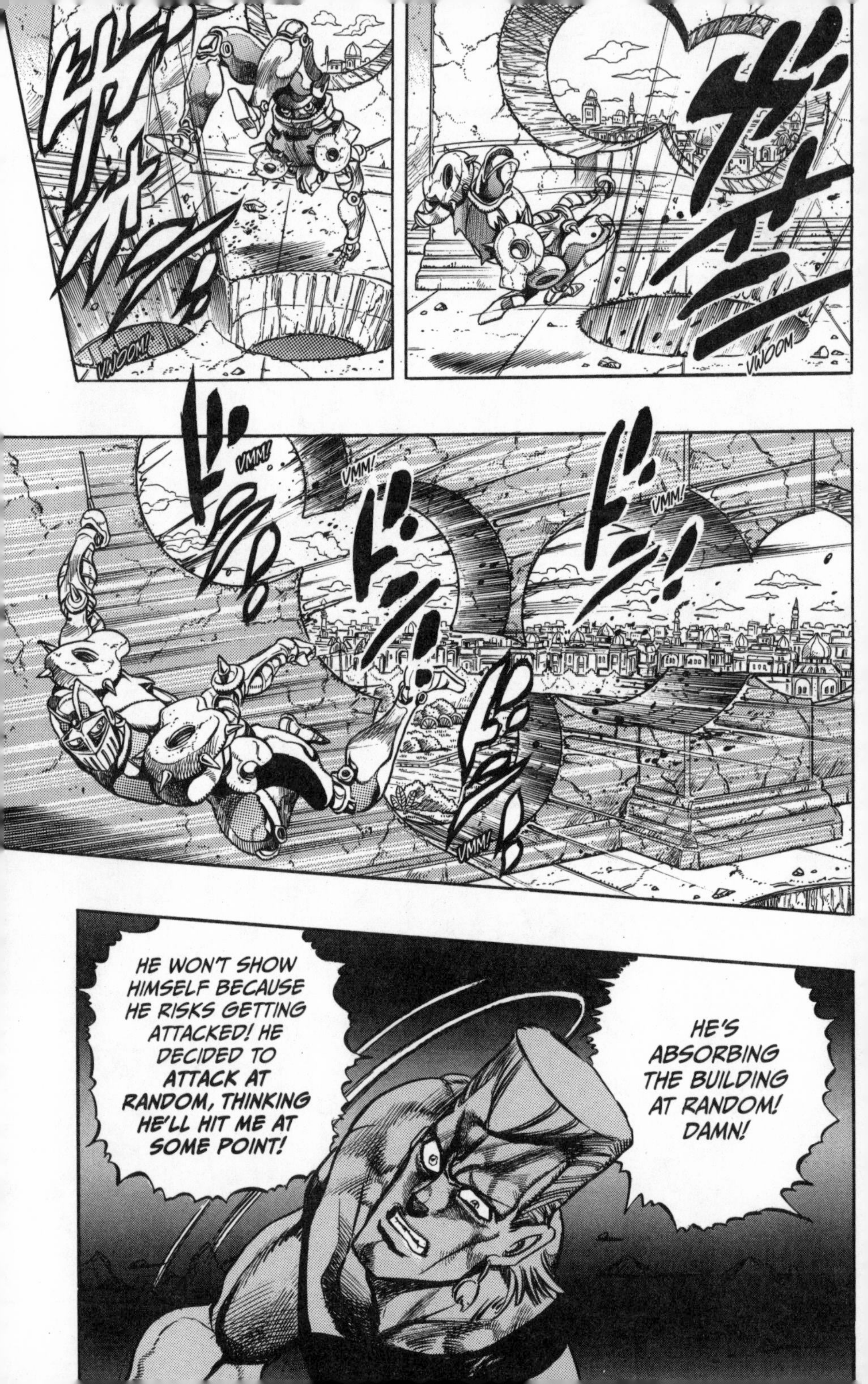
VWOOM
VWOOM!
VMM!
VMM!
VMM!
VMM!
HE'S ABSORBING THE BUILDING AT RANDOM! DAMN!
HE WON'T SHOW HIMSELF BECAUSE HE RISKS GETTING ATTACKED! HE DECIDED TO ATTACK AT RANDOM, THINKING HE'LL HIT ME AT SOME POINT!

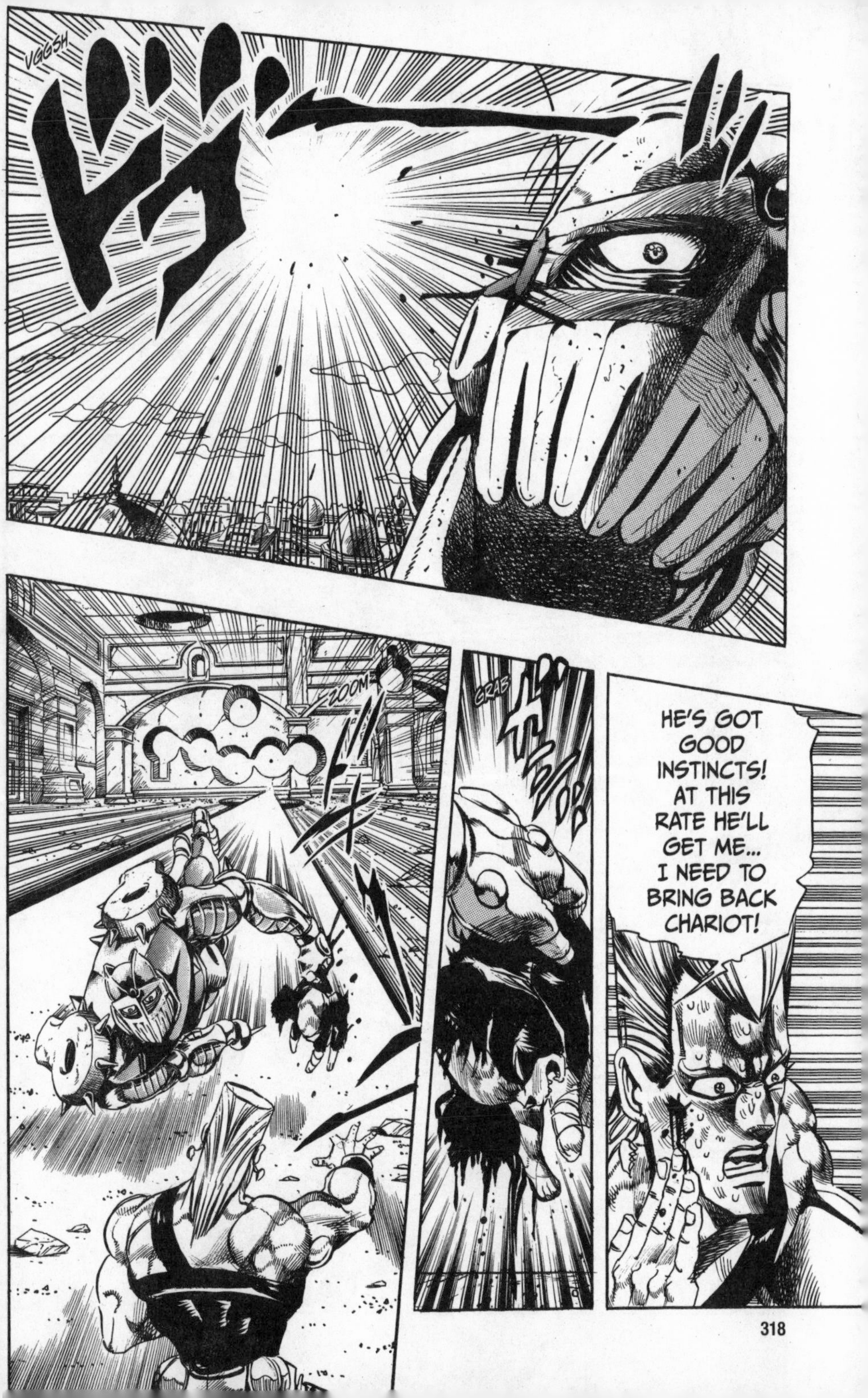
VGGGSH
HE'S GOT GOOD INSTINCTS! AT THIS RATE HE'LL GET ME... I NEED TO BRING BACK CHARIOT!
GRAB
ZOOM

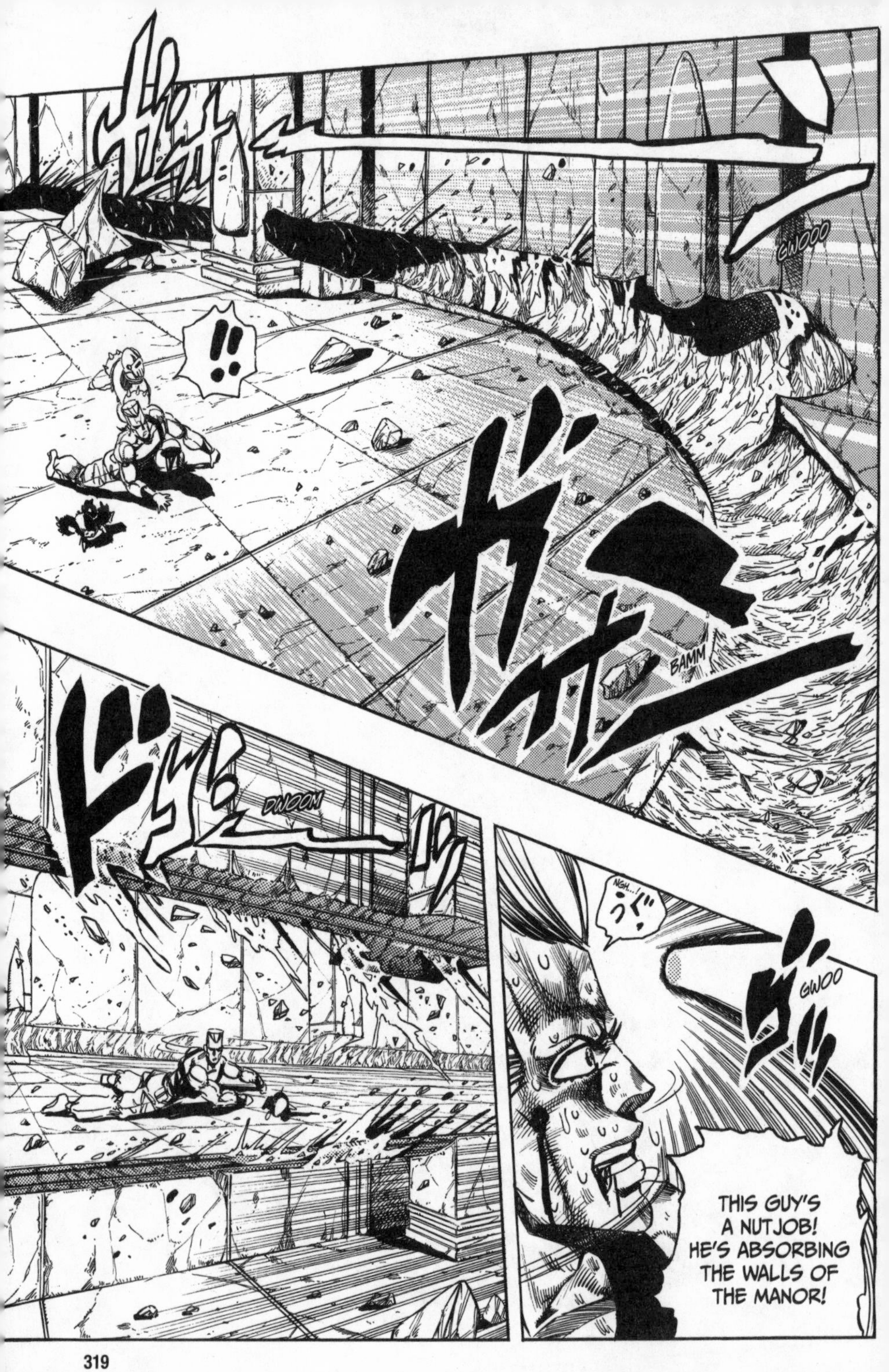
GWOOO
BAMM
!!
NGH...! うぐ
GWOO
THIS GUY'S A NUTJOB! HE'S ABSORBING THE WALLS OF THE MANOR!
DWOON

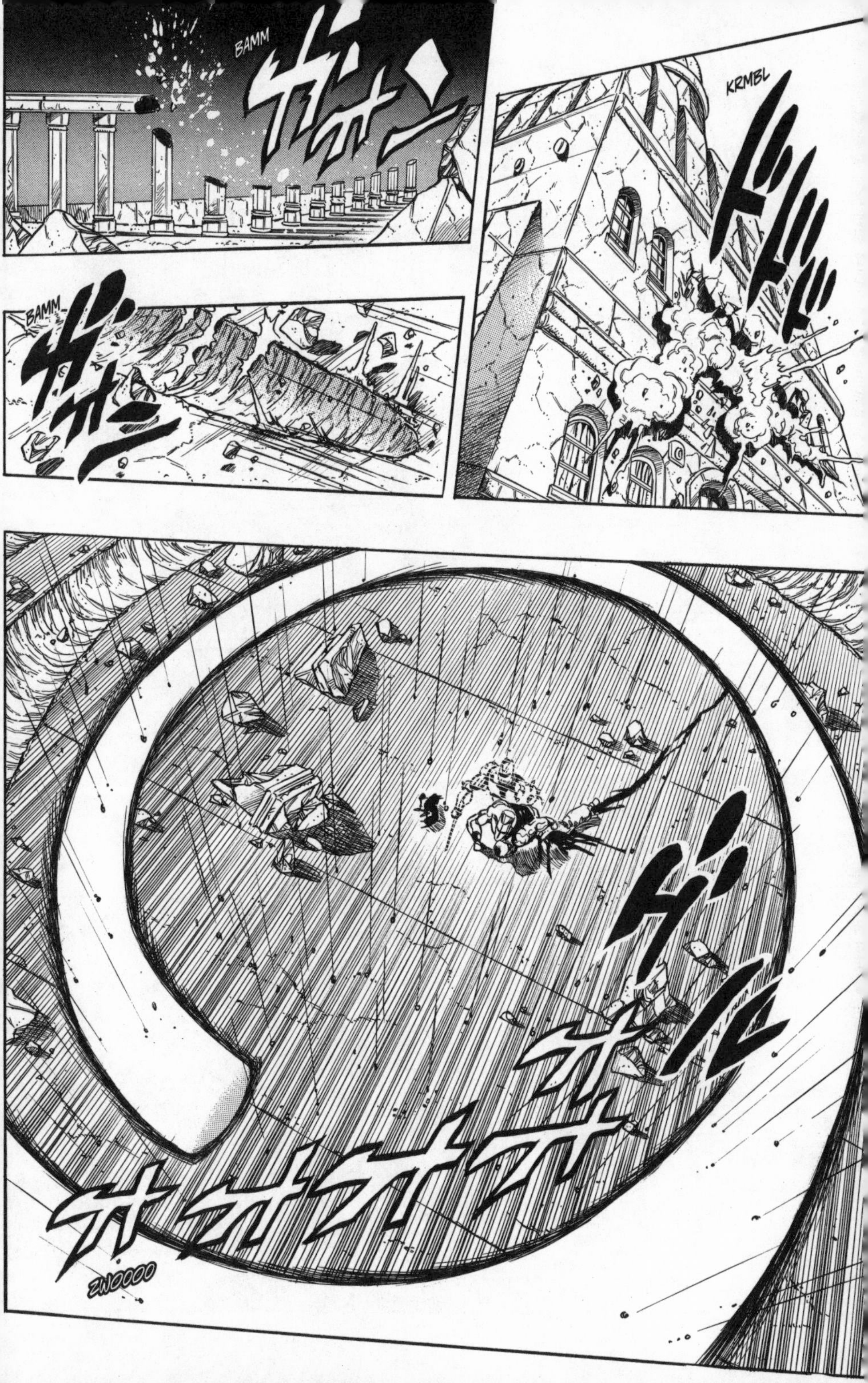
KRMBL
BAMM
BAMM
ZWOOOO

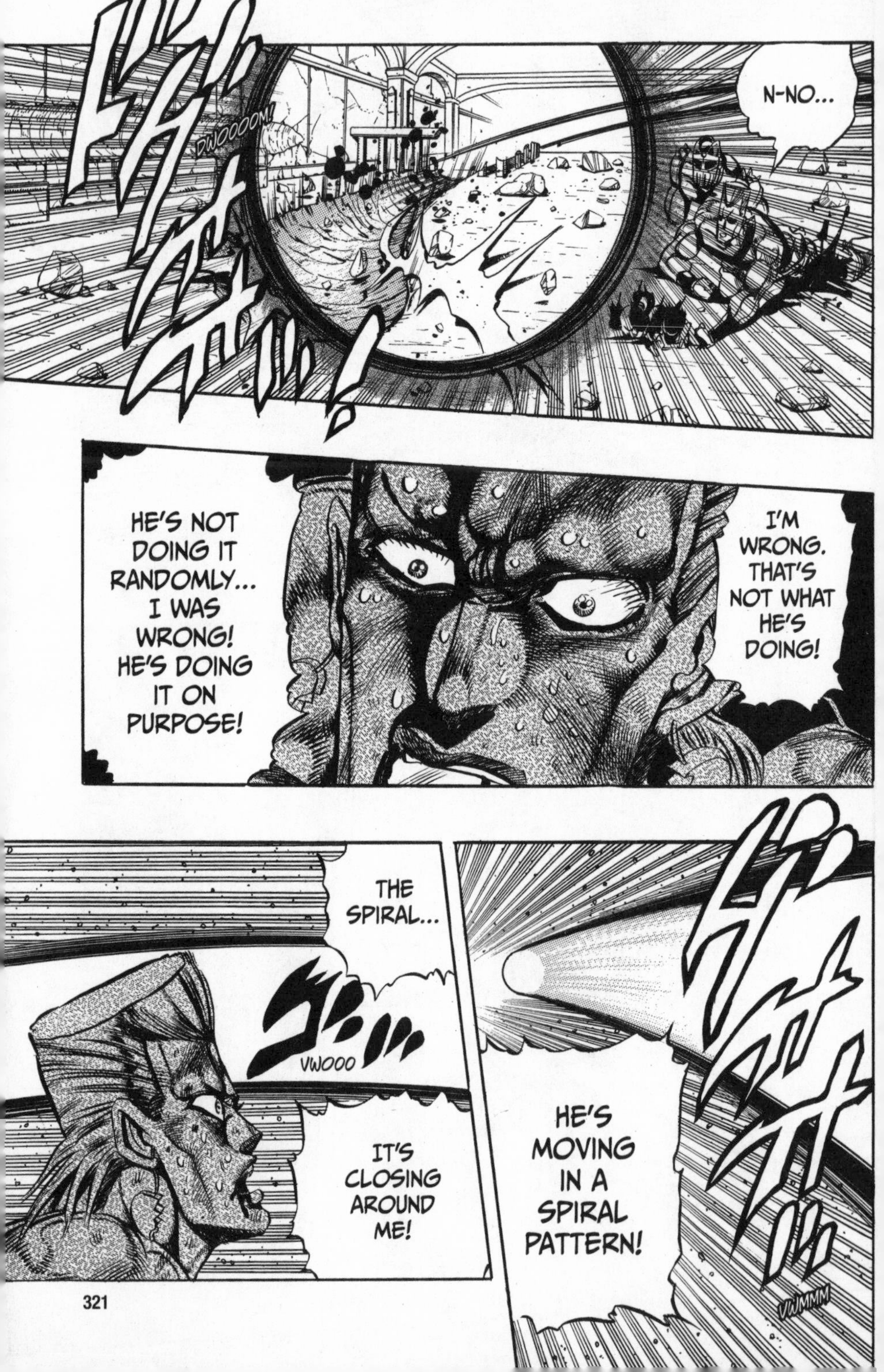
N-NO...
DWOOOOM!
I'M WRONG. THAT'S NOT WHAT HE'S DOING!
HE'S NOT DOING IT RANDOMLY... I WAS WRONG! HE'S DOING IT ON PURPOSE!
HE'S MOVING IN A SPIRAL PATTERN!
VWMMM
THE SPIRAL...
VWOOO
IT'S CLOSING AROUND ME!

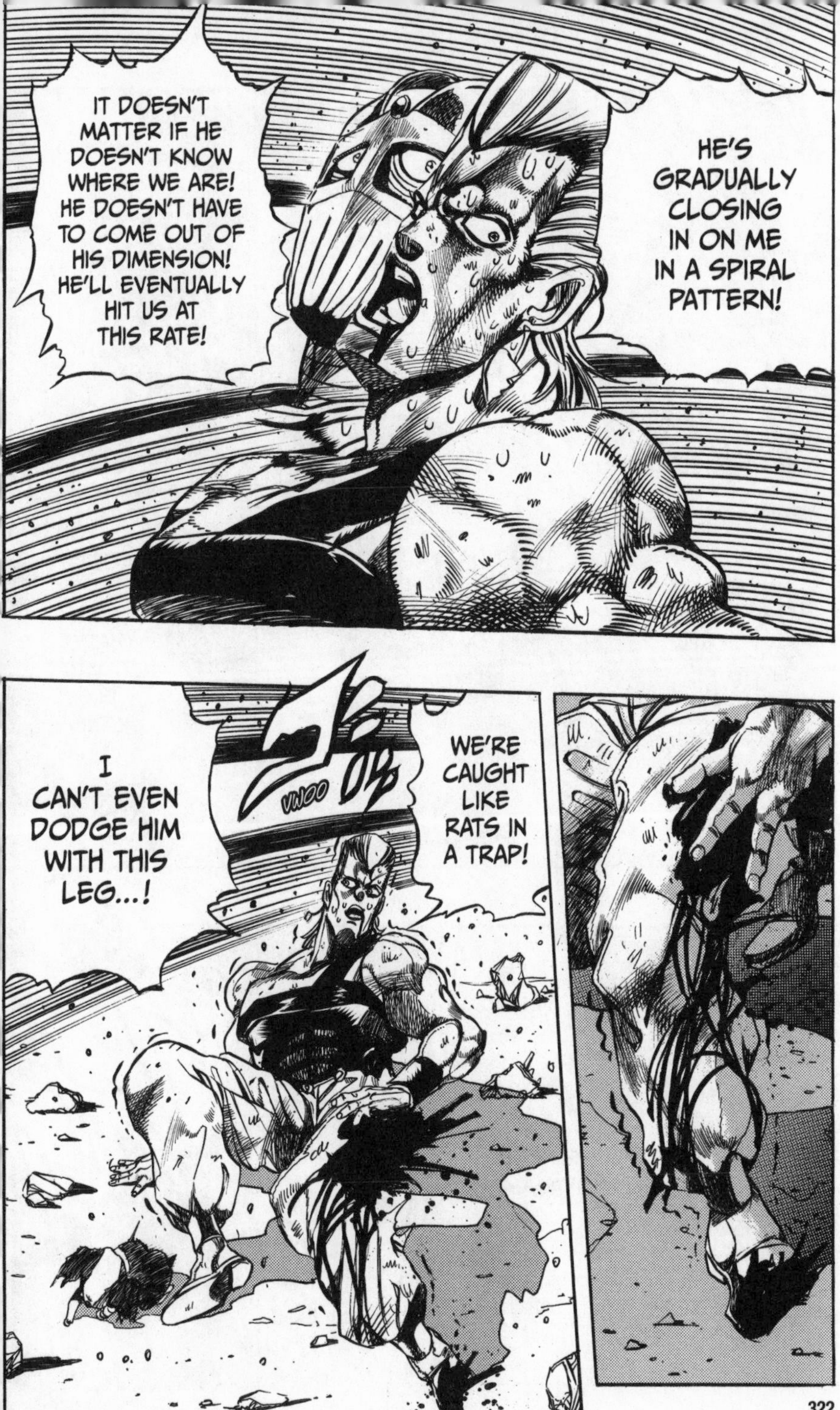
HE'S GRADUALLY CLOSING IN ON ME IN A SPIRAL PATTERN!
IT DOESN'T MATTER IF HE DOESN'T KNOW WHERE WE ARE! HE DOESN'T HAVE TO COME OUT OF HIS DIMENSION! HE'LL EVENTUALLY HIT US AT THIS RATE!
WE'RE CAUGHT LIKE RATS IN A TRAP!
VWOO
I CAN'T EVEN DODGE HIM WITH THIS LEG...!

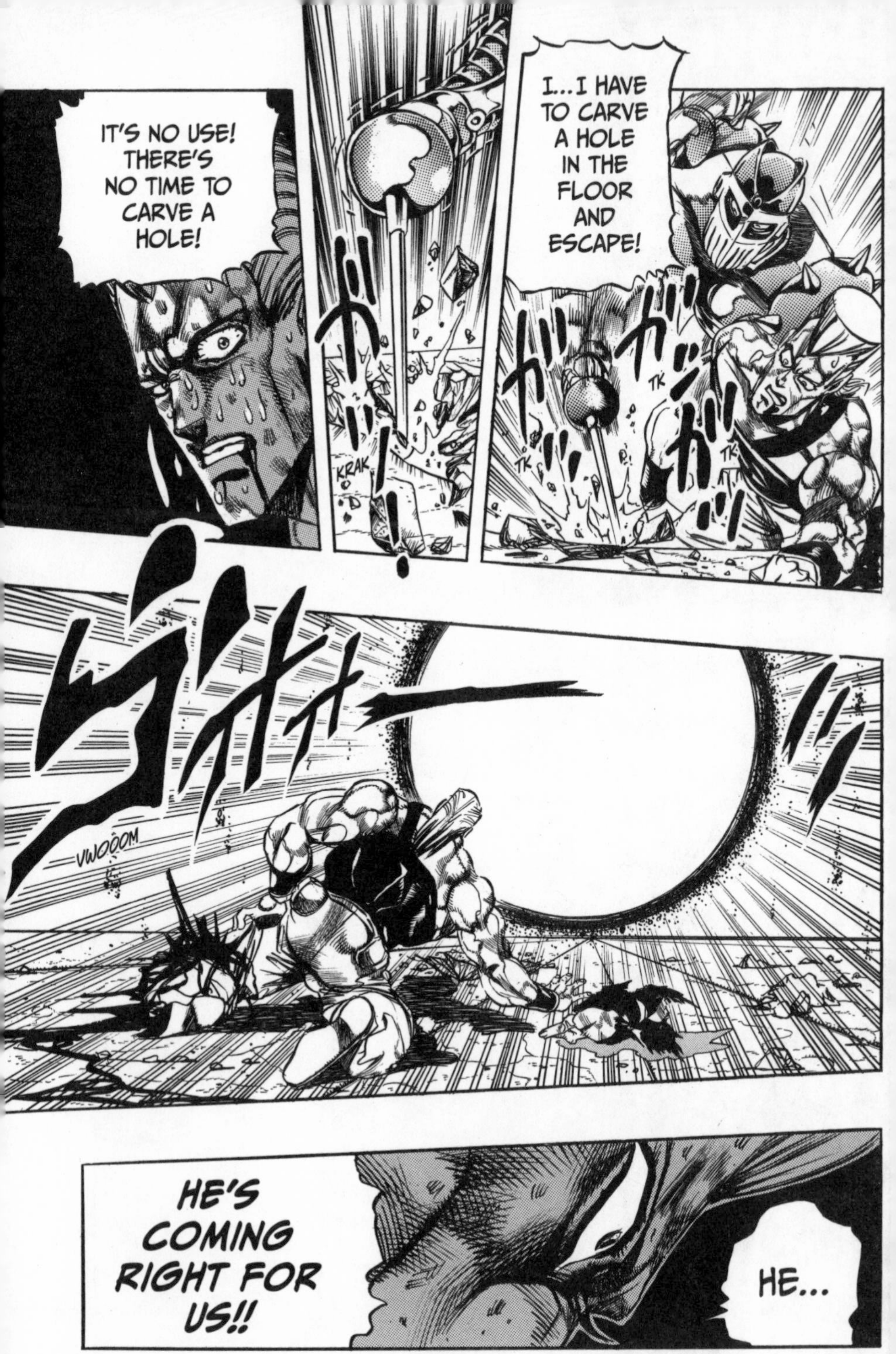
I...I HAVE TO CARVE A HOLE IN THE FLOOR AND ESCAPE!
TK
TK
TK
KRAK
IT'S NO USE! THERE'S NO TIME TO CARVE A HOLE!
VWOOOM
HE...
HE'S COMING RIGHT FOR US!!

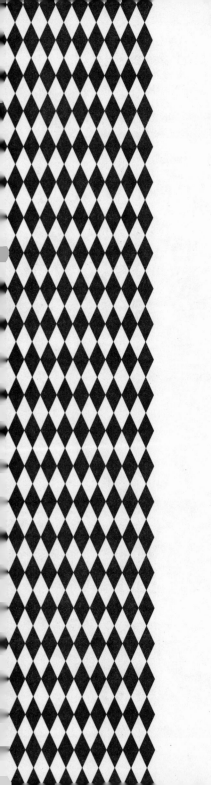

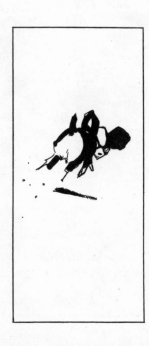

CHAPTER 131: The Dark Void of Cool Ice PART 7

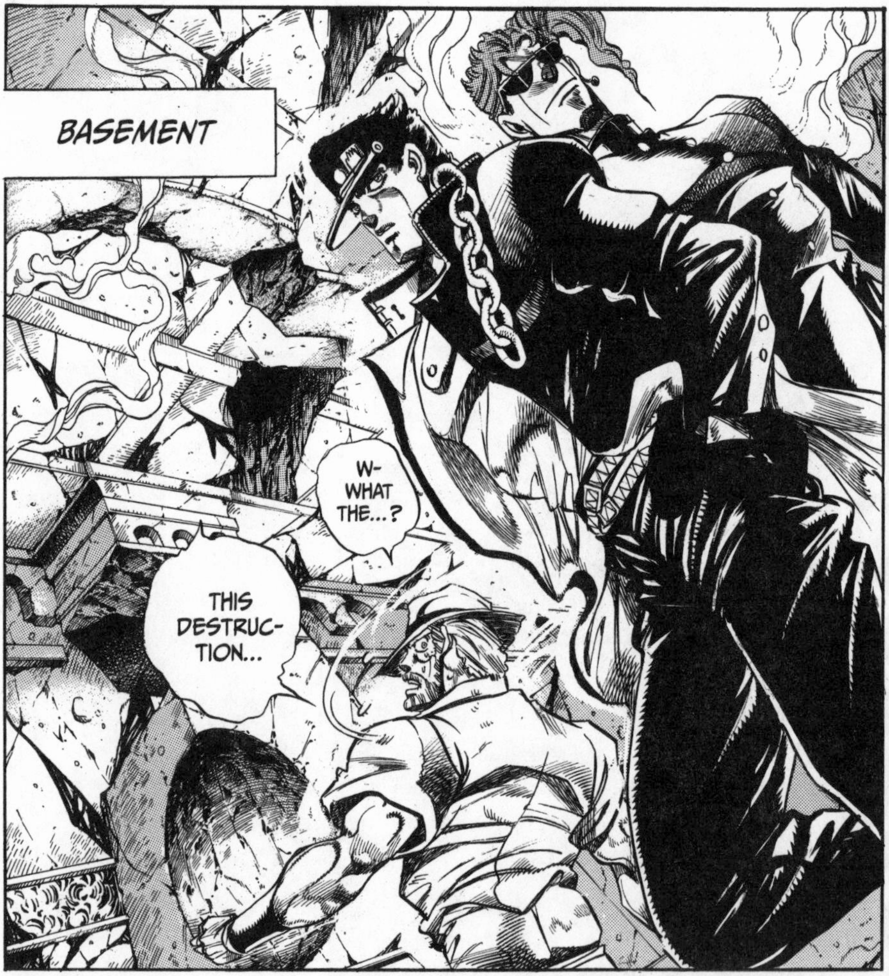
BASEMENT
W-WHAT THE...?
THIS DESTRUCTION...

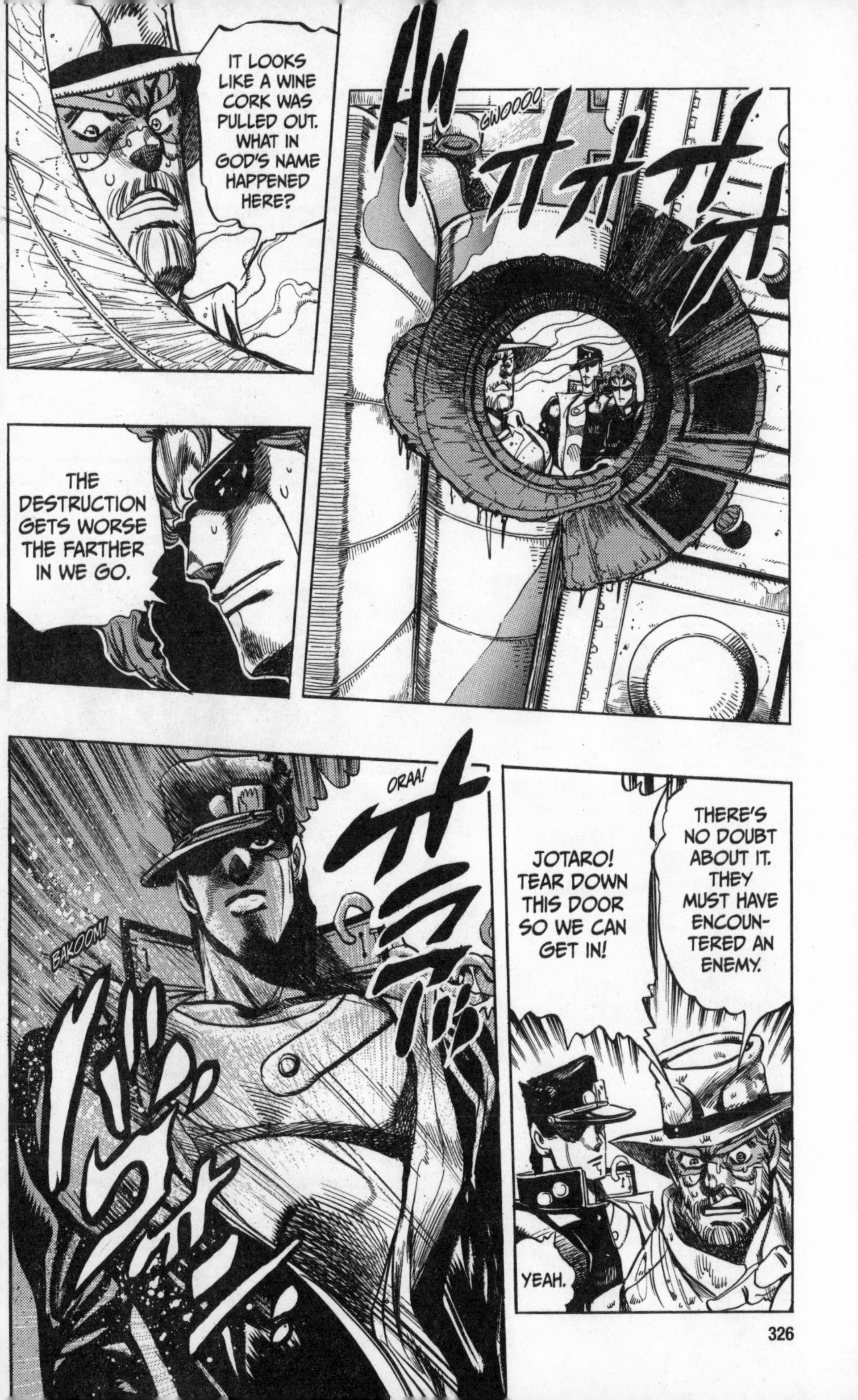
GWOOOO
IT LOOKS LIKE A WINE CORK WAS PULLED OUT. WHAT IN GOD'S NAME HAPPENED HERE?
THE DESTRUCTION GETS WORSE THE FARTHER IN WE GO.
THERE'S NO DOUBT ABOUT IT. THEY MUST HAVE ENCOUNTERED AN ENEMY.
JOTARO! TEAR DOWN THIS DOOR SO WE CAN GET IN!
YEAH.
ORAA!
BAKOOM!

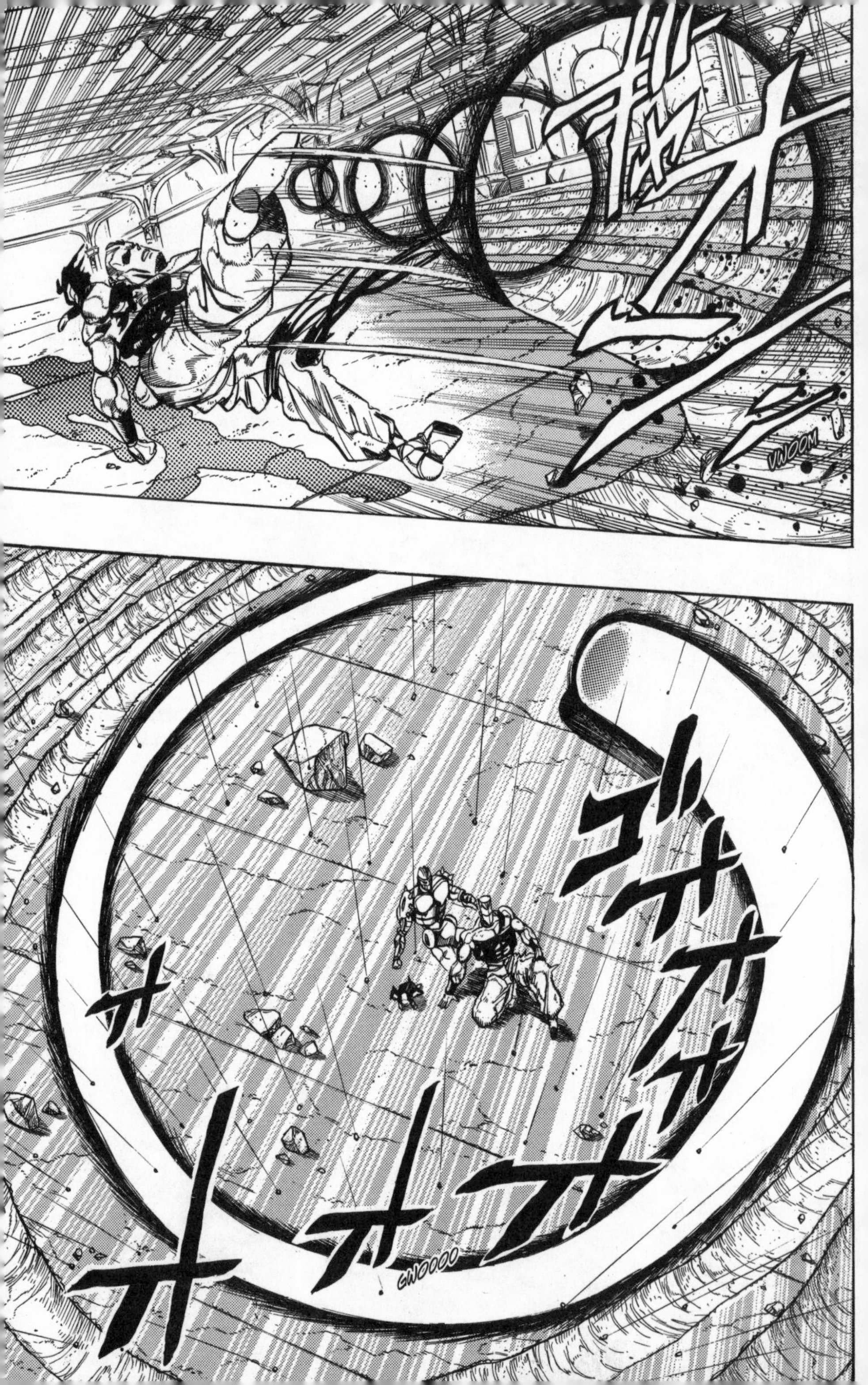
VWOOM
GWOOOO

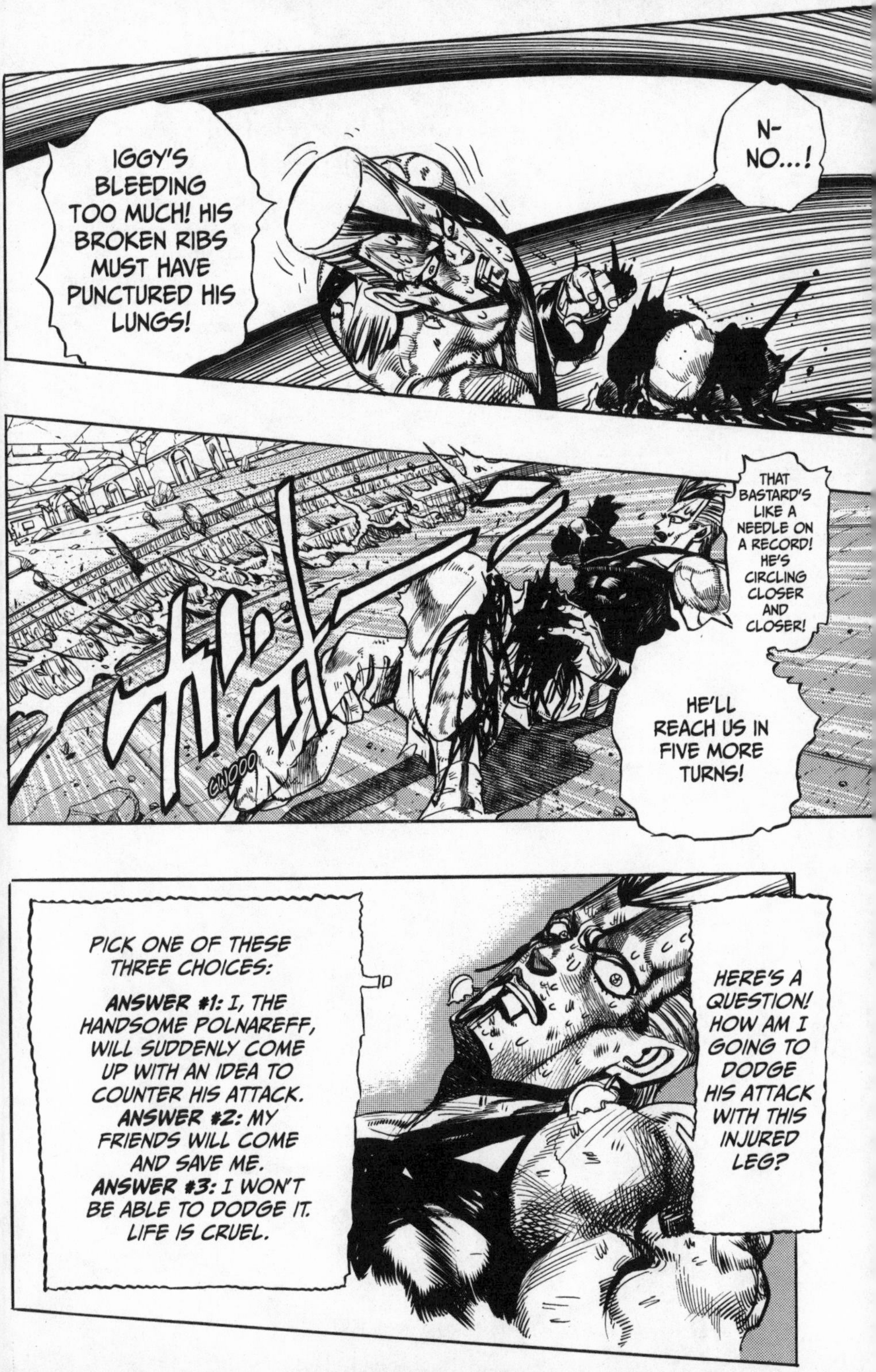
N-NO...!
IGGY'S BLEEDING TOO MUCH! HIS BROKEN RIBS MUST HAVE PUNCTURED HIS LUNGS!
THAT BASTARD'S LIKE A NEEDLE ON A RECORD! HE'S CIRCLING CLOSER AND CLOSER!
HE'LL REACH US IN FIVE MORE TURNS!
GWOOO
HERE'S A QUESTION! HOW AM I GOING TO DODGE HIS ATTACK WITH THIS INJURED LEG?
PICK ONE OF THESE THREE CHOICES:
ANSWER #1: I, THE HANDSOME POLNAREFF, WILL SUDDENLY COME UP WITH AN IDEA TO COUNTER HIS ATTACK.
ANSWER #2: MY FRIENDS WILL COME AND SAVE ME.
ANSWER #3: I WON'T BE ABLE TO DODGE IT. LIFE IS CRUEL.

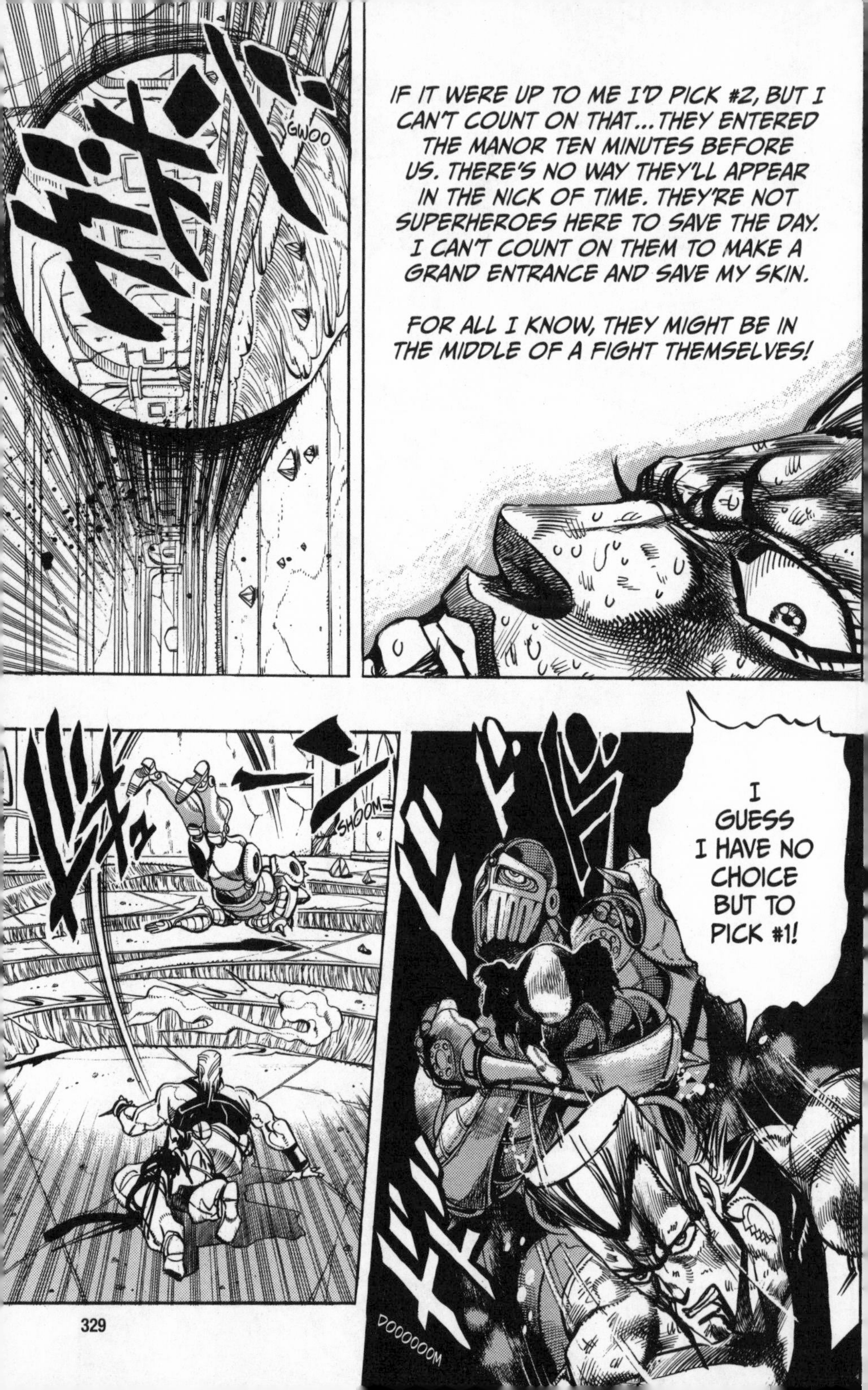
IF IT WERE UP TO ME I'D PICK #2, BUT I CAN'T COUNT ON THAT...THEY ENTERED THE MANOR TEN MINUTES BEFORE US. THERE'S NO WAY THEY'LL APPEAR IN THE NICK OF TIME. THEY'RE NOT SUPERHEROES HERE TO SAVE THE DAY. I CAN'T COUNT ON THEM TO MAKE A GRAND ENTRANCE AND SAVE MY SKIN.
FOR ALL I KNOW, THEY MIGHT BE IN THE MIDDLE OF A FIGHT THEMSELVES!
GWOO
I GUESS I HAVE NO CHOICE BUT TO PICK #1!
DOOOOOOM
SHOOM

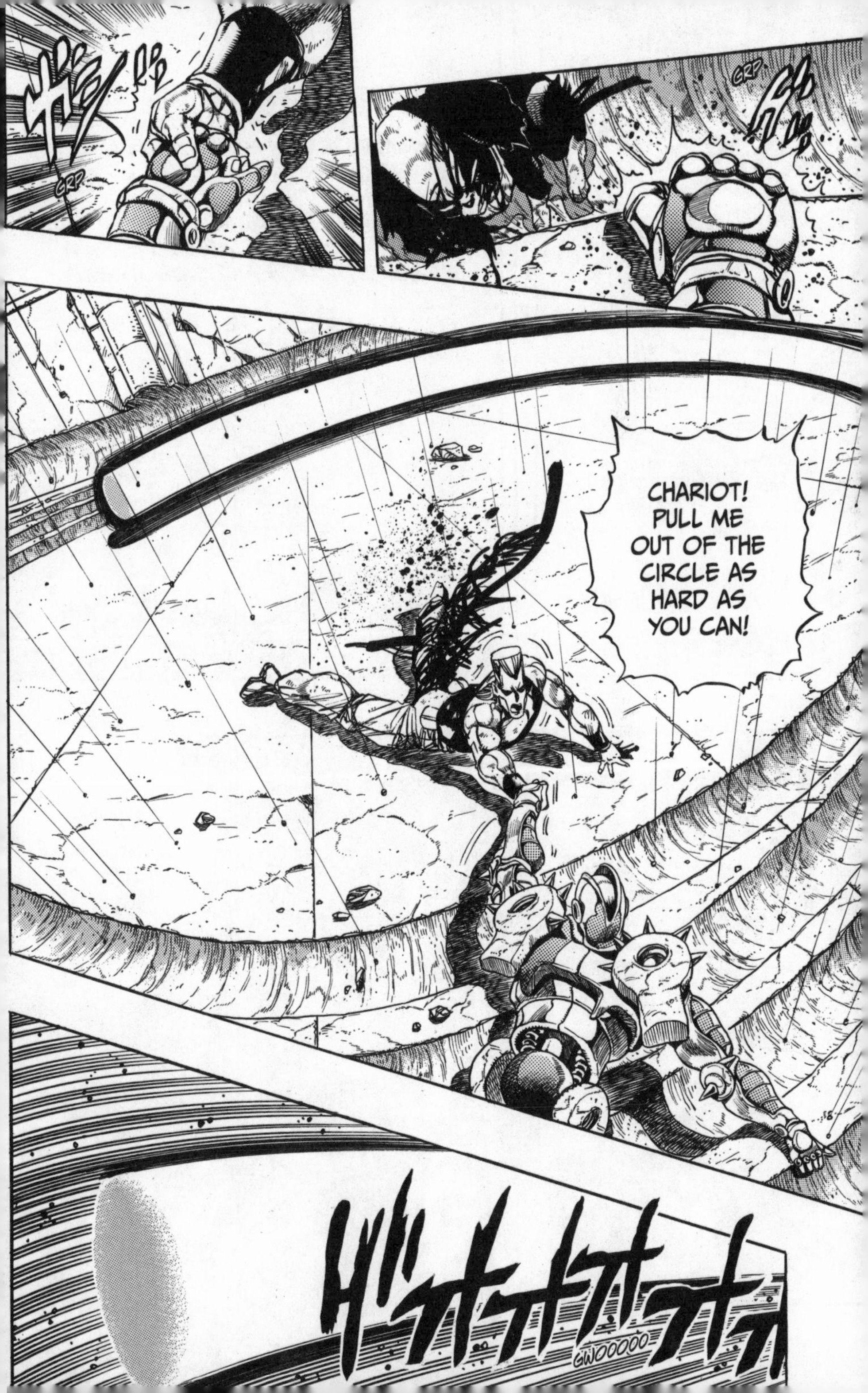
GRP
GRP
CHARIOT! PULL ME OUT OF THE CIRCLE AS HARD AS YOU CAN!
GWOOOOO

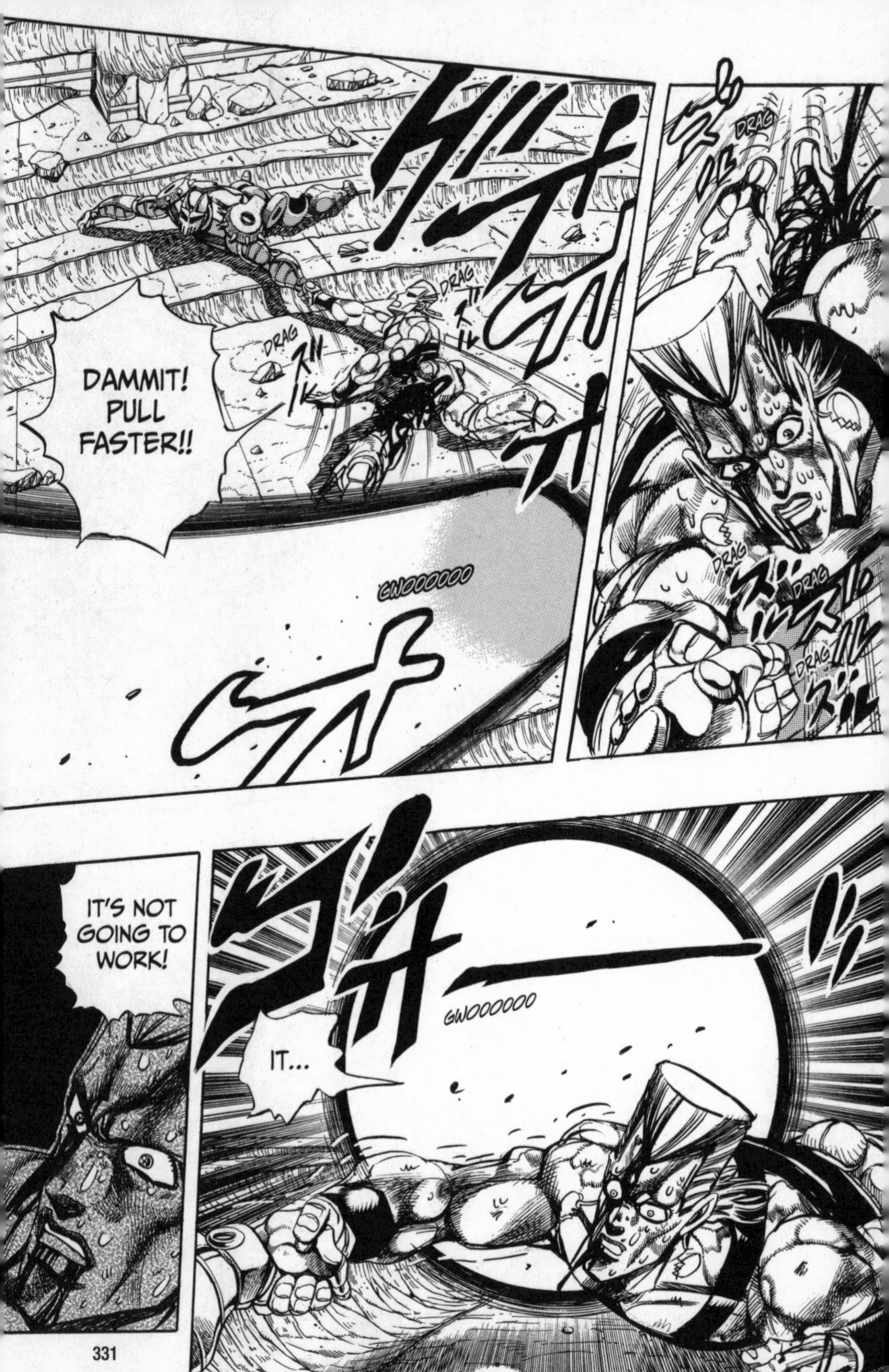
DRAG
DRAG
DRAG
DRAG
DRAG
DRAG
DAMMIT! PULL FASTER!!
GWOOOOOO
GWOOOOOO
IT...
IT'S NOT GOING TO WORK!

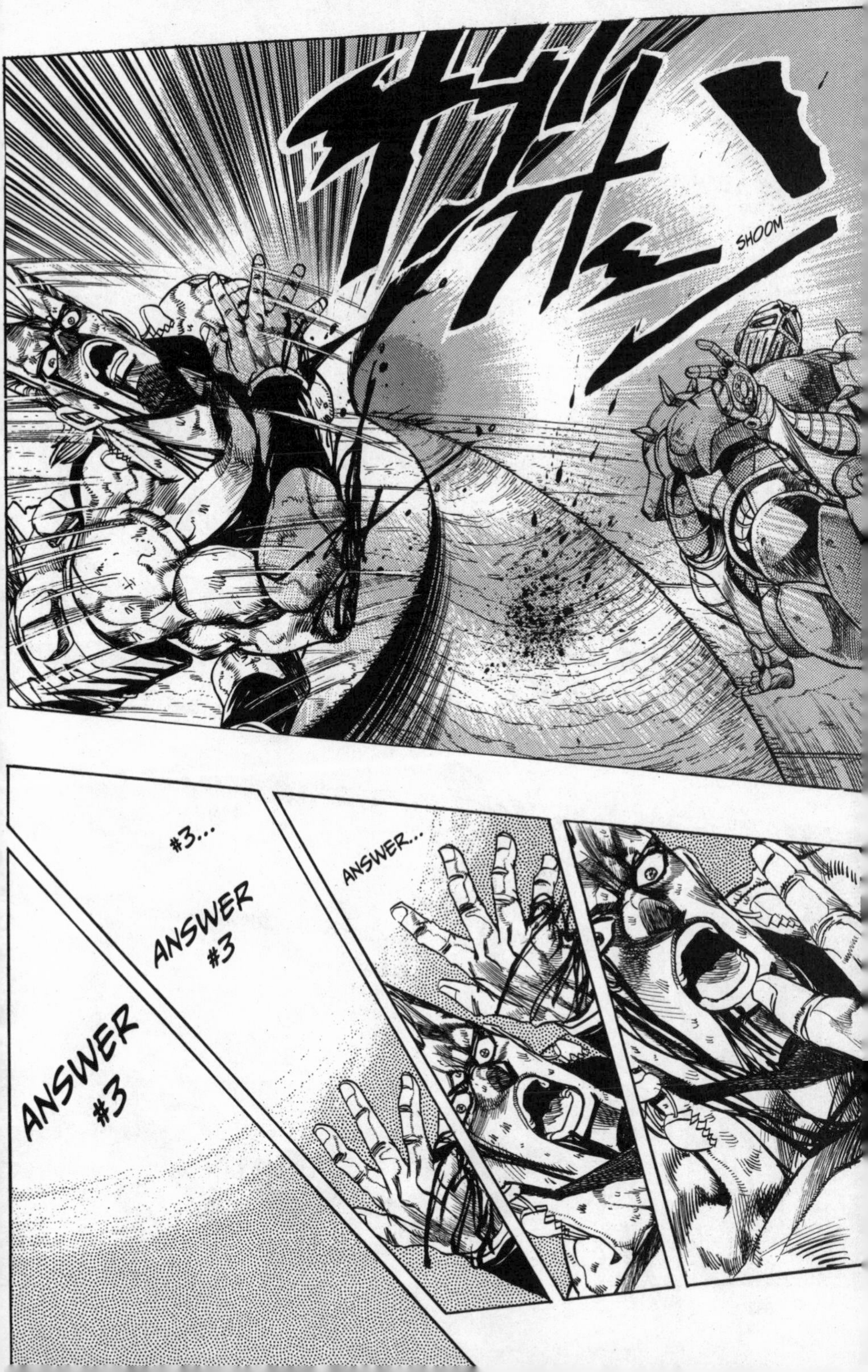
SHOOM
ANSWER...
#3...
ANSWER #3
ANSWER #3

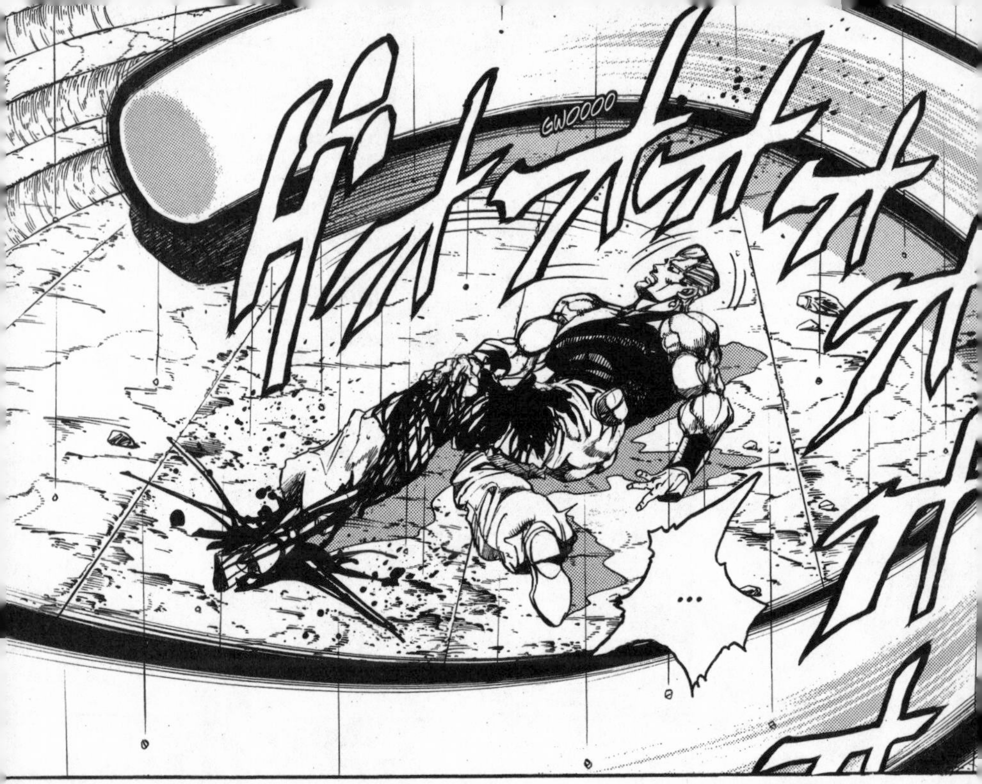
GWOOOO
...
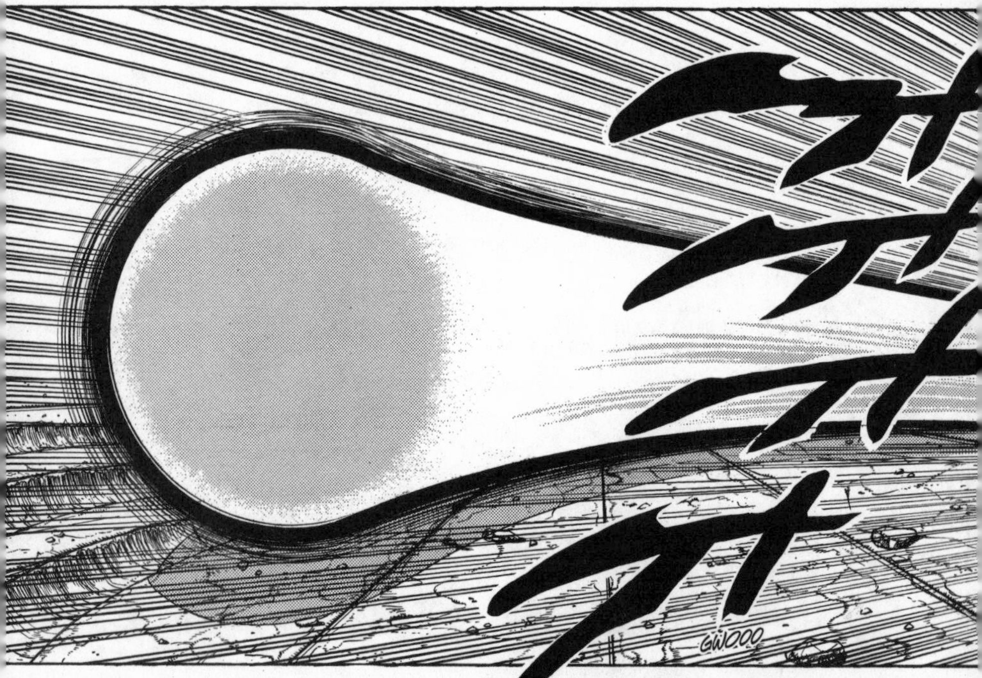
GWOOO

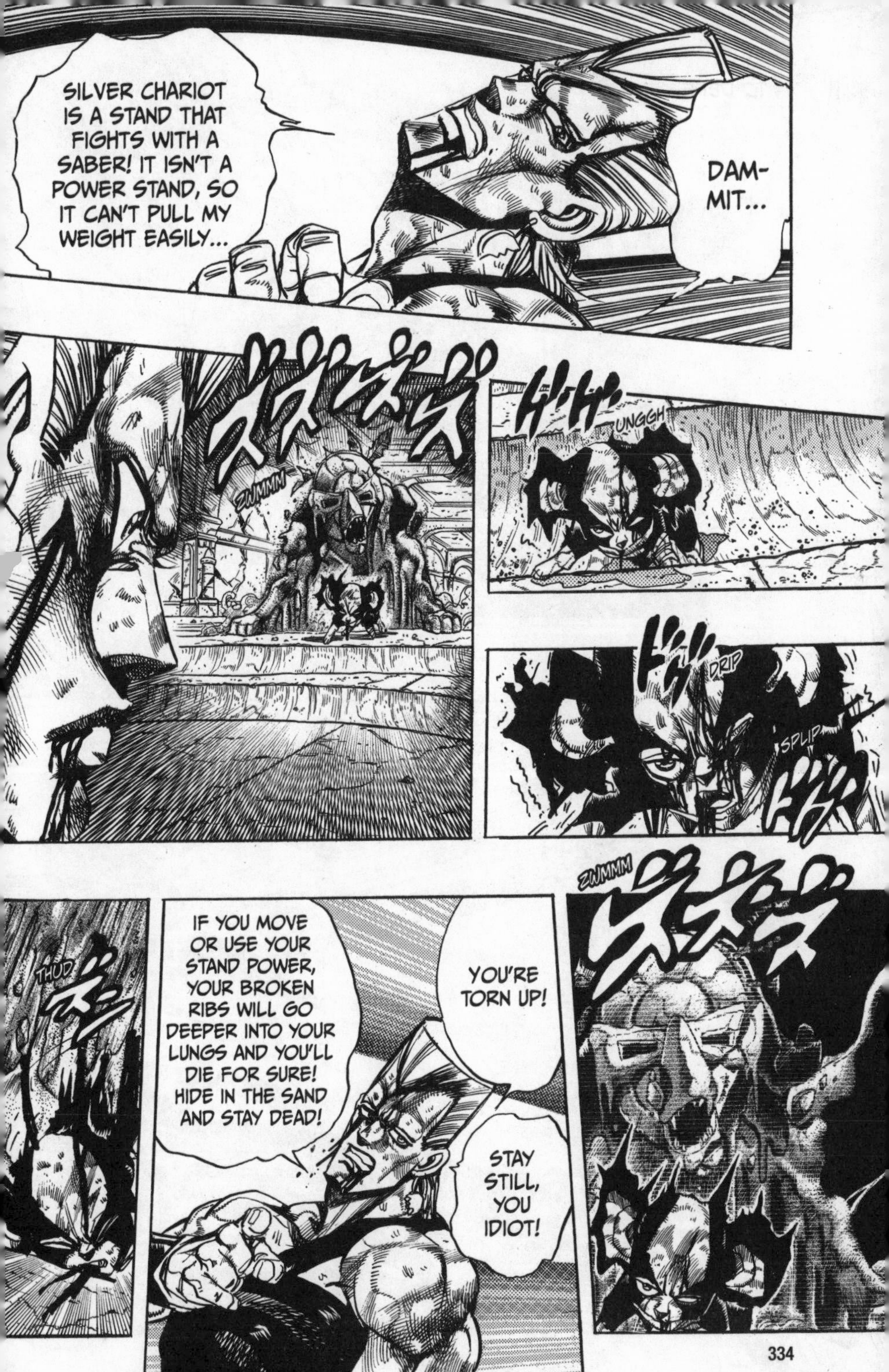
DAM-
MIT...
SILVER CHARIOT IS A STAND THAT FIGHTS WITH A SABER! IT ISN'T A POWER STAND, SO IT CAN'T PULL MY WEIGHT EASILY...
UNGGH
DRIP
SPLIP
ZWMMM
ZWMMM
YOU'RE TORN UP!
IF YOU MOVE OR USE YOUR STAND POWER, YOUR BROKEN RIBS WILL GO DEEPER INTO YOUR LUNGS AND YOU'LL DIE FOR SURE! HIDE IN THE SAND AND STAY DEAD!
STAY STILL, YOU IDIOT!
THUD

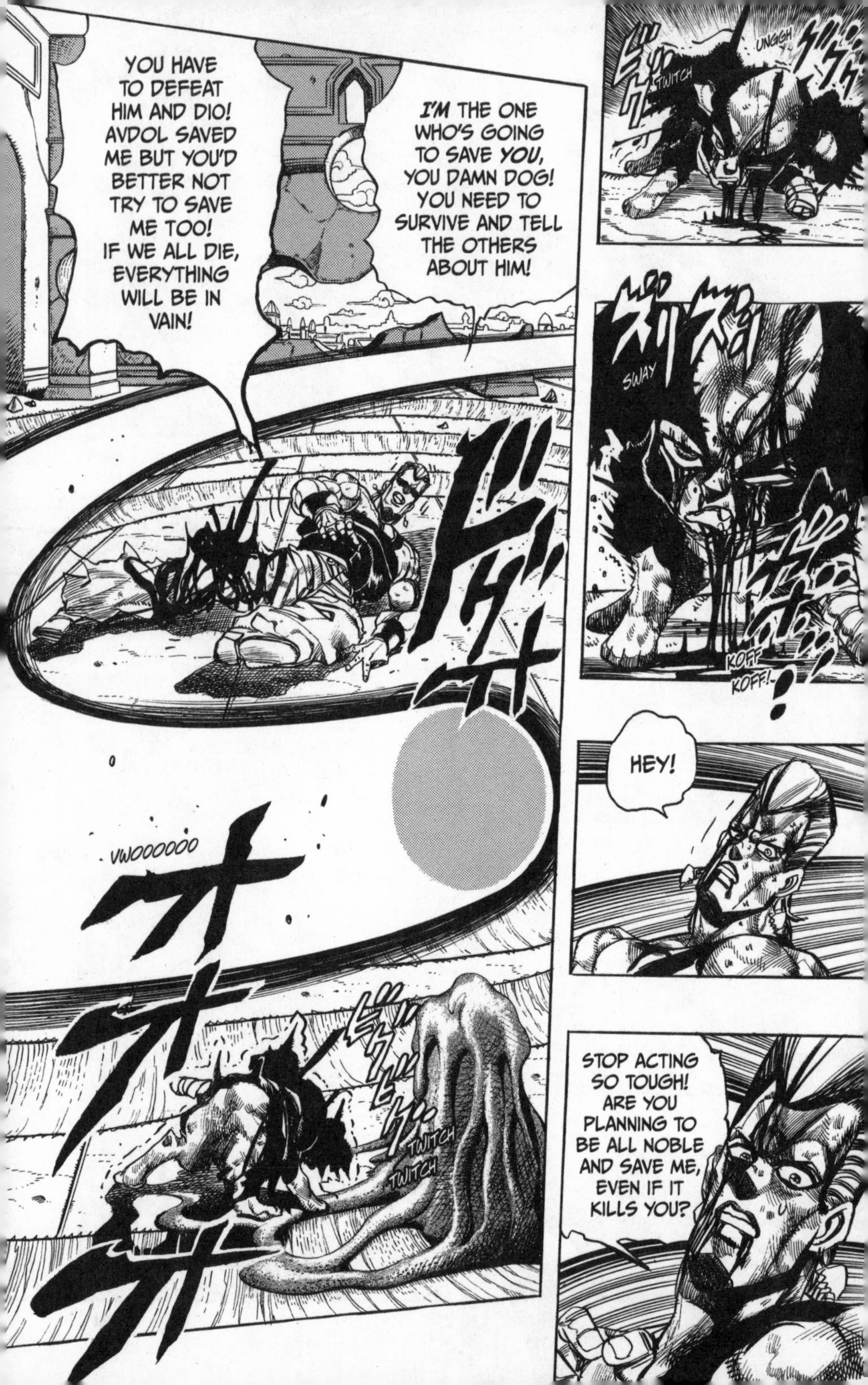

UNGGH
TWITCH
SWAY
KOFF KOFF!
HEY!
STOP ACTING SO TOUGH! ARE YOU PLANNING TO BE ALL NOBLE AND SAVE ME, EVEN IF IT KILLS YOU?
YOU HAVE TO DEFEAT HIM AND DIO! AVDOL SAVED ME BUT YOU'D BETTER NOT TRY TO SAVE ME TOO! IF WE ALL DIE, EVERYTHING WILL BE IN VAIN!
I'M THE ONE WHO'S GOING TO SAVE YOU, YOU DAMN DOG! YOU NEED TO SURVIVE AND TELL THE OTHERS ABOUT HIM!
VWOOOOOO
TWITCH
TWITCH

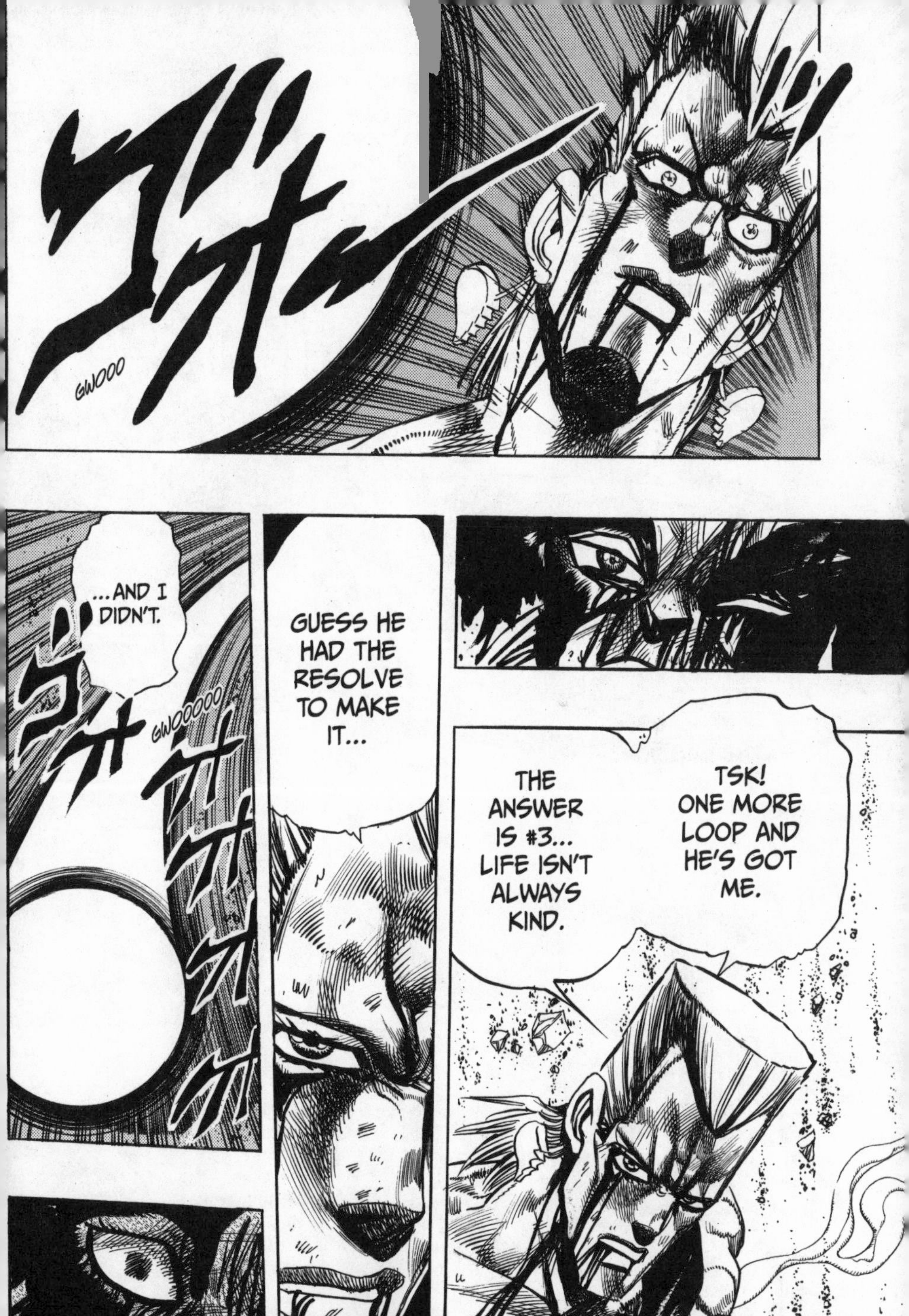
GWOOO
TSK! ONE MORE LOOP AND HE'S GOT ME.
THE ANSWER IS #3... LIFE ISN'T ALWAYS KIND.
GUESS HE HAD THE RESOLVE TO MAKE IT...
...AND I DIDN'T.
GWOOOOO

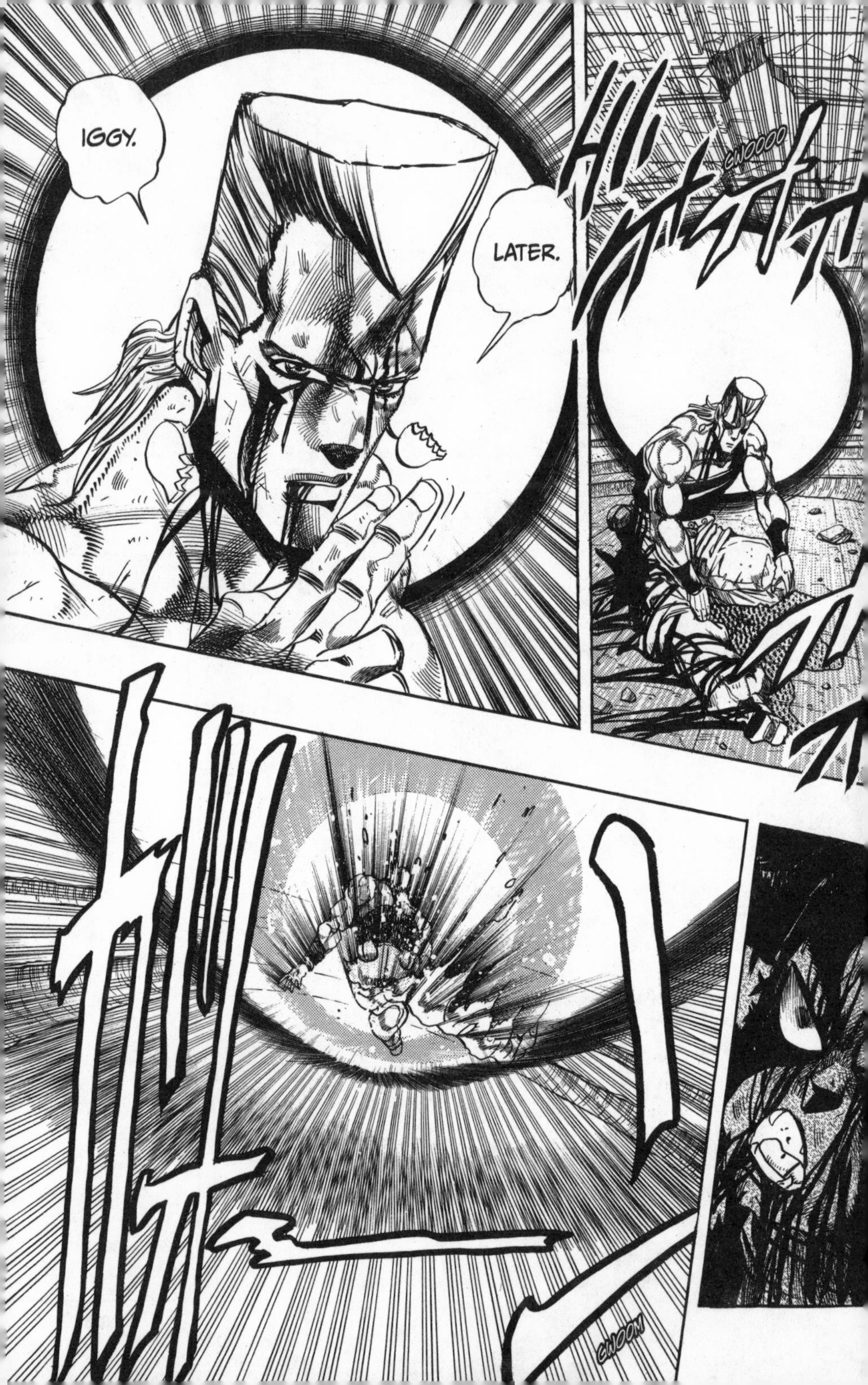
CWOOOO
IGGY.
LATER.
CWOOM

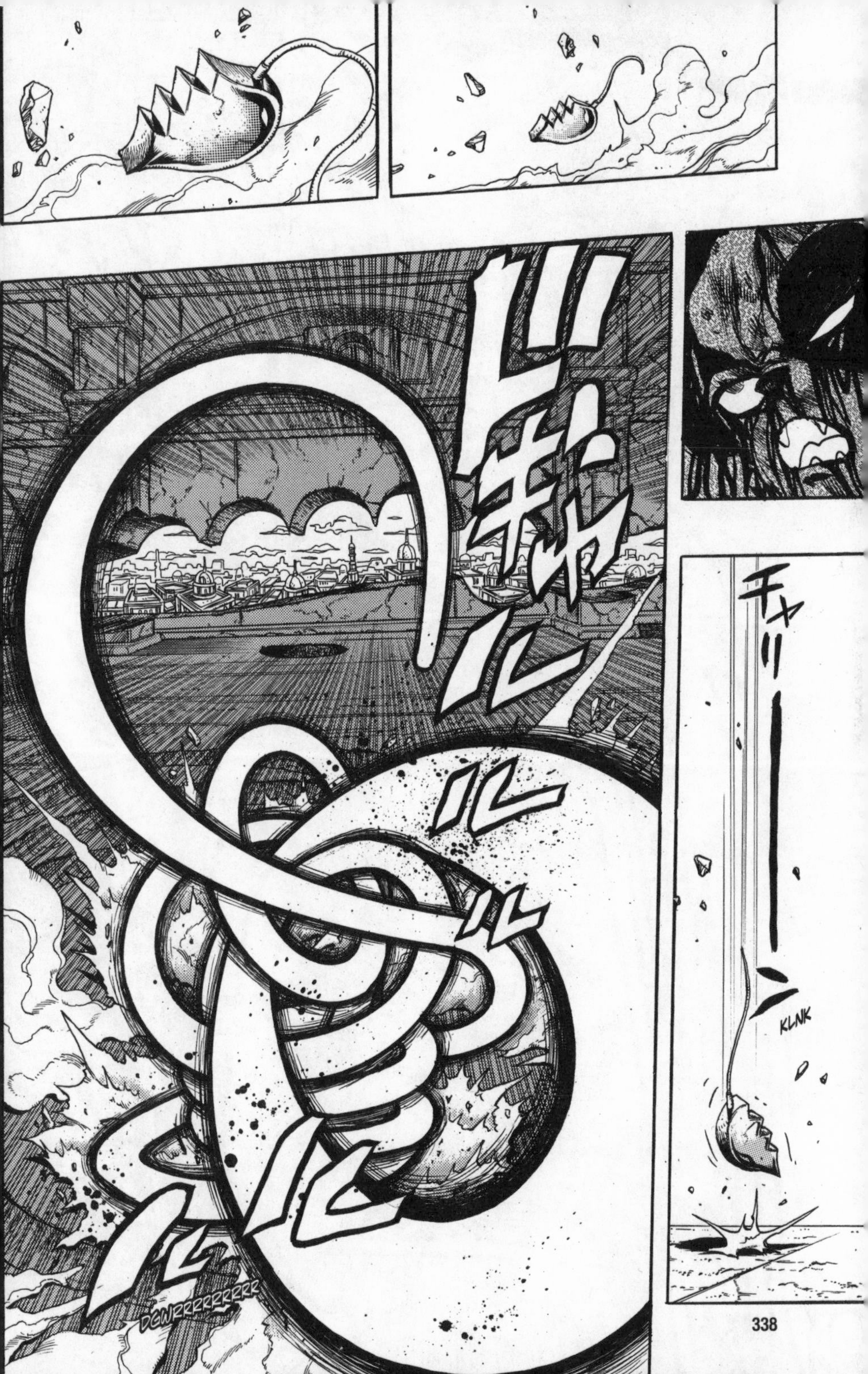
チャリーン
KLNK
ギュルルルルル
DGWRRRRRRRRR

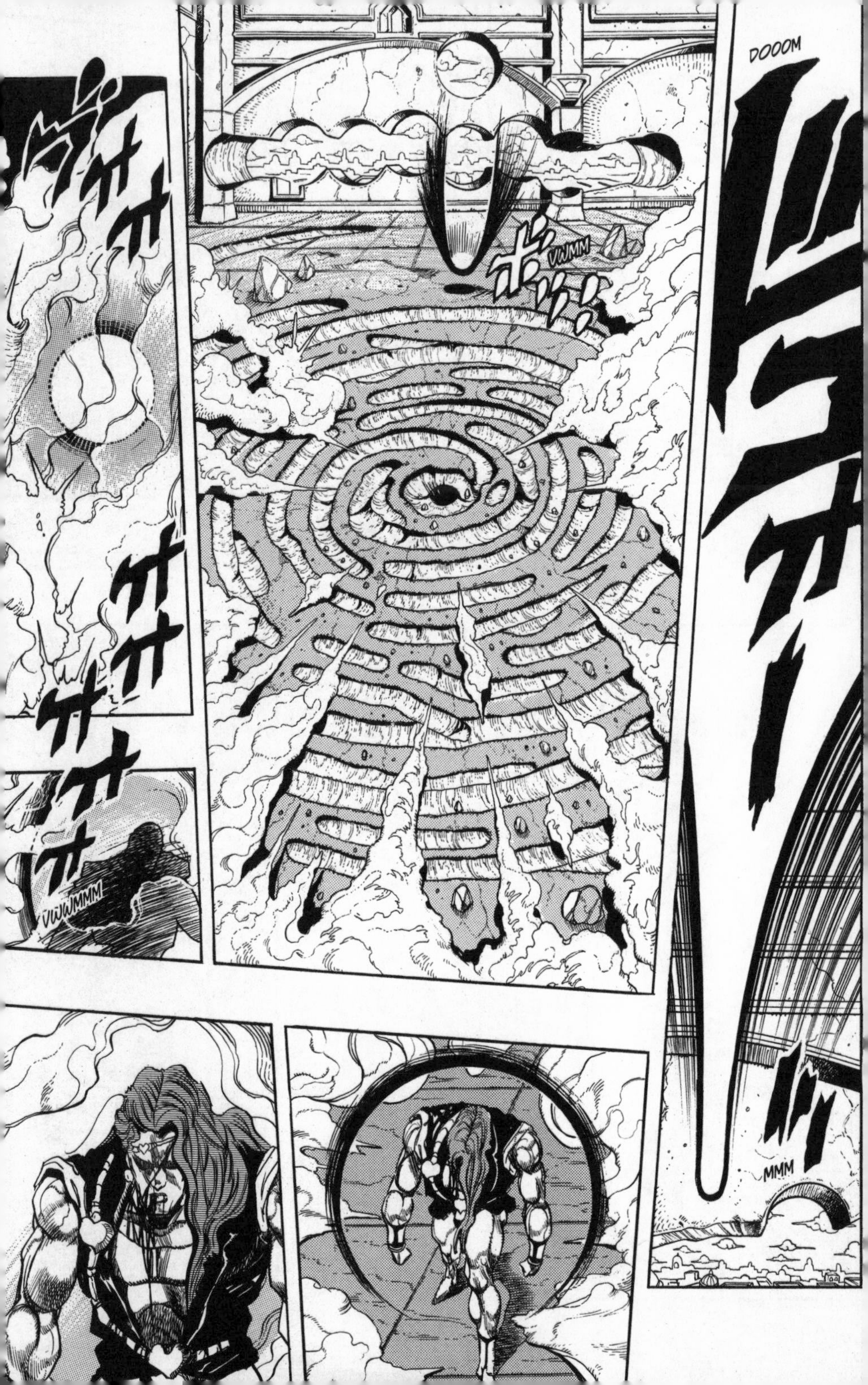
DOOOM
MMM
VWMM
VWWMMM

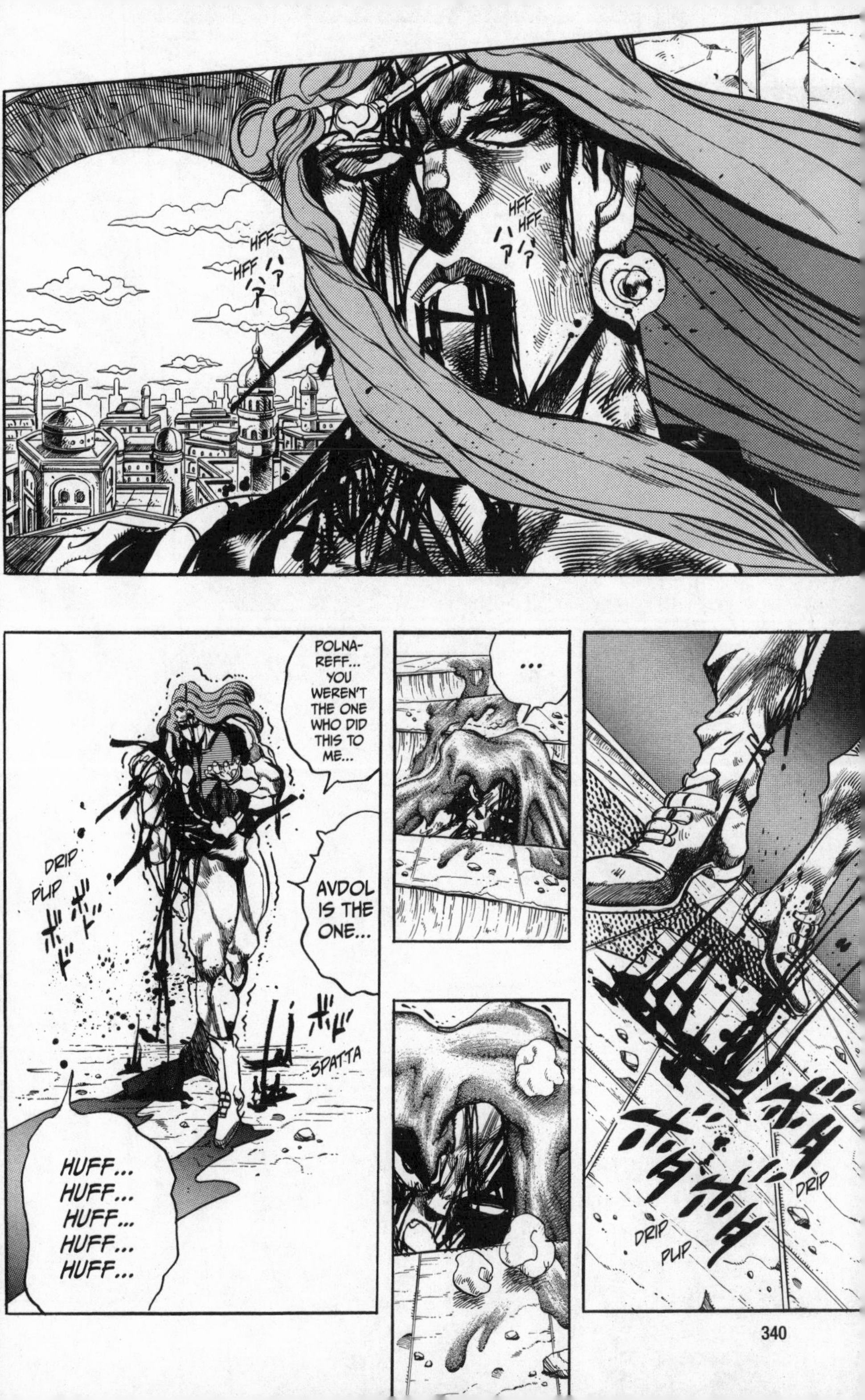
HFF HFF
HFF HFF
DRIP
DRIP PLIP
...
POLNA-REFF... YOU WEREN'T THE ONE WHO DID THIS TO ME...
AVDOL IS THE ONE...
SPATTA
DRIP PLIP
HUFF... HUFF... HUFF... HUFF... HUFF...

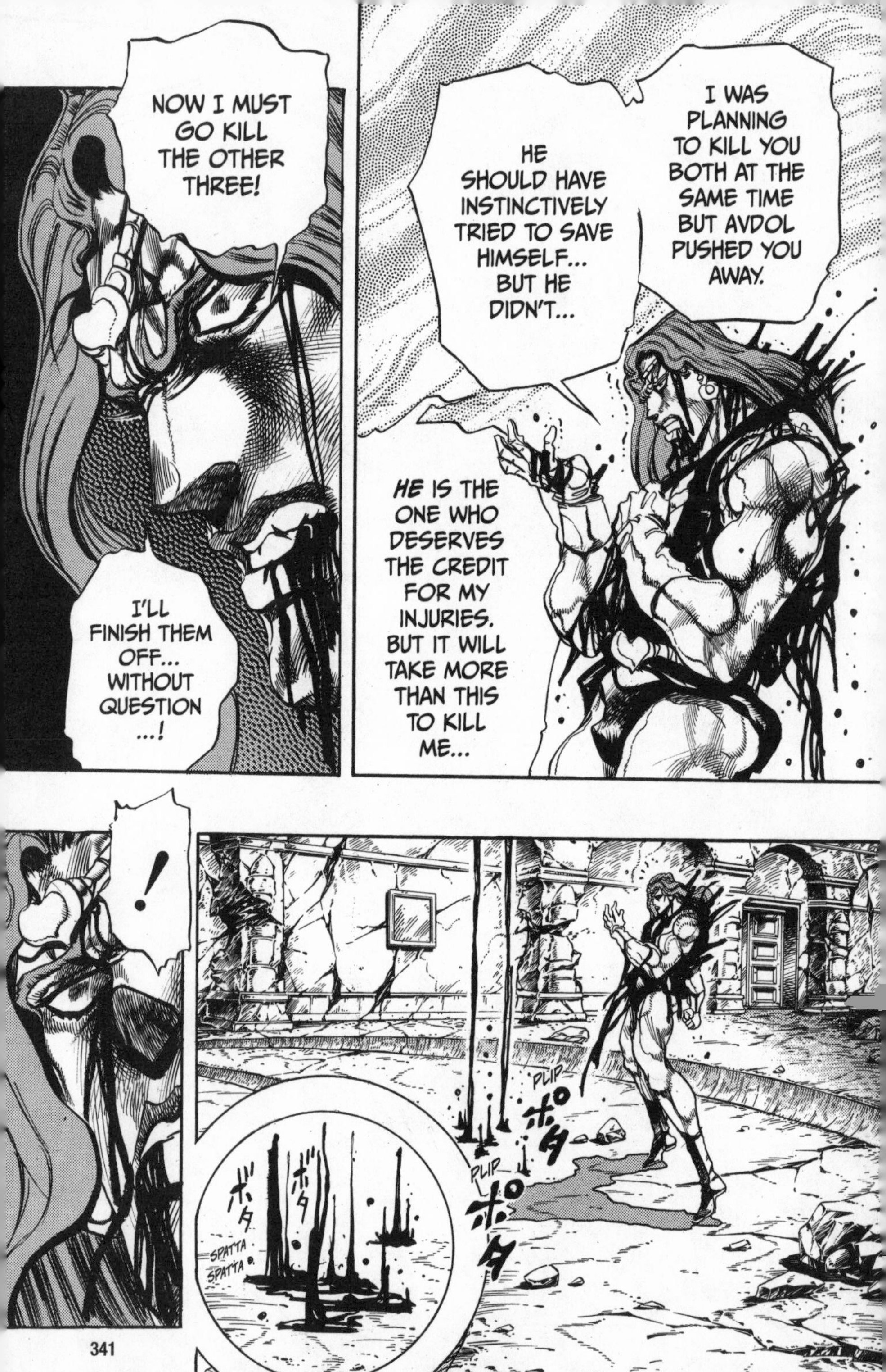

I WAS PLANNING TO KILL YOU BOTH AT THE SAME TIME BUT AVDOL PUSHED YOU AWAY.
HE SHOULD HAVE INSTINCTIVELY TRIED TO SAVE HIMSELF... BUT HE DIDN'T...
HE IS THE ONE WHO DESERVES THE CREDIT FOR MY INJURIES. BUT IT WILL TAKE MORE THAN THIS TO KILL ME...
NOW I MUST GO KILL THE OTHER THREE!
I'LL FINISH THEM OFF... WITHOUT QUESTION ...!
PLIP
ポタ
PLIP
ポタ
ボタ
ボタ
SPATTA
SPATTA
!

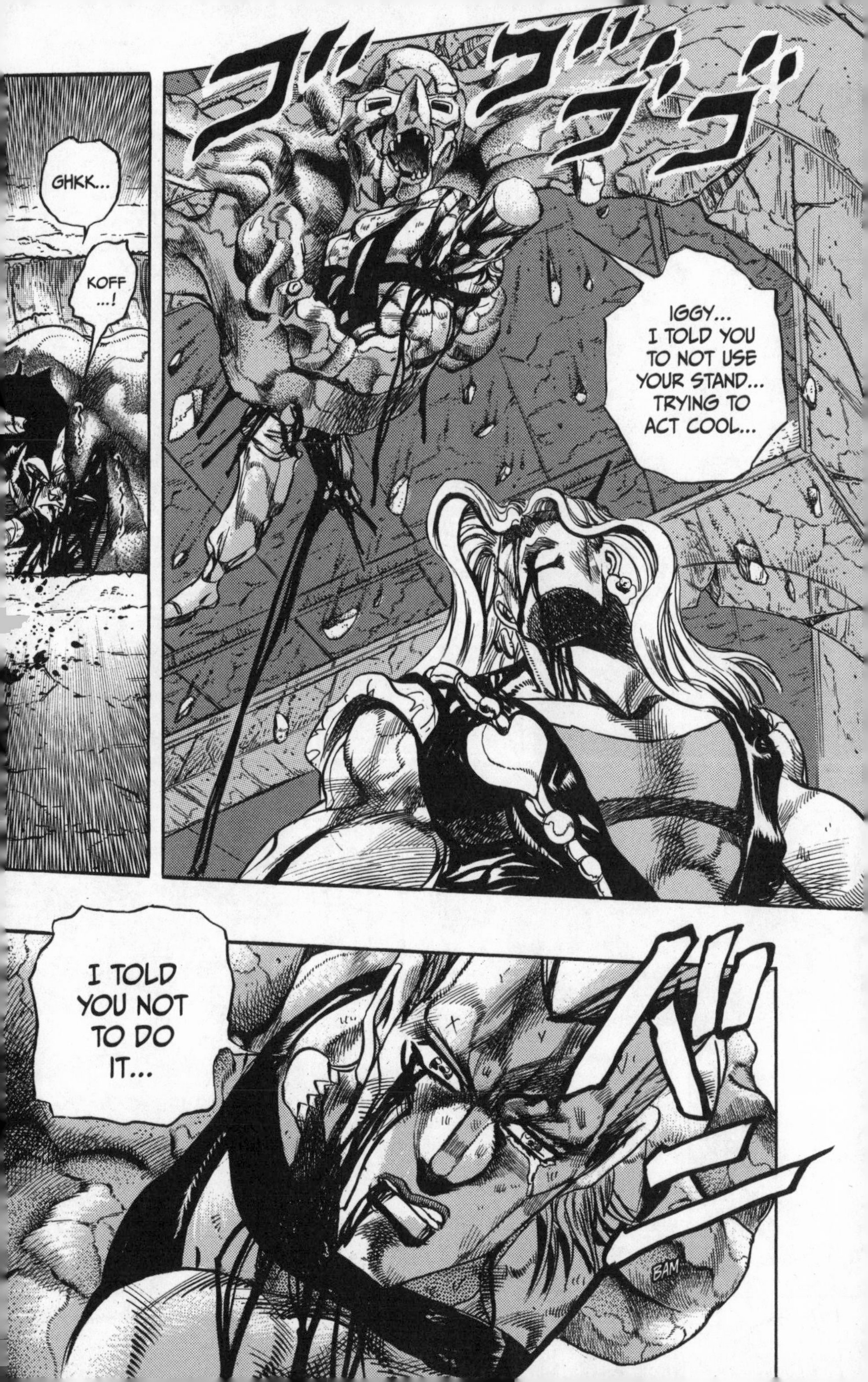
ゴゴゴゴ
IGGY... I TOLD YOU TO NOT USE YOUR STAND... TRYING TO ACT COOL...
GHKK...
KOFF ...!
I TOLD YOU NOT TO DO IT...
BAM

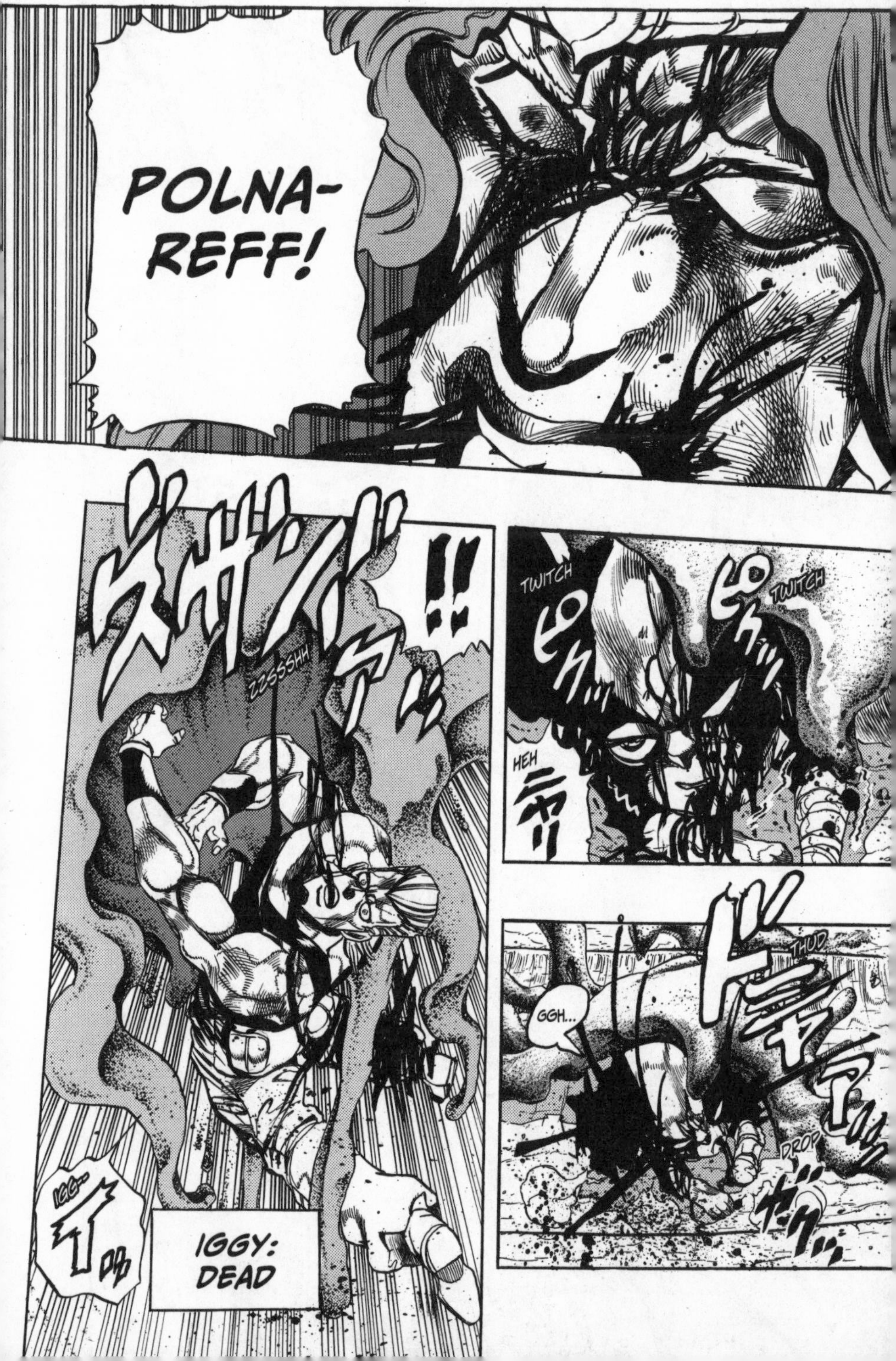
POLNA-
REFF!
TWITCH
TWITCH
HEH
THUD
GGH...
DROP
ZZSSSHH!
IGGY:
DEAD
IGG-

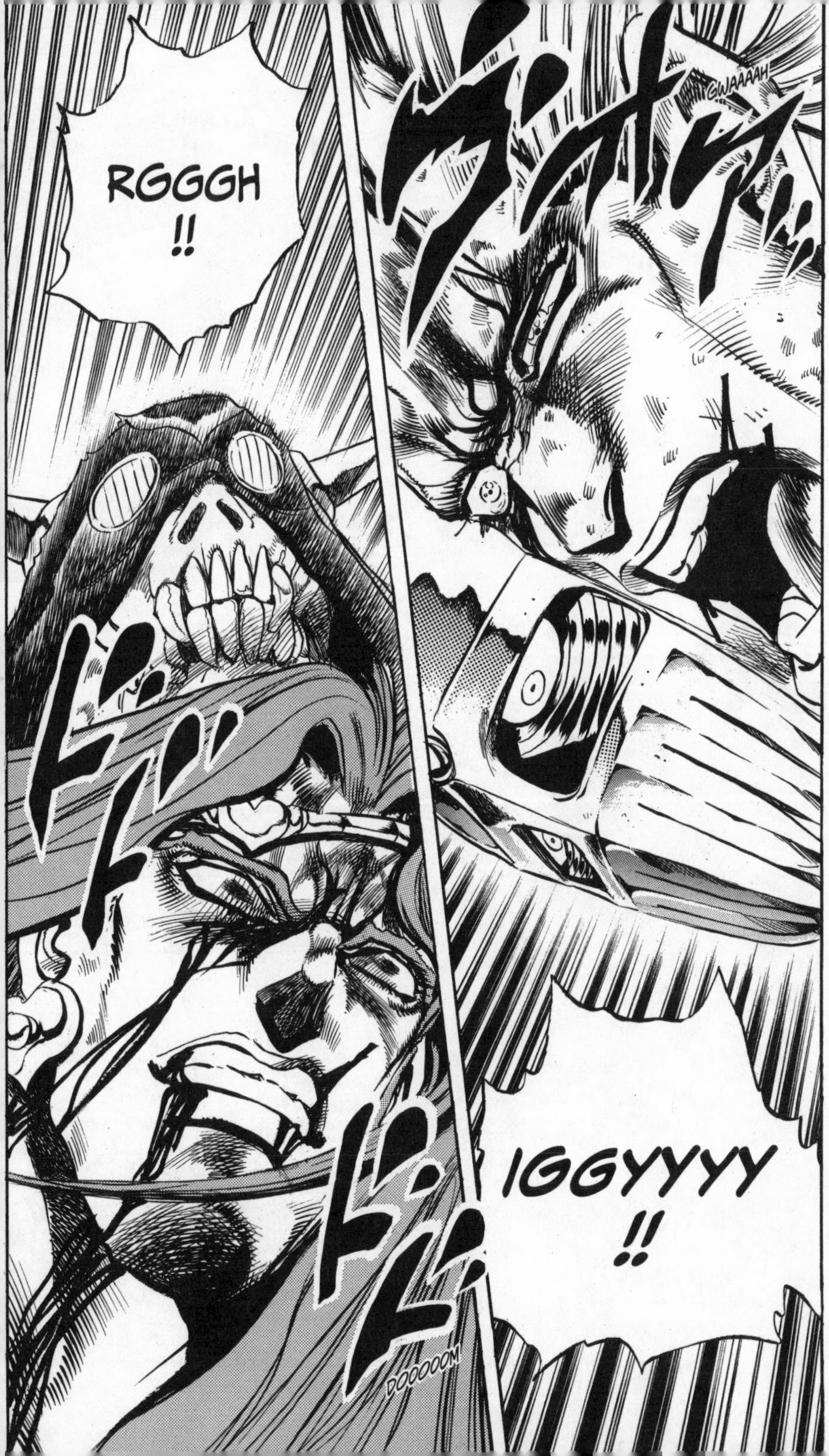
GWAAAAH
IGGYYYY!!
RGGGH!!
DOOOOOM

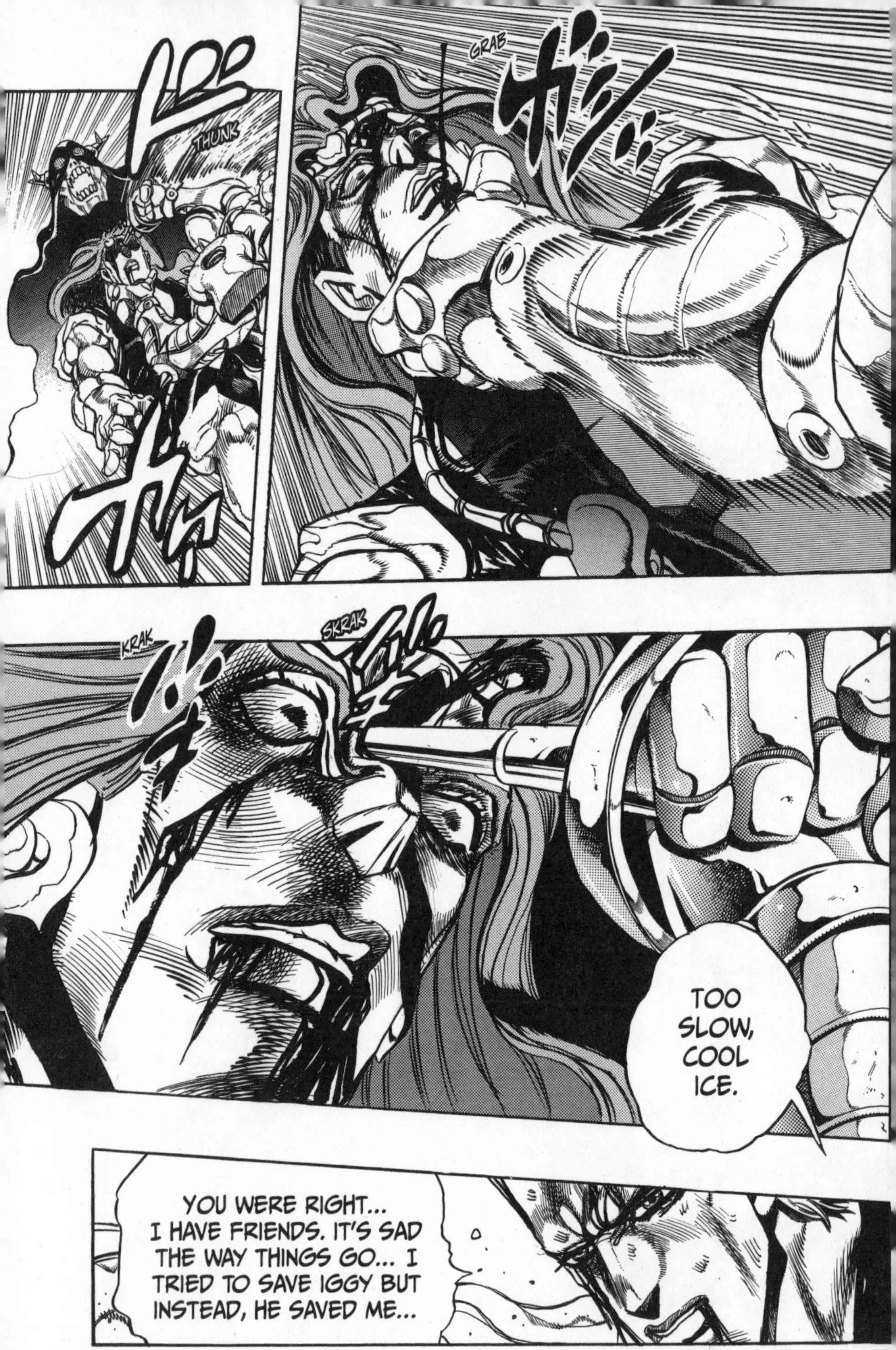
GRAB
THUNK
SKRAK
KRAK
TOO SLOW, COOL ICE.
YOU WERE RIGHT... I HAVE FRIENDS. IT'S SAD THE WAY THINGS GO... I TRIED TO SAVE IGGY BUT INSTEAD, HE SAVED ME...

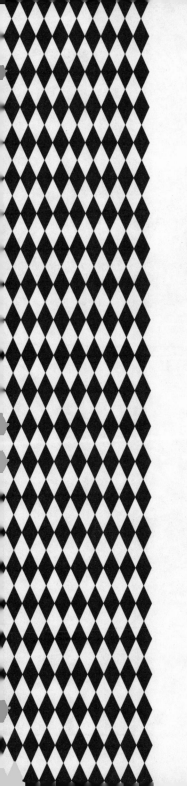

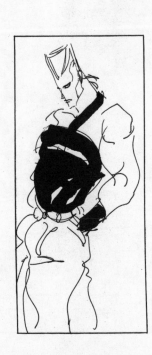

CHAPTER 132: The Dark Void of Cool Ice PART 8

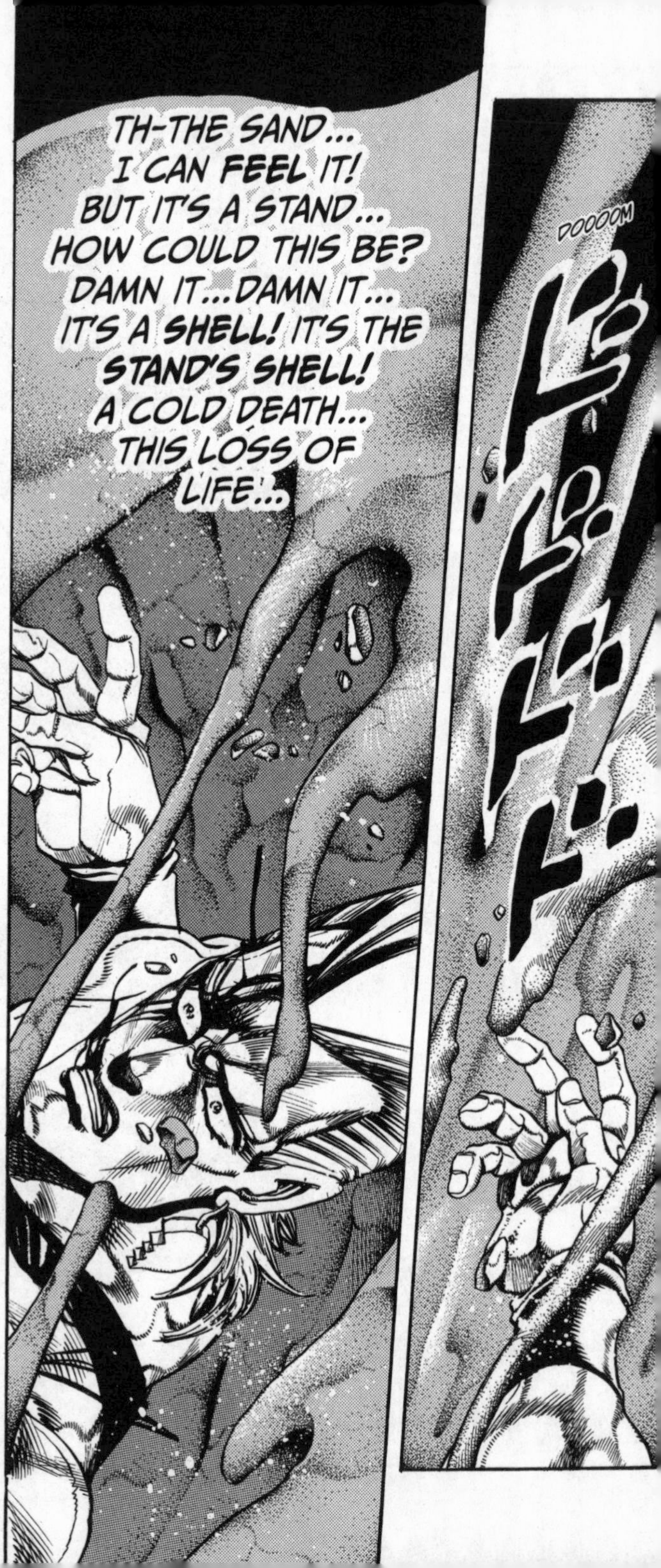
DOOOOM
TH-THE SAND... I CAN FEEL IT! BUT IT'S A STAND... HOW COULD THIS BE? DAMN IT...DAMN IT... IT'S A SHELL! IT'S THE STAND'S SHELL! A COLD DEATH... THIS LOSS OF LIFE...

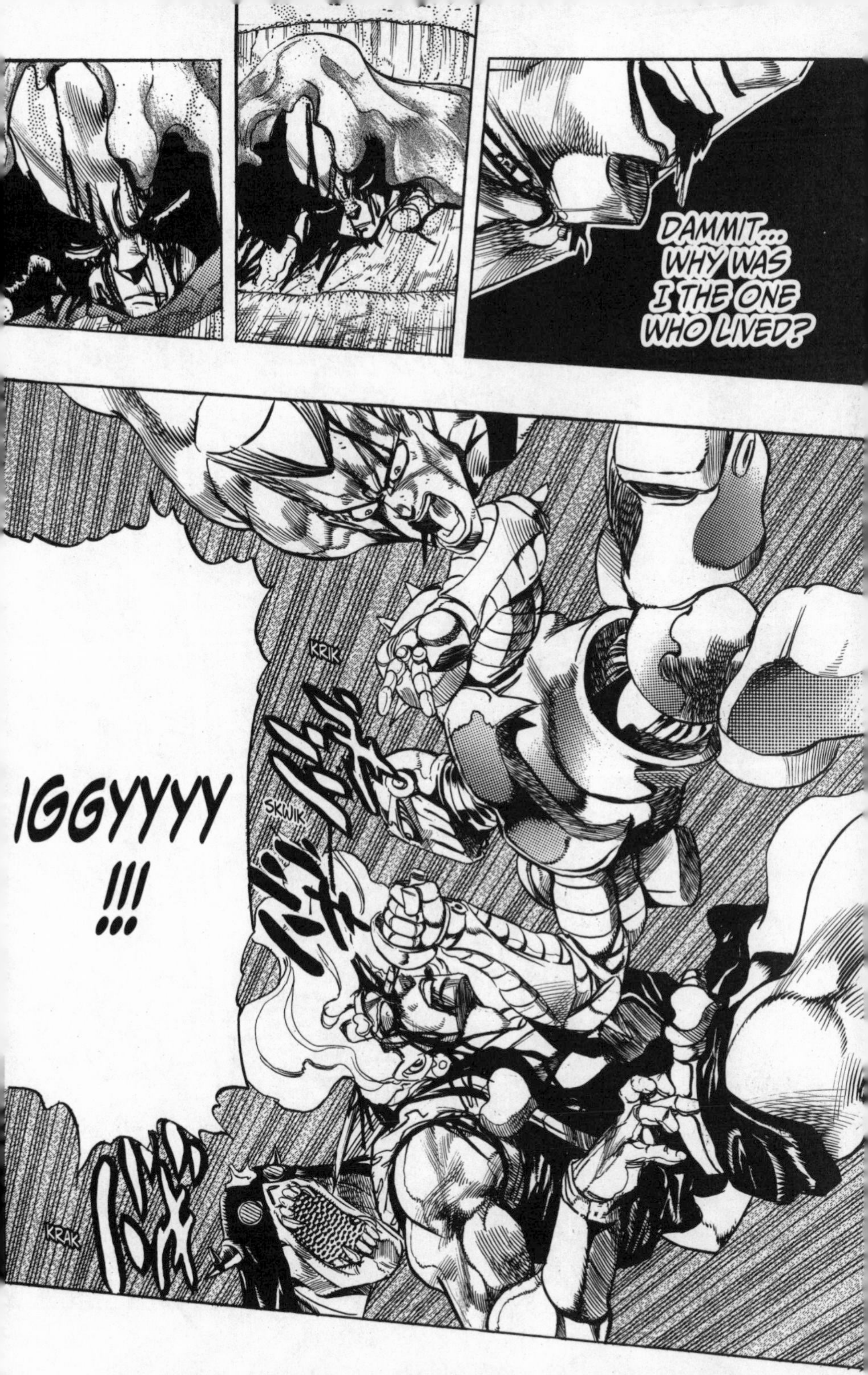
DAMMIT... WHY WAS I THE ONE WHO LIVED?
KRIK
IGGYYYY !!!
SKWIK
KRAK

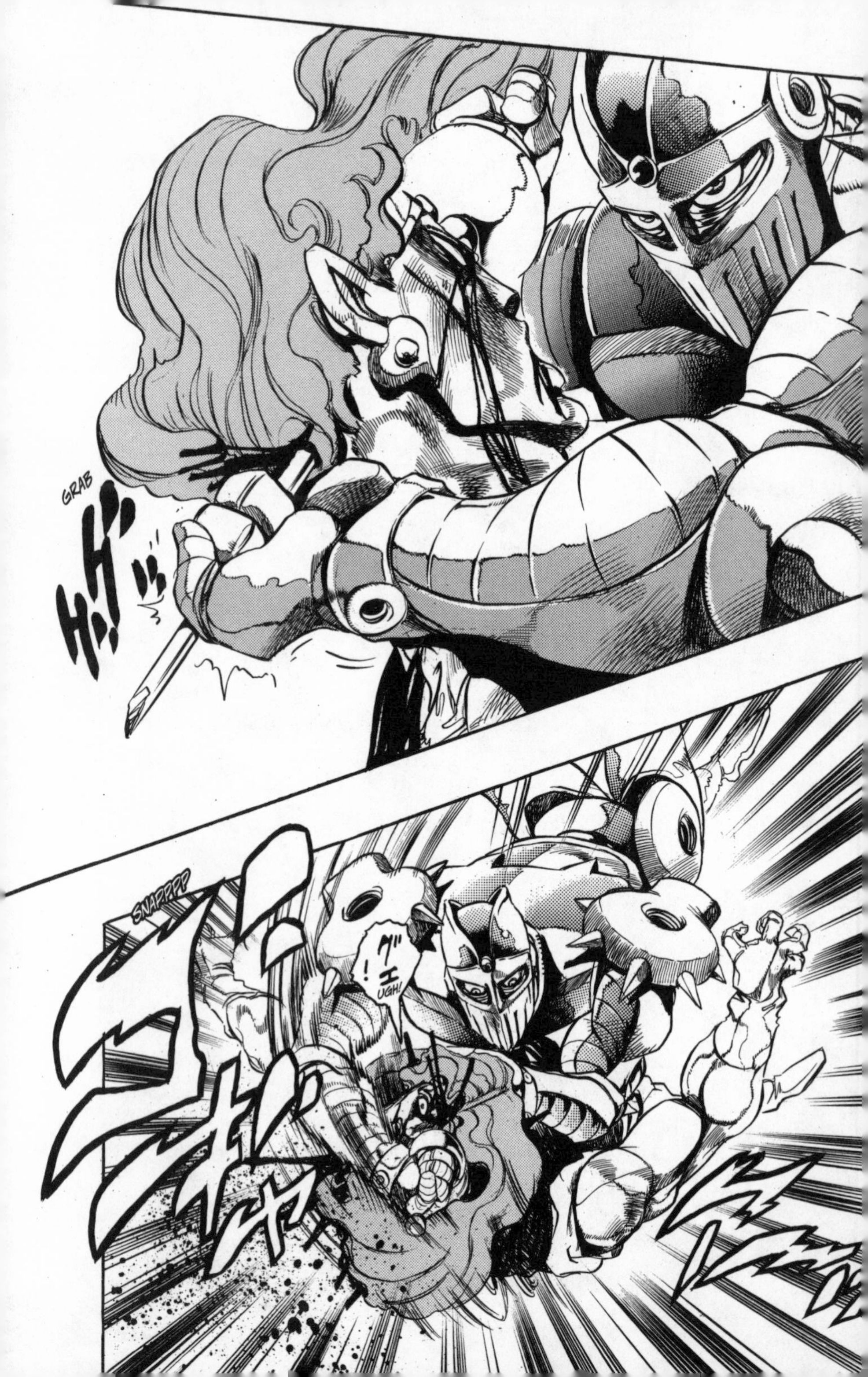
GRAB
SNAPPPP
グエ!
UGH!

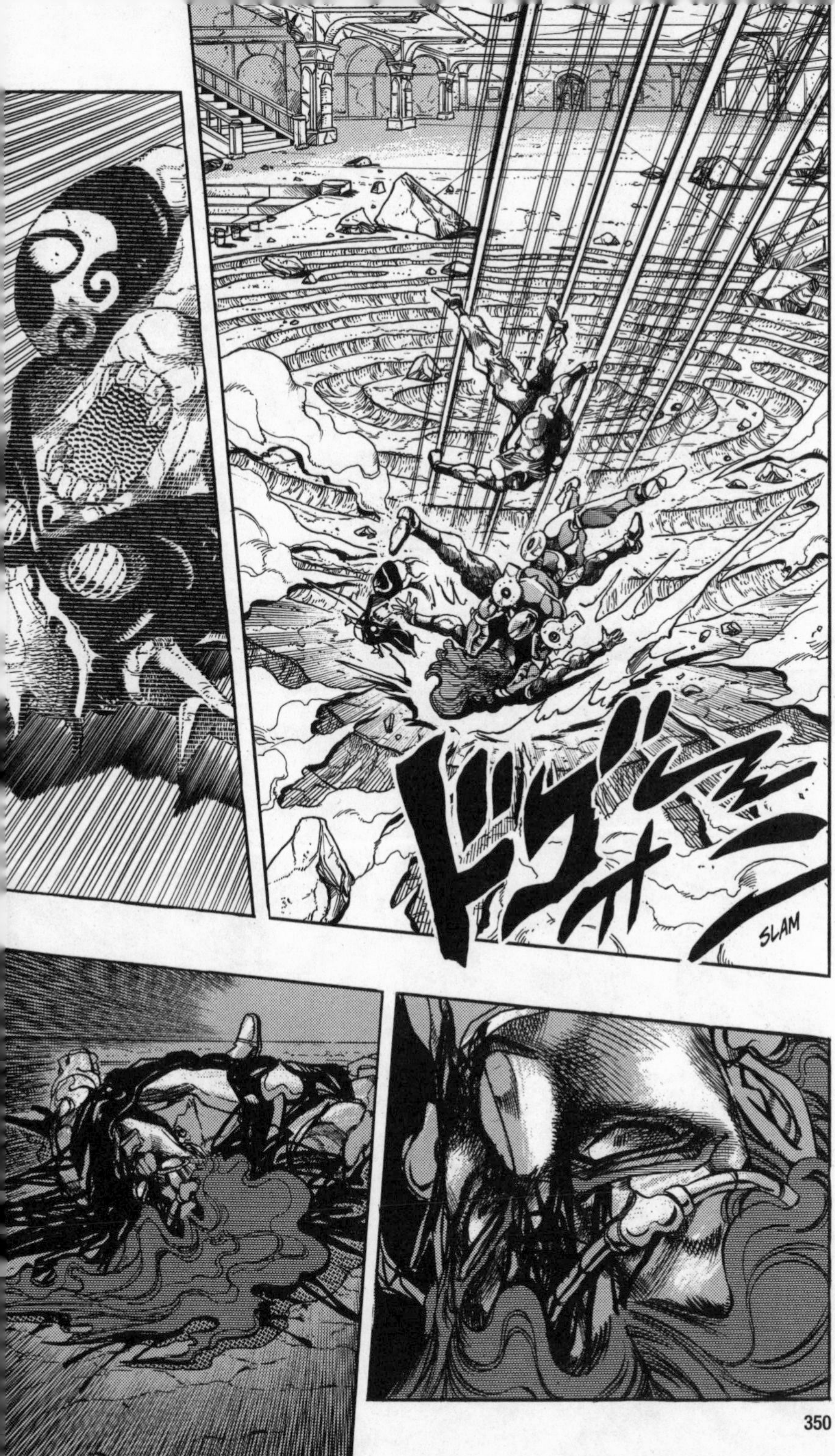
SLAM

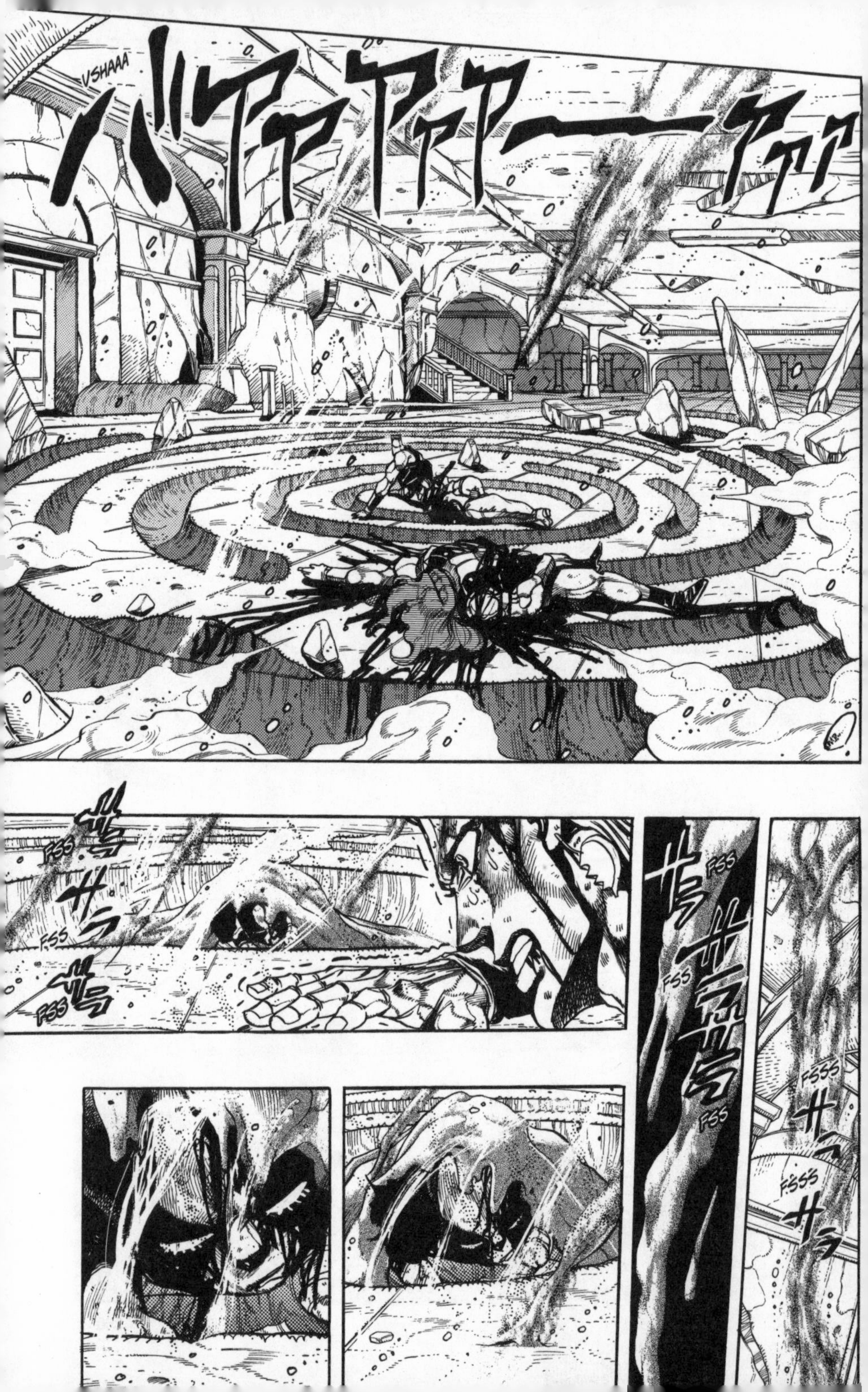
VSHAAA
バシャアァアァアーーアァア
FSSS
サラ
FSSS
サラ
サラ
FSS
サラサラ
FSS
サラ
FSS
サラ
FSS
サラ
FSS

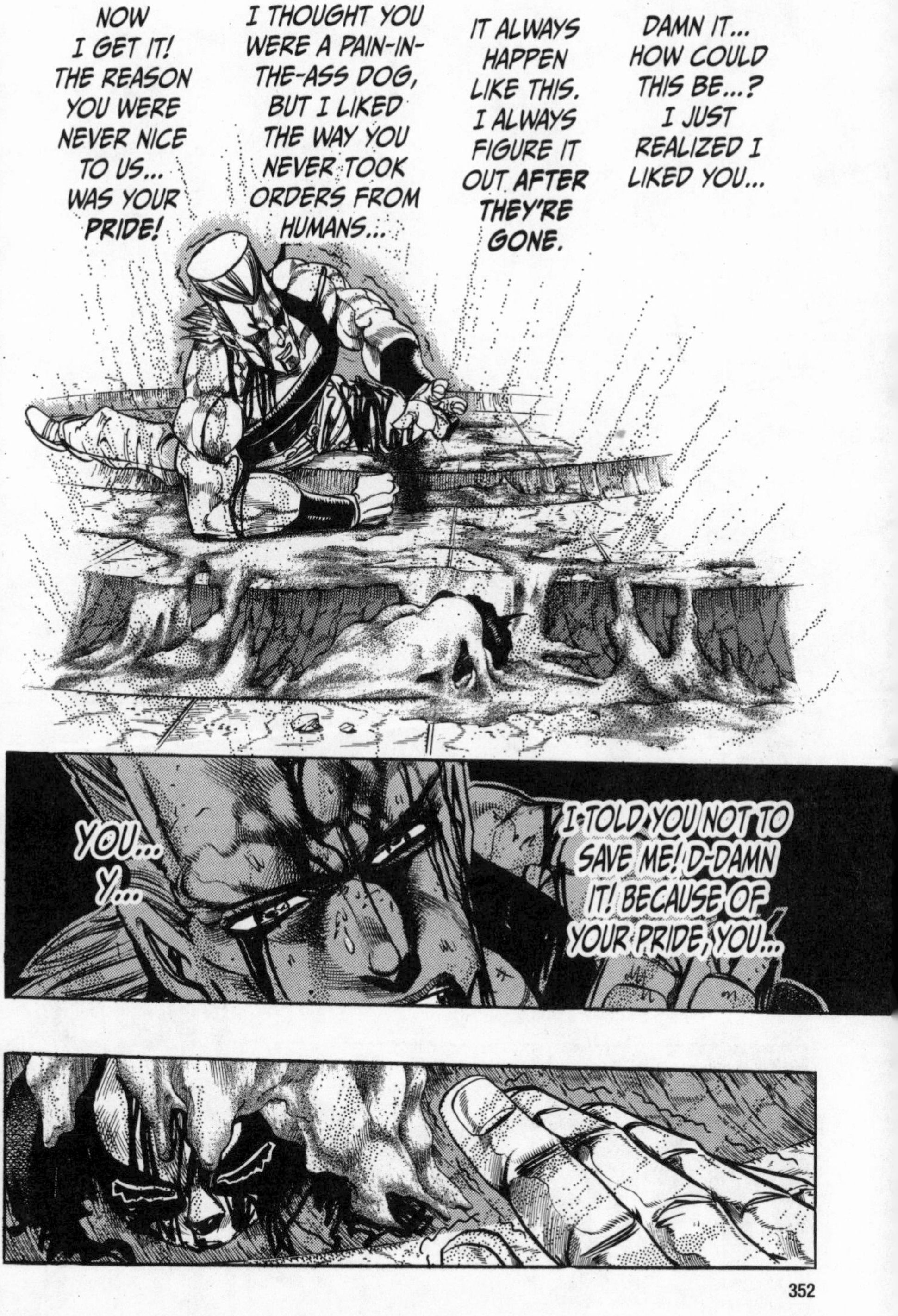
DAMN IT... HOW COULD THIS BE...? I JUST REALIZED I LIKED YOU...
IT ALWAYS HAPPEN LIKE THIS. I ALWAYS FIGURE IT OUT AFTER THEY'RE GONE.
I THOUGHT YOU WERE A PAIN-IN-THE-ASS DOG, BUT I LIKED THE WAY YOU NEVER TOOK ORDERS FROM HUMANS...
NOW I GET IT! THE REASON YOU WERE NEVER NICE TO US... WAS YOUR PRIDE!
I TOLD YOU NOT TO SAVE ME! D-DAMN IT! BECAUSE OF YOUR PRIDE, YOU...
YOU... Y...

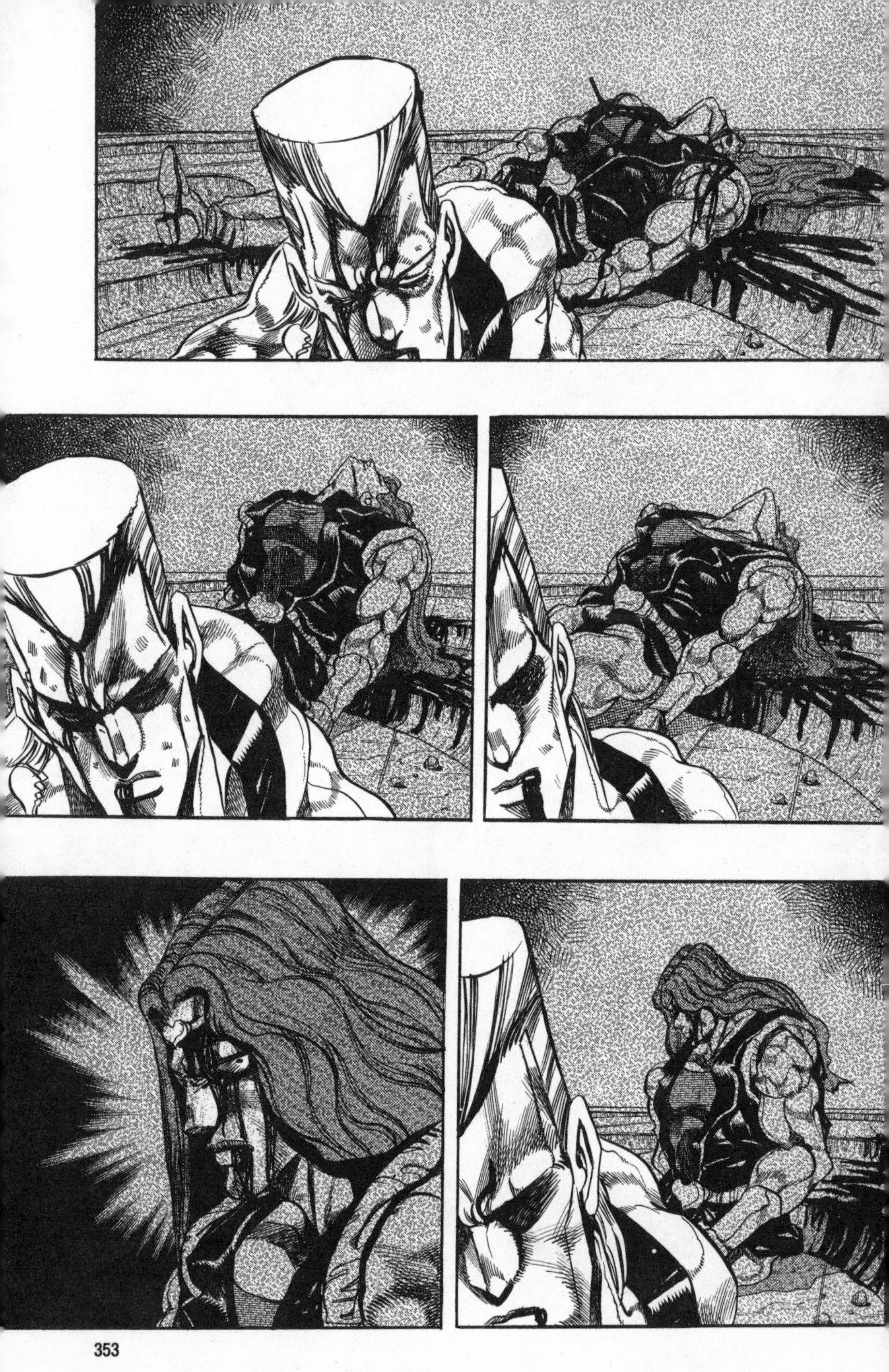

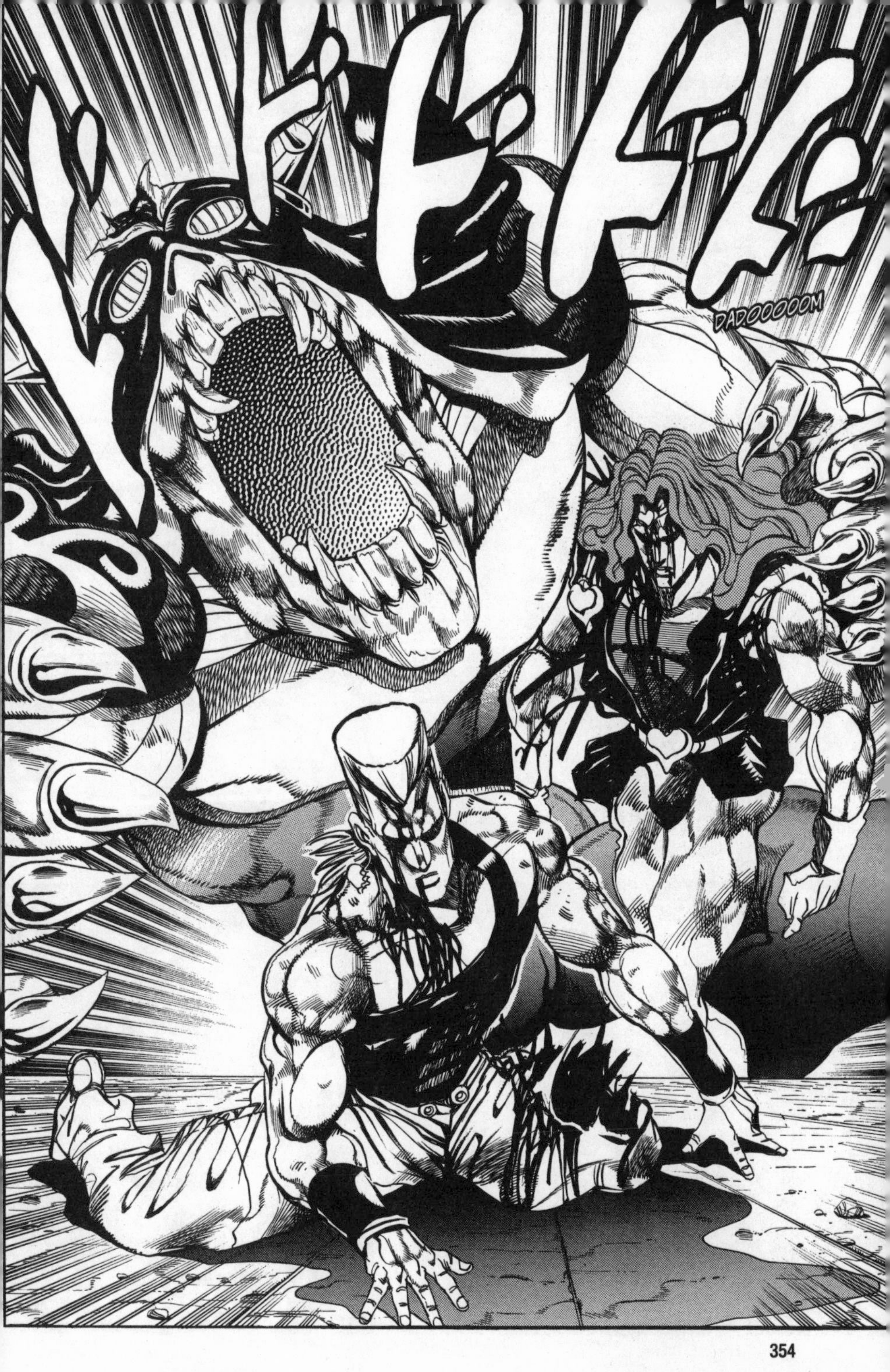
DADOOOOOOM

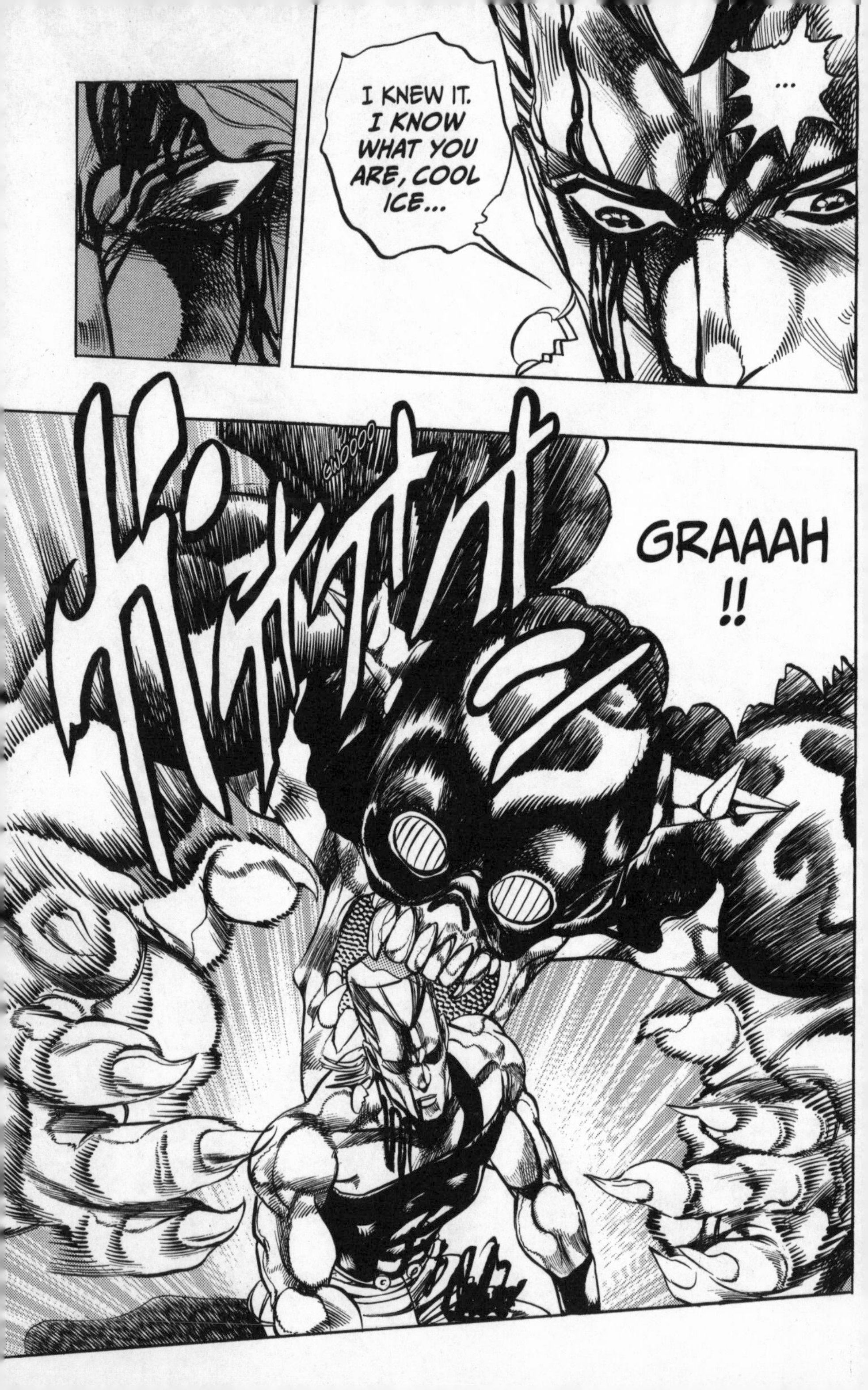
...
I KNEW IT. I KNOW WHAT YOU ARE, COOL ICE...
GRAAAH !!
GWOOOO

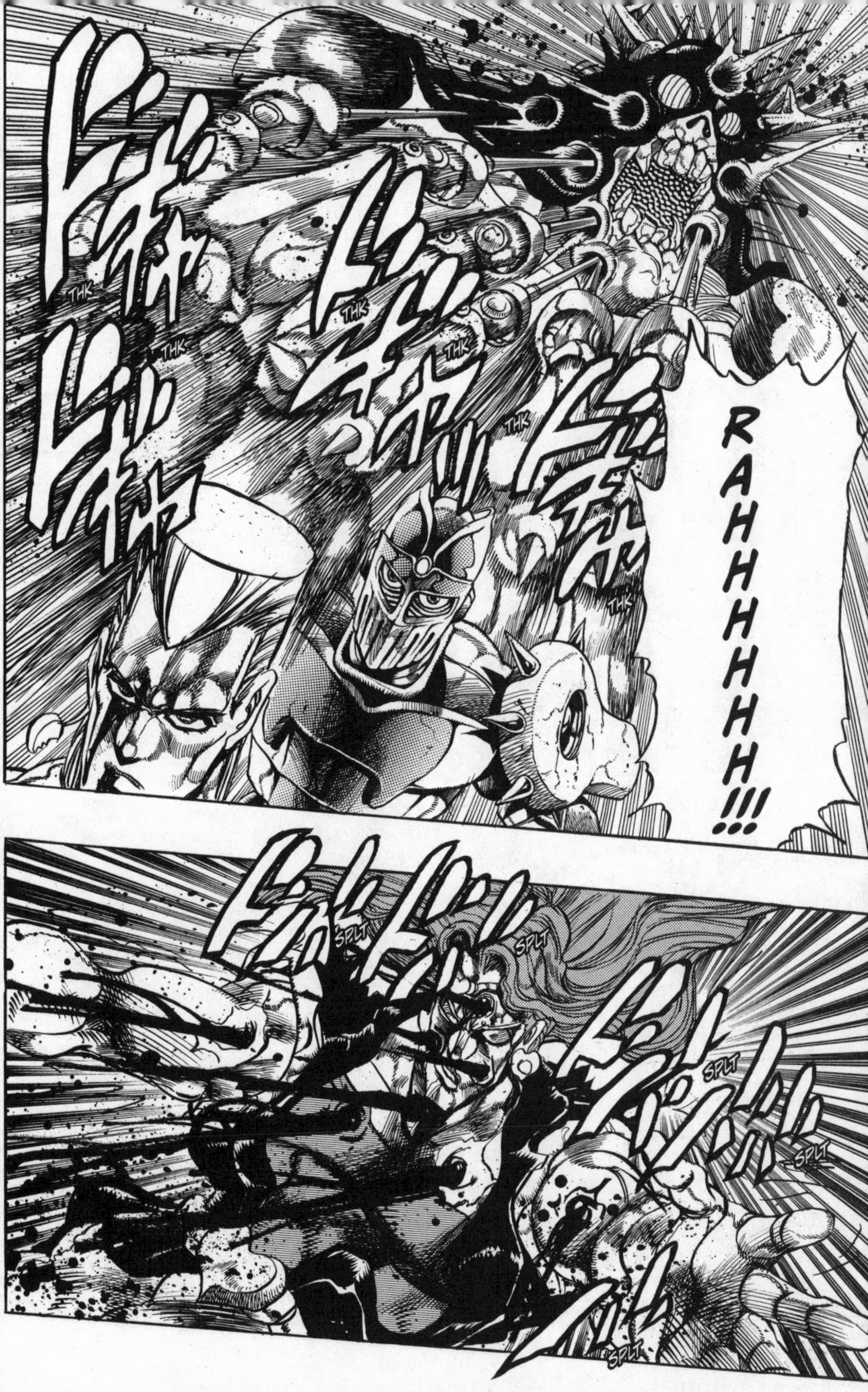
THK
THK
THK
THK
THK
THK
RAHHHHHH!!!
SPLT
SPLT
SPLT
SPLT
SPLT

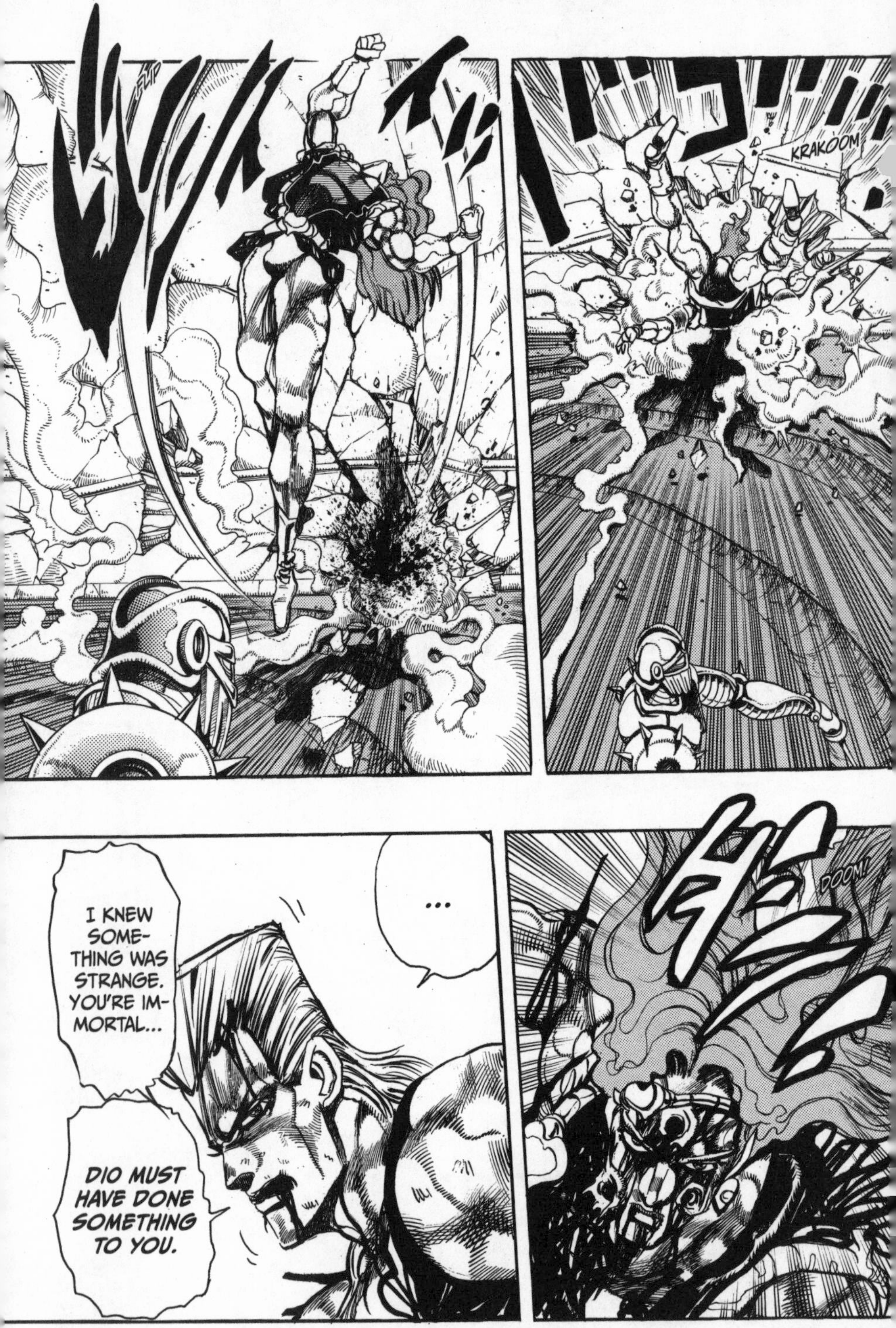
KRAKOOM
FLIP
DOOM!
...
I KNEW SOMETHING WAS STRANGE. YOU'RE IMMORTAL...
DIO MUST HAVE DONE SOMETHING TO YOU.

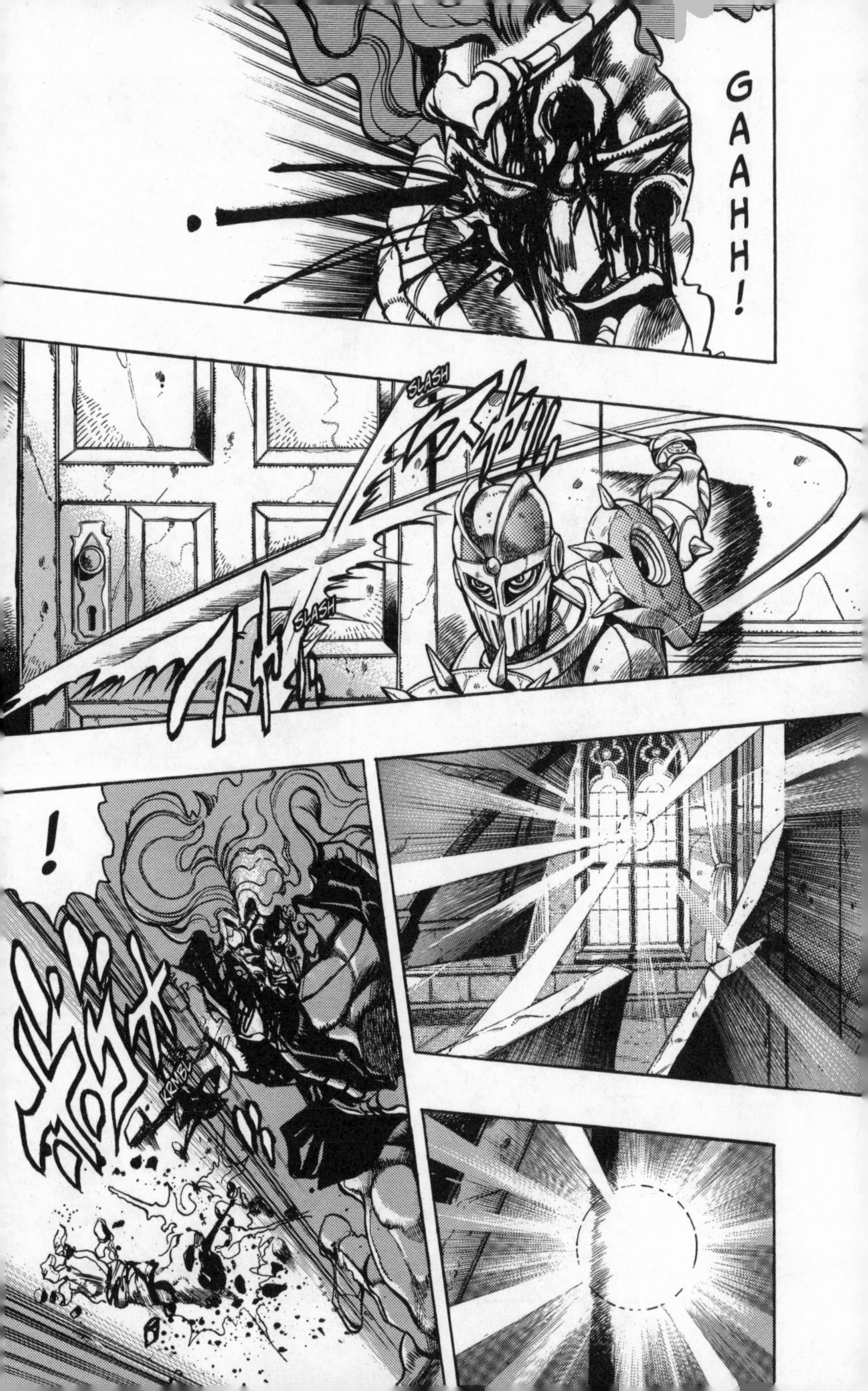
GAAHH!
SLASH
SLASH
!
KRMBL

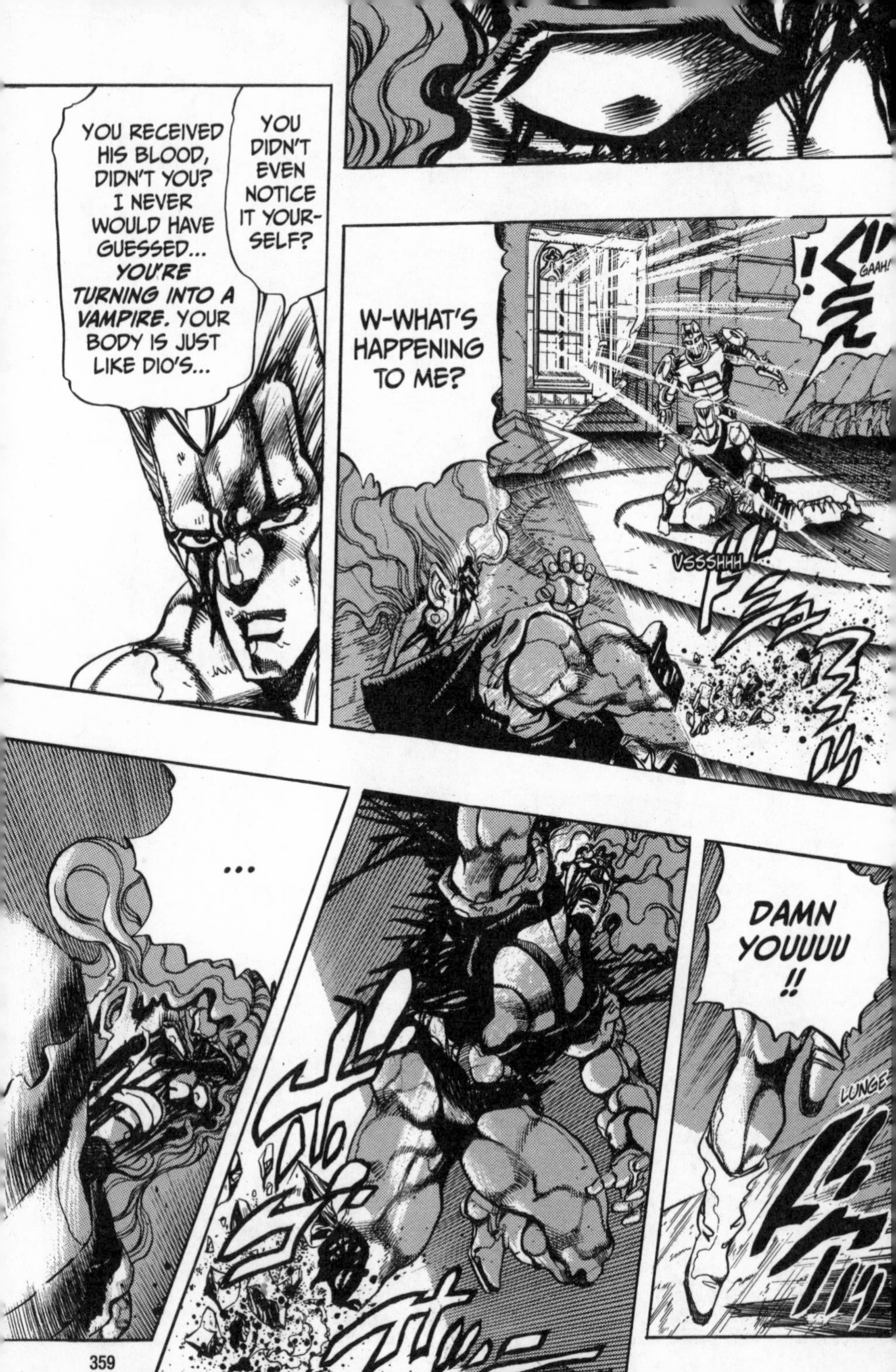
W-WHAT'S HAPPENING TO ME?
GAAH!
VSSSHHH
YOU DIDN'T EVEN NOTICE IT YOURSELF?
YOU RECEIVED HIS BLOOD, DIDN'T YOU? I NEVER WOULD HAVE GUESSED... YOU'RE TURNING INTO A VAMPIRE. YOUR BODY IS JUST LIKE DIO'S...
DAMN YOUUUU!!
LUNGE
SKRSSSSH
...

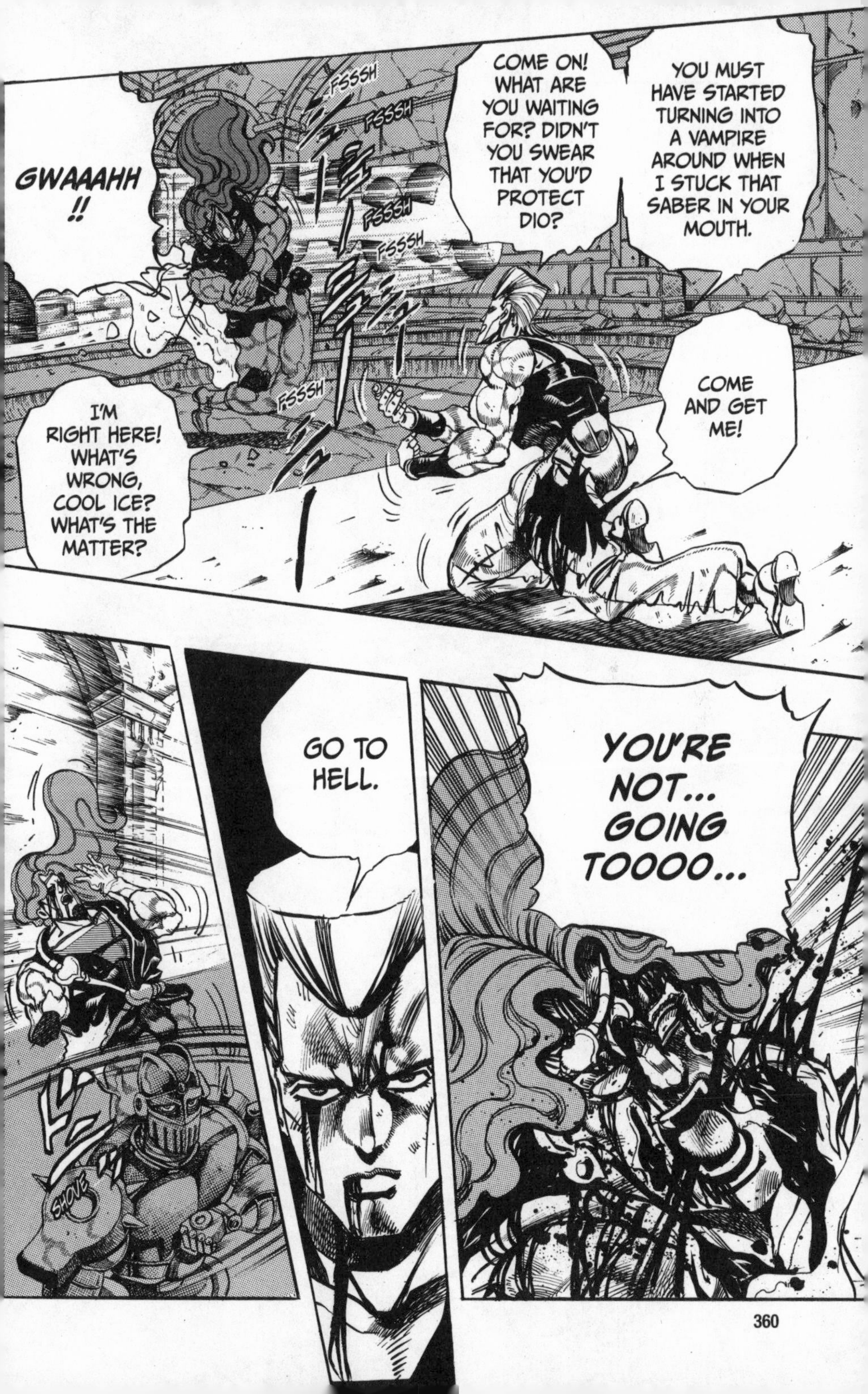
YOU MUST HAVE STARTED TURNING INTO A VAMPIRE AROUND WHEN I STUCK THAT SABER IN YOUR MOUTH.
COME ON! WHAT ARE YOU WAITING FOR? DIDN'T YOU SWEAR THAT YOU'D PROTECT DIO?
FSSSH
FSSSH
FSSSH
FSSSH
GWAAAHH!!
COME AND GET ME!
FSSSH
I'M RIGHT HERE! WHAT'S WRONG, COOL ICE? WHAT'S THE MATTER?
YOU'RE NOT... GOING TOOOO...
GO TO HELL.
SHOVE

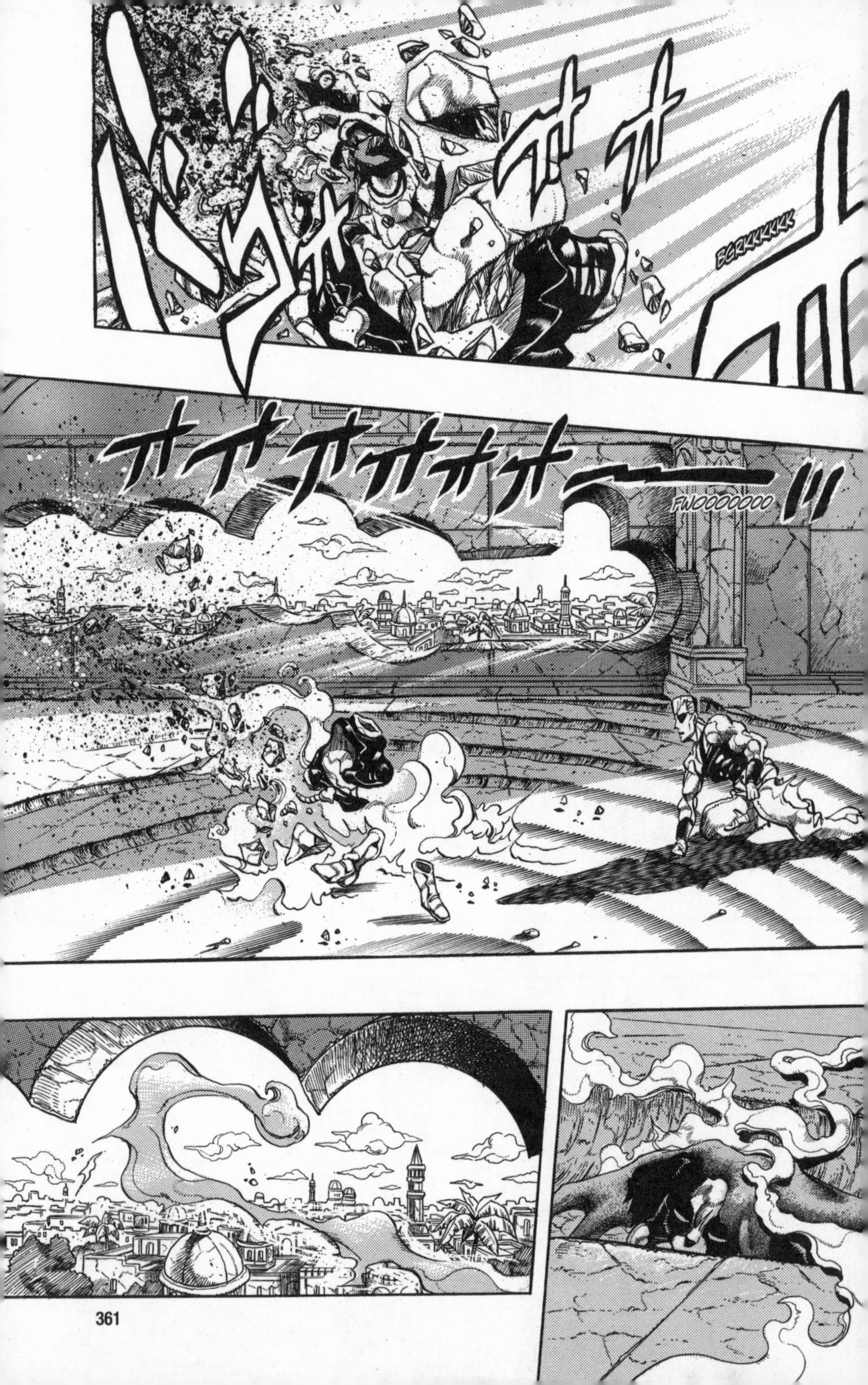
BCRKKKKKK
FWOOOOOOOO

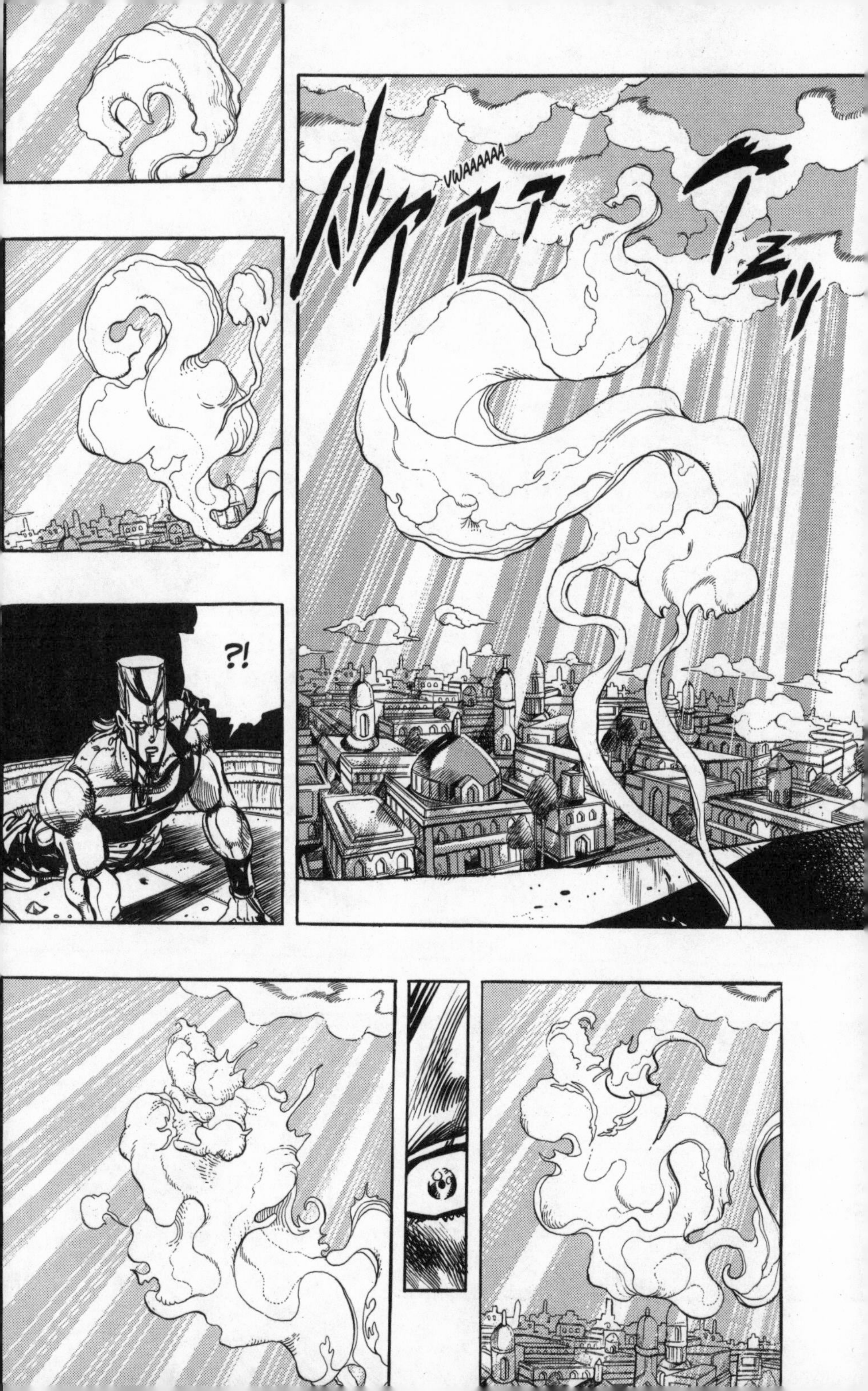
VWAAAAAA
?!

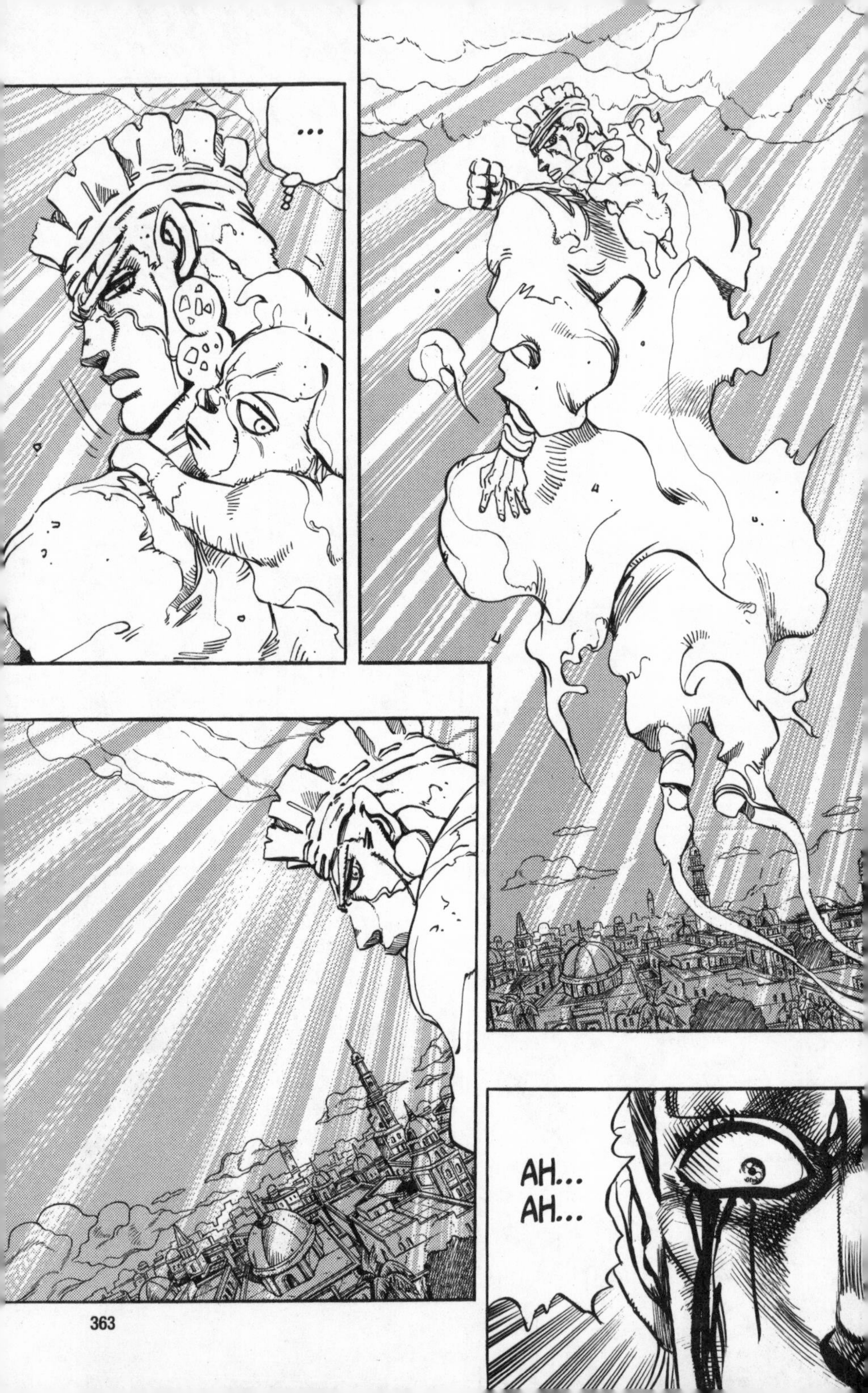
...
AH... AH...

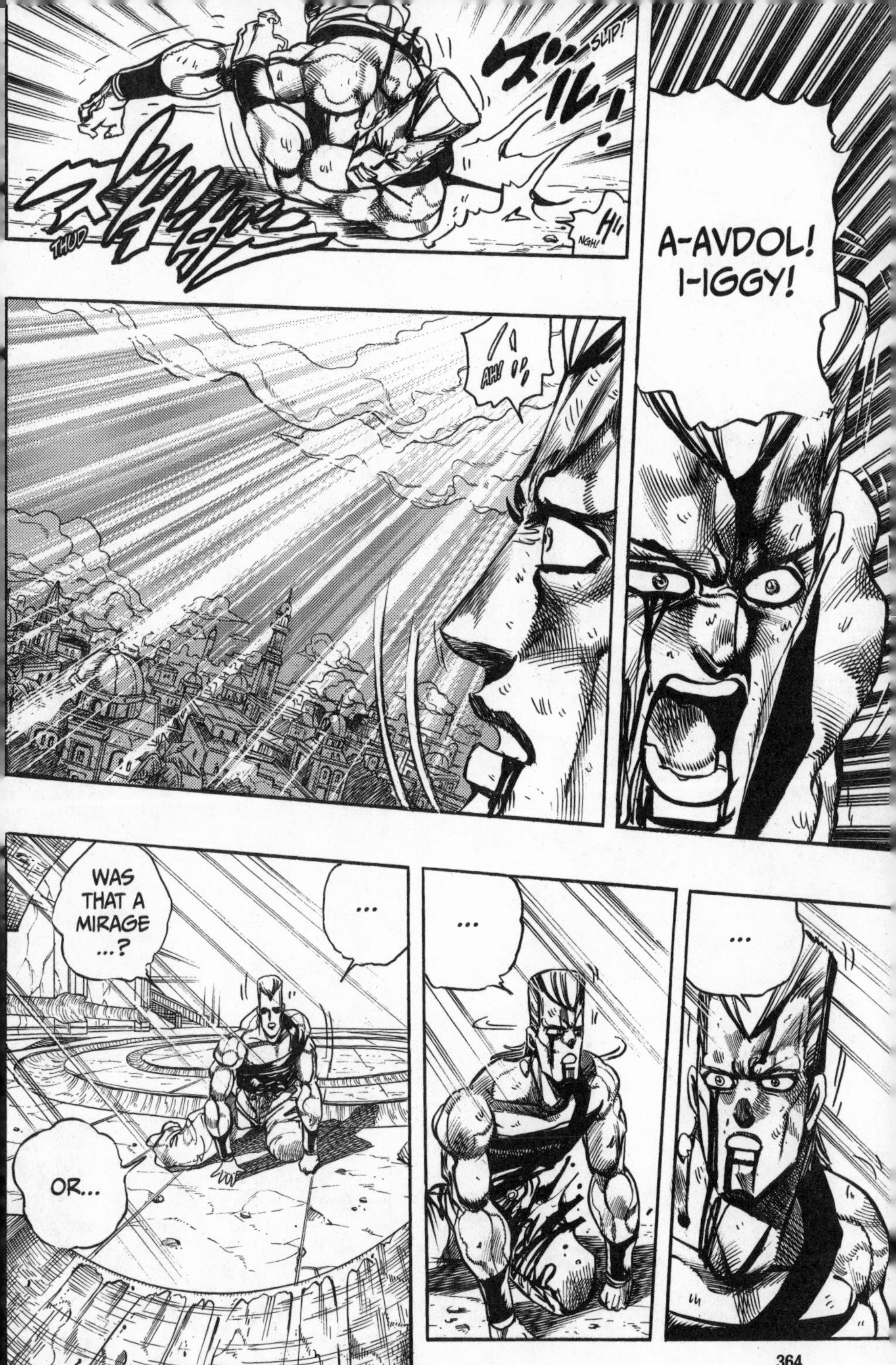
A-AVDOL!
I-IGGY!
SLIP!
NGH!
THUD
AH!
...
...
...
WAS THAT A MIRAGE ...?
OR...

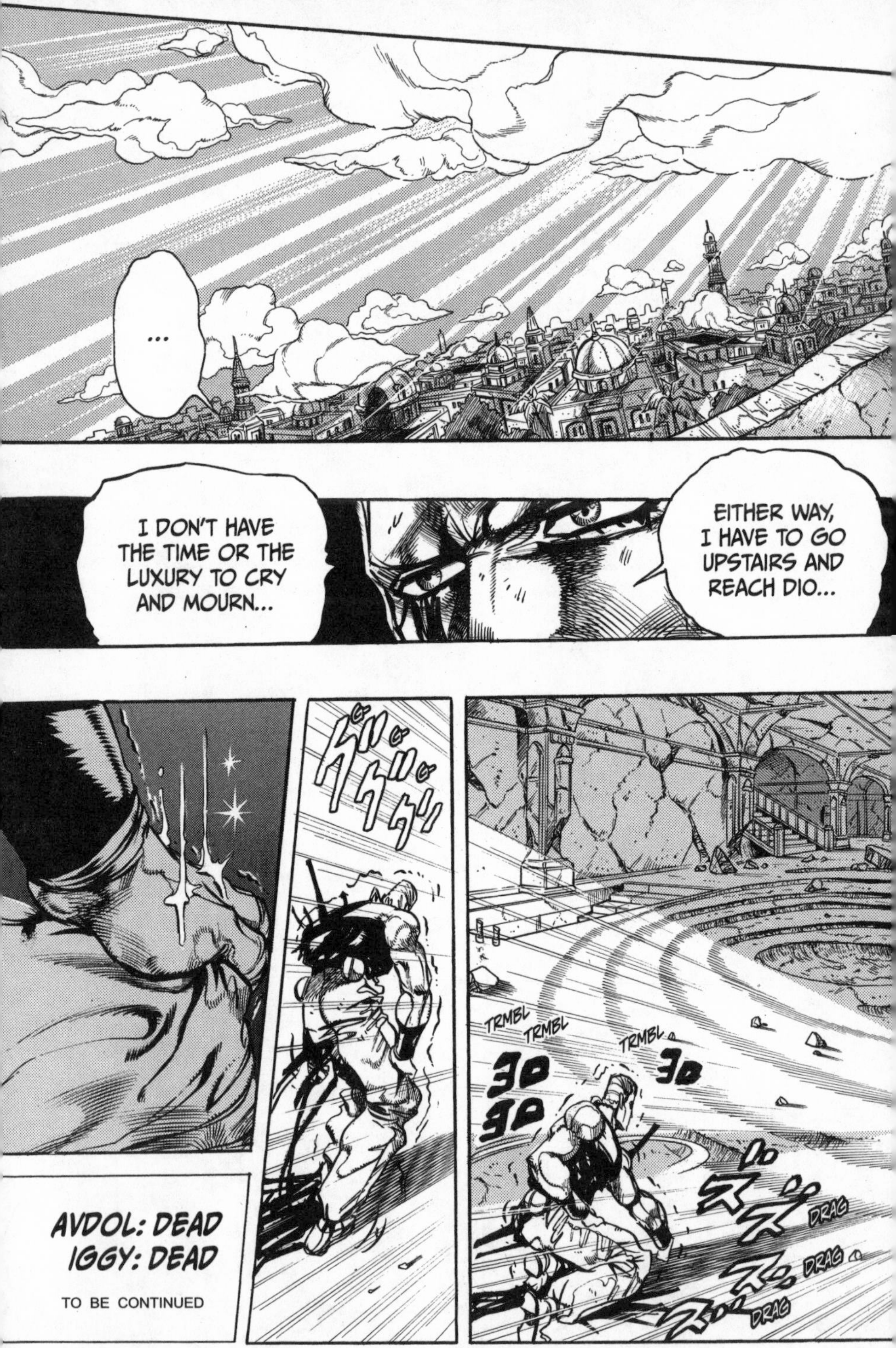
...
EITHER WAY, I HAVE TO GO UPSTAIRS AND REACH DIO...
I DON'T HAVE THE TIME OR THE LUXURY TO CRY AND MOURN...
TRMBL
TRMBL
TRMBL
DRAG
DRAG
DRAG
AVDOL: DEAD
IGGY: DEAD
TO BE CONTINUED

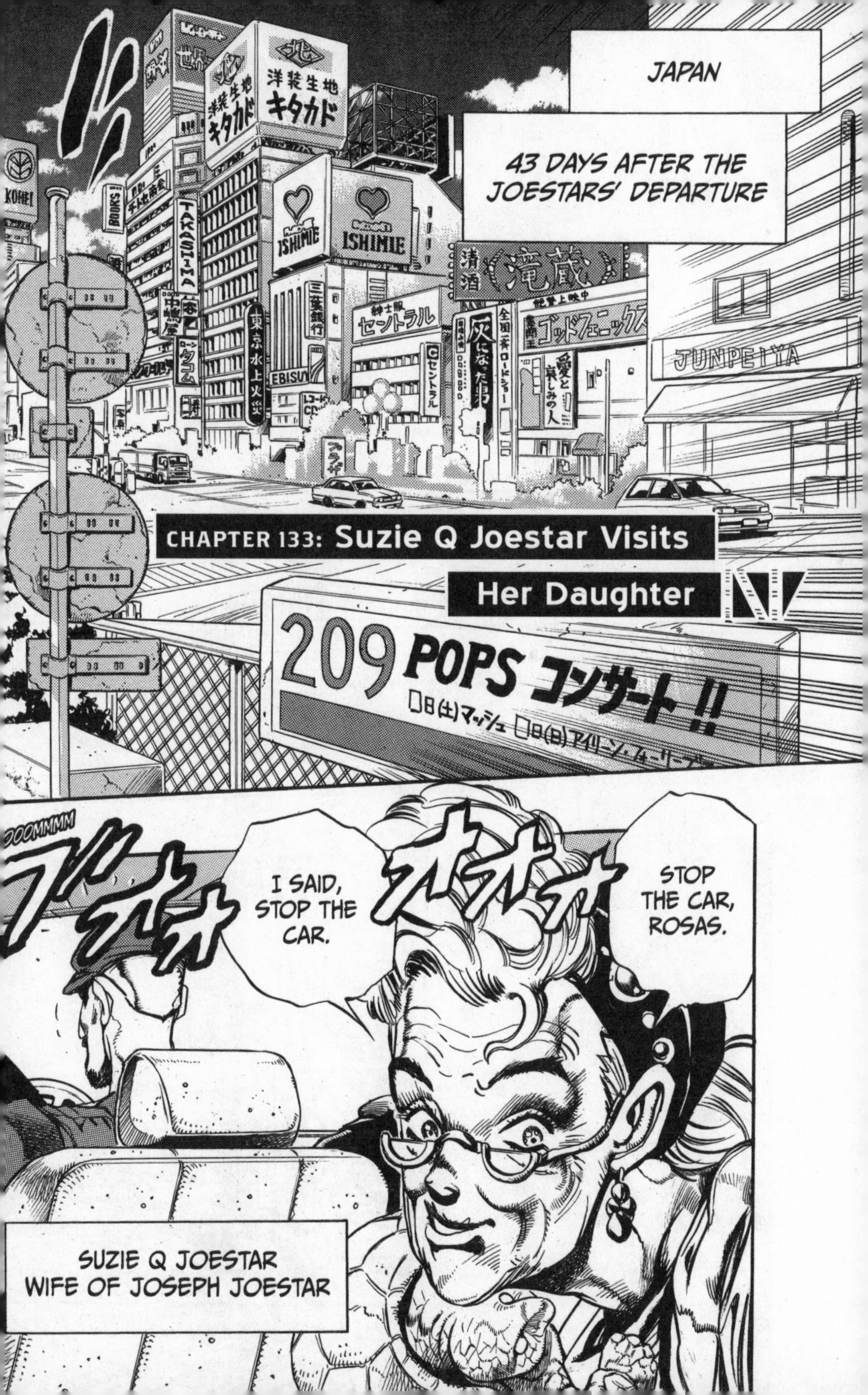
JAPAN
43 DAYS AFTER THE JOESTARS' DEPARTURE
CHAPTER 133: Suzie Q Joestar Visits Her Daughter
209 POPS コンサート!!
STOP THE CAR, ROSAS.
I SAID, STOP THE CAR.
DOOMMMM
SUZIE Q JOESTAR
WIFE OF JOSEPH JOESTAR

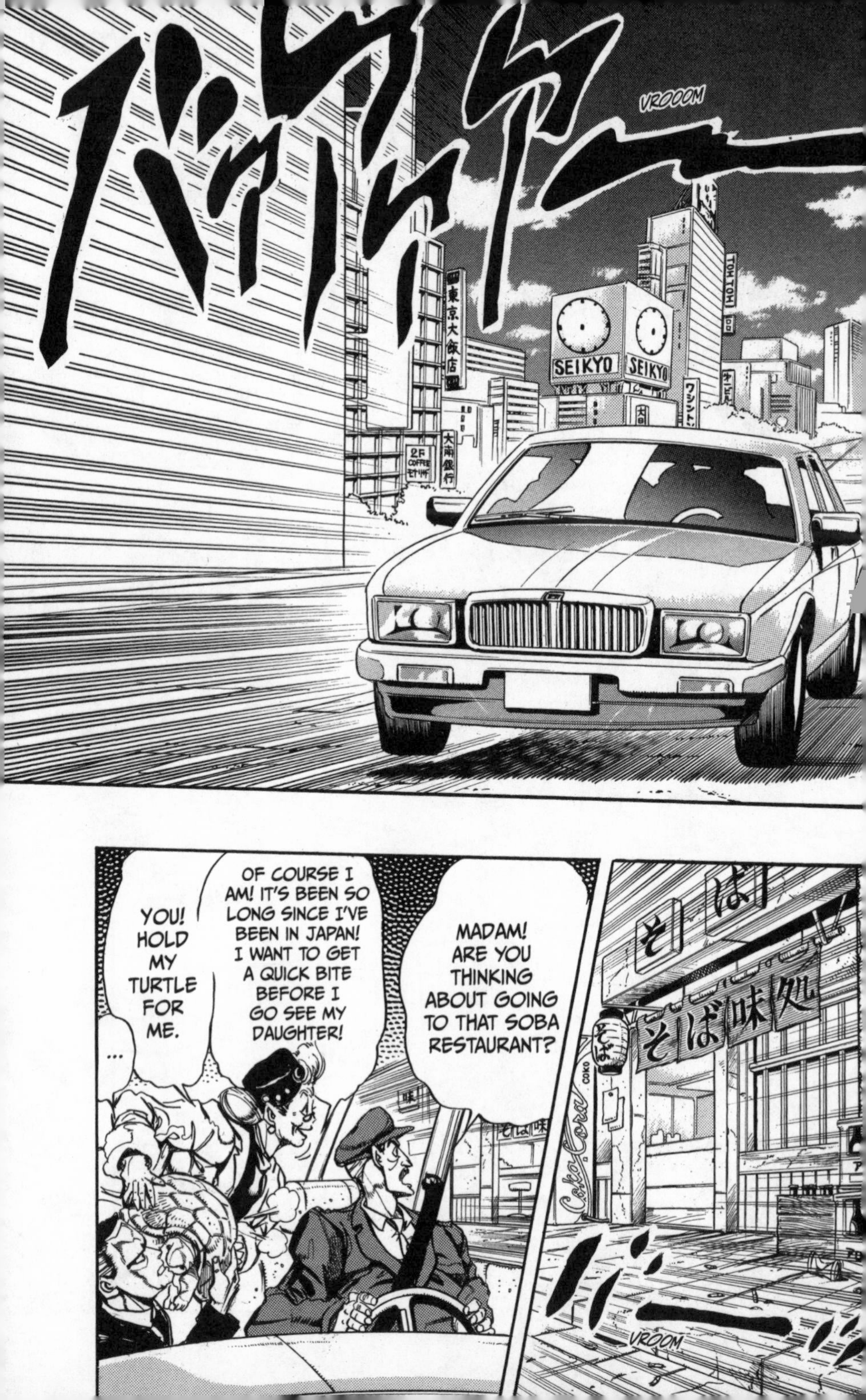
VROOOM
東京大飯店
SEIKYO
SEIKYO
TOM TOM
2F COFFEE
大南銀行
そば
そば味処
VROOM
MADAM! ARE YOU THINKING ABOUT GOING TO THAT SOBA RESTAURANT?
OF COURSE I AM! IT'S BEEN SO LONG SINCE I'VE BEEN IN JAPAN! I WANT TO GET A QUICK BITE BEFORE I GO SEE MY DAUGHTER!
YOU! HOLD MY TURTLE FOR ME.
...

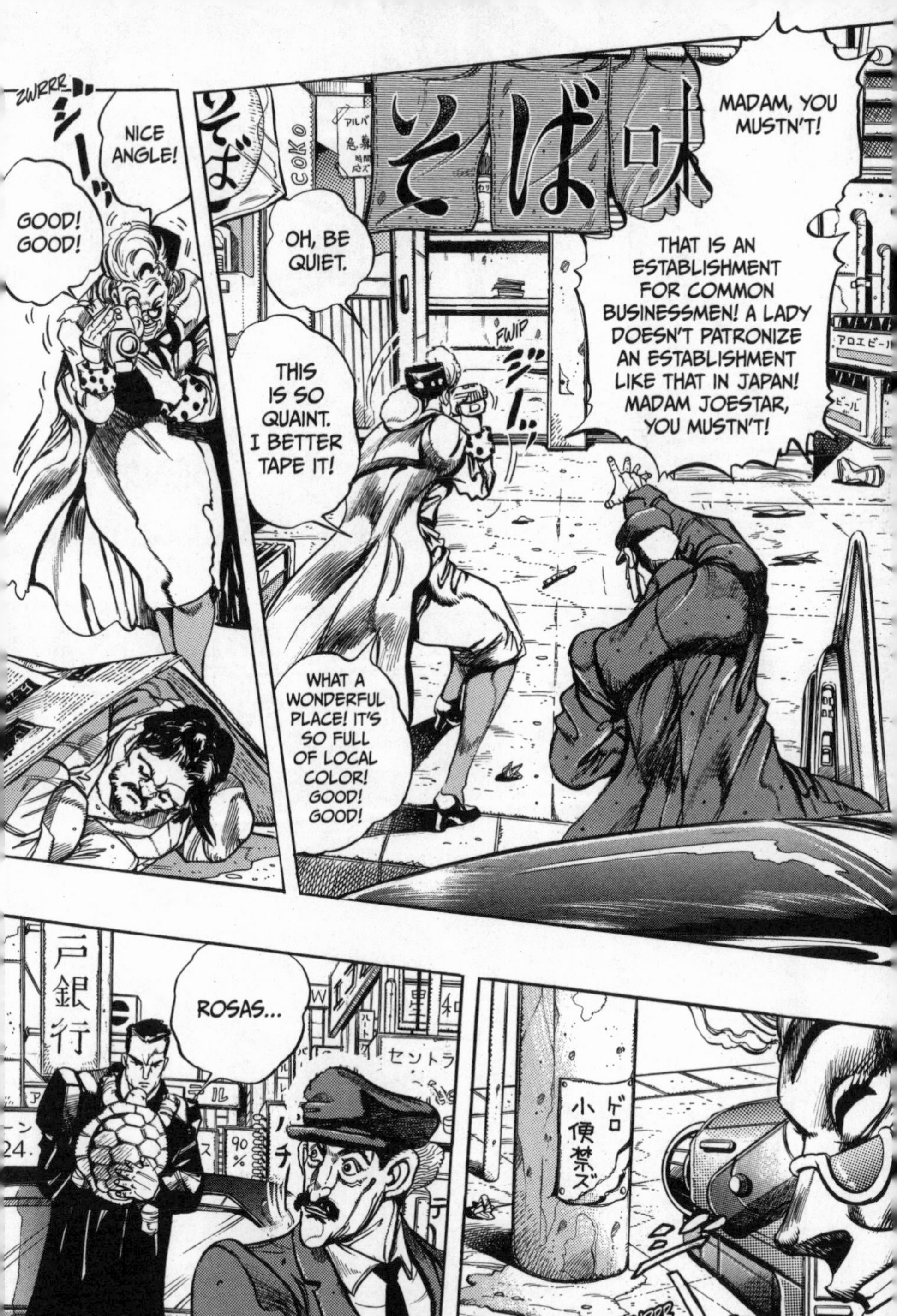
MADAM, YOU MUSTN'T!
THAT IS AN ESTABLISHMENT FOR COMMON BUSINESSMEN! A LADY DOESN'T PATRONIZE AN ESTABLISHMENT LIKE THAT IN JAPAN! MADAM JOESTAR, YOU MUSTN'T!
FWIP
OH, BE QUIET.
THIS IS SO QUAINT. I BETTER TAPE IT!
WHAT A WONDERFUL PLACE! IT'S SO FULL OF LOCAL COLOR! GOOD! GOOD!
ZWRRR
NICE ANGLE!
GOOD! GOOD!
ZWRRR
ROSAS...

*SIGN: NO BARFING OR PEEING

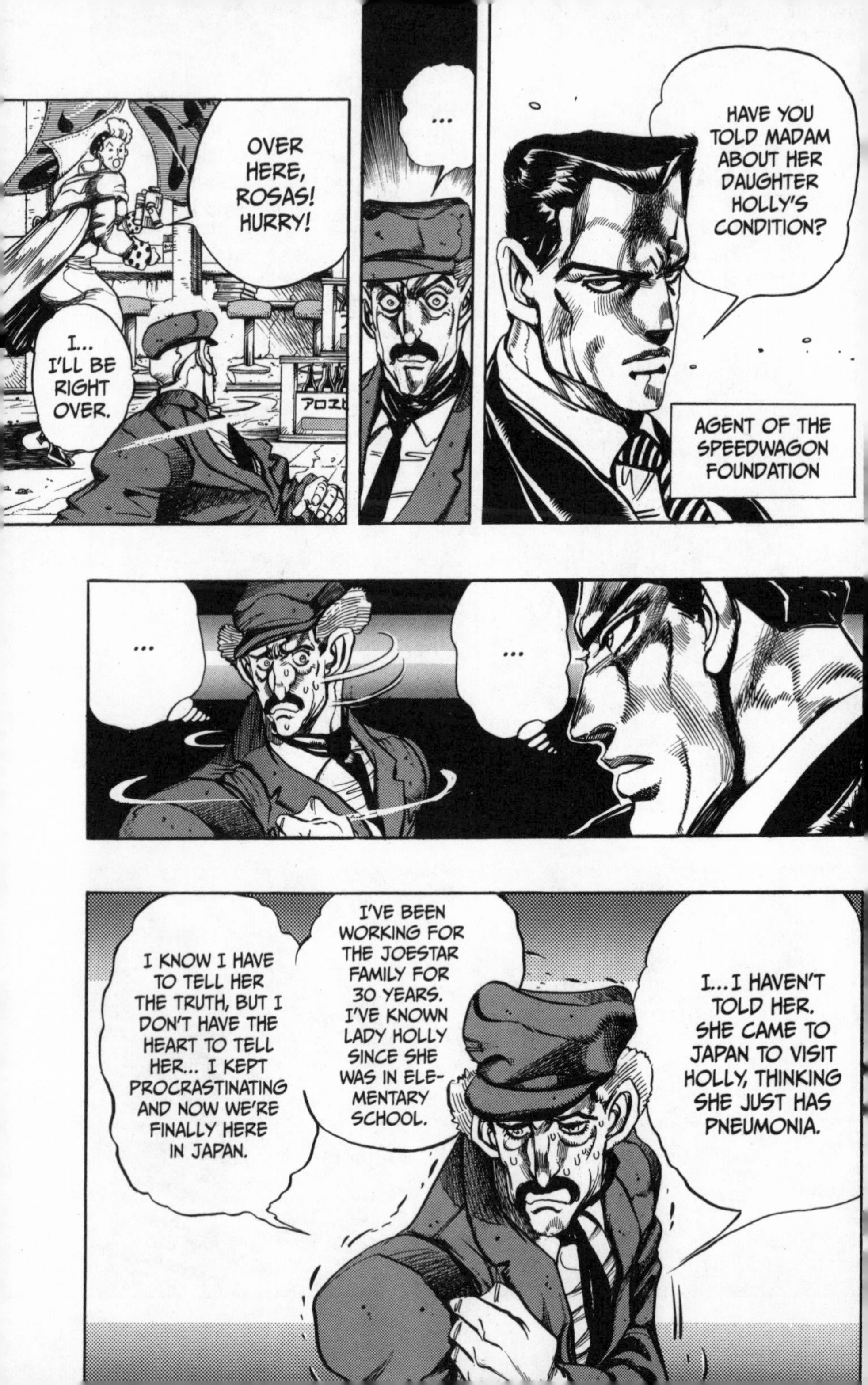
HAVE YOU TOLD MADAM ABOUT HER DAUGHTER HOLLY'S CONDITION?
AGENT OF THE SPEEDWAGON FOUNDATION
...
OVER HERE, ROSAS! HURRY!
I... I'LL BE RIGHT OVER.
...
...
I...I HAVEN'T TOLD HER. SHE CAME TO JAPAN TO VISIT HOLLY, THINKING SHE JUST HAS PNEUMONIA.
I'VE BEEN WORKING FOR THE JOESTAR FAMILY FOR 30 YEARS. I'VE KNOWN LADY HOLLY SINCE SHE WAS IN ELE-MENTARY SCHOOL.
I KNOW I HAVE TO TELL HER THE TRUTH, BUT I DON'T HAVE THE HEART TO TELL HER... I KEPT PROCRASTINATING AND NOW WE'RE FINALLY HERE IN JAPAN.

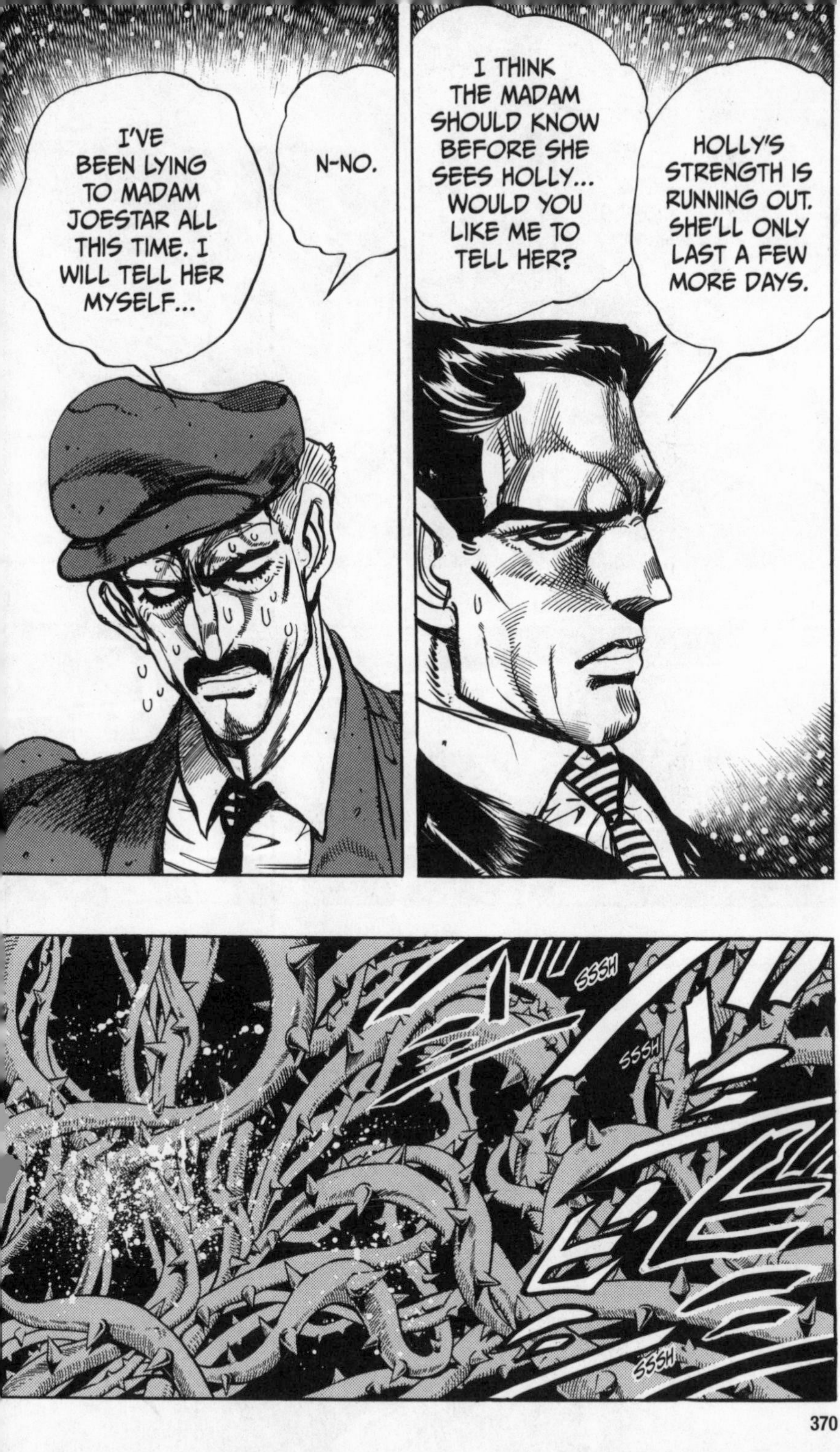
HOLLY'S STRENGTH IS RUNNING OUT. SHE'LL ONLY LAST A FEW MORE DAYS.
I THINK THE MADAM SHOULD KNOW BEFORE SHE SEES HOLLY... WOULD YOU LIKE ME TO TELL HER?
N-NO.
I'VE BEEN LYING TO MADAM JOESTAR ALL THIS TIME. I WILL TELL HER MYSELF...
SSSH
SSSH
SSSH

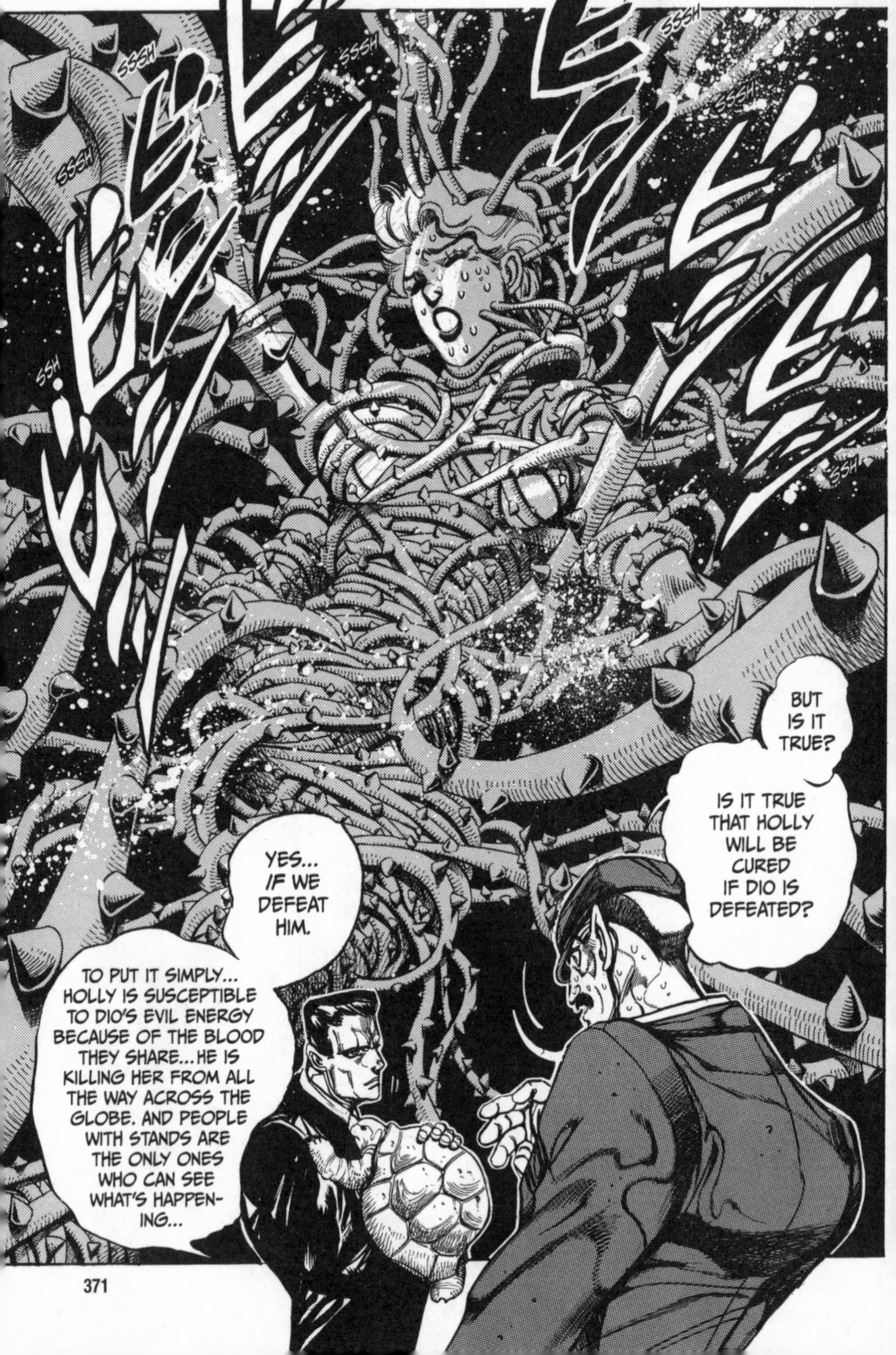
SSSH
SSSH
SSSH
SSSH
SSSH
SSH
SSH
BUT IS IT TRUE?
IS IT TRUE THAT HOLLY WILL BE CURED IF DIO IS DEFEATED?
YES... IF WE DEFEAT HIM.
TO PUT IT SIMPLY... HOLLY IS SUSCEPTIBLE TO DIO'S EVIL ENERGY BECAUSE OF THE BLOOD THEY SHARE... HE IS KILLING HER FROM ALL THE WAY ACROSS THE GLOBE. AND PEOPLE WITH STANDS ARE THE ONLY ONES WHO CAN SEE WHAT'S HAPPEN-ING...

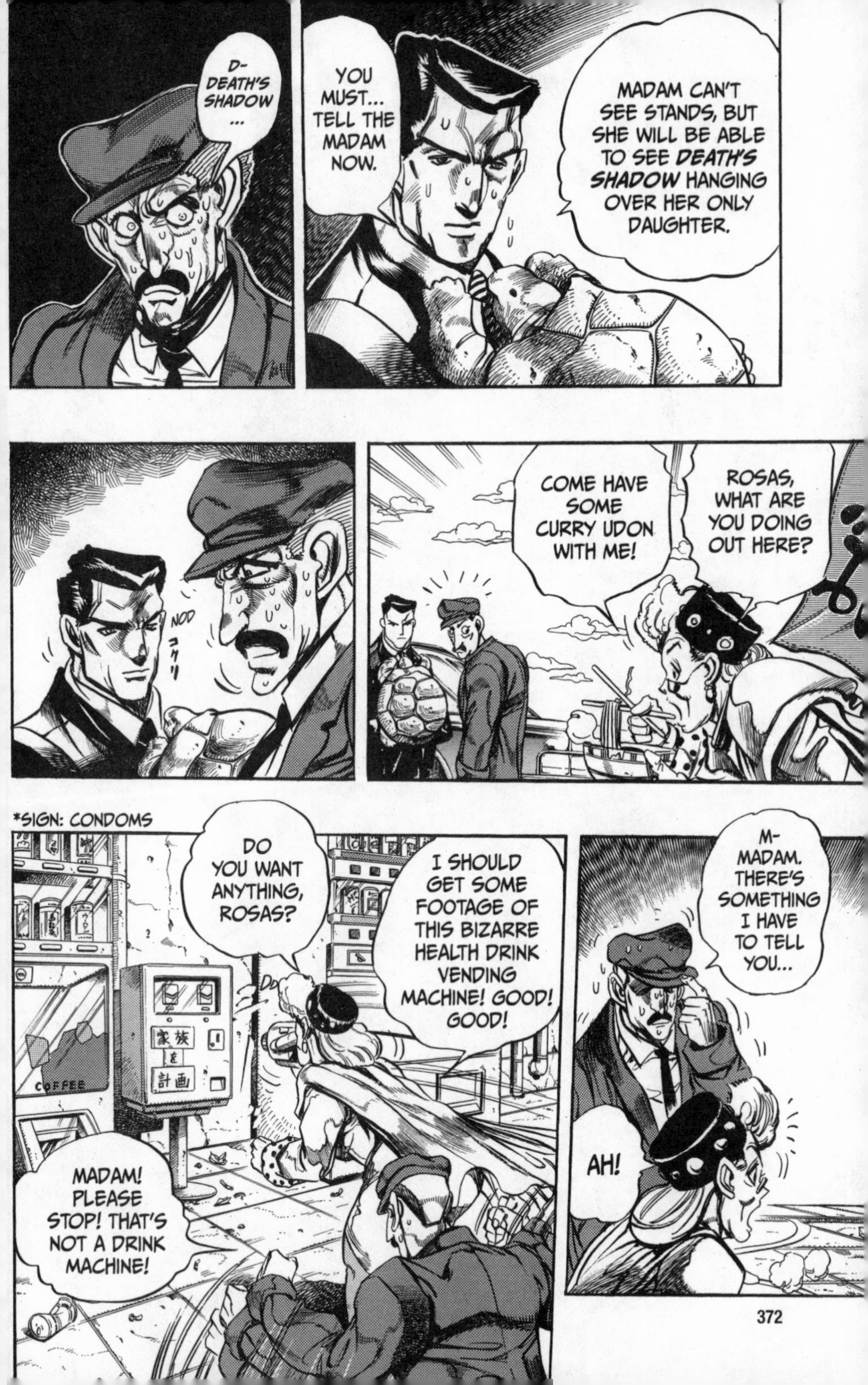
MADAM CAN'T SEE STANDS, BUT SHE WILL BE ABLE TO SEE *DEATH'S SHADOW* HANGING OVER HER ONLY DAUGHTER.
YOU MUST... TELL THE MADAM NOW.
D- DEATH'S SHADOW ...
ROSAS, WHAT ARE YOU DOING OUT HERE?
COME HAVE SOME CURRY UDON WITH ME!
NOD
M- MADAM. THERE'S SOMETHING I HAVE TO TELL YOU...
AH!
*SIGN: CONDOMS
I SHOULD GET SOME FOOTAGE OF THIS BIZARRE HEALTH DRINK VENDING MACHINE! GOOD! GOOD!
DO YOU WANT ANYTHING, ROSAS?
家族を計画
COFFEE
MADAM! PLEASE STOP! THAT'S NOT A DRINK MACHINE!

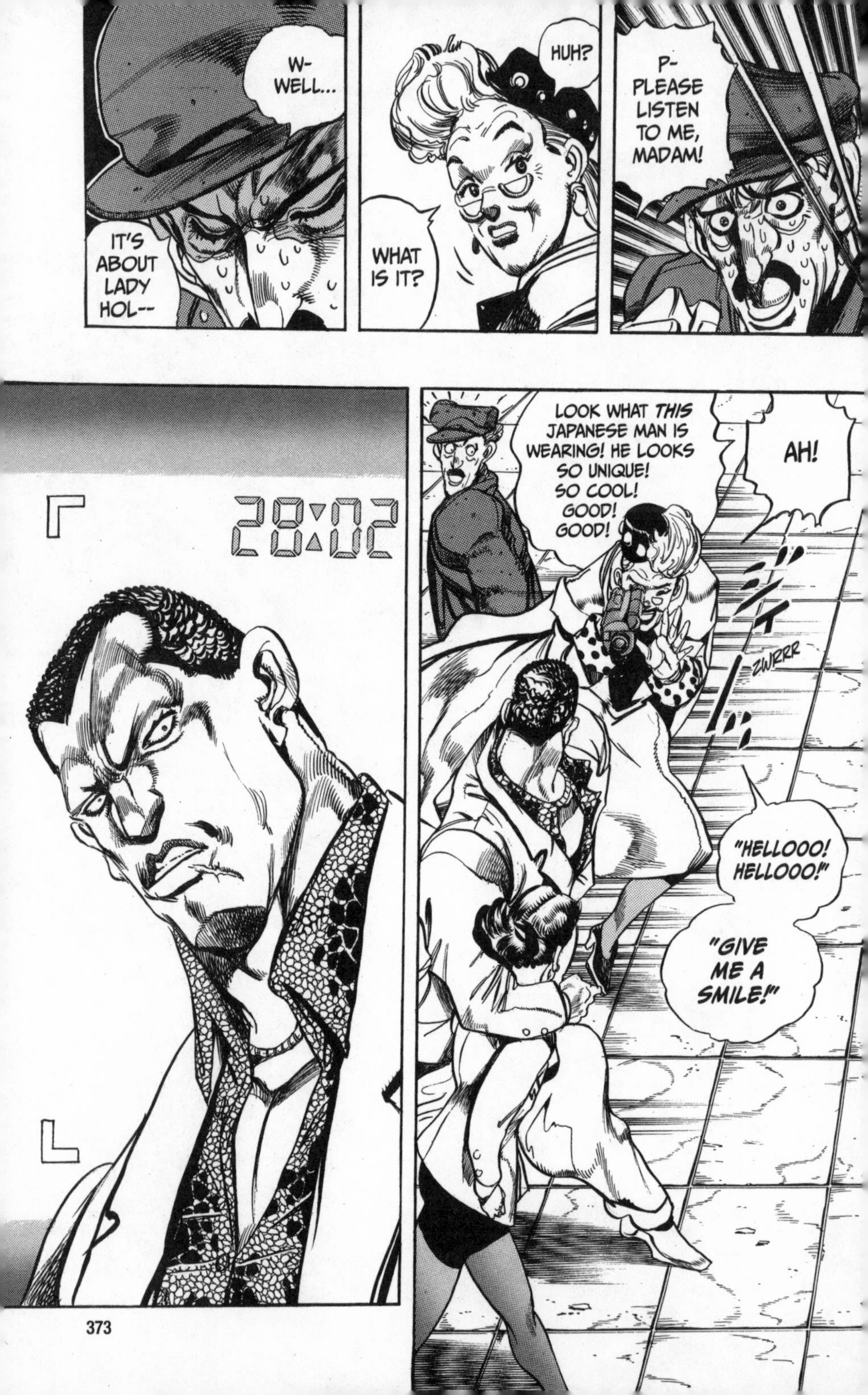
P-PLEASE LISTEN TO ME, MADAM!
HUH?
WHAT IS IT?
W-WELL...
IT'S ABOUT LADY HOL--
AH!
LOOK WHAT THIS JAPANESE MAN IS WEARING! HE LOOKS SO UNIQUE! SO COOL! GOOD! GOOD!
ZWRRR
"HELLOOO! HELLOOO!"
"GIVE ME A SMILE!"
28:02

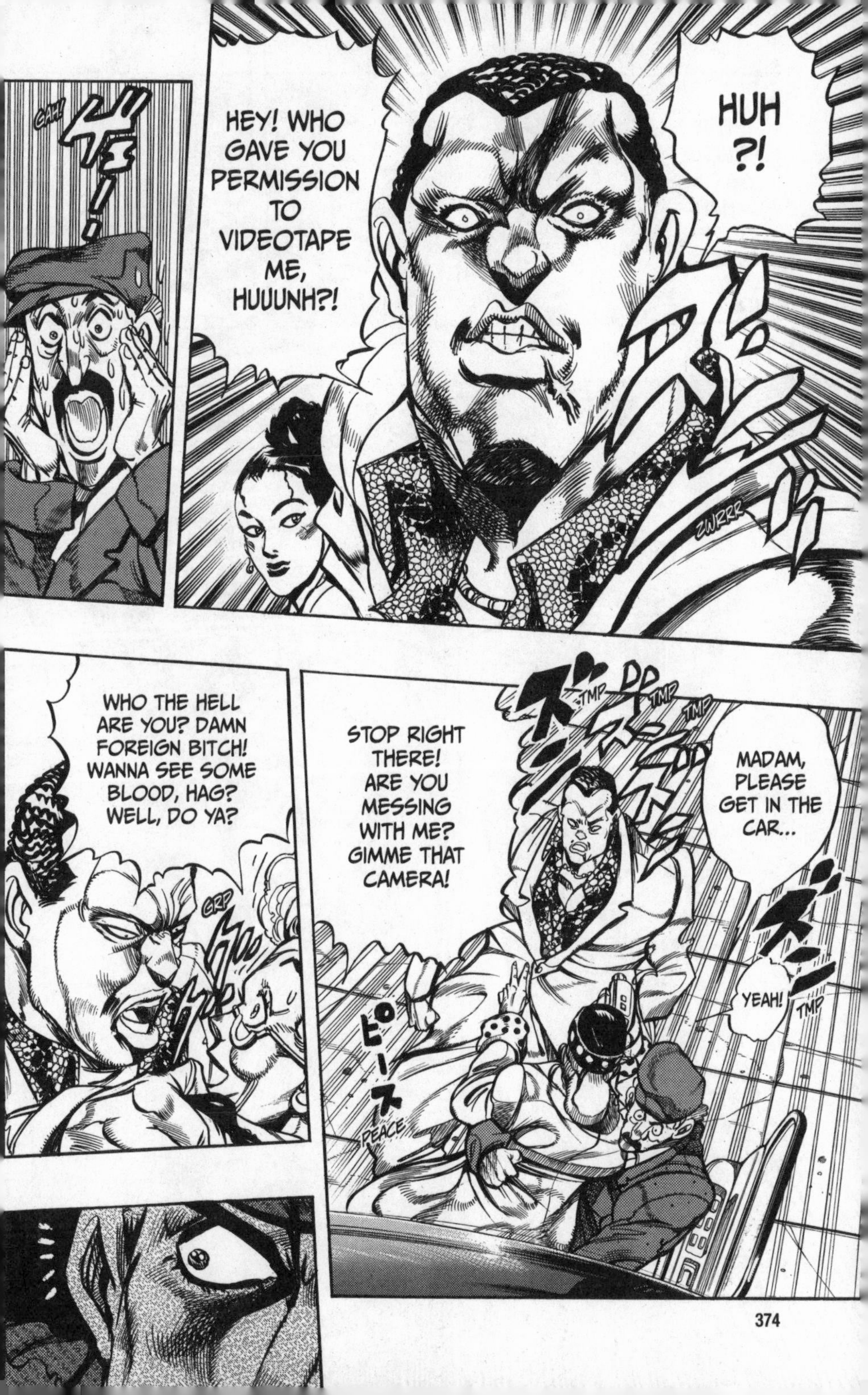
HUH ?!
HEY! WHO GAVE YOU PERMISSION TO VIDEOTAPE ME, HUUUNH?!
ZWRRR
GAH!
TMP
TMP
TMP
MADAM, PLEASE GET IN THE CAR...
STOP RIGHT THERE! ARE YOU MESSING WITH ME? GIMME THAT CAMERA!
YEAH!
TMP
PEACE
WHO THE HELL ARE YOU? DAMN FOREIGN BITCH! WANNA SEE SOME BLOOD, HAG? WELL, DO YA?
GRP

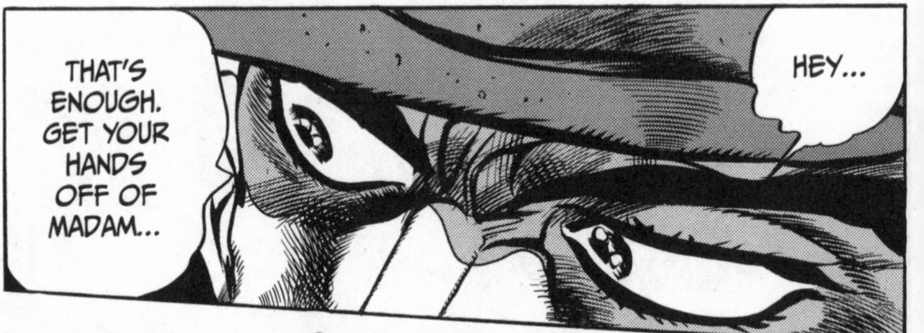
HEY...
THAT'S ENOUGH. GET YOUR HANDS OFF OF MADAM...
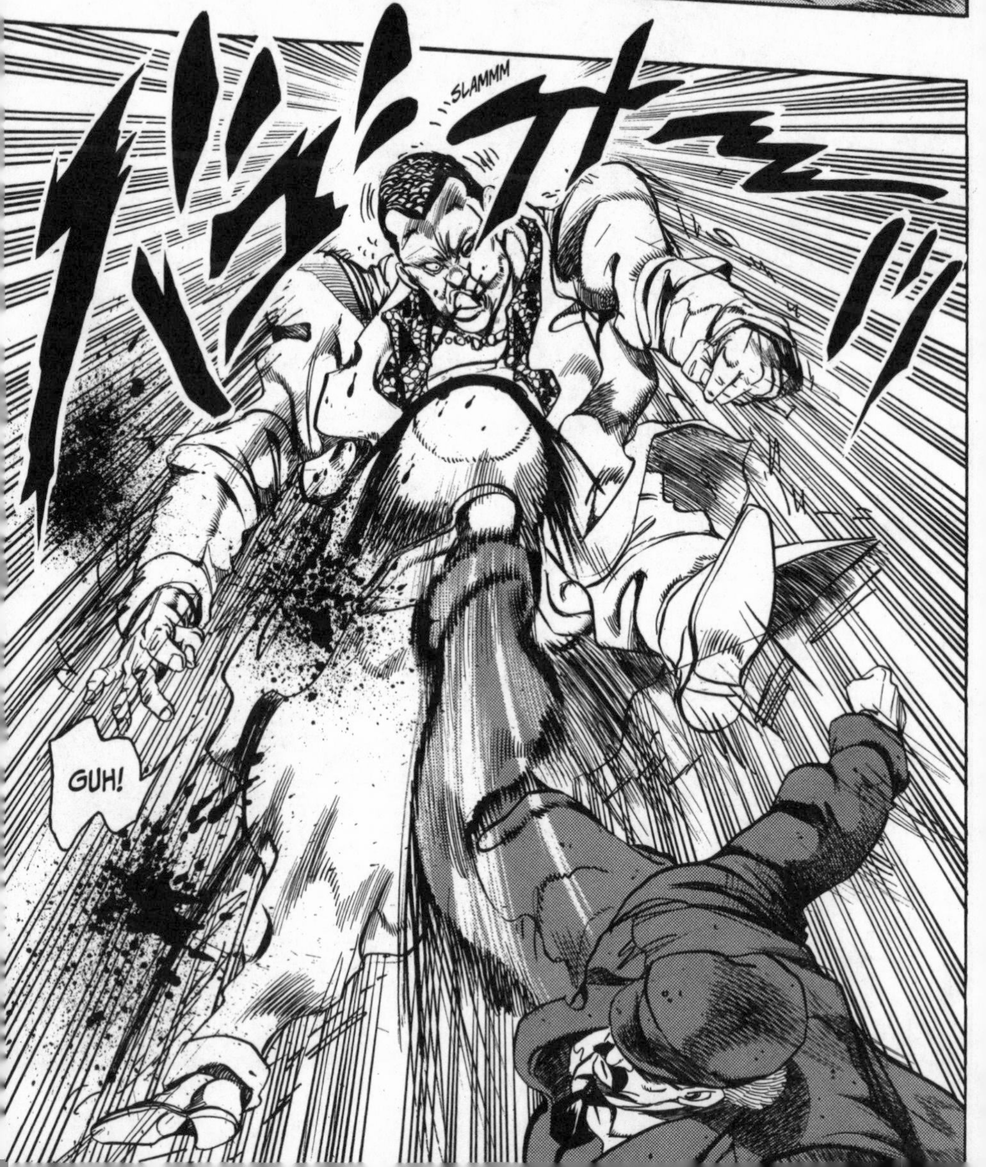
SLAMMM
GUH!

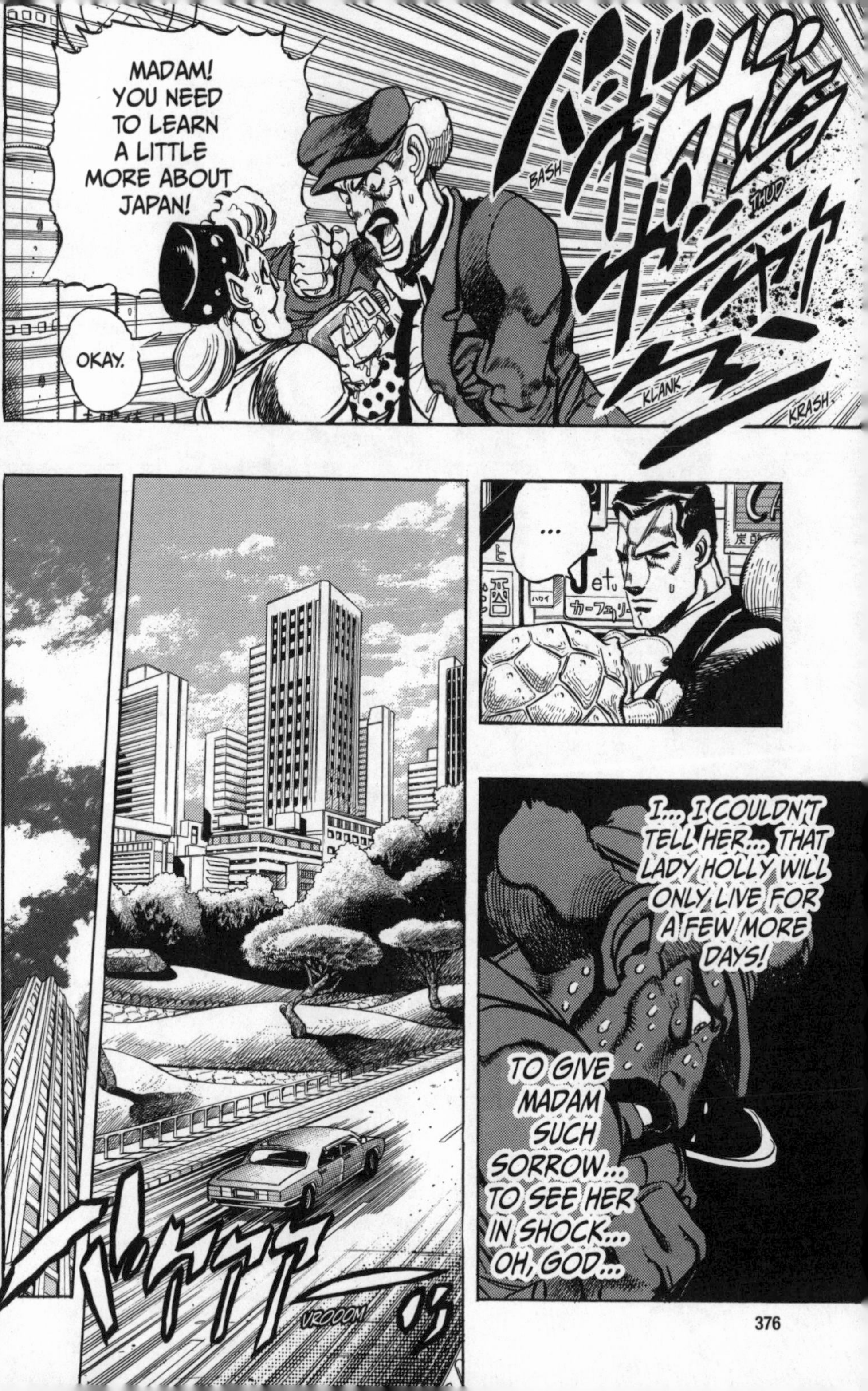
MADAM! YOU NEED TO LEARN A LITTLE MORE ABOUT JAPAN!
BASH
THUD
KLANK
KRASH
OKAY.
...
I... I COULDN'T TELL HER... THAT LADY HOLLY WILL ONLY LIVE FOR A FEW MORE DAYS!
TO GIVE MADAM SUCH SORROW... TO SEE HER IN SHOCK... OH, GOD...
VROOOM

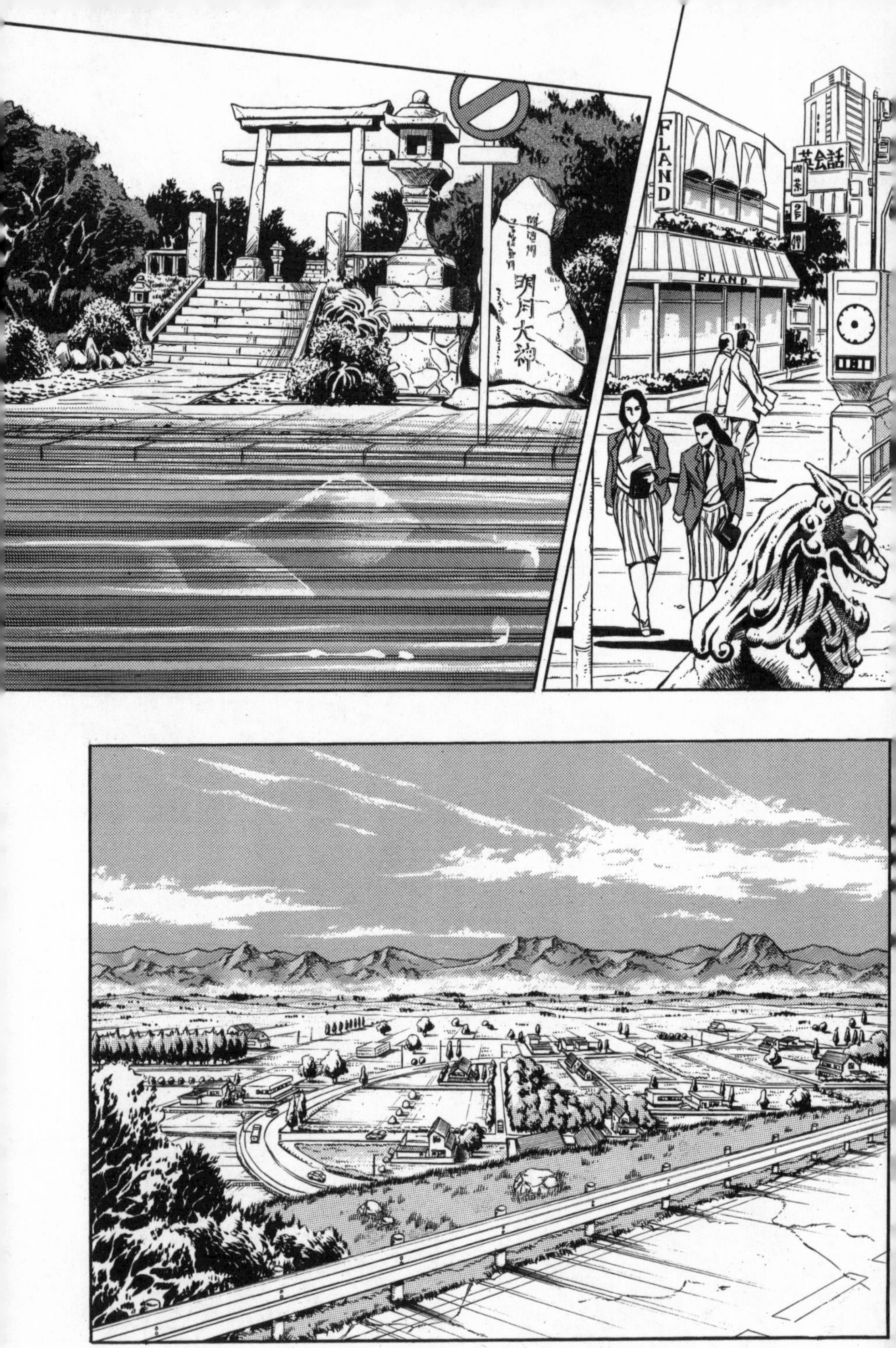
FLAND
英会話
FLAND
明月大神

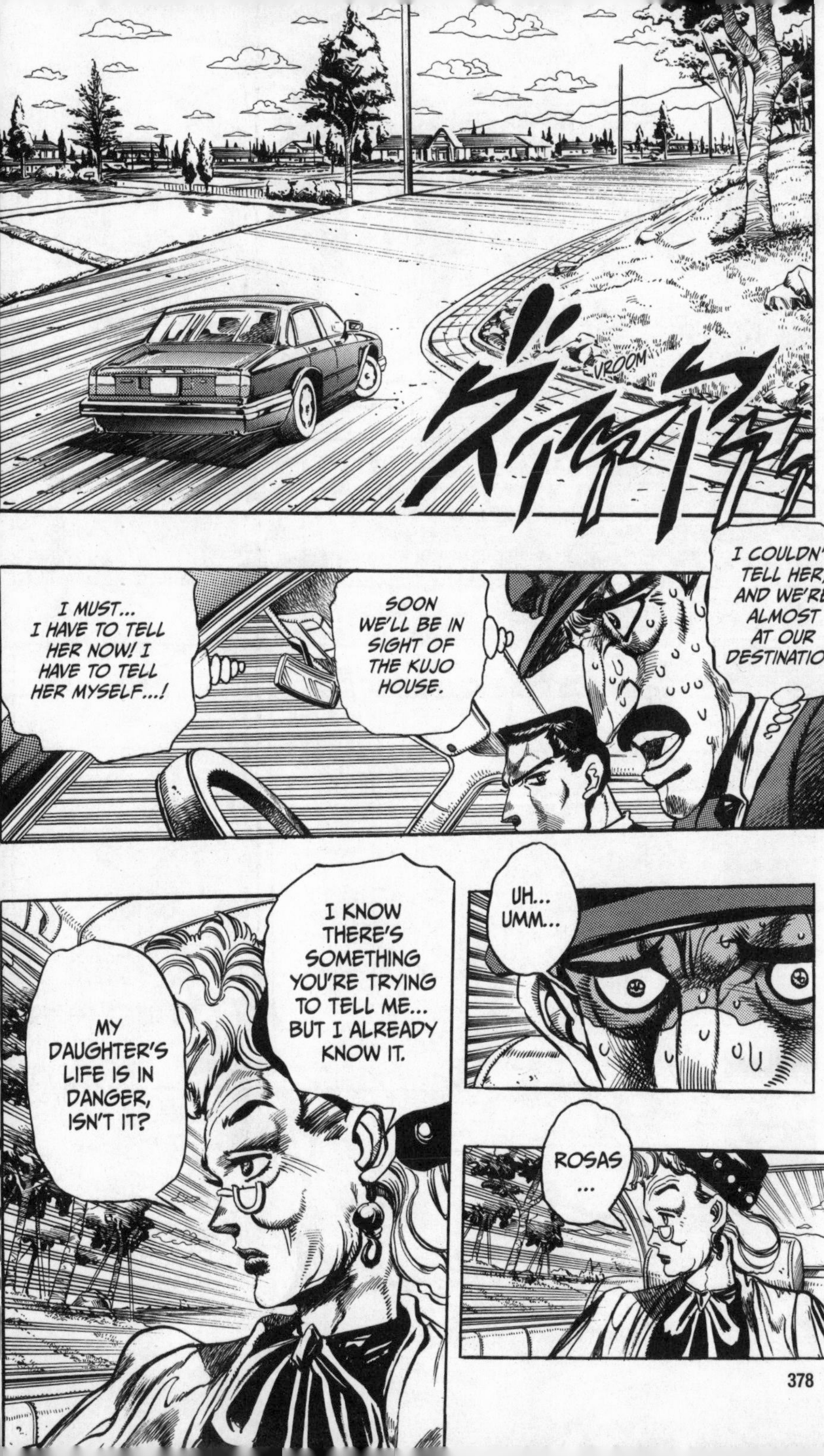
VROOM
I COULDN'T TELL HER, AND WE'RE ALMOST AT OUR DESTINATION.
SOON WE'LL BE IN SIGHT OF THE KUJO HOUSE.
I MUST... I HAVE TO TELL HER NOW! I HAVE TO TELL HER MYSELF...!
UH... UMM...
ROSAS ...
I KNOW THERE'S SOMETHING YOU'RE TRYING TO TELL ME... BUT I ALREADY KNOW IT.
MY DAUGHTER'S LIFE IS IN DANGER, ISN'T IT?

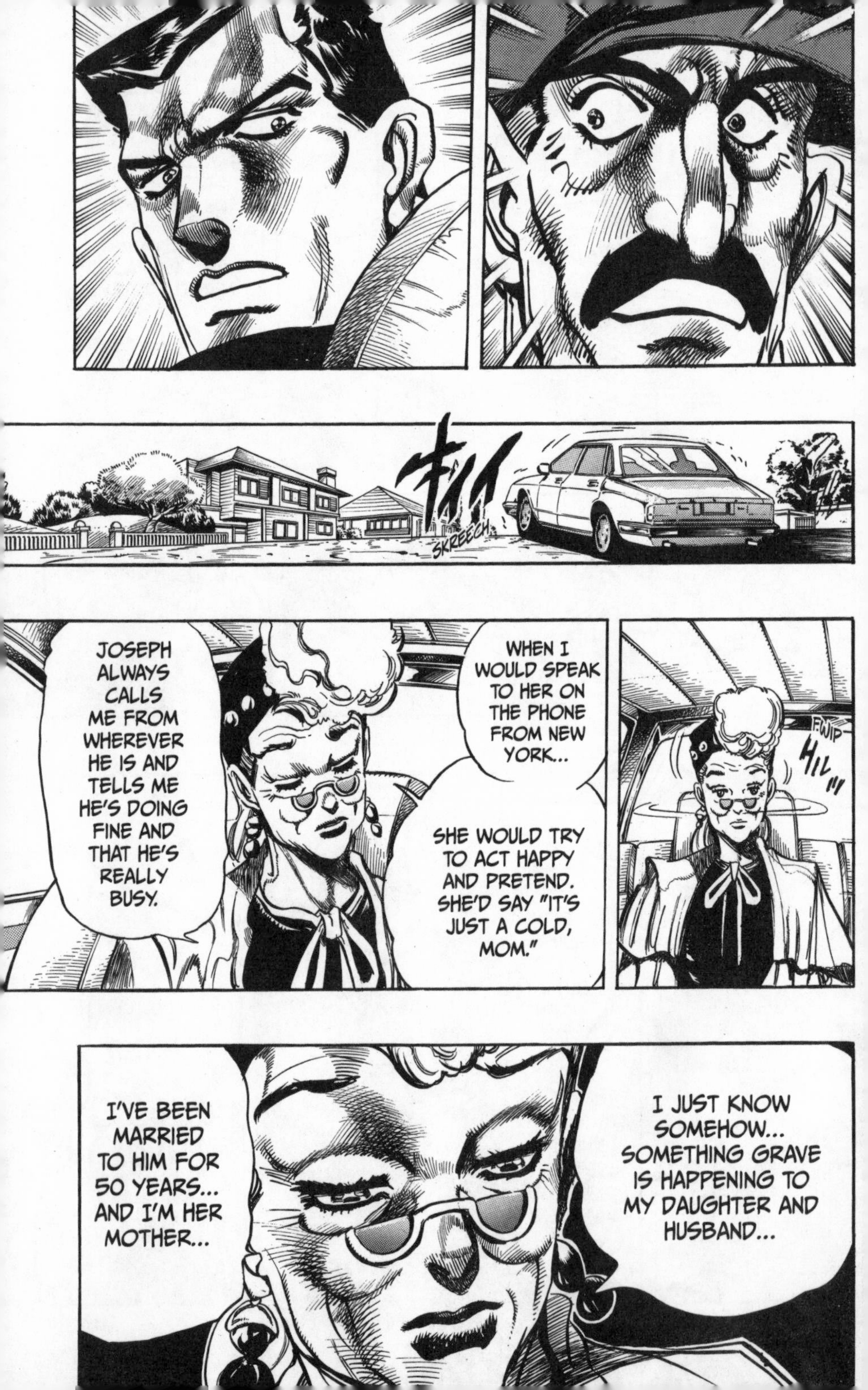
SKREECH
FWIP
WHEN I WOULD SPEAK TO HER ON THE PHONE FROM NEW YORK...
SHE WOULD TRY TO ACT HAPPY AND PRETEND. SHE'D SAY "IT'S JUST A COLD, MOM."
JOSEPH ALWAYS CALLS ME FROM WHEREVER HE IS AND TELLS ME HE'S DOING FINE AND THAT HE'S REALLY BUSY.
I JUST KNOW SOMEHOW... SOMETHING GRAVE IS HAPPENING TO MY DAUGHTER AND HUSBAND...
I'VE BEEN MARRIED TO HIM FOR 50 YEARS... AND I'M HER MOTHER...

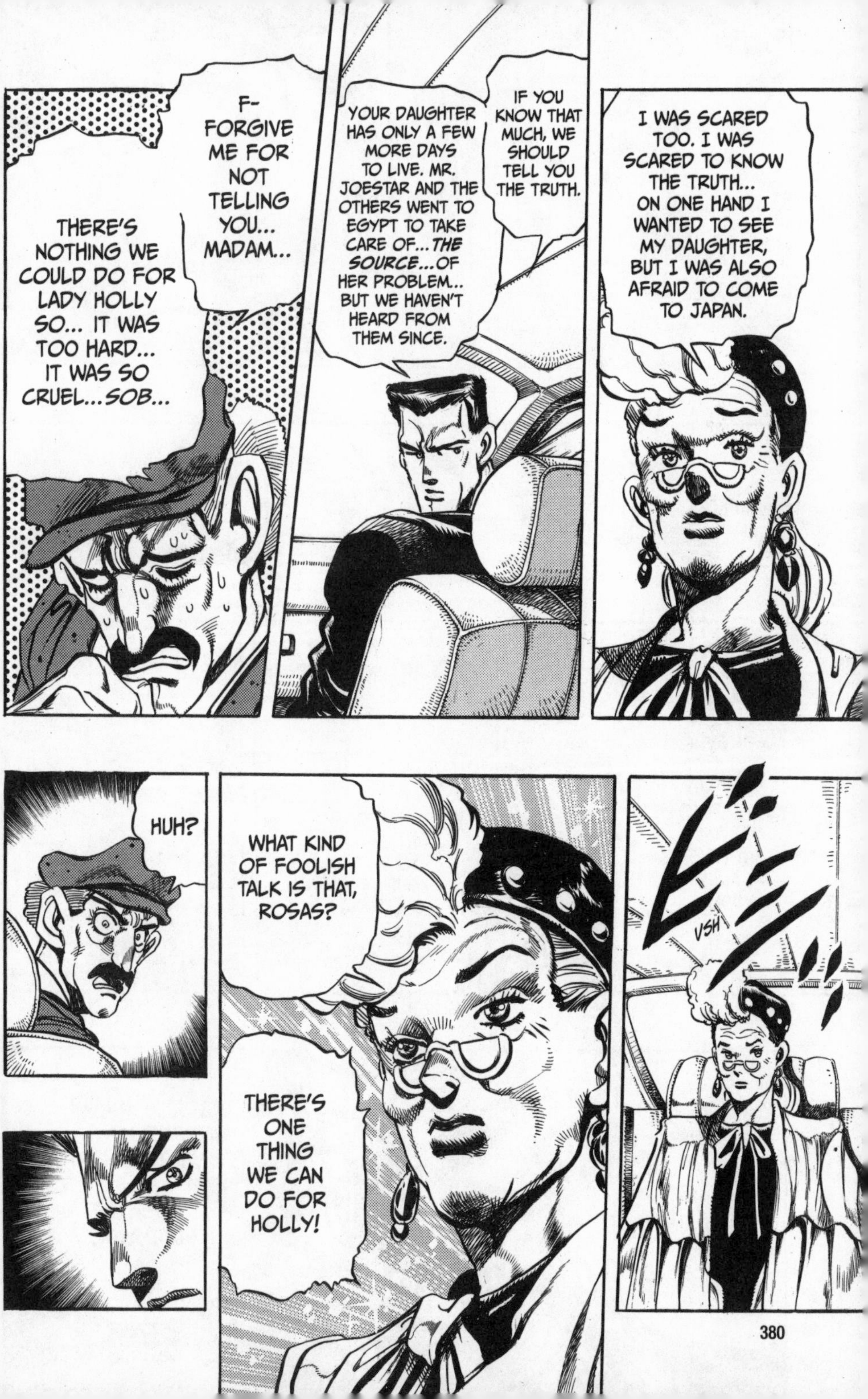
I WAS SCARED TOO. I WAS SCARED TO KNOW THE TRUTH... ON ONE HAND I WANTED TO SEE MY DAUGHTER, BUT I WAS ALSO AFRAID TO COME TO JAPAN.
IF YOU KNOW THAT MUCH, WE SHOULD TELL YOU THE TRUTH.
YOUR DAUGHTER HAS ONLY A FEW MORE DAYS TO LIVE. MR. JOESTAR AND THE OTHERS WENT TO EGYPT TO TAKE CARE OF...*THE SOURCE*...OF HER PROBLEM... BUT WE HAVEN'T HEARD FROM THEM SINCE.
F-FORGIVE ME FOR NOT TELLING YOU... MADAM...
THERE'S NOTHING WE COULD DO FOR LADY HOLLY SO... IT WAS TOO HARD... IT WAS SO CRUEL...*SOB*...
VSH
WHAT KIND OF FOOLISH TALK IS THAT, ROSAS?
THERE'S ONE THING WE CAN DO FOR HOLLY!
HUH?

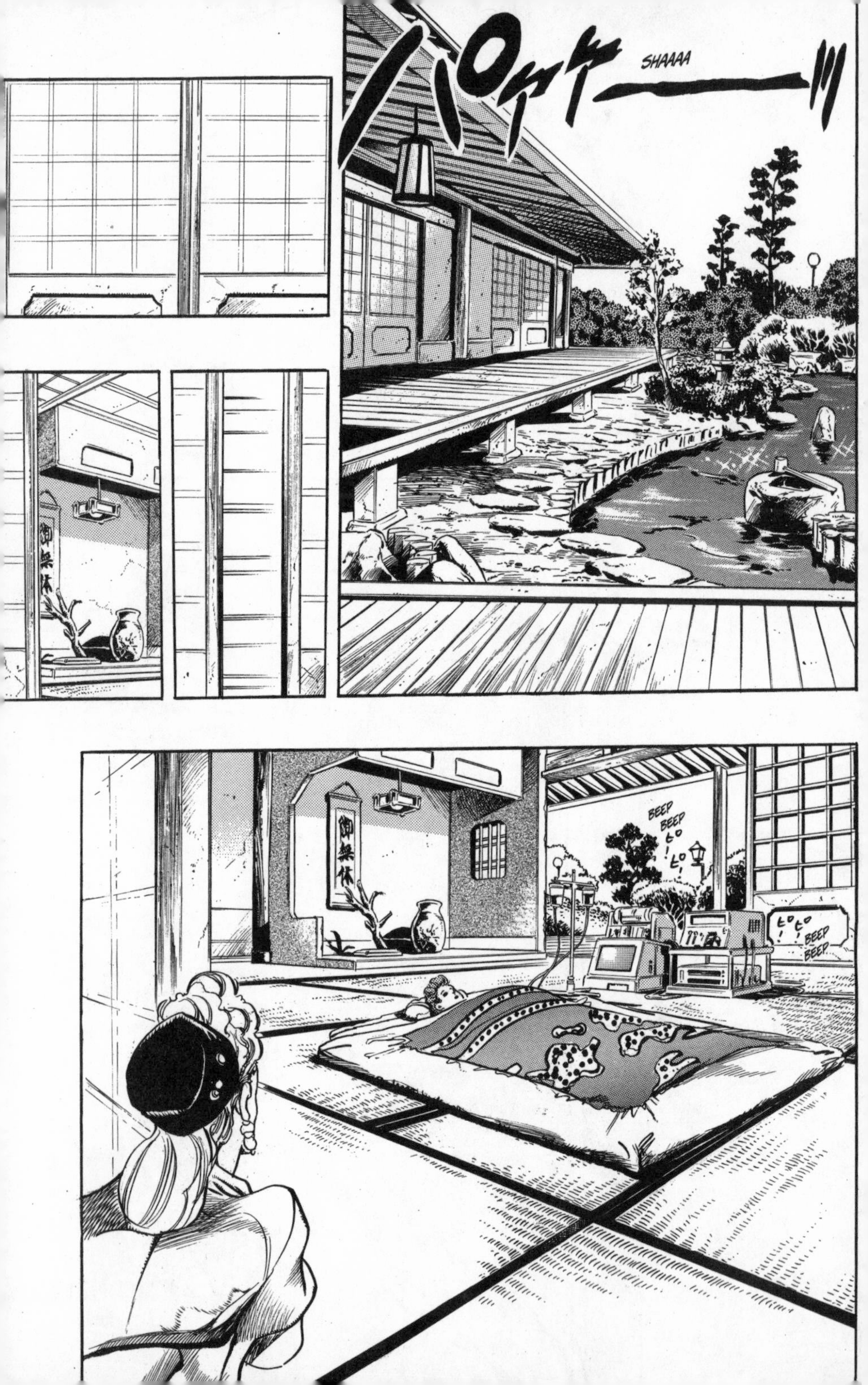
SHAAAA
BEEP BEEP
ピ! ピ!
ピ! ピ!
BEEP BEEP

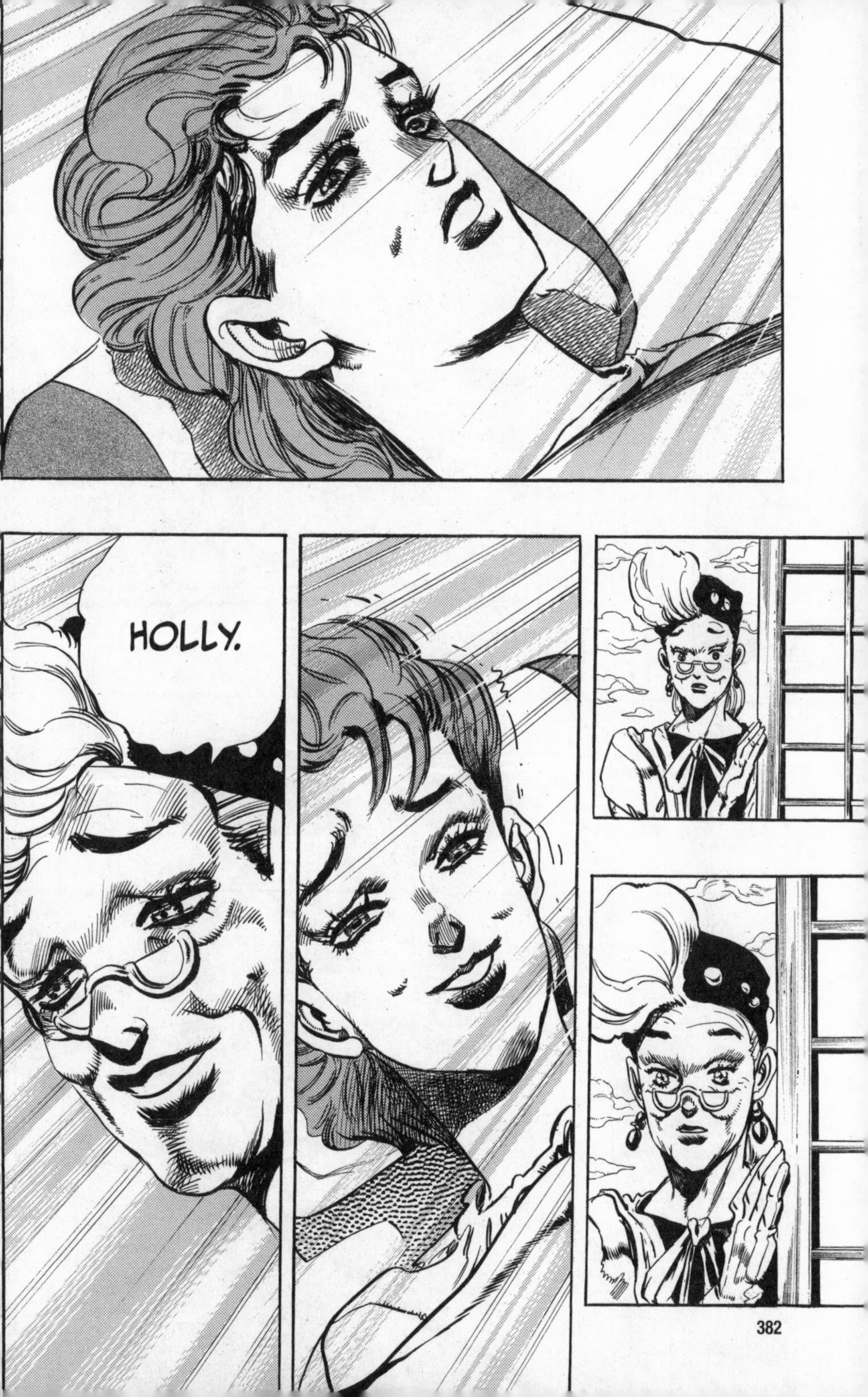
HOLLY.

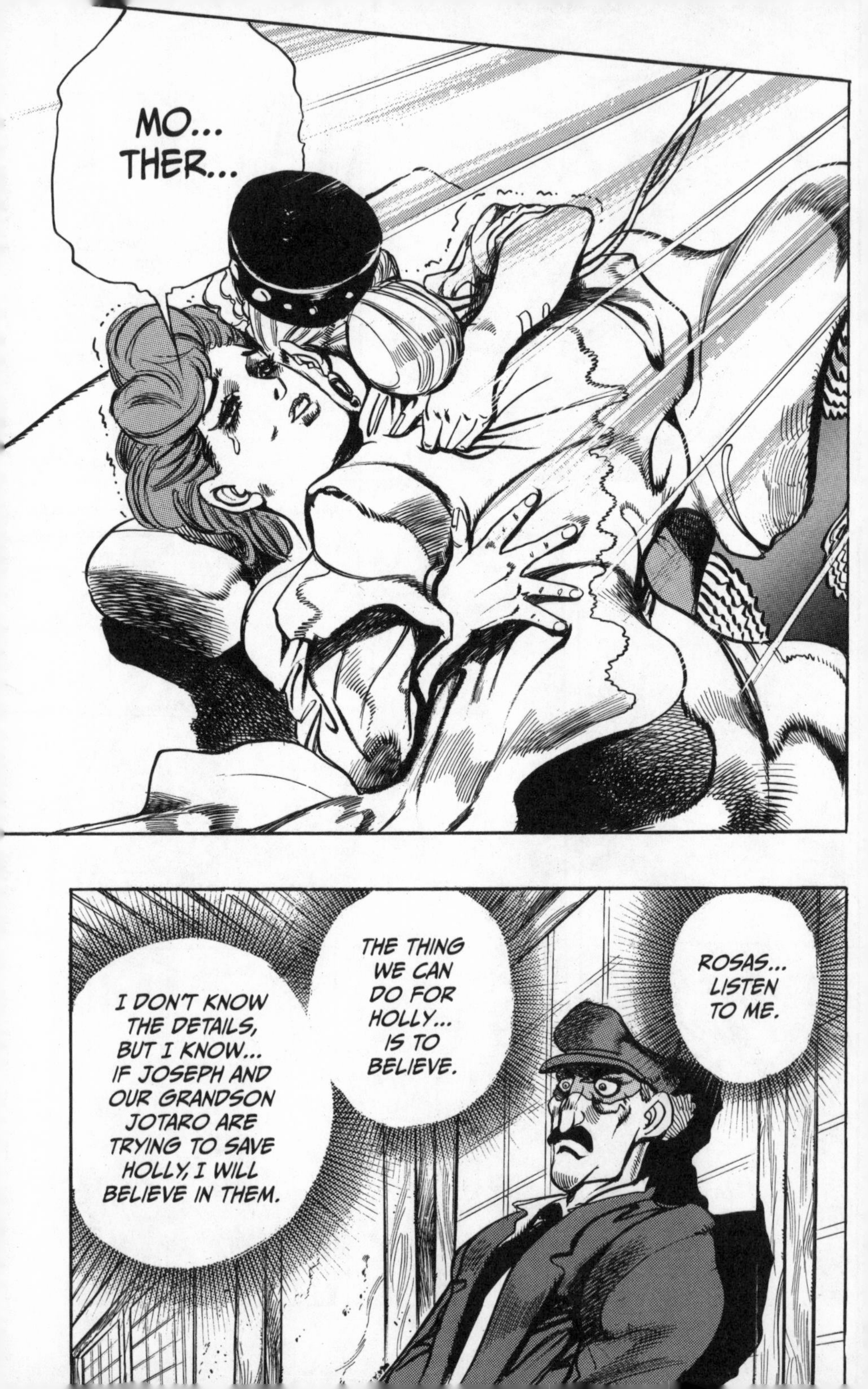
MO... THER...
ROSAS... LISTEN TO ME.
THE THING WE CAN DO FOR HOLLY... IS TO BELIEVE.
I DON'T KNOW THE DETAILS, BUT I KNOW... IF JOSEPH AND OUR GRANDSON JOTARO ARE TRYING TO SAVE HOLLY, I WILL BELIEVE IN THEM.

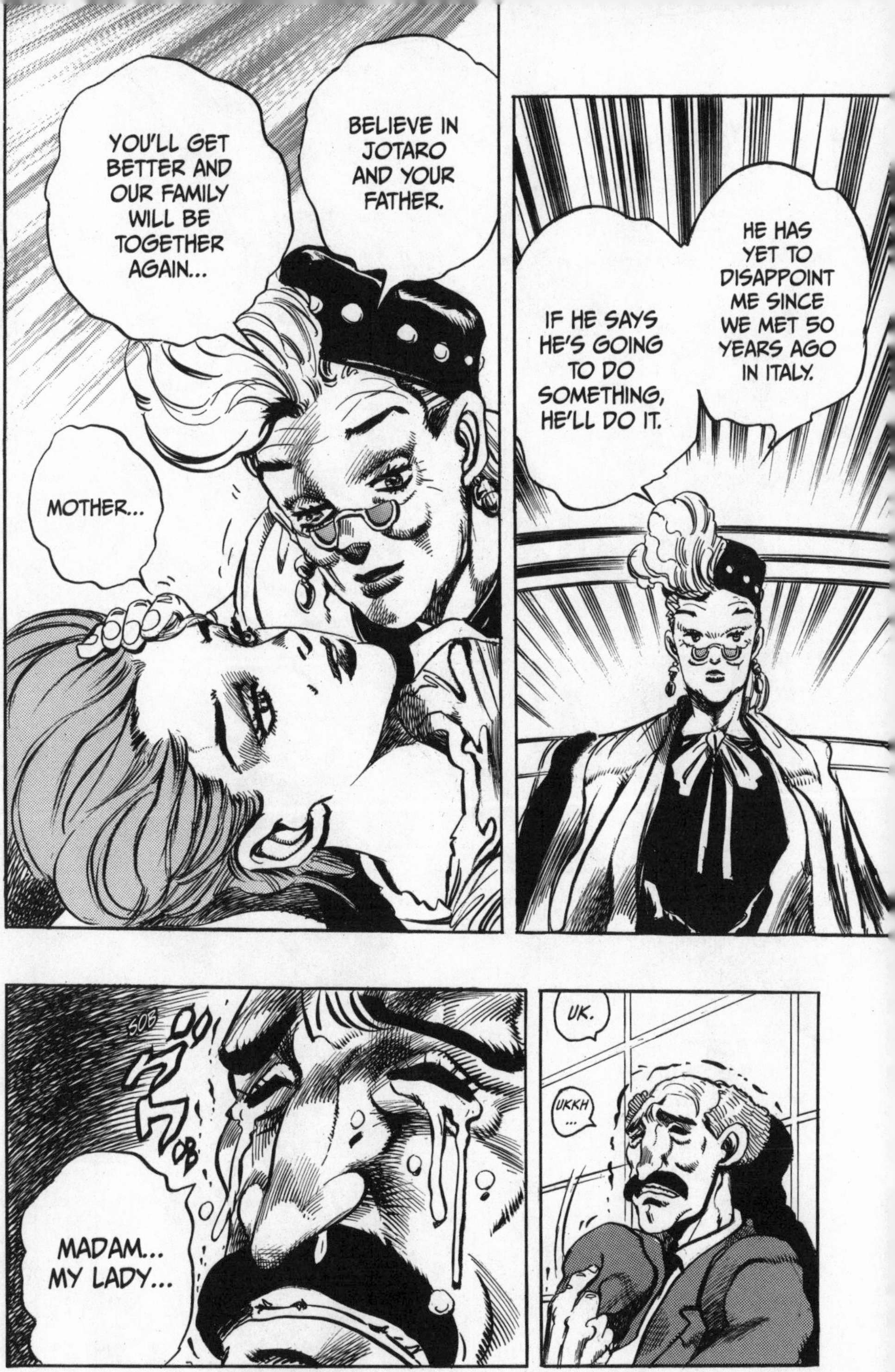
HE HAS YET TO DISAPPOINT ME SINCE WE MET 50 YEARS AGO IN ITALY.
IF HE SAYS HE'S GOING TO DO SOMETHING, HE'LL DO IT.
BELIEVE IN JOTARO AND YOUR FATHER.
YOU'LL GET BETTER AND OUR FAMILY WILL BE TOGETHER AGAIN...
MOTHER...
UK.
UKKH...
SOB
SOB
MADAM... MY LADY...

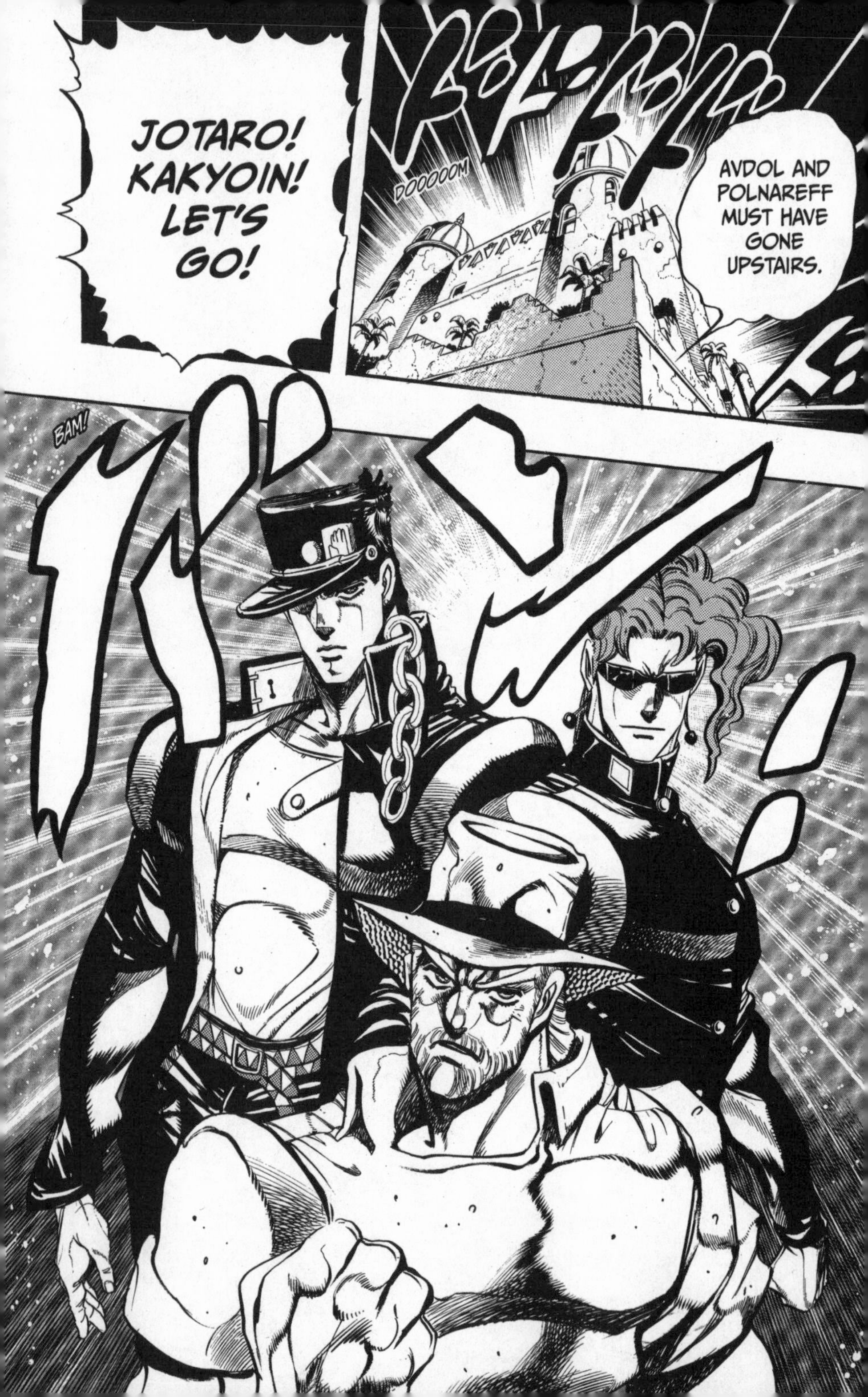
DOOOOOM
AVDOL AND POLNAREFF MUST HAVE GONE UPSTAIRS.
JOTARO! KAKYOIN! LET'S GO!
BAM!

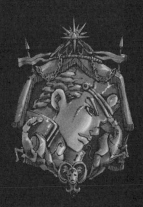

JoJo's
BIZARRE ADVENTURE

(09)
END

To Be Continued

JoJo's BIZARRE ADVENTURE

09

Po

荒木飛呂彦が
語る
キャラクター
誕生秘話

Hirohiko Araki talks about character creation!

JoJo's BIZARRE ADVENTURE
PART 3
STARDUST CRUSADERS

Pierre Polnareff

09

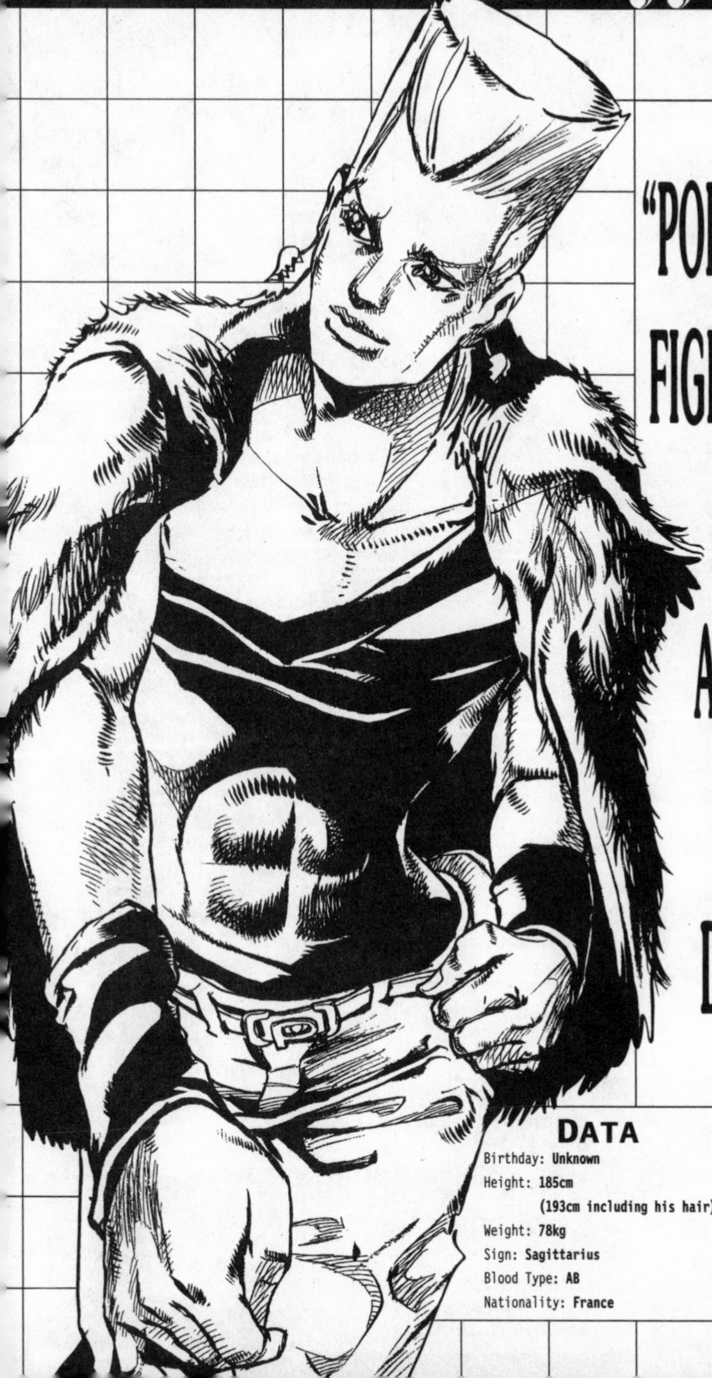

"POLNAREFF'S FIGHTS WERE ALWAYS A BRUSH WITH DEATH"

DATA

Birthday: **Unknown**

Height: **185cm**
(193cm including his hair)

Weight: **78kg**

Sign: **Sagittarius**

Blood Type: **AB**

Nationality: **France**

PO

Jea

If you asked me which character grew the most on the journey to defeat DIO, the first one who comes to mind is Polnareff. He started out as a lone wolf who was only out to avenge his little sister and evolved into a true companion who supported the Joestar party until the end. It was a lot of fun to have him grow along the way to Egypt as he battled enemy Stands. His lines tend to stand out, for better or for worse, so I'm sure many readers feel as if he was one of the more prominent characters. However, the main character is still Jotaro, with Joseph serving as the navigator. In order to not have him overlap with them, I gave him a distinctive look and personality, which by contrast allowed him to shine on his own. He could cover what the Joestars themselves couldn't…which could be why I gave him special treatment *(laughs wryly)*.

For example, when he's with Jotaro and Joseph, I could have him spout both goofy lines and serious ones, making him a very versatile character to employ. From bathroom-related issues to traps set by enemy Stands, Polnareff is the first one in the group to tackle them. It wouldn't be as fun if the aloof Jotaro were to do so instead. As such, naturally, Polnareff needed to make more appearances. Polnareff is straightforward and a bit of a rubbernecker compared to Kakyoin or Avdol, which allows him to get into all sorts of hijinks. As such, he may have had an advantage as to how often he appeared in the series. Also, from my perspective as the artist, he also had the most memorable silhouette out of the good guys by far. I used foreign models as reference for his hair. I sort of drew it like Stroheim's from Part 2, but done up.

More appearances in the story means more fights for him to take part in. Soul Sacrifice, Centerfold, Alessi, Cool Ice…he ended up fighting many of DIO's underlings, all with very different abilities. Back when this was being serialized, I was always writing those fights with the intention that Polnareff could lose and face death at any given moment. Like in the movie *The Magnificent Seven*, I wanted the reader to never know who would survive until the end--to experience the thrill of lives being on the line--and I think his fights definitely had that in them. I think it's because he made it through so many life-or-death situations that I feel like he grew the most along the way.

Lastly, as for the origin behind his name, Jean P. Polnareff: my three favorite French people are the actors Alain Delon and Jean-Paul Belmondo, and the musician Michel Polnareff, so naturally, I drew inspiration from their names. The character is French, so naturally, his name would have to be Jean P.! Now there's also the famous chocolatier, Jean-Paul Hévin, so I think I would think the same way, even now.

The story behind the new illustration for JoJo Part 3 09!

Q. He doesn't usually have a coat. Why does he have one now?

A. I imagined him like a supermodel or a rock star.

His original outfit was pretty simple, and I mean, he's going to be on the cover, so why not have him dress up for it? Also, the reason why Silver Chariot is purple is

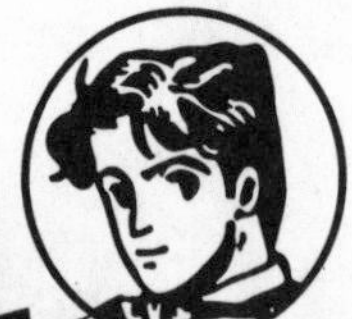

Hirohiko Araki

09

JoJo's Bizarre Adventure

Part 3 Stardust Crusaders

BY

HIROHIKO ARAKI

SHONEN JUMP ADVANCED EDITION
Translation ☆ Mayumi Kobayashi
Editor ☆ Jason Thompson

DELUXE HARDCOVER EDITION
Translation ☆ Evan Galloway
Touch-Up Art & Lettering ☆ Mark McMurray
Design ☆ Adam Grano
Editor ☆ David Brothers

Original Japanese cover design by
MITSURU KOBAYASHI (GENI A LÒIDE)

Printed in the U.S.A.

Published by VIZ Media, LLC
P.O. Box 77010
San Francisco, CA 94107

10 9 8 7 6 5 4 3 2 1
First printing, November 2018

RATED T+ FOR OLDER TEEN ratings.viz.com

PARENTAL ADVISORY
JOJO'S BIZARRE ADVENTURE PART THREE STARDUST CRUSADERS
is rated T+ for Older Teen and is recommended for ages 16 and up.
This volume contains graphic violence and some mature themes.

VIZ media
www.viz.com

SHONEN JUMP ADVANCED
www.shonenjump.com

Jo

JoJo's BIZARRE ADVENTURE
PART 3 STARDUST CRUSADERS

THIS IS THE LAST PAGE

ドドド

JoJo's Bizarre Adventure
has been printed in the original Japanese format in order to preserve the orientation of the original artwork.

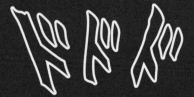

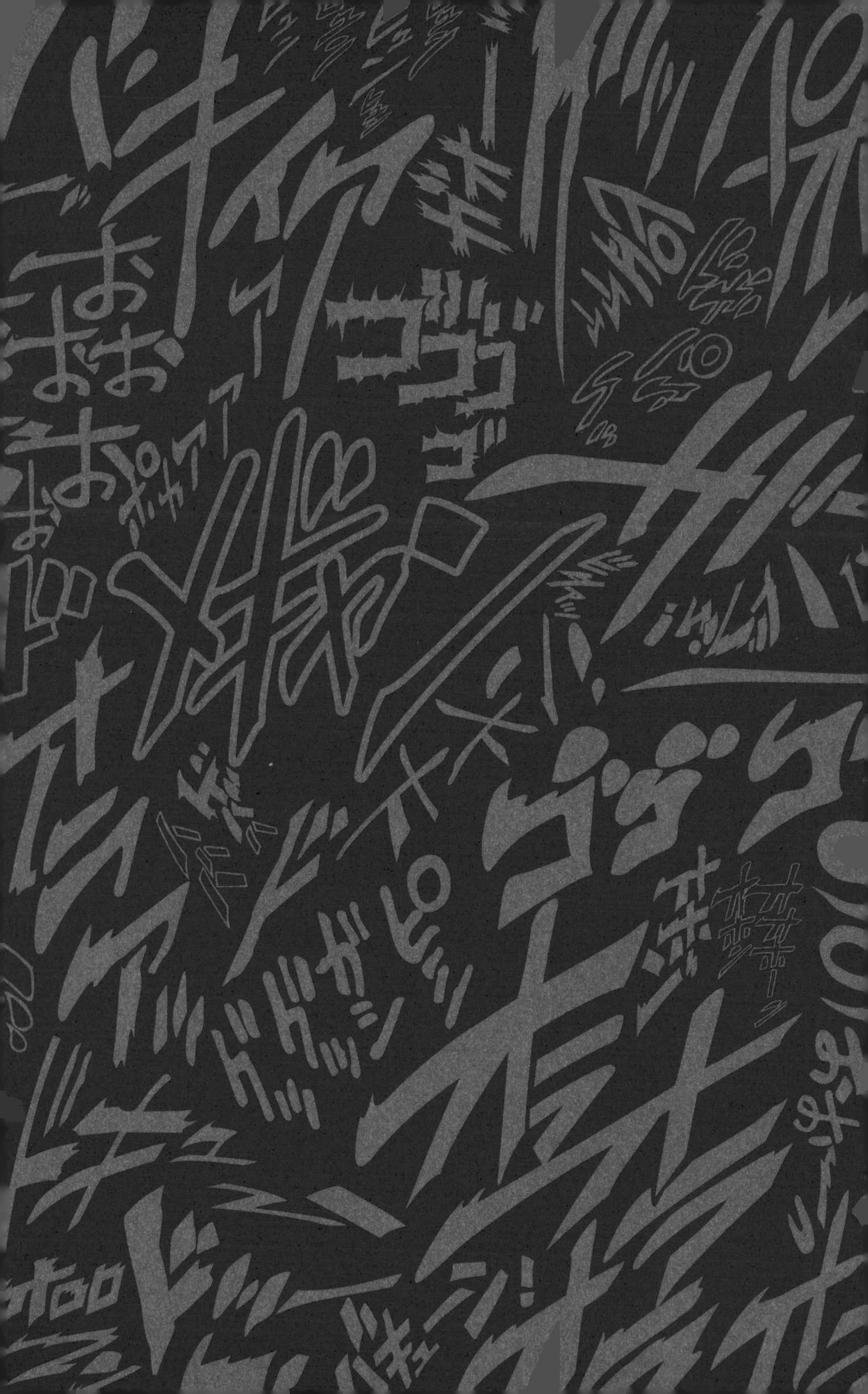
ゴゴゴ
バキューン!